Contemporary Sociological Theory

Contemporary Sociological Theory

Third Edition

Edited by

Craig Calhoun, Joseph Gerteis, James Moody,
Steven Pfaff, and Indermohan Virk

WILEY-BLACKWELL
A John Wiley & Sons, Ltd., Publication

This edition first published 2012
Editorial material and organization © 2012 John Wiley & Sons, Ltd

Edition history: Blackwell Publishing Ltd (1e, 2002 and 2e, 2007)

Wiley-Blackwell is an imprint of John Wiley & Sons formed by the merger of Wiley's global Scientific, Technical and Medical business with Blackwell Publishing.

Registered Office
John Wiley & Sons, Ltd, The Atrium, Southern Gate, Chichester, West Sussex, PO19 8SQ, United Kingdom

Editorial Offices
350 Main Street, Malden, MA 02148-5020, USA
9600 Garsington Road, Oxford, OX4 2DQ, UK
The Atrium, Southern Gate, Chichester, West Sussex, PO19 8SQ, UK

For details of our global editorial offices, for customer services, and for information about how to apply for permission to reuse the copyright material in this book please see our website at www.wiley.com/wiley-blackwell.

The right of Craig Calhoun, Joseph Gerteis, James Moody, Steven Pfaff, and Indermohan Virk to be identified as the editors of the editorial material in this work has been asserted in accordance with the UK Copyright, Designs and Patents Act 1988.

All rights reserved. No part of this publication may be reproduced, stored in a retrieval system, or transmitted, in any form or by any means, electronic, mechanical, photocopying, recording or otherwise, except as permitted by the UK Copyright, Designs and Patents Act 1988, without the prior permission of the publisher.

Wiley also publishes its books in a variety of electronic formats. Some content that appears in print may not be available in electronic books.

Designations used by companies to distinguish their products are often claimed as trademarks. All brand names and product names used in this book are trade names, service marks, trademarks or registered trademarks of their respective owners. The publisher is not associated with any product or vendor mentioned in this book. This publication is designed to provide accurate and authoritative information in regard to the subject matter covered. It is sold on the understanding that the publisher is not engaged in rendering professional services. If professional advice or other expert assistance is required, the services of a competent professional should be sought.

Library of Congress Cataloging-in-Publication Data
Contemporary sociological theory / edited by Craig Calhoun ... [et al.].
    p. cm.
  Complements Classical sociological theory.
  Includes bibliographical references and index.
  ISBN 978-0-470-65566-5 (pbk.)
 1. Sociology–History–20th century.   2. Sociology–Philosophy.   I. Calhoun, Craig, 1952–
 II. Classical sociological theory.
  HM447.C66 2012
  301.01–dc23
                                                                    2011036064
A catalogue record for this book is available from the British Library.

Set in 10.5/13pt Minion by SPi Publisher Services, Pondicherry, India

1   2012

Contents

Notes on the Editors xi
Acknowledgments xii

Introduction 1

Part I Micro-Sociological Analysis 25

Introduction to Part I 27
1 The Phenomenology of the Social World
   (from *The Phenomenology of the Social World*) 35
   Alfred Schutz
2 The Presentation of Self in Everyday Life
   (from *The Presentation of Self in Everyday Life*) 46
   Erving Goffman
3 Symbolic Interactionism (from *Symbolic Interactionism:
   Perspective and Method*) 62
   Herbert Blumer
4 "Interaction Ritual Chains" (from *Interaction Ritual Chains*) 75
   Randall Collins

Part II Exchange and Rationality 91

Introduction to Part II 93
5 Social Behavior as Exchange
   (from *American Journal of Sociology*) 100
   George C. Homans

6. Exchange and Power in Social Life (from *Exchange and Power in Social Life*) 112
Peter M. Blau

7. The Logic of Collective Action (from *The Logic of Collective Action: Public Goods and the Theory of Groups*) 124
Mancur Olson

8. A Theory of Group Solidarity (from *Principles of Group Solidarity*) 129
Michael Hechter

9. Cooperation without Law or Trust (from *Cooperation without Trust?*) 142
Karen S. Cook, Russell Hardin, and Margaret Levi

Part III Institutions and Networks   157

Introduction to Part III   159

10. Economic Embeddedness (from "*Economic Action and Social Structure: The Problem of Embeddedness*") 165
Mark Granovetter

11. The Iron Cage Revisited: Institutional Isomorphism and Collective Rationality in Organizational Fields (from "*The Iron Cage Revisited: Institutional Isomorphism and Collective Rationality in Organizational Fields*") 175
Paul J. DiMaggio and Walter W. Powell

12. Catnets (from *Notes on the Constituents of Social Structure*) 193
Harrison White

13. Structural Holes (from *Stuctural Holes: The Social Structure of Competition*) 204
Ronald S. Burt

Part IV Power and Inequality   221

Introduction to Part IV   223

14. The Power Elite (from *The Power Elite*) 229
C. Wright Mills

15. On Hegemony (from *Selections From the Prison Notebooks of Antonio Gramsci*) 237
Antonio Gramsci

16. Coercion, Capital, and European States (from *Coercion, Capital and European States, AD 990–1990*) 251
Charles Tilly

17. Power: A Radical View (from *Power: A Radical View*) 266
Steven Lukes

	18 State, Society and Modern History (from *The Nation-State and Violence Volume Two of A Contemporary Critique of Historical Materialism*) *Anthony Giddens*	277
Part V	**The Sociological Theory of Michel Foucault**	**287**
	Introduction to Part V	289
	19 The History of Sexuality (from *The History of Sexuality*, vol. I: *An Introduction*) *Michel Foucault*	295
	20 Truth and Power (from *Power/Knowledge: Selected Interviews and Other Writings, 1972–1977*) *Michel Foucault*	305
	21 Discipline and Punish (from *Discipline and Punish: The Birth of the Prison*) *Michel Foucault*	314
Part VI	**The Sociological Theory of Pierre Bourdieu**	**323**
	Introduction to Part VI	325
	22 Social Space and Symbolic Space (from "*Social Space and Symbolic Space: Introduction to a Japanese Reading of Distinction*") *Pierre Bourdieu*	335
	23 Structures, *Habitus*, Practices (from *The Logic of Practice*) *Pierre Bourdieu*	345
	24 The Field of Cultural Production, or: The Economic World Reversed (from *Poetics*) *Pierre Bourdieu*	359
	25 Rethinking the State: Genesis and Structure of the Bureaucratic Field (from *Rethinking the State: Genesis and Structure of the Bureaucratic Field*) *Pierre Bourdieu*	375
Part VII	**Race, Gender, Difference**	**387**
	Introduction to Part VII	389
	26 The Conceptual Practices of Power (from *The Conceptual Practices of Power: A Feminist Sociology of Knowledge*) *Dorothy E. Smith*	398
	27 Black Feminist Epistemology (from *Black Feminist Thought: Knowledge, Consciousness, and the Politics of Empowerment*) *Patricia Hill Collins*	407

28	Black Skin, White Masks (from *Black Skin, White Masks*) Frantz Fanon	417
29	The Paradoxes of Integration (from *The Ordeal of Integration: Progress and Resentment in America's "Racial" Crisis*) Orlando Patterson	426

Part VIII Sociological Theory of Jürgen Habermas — 435

	Introduction to Part VIII	437
30	Modernity: An Unfinished Project (from *Habermas and the Unfinished Project of Modernity*) Jürgen Habermas	444
31	The Rationalization of the Lifeworld (from *The Theory of Communicative Action Volume 2: Lifeworld and System: A Critique of Functionalist Reason*) Jürgen Habermas	451
32	Civil Society and the Political Public Sphere (from *Between Facts and Norms: Contributions to a Discourse Theory of Law and Democracy*) Jürgen Habermas	469

Part IX Modernity — 491

	Introduction to Part IX	493
33	The Social Constraint towards Self-Constraint (from *The Civilizing Process: The History of Manners and State Formation and Civilization*) Norbert Elias	499
34	Modernity and the Holocaust (from *Modernity and the Holocaust*) Zygmunt Bauman	510
35	The Consequences of Modernity (from *The Consequences of Modernity*) Anthony Giddens	531
36	We Have Never Been Modern (from *We Have Never Been Modern*) Bruno Latour	546

| Part X | Crisis and Change | **561** |

Introduction to Part X — 563

37 Systemic and Antisystemic Crises (from *Adam Smith in Beijing: Lineages of the Twenty-First Century*) — 569
   Giovanni Arrighi

38 Reconfiguring Territory, Authority, and Rights (from *Territory. Authority. Rights: From Medieval to Global Assemblages*) — 579
   Saskia Sassen

39 The Modern World-System in Crisis (from *World-Systems Analysis: An Introduction*) — 587
   Immanuel Wallerstein

Index — 000

Notes on the Editors

Craig Calhoun is University Professor of the Social Sciences at New York University and President of the Social Science Research Council. His books include *The Roots of Radicalism* (2011), *Nations Matter: Culture, History and the Cosmopolitan Dream* (2007), *Nationalism* (1997), and *Critical Social Theory: Culture, History, and the Challenge of Difference* (1995). For the Centennial of the American Sociological Association, he edited *Sociology in America: A History* (2006). He was also editor-in-chief of the *Oxford Dictionary of the Social Sciences* (2002), and he recently published the three volume collection *Possible Futures* (2011) looking at the financial crisis, its aftermath, and other global challenges.

Joseph Gerteis is Associate Professor of Sociology at the University of Minnesota, Twin Cities. His work explores the race, class and the complexities of American national identity in politics and social movements. He is author of *Class and the Color Line: Interracial Class Coalition in the Knights of Labor and the Populist Movement* (2007) and is co-investigator of the American Mosaic Project at the University of Minnesota.

James Moody is Robert O. Keohane Professor of Sociology at Duke University, Durham, North Carolina. His work examines social networks, with an emphasis on social cohesion, diffusion, and network dynamics.

Steven Pfaff is Associate Professor of Sociology at the University of Washington where he is also affiliated with European Studies. He has published articles in journals such the *American Journal of Sociology, Theory & Society, Social Forces, Comparative Political Studies,* and *Journal for the Scientific Study of Religion*. His first monograph, *Exit-Voice Dynamics and the Collapse of East Germany* (2006), reflects his interests in comparative and historical sociology, political sociology, religion, and social movements.

Indermohan Virk is a lecturer in Sociology and Executive Director of the Patten Foundation at Indiana University. She teaches courses on sociological theory and race and ethnicity.

Acknowledgments

The editors and publisher gratefully acknowledge the permission granted to reproduce the copyright material in this book.

Chapter 1
Alfred Schutz, "The Phenomenology of the Social World," pp. 107, 113–16, 126–36 from Albert Schutz, *The Phenomenology of the Social World*. Evanston, IL: Northwestern University Press, 1967. Copyright © 1967. Reprinted by permission of Northwestern University Press.

Chapter 2
Erving Goffman, "The Presentation of Self in Everyday Life," pp. 17–25 from Erving Goffman, *The Presentation of Self in Everyday Life* (New York: Doubleday, 1959). Copyright © 1959 by Erving Goffman, used by permission of Doubleday, a division of Random House, Inc. and Penguin Books, UK.

Chapter 3
Herbert Blumer, "Symbolic Interactionism," pp. 46–8, 50–2, 78–89 from Herbert Blumer, *Symbolic Interactionism: Perspective and Method*, 1st edn. Upper Saddle River, NJ: Prentice-Hall, 1998. Copyright © 1969. Reprinted by permission of Pearson Education, Inc., Upper Saddle River, NJ.

Chapter 4
Randall Collins, "Interaction Ritual Chains," pp. 3–4, 5, 15, 42–5, 47–54, 55–61, 62–3, 81–3, 87 from Randall Collins, *Interaction Ritual Chains*. Oxford: Princeton University Press, 2004. © 2004 by Princeton University Press. Reprinted by permission of Princeton University Press.

Chapter 5
George C. Homans, "Social Behavior as Exchange," pp. 598–606 from George C. Homans, *American Journal of Sociology* 63: 6. Copyright © 1958 by American Journal of Sociology. Reprinted by permission of The University of Chicago Press.

Chapter 6
Peter M. Blau, "Exchange and Power in Social Life," pp. 19–31, 91–5 from Peter M. Blau, *Exchange and Power in Social Life*. New York: John Wiley and Sons, 1964. Copyright © 1964 by Peter M. Blau. Reprinted by permission of Judith Blau.

Chapter 7
Mancur Olson, "The Logic of Collective Action," pp. 9–16 from Mancur Olson, *The Logic of Collective Action: Public Goods and the Theory of Groups*. Cambridge, MA: Harvard University Press, 1965. Copyright © 1965, 1971 by the President and Fellows of Harvard College. Reprinted by permission of Harvard University Press.

Chapter 8
Michael Hechter, "A Theory of Group Solidarity," pp. 40–54 from Michael Hechter, *Principles of Group Solidarity*. Berkeley, CA: University of California Press, 1987. Reprinted with permission.

Chapter 9
Karen S. Cook, Russell Hardin, and Margaret Levi, "Cooperation without Law or Trust," pp. 83–5, 86–7, 87–8, 89–94, 98–100, 101–3 from Karen S. Cook, Russell Hardin, and Margaret Levi, *Cooperation Without Trust?* New York: Russell Sage Foundation, 2005. Copyright © 2005 Russell Sage Foundation, 112 East 64th Street, New York, NY 10021. Reprinted with permission.

Chapter 10
Mark Granovetter, "Economic Embeddedness," pp. 481–2, 482–8, 488–9, 490–2, 492–3, 508–10 from Mark Granovetter "Economic Action and Social Structure: The Problem of Embeddedness," *American Journal of Sociology*, 91: 3 (November, 1985). Copyright © 1985 by American Journal of Sociology. Reprinted by permission of The University of Chicago Press.

Chapter 11
Paul J. DiMaggio and Walter W. Powell, "The Iron Cage Revisited," pp. 147–60 from Paul J. DiMaggio and Walter W. Powell, "The Iron Cage Revisited: Institutional Isomorphism and Collective Rationality in Organizational Fields," *American Sociological Review*, 48: 2 (1983). Copyright © 1983 by American Sociological Review. Reprinted by permission of the authors and the American Sociological Association.

Chapter 12
Harrison White, "Catnets," from *Notes on the Constituents of Social Structure* (unpublished manuscript, 1966).

Chapter 13
Ronald S. Burt. "Structural Holes," pp. 8–10, 15–23, 30–4, 38–40, 44–5, 46 from Ronald S. Burt, *Structural Holes: The Social Structure of Competition*. Cambridge, MA: Harvard University Press, 1992. Copyright © 1992 by the President and Fellows of Harvard College. Reprinted with permission of Harvard University Press.

Chapter 14
C. Wright Mills, "The Power Elite," pp. 3–4, 6, 7–11, 287–9, 296 from C. Wright Mills, *The Power Elite*. Oxford: Oxford University Press, 1956. © 1956 Oxford University Press Inc. Reprinted with permission of Oxford University Press.

Chapter 15
Antonio Gramsci, "On Hegemony," pp. 326–31, 333–5, 338–43, 348–51 from Antonio Gramsci, *Selections from the Prison Notebooks of Antonio Gramsci*, edited and translated by Quentin Hoare and Geoffrey Nowell-Smith. New York: International Publishers, 1971. Reprinted with permission of International Publishers.

Chapter 16
Charles Tilly, "Coercion, Capital, and European States," pp. 1–5, 16–23, 96–9 from Charles Tilly, *Coercion, Capital and European States, AD 990–1990*. Oxford: Basil Blackwell Ltd., 1990. Reprinted with permission of Wiley-Blackwell.

Chapter 17
Steven Lukes, "Power: A Radical View," pp. 16–17, 19–21, 25–30, 34–8, 58–9 from Steven Lukes, *Power: A Radical View*, 2nd Edition. Basingstoke: Palgrave Macmillan, 2005. Reprinted with permission of Palgrave Macmillan.

Chapter 18
Anthony Giddens, "State Society and Modern History," pp. 7–17 from Anthony Giddens, *The Nation-State and Violence*, Volume Two of *A Contemporary Critique of Historical Materialism*. Palgrave Macmillan 1987. Reprinted with permission of Palgrave Macmillan.

Chapter 19
Michel Foucault, "The History of Sexuality," pp. 135–50 from Michel Foucault, *The History of Sexuality*, vol. I: *An Introduction*, translated from French by Robert Hurley. New York: Random House, Vintage Books, 1980. Copyright © 1978 by Random House, Inc., New York. Originally published in France as *La Volenté de Savoir*. Copyright © 1976 by Éditions Gallimard. Translation copyright © 1978 by Random House, Inc. Reprinted by permission of Georges Borchardt, Inc., for Éditions Gallimard, and Penguin Books Ltd.

Chapter 20
Michel Foucault, "Truth and Power," pp. 113, 115–17, 118–26, 131–3 from Michel Foucault, *Power/Knowledge: Selected Interviews and Other Writings, 1972–1977*, edited by

Colin Gordon. New York: Random House, Pantheon Books, 1972. Copyright © 1972, 1975, 1976, 1977 by Michel Foucault. Preface and Afterword © 1980 by Colin Gordon. Bibliography © 1980 by Colin Gordon. This collection © 1980 by The Harvester Press. Used by permission of Pantheon Books, a division of Random House, Inc.

Chapter 21
Michel Foucault, "Discipline and Punish," pp. 200–2, 215–16, 218–24 from Michel Foucault, *Discipline and Punish: The Birth of the Prison*. New York: Penguin Books, 1975. English translation copyright © 1977 by Alan Sheridan (New York: Pantheon). Originally published in French as *Surveiller et Punir: Naissance de la prison* (by Éditions Gallimard 1975, Allen Lane 1975). Copyright © 1975 by Éditions Gallimard. Reprinted by permission of Georges Borchardt, Inc., for Éditions Gallimard, and Penguin Books Ltd.

Chapter 22
Pierre Bourdieu, "Social Space and Symbolic Space," pp. 627–38 from Pierre Bourdieu, "Social Space and Symbolic Space: Introduction to a Japanese Reading of Distinction," *Poetics Today*, 12: 4 (1991). Copyright © 1991 by the Porter Institute for Poetics and Semiotics, Tel Aviv University. All rights reserved. Used by permission of the publisher, Duke University Press.

Chapter 23
Pierre Bourdieu, "Structures, *Habitus*, Practice," from Pierre Bourdieu, *The Logic of Practice*. Cambridge: Polity Press, in association with Blackwell Publishers, 1990. English translation copyright © 1990 by Polity Press. Originally published in French as *Le Sens Pratique* by Les Éditions des Minuit. Original French text copyright © 1980 Les Éditions des Minuit. Reprinted by permission of Stanford University Press and Georges Borchardt.

Chapter 24
Pierre Bourdieu, "The Field of Cultural Production, or: The Economic World Reversed," pp. 312–13, 315–16, 319–26, 341–6, 349–50, 353–6 from Pierre Bourdieu, *Poetics*, 12. Elsevier Science Publishers, B.V. (1983). Copyright © 1983 by Poetics. Reprinted by permission of Elsevier.

Chapter 25
Pierre Bourdieu, "Rethinking the State: Genesis and Structure of the Bureaucratic Field," pp. 1–5, 12–18 from Pierre Bourdieu, "Rethinking the State: Genesis and Structure of the Bureaucratic Field," translated by Loïc J. D. Wacquant and Samar Farage. *Sociological Theory*, vol. 12, no. 1 (Mar., 1994). Reprinted with permission of the American Sociological Association.

Chapter 26
Dorothy E. Smith, "The Conceptual Practices of Power," pp. 12–19, 21–7 from Dorothy E. Smith, *The Conceptual Practices of Power: A Feminist Sociology of Knowledge*.

Boston, MA: Northeastern University Press, 1990. Copyright © 1990 by Dorothy E. Smith. Reprinted by permission of University Press of New England, Hanover, NH.

Chapter 27
Patricia Hill Collins, "Black Feminist Epistemology," pp. 251–6, 266–71 from Patricia Hill Collins, *Black Feminist Thought: Knowledge, Consciousness, and the Politics of Empowerment*, 2nd edn. New York: Routledge, Taylor & Francis, 2000. Copyright © 2000. Reproduced by permission of the author and Routledge/Taylor & Francis Group, LLC.

Chapter 28
Frantz Fanon, "Black Skin, White Masks," pp. 17–8, 109–16, 216–22 from Frantz Fanon, *Black Skin, White Masks*. New York: Grove Press, 1967. Translated from the French by Charles Lam Markmann. Copyright © 1967. Reprinted by permission of Grove Press, Inc.

Chapter 29
Orlando Patterson, "The Paradoxes of Integration," pp. 15–6, 64–6, 68–74, 76–7 from Orlando Patterson, *The Ordeal of Integration: Progress and Resentment in America's "Racial" Crisis*. Washington, DC: Perseus Books, LLC, Counterpoint Press, 1997. Copyright © 1997 by Orlando Patterson. Reprinted by permission of Basic Civitas Books, a member of The Perseus Books Group.

Chapter 30
Jürgen Habermas, "Modernity: An Unfinished Project," pp. 39–40, 42–6, 53–5 from Jürgen Habermas, *Habermas and the Unfinished Project of Modernity*, edited by Maurizio Passerin d'Entrèves and Seyla Benhabib. Cambridge: Polity Press, 1996. Copyright © 1996. Reprinted by permission of The MIT Press and Polity Press.

Chapter 31
Jürgen Habermas, "The Rationalization of the Lifeworld," pp. 119–26, 136–45, 147–8, 150–2 from Jürgen Habermas, *The Theory of Communicative Action*, vol. 2: *Lifeworld and System: A Critique of Functionalist Reason*. Boston, MA: Beacon Press, 1981 by Jürgen Habermas. Translator's preface and translation © 1987 by Beacon Press. Originally published as *Theorie des kommunikativen Handelns, Band 2: Zur Kritik der funktionalistischen Vernunft*. © 1981 by Suhrkamp Verlag, Frankfurt am Main. Reprinted with permission of Beacon Press, Boston and Polity Press UK.

Chapter 32
Jürgen Habermas, "Civil Society and the Political Public Sphere," pp. 359–87 from Jürgen Habermas, *Between Facts and Norms: Contributions to a Discourse Theory of Law and Democracy*. Cambridge, MA: MIT Press, 1996. Copyright © 1996 Massachusetts Institute of Technology. This book was originally published as *Faktizität und Geltung. Beiträge zur Diskurstheorie des Rechts and des demokratischen Rechtsstaats*. Copyright © 1992 Suhrkamp Verlag, Frankfurt am Main, Germany. Reprinted with permission of MIT Press and Polity Press.

Chapter 33
Norbert Elias, "The Social Constraint towards Self-Constraint," pp. 443–8, 450–6 from Norbert Elias, *The Civilizing Process: The History of Manners and State Formation and Civilization*. Oxford: Basil Blackwell, 1978. Originally translated by Edmund Jephcott. Copyright © 1978 by Norbert Elias. Reprinted by permission of Blackwell Publishing Ltd.

Chapter 34
Zygmunt Bauman, "Modernity and the Holocaust," pp. 83–6, 86–95, 95–102, 103–4, 106–9, 111–13, 217–18 from Zygmunt Bauman, *Modernity and the Holocaust*. Ithaca, NY: Cornell University Press, 1989. Copyright © 1989 by Zygmunt Bauman. Reprinted by permission of Polity Press and Cornell University Press.

Chapter 35
Anthony Giddens, "The Consequences of Modernity," pp. 112–14, 120–5, 131–4, 137–50 from Anthony Giddens, *The Consequences of Modernity*. Stanford, CA: Stanford University Press, 1990. Copyright © 1990 by the Board of Trustees of the Leland Stanford Jr. University. Used with permission of the Leland Stanford Jr. University and Polity Press.

Chapter 36
Bruno Latour, "We Have Never Been Modern," pp. 130–45 from Bruno Latour, *We Have Never Been Modern*. Cambridge, MA: Harvard University Press, 1993. Copyright © 1993 by Harvester Wheatsheaf and the President and Fellows of Harvard College. Reprinted by permission of Harvard University Press. Originally translated by Catherine Porter.

Chapter 37
Giovanni Arrighi, "Systemic and Antisystemic Crises," pp. 1–2, 379–89 from Giovanni Arrighi, *Adam Smith in Beijing: Lineages of the Twenty-First Century*. (London: Verso, 2007). Reprinted with the permission of Verso.

Chapter 38
Saskia Sassen, "Reconfiguring Territory, Authority, and Rights," pp. 415–23 from Saskia Sassen, *Territory. Authority. Rights: From Medieval to Global Assemblages*. (Princeton: Princeton University Press, 2006). Reprinted with permission of Princeton University Press.

Chapter 39
Immanuel Wallerstein, "The Modern World-System in Crisis," pp. 76–90 from Immanuel Wallerstein, *World-Systems Analysis: An Introduction*. Durham, NC: Duke University Press, 2004. Copyright © 2004 Duke University Press. Reprinted by permission of the author.

Introduction

It is common to distinguish between "classical" and "contemporary" sociological theory, but the demarcation is vague. Perhaps most significantly, the dividing line continually shifts. In the 1930s, for example, the great American sociological theorist Talcott Parsons set out to synthesize what he regarded as crucial in the "classical" tradition. In his view, Max Weber and Emile Durkheim were among the most important classics. Each wrote during the late nineteenth and early twentieth centuries. Parsons saw himself as continuing work they had started. Part of what made them classical was precisely this continuing importance their work had for later analyses. But Parsons also saw himself as the new kid on the block, an innovator in his contemporary scene. He continued to produce influential original work through the 1960s and remained active until his death in 1979. Today, however, *his* work seems "classical". This has four meanings:

First, calling work "classical" means that it has stood the test of time and we are still interested in it. It is the opposite of "best forgotten". In this sense, Parsons surely aspired to have his work become classical.

Second, work we call classical tends to define broad orientations in the field of sociology. Reference to classical sociological theory is used to signal analytic approaches; it offers signposts to guide readers in seeing the intellectual heritage on which new theorists are drawing. Reference to Parsons signals, for example, a concern for "functionalist" approaches to questions of social integration, that is for understanding different social institutions and practices in terms of how they contribute to the successful workings of the whole.

Third, we term work "classical" when we acknowledge that there have been major new developments since it was written. This doesn't mean that the "classical" work has been superseded. What it means is that new perspectives and debates have been introduced to which the classical social theorist has not been able to respond.

Contemporary Sociological Theory, Third Edition. Edited by Craig Calhoun, Joseph Gerteis, James Moody, Steven Pfaff, and Indermohan Virk. Editorial material and organization © 2012 John Wiley & Sons, Ltd. Published 2012 by John Wiley & Sons, Ltd.

2 Introduction

In Parsons' case, a variety of innovations began to come to the fore in and after the 1960s. Some of these were directly criticisms of or challenges to Parsons' functionalism. He did respond to many, defending his perspective most of the time but also modifying it where he saw potential for improvement. Other parts of the new work, however, represented approaches that Parsons didn't consider. Jürgen Habermas, for example, combined some of Parsons' concerns with Marxism, critical theory, and symbolic interactionism in a way that Parsons had never anticipated.[1] Jeffrey Alexander led the way in developing a "neofunctionalism" that not only built on Parsons and Durkheim, but shifted the emphases of their theories in much more cultural directions, away from the sides of their work that emphasized economic organization and social institutions, and away from strong presumptions of value consensus.[2] Niklas Luhmann pioneered a systems analysis intended to correct some of the weaknesses of Parsons' functionalism and establish greater continuities between analysis of social and natural systems.[3] Classical theory still matters, thus, but we see it in new ways based on new ideas and interests.

Fourth, in order to understand classical social theory we make a special effort to understand its distinctive historical context. In fact all theory needs to be understood in historical context, but part of what we mean when we identify certain theories as "contemporary" is that we share the same broad historical situation with their authors. This is a key reason why what counts as "classical" keeps shifting.

Mid-Twentieth Century Transformations in Sociological Theory's Historical Context

When Parsons started writing his great synthetic work, *The Structure of Social Action*, in the 1930s, World War I was the biggest historical watershed separating the classical theories from the contemporary. Soon, though, the Great Depression of the 1930s – which was contemporary to Parsons – loomed larger as a divide. This was not just because of its historical importance but because of its theoretical importance. It led to work like that of the economist John Maynard Keynes and the sociologist T.H. Marshall. Keynes' theory played a central role in changing the way both social scientists and policy-makers thought about the relationship of the state to the economy. Keynes held notably that states could use their financial clout as major purchasers of goods and services to help to stimulate the economy and smooth out the business cycle and the tendency Marx had noted for capitalism to suffer recurrent crises of overproduction.[4] His theories influenced the New Deal in the United States and the rise of the welfare state in Europe – both projects that shaped social life and changed the issues with which social theory had to deal. Marshall's theory of citizenship also responded to the Great Depression (and to the new sorts of state responses), suggesting that citizenship needed to be reconceptualized as referring not merely to political rights, but to social and economic rights as well.[5]

In addition to the Great Depression – and recovery from it – fascism and World War II and the Cold War between the Communist East and the Capitalist West were shaping influences on social theory during the course of Talcott Parsons' career. There is debate about how they influenced his writing – for example, about the extent to which he was an advocate for what he saw as American values in a specifically Cold War framework – but there is no doubt that the historical context shaped his work.

These factors also shaped the work of most social theorists writing between the 1930s and 1960s. They posed big questions – like what enabled some societies to develop democratic institutions while others were prone to dictatorship. As the American sociologist Barrington Moore famously argued, this was a matter of different paths to modernization and of some very old historical conditions – like whether the premodern agriculture of a country involved serfs who were tied to the land in near slavery, or was based on more or less independent peasants.[6] The Cold War pitting the US against the Soviet Union influenced the ways in which American sociologists looked at other societies in the world. This was not just a matter of theoretical orientation but of financial support. Much new research was made possible by the fact that the US government gave grants for "foreign area studies," including help to social scientists to learn non-Western languages and engage in detailed studies of other ways of life. The government was concerned that in order to compete effectively with the Soviet Union in the Cold War, America needed experts on other societies. This provided the basis for a great expansion in social knowledge. At the same time, this knowledge was often guided by theories that asked whether other societies were likely to become "modern" in the European and American way – that is, as capitalist democracies – or in the problematic communist way. It took some time before people began to consider that there might be other ways of becoming modern that didn't fit either of those models – or that the economic and political power of the US and Europe might stand in the way of development in other countries as often as it helped it.

Especially from the 1960s forward, the historical context started to change in important ways. Not least of all, young sociologists began their careers who had been born after World War II and had never experienced the Great Depression. This doesn't mean that there was a sharp break. Many of the sociologists who became important leaders of the field in the 1960s and 1970s were old enough to remember the war (if not very much the Depression). New historical perspectives were important, though, both in leading to new theoretical ideas and in encouraging different uses of resources offered by classical theory. Immanuel Wallerstein, for example, emerged as one of the most important revitalizers of the Marxist tradition, and moved it forward in new and distinctive ways with his "world systems theory."[7] One of Wallerstein's central points was that in a world dominated by capitalist trade, poorer countries could not grow wealthy simply by following the example of those who had done so earlier. Because European and American countries already dominated the core of the capitalist world economy – the industries that innovated most rapidly and brought the most return on investment – the fate of other countries was not simply based on how "modern" they were, but whether and how they could compete in capitalist trade. Countries with less advanced technology and industry countries were always at a disadvantage in this. The likelihood that they would suffer under dictatorships rather than democracies was also explicable not just by internal factors, but by the influence of more powerful countries – including the US and the USSR.

Of course, core countries could lose their leading positions by failing to innovate or failing to invest enough in renewing their base in core sectors. Since the 1970s the US has been hampered by the proportion of its capital tied up in finance (and leveraged real estate investments), rather than more directly productive investments, by the cost of imported energy, and by the cost of its international military activities. This (and even greater weaknesses in some other core economies) has created room for other countries could move into increasingly core positions – as for example China and Korea have done. But world-systems analysis indicates that this is not just a matter of development, but of social relations among countries: in order for some to enter the core of the capitalist system others must be pushed out. The financial crisis of 2008 brought the issue of a change in the world system to prominence in newspapers, TV, and public debates – but it was produced not just by short-term miscalculations of bankers but also by social changes that had been going on since the 1960s (and that had shaped an earlier crisis in the 1970s).[8]

To draw a dividing line in the 1960s is partly symbolic but not arbitrary. It reflects the importance of the baby boom generation born after World War II, the renewed attention to internationalism and globalization that flourished in that decade after relative isolationism in the 1950s, the emergence of important new voices from the global South or Third World, the beginnings of the greatest phase so far of the modern women's movement, a variety of other social movements from environment to gay rights, and the impact of the American war in Vietnam. The 1970s crisis ushered in an era of financialization, intensified inequality, and competition for oil. The events of the 1960s and 1970s reshaped what social theorists saw as most significant in the social world – even if they did not always see these things in the same way. The 1960s and 1970s pushed sociological theorists to focus more on processes of social change (and resistance to change), on social inequality and on processes of marginalization and exploitation that shape it, on power relations and social movements that contest them, and on cultural and other differences among individuals and groups. These themes animate the work of many of the authors included in this volume. Of course, social change continues, and social theorists grapple with new issues including globalization and financial and political crises, as we see in the last sections of this book.

Individual and Society

Among the themes that came to the fore, none was more important than the relationship between the individual and society. This was obviously not all new, but it became newly unsettled and demanded attention. Erving Goffman, a pivotal American sociologist who changed forever the way in which people understood interpersonal relations, was only a few years younger than Parsons and began to publish important work in the 1950s, but his analyses did not become widely influential until the 1960s. By then they were pivotal, however, in calling attention to the way in which ritual and strategy intertwined in everyday phenomena like dating.[9] A date is like theater, in that each person has a role to play, and can play it better or worse. To some extent everyone knows that they are playing roles, not simply expressing themselves openly. At the same time, a date – like all social interaction – calls for improvisation. Participants seek to manage the impressions others form of them. But in order to do this successfully, they have to accept the social roles at least to some extent. Among other things, the popularity of Goffman's work reflected a new critical perspective on the social conformity of the 1950s.

One feature in the changed context was a widespread sense that people had more choice about their lives and the social roles they would assume. This reflected the new opportunities opening up in societies that were rapidly growing wealthier. In the US, for example, the percentage of the population going to college more than tripled, reflecting not only wealth but the growing shift from an industrial to an information society. As the American sociologist Daniel Bell wrote in one of the first books to analyze this change, to an ever-greater extent society was being organized around the production of knowledge, not only material goods.[10] Renewed attention to individuals and how they might fit into society was also shaped by what another American social theorist, Philip Rieff, called "the triumph of the therapeutic."[11] By this, Rieff meant the prominent place that both introspection and attempts at reformation of the self had assumed in modern culture. People not only went to therapists, they expected therapeutic work from ministers, teachers, and even television. This encouraged sociologists not only to analyze therapy, but to ask what was behind the change in culture.

The critical theorist Herbert Marcuse noted that capitalism had long seemed to require a certain repression of impulses. In *The Protestant Ethic and the Spirit of Capitalism*, for example, Weber had described the importance of saving and reinvestment, both dependent on resisting impulses to enjoy luxuries. Equally, it was important for workers and managers alike to be committed to hard work, disciplined, and rationalistic. This extended from strictly economic realms, Marcuse suggested, to sexuality and artistic creativity. (This is one reason why the Bohemian artist had long seemed such an affront to capitalism and to businessmen's understanding of rationalism.) The more consumer-oriented capitalism of the late 1950s and 1960s, however, brought with it a loosening of repression.[12] Not least, Marcuse argued, disciplining workers was no longer the main issue for capitalists; it was increasingly supplanted by motivating consumers. This could be a matter of irrational eroticism – selling cars by showing them with sexy models draped over the hood. Tolerance for new levels of aesthetic and erotic expression not only encouraged consumption, it muted tendencies to challenge the established order. In the era of the Keynesian welfare state, the established system of power and wealth was better able to manage the resistance and rebellions of ordinary people. This very idea is an indication of why we see this period as "contemporary" in regard to society and social theory, even though there have obviously been significant changes.

There were many different ways in which sociologists explored the relationship between individual and society. These drew on different roots in earlier, "classical" social theory. What the new theorists shared was a sense that there was a tension in this relationship. Although most agreed that there was no such thing as "pure individuality" outside of society, and that human beings developed personhood only as parties to social relationships, they did not take this to mean that the relationship between individuals and actually existing forms of society was harmonious – let along, as fulfilling as it could be. On the contrary, in various ways these theorists pointed to the ways in which people found themselves limited by the social conditions in which they found themselves. This was not just a matter of blockages in their way, of course, but often also of the absence of support systems. At the same time, people's aspirations did not simply come from within them; they were socially produced. Whether it was a matter of wanting faster cars, bigger TVs, or more fashionable clothes, this could not be understood simply from looking inside individuals but had to be understood at a sociological level. Likewise, the means people chose to pursue their goals were not automatic. Some would drop out of school to enjoy consumer goods immediately, even though this hurt their long-term prospects. Others would study hard in order to get into competitive colleges and graduate schools. Some would stick completely to legal means, others would turn to crime. Who did what was based on an interaction between personal characteristics and social organization.

One important approach to these questions focused on the ways in which people developed identities – for themselves and for others. "Labeling theory" was rooted in the symbolic interactionism of George Herbert Mead and his followers.[13] It started with the commonplace observation that many children steal but few become professional thieves (and conversely, most do homework but few become real scholars). Labeling theorists acknowledged that differences in talent and opportunity were and are important. For example, having parents wealthy enough to be able to send their children to college is a big predictor of whether those children become well-educated. But they added that what happens is also shaped by the labels that others come to apply (and individuals sometimes accept for themselves). Thus a youth who is caught and punished repeatedly for theft may come to be known as a thief (while one who gets away does not). Having the identity "thief" may close some doors, making it harder for example to get an honest job. Accepting the label for oneself may reduce inhibitions against stealing in the future. In short, the identity of the person and the social role ("thief," in this example) are both socially constructed. They do not exist "objectively," separate from social life and culture.

The Social and Cultural Construction of Knowledge

Many of the new explorations of the individual/society relationship were guided by attention to the capacities that individuals have for constructing the social world in new ways. As Alfred Schutz emphasized, for example, the ways in which people share understanding of their social world – what he called intersubjectivity – are effective in shaping that world itself as well as their identities as individuals within it.[14] Peter Berger and Thomas Luckman drew on Schutz's work to explore the ways in which the very construction of social knowledge was itself analyzable not simply as a matter of externally verifiable discovery but a reflection of social relations and everyday life concerns.[15] These theorists drew on phenomenology, a theoretical approach that had developed largely outside of sociology as a form of attention to individual consciousness, to develop a new sociology of knowledge and intersubjective understanding. Durkheim had been interested in phenomenology and some sociologists – like Goffman and Harold Garfinkel – combined Durkheimian attention to social structure with phenomenological concern for the ways in which individuals construct their social lives and their knowledge of the everyday social world.

The classical social theory of George Herbert Mead addressed similar questions and provided an alternative approach for many of the new generation of thinkers. Mead's theory was rooted in pragmatism, an American approach to philosophy that emphasized the extent to which all knowledge was grounded in practical experience and communication – not based simply on holding up a mirror to objective reality.[16] There are many different ways to understand any specific object in the world, the pragmatists suggested; which ones become important to people will depend on the tasks they are engaged in and the ways others they care about grasp the same objects. What this implied is that there is no way that anyone simply and directly gets reality right. Different cultures and even different scientific theories can with equal validity understand similar phenomena differently.

Questions about the social construction of knowledge – whether everyday or scientific – have become one of the major themes of the post-1960s period. Here the work of theorists reflects both struggles to come to terms with history and new awareness of cross-cultural diversity. For example, a number of social theorists have addressed the transformations in Western culture. Some of their work was shaped by a concern to understand how what had seemed in the nineteenth century to be a straightforward march of reason and progress could issue in the twentieth century in Naziism – or for that matter Stalinism. Their explorations involved not just research on the fascism or communism as special cases, but inquiries into how there might be potential for such disasters built into Western culture more generally.[17]

Michel Foucault, for example, sought to uncover the different characteristic approaches to knowledge of different epochs and emphasized the dramatic differences between them.[18] He saw the modern period as shaped by the rise of the individual, both as the basis of epistemology – the source of knowledge understood as empirical observation and philosophical reflection – and as a basic value – the independent actor. But instead of presenting this simply as progress, looking at it from within an individualistic point of view, he presented this as opening up a new set of problems. Individualism was a way of seeing the world and living in it, Foucault argued, and as such it was not a starting point for analysis but an effect to be explained. What produced this effect, he suggested, was more than anything else a set of disciplinary practices. The modern individual was ideologically understood as the fount of freedom – the self-craving free expression – but in fact was produced by demanding of people that they take on the task of self-discipline. The new individual was a person constantly aware of the gaze of others, including especially the gaze of authority. This was produced by the development of medical examinations, of schooling, of government statistics. It was reflected in an approach to law and morality that emphasized not just what people did – the external manifestations of wrongdoing – but their inner intentions. Even sexuality, Foucault suggested, was not simply a natural self-expression but a social phenomenon. It was shaped by ideas about "normality" and "performance" that were reflected not just in hostility towards homosexuals or other "deviants" but in anxieties to conform to expectations, the proliferation of "self-help" and "how-to" books and comparisons of each individual's own experience to that in movies or literature.[19] Individualism raised as many questions as it answered, and it called for a new focus on discipline as well as new kinds of "care of the self."[20] Everything from producing a sexual identity to maintaining a desirable weight became implicated in a new culture of bodily discipline.

Foucault was one of the most important social theorists to emerge in an initially French intellectual movement commonly called "structuralism" and later "poststructuralism."[21] Structuralism shared some of its classical roots with the sociology of Emile Durkheim, especially in his examination of the social sources of knowledge and intellectual categories.[22] Influenced by the linguist Ferdinand de Saussure, structuralism stressed the extent to which systems of meaning (language or culture) were based on the reference of terms to each other. Thus words get their meaning from relations to other words, not simply by pointing to things, nor from historical origins. The Austrian philosopher Ludwig Wittgenstein developed similar notions in his later work.[23] Both structuralism and Wittgenstein influenced social theory in and after the 1960s. They challenged not only ideas about language but underlying theories of knowledge that approached it as a more or less transparent mental representation of external reality. Some structuralists, like the French anthropologist Claude Lévi-Strauss, endeavored to decode universal patterns of meaning – possibly rooted in the brain itself.[24] Others, including Foucault, focused increasingly on the ways power and historical change shaped knowledge; this was what led to the label of "poststructuralism." Poststructuralists emphasized the difficulties of transcending specific cultures or systems of meaning without the dominance of one over another. They also urged attention to the ways in which each system of knowledge blocked attention to some kinds of understanding, imposing silences as well as enabling speech. Together these influences led to a new concern with culture not – as it had been for Parsons – as a source of values that unite a society but as an arena of contestation and difference.

Another poststructuralist sociologist, Pierre Bourdieu emphasized "symbolic violence" and the "struggle over classification."[25] Even within one society, he argued, culture was used not only to unite but also to dominate. Widespread ideology claimed that culture was simply a matter of meaning, thought, or aesthetic taste. This suggested that it was somehow the opposite of power and economic determination. But clearly, claims to have highly cultivated taste could be used to exclude those with "baser" tastes. Moreover, ideas like "art for art's sake" might seem to represent the reversal of the economic world but in fact they revealed economies of their own in which participants struggled over "cultural capital" rather than material, monetary capital. The logic of the competition was different, but it was still a competition. Indeed, to gain prestige as an artist, it was necessary to demonstrate that one put creativity ahead of material gain, to show individual "genius" required not producing art that found too easy and widespread a popular acceptance. To be seen as a literary artist and not just a writer, thus, a novelist had to differentiate himself from a journalist.[26] Outside the specialized field of art, the state and other powerful actors used cultural goods – like diplomas and public honors – to supplement the direct workings of the monetary economy. The operation of schemes of classification by race, gender, class, sexual orientation, artistic taste or other criteria offered a way to uphold social hierarchies that granted privilege to those on top. And the other side of classification and the development of fields shaped by status hierarchies was a demand for individuals to develop capacities to navigate in these complex environments – capacities (Bourdieu analyzed with the idea of the "habitus") that were embodied at a mostly unconscious level, hard to change, and thus a factor in reproducing inequality.

Inequality, Power, and Difference

One of the big issues that changed sociological theory in and after the 1960s was a new level of attention to class, race, ethnicity, gender, and sexual orientation. Of course these had been noticed by earlier generations. Class was a central theme for both Marx and Weber. The Chicago School that helped to pioneer American sociology had studied ethnicity both as a feature of urban life and as one of the issues resulting from immigration to the United States.[27] Chicago sociologists had also addressed race, though the most important classic work was that of America's first great Black sociologist, W.E.B. Dubois.[28] Despite the fact that sociologists had always been attentive to issues of social inequality and difference, though, during the period of functionalist dominance after World War II the theoretical emphasis had fallen overwhelmingly on social integration, consensus, and factors that held society together. The development of new social movements and conflicts during the 1960s and 1970s brought inequality, difference and struggle to center stage.

One symptom of this was that when Talcott Parsons produced his account of classical social theory, Marx was not an important figure. Each new generation has the opportunity to redefine what it finds useful in the classics, though, and during the 1960s and 1970s Marx, later Marxists like the Italian Antonio Gramsci, and the German critical theorists were rediscovered. They had always been better known in Europe than in the US (and indeed, functionalism was more dominant in the US). Younger sociologists were looking for different classics largely in order to analyze better the inequalities and conflicts they saw in contemporary society. Influenced by Marx and by actual social conflicts presented a model of society in which tensions and struggles were basic and unity was largely maintained by power. Parsons, by contrast, had paid little attention to the ways in which some people wielded power over others and controlled aspects of social organization. When he used the word "power" his emphasis was on the overall capacity of a society, not on the dominance of some members by others.[29]

Parsons and other functionalists emphasized the "systemic" character of social life, the extent to which social organization fit together so that every feature was necessary to the whole. The new generation of theorists criticized the implicit conservatism in this. They asked more frequently how society could change, how individuals could have an impact on the whole, and whether the functionalist model of the system masked real differences among members of a society. When functionalists said that the social system "worked," critics asked "worked for whom?" In both Europe and America, younger sociologists pointed out that society might successfully educate workers to have the skills needed for its industry but that didn't mean it educated students in all social classes equally, or gave them equal opportunities for creativity. They argued that the if generating wealth was one indicator of a society "working" than how equally or fairly that wealth was distributed should be another. Leading functionalists had argued that differences in wages and salaries mainly reflected a necessary incentive system.[30] The critics charged that it had more to do with power, with what class someone happened to be borne into, with privileges based unfairly on sex, race, ethnicity, and similar characteristics, and with the needs of capitalism rather than of society as such.

Starting with the premise that social inequalities were not always necessary or fair, theorists set out to understand what form they took, why they existed, how they could change and what power structures resisted change. This applied both domestically and internationally. Rather than assuming that "modernization" would bring about a convergence of all societies in which these would necessarily develop on a European-American model, researchers analyzed the structures of global inequality, who benefited from them, and how they were produced and maintained. Central to the new theoretical orientations were attention to power and to historical change and variability. These encouraged more critical perspectives because they shared the ideas that society could be different, that choices could be made.[31] It was necessary, in other words, to avoid equating the actually existing with the necessary or normal.

For example, many sociologists (and others) had long assumed that assimilation and integration were the necessary end results of migration (including the forced migration that brought Africans to America as slaves). Sociologists, like anthropologists, had long questioned the scientific status of racial distinctions. They argued that using skin color to classify human populations was arbitrary and a result of historical circumstance and pseudo-science (a view that genetic research has more recently supported). But during the 1960s, influenced by the Black Power movement, many sociologists began to go beyond this, questioning the goals of assimilation and racial integration. The basic question was how much of their own culture, identity, and claims to respect did African-Americans have to surrender to assimilate. It appeared to many that ending forced segregation (a main goal of the civil rights movement) only addressed half the issue. It questioned keeping Blacks out of white neighborhoods and other preserves, but didn't question whiteness as such, or the extent to which integration was only offered on the condition that Blacks act like whites. It appeared, in other words, as if greater economic and political equality for Blacks was offered at the expense of Black pride – that is, of recognition of the cultural achievements and self-understanding of Blacks themselves.

The issue, in other words, was not only one of equality but also one of recognizing cultural difference. This remains controversial, not least with regard to how much of their older culture new immigrants should retain. How rapidly, for example, should Spanish-speaking immigrants be expected to learn English? The other side of the question, of course, involves change in American society – including the growth in how many other Americans can speak Spanish. Immigration has also changed American religious life, both by bringing new religions and by changing the ethnic makeup of the members of different religious groups (as Latinos have become prominent in the American Catholic church). Church membership is also a way in which immigrants assimilate into American society, finding help with issues from jobs to housing as well as worshipping. Similar issues have arisen in Europe, both with regard to non-European immigrants, especially from Muslim countries, and with regard to internal migrations facilitated by European integration. Sociological theory is at the center of debates about how to preserve social solidarity while including people of different races, cultures, and backgrounds.

Some societies, like the United States and Canada, have found it much easier to be "multicultural." This is based in part on their immigrant histories, but also reflects other parts of national culture – like a sense that there is open land and room for everyone. But as basic as immigration has been to American society and its growth, it has always been controversial. Immigration is also highly controversial in European societies today. In order to understand what is going on, sociological theory focuses our attention not only on the characteristics of immigrants, but also on the characteristics of host societies.

American culture, for example, tends always to emphasize race. Out of its history of dealings with Native Americans and African Americans, the United States produced a distinctive racial formation.[32] Old categories were extended to new groups; for example, when Asian immigrants became more numerous Americans struggled to fit them into pre-existing racial categories and hierarchies. This process involved not merely the recognition of objective differences, but the racialization of social groups, the use of race to construct them in specific ways. Although this was most obvious in the case of minority groups against which there was discrimination, it was true also of whites. Whiteness was treated as a kind of "normal" characteristic, as simply American. Sociological research, however, helped people recognize that being white was also one particular – racialized – category, and that it was being given hierarchical privilege.

Similar concerns were raised in relation to gender, sexual orientation, ethnicity and other lines of difference. Rather than seeing differences between male and female as simply natural, for example, sociologists increasingly focused on the processes by which such differences were culturally constructed.[33] They did not treat this as a neutral feature of cultural difference, but went on to examine the ways in which the subordination of women was reproduced and maintained. The question was both one of cultural differentiation (women were more likely to become nurses, men more likely to drive trucks) and one of economic hierarchy (truck drivers were paid more than nurses).

The issue of difference was not just a matter of groups defined by a specific identity like race or gender. It applied to a whole variety of social practices. Consider family. The term "nuclear family" was coined in 1949 by the anthropologist George Peter Murdoch. Murdoch described it as a basic building block of larger structures – lineages, clans, and "extended families." He acknowledged, though, that America was unusual because it was commonly expected for the nuclear family to stand alone. This expectation took on the force of normalization. Television shows like *Ozzie and Harriett* and *Leave it to Beaver* presented this as simply the way families were. But as the sociologist Stephanie Coontz pointed out, this is not how most families ever really were.[34] And in fact, starting in the 1960s, nuclear families began to account for a smaller and smaller percentage of American households. From 45% in 1960 the proportion fell to 23.5% by 2000.[35] Even as this happened, the nuclear family continued to be treated by many as what was both morally right and normal – an implicit denigration of the actual – and often stable and supportive – living situations of others. From a functionalist point of view, this sometimes appeared as a breakdown in the normal pattern of social organization. To others, it didn't signify anything good or bad in itself; the questions were whether the other living arrangements brought people satisfaction, support, or other desirable results. Many pointed out that part of the rise of other living arrangements was in fact made possible by new levels of affluence and freedom of choice.

Theoretically, the most important of the new orientations emphasizing difference was feminism. Women's struggles for social equality entered a new phase of growth in the 1960s and theory was closely linked to the practical movement. This reflected in part the need to explain why gender inequality was as pervasive as it was – and simultaneously why this was not inevitable (as functionalist theory suggested) but open to change. Feminist theory simultaneously addressed two crucial themes: the material inequality between men and women, and the implications of the conceptual construction of gender categories. Sociologists studying class had often compared the incomes or wealth of men without attention to that of women; many reasoned that this was necessary because men were the main breadwinners in families. Especially in and after the 1960s, research focused on questions like what men and women earned when they had similar jobs or levels of education – and what explained the substantial inequalities that were found. As in the case of race and ethnicity, many of the newer sociological theories emphasized the role of power. This was often physical power, sometimes backed up by law. But it was also often the power of dominant culture. This raised the second major theme. The Canadian sociologist Dorothy Smith, for example, drew on both ethnomethodology and Marxism to construct a theory of the "conceptual practices of power."[36] Work like this drew attention to the ways in which seemingly neutral classifications like those of law courts and welfare agencies, censuses and indeed sociological surveys reproduced and helped to enforce certain normative understandings of how the world *should* work. These normative understandings commonly benefited men at the expense of women – for example by associating housework "naturally" with childbearing.

Feminist theory generally argued that material equality would be hard to achieve so long as cultural categories remained biased against women. This left open a major question, though. Did the elimination of bias necessarily mean seeing men and women as essentially the same? Or could it mean recognizing gender differences but valuing men and women equally? The issue was similar to that of whether the elimination of ethnic and racial discrimination necessarily depended on the assimilation of immigrants into host cultures – or, in the case of US race relations, on making blacks more like whites. An influential strand of theory in both racial and gender studies argued that such assimilationist thinking was a further reflection of inequality and power, not a way around it. Why should women need to become more like men in order to gain equivalent political or economic rights? While much of the empirical research in sociology continued to focus on material dimensions of gender inequality – in workplaces, political institutions, and families – a major strand of feminist theory focused more on questions of the cultural construction of difference. This was influenced by both the critical theory tradition and by French poststructuralist theory. Feminist theory of this sort also influenced the development of critical theories of sexuality. Linking these theories was concern to avoid assuming that there was one correct model for human identity or social life. Rather, theorists suggested, theory needed to address the ways in which differences could be recognized without unjust discrimination.

On an international scale, paying attention to power, inequality, and cultural difference meant reconceptualizing the ideas of progress and development. Much earlier work was based on evolutionary assumptions about social change and indeed (unlike most biological theories of evolution) suggested that historical change moved "forwards," that societies "advanced," and therefore that the conditions of the "leading" societies of any one period would reveal the future of others.[37] It was this sort of thinking that led Alexis de Tocqueville to travel to America to see Europe's future and Friedrich Engels to go to England during the industrial revolution to see what lay in store for Germany. Neither Tocqueville nor Engels was strictly an evolutionary theorist; Tocqueville stressed political choices that Europeans could make about how to democratize (though he thought democracy a trend of the age); Engels stressed conflict and struggle as shapers of social change. Many other theorists placed a greater emphasis on the "natural" ways in which they thought society would develop. The most influential of these in the twentieth century were "modernization" theorists.

Modernization theory drew on the actual social conditions of the richer Western European countries and the United States to construct a model of modernity. Then followers analyzed the paths by which other countries and parts of the world could become more modern – emphasizing the lessons offered by past "successful modernizers" like Britain and the United States. A common concern was for how poor countries – conceived as "traditional" – could achieve the developmental momentum to "take off" into a process of self-sustaining economic growth and modernization.[38] Modernization theory guided a range of important research projects which did indeed produce useful knowledge. However, especially in and after the 1960s, it was challenged on several fronts. Among the most important was the unilinear concept of social change widespread within it. Modernization was understood as a process moving in one pre-determined direction. Closely related was the criticism that modernization theory neglected power, including the power by which some societies dominated others and also the power by which elites within societies shaped the course of their growth and change. Third was the argument that modernization theory lumped all manner of very different cultural and social formations together into the category of "traditional" or pre-modernity.

As we noted above, more recent thinkers often argued that it was difficult for newly developing countries to follow the paths of those that industrialized in the nineteenth century precisely because they had to compete with these already technologically and economically advanced countries. Some have also questioned whether "modern" is a sufficiently precise concept. If one means "capitalism" or "democracy," these theorists suggest, it is best to say so clearly and study when and how they are linked rather than assuming that they automatically combine in "modernity." In the same vein, many hold that it is important to ask whether there might be multiple versions of modernity, different projects of modernization rather than a single path. For example, is socialism an alternative form of modern economy to capitalism? Is it right to see religious conservatives as always anti-modern? Or, are some Islamists, Hindu fundamentalists, and many Catholics and Protestants seeking to shape versions of modernity that accord with their values? These questions have come to the fore recently in response to the renewed pace of globalization of the 1990s and early 2000s. What it means to be a part of the modern world system has become an even more important questions with expansion of market relations, globalization of media, and farflung migrations. But fights over the World Trade Organization, exploitation of the environment, human rights, and other questions all suggest that there are diverse visions of modernity. Power and struggle, not just a natural course of development, shape which ones are realized. One of the advantages of recent sociological theory is the opportunity to learn from the history of the twentieth century.

Empirical Research

When Karl Marx and Friedrich Engels began to develop their sociological theory in the 1840s, empirical research was also in its infancy. Marx relied heavily on government reports and investigations into industrial conditions undertaken by British Parliamentary Commissions. These were not products of scientific research but rather interviews undertaken by officials, physicians, and others concerned about public welfare. Engels actually conducted one of the first sociological investigations into urban life. He walked several routes through Manchester and its environs and systematically recorded what he saw, and what he learned from those he talked to. Along with other data garnered mainly from businesses, this became a crucial basis for his book, *The Condition of the Working Class in England in 1844*.

At roughly the same time, a few other social scientists were pioneering empirical research methods. Economics was in the lead, with sociology second and close behind. Frédéric Le Play, for example, set out to examine the conditions of family life, systematically comparing different communities and economic conditions to see how they affected the organization of households.[39] Though he himself did not conduct significant empirical research, Auguste Comte heralded the significance of empirical evidence in his designation of a new "positivist" epoch in the organization of human affairs, in which science could truly guide practical organization.[40] Herbert Spencer relied on systematic examination of the reports of missionaries, colonial administrators and occasionally scientists to describe the social organization of different peoples around the world and construct his evolutionary theory.[41] His contemporary Charles Darwin had the advantage of personal participation in documenting biological diversity, but also relied on similar analyses of the reports of others, including substantially lay observers.[42]

The situation was only modestly better at the end of the nineteenth century and beginning of the twentieth, when Max Weber and Emile Durkheim produced their pioneering sociological analyses. Governments had begun to collect information about the population of most European countries on regular intervals – the modern census was basically created during the nineteenth century. Censuses were supplemented by labor statistics, mortality statistics, and a host of other indicators of the social experience of populations. Economic data on trade, business organizations, taxes and the like led the way, but widespread concern for the possible effects of industrialization and other social changes pressed the collective of other sorts of social data to the fore as well. When Durkheim set out in the 1890s to examine the social causes of suicide, he was able to rely on data about deaths collected by government agencies in several countries.[43] This improved the record-keeping that had long been undertaken by churches as they recorded births, marriages, deaths and similar information in different parishes. It was not yet fully scientific data – insofar as there was relatively little research underpinning techniques of data collection – but it was increasingly systematic data. Indeed, the growth of the state – and especially of a variety of government agencies charged with specific administrative tasks from education to defense to regulating the quality of food – was basic to the development of systematic data collection. The data gathered, in turn, were basic to helping sociology (and other social sciences) become more scientific.

At the same time, sociological theorists began to see the need to collect their own data. Max Weber was not satisfied with the information publicly available when he set out to analyze property relations and economic conditions in Germany's East Elbian district; he organized the collective of new data on "Junker capitalism" and the proletarianization of German peasants.[44] George Herbert Mead conducted both systematic observations of children and rudimentary experiments.[45] In each case, the developments of their theories led these pioneering sociologists to ask questions that previously available data couldn't answer.

From the seventeenth century on, but especially in the twentieth century, the simple availability of more reliable data was supplemented by improvements in statistics – quantitative techniques for the analysis of data.[46] Indeed, in many early cases the development of statistical techniques outstripped the availability of rigorous data. It was especially hard to gather certain sorts of data because they were controversial. Early sociologists wanted to know, for example, how employers treated their workers, how many hours child laborers worked, and what occupational injuries workers in different crafts suffered. They were not able to go directly to factories and survey employees; they relied instead on those who came forward as voluntary witnesses. Early social scientists also pioneered ways of collecting data systematically even when it could not be rendered in quantitative form. Anthropologists carefully documented kinship systems, for example, while at the same time sociologists set out to describe the forms of life in Europe's and America's rapidly growing cities or to record how immigrants adjusted.

What is most important to see here is the extent to which the growth of social theory was intertwined with the development of new approaches to empirical social research. If this was a factor in the nineteenth century, it became even more vitally important in the twentieth. The development of sociological theory was more clearly separated from the normative concerns of political philosophy; explanation became increasingly its goal. Theory also became part of a shared sociological enterprise with empirical research. Attention centered increasingly on the way the two came together in analyzing specific phenomena, and answering specific questions. Not only how did society work in general, but how did cities grow – and why in those patterns? Why did people migrate from one country to another – and what determined their success or integration into new settings? What kinds of social groups stuck together under pressure, which ones tended to split up, and why? How sociologists posed these questions, which ones they thought were important, and how they went about answering them were all shaped by theory. But at the same time, the theories offered predictions and explanations that either fit with available data or didn't – and contradictory data could drive the theorists back to the drawing board.

New data didn't change overall perspectives on society, but it changed the ways in which theorists explained specific aspects of social life within each perspective. For example, there was no datum that could prove it right to follow Weber in a more individualistic approach to social action or Durkheim in a more holistic approach to society as a separate level of analysis. But from either perspective, theorists struggled to explain new information about how society worked. This included both the results of empirical research into the relationship between specific variables and empirical observations of new events and historical developments. For example, the rise of fascism in the 1930s involved something new in history; it had not existed before and it challenged theories based on previous experience. But Weber's and Durkheim's theories were able to contribute to the analysis of fascism because they helped sociologists grasp important features. Weber's account of charismatic leadership could help explain Hitler's or Mussolini's roles in German and Italian mass movements. Durkheim's account of how large-scale rituals bind people together could help to explain why the grand spectacles staged by fascists were effective not just in spreading ideology or offering entertainment but in leading individuals to accept that the social whole was more important than any of its parts. But new research also added new dimensions that neither theoretical perspective completely anticipated. In their research on "the authoritarian personality," for example, Adorno and his colleagues showed that how individually rational people would be, and how they would respond to charismatic leadership, depended on their upbringing and experience of work and other relationships. This new research didn't overturn either Weber's or Durkheim's theory, but it pushed followers of each to add new dimensions, and to make general arguments about the nature of human beings and social life more attentive to variations in historical circumstances and culture. It also pressed for better integration between sociological and psychological analysis.

It was mainly in the 1950s and 1960s that quantitative empirical research in sociology took on its modern form and became a large-scale enterprise. The US was in the vanguard of this development.[47] The Depression and World War II played decisive roles as social science research was mobilized to aid first the New Deal and similar projects of social reconstruction elsewhere and then the war effort. On topics from social stratification and mobility to formal organizations, demography and group dynamics this produced important new knowledge and more precise tests of hypotheses. Techniques for data collection, data organization, and data analysis also grew more powerful. Sociology was based increasingly on the analysis of large-scale surveys and census data as well as ethnographic observation. Computers have contributed to different abilities to collect data – for example, now it is possible to study consumers' actual purchases not just ask them what they bought. And computers have contributed to the ability to use more complex statistics and models, and also to search more effectively in texts.

At the same time, the advances in research contributed to a differentiation between two senses of theory. On the one hand, some theory was very close to empirical research projects; it consisted largely of relatively formalized structures of hypotheses and confirmations. On the other hand, much of the classical tradition of sociological theory tried to offer large-scale perspectives on social life in general. Writing in the late 1950s, the American sociologist C. Wright Mills contrasted what he called "grand theory" and "abstracted empiricism."[48] The "grand theory" to which he referred was the attempt to build an all-encompassing theory of society exemplified by Talcott Parsons' functionalism. The "abstracted empiricism" was the practice of social research more and more concerned with technique, especially statistical technique. Mills was unhappy about both. While they took opposite paths, they complimented each other because neither encouraged the kind of critical awareness of social life that Mills thought important. Moreover, neither engaged adequately with the challenge of understanding specific patterns of historical change. They didn't help as much as the classical traditions of Marx, Weber, and Durkheim to connect the social issues people experienced in their everyday lives to an analysis of large-scale social patterns. Unemployment, divorce, and military service, for example, were biographical experiences of millions of individuals. The job of sociology, Mills contended, was to help people see how these were also organized on a society-wide scale: who was most likely to experience each? How did this reflect the class structure or the nature of political power?

Mills' Columbia University colleague Robert Merton was also concerned about the gap between the broadest theoretical perspectives that illuminated social life in general and the specific hypotheses and tests of empirical research. His suggestion was to emphasize what he called "theories of the middle range."[49] By these he meant theories which attempted to explain social phenomena which occurred in many different situations. They were thus more general than specific empirical findings about particular cases and less all-encompassing than broad theoretical perspectives like functionalism, Marxism, or symbolic interactionism. Merton thought these broad perspectives valuable as orientations, aids to thinking through more specific analyses. But he thought it crucial for a relatively young science like sociology to seek rigorous explanations of phenomena that were concrete but generalizable. His examples included theories of social roles, deviance, and reference groups. The last, for example, refers to analysis of the ways in which people compare themselves to others. Everyone derives a sense of his or her particular identity, level of success in life, and other characteristics largely through comparisons to other people. But no one compares himself to everyone; a key sociological question is how people determine who are the relevant comparisons. In the army, for example, sergeants are apt to compare themselves to lieutenants and corporals but not to generals. In high schools, football players are likely to compare themselves to other athletes more than to students in general – but to other students more than to drop-outs or adults. This and other examples yield the generalizable finding that the most meaningful comparisons are those to fairly similar and local others. There is more to reference group theory, but this illustrates the idea of identifying a generalizable phenomenon – comparisons within specific groups – that is neither a general theory of society nor a research finding specific to one case, merely a single tested hypothesis. Reference groups are influential in dating behavior (as people judge who is likely to go out with them or how others view their partners), in job satisfaction (as people judge their salaries and their treatment by peers and superiors), and even in job performance (as people look at others to see whether they are working hard enough, or harder than they have to).

The connection between empirical research and sociological theory is often strongest and most balanced at the level of theories of the middle range. These may focus on a wide variety of phenomena from revolutions to consumer behavior. Two of the most important lines of development of middle-range theories address structures of social relations (networks) and the way social actors make decisions (exchange and rational choice theories). In the work of the most ambitious advocates for each theory, these may look like grand theoretical perspectives like Parsons' functionalism – i.e., a few passionate theorists claim that *everything* is a matter of either network structures or rational choice. But though these theories like others are shaped by broad perspectives and orientations, they are at their most productive in abstracting certain generalizable features of social life and concentrating on how they operate in many different kinds of social circumstances. Rational choice theorists know that no one is perfectly rational and network theorists know that structural patterns are only part of what makes social relationships meaningful. But each of these theories makes it possible to abstract from particular cases and compare aspects of social life across diverse contexts.

The central idea in network approaches to social structure, for example, is to abstract the *form* of social relationships from their *content* and then to compare formal structures and analyze the effects of variation. For example, within any collection of people, we could start by asking what is their density of their interrelationships (i.e., how many of any specific type of possible connections between them actually exist). How many of the brothers in a fraternity are actually close friends, for example? Then one can go on to ask what factors explain where the connections exist and where they are absent (is it, for example, a matter of which year in school the men are, or what they study, or where their rooms in a shared house are located)? Then, one could compare many fraternities and ask what are the differences in the patterns of relationships found. The same sort of analysis has been applied not only to friendship groups but to structures like those linking corporations through their boards of directors; those linking banks or law firms to particular clients; those shaping the organizations and recruitment of participants to protest movements; and those determining the spread of sexually transmitted diseases. In developing such analyses it is as important to see where relationships are absent as where they are present. For example, in groups of equivalent density, there are usually some members densely knit into social relationships and others relatively isolated from them. Analysts ask whether there are consistent, predicable patterns to the behavior of these social isolates or to those more strongly integrated into networks.

While the phenomenological and symbolic interactionist (or pragmatist) approaches to relations of individual and society emphasized the construction of meaningful relationships, others emphasized pursuit of strategic advantage. People did not simply adapt to social norms or follow cultural rules, theorists suggested. Rather, social actors chose strategies for trying to present themselves in the most favorable light, trying to get the best possible response from other people, trying to come out ahead in interpersonal relationships even while preserving the illusion of equality or reciprocity. Drawing on economics and on behavioral psychology, theorists like Peter Blau and George Homans approached social interactions as exchanges.[50] Later theorists expanded these approaches into "rational choice theory," continuing to draw on interdisciplinary collaboration with psychology and especially economics.[51] They stressed Weberian methodological individualism, but for the most part abandoned Weber's interpretative search for the meaning actors attach to their social actions. Instead, rational choice theorists tried to develop models that predicted what rational, self-interested actors would do to pursue their advantage in any situation. When would it be rational to cooperate, for example, and when not? The answer would depend, of course, not just on the characteristics of the actors but on the structure of opportunities and constraints open to them. These models could then be used to explain actual behavior – or to identify deviations from rational action in order to seek explanations for these.

Examining the relationship between individual and society is one of the sources of intellectual excitement in modern sociology, and also one of the reasons why it is perennially controversial. This is partly simply because sociology challenges a widespread everyday individualism in contemporary society – an individualism that is particularly extreme in the US. Sociology reminds people who like to think they are in complete control of their own lives that they are not; it reminds people who say they are completely independent that they in fact depend on others and on a whole social system. It even reveals that when we make our own choices they do not simply express our individual distinctiveness but predictable sociological patterns. Much in our contemporary world is set up to encourage people to think in terms of the uniqueness of individual identity and the complete freedom of choice – people sometimes resist recognizing limits to these.

Controversy and Resistance

Sociological theory has often been controversial. Perhaps no reason is more basic than the efforts of sociologists to make explicit and openly understandable social phenomena that many people have strong interests in keeping implicit and inaccessible. Certainly this includes issues like who benefits from social inequality and injustice. Call them the "big issues"; there are certainly big interests behind keeping them obscure. But the resistance to clear sociological understanding comes not only from the rich and the powerful but from all of us.

We all invest ourselves in social misunderstandings, and some of these actually help to make social relationships work. We say, for example, that we give gifts out of a pure spirit of love or generosity. In fact, however, most people modulate their giving to match gifts they receive from others. The American sociological theorist Alvin Gouldner attributed this to the "norm of reciprocity," the idea that social relationships depend on exchanges that people judge to be appropriate.[52] This applies even in conversation itself. If I say "hello," the norm of reciprocity requires you to respond in kind. But, as the French sociological theorist Pierre Bourdieu points out, this is a more complex game. It depends not only on a good sense of what is appropriate (how to play the game) but on shared and socially reproduced "misrecognitions."[53] We say the gift requires no response, but in fact expect one – either a matching gift in a kind of exchange or appropriate thanks and deference. But we resent having this pointed out. We prefer to think of ourselves simply as being generous, and the gift only does its work in cementing relationships if the norm of reciprocity does not become too obvious. If giving is seen as too transparent an attempt to curry favor, to get something in response, it is less valuable.

From the relatively humble example of gifts, we can see sources of resistance to sociological analysis, to attempts to expose the real interests behind accepted social practices and arrangements. And this extends through the build of personal relationships (e.g., dating and marriage), the building of complex organizations (like businesses or political parties), to the creation of states, governments and whole societies. People getting married say that it is "until death do us part" even though they know that nearly half of marriages end in divorce. They often really mean it, and meaning it may help nurture commitment and make marriages last. A variety of social factors influence whether marriages actually last – financial circumstances, career pressures, children, support groups. Love and commitment between two individuals are important, but not the whole story. Yet, we tend to resist the message that something so personal could be explained by generalizable social factors – or at least, we resist applying those generalizations to ourselves.

Take a different example: is rap music an expression of individual artistic creativity, Black culture, or corporate capitalism? Rappers have an investment in the first and they and their listeners often have an investment in both the first and the second. But rappers, audiences, and music companies all have an interest in the last not being too apparent. As West-Indian born sociologist Paul Gilroy observes, rappers may appear as sexual rebels and as Black men challenging authority, but the organization of the music industry channels this for profit and the organization of actual politics makes this form of challenge much less radical than some other forms of Black Power movements. Gilroy worries that a musical tradition that was genuinely creative and politically challenging is being reduced to "marketing hollow defiance."[54] But listeners who want to hear a deeper politics, or fit into a fashion, or simply have a good time all have an interest in not considering the question – as do rappers who want to stay popular and music companies that want to make money.

This is not simply a matter of deceit. Rappers and media companies may both be honest about being in the business for the money. It is a matter of how people construct meaning in social life and resist disruptions to it. This works on a larger scale too. Many people believe that their ethnic, racial, or national identities are clear-cut and natural. They resist sociological analyses showing how blurred the boundaries are, how much the categories are invented, and how often they are manipulated. Within each group, people may have an ideology that stresses community and sharing – a common fate – and obscures how some members of the group take advantage of others. They resist sociological analyses demonstrating how deeply members of the same race or nation are divided by class or how appeals to upholding traditional ethnicity may carry a gender bias.

Or again, take the question of whether "society" is defined by or epitomized by the nation-state. It is common to speak of Chinese society, Indian society, or Egyptian society. But each of these focuses on a particular set of boundaries produced by the formation of a nation-state and raises various questions. First, what about people of the same or similar ethnic backgrounds that are outside the state (as many Taiwanese consider themselves outside the People's Republic of China)? Second, what about changes in definition, as for example India was partitioned in 1949 to produce Pakistan and Pakistan was later divided to produce Bangladesh? Third, states are organizations of power and bureaucracy, but nations are largely matters of cultural identity and society is a web of social relationships, interactions, and interdependence. These all extend across the borders of states and nations. This creates new issues of diversity but also new conflicts and challenges as for example immigration has become a political issue in many countries. Sociologists have analyzed these questions for years, showing the importance of both power relations and interdependence organized by markets and also by communities, religions, families and other kinds of social institutions. Power may stabilize social relations, but is also subject to revolutions and upheavals. We have only to think of how several dictatorships in the Arab world were toppled by popular movements in the Spring of 2011; national identities like Egyptian were complemented by transnational identities like 'Arab' and 'Muslim'. At the same time, markets organize much of our lives but sometimes are disrupted in periods of crisis, as during the financial crisis that gripped the world in and after 2008. Whether these produce a return to some pre-existing "normal" state or lead to larger transformations is a question of basic importance.

Conclusion

Contemporary sociological theory is enormously diverse and multifaceted. It includes macroscopic studies of the structures of power, production, and trade that link and separate countries. It includes studies of interpersonal relations that emphasize both the process of communication and the formal structure of networks. And it includes a variety of levels of analysis in between.

No single theory or perspective is dominant. Contemporary sociological theory includes a variety of contending but also often complementary perspectives and is informed by work in various neighboring disciplines and interdisciplinary fields. While any particular sociologist may make more use of feminist theory or rational choice theory or some other specific approach in his or her analyses, almost all draw on several theoretical traditions. These include both classical and more recent theoretical writings. Indeed, all contemporary theories draw on some combination of classical influences, though some of today's theorists follow more in the line of Marx, others Weber, and still others Durkheim or Mead.

That different theories can complement each other doesn't mean that they always fit neatly together. On the contrary, theories often start with different assumptions about human nature, or about the nature of knowledge (epistemology); they frequently focus on different levels of social reality. These differences mean that fitting them together in any specific analysis always requires creative work and decisions. Theory is something to do, not simply to read. The theoretical resources available to today's sociologists are enormous, but this doesn't mean that theoretical work can stop.

NOTES

1 Habermas, Jürgen. 1984, 1988. *The Theory of Communicative Action*. Boston, MA: Beacon.
2 Alexander, Jeffrey. 1998. *Neofunctionalism and After*. Cambridge, MA: Blackwell.
3 Luhmann, Niklas. 1982. *The Differentiation of Society*. New York: Columbia University Press.

4   Keynes, John Maynard. 1935. *General Theory of Employment, Interest, and Money*. New York: Harvest.
5   Marshall, Thomas. 1970 [1950]. *Citizenship and Social Class*. London: Pluto.
6   Moore, Barrington. 1966. *Social Origins of Dictatorship and democracy*. Boston, MA: Beacon.
7   Wallerstein, Immanuel. 1974. *The Modern World System*, vol. 1. New York: Academic Press.
8   See Calhoun, Craig, ed. 2011. *Business as Usual: The Roots of the Global Financial Meltdown*. New York: New York University Press.
9   Goffman, Erving. 1961. *The Presentation of Self in Everyday Life*. New York: Doubleday.
10 Bell, Daniel. 1974. *The Coming of Post Industrial Society*. New York: Basic Books.
11 Rieff, Philip. 1987. *The Triumph of the Therapeutic*. Chicago, IL: University of Chicago Press.
12 Marcuse, Herbert. 1964. *One-Dimensional Man*. Boston, MA: Beacon.
13 Becker, Howard. 1963. *Outsiders: Studies in the Sociology of Deviance*. New York: Free Press; Lemert, Edwin. 1951. *Social Pathology*. New York: McGraw-Hill.
14 Schutz, Alfred. 1960. *Phenomenology of the Social World*. Evanston, IL: Northwestern University Press.
15 Berger, Peter and Luckman, Thomas. 1967. *The Social Construction of Knowledge*. New York: New American Library.
16 Richard Rorty clarifies the difference between pragmatism and more conventional philosophical epistemology in *Philosophy and the Mirror of Nature* (Princeton: Princeton University Press, 1977).
17 This was an important theme for the critical theory of Max Horkheimer and Theodore Adorno, e.g., *Dialectic of Enlightenment* (New York: Herder and Herder, 1972; orig. 1946). This enjoyed a surge of popularity in the 1960s and 1970s.
18 Foucault, Michel. 1977. *Discipline and Punish*. New York: Pantheon and *The Order of Things* (New York: Random House, 1966) among many other works.
19 Foucault, Michel. 1976–88. *The History of Sexuality*. New York: Pantheon, 3 vols.
20 Foucault, Michel. 1988. *Care of the Self*. New York: Vintage.
21 See Dosse, Francois. 1997. *History of Structuralism*. Minneapolis, MN: University of Minnesota Press. Though related, this is distinct from the structural approach to the study of social relationships and networks prominent American sociologists (see below).
22 Durkheim, Emile. 1976 [1912]. *The Elementary Forms of Religious Life*. Glencoe, IL: Free Press.
23 Wittgenstein, Ludwig. 1999. *Philosophical Investigations*. Englewood Cliffs, NJ: Prentice-Hall.
24 Levi-Strauss, Claude. 1970. *Structural Anthropology*. New York: Basic Books; 1967. *The Raw and the Cooked*. Chicago, IL: University of Chicago Press.
25 Bourdieu, Pierre. 1976. *Outline of a Theory of Practice*. Cambridge: Cambridge University Press; 1998. *Practical Reason*. Stanford, CT: Stanford University Press.
26 Bourdieu, Pierre. 1984. *Distinction*. Cambridge, MA: Harvard University Press; 1996. *The Rules of Art*. Stanford, CT: Stanford University Press.
27 Thomas, William I. and Znaniecki Florian. 1995. *The Polish Peasant in Europe and America*. Urbana, IL: University of Illinois Press.
28 See especially DuBois, W.E.B. 1989 [1903]. The Souls of Black Folk. New York. Dover.
29 Parsons, Talcott. 1951. *The Social System*. Glencoe, IL: Free Press; Anthony Giddens, "The Concept of 'Power' in the Writings of Talcott Parsons," in *Studies in Social and Political Theory* (New York: Basic Books, orig. 1967).
30 In the words of Kingsley Davis and Wilbert E. Moore "Social inequality is … an unconsciously evolved device by which societies ensure that the most important positions are conscientiously filled by the most qualified persons," "Some Principles of Stratification," *American Sociological Review*, 10 (2) (1945): 242–9, p. 248.

31 This is the basic premise of critical theory in contrast to what is often called "positivism". See Craig Calhoun, "The Critical Dimension in Social Theory," in J. Turner, ed., *Sociological Theory Today* (Beverly Hills, CA: Sage).
32 See, for an influential theoretical synthesis of this line of analysis, Omi, Michael and Winant, Howard. 1991. *Racial Formation in the United States*, 2nd edn. New York: Routledge.
33 This focus had its own classics to draw on, of course, including not least of all Margaret Mead's *Sex and Temperament in Three Primitive Societies* (New York: Morrow, 1988; orig. 1935).
34 Coontz, Stephanie. 1992. *The Way We Never Were*. New York.
35 US Bureau of the Census, preliminary reports on the US Census for 2000; *Statistical Abstract of the United States, 2000*. Note that these statistics involve a fairly strict definition of the nuclear family – two parents living together with children. While this arrangement has become less common it still reflects a social ideal. Moreover, alternatives are not simply "non-families" but different arrangements: single parents with children; married couples who live with one or more of their parents, etc.
36 Smith, Dorothy. 1990. *The Conceptual Practices of Power*. Boston, MA: Northeastern University Press.
37 For a critique of the confusion of development with evolution, see Nisbet, Robert. 1969. *Social Change and History*. New York: Oxford University Press.
38 See notably Walter W. Rostor, *The Stages of Economic Growth* (Cambridge: Cambridge University Press 1960).
39 LePlay, Frederic. 1870. *L'Organisation de la famille selon le vrai modele signale par l'histoire de toutes les races et de tous les temps*. Tours: Mame.
40 Comte, Auguste. 1987. *The Positive Philosophy*. New York: AMS Press.
41 Spencer, Herbert. 2001. *The Principles of Sociology*. New Brunswick, NJ: Transaction Publishers.
42 Darwin, Charles. 1982. *Origin of Species*. New York: Viking.
43 Durkheim, Emile. 1951 [1897]. *Suicide*. New York: Free Press.
44 Weber, Max. 1924. "Die landliche Arbeitsverfassung," in *Gesammelte Aufsatze zur Sozial und Wirtschaftugeschichte*. Tubingen: J.C.B. Mohr.
45 Mead, George Herbert. 1898. "The Child and His Environment", *Transactions of the Illinois Society for Child Study* 3: 1–11.
46 See Stigler, Stephen M. 1990. *The History of Statistics: The Measurement of Uncertainty before 1900*. Cambridge, MA: Harvard University Press.
47 On the history of American sociology, see Calhoun, Craig, ed. 2006. *Sociology in America*. Chicago, IL: University of Chicago Press.
48 Mills, C. Wright. 1959. *The Sociological Imagination*. Harmondsworth: Penguin.
49 Merton, Robert. 1968. *Social Theory and Social Structure*, 3rd edn. Glencoe, IL: Free Press.
50 Blau, Peter. 1964. *Exchange and Power in Social Life*. New York: Wiley; Homans, George. 1961. *Social Behavior: Its Elementary Forms*. New York: Harcourt, Brace, and World.
51 The single most influential and broadly developed sociological contribution to rational choice theory is James Coleman's *Foundations of Social Theory* (Cambridge, MA: Harvard University Press, 1990).
52 Gouldner, Alvin. 1960. "The Norm of Reciprocity," *American Sociological Review* 25: 161–78.
53 Bourdieu, Pierre. 1988 [1980]. *The Logic of Practice*. Stanford, CT: Stanford University Press.
54 Gilroy, Paul. 2000. *Against Race: Imagining Political Culture beyond the Color Line*. Cambridge, MA: Harvard University Press.

Part I

Micro-Sociological Analysis

Introduction to Part I
1 The Phenomenology of the Social World
2 The Presentation of Self in Everyday Life
3 Symbolic Interactionism
4 "Interaction Ritual Chains"

Introduction to Part I

Social life is part of every individual and every interaction, not only of the large-scale affairs of governments, economies, and complex organizations. Sociology that focuses primarily on persons and interpersonal relations is called "micro-sociology." This can be relevant on a large scale: how members of a corporation's board of directors interact, for example, can determine whether 10,000 people lose their jobs or an entire country experiences an economic crisis. Micro-level decisions are the basis of many macro-sociological phenomena; individual decisions, each small in themselves, can also be aggregated to have huge effects. Consider how decisions to have children, or to migrate, to invest in education, or what and how much to buy, combine to produce population crises, "brain drains," burgeoning college enrollments, or recession. Even without attention to their large-scale effects, micro-sociological phenomena matter to us because we can see their effects on people involved in everyday life. Indeed, it is often easiest for us to see ourselves in the "micro" part of sociology.

There are many different approaches to micro-sociological analysis. Perhaps the most prominent is symbolic interactionism, developed on the basis of work by George Herbert Mead in the early twentieth century and pioneered by Herbert Blumer. This approach emphasizes that people develop their identities and their senses of how society works and what constitutes fair play in the course of their interaction with each other. It is linked theoretically to the pragmatist school of American philosophy, which emphasizes the ways that not only social order but all knowledge is achieved in practically situated action.

A second major line of micro-sociological analysis is rooted in the European philosophical tradition called phenomenology. This emphasizes close observation of human experience and especially the ways that the basic categories of understanding are formed. This has been developed directly in the social phenomenology of Alfred

Schutz and followers like Peter Berger and Thomas Luckmann, and has been a major influence on "ethnomethodology," an approach developed especially by Harold Garfinkel and colleagues in California. Ethnomethodology refers to the methods ordinary people use to construct their own everyday understandings of social life, confronting practical challenges and shaping reality through the ways in which they conceptualize it. In this sense, it is a bottom-up rather than top-down approach to the study of culture (*ethnos*).

Still a third approach reveals some similarities to each of the others but is also distinct. This is the idiosyncratic but highly influential sociology of Erving Goffman. Goffman built his approach to micro-analysis on the basis of Durkheim's social theory, trying to show how the sort of large-scale phenomena Durkheim analyzed were produced and reproduced in interpersonal interaction. Much interaction is ritualized, he suggested, in ways that make it reinforce the social order and prevent it from becoming highly disruptive. Goffman also developed theoretical approaches to aspects of communication, institutional analysis, and perhaps most famously the presentation of self in everyday life – how we show ourselves to others (and simultaneously determine which aspects are visible and which hidden).

Challenges of Micro-Sociological Analysis

Micro-sociological theory grew, in large part, as a counterpoint to the dominance of structural functionalism in the mid-twentieth century, although its antecedents had been present in sociological theory, and in philosophy, far earlier. Structural-functionalism, and the Durkheimian tradition in sociology more generally, focused on the social system as a whole, its functional requirements, and the ways that these requirements are met (see *Classical Sociological Theory*, the sister volume to this reader). In doing so, it tended to treat human agents as cogs in the machine of social forces. Even the early work of Talcott Parsons, which was greatly concerned with social action, was more clearly about action *systems* than about *actors* and their subjective orientation to the action at hand and to the other actors it involved.

Micro-sociologists, by contrast, emphasized the other side of social existence. Just as humans are shaped by the social system in which they act, the micro-sociologists emphasized that the social system was also a human creation. Rather than order being imposed on individuals by the system, micro-sociologists see social order as produced from below – either as an emergent phenomenon produced through human interaction or as the result of discrete, self-interested action and exchange. It is created and maintained, they claim, by the institutions that we actively produce, even when we are not aware of them. Because of this, society itself rests on the ability of human agents to communicate with one another through the use of symbols to signify particular meanings. This highly evolved capacity for communication based on complex, abstract symbolic systems, is, in fact, one of the features that distinguish humans from other species. Although there are different theoretical traditions in micro-sociology, some of which will be discussed more fully below, in a general sense it can be said that micro-sociology is characterized by at least three common elements.

First, micro-sociologists place emphasis on the face-to-face social interaction of human agents rather than on the workings of the social system as an abstract entity. It is not quite correct to say that they focus on individuals, since it is really the creation and maintenance of stable systems of meaning *between* individuals that micro-sociologists find fascinating. But it is true that micro-sociologists generally focus on the interactions of concrete human agents or sets of agents rather than abstract social units such as classes.

Second, micro-sociologists place emphasis on meanings rather than functions. Here the influence of Max Weber and George Herbert Mead are evident in later micro-sociology. For Weber, sociology was the study of social action. Because it is individuals who carry on social action, Weber stressed that sociology had to be an interpretive science. That is, we should strive to provide *objective* accounts of the *subjective* motivations of the actions of individuals. Doing this necessarily involved taking into account the meanings that people assigned to their actions. Weber's own empirical analyses tended to examine highly routine forms of social action, however. Later micro-sociologists began to examine the way that even everyday interactions are supported by the meanings produced and maintained in social interaction. Here Mead's emphasis on the role of verbal and non-verbal symbols in the creation of meaning becomes central to micro-sociology. Although we are all born with the capacity to interpret symbols, it is only through the use of such symbols in interaction that humans acquire a "self" – a sense of who we are in the world. In this way, the micro-sociologists stress the *intersubjective* aspects of human existence.

Third, micro-sociologists emphasize lived experience rather than an abstracted (or reified) concept of "society." The authors in this section generally grant that social institutions, once produced, do confront us as external and "objective" realities. Nevertheless, they focus on the way that human agents experience regularized patterns of social interaction (or "institutions") and how they support them in both big and small ways. The exchange of symbols allows us to form solidarity with others by allowing us to come to common definitions of the world. Even seemingly banal social institutions such as greeting rituals have important symbolic meanings. As the sociologist Harold Garfinkel showed, we rarely recognize the importance of such institutions until they break down.[1] When we cannot take such minor routines for granted in our interactions, we have to do a great deal of interpretive work to figure out how to understand each interaction we face. Additionally, as the readings below will argue, our past experiences matter in how we interpret the world. This is why people who meet for the first time, especially when they come from very different backgrounds, have to spend so much more energy to understand one another than do people who see each other every day.

The Development of Micro-Sociological Analysis

Micro-sociology did not develop all at once, and it did not all develop in the same way. While the core concerns of the authors presented below are common enough to warrant including them in one section, we must take some care to note some of the different traditions of micro-sociological analysis as well. Loosely speaking, the authors in this section may be grouped into three headings – phenomenology, symbolic interactionism, and the "dramaturgical" approach of Erving Goffman.

Phenomenology is the oldest of the traditions. Originally a branch of social philosophy, its modern form was related to the existentialist thought of Kierkegaard, Heidegger, and later Sartre. It became a more properly sociological tradition with the work of Alfred Schutz (1899–1959) and others. Sociological versions of phenomenology were influenced by several sources, including Marx and the Frankfurt School critical theorists (see *Classical Sociological Theory*). Schutz's version, unquestionably the most prominent, was deeply influenced by Weber's conception of a sociology based on interpretive understanding, as will become clear in the reading below.

In all its forms, phenomenology was concerned with an old question – what makes things knowable? Phenomenologists were strongly concerned with the idea of "situatedness" in the world, claiming that the possibility for knowledge was based in empirical sensory perception, rather than in abstract categories of knowledge such as general conceptions of "Man" (in the case of some versions of philosophy) or "society" (in the case of some sociological traditions).

Schutz emphasized the everyday world of lived experience, which is predicated first on our physical being and therefore our sensory knowledge of the world, but second on the socially constructed concepts that we use to organize and interpret our experiences. The reading provided here, from his key work *The Phenomenology of the Social World* (1967 [1932]), is most centrally concerned with the concept of "intersubjective understanding." Schutz argues that subjectivity is not just something that is isolated in individuals; rather, it grows in social relationships. To illustrate the problem of how we understand another person, Schutz revisits a famous example from Weber of a man cutting wood. To know what the woodcutter is doing, we have to make an interpretive leap – to put ourselves in his place, as it were, by drawing on our past experience. This process is much facilitated by the use of language and other meaningful signs. Such signs are conventions that act as a sort of bridge between minds, allowing people to connect their own experiences to those of others. Once created and put into use, they act as data that allow us to interpret others' meaning and motives. Schutz notes that such communication is also crucial to our reflective understanding of ourselves – we are not consciously aware of our own motives until we try to interpret them as we would interpret those of another person.

The second major tradition of micro-sociology represented in this section is known as symbolic interactionism, a term coined by Herbert Blumer (1900–87).

For much of his career a professor at the University of Chicago, Blumer's work was deeply indebted to Mead, as well as to his colleagues Robert E. Park and W.I. Thomas. Particularly important for Blumer was Mead's emphasis on the role of symbols in the maintenance of social interaction and the constitution of the self as a social process. In the same manner as Schutz's phenomenology, symbolic interactionists place a strong emphasis on empiricism rather than the social realism typified by Durkheimian and functionalist sociology.

The reading included here is from Blumer's best-known work, *Symbolic Interactionism* (1969). Blumer begins by defining symbolic interaction as an approach that studies the "natural world of human group life and human conduct." The reading uses this concept of "naturalistic" studies of social life to issue an extremely sharp critique of functionalist methods. Nestled within this critique is Blumer's statement about how social analysis ought to be done. Blumer lays out four central claims: people act (in relation to things and each other) on the basis of the meanings attached to them; human interaction ("association") is necessary for the making of meaning; social acts are necessarily embedded, therefore, in an interpretive process; and because of this, social networks, institutions and other things are inherently fluid, and are always being renegotiated to some extent.

The work of Erving Goffman (1922–82) is often considered to be part of the tradition of symbolic interactionism (and indeed, "symbolic interactionism" is often used misleadingly as a term for almost all micro-sociological analysis). Goffman's graduate work at Chicago overlapped with the last part of Blumer's stay there, and Goffman later joined Blumer as a colleague at Berkeley.[2] Nevertheless, Goffman built a body of work distinct from that of Blumer, and indeed distinct from just about everything else in the discipline. His work emphasized how people used symbols in the performance of their social roles. This is often called the "dramaturgical approach" because it suggests that people are always staging their performances for others and analyzes how such performances play out to others. A central concern of Goffman's work is the tactical repertoire that actors develop in order to manage their social identities and to defend themselves from unwanted scrutiny and the negative appraisal of others. Sometimes this leads them to act together, as when members of a group put on a team performance to gain what they want from others or when those sharing a common "stigma" (or a marker of an undesirable social identity) frame themselves in less damaging terms.

Like the other authors in this section, Goffman focused on the way that human social interaction makes the social possible. But in contrast to the other authors in this section, Goffman had a certain affinity with the work of Durkheim. He saw himself as a sort of Durkheimian working on the "micro" side of the social equation. More than any of the other authors in this section, Goffman emphasized the importance of integration in the social process. To be an actor on the social stage requires not only that one claim a role, it also requires that others recognize the claim, grant it, and act accordingly. Goffman also emphasized the fact that social performances serve broader functional needs. Our performances are done in such a way as to keep social life going smoothly. For example, even when we fail in our performances, others are likely to overlook our mistakes so as not to disrupt everyone's performances.

The reading included here is from *The Presentation of Self in Everyday Life*. One of the central concepts in the reading is that of "front" – the part of a person's performance that serves to define a relevant context for the "audience." It therefore includes the props that go along with the physical setting, as well as the clothes, manners, and other symbols that can be used to corroborate the impression that one wishes to convey. The concept is important for pointing out not only the way that performances are realized, but also the degree to which they are situational. For example, it is easy for a person to put on a convincing performance as a serious professor or a diligent student in the context of a classroom – but it is difficult and awkward to maintain the same relation when the professor and a student notice each other in a supermarket or in a tavern.

The contemporary vitality of micro-sociological theory is reflected well in the work of Randall Collins (b. 1941), one of today's leading sociologists. Collins has made a number of important contributions to sociological theory, particularly in studies of social order, conflict, historical sociology, and social change. Recently, Collins has proposed a bold theoretical synthesis that builds upon Durkheim's theory of moral integration through ritual and Goffman's situational analysis. In his book *Interaction Ritual Chains* (2004), from which a reading is taken, Collins contends that rituals are powerful because they instigate social interaction based on bodily co-presence and mutual emotional attunement. When engaged in rituals, individuals feel solidarity with one another and imagine themselves to be members of a common undertaking; they become infused with emotional energy and exhilaration; they establish and reinforce collective symbols, moral representations of the group that ought to be defended and reinforced; and they react angrily to insults toward or the profanation of these symbols. Yet this is not a functional account of social order; drawing on Goffman, Collins shows how actors are obliged to perform in chains of ritual encounters which they can attempt to manipulate but which may also fail to produce emotional energy and attachment.

In analyzing a diverse range of social behaviors from the veneration of the 9–11 "ground zero" site, to the enactment of social status differences, to drug consumption to sexual intercourse, Collins observes similar features of common emotional entrainment, the production of symbolic focal objects that become invested with the emotional energy of ritual participants, and the continuation or transformation of social relations as rituals either link performances into chains of interaction into the future or produce dissonant emotions that lead social relations to decay. Ritual participation does not always perpetuate social order – Collins observes that formal rituals sometimes fail, or decay over time, such that they produce "little or no feeling of group solidarity; no sense of one's identity affirmed or changed; no respect for the group's symbols; no heightened emotional energy" (2004, p. 51). The decay of rituals provokes a sense of stale ceremonialism, inappropriateness, or even "strong abhorrence." When rituals feel imposed, rather than spontaneously joined, they usually provoke resentment and disgust. The rejection of imposed rituals and the destruction of symbols associated with them seems to be a typical elements in the collapse of social orders, a violent reaction to "kind of formality that one wishes never to go through again" (p. 51).

Legacy of Micro-Sociological Analysis

All the different approaches to micro-sociological analysis presented here remain active in contemporary sociology. They are sometimes joined together with each other, or with various macro-sociological theories. For example, in developing Marx's theory of alienation, several sociologists have drawn on social phenomenology. Jürgen Habermas relies significantly on symbolic interactionism in his theory of communicative action and how it shapes modern law and politics (see Part VIII of this volume). Pierre Bourdieu has drawn on ethnomethodology and especially the work of Erving Goffman in his theory of social practice (Part VI). Ethnomethodology also informs Anthony Giddens' analyses of reflexive modernization with its new consciousness of risk and new kinds of individualism (Part IV). The various micro-analytic approaches have also influenced theories that are not specifically either macro- or micro-. Feminism and gender studies, for example, have benefited from symbolic interactionism and especially the analysis of 'otherness' developed in that tradition (Part VII). Another example is the importance of Blumer's work for exchange theory (Part II).

The micro-sociological theories are especially influential in the tradition of qualitative sociology. This refers mainly to methodological approaches that emphasize direct communication with social actors and observation of everyday social life. Ethnography, participant observation, interviews and other methodological strategies are all examples. A key link to the micro-sociological theories presented in this Part is that these methods are used most often when sociologists want to develop analyses that make sense of the ways in which ordinary people understand their lives and the social world. This need not mean claiming that everyone already understands social interaction adequately, or that everyday concepts can serve without modification as scientific ones. But it does mean trying to grasp how everyday understanding and concepts work and how actors help to shape the reality in which they act.

NOTES

1 Harold Garfinkel, *Studies in Ethnomethodology*. (Englewood Cliffs, NJ: Prentice-Hall, 1967).
2 George Ritzer, *Modern Sociological Theory*, 4th edn (New York: McGraw Hill, 1996, p. 74).

SELECTED BIBLIOGRAPHY

Berger, Peter and Luckmann, Thomas. 1967. *The Social Construction of Reality: A Treatise in the Sociology of Knowledge*. New York: Doubleday Anchor. (Applies the methods of Schutz's phenomenology to problems in the sociology of knowledge. This has been one of the most important introductions to social phenomenology for English-language readers.)

Blumer, Herbert. 1969. *Symbolic Interactionism: Perspective and Method*. Englewood Cliffs, NJ: Prentice-Hall. (Blumer's own introductory overview to the approach he helped to create.)

Collins, Randall. 1981. "On the Micro-foundations of Macro-Sociology," *American Journal of Sociology* 80: 984–1014. (A classic article on the ways in which micro-sociological analysis can support larger scale theory-building.)

Collins, Randall. 2004. *Interaction Ritual Chains*. Princeton, NJ: Princeton University Press.

Coulter, Jeff. 1989. *Mind in Action*. Cambridge: Polity Press. (Provides a useful link between ethnomethodology and cognitive approaches to sociological analysis.)

Fine, Gary Alan, House, James B., and Cook, Karen. 1995. *Sociological Perspectives on Social Psychology*. Boston, MA: Allyn and Bacon. (Includes chapters on each of the theories presented here, and on different themes in which they are important.)

Garfinkel, Harold. 1967. *Studies in Ethnomethodology*. Englewood Cliffs, NJ: Prentice Hall. (The classic foundation of ethnomethodology, based on several case studies disruptions in the established order of mutual understanding. Some of these were produced by Garfinkel's famous "breeching method" of introducing clashes of categories.)

Goffman, Erving. 1959. *The Presentation of Self in Everyday Life*. New York: Anchor. (Probably Goffman's most famous book, a fascinating account of the ways in which people seek – consciously or unconsciously – to control the ways in which other people see them.)

Goffman, Erving. 1982. *Interaction Ritual: Essays on Face-to-Face Behavior*. New York: Pantheon. (Contains several of Goffman's most famous studies of the ways interpersonal interaction is socially organized.)

Goffman, Erving. 1988. *Frame Analysis: An Essay on the Organization of Experience*. (One of Goffman's last major books, this provides an approach to studying the ways in which experience is structured by the frames – social or "natural" – through which we grasp it.)

Joas, Hans. 1997. *G.H. Mead: A Contemporary Re-Examination of His Thought*. Cambridge, MA: MIT Press. (The most substantial reinterpretation and representation of Mead's thought and the theoretical foundations of symbolic interactionism for modern readers.)

Manning, Philip. 1993. *Erving Goffman and Modern Sociology*. Stanford, CA: Stanford University Press. (A brief but clear introductory overview of Goffman's thought and legacy.)

Schutz, Alfred. 1967. *The Phenomenology of the Social World*. Evanston, IL: Northwestern University Press. (The major synthetic statement of Schutz's approach to the basic categories through which we gain consciousness of the social world.)

Schutz, Alfred and Luckmann, Thomas. 1989. *The Structures of the Lifeworld*. (Schutz and his most important student collaborate to present a phenomenological approach to the world of direct experience in everyday life.)

Stryker, Sheldon. 1980. *Symbolic Interactionism: A Social Structural Version*. Menlo Park, CA: Benjamin Cummings. (An attempt to connect micro- and macro-order based on symbolic interactions.)

Chapter 1

The Phenomenology of the Social World* [1932]

Alfred Schutz

The Ambiguities in the Ordinary Notion of Understanding the Other Person

Before we proceed further, it would be well to note that there are ambiguities in the ordinary notion of understanding another person. Sometimes what is meant is intentional Acts directed toward the other self; in other words, my lived experiences of you. At other times what is in question is *your* subjective experiences. Then, the arrangements of all such experiences into meaning-contexts (Weber's comprehension of intended meaning) is sometimes called "understanding of the other self," as is the classification of others' behavior into motivation contexts. The number of ambiguities associated with the notion of "understanding another person" becomes even greater when we bring in the question of understanding the signs he is using. On the one hand, what is understood is the sign itself, then again *what* the other person means by using this sign, and finally the significance of the fact *that* he is using the sign, here, now, and in this particular context. [...]

---

* Originally translated by George Walsh and Frederick Lehnert.

Alfred Schutz, "The Phenomenology of the Social World," pp. 107, 113–16, 126–36 from Albert Schutz, *The Phenomenology of the Social World*. Evanston, IL: Northwestern University Press, 1967. Copyright © 1967. Reprinted by permission of Northwestern University Press.

Contemporary Sociological Theory, Third Edition. Edited by Craig Calhoun, Joseph Gerteis, James Moody, Steven Pfaff, and Indermohan Virk. Editorial material and organization © 2012 John Wiley & Sons, Ltd. Published 2012 by John Wiley & Sons, Ltd.

The Nature of Genuine Intersubjective Understanding

Having established that all genuine understanding of the other person must start out from Acts of explication performed by the observer on his own lived experience, we must now proceed to a precise analysis of this genuine understanding itself. From the examples we have already given, it is clear that our inquiry must take two different directions. First we must study the genuine understanding of actions which are performed *without any communicative intent*. The action of the woodcutter would be a good example. Second we would examine cases where such communicative intent was present. The latter type of action involves a whole new dimension, the using and interpreting of signs.

Let us first take actions performed without any communicative intent. We are watching a man in the act of cutting wood and wondering what is going on in his mind. Questioning him is ruled out, because that would require entering into a social relationship with him, which in turn would involve the use of signs.

Let us further suppose that we know nothing about our woodcutter except what we see before our eyes. By subjecting our own perceptions to interpretation, we know that we are in the presence of a fellow human being and that his bodily movements indicate he is engaged in an action which we recognize as that of cutting wood.

Now how do we know what is going on in the woodcutter's mind? Taking this interpretation of our own perceptual data as a starting point, we can plot out in our mind's eye exactly how *we* would carry out the action in question. Then we can actually imagine ourselves doing so. In cases like this, then, we project the other person's goal as if it were our own and fancy ourselves carrying it out. Observe also that we here project the action in the future perfect tense as completed and that our imagined execution of the action is accompanied by the usual retentions and reproductions of the project, although, of course, only in fancy. Further, let us note that the imagined execution may fulfill or fail to fulfill the imagined project.

Or, instead of imagining for ourselves an action wherein we carry out the other person's goal, we may recall in concrete detail how we once carried out a similar action ourselves. Such a procedure would be merely a variation on the same principle.

In both these cases, we put ourselves in the place of the actor and identify our lived experiences with his. It might seem that we are here repeating the error of the well-known "projective" theory of empathy. For here we are reading our own lived experiences into the other person's mind and are therefore only discovering our own experiences. But, if we look more closely, we will see that our theory has nothing in common with the empathy theory except for one point. This is the general thesis of the Thou as the "other I," the one whose experiences are constituted in the same fashion as mine. But even this similarity is only apparent, for we start out from the general thesis of the other person's flow of duration, while the projective theory of empathy jumps from the mere fact of empathy to the belief in other minds by an act of blind faith. Our theory only brings out the implications of what is already present in the self-explicative judgment "I am experiencing a fellow human being." We know with certainty that the other person's subjective experience of his own action is in principle different from our own imagined picture of what we would do in the same situation. The reason, as we have already pointed out, is that the intended meaning of an action is always in principle subjective and accessible only to the actor. The error in the empathy theory is twofold. First, it naïvely tries to trace back the constitution of the other self within the ego's consciousness to empathy, so that the latter becomes the direct source of knowledge of the other. Actually, such a task of discovering the constitution of the other self can only be carried out in a transcendentally phenomenological manner. Second, it pretends to a knowledge of the other person's mind that goes far beyond the establishment of a structural parallelism between that mind and my own. In fact, however, when we are dealing with actions having no communicative intent, all that we can assert about their meaning is already contained in the general thesis of the alter ego.

It is clear, then, that we imaginatively project the in-order-to motive of the other person as if it were our own and then use the fancied carrying-out of such an action as a scheme in which to interpret his lived experiences. However, to prevent misunderstanding, it should be added that what is involved here is only a reflective analysis of another person's completed act. It is an interpretation carried out after the fact. When an observer is directly watching someone else to whom he is attuned in simultaneity, the situation is different. Then the observer's living intentionality carries him along without having to make constant playbacks of his own past or imaginary experiences. The other person's action unfolds step by step before his eyes. In such a situation, the identification of the observer with the observed person is not carried out by starting with the goal of the act as already given and then proceeding to reconstruct the lived experiences which must have accompanied it. Instead, the observer keeps pace, as it were, with each step of the observed person's action, identifying himself with the latter's experiences within a common "we-relationship." We shall have much more to say about this later.

So far we have assumed the other person's bodily movement as the only datum given to the observer. It must be emphasized that, if the bodily movement is taken by itself in this way, it is necessarily isolated from its place within the stream of the observed person's living experience. And this context is important not only to the observed person but to the observer as well. He can, of course, if he lacks other data, take a mental snapshot of the observed bodily movement and then try to fit it into a fantasied filmstrip in accordance with the way he thinks he would act and feel in a similar situation. However, the observer can draw much more reliable conclusions about his subject if he knows something about his past and something about the overall plan into which this action fits. To come back to Max Weber's example, it would be important for the observer to know whether the woodcutter was at his regular job or just chopping wood for physical exercise. An adequate model of the observed person's subjective experiences calls for just this wider context. We have already seen, indeed, that the unity of the action is a function of the project's span. From the observed bodily movement, all the observer can infer is the single course of action which has directly led to it. If, however, I as the observer wish to avoid an inadequate interpretation of what I see another person doing, I must "make my own" all those meaning-contexts which make sense of this action on the basis of my past knowledge of this particular person. We shall come back later on to this concept of "inadequacy" and show its significance for the theory of the understanding of the other person.

Meaning-Establishment and Meaning-Interpretation

We have now seen that the sign has two different functions. First it has a *significative function*. By this we mean that it can be ordered by an interpreter within a previously learned sign system of his own. What he is doing here is interpreting the sign as an item of his own experience. His act is just another example of what we call self-interpretation. But there is a second kind of interpretation in which he can engage. He can inquire into the subjective and occasional meaning of the sign, in short, the *expressive* function which it acquires within the context of discourse. This subjective meaning can be his own, in which case he must go back in memory to the experiences he had at the moment of using the sign and establishing its meaning. Or it can be someone else's, in which case he must try to find out about the other person's subjective experiences when *he* used the sign. But in any case, when interpreting signs used by others, we will find two components involved, the objective and the subjective. Objective meaning is the meaning of the sign as such, the kernel, so to speak; whereas subjective meaning is the fringe or aura emanating from the subjective context in the mind of the sign-user.

Let us take a conversation between two people as an example. As one person speaks, thoughts are building up in his mind, and his listener is following him every step of the way just as the thoughts occur. In other words, none of the thoughts comes out as prefabricated unities. They are constructed gradually, and they are interpreted gradually. Both speaker and listener live through the conversation in such a manner that on each side Acts of meaning-establishment or meaning-interpretation are filled in and shaded with memories of what has been said and anticipations of what is yet to be said. Each of these Acts can in turn be focused upon introspectively and analyzed as a unit in itself. The meaning of the speaker's discourse consists for him *and* for his listener in his individual sentences and these, in turn, in their component words as they come, one after another. The sentences for both of them serve as the meaning-contexts of the words, and the whole discourse as the meaning-context of the separate sentences.

Understanding the conscious Acts of another person who is communicating by means of signs does not differ in principle from understanding his other Acts. Like the latter, it occurs in the mode of simultaneity or quasi-simultaneity. The interpreter puts himself in the place of the other person and imagines that he himself is selecting and using the signs. He interprets the other person's subjective meaning as if it were his own. In the process he draws upon his whole personal knowledge of the speaker, especially the latter's ways and habits of expressing himself. Such personal knowledge continues to build itself up in the course of a conversation.

The same process goes on in the mind of the speaker. His words will be selected with a view to being understood by his listener. And the meaning he seeks to get across will not only be objective meaning, for he will seek to communicate his personal attitude as well. He will sketch out his communicative aim in the future perfect tense, just as he does the project of any other act. His choice of words will depend on the habits he has built up in interpreting the words of others, but it will, of course, also be influenced by his knowledge of his listener.

However, if the speaker is focused on what is going on in the mind of his listener, his knowledge of the latter is still quite uncertain. He can only estimate how much he is actually getting across. Any such estimate is necessarily vague, especially considering the fact that the listener's interpretation is always subsequent to the choice of words and fulfills or fails to fulfill the speaker's project in making that choice.

The listener is in a different position. For him the actual establishment of the meaning of the words has already occurred. He can start out with the objective meaning of the words he has heard and from there try to discover the subjective meaning of the speaker. In order to arrive at that subjective meaning, he imagines the project which the speaker must have had in mind. However, this picturing of the project starts out from the speaker's already spoken words. Contrary to the case of the speaker who is picturing something future on the basis of something present, the listener is picturing something pluperfect on the basis of something past. Another difference is that he is starting from words which have either succeeded or failed in fulfilling the speaker's project, and he is trying to uncover that project. The speaker, on the other hand, starts out with his own project as datum and tries to estimate whether it is going to be fulfilled by the listener's future interpretation.

Now since the words chosen by the speaker may or may not express his meaning, the listener can always doubt whether he is understanding the speaker adequately. The project of the speaker is always a matter of imaginative reconstruction for his interpreter and so is attended by a certain vagueness and uncertainty.

To illustrate what we mean, consider the fact that, in a conversation, thoughts like the following may run through the heads of the participants. The person about to speak will say to himself, "Assuming that this fellow speaks my kind of language, I must use such and such words." A moment later his listener will be saying to himself, "If this other fellow is using words the way I understand them, then he must be telling me such and such." The first statement shows how the speaker always chooses his words with the listener's interpretation in mind. The second statement shows how the listener always interprets with the speaker's subjective meaning in mind. In either case an intentional reference to the other person's scheme is involved, regardless of whether the scheme is interpretive or expressive.

As the speaker chooses his words, he uses, of course, his own interpretive scheme. This depends partly upon the way he himself usually interprets words and partly upon his knowledge of his listener's interpretive habits. When I read over a letter I have written to someone, I tend to interpret it just as if I were the receiver and not the sender. Now, my purpose in writing the letter was not merely to communicate an objective meaning to the reader but my subjective meaning as well. To put it in another way, I want him to rethink my thoughts. It may very well be, therefore, that when I read over my letter I shall decide that it falls short of this purpose. Knowing the person to whom I am writing and knowing his customary reactions to certain words and phrases, I may decide that this or that expression is open to misinterpretation or that he will not really be in a position to understand this or that thought of mine. Or I may fear that he will, as he reads, miss the point I am trying to make due to some subjective bias or some failure of attention on his part.

On the other hand, the recipient of the letter can carry out the opposite process. He can take a sentence and imagine that he himself wrote it. He can try to reconstruct the intention of the writer by guessing at some possible intentions and then comparing them with the actual propositional content of the sentence. He may conclude, "I see what he was trying to say, but he really missed his mark and said something else. If I had been he, I should have put it in such and such a way." Or the reader may say to himself instead, "My friend always uses that term in an odd way, but I see what he means, since I know the way he thinks. It's lucky that I am the one reading the letter. A third party would have been thrown off the track entirely at this point." In the last case, the reader really carries out a threefold interpretation. First, he interprets the sentence objectively on the basis of his ordinary habits of interpretation. Second, from his knowledge of the writer, he reconstructs what must be the latter's real meaning. Third, he imagines how the ordinary reader would understand the sentence in question.

These considerations hold true quite generally for all cases in which signs are either used or interpreted. This being the case, it ought to be clear that in interpreting the subjective meaning of the signs used by someone else, or in anticipating someone else's interpretation of the subjective meaning of our own signs, we must be guided by our knowledge of that person. Naturally, therefore, the degree of intimacy or anonymity in which the person stands to us will have a great deal to do with the matter. The examples we have just used were all cases where knowledge of the other person was derived from direct contact; they belong to what we call the domain of directly experienced social reality. However, the use and interpretation of signs are to be found in the other areas of social life as well, such as the worlds of contemporaries and of predecessors, where direct knowledge of the people with whom we are dealing is minimal or even absent. Our theory of the establishment and interpretation of the meaning of signs will naturally undergo various modifications as it is applied to these areas. Even in the direct social relations we have used as examples, it was obviously impossible for the participants to "carry out the postulate of grasping each other's intended meaning," a point that we discussed earlier. The subjective meaning that the interpreter *does* grasp is at best an approximation to the sign-user's intended meaning, but never that meaning itself, for one's knowledge of another person's perspective is always necessarily limited. For exactly the same reason, the person who expresses himself in signs is never quite sure of how he is being understood.

What we have been discussing is the content of communication. But we must remember that the actual *communicating* is itself a meaningful act and that we must interpret that act and the way it is done as things in their own right.

The Meaning-Context of Communication. Recapitulation

Once the interpreter has determined both the objective and subjective meanings of the content of any communication, he may proceed to ask why the communication was made in the first place. He is then seeking the in-order-to motive of the person communicating. For it is essential to every act of communication that it have an extrinsic goal. When I say something to you, I do so for a reason, whether to evoke a particular attitude on your part or simply to explain something to you. Every act of communication has, therefore, as its in-order-to motive the aim that the person being addressed take cognizance of it in one way or another.

The person who is the object or recipient of the communication is frequently the one who makes this kind of interpretation. Having settled what are the objective and subjective meanings of the content of the communication by finding the corresponding interpretive or expressive schemes, he proceeds to inquire into the reason why the other person said this in the first place. In short, he seeks the "plan" behind the communication.

However, the seeker of the in-order-to motive need not be the person addressed at all. A nonparticipant observer may proceed to the same kind of interpretation. I can, indeed I must, seek the in-order-to motive of the communication if I am ever to know the goal toward which the communication is leading. Furthermore, it is self-evident that one can seek the in-order-to motives even of those acts of other people which have no communicative intent. What an actor's subjective experience actually is we can only grasp if we find his in-order-to motive. We must first light upon his project and then engage in a play-by-play fantasy of the action which would fulfill it. In the case of action without communicative intent, the completed act itself is properly interpreted as the fulfillment of the in-order-to motive. However, if I happen to know that the completed act is only a link in a chain of means leading to a further end, then what I must do is interpret the subjective experiences the other person has of that further goal itself.

Now, we have already seen that we can go beyond the in-order-to motive and seek out the because-motive. Of course, knowledge of the latter presupposes in every case knowledge of the former. The subjective meaning-context which is the in-order-to motive must first be seen and taken for granted as an already constituted object in itself before any venture into deeper levels is undertaken. To speak of such deeper levels *as existing* by no means implies that the actor actually experiences them subjectively as meaning-contexts of his action. Nor does it mean that he can become aware even retrospectively of those polythetic Acts which, according to my interpretation, have constituted the in-order-to motive. On the contrary, there is every evidence against the view that the actor ever has any awareness of the because-motive of his action. This applies to one who is establishing a meaning as well as to any other actor. To be sure, he lives through the subjective experiences and intentional Acts which I have interpreted as his because-motive. However, he is not as a rule aware of them, and, when he is, it is no longer as actor. Such awareness, when it occurs, is a separate intentional Act independent of and detached from the action it is interpreting. It is then that a man can be said to understand himself. Such self-understanding is essentially the same as understanding others, with this difference – that usually, but not always, we have at our disposal a much richer array of information about ourselves and our past than others do.

Later on we shall describe the relation of the in-order-to motive to the because-motives in the various regions of the social world. At this point we shall merely try to recapitulate the complex structures involved in understanding another person insofar as these bear on communication and the use of signs. For to say, as we do, that for the user of the sign the sign stands in a meaning-context involves a number of separate facts which must be disentangled.

First of all, whenever I make use of a sign, those lived experiences signified by that sign stand for me in a meaning-context. For they have already been constituted into a synthesis, and I look upon them as a unit.

In the second place, for me the sign must already be part of a sign system. Otherwise I would not be able to use it. A sign must already have been interpreted before it can be used. But the understanding of a sign is a complicated synthesis of lived experiences resulting in a special kind of meaning-context. This meaning-context is a configuration involving two elements: the sign as object in itself and the *signatum*, each of which, of course, involves separate meaning-contexts in its own right. The total new meaning-context embracing them both we have called the "coordinating scheme" of the sign.

Third, the Act of selecting and using the sign is a special meaning-context for the sign-user to the extent that each use of a sign is an expressive action. Since every action comprises a meaning-context by virtue of the fact that the actor visualizes all the successive lived experiences of that action as one unified act, it follows that every expressive action is therefore a meaning-context. This does not mean that every case of sign-using is *ipso facto* a case of communication. A person may, talking to himself for instance, use a sign purely as an act of self-expression without any intention of communication.

Fourth, the meaning-context "sign-using as act" can serve as the basis for a superimposed meaning-context "sign-using as communicative act" without in any way taking into account the particular person addressed.

Fifth, however, this superimposed meaning-context can enter into a still higher and wider meaning-context in which the addressee *is* taken into account. In this case the communicating act has as its goal not merely that someone take cognizance of it but that its message should motivate the person cognizing to a particular attitude or piece of behavior.

Sixth, the fact that this particular addressee is communicated with *here*, *now*, and *in this way* can be placed within a still broader context of meaning by finding the in-order-to motive of that communicative act.

All these meaning-contexts are in principle open to the interpreter and can be uncovered systematically by him. Just which ones he does seek to inquire into will depend upon the kind of interest he has in the sign.

However, the statement that all these meaning-contexts in principle lie open to interpretation requires some modification. As we have said repeatedly, the structure of the social world is by no means homogeneous. Our fellow men and the signs they use can be given to us in different ways. There are different approaches to the sign and to the subjective experience it expresses. Indeed, we do not even need a sign in order to gain access to another person's mind; a mere indication can offer us the opening. This is what happens, for instance, when we draw inferences from artifacts concerning the experiences of people who lived in the past.

Subjective and Objective Meaning. Product and Evidence

We have now seen the different approaches to the genuine understanding of the other self. The interpreter starts with his own experience of the animate body of the other person or of the artifacts which the latter has produced. In either case he is interpreting Objectivations in which the other's subjective experiences manifest themselves. If it is the body of the other that is in question, he concerns himself with act-objectifications, i.e., movements, gestures, or the results of action. If it is artifacts that are in question, these may be either signs in the narrower sense or manufactured external objects such as tools, monuments, etc. All that these Objectivations have in common is that they exist only as the result of the action of rational beings. Because they are products of action, they are *ipso facto* evidence of what went on in the minds of the actors who made them. It should be noted that *not all evidences are signs*, but all signs are evidences. For an evidence to be a sign, it must be capable of becoming an element in a sign system with the status of coordinating scheme. This qualification is lacking in some evidence. A tool, for instance, although it is an evidence of what went on in the mind of its maker, is surely no sign. However, under "evidences" we mean to include not only equipment that has been produced by a manufacturing process, but judgment that has been produced by thought, or the message content which has been produced by an act of communication.

The problematic of subjective and objective meaning includes evidences of all sorts. That is to say, anyone who encounters a given product can proceed to interpret it in two different ways. First, he can focus his attention on its status as an object, either real or ideal, but at any rate independent of its maker. Second, he can look upon it as evidence for what went on in the mind of its makers at the moment it was being made. In the former case the interpreter is subsuming his own experiences (*erfahrende Akte*) of the object under the interpretive schemes which he has at hand. In the latter case, however, his attention directs itself to the constituting Acts of consciousness of the producer (these might be his own as well as those of another person).

This relation between objective and subjective meaning will be examined in a more detailed way at a later point. *We speak, then, of the subjective meaning of the product if we have in view the meaning-context within which the product stands or stood in the mind of the producer. To know the subjective meaning of the product means that we are able to run over in our own minds in simultaneity or quasi-simultaneity the polythetic Acts which constituted the experience of the producer.*

We keep in view, then, the other person's lived experiences as they are occurring; we observe them being constituted step by step. For us, the other person's products are indications of those lived experiences. The lived experiences stand for him, in turn, within a meaning context. We know this by means of a particular evidence, and we can in an act of genuine understanding be aware of the constituting process in his mind.

Objective meaning, on the contrary, we can predicate only of the product as such, that is, of the already constituted meaning-context of the thing produced, whose actual production we meanwhile disregard. The product is, then, in the fullest sense the end result of the process of production, something that is finished and complete. It is no longer part of the process but merely points back to it as an event in the past. The product itself is, however, not an event but an entity (*ein Seiendes*) which is the sediment of past events within the mind of the producer. To be sure, even the interpretation of the objective meaning of the product occurs in step-by-step polythetic Acts. Nevertheless, it is exhausted in the ordering of the interpreter's experiences of the product within the total meaning-context of the interpretive act. And, as we have said, the interpreter leaves the original step-by-step creation of the product quite out of account. It is not that he is unaware that it has occurred; it is just that he pays no attention to it. Objective meaning therefore consists only in a meaning-context within the mind of the interpreter, whereas subjective meaning refers beyond it to a meaning-context in the mind of the producer.

A subjective meaning-context, then, is present if what is given in an objective meaning-context was created as a meaning-context by a Thou on its own part. Nothing, however, is thereby implied either about the particular kind of meaning-context into which the Thou orders its lived experiences or about the quality of those experiences themselves.

We have already noted that the interpreter grasps the other person's conscious experiences in the mode of simultaneity or quasi-simultaneity. Genuine simultaneity is the more frequent, even though it is a special case of the process. It is tied to the world of directly experienced social reality and presupposes that the interpreter witnesses the actual bringing-forth of the product. An example would be a conversation, where the listener is actually present as the speaker performs Acts that bring forth meaningful discourse and where the listener performs these Acts with and after the speaker. A case of quasi-simultaneous interpretation would be the reading of a book. Here the reader relives the author's choice of words as if the choice were made before his very eyes. The same would hold for a person inspecting some artifacts, such as tools, and imagining to himself how they were made. However, in saying that we can observe such subjective experiences on the part of the producer, we only meant that we can grasp the fact *that* they occur. We have said nothing about how we understand *what* experiences occur, nor how we understand *the way* in which they are formed. We shall deal with these problems when we analyze the world of contemporaries, the world of direct social experience, and the world of the genuine We-relationship. Still, it can be said even at this point that what is essential to this further knowledge is a knowledge of the person being interpreted. When we ask what the subjective meaning of a product is, and therefore what conscious experiences another person has, we are asking what particular polythetically constructed lived experiences are occurring or have occurred in a particular other person. This other person, this Thou, has his own unique experiences and meaning-contexts. No other person, not even he himself at another moment, can stand in his shoes at this moment.

The objective meaning of a product that we have before us is, on the other hand, by no means interpreted as evidence for the particular lived experience of a particular Thou. Rather, it is interpreted as already constituted and established, abstracted from every subjective flow of experience and every subjective meaning-context that could exist in such a flow. It is grasped as an objectification endowed with "universal meaning." Even though we implicitly refer to its author when we call it a "product," still we leave this author and everything personal about him out of account when we are interpreting objective meaning. He is hidden behind the impersonal "one" (someone, someone or other). This anonymous "one" is merely the linguistic term for the fact that a Thou exists, or has once existed, of whose particularity we take no account. I myself or you or some ideal type or Everyman could step into its shoes without in any way altering the subjective meaning of the product. We can say nothing about the subjective processes of this anonymous "one," for the latter has no duration, and the temporal dimension we ascribe to it, being a logical fiction, is in principle incapable of being experienced. But precisely for this reason the objective meaning remains, from the point of view of the interpreter, invariant for all possible creators of the meaningful object. Insofar as that object contains within its very meaning the ideality of the "and so forth" and of the "I can do it again," to that extent is that meaning independent of its maker and the circumstances of its origination. The product is abstracted from every individual consciousness and indeed from every consciousness as such. Objective meaning is merely the interpreter's ordering of his experiences of a product into the total context of his experience.

It follows from all we have said that every interpretation of subjective meaning involves a reference to a particular person. Furthermore, it must be a person of whom the interpreter has some kind of experience (*Erfahrung*) and whose subjective states he can run through in simultaneity or quasi-simultaneity, whereas objective meaning is abstracted from and independent of particular persons. Later we shall study this antithesis in greater detail, treating it as a case of polar opposition. Between the understanding of subjective meaning and the understanding of pure objective meaning there is a whole series of intermediate steps based on the fact that the social world has its own unique structure derived, as it is, from the worlds of direct social experience, of contemporaries, of predecessors, and of successors.

Chapter 2

The Presentation of Self in Everyday Life [1959]

Erving Goffman

Masks are arrested expressions and admirable echoes of feeling, at once faithful, discreet, and superlative. Living things in contact with the air must acquire a cuticle, and it is not urged against cuticles that they are not hearts; yet some philosophers seem to be angry with images for not being things, and with words for not being feelings. Words and images are like shells, no less integral parts of nature than are the substances they cover, but better addressed to the eye and more open to observation. I would not say that substance exists for the sake of appearance, or faces for the sake of masks, or the passions for the sake of poetry and virtue. Nothing arises in nature for the sake of anything else; all these phases and products are involved equally in the round of existence.

George Santayana, *Soliloquies in England and Later Soliloquies* (New York: Scribner's, 1922), pp. 131–2

Belief in the Part One is Playing

When an individual plays a part he implicitly requests his observers to take seriously the impression that is fostered before them. They are asked to believe that the character they see actually possesses the attributes he appears to possess, that the task he performs will have the consequences that are implicitly claimed for it, and that, in general, matters are what they appear to be. In line with this, there is the popular view that the individual offers his performance and puts on his show "for the benefit of other people." It will be convenient to begin a consideration of performances by turning the question around and looking at the individual's own belief in the impression of reality that he attempts to engender in those among whom he finds himself.

At one extreme, one finds that the performer can be fully taken in by his own act; he can be sincerely convinced that the impression of reality which he stages is the real reality. When his audience is also convinced in this way about the show he puts on – and this seems to be the typical case – then for the moment at least, only the sociologist or the socially disgruntled will have any doubts about the "realness" of what is presented.

At the other extreme, we find that the performer may not be taken in at all by his own routine. This possibility is understandable, since no one is in quite as good an observational position to see through the act as the person who puts it on. Coupled with this, the performer may be moved to guide the conviction of his audience only as a means to other ends, having no ultimate concern in the conception that they have of him or of the situation. When the individual has no belief in his own act and no ultimate concern with the beliefs of his audience, we may call him cynical, reserving the term "sincere" for individuals who believe in the impression fostered by their own performance. It should be understood that the cynic, with all his professional disinvolvement, may obtain unprofessional pleasures from his masquerade, experiencing a kind of gleeful spiritual aggression from the fact that he can toy at will with something his audience must take seriously.

It is not assumed, of course, that all cynical performers are interested in deluding their audiences for purposes of what is called "self-interest" or private gain. A cynical individual may delude his audience for what he considers to be their own good, or for the good of the community, etc. For illustrations of this we need not appeal to sadly enlightened showmen such as Marcus Aurelius or Hsun Tzǔ. We know that in service occupations practitioners who may otherwise be sincere are sometimes forced to delude their customers because their customers show such a heartfelt demand for it. Doctors who are led into giving placebos, filling station attendants who resignedly check and recheck tire pressures for anxious women motorists, shoe clerks who sell a shoe that fits but tell the customer it is the size she wants to hear – these are cynical performers whose audiences will not allow them to be sincere. Similarly, it seems that sympathetic patients in mental wards will sometimes feign bizarre symptoms so that student nurses will not be subjected to a disappointingly sane performance. So also, when inferiors extend their most lavish reception for visiting superiors, the selfish desire to win favor may not be the chief motive; the inferior may be tactfully attempting to put the superior at ease by simulating the kind of world the superior is thought to take for granted.

I have suggested two extremes: an individual may be taken in by his own act or be cynical about it. These extremes are something a little more than just the ends of a continuum. Each provides the individual with a position which has its own particular securities and defenses, so there will be a tendency for those who have traveled close to one of these poles to complete the voyage. Starting with lack of inward belief in one's role, the individual may follow the natural movement described by Park:

> It is probably no mere historical accident that the word person, in its first meaning, is a mask. It is rather a recognition of the fact that everyone is always and everywhere, more or less consciously, playing a role ... It is in these roles that we know each other; it is in these roles that we know ourselves.[1]

In a sense, and in so far as this mask represents the conception we have formed of ourselves – the role we are striving to live up to – this mask is our truer self, the self we would like to be. In the end, our conception of our role becomes second nature and an integral part of our personality. We come into the world as individuals, achieve character, and become persons.[2]

This may be illustrated from the community life of Shetland. For the last four or five years the island's tourist hotel has been owned and operated by a married couple of crofter origins. From the beginning, the owners were forced to set aside their own conceptions as to how life ought to be led, displaying in the hotel a full round of middle-class services and amenities. Lately, however, it appears that the managers have become less cynical about the performance that they stage; they themselves are becoming middle class and more and more enamored of the selves their clients impute to them.

Another illustration may be found in the raw recruit who initially follows army etiquette in order to avoid physical punishment and eventually comes to follow the rules so that his organization will not be shamed and his officers and fellow soldiers will respect him.

As suggested, the cycle of disbelief-to-belief can be followed in the other direction, starting with conviction or insecure aspiration and ending in cynicism. Professions which the public holds in religious awe often allow their recruits to follow the cycle in this direction, and often recruits follow it in this direction not because of a slow realization that they are deluding their audience – for by ordinary social standards the claims they make may be quite valid – but because they can use this cynicism as a means of insulating their inner selves from contact with the audience. And we may even expect to find typical careers of faith, with the individual starting out with one kind of involvement in the performance he is required to give, then moving back and forth several times between sincerity and cynicism before completing all the phases and turning-points of self-belief for a person of his station. Thus, students of medical schools suggest that idealistically oriented beginners in medical school typically lay aside their holy aspirations for a period of time. During the first two years the students find that their interest in medicine must be dropped that they may give all their time to the task of learning how to get through examinations. During the next two years they are too busy learning about diseases to show much concern for the persons who are diseased. It is only after their medical schooling has ended that their original ideals about medical service may be reasserted.

While we can expect to find natural movement back and forth between cynicism and sincerity, still we must not rule out the kind of transitional point that can be sustained on the strength of a little self-illusion. We find that the individual may attempt to induce the audience to judge him and the situation in a particular way, and he may seek this judgment as an ultimate end in itself, and yet he may not completely believe that he deserves the valuation of self which he asks for or that the impression of reality which he fosters is valid. [...]

Front

I have been using the term "performance" to refer to all the activity of an individual which occurs during a period marked by his continuous presence before a particular set of observers and which has some influence on the observers. It will be convenient to label as "front" that part of the individual's performance which regularly functions in a general and fixed fashion to define the situation for those who observe the performance. Front, then, is the expressive equipment of a standard kind intentionally or unwittingly employed by the individual during his performance. For preliminary purposes, it will be convenient to distinguish and label what seem to be the standard parts of front.

First, there is the "setting," involving furniture, décor, physical layout, and other background items which supply the scenery and stage props for the spate of human action played out before, within, or upon it. A setting tends to stay put, geographically speaking, so that those who would use a particular setting as part of their performance cannot begin their act until they have brought themselves to the appropriate place and must terminate their performance when they leave it. It is only in exceptional circumstances that the setting follows along with the performers; we see this in the funeral cortège, the civic parade, and the dream-like processions that kings and queens are made of. In the main, these exceptions seem to offer some kind of extra protection for performers who are, or who have momentarily become, highly sacred. These worthies are to be distinguished, of course, from quite profane performers of the peddler class who move their place of work between performances, often being forced to do so. In the matter of having one fixed place for one's setting, a ruler may be too sacred, a peddler too profane.

In thinking about the scenic aspects of front, we tend to think of the living room in a particular house and the small number of performers who can thoroughly identify themselves with it. We have given insufficient attention to assemblages of sign-equipment which large numbers of performers can call their own for short periods of time. It is characteristic of Western European countries, and no doubt a source of stability for them, that a large number of luxurious settings are available for hire to anyone of the right kind who can afford them. [...]

If we take the term "setting" to refer to the scenic parts of expressive equipment, one may take the term "personal front" to refer to the other items of expressive equipment, the items that we most intimately identify with the performer himself and that we naturally expect will follow the performer wherever he goes. As part of personal front we may include: insignia of office or rank; clothing; sex, age, and racial characteristics; size and looks; posture; speech patterns; facial expressions; bodily gestures; and the like. Some of these vehicles for conveying signs, such as racial characteristics, are relatively fixed and over a span of time do not vary for the individual from one situation to another. On the other hand, some of these sign vehicles are relatively mobile or transitory, such as facial expression, and can vary during a performance from one moment to the next.

It is sometimes convenient to divide the stimuli which make up personal front into "appearance" and "manner," according to the function performed by the information that these stimuli convey. "Appearance" may be taken to refer to those stimuli which function at the time to tell us of the performer's social statuses. These stimuli also tell us of the individual's temporary ritual state, that is, whether he is engaging in formal social activity, work, or informal recreation, whether or not he is celebrating a new phase in the season cycle or in his life-cycle. "Manner" may be taken to refer to those stimuli which function at the time to warn us of the interaction role the performer will expect to play in the oncoming situation. Thus a haughty, aggressive manner may give the impression that the performer expects to be the one who will initiate the verbal interaction and direct its course. A meek, apologetic manner may give the impression that the performer expects to follow the lead of others, or at least that he can be led to do so.

We often expect, of course, a confirming consistency between appearance and manner; we expect that the differences in social statuses among the interactants will be expressed in some way by congruent differences in the indications that are made of an expected interaction role. […] But, of course, appearance and manner may tend to contradict each other, as when a performer who appears to be of higher estate than his audience acts in a manner that is unexpectedly equalitarian, or intimate, or apologetic, or when a performer dressed in the garments of a high position presents himself to an individual of even higher status.

In addition to the expected consistency between appearance and manner, we expect, of course, some coherence among setting, appearance, and manner. Such coherence represents an ideal type that provides us with a means of stimulating our attention to and interest in exceptions. […]

Dramatic Realization

While in the presence of others, the individual typically infuses his activity with signs which dramatically highlight and portray confirmatory facts that might otherwise remain unapparent or obscure. For if the individual's activity is to become significant to others, he must mobilize his activity so that it will express *during the interaction* what he wishes to convey. In fact, the performer may be required not only to express his claimed capacities during the interaction but also to do so during a split second in the interaction. Thus, if a baseball umpire is to give the impression that he is sure of his judgment, he must forgo the moment of thought which might make him sure of his judgment; he must give an instantaneous decision so that the audience will be sure that he is sure of his judgment.

It may be noted that in the case of some statuses dramatization presents no problem, since some of the acts which are instrumentally essential for the completion of the core task of the status are at the same time wonderfully adapted, from the point of view of communication, as means of vividly conveying the qualities and attributes claimed by the performer. The roles of prizefighters, surgeons, violinists, and policemen are cases in point. These activities allow for so much dramatic self-expression that exemplary practitioners – whether real or fictional – become famous and are given a special place in the commercially organized fantasies of the nation.

In many cases, however, dramatization of one's work does constitute a problem. An illustration of this may be cited from a hospital study where the medical nursing staff is shown to have a problem that the surgical nursing staff does not have:

> The things which a nurse does for post-operative patients on the surgical floor are frequently of recognizable importance, even to patients who are strangers to hospital activities. For example, the patient sees his nurse changing bandages, swinging orthopedic frames into place, and can realize that these are purposeful activities. Even if she cannot be at his side, he can respect her purposeful activities.
>
> Medical nursing is also highly skilled work. [...] The physician's diagnosis must rest upon careful observation of symptoms over time where the surgeon's are in larger part dependent on visible things. The lack of visibility creates problems on the medical. A patient will see his nurse stop at the next bed and chat for a moment or two with the patient there. He doesn't know that she is observing the shallowness of the breathing and color and tone of the skin. He thinks she is just visiting. So, alas, does his family who may thereupon decide that these nurses aren't very impressive. If the nurse spends more time at the next bed than at his own, the patient may feel slighted. [...] The nurses are "wasting time" unless they are darting about doing some visible thing such as administering hypodermics.[3]

Similarly, the proprietor of a service establishment may find it difficult to dramatize what is actually being done for clients because the clients cannot "see" the overhead costs of the service rendered them. Undertakers must therefore charge a great deal for their highly visible product – a coffin that has been transformed into a casket – because many of the other costs of conducting a funeral are ones that cannot be readily dramatized. Merchants, too, find that they must charge high prices for things that look intrinsically expensive in order to compensate the establishment for expensive things like insurance, slack periods, etc., that never appear before the customers' eyes.

The problem of dramatizing one's work involves more than merely making invisible costs visible. The work that must be done by those who fill certain statuses is often so poorly designed as an expression of a desired meaning, that if the incumbent would dramatize the character of his role, he must divert an appreciable amount of his energy to do so. And this activity diverted to communication will often require different attributes from the ones which are being dramatized. Thus to furnish a house so that it will express simple, quiet dignity, the householder may have to race to auction sales, haggle with antique dealers, and doggedly canvass all the local shops for proper wallpaper and curtain materials. To give a radio talk that will sound genuinely informal, spontaneous, and relaxed, the speaker may have to design his script with painstaking care, testing one phrase after another, in order to follow the content, language, rhythm, and pace of everyday talk. Similarly, a *Vogue* model, by her clothing, stance, and facial expression, is able expressively to portray a cultivated understanding of the book she poses in her hand; but those who trouble to express themselves so appropriately will have very little time left over for reading. As Sartre suggested: "The attentive pupil who wishes to *be* attentive, his eyes riveted on the teacher, his ears open wide, so exhausts himself in playing the attentive role that he ends up by no longer hearing anything."[4] And so individuals often find themselves with the dilemma of expression *versus* action. Those who have the time and talent to perform a task well may not, because of this, have the time or talent to make it apparent that they are performing well. It may be said that some organizations resolve this dilemma by officially delegating the dramatic function to a specialist who will spend his time expressing the meaning of the task and spend no time actually doing it.

If we alter our frame of reference for a moment and turn from a particular performance to the individuals who present it, we can consider an interesting fact about the round of different routines which any group or class of individuals helps to perform. When a group or class is examined, one finds that the members of it tend to invest their egos primarily in certain routines, giving less stress to the other ones which they perform. Thus a professional man may be willing to take a very modest role in the street, in a shop, or in his home, but, in the social sphere which encompasses his display of professional competency, he will be much concerned to make an effective showing. In mobilizing his behavior to make a showing, he will be concerned not so much with the full round of the different routines he performs but only with the one from which his occupational reputation derives. It is upon this issue that some writers have chosen to distinguish groups with aristocratic habits (whatever their social status) from those of middle-class character. The aristocratic habit, it has been said, is one that mobilizes all the minor activities of life which fall outside the serious specialities of other classes and injects into these activities an expression of character, power, and high rank. […]

Idealization

It was suggested earlier that a performance of a routine presents through its front some rather abstract claims upon the audience, claims that are likely to be presented to them during the performance of other routines. This constitutes one way in which a performance is "socialized," molded, and modified to fit into the understanding and expectations of the society in which it is presented. I want to consider here another important aspect of this socialization process – the tendency for performers to offer their observers an impression that is idealized in several different ways.

The notion that a performance presents an idealized view of the situation is, of course, quite common. Cooley's view may be taken as an illustration:

> If we never tried to seem a little better than we are, how could we improve or "train ourselves from the outside inward?" And the same impulse to show the world a better or idealized aspect of ourselves finds an organized expression in the various professions and classes, each of which has to some extent a cant or pose, which its members assume unconsciously, for the most part, but which has the effect of a conspiracy to work upon the credulity of the rest of the world. There is a cant not only of theology and of philanthropy, but also of law, medicine, teaching, even of science – perhaps especially of science, just now, since the more a particular kind of merit is recognized and admired, the more it is likely to be assumed by the unworthy.[5]

Thus, when the individual presents himself before others, his performance will tend to incorporate and exemplify the officially accredited values of the society, more so, in fact, than does his behavior as a whole.

To the degree that a performance highlights the common official values of the society in which it occurs, we may look upon it, in the manner of Durkheim and Radcliffe-Brown, as a ceremony – as an expressive rejuvenation and reaffirmation of the moral values of the community. Furthermore, in so far as the expressive bias of performances comes to be accepted as reality, then that which is accepted at the moment as reality will have some of the characteristics of a celebration. To stay in one's room away from the place where the party is given, or away from where the practitioner attends his client, is to stay away from where reality is being performed. The world, in truth, is a wedding. [...]

The expressive coherence that is required in performances points out a crucial discrepancy between our all-too-human selves and our socialized selves. As human beings we are presumably creatures of variable impulse with moods and energies that change from one moment to the next. As characters put on for an audience, however, we must not be subject to ups and downs. As Durkheim suggested, we do not allow our higher social activity "to follow in the trail of our bodily states, as our sensations and our general bodily consciousness do."[6] A certain bureaucratization of the spirit is expected so that we can be relied upon to give a perfectly homogeneous performance at every appointed time. As Santayana suggests, the socialization process not only transfigures, it fixes:

> But whether the visage we assume be a joyful or a sad one, in adopting and emphasizing it we define our sovereign temper. Henceforth, so long as we continue under the spell of this self-knowledge, we do not merely live but act; we compose and play our chosen character, we wear the buskin of deliberation, we defend and idealize our passions, we encourage ourselves eloquently to be what we are, devoted or scornful or careless or austere; we soliloquize (before an imaginary audience) and we wrap ourselves

gracefully in the mantle of our inalienable part. So draped, we solicit applause and expect to die amid a universal hush. We profess to live up to the fine sentiments we have uttered, as we try to believe in the religion we profess. The greater our difficulties the greater our zeal. Under our published principles and plighted language we must assiduously hide all the inequalities of our moods and conduct, and this without hypocrisy, since our deliberate character is more truly ourself than is the flux of our involuntary dreams. The portrait we paint in this way and exhibit as our true person may well be in the grand manner, with column and curtain and distant landscape and finger pointing to the terrestrial globe or to the Yorick-skull of philosophy; but if this style is native to us and our art is vital, the more it transmutes its model the deeper and truer art it will be. The severe bust of an archaic sculpture, scarcely humanizing the block, will express a spirit far more justly than the man's dull morning looks or casual grimaces. Everyone who is sure of his mind, or proud of his office, or anxious about his duty assumes a tragic mask. He deputes it to be himself and transfers to it almost all his vanity. While still alive and subject, like all existing things, to the undermining flux of his own substance, he has crystallized his soul into an idea, and more in pride than in sorrow he has offered up his life on the altar of the Muses. Self-knowledge, like any art or science, renders its subject-matter in a new medium, the medium of ideas, in which it loses its old dimensions and its old place. Our animal habits are transmuted by conscience into loyalties and duties, and we become "persons" or masks.[7]

Through social discipline, then, a mask of manner can be held in place from within. But, as Simone de Beauvoir suggests, we are helped in keeping this pose by clamps that are tightened directly on the body, some hidden, some showing:

Even if each woman dresses in conformity with her status, a game is still being played: artifice, like art, belongs to the realm of the imaginary. It is not only that girdle, brassiere, hair-dye, make-up disguise body and face; but that the least sophisticated of women, once she is "dressed," does not present *herself* to observation; she is, like the picture or the statue, or the actor on the stage, an agent through whom is suggested someone not there – that is, the character she represents, but is not. It is this identification with something unreal, fixed, perfect as the hero of a novel, as a portrait or a bust, that gratifies her; she strives to identify herself with this figure and thus to seem to herself to be stabilized, justified in her splendor.[8]

Misrepresentation

It was suggested earlier that an audience is able to orient itself in a situation by accepting performed cues on faith, treating these signs as evidence of something greater than or different from the sign-vehicles themselves. If this tendency of the audience to accept signs places the performer in a position to be misunderstood and makes it necessary for him to exercise expressive care regarding everything he does when before the audience, so also this sign-accepting tendency puts the audience in a position to be duped and misled, for there are few signs that cannot be used to attest to the presence of something that is not really there. And it is plain that many performers have ample capacity and motive to misrepresent the facts; only shame, guilt, or fear prevent them from doing so.

As members of an audience it is natural for us to feel that the impression the performer seeks to give may be true or false, genuine or spurious, valid or "phony." So common is this doubt that, as suggested, we often give special attention to features of the performance that cannot be readily manipulated, thus enabling ourselves to judge the reliability of the more misrepresentable cues in the performance. (Scientific police work and projective testing are extreme examples of the application of this tendency.) And if we grudgingly allow certain symbols of status to establish a performer's right to a given treatment, we are always ready to pounce on chinks in his symbolic armor in order to discredit his pretensions.

When we think of those who present a false front or "only" a front, of those who dissemble, deceive, and defraud, we think of a discrepancy between fostered appearances and reality. We also think of the precarious position in which these performers place themselves, for at any moment in their performance an event may occur to catch them out and baldly contradict what they have openly avowed, bringing them immediate humiliation and sometimes permanent loss of reputation. We often feel that it is just these terrible eventualities, which arise from being caught out *flagrante delicto* in a patent act of misrepresentation, that an honest performer is able to avoid. This common-sense view has limited analytical utility.

Sometimes when we ask whether a fostered impression is true or false we really mean to ask whether or not the performer is authorized to give the performance in question, and are not primarily concerned with the actual performance itself. When we discover that someone with whom we have dealings is an impostor and out-and-out fraud, we are discovering that he did not have the right to play the part he played, that he was not an accredited incumbent of the relevant status. We assume that the impostor's performance, in addition to the fact that it misrepresents him, will be at fault in other ways, but often his masquerade is discovered before we can detect any other difference between the false performance and the legitimate one which it simulates. Paradoxically, the more closely the impostor's performance approximates to the real thing, the more intensely we may be threatened, for a competent performance by someone who proves to be an impostor may weaken in our minds the moral connection between legitimate authorization to play a part and the capacity to play it. (Skilled mimics, who admit all along that their intentions are unserious, seem to provide one way in which we can "work through" some of these anxieties.)

The social definition of impersonation, however, is not itself a very consistent thing. For example, while it is felt to be an inexcusable crime against communication to impersonate someone of sacred status, such as a doctor or a priest, we are often less concerned when someone impersonates a member of a disesteemed, non-crucial, profane status, such as that of a hobo or unskilled worker. When a disclosure shows that we have been participating with a performer who has a higher status than he led us to believe, there is good Christian precedent for our reacting with wonderment and chagrin rather than with hostility. Mythology and our popular magazines, in fact, are full of romantic stories in which the villain and the hero both make fraudulent claims that are discredited in the last chapter, the villain proving not to have a high status, the hero proving not to have a low one.

Further, while we may take a harsh view of performers such as confidence men who knowingly misrepresent every fact about their lives, we may have some sympathy for those who have but one fatal flaw and who attempt to conceal the fact that they are, for example, ex-convicts, deflowered, epileptic, or racially impure, instead of admitting their fault and making an honorable attempt to live it down. Also, we distinguish between impersonation of a specific, concrete individual, which we usually feel is quite inexcusable, and impersonation of category membership, which we may feel less strongly about. So, too, we often feel differently about those who misrepresent themselves to forward what they feel are the just claims of a collectivity, or those who misrepresent themselves accidentally or for a lark, than about those who misrepresent themselves for private psychological or material gain.

Finally, since there are senses in which the concept of "a status" is not clear-cut, so there are senses in which the concept of impersonation is not clear either. For example, there are many statuses in which membership obviously is not subject to formal ratification. Claims to be a law graduate can be established as valid or invalid, but claims to be a friend, a true believer, or a music-lover can be confirmed or disconfirmed only more or less. Where standards of competence are not objective, and where *bona fide* practitioners are not collectively organized to protect their mandate, an individual may style himself an expert and be penalized by nothing stronger than sniggers. [...]

In previous sections of this chapter some general characteristics of performance were suggested: activity oriented towards work-tasks tends to be converted into activity oriented towards communication; the front behind which the routine is presented is also likely to be suitable for other, somewhat different routines and so is likely not to fit completely any particular routine; sufficient self-control is exerted so as to maintain a working consensus; an idealized impression is offered by accentuating certain facts and concealing others; expressive coherence is maintained by the performer taking more care to guard against minor disharmonies than the stated purpose of the performance might lead the audience to think was warranted. All of these general characteristics of performances can he seen as interaction constraints which play upon the individual and transform his activities into performances. Instead of merely doing his task and giving vent to his feelings, he will express the doing of his task and acceptably convey his feelings. In general, then, the representation of an activity will vary in some degree from the activity itself and therefore inevitably misrepresent it. And since the individual will be required to rely on signs in order to construct a representation of his activity, the image he constructs, however faithful to the facts, will be subject to all the disruptions that impressions are subject to.

While we could retain the common-sense notion that fostered appearances can be discredited by a discrepant reality, there is often no reason for claiming that the facts discrepant with the fostered impression are any more the real reality than is the fostered reality they embarrass. A cynical view of everyday performances can be as one-sided as the one that is sponsored by the performer. For many sociological issues it may not even be necessary to decide which is the more real, the fostered impression or the one the performer attempts to prevent the audience from receiving. The crucial sociological consideration, for this report at least, is merely that impressions fostered in everyday performances are subject to disruption. We will want to know what kind of impression of reality can shatter the fostered impression of reality, and what reality really is can be left to other students. We will want to ask, "What are the ways in which a given impression can be discredited?" and this is not quite the same as asking, "What are the ways in which the given impression is false?"

We come back, then, to a realization that while the performance offered by impostors and liars is quite flagrantly false and differs in this respect from ordinary performances, both are similar in the care their performers must exert in order to maintain the impression that is fostered. Thus, for example, we know that the formal code of British civil servants and of American baseball umpires obliges them not only to desist from making improper "deals" but also to desist from innocent action which might possibly give the (wrong) impression that they are making deals. Whether an honest performer wishes to convey the truth or whether a dishonest performer wishes to convey a falsehood, both must take care to enliven their performances with appropriate expressions, exclude from their performances expressions that might discredit the impression being fostered, and take care lest the audience impute unintended meanings. Because of these shared dramatic contingencies, we can profitably study performances that are quite false in order to learn about ones that are quite honest. [...]

Reality and Contrivance

In our own Anglo-American culture there seems to be two common-sense models according to which we formulate our conceptions of behavior: the real, sincere, or honest performance; and the false one that thorough fabricators assemble for us, whether meant to be taken unseriously, as in the work of stage actors, or seriously, as in the work of confidence men. We tend to see real performances as something not purposely put together at all, being an unintentional product of the individual's unselfconscious response to the facts in his situation. And contrived performances we tend to see as something painstakingly pasted together, one false item on another, since there is no reality to which the items of behavior could be a direct response. It will be necessary to see now that these dichotomous conceptions are by way of being the ideology of honest performers, providing strength to the show they put on, but a poor analysis of it.

First, let it be said that there are many individuals who sincerely believe that the definition of the situation they habitually project is the real reality. In this report I do not mean to question their proportion in the population but rather the structural relation of their sincerity to the performances they offer. If a performance is to come off, the witnesses by and large must be able to believe that the performers are sincere.

This is the structural place of sincerity in the drama of events. Performers may be sincere – or be insincere but sincerely convinced of their own sincerity – but this kind of affection for one's part is not necessary for its convincing performance. There are not many French cooks who are really Russian spies, and perhaps there are not many women who play the part of wife to one man and mistress to another; but these duplicities do occur, often being sustained successfully for long periods of time. This suggests that while persons usually are what they appear to be, such appearances could still have been managed. There is, then, a statistical relation between appearances and reality, not an intrinsic or necessary one. In fact, given the unanticipated threats that play upon a performance, and given the need (later to be discussed) to maintain solidarity with one's fellow performers and some distance from the witnesses, we find that a rigid incapacity to depart from one's inward view of reality may at times endanger one's performance. Some performances are carried off successfully with complete dishonesty, others with complete honesty; but for performances in general neither of these extremes is essential and neither, perhaps, is dramaturgically advisable.

The implication here is that an honest, sincere, serious performance is less firmly connected with the solid world than one might first assume. And this implication will be strengthened if we look again at the distance usually placed between quite honest performances and quite contrived ones. In this connection take, for example, the remarkable phenomenon of stage acting. It does take deep skill, long training, and psychological capacity to become a good stage actor. But this fact should not blind us to another one: that almost anyone can quickly learn a script well enough to give a charitable audience some sense of realness in what is being contrived before them. And it seems this is so because ordinary social intercourse is itself put together as a scene is put together, by the exchange of dramatically inflated actions, counter-actions, and terminating replies. Scripts even in the hands of unpracticed players can come to life because life itself is a dramatically enacted thing. All the world is not, of course, a stage, but the crucial ways in which it isn't are not easy to specify.

The recent use of "psychodrama" as a therapeutic technique illustrates a further point in this regard. In these psychiatrically staged scenes patients not only act out parts with some effectiveness, but employ no script in doing so. Their own past is available to them in a form which allows them to stage a recapitulation of it. Apparently a part once played honestly and in earnest leaves the performer in a position to contrive a showing of it later. Further, the parts that significant others played to him in the past also seem to be available, allowing him to switch from being the person that he was to being the persons that others were for him. This capacity to switch enacted roles when obliged to do so could have been predicted; everyone apparently can do it. For in learning to perform our parts in real life we guide our own productions by not too consciously maintaining an incipient familiarity with the routine of those to whom we will address ourselves. And when we come to be able properly to manage a real routine we are able to do this in part because of "anticipatory socialization,"[9] having already been schooled in the reality that is just coming to be real for us.

When the individual does move into a new position in society and obtains a new part to perform, he is not likely to be told in full detail how to conduct himself, nor will the facts of his new situation press sufficiently on him from the start to determine his conduct without his further giving thought to it. Ordinarily he will be given only a few cues, hints, and stage directions, and it will be assumed that he already has in his repertoire a large number of bits and pieces of performances that will be required in the new setting. The individual will already have a fair idea of what modesty, deference, or righteous indignation looks like, and can make a pass at playing these bits when necessary. He may even be able to play out the part of a hypnotic subject or commit a "compulsive" crime on the basis of models for these activities that he is already familiar with.

A theatrical performance or a staged confidence game requires a thorough scripting of the spoken content of the routine; but the vast part involving "expression given off" is often determined by meager stage directions. It is expected that the performer of illusions will already know a good deal about how to manage his voice, his face, and his body, although he – as well as any person who directs him – may find it difficult indeed to provide a detailed verbal statement of this kind of knowledge. And in this, of course, we approach the situation of the straightforward man in the street. Socialization may not so much involve a learning of the many specific details of a single concrete part – often there could not be enough time or energy for this. What does seem to be required of the individual is that he learn enough pieces of expression to be able to "fill in" and manage, more or less, any part that he is likely to be given. The legitimate performances of everyday life are not "acted" or "put on" in the sense that the performer knows in advance just what he is going to do, and does this solely because of the effect it is likely to have. The expressions it is felt he is giving off will be especially "inaccessible" to him. But as in the case of less legitimate performers, the incapacity of the ordinary individual to formulate in advance the movements of his eyes and body does not mean that he will not express himself through these devices in a way that is dramatized and pre-formed in his repertoire of actions. In short, we all act better than we know how.

When we watch a television wrestler gouge, foul, and snarl at his opponent we are quite ready to see that, in spite of the dust, he is, and knows he is, merely playing at being the "heavy," and that in another match he may be given the other role, that of clean-cut wrestler, and perform this with equal verve and proficiency. We seem less ready to see, however, that while such details as the number and character of the falls may be fixed beforehand, the details of the expressions and movements used do not come from a script but from command of an idiom, a command that is exercised from moment to moment with little calculation or forethought.

In reading of persons in the West Indies who become the "horse" or the one possessed of a voodoo spirit, it is enlightening to learn that the person possessed will be able to provide a correct portrayal of the god that has entered him because of "the knowledge and memories accumulated in a life spent visiting congregations of the cult"; that the person possessed will be in just the right social relation to those who are watching; that possession occurs at just the right moment in the ceremonial undertakings, the possessed one carrying out his ritual obligations to the point of participating in a kind of skit with persons possessed at the time with other spirits. But in learning this, it is important to see that this contextual structuring of the horse's role still allows participants in the cult to believe that possession is a real thing and that persons are possessed at random by gods whom they cannot select.

And when we observe a young American middle-class girl playing dumb for the benefit of her boyfriend, we are ready to point to items of guile and contrivance in her behavior. But like herself and her boyfriend, we accept as an unperformed fact that this performer *is* a young American middle-class girl. But surely here we neglect the greater part of the performance. It is commonplace to say that different social groupings express in different ways such attributes as age, sex, territory, and class status, and that in each case these bare attributes are elaborated by means of a distinctive complex cultural configuration of proper ways of conducting oneself. To *be* a given kind of person, then, is not merely to possess the required attributes, but also to sustain the standards of conduct and appearance that one's social grouping attaches thereto. The unthinking ease with which performers consistently carry off such standard-maintaining routines does not deny that a performance has occurred, merely that the participants have been aware of it.

A status, a position, a social place is not a material thing, to be possessed and then displayed; it is a pattern of appropriate conduct, coherent, embellished, and well articulated. Performed with ease or clumsiness, awareness or not, guile or good faith, it is none the less something that must be enacted and portrayed, something that must be realized. Sartre, here, provides a good illustration:

> Let us consider this waiter in the café. His movement is quick and forward, a little too precise, a little too rapid. He comes toward the patrons with a step a little too quick. He bends forward a little too eagerly; his voice, his eyes express an interest a little too solicitous for the order of the customer. Finally there he returns, trying to imitate in his walk the inflexible stiffness of some kind of automaton while carrying his tray with the recklessness of a tightrope-walker by putting it in a perpetually unstable, perpetually broken equilibrium which he perpetually re-establishes by a light movement of the arm and hand. All his behavior seems to us a game. He applies himself to chaining his movements as if they were mechanisms, the one regulating the other; his gestures and even his voice seem to be mechanisms; he gives himself the quickness and pitiless rapidity of things. He is playing, he is amusing himself. But what is he playing? We need not watch long before we can explain it: he is playing at being a waiter in a café. There is nothing there to surprise us. The game is a kind of marking out and investigation. The child plays with his body in order to explore it, to take inventory of it; the waiter in the café plays with his condition in order to *realize* it. This obligation is not different from that which is imposed on all tradesmen. Their condition is wholly one of ceremony. The public demands of them that they realize it as a ceremony; there is the dance of the grocer, of the tailor, of the auctioneer, by which they endeavor to persuade their clientele that they are nothing but a grocer, an auctioneer, a tailor. A grocer who dreams is offensive to the buyer, because such a grocer is not wholly a grocer. Society demands that he limit himself to his function as a grocer, just as the soldier at attention makes himself into a soldier-thing with a direct regard which does

not see at all, which is no longer meant to see, since it is the rule and not the interest of the moment which determines the point he must fix his eyes on (the sight "fixed at ten paces"). There are indeed many precautions to imprison a man in what he is, as if we lived in perpetual fear that he might escape from it, that he might break away and suddenly elude his condition.[10]

NOTES

1. Robert Ezra Park, *Race and Culture* (Glencoe, IL: The Free Press, 1950), p. 249.
2. Ibid., p. 250.
3. Edith Lentz, "A Comparison of Medical and Surgical Floors" (Mimeo: New York State School of Industrial and Labor Relations, Cornell University, 1954), pp. 2–3.
4. Jean-Paul Sartre, *Being and Nothingness*, trans. Hazel E. Barnes (New York: Philosophical Library, 1956), p. 60.
5. Charles H. Cooley, *Human Nature and the Social Order* (New York: Scribner's, 1922), pp. 352–3.
6. Emile Durkheim, *The Elementary Forms of the Religious Life*, trans. J. W. Swain (London: Allen & Unwin, 1926), p. 272.
7. George Santayana, *Soliloquies in England and Later Soliloquies* (New York: Scribner's, 1922), pp. 133–4.
8. Simone de Beauvoir, *The Second Sex*, trans. H. M. Parshley (New York: Knopf, 1953), p. 533.
9. See R. K. Merton, *Social Theory and Social Structure* (Glencoe, IL: The Free Press, revised and enlarged edition, 1957), p. 265ff.
10. Sartre, *Being and Nothingness*, p. 59.

Chapter 3

Symbolic Interactionism [1969]

Herbert Blumer

The Methodological Position of Symbolic Interactionism

Exploration and inspection, representing respectively depiction and analysis, constitute the necessary procedure in direct examination of the empirical social world. They comprise what is sometimes spoken of as "naturalistic" investigation – investigation that is directed to a given empirical world in its natural, ongoing character instead of to a simulation of such a world, or to an abstraction from it (as in the case of laboratory experimentation), or to a substitute for the world in the form of a preset image of it. The merit of naturalistic study is that it respects and stays close to the empirical domain. This respect and closeness is particularly important in the social sciences because of the formation of different worlds and spheres of life by human beings in their group existence. Such worlds both represent and shape the social life of people, their activities, their relations, and their institutions. Such a world or sphere of life is almost always remote and unknown to the research scholar; this is a major reason why he wants to study it. To come to know it he should get close to it in its actual empirical character. Without doing this he has no assurance that his guiding imagery of the sphere or world, or the problem he sets forth for it, or the leads he lays down, or the data he selects, or the kinds of relations that he prefigures between them, or the theoretical views that guide his interpretations are empirically valid. Naturalistic inquiry, embracing the dual

Herbert Blumer, "Symbolic Interactionism," pp. 46–8, 50–2, 78–89 from Herbert Blumer, *Symbolic Interactionism: Perspective and Method*, 1st edn. Upper Saddle River, NJ: Prentice-Hall, 1998. Copyright © 1969. Reprinted by permission of Pearson Education, Inc., Upper Saddle River, NJ.

Contemporary Sociological Theory, Third Edition. Edited by Craig Calhoun, Joseph Gerteis, James Moody, Steven Pfaff, and Indermohan Virk. Editorial material and organization © 2012 John Wiley & Sons, Ltd. Published 2012 by John Wiley & Sons, Ltd.

procedures of exploration and inspection, is clearly necessary in the scientific study of human group life. It qualifies as being "scientific" in the best meaning of that term.

My presentation has set forth rather sharply the opposition between naturalistic inquiry, in the form of exploration and inspection, and the formalized type of inquiry so vigorously espoused in current methodology. This opposition needs to be stressed in the hope of releasing social scientists from unwitting captivity to a format of inquiry that is taken for granted as the naturally proper way in which to conduct scientific study. The spokesmen for naturalistic inquiry in the social and psychological sciences today are indeed very few despite the fact that many noteworthy studies in the social sciences are products of naturalistic study. The consideration of naturalistic inquiry scarcely enters into the content of present-day methodology. Further, as far as I can observe, training in naturalistic inquiry is soft-pedaled or not given at all in our major graduate departments. There is a widespread ignorance of it and an accompanying blindness to its necessity. This is unfortunate for the social and psychological sciences since, as empirical sciences, their mission is to come to grips with their empirical world.

Methodological orientation

Symbolic interactionism is a down-to-earth approach to the scientific study of human group life and human conduct. Its empirical world is the natural world of such group life and conduct. It lodges its problems in this natural world, conducts its studies in it, and derives its interpretations from such naturalistic studies. If it wishes to study religious cult behavior it will go to actual religious cults and observe them carefully as they carry on their lives. If it wishes to study social movements it will trace carefully the career, the history, and the life experiences of actual movements. If it wishes to study drug use among adolescents it will go to the actual life of such adolescents to observe and analyze such use. And similarly with respect to other matters that engage its attention. Its methodological stance, accordingly, is that of direct examination of the empirical social world – the methodological approach that I have discussed above. It recognizes that such direct examination permits the scholar to meet all of the basic requirements of an empirical science: to confront an empirical world that is available for observation and analysis; to raise abstract problems with regard to that world; to gather necessary data through careful and disciplined examination of that world; to unearth relations between categories of such data; to formulate propositions with regard to such relations; to weave such propositions into a theoretical scheme; and to test the problems, the data, the relations, the propositions, and the theory by renewed examination of the empirical world. Symbolic interactionism is not misled by the mythical belief that to be scientific it is necessary to shape one's study to fit a pre-established protocol of empirical inquiry, such as adopting the working procedure of advanced physical science, or devising in advance a fixed logical or mathematical model, or forcing the study into the mould of laboratory experimentation, or imposing a statistical or mathematical framework on the study, or organizing it in terms of preset variables, or restricting it to a particular standardized procedure such as survey research. Symbolic interactionism recognizes that the genuine mark of an empirical science is to respect the nature of its empirical world – to fit its problems, its guiding conceptions, its procedures of inquiry, its techniques of study, its concepts, and its theories to that world. It believes that this determination of problems, concepts, research techniques, and theoretical schemes should be done by the *direct* examination of the actual empirical social world rather than by working with a simulation of that world, or with a preset model of that world, or with a picture of that world derived from a few scattered observations of it, or with a picture of that world fashioned in advance to meet the dictates of some imported theoretical scheme or of some scheme of "scientific" procedure, or with a picture of the world built up from partial and untested accounts of that world. For symbolic interactionism the nature of the empirical social world is to be discovered, to be dug out by a direct, careful, and probing examination of that world. […]

Granted that human group life has the character that is stated by the premises of symbolic interactionism, the general topic I wish to consider is how does one study human group life and social action. I do not have in mind an identification and analysis of the numerous separate procedures that may be employed at one or another point in carrying on exploration and inspection. There is a sizeable literature, very uneven to be true, on a fair number of such separate procedures, such as direct observation, field study, participant observation, case study, interviewing, use of life histories, use of letters and diaries, use of public documents, panel discussions, and use of conversations. There is great need, I may add, of careful circumspective study of such procedures, not to bring them inside a standardized format but to improve their capacity as instruments for discovering what is taking place in actual group life. My current concern, however, lies in a different direction, namely, to point out several of the more important methodological implications of the symbolic interactionist's view of human group life and social action. I want to consider such implications in the case of each of four central conceptions in symbolic interactionism. These four central conceptions are: (1) people, individually and collectively, are prepared to act on the basis of the meanings of the objects that comprise their world; (2) the association of people is necessarily in the form of a process in which they are making indications to one another and interpreting each other's indications; (3) social acts, whether individual or collective, are constructed through a process in which the actors note, interpret, and assess the situations confronting them; and (4) the complex interlinkages of acts that comprise organization, institutions, division of labor, and networks of interdependency are moving and not static affairs. I wish to discuss each of these in turn.

(1) The contention that people act on the basis of the meaning of their objects has profound methodological implications. It signifies immediately that if the scholar wishes to understand the action of people it is necessary for him to see their objects as they see them. Failure to see their objects as they see them, or a substitution

of his meanings of the objects for their meanings, is the gravest kind of error that the social scientist can commit. It leads to the setting up of a fictitious world. Simply put, people act toward things on the basis of the meaning that these things have for them, not on the basis of the meaning that these things have for the outside scholar. Yet we are confronted right and left with studies of human group life and of the behavior of people in which the scholar has made no attempt to find out how the people see what they are acting toward. This neglect is officially fostered by two pernicious tendencies in current methodology: (1) the belief that mere expertise in the use of scientific techniques plus facility in some given theory are sufficient equipment to study an unfamiliar area; and (2) the stress that is placed on being objective, which all too frequently merely means seeing things from the position of the detached outside observer. We have multitudes of studies of groups such as delinquents, police, military elites, restless students, racial minorities, and labor unions in which the scholar is unfamiliar with the life of the groups and makes little, if any, effort to get inside their worlds of meanings. We are compelled, I believe, to recognize that this is a widespread practice in the social sciences.

To try to identify the objects that comprise the world of an individual or a collectivity is not simple or easy for the scholar who is not familiar with that world. It requires, first of all, ability to place oneself in the position of the individual or collectivity. This ability to take the roles of others, like any other potential skill, requires cultivation to be effective. By and large, the training of scholars in the social sciences today is not concerned with the cultivation of this ability nor do their usual practices in research study foster its development. Second, to identify the objects of central concern one must have a body of relevant observations. These necessary observations are rarely those that are yielded by standard research procedure such as questionnaires, polls, scales, use of survey research items, or the setting of predesignated variables. Instead, they are in the form of descriptive accounts from the actors of how they see the objects, how they have acted toward the objects in a variety of different situations, and how they refer to the objects in their conversations with members of their own group. The depiction of key objects that emerge from such accounts should, in turn, be subject to probing and critical collective discussion by a group of well-informed participants in the given world. This latter procedure is a genuine "must" to guard against the admitted deficiencies of individual accounts. Third, as mentioned in earlier discussion, research scholars, like human beings in general, are slaves to their own pre-established images and thus are prone to assume that other people see the given objects as they, the scholars, see them. Scholars need to guard against this proneness and to give high priority to deliberate testing of their images.

All these observations make clear the need for a different methodological approach if one takes seriously the proposition that people act toward objects on the basis of the meaning of such objects for them. This proposition calls for kinds of inquiry significantly different from those generally sanctioned and encouraged today. Since people everywhere and in all of their groups live in worlds of objects and act in terms of the meaning of these objects to them, it is a matter of simple sense that one has to identify the objects and their meaning. The research position of symbolic interaction is predicated on this recognition. [...]

Society as Symbolic Interaction

The term "symbolic interaction" refers, of course, to the peculiar and distinctive character of interaction as it takes place between human beings. The peculiarity consists in the fact that human beings interpret or "define" each other's actions instead of merely reacting to each other's actions. Their "response" is not made directly to the actions of one another but instead is based on the meaning which they attach to such actions. Thus, human interaction is mediated by the use of symbols, by interpretation, or by ascertaining the meaning of one another's actions. This mediation is equivalent to inserting a process of interpretation between stimulus and response in the case of human behavior.

The simple recognition that human beings interpret each other's actions as the means of acting toward one another has permeated the thought and writings of many scholars of human conduct and of human group life. Yet few of them have endeavored to analyze what such interpretation implies about the nature of the human being or about the nature of human association. They are usually content with a mere recognition that "interpretation" should be caught by the student, or with a simple realization that symbols, such as cultural norms or values, must be introduced into their analyses. Only G. H. Mead, in my judgment, has sought to think through what the act of interpretation implies for an understanding of the human being, human action, and human association. The essentials of his analysis are so penetrating and profound and so important for an understanding of human group life that I wish to spell them out, even though briefly.

The key feature in Mead's analysis is that the human being has a self. This idea should not be cast aside as esoteric or glossed over as something that is obvious and hence not worthy of attention. In declaring that the human being has a self, Mead had in mind chiefly that the human being can be the object of his own actions. He can act toward himself as he might act toward others. Each of us is familiar with actions of this sort in which the human being gets angry with himself, rebuffs himself, takes pride in himself, argues with himself, tries to bolster his own courage, tells himself that he should "do this" or not "do that," sets goals for himself, makes compromises with himself, and plans what he is going to do. That the human being acts toward himself in these and countless other ways is a matter of easy empirical observation. To recognize that the human being can act toward himself is no mystical conjuration.

Mead regards this ability of the human being to act toward himself as the central mechanism with which the human being faces and deals with his world. This mechanism enables the human being to make indications to himself of things in his surroundings and thus to guide his actions by what he notes. Anything of which a human being is conscious is something which he is indicating to himself – the ticking of a clock, a knock at the door, the appearance of a friend, the remark made by a companion, a recognition that he has a task to perform, or the realization that he has a cold. Conversely, anything of which he is not conscious is, *ipso facto*, something which he is not indicating to himself. The conscious life of the human being, from the time that he awakens until he falls asleep, is a continual flow of self-indications – notations of the things with which he deals and takes into account. We are given, then, a picture of the human being as an organism which confronts its world with a mechanism for making indications to itself. This is the mechanism that is involved in interpreting the actions of others. To interpret the actions of another is to point out to oneself that the action has this or that meaning or character.

Now, according to Mead, the significance of making indications to oneself is of paramount importance. The importance lies along two lines. First, to indicate something is to extricate it from its setting, to hold it apart, to give it a meaning or, in Mead's language, to make it into an object. An object – that is to say, anything that an individual indicates to himself – is different from a stimulus; instead of having an intrinsic character which acts on the individual and which can be identified apart from the individual, its character or meaning is conferred on it by the individual. The object is a product of the individual's disposition to act instead of being an antecedent stimulus which evokes the act. Instead of the individual being surrounded by an environment of pre-existing objects which play upon him and call forth his behavior, the proper picture is that he constructs his objects on the basis of his on-going activity. In any of his countless acts – whether minor, like dressing himself, or major, like organizing himself for a professional career – the individual is designating different objects to himself, giving them meaning, judging their suitability to his action, and making decisions on the basis of the judgment. This is what is meant by interpretation or acting on the basis of symbols.

The second important implication of the fact that the human being makes indications to himself is that his action is constructed or built up instead of being a mere release. Whatever the action in which he is engaged, the human individual proceeds by pointing out to himself the divergent things which have to be taken into account in the course of his action. He has to note what he wants to do and how he is to do it; he has to point out to himself the various conditions which may be instrumental to his action and those which may obstruct his action; he has to take account of the demands, the expectations, the prohibitions, and the threats as they may arise in the situation in which he is acting. His action is built up step by step through a process of such self-indication. The human individual pieces together and guides his action by taking account of different things and interpreting their significance for his prospective action. There is no instance of conscious action of which this is not true.

The process of constructing action through making indications to oneself cannot be swallowed up in any of the conventional psychological categories. This process is distinct from and different from what is spoken of as the "ego" – just as it is different from any other conception which conceives of the self in terms of composition or organization. Self-indication is a moving communicative process in which the individual notes things, assesses them, gives them a meaning, and decides to act on the basis of the meaning. The human being stands over against the world, or against "alters," with such a process and not with a mere ego. Further, the process of self-indication cannot be subsumed under the forces, whether from the outside or inside, which are presumed to play upon the individual to produce his behavior. Environmental pressures, external stimuli, organic drives, wishes, attitudes, feelings, ideas, and their like do not cover or explain the process of self-indication. The process of self-indication stands over against them in that the individual points out to himself and interprets the appearance or expression of such things, noting, a given social demand that is made on him, recognizing a command, observing that he is hungry, realizing that he wishes to buy something, aware that he has a given feeling, conscious that he dislikes eating with someone he despises, or aware that he is thinking of doing some given thing. By virtue of indicating such things to himself, he places himself over against them and is able to act back against them, accepting them, rejecting them, or transforming them in accordance with how he defines or interprets them. His behavior, accordingly, is not a result of such things as environmental pressures, stimuli, motives, attitudes, and ideas but arises instead from how he interprets and handles these things in the action which he is constructing. The process of self-indication by means of which human action is formed cannot be accounted for by factors which precede the act. The process of self-indication exists in its own right and must be accepted and studied as such. It is through this process that the human being constructs his conscious action.

Now Mead recognizes that the formation of action by the individual through a process of self-indication always takes place in a social context. Since this matter is so vital to an understanding of symbolic interaction it needs to be explained carefully. Fundamentally, group action takes the form of a fitting together of individual lines of action. Each individual aligns his action to the action of others by ascertaining what they are doing or what they intend to do – that is, by getting the meaning of their acts. For Mead, this is done by the individual "taking the role" of others – either the role of a specific person or the role of a group (Mead's "generalized other"). In taking such roles the individual seeks to ascertain the intention or direction of the acts of others. He forms and aligns his own action on the basis of such interpretation of the acts of others. This is the fundamental way in which group action takes place in human society.

The foregoing are the essential features, as I see them, in Mead's analysis of the bases of symbolic interaction. They presuppose the following: that human society is made up of individuals who have selves (that is, make indications to themselves); that individual action is a construction and not a release, being built up by the individual through noting and interpreting features of the situations in which he acts; that group or collective action consists of the aligning of individual actions, brought about by the individuals' interpreting or taking into account each other's actions. Since my purpose is to present and not to defend the position of symbolic interaction I shall not endeavor in this essay to advance support for the three premises which I have just indicated. I wish merely to say that the three premises can be easily verified empirically. I know of no instance of human group action to which the three premises do not apply. The reader is challenged to find or think of a single instance which they do not fit.

I wish now to point out that sociological views of human society are, in general, markedly at variance with the premises which I have indicated as underlying symbolic interaction. Indeed, the predominant number of such views, especially those in vogue at the present time, do not see or treat human society as symbolic interaction. Wedded, as they tend to be, to some form of sociological determinism, they adopt images of human society, of individuals in it, and of group action which do not square with the premises of symbolic interaction. I wish to say a few words about the major lines of variance.

Sociological thought rarely recognizes or treats human societies as composed of individuals who have selves. Instead, they assume human beings to be merely organisms with some kind of organization, responding to forces which play upon them. Generally, although not exclusively, these forces are lodged in the make-up of the society, as in the case of "social system," "social structure," "culture," "status position," "social role," "custom," "institution," "collective representation," "social situation," "social norm," and "values." The assumption is that the behavior of people as members *of a society* is an expression of the play on them of these kinds of factors or forces. This, of course, is the logical position which is necessarily taken when the scholar explains their behavior or phases of their behavior in terms of one or another of such social factors. The individuals who compose a human society are treated as the media through which such factors operate, and the social action of such individuals is regarded as an expression of such factors. This approach or point of view denies, or at least ignores, that human beings have selves – that they act by making indications to themselves. Incidentally, the "self" is not brought into the picture by introducing such items as organic drives, motives, attitudes, feelings, internalized social factors, or psychological components. Such psychological factors have the same status as the social factors mentioned: they are regarded as factors which play on the individual to produce his action. They do not constitute the process of self-indication. The process of self-indication stands over against them, just as it stands over against the social factors which play on the human being. Practically all sociological conceptions of human society fail to recognize that the individuals who compose it have selves in the sense spoken of.

Correspondingly, such sociological conceptions do not regard the social actions of individuals in human society as being constructed by them through a process of interpretation. Instead, action is treated as a product of factors which play on and through individuals. The social behavior of people is not seen as built up by them through an interpretation of objects, situations, or the actions of others. If a place is given to "interpretation," the interpretation is regarded as merely an expression of other factors (such as motives) which precede the act, and accordingly disappears as a factor in its own right. Hence, the social action of people is treated as an outward flow or expression of forces playing on them rather than as acts which are built up by people through their interpretation of the situations in which they are placed.

These remarks suggest another significant line of difference between general sociological views and the position of symbolic interaction. These two sets of views differ in where they lodge social action. Under the perspective of symbolic interaction, social action is lodged in acting individuals who fit their respective lines of action to one another through a process of interpretation; group action is the collective action of such individuals. As opposed to this view, sociological conceptions generally lodge social action in the action of society or in some unit of society. Examples of this are legion. Let me cite a few. Some conceptions, in treating societies or human groups as "social systems," regard group action as an expression of a system, either in a state of balance or seeking to achieve balance. Or group action is conceived as an expression of the "functions" of a society or of a group. Or group action is regarded as the outward expression of elements lodged in society or the group, such as cultural demands, societal purposes, social values, or institutional stresses. These typical conceptions ignore or blot out a view of group life or of group action as consisting of the collective or concerted actions of individuals seeking to meet their life situations. If recognized at all, the efforts of people to develop collective acts to meet their situations are subsumed under the play of underlying or transcending forces which are lodged in society or its parts. The individuals composing the society or the group become "carriers," or media for the expression of such forces; and the interpretative behavior by means of which people form their actions is merely a coerced link in the play of such forces.

The indication of the foregoing lines of variance should help to put the position of symbolic interaction in better perspective. In the remaining discussion I wish to sketch somewhat more fully how human society appears in terms of symbolic interaction and to point out some methodological implications.

Human society is to be seen as consisting of acting people, and the life of the society is to be seen as consisting of their actions. The acting units may be separate individuals, collectivities whose members are acting together on a common quest, or organizations acting on behalf of a constituency. Respective examples are individual purchasers in a market, a play group or missionary band, and a business corporation or a national professional association. There is no empirically observable activity in a human society that does not spring from some acting unit. This banal statement needs to be stressed in light of the common practice of sociologists of reducing human society to social units that do not act – for example, social classes in modern society. Obviously, there are ways of viewing human society other than in terms of the acting units that compose it. I merely wish to point out that in respect to concrete or empirical activity human society must necessarily be seen in terms of the acting units that form it. I would add that any scheme of human society claiming to be a realistic analysis has to respect and be congruent with the empirical recognition that a human society consists of acting units.

Corresponding respect must be shown to the conditions under which such units act. One primary condition is that action takes place in and with regard to a situation. Whatever be the acting unit – an individual, a family, a school, a church, a business firm, a labor union, a legislature, and so on – any particular action is formed in the light of the situation in which it takes place. This leads to the recognition of a second major condition, namely, that the action is formed or constructed by interpreting the situation. The acting unit necessarily has to identify the things which it has to take into account – tasks, opportunities, obstacles, means, demands, discomforts, dangers, and the like; it has to assess them in some fashion and it has to make decisions on the basis of the assessment. Such interpretative behavior may take place in the individual guiding his own action, in a collectivity of individuals acting in concert, or in "agents" acting on behalf of a group or organization. Group life consists of acting units developing acts to meet the situations in which they are placed.

Usually, most of the situations encountered by people in a given society are defined or "structured" by them in the same way. Through previous interaction they develop and acquire common understandings or definitions of how to act in this or that situation. These common definitions enable people to act alike. The common repetitive behavior of people in such situations should not mislead the student into believing that no process of interpretation is in play; on the contrary, even though fixed, the actions of the participating people are constructed by them through a process of interpretation. Since ready-made and commonly accepted definitions are at hand, little strain is placed on people in guiding and organizing their acts. However, many other situations may not be defined in a single way by the participating people. In this event, their lines of action do not fit together readily and collective action is blocked. Interpretations have to be developed and effective accommodation of the participants to one another has to be worked out. In the case of such "undefined" situations, it is necessary to trace and study the emerging process of definition which is brought into play.

Insofar as sociologists or students of human society are concerned with the behavior of acting units, the position of symbolic interaction requires the student to catch the process of interpretation through which they construct their actions. This process is not to be caught merely by turning to conditions which are antecedent to the process. Such antecedent conditions are helpful in understanding the process insofar as they enter into it, but as mentioned previously they do not constitute the process. Nor can one catch the process merely by inferring its nature from the overt action which is its product. To catch the process, the student must take the role of the acting unit whose behavior he is studying. Since the interpretation is being made by the acting unit in terms of objects designated and appraised, meanings acquired, and decisions made, the process has to be seen from the standpoint of the acting unit. It is the recognition of this fact that makes the research work of such scholars as R. E. Park and W. I. Thomas so notable. To try to catch the interpretative process by remaining aloof as a so-called "objective" observer and refusing to take the role of the acting unit is to risk the worst kind of subjectivism – the objective observer is likely to fill in the process of interpretation with his own surmises in place of catching the process as it occurs in the experience of the acting unit which uses it.

By and large, of course, sociologists do not study human society in terms of its acting units. Instead, they are disposed to view human society in terms of structure or organization and to treat social action as an expression of such structure or organization. Thus, reliance is placed on such structural categories as social system, culture, norms, values, social stratification, status positions, social roles and institutional organization. These are used both to analyze human society and to account for social action within it. Other major interests of sociological scholars center around this focal theme of organization. One line of interest is to view organization in terms of the functions it is supposed to perform. Another line of interest is to study societal organization as a system seeking equilibrium; here the scholar endeavors to detect mechanisms which are indigenous to the system. Another line of interest is to identify forces which play upon organization to bring about changes in it; here the scholar endeavors, especially through comparative study, to isolate a relation between causative factors and structural results. These various lines of sociological perspective and interest, which are so strongly entrenched today, leap over the acting units of a society and bypass the interpretative process by which such acting units build up their actions.

These respective concerns with organization on one hand and with acting units on the other hand set the essential difference between conventional views of human society and the view of it implied in symbolic interaction. The latter view recognizes the presence of organization to human society and respects its importance. However, it sees and treats organization differently. The difference is along two major lines. First, from the standpoint of symbolic interaction the organization of a human society is the framework inside of which social action takes place and is not the determinant of that action. Second, such organization and changes in it are the product of the activity of acting units and not of "forces" which leave such acting units out of account. Each of these two major lines of difference should be explained briefly in order to obtain a better understanding of how human society appears in terms of symbolic interaction.

From the standpoint of symbolic interaction, social organization is a framework inside of which acting units develop their actions. Structural features, such as "culture," "social systems," "social stratification," or "social roles," set conditions for their action but do not determine their action. People – that is, acting units – do not act toward culture, social structure or the like; they act toward situations. Social organization enters into action only to the extent to which it shapes situations in which people act, and to the extent to which it supplies fixed sets of symbols which people use in interpreting their situations. These two forms of influence of social organization are important. In the case of settled and stabilized societies, such as isolated primitive tribes and peasant communities, the influence is certain to be profound. In the case of human societies, particularly modern societies, in which streams of new situations arise and old situations become unstable, the influence of organization decreases. One should bear in mind that the most important element confronting an acting unit in situations is the actions of other acting units. In modern society, with its increasing criss-crossing of lines of action, it is common for situations to arise in which the actions of participants are not previously regularized and standardized. To this extent, existing social organization does not shape the situations. Correspondingly, the symbols or tools of interpretation used by acting units in such situations may vary and shift considerably. For these reasons, social action may go beyond, or depart from, existing organization in any of its structural dimensions. The organization of a human society is not to be identified with the process of interpretation used by its acting units; even though it affects that process, it does not embrace or cover the process.

Perhaps the most outstanding consequence of viewing human society as organization is to overlook the part played by acting units in social change. The conventional procedure of sociologists is (a) to identify human society (or some part of it) in terms of an established or organized form, (b) to identify some factor or condition of change playing upon the human society or the given part of it, and (c) to identify the new form assumed by the society following upon the play of the factor of change. Such observations permit the student to couch propositions to the effect that a given factor of change playing upon a given organized form results in a given new organized form. Examples ranging from crude to refined statements are legion, such as that an economic depression increases solidarity in the families of working-men or that industrialization replaces extended families by nuclear families. My concern here is not with the validity of such propositions but with the methodological position which they presuppose. Essentially, such propositions either ignore the role of the interpretative behavior of acting units in the given instance of change, or else regard the interpretative behavior as coerced by the factor of change. I wish to point out that any line of social change, since it involves change in human action, is necessarily mediated by interpretation on the part of the people caught up in the change – the change appears in the form of new situations in which people have to construct new forms of action. Also, in line with what has been said previously, interpretations of new situations are not predetermined by conditions antecedent to the situations but depend on what is taken into account and assessed in the actual situations in which behavior is formed. Variations in interpretation may readily occur as different acting units cut out different objects in the situation, or give different weight to the objects which they note, or piece objects together in different patterns. In formulating propositions of social change, it would be wise to recognize that any given line of such change is mediated by acting units interpreting the situations with which they are confronted.

Students of human society will have to face the question of whether their preoccupation with categories of structure and organization can be squared with the interpretative process by means of which human beings, individually and collectively, act in human society. It is the discrepancy between the two which plagues such students in their efforts to attain scientific propositions of the sort achieved in the physical and biological sciences. It is this discrepancy, further, which is chiefly responsible for their difficulty in fitting hypothetical propositions to new arrays of empirical data. Efforts are made, of course, to overcome these shortcomings by devising new structural categories, by formulating new structural hypotheses, by developing more refined techniques of research, and even by formulating new methodological schemes of a structural character. These efforts continue to ignore or to explain away the interpretative process by which people act, individually and collectively, in society. The question remains whether human society or social action can be successfully analyzed by schemes which refuse to recognize human beings as they are, namely, as persons constructing individual and collective action through an interpretation of the situations which confront them.

Chapter 4

"Interaction Ritual Chains" [2004]

Randall Collins

Chapter 1

A THEORY OF INTERACTION ritual is the key to microsociology, and microsociology is the key to much that is larger. The smallscale, the here-and-now of face-to-face interaction, is the scene of action and the site of social actors. If we are going to find the agency of social life, it will be here. Here reside the energy of movement and change, the glue of solidarity, and the conservatism of stasis. Here is where intentionality and consciousness find their places; here, too, is the site of the emotional and unconscious aspects of human interaction. In whatever idiom, here is the empirical/experiential location for our social psychology, our symbolic or strategic interaction, our existential phenomenology or ethnomethodology, our arena of bargaining, games, exchange, or rational choice. Such theoretical positions may already seem to be extremely micro, intimate, and small scale. Yet we shall see they are for the most part not micro enough; some are mere glosses over what happens on the micro-interactional level. If we develop a sufficiently powerful theory on the micro-level, it will unlock some secrets of large-scale macrosociological changes as well.

Let us begin with two orienting points. First, the center of microsociological explanation is not the individual but the situation. Second, the term "ritual" is used in a confusing variety of ways; I must show what I will mean by it and why this approach yields the desired explanatory results.

Randall Collins, "Interaction Ritual Chains," pp. 3–4, 5, 15, 42–5, 47–54, 55–61, 62–3, 81–3, 87 from Randall Collins, *Interaction Ritual Chains*. Oxford: Princeton University Press, 2004. © 2004 by Princeton University Press. Reprinted by permission of Princeton University Press.

Contemporary Sociological Theory, Third Edition. Edited by Craig Calhoun, Joseph Gerteis, James Moody, Steven Pfaff, and Indermohan Virk. Editorial material and organization © 2012 John Wiley & Sons, Ltd. Published 2012 by John Wiley & Sons, Ltd.

[...]

Selecting an analytical starting point is a matter of strategic choice on the part of the theorist. But it is not merely an unreasoning *de gustibus non disputandum est*. I will attempt to show why we get more by starting with the situation and developing the individual, than by starting with individuals; and we get emphatically more than by the usual route of skipping from the individual to the action or cognition that ostensibly belongs to him or her and bypassing the situation entirely.

A theory of interaction ritual (IR) and interaction ritual chains is above all a theory of situations. It is a theory of momentary encounters among human bodies charged up with emotions and consciousness because they have gone through chains of previous encounters. What we mean by the social actor, the human individual, is a quasi-enduring, quasi-transient flux in time and space. Although we valorize and heroize this individual, we ought to recognize that this way of looking at things, this keyhole through which we peer at the universe, is the product of particular religious, political, and cultural trends of recent centuries. It is an ideology of how we regard it proper to think about ourselves and others, part of the folk idiom, not the most useful analytical starting point for microsociology.

This is not to say that the individual does not exist. But an individual is not simply a body, even though a body is an ingredient that individuals get constructed out of. My analytical strategy (and that of the founder of interaction ritual analysis, Erving Goffman), is to start with the dynamics of situations; from this we can derive almost everything that we want to know about individuals, as a moving precipitate across situations.

[...]

In a strong sense, the individual is the interaction ritual chain. The individual is the precipitate of past interactional situations and an ingredient of each new situation. An ingredient, not the determinant, because a situation is an emergent property. A situation is not merely the result of the individual who comes into it, nor even of a combination of individuals (although it is that, too). Situations have laws or processes of their own; and that is what IR theory is about.

Goffman concluded: "not men and their moments, but moments and their men." In gender-neutral language: not individuals and their interactions, but interactions and their individuals; not persons and their passions, but passions and their persons. "Every dog will have its day" is more accurately "every day will have its dog." Incidents shape their incumbents, however momentary they may be; encounters make their encountees. It is games that make sports heroes, politics that makes politicians into charismatic leaders, although the entire weight of record-keeping, news-story-writing, award-giving, speech-making, and advertising hype goes against understanding how this comes about. To see the common realities of everyday life sociologically requires a gestalt shift, a reversal of perspectives. Breaking such deeply ingrained conventional frames is not easy to do; but the more we can discipline ourselves to think everything through the sociology of the situation, the more we will understand why we do what we do.

[...]

One frequent criticism of ritual analysis is that it is overgeneralized. Rituals are held to be omnipresent; but if everything is a ritual, what isn't? In that case, the concept is useless to discriminate among the different kinds of things that happen. The criticism holds up best against a notion of ritual as serving functionally to equilibrate society, operating as a pressure-valve to let off hostilities, or as a celebration of shared values, in either case acting to sustain and restore social order. When things go wrong there are rituals; when things go right there are rituals. Ritual analysis just seems to illustrate, on a micro-level, the conservative bias of functionalism: everything is interpreted as part of the tendency of society automatically to produce social integration. But the problem here is functionalism, not ritual analysis. If we take rituals out of the functionalist context, we still have a clear model of what social ingredients go into making a ritual, and what outcomes occur; and the strength of those ingredients are variables, which determines just how much solidarity occurs. Rituals can fail, or they can succeed at different degrees of intensity. We can predict and test just what should result from these variable conditions. Such ritual analysis is not a tautology.

[...]

The central mechanism of interaction ritual theory is that occasions that combine a high degree of mutual focus of attention, that is, a high degree of intersubjectivity, together with a high degree of emotional entrainment – through bodily synchronization, mutual stimulation / arousal of participants' nervous systems – result in feelings of membership that are attached to cognitive symbols; and result also in the emotional energy of individual participants, giving them feelings of confidence, enthusiasm, and desire for action in what they consider a morally proper path. These moments of high degree of ritual intensity are high points of experience. They are high points of collective experience, the key moments of history, the times when significant things happen. These are moments that tear up old social structures or leave them behind, and shape new social structures. As Durkheim notes, these are moments like the French Revolution in the summer of 1789. We could add, they are moments like the key events of the Civil Rights movement in the 1960s; like the collapse of communist regimes in 1989 and 1991; and to a degree of significance that can be ascertained only in the future, as in the national mobilization in the United States following September 11, 2001. These examples are drawn from large-scale ritual mobilizations, and examples of a smaller scale could be drawn as we narrow our attention to smaller arenas of social action.

Interaction ritual theory is a theory of social dynamics, not merely of statics. Among social theorists there is a tendency to regard ritual analysis as conservative, a worship of traditions laid down in the past, a mechanism for reproducing social structure as it always existed. True enough, ritual analysis has often been used in this vein; and even theories like Bourdieu's, which combine Durkheim with Marx, see a mutually supporting interplay between the cultural or symbolic order and the order of economic power. For Bourdieu, ritual reproduces the cultural and therefore the economic fields. But this is to miss the transformative power of ritual mobilization. Intense ritual experience creates new symbolic objects and generates energies that fuel the major social changes. Interactional ritual is a mechanism of change. As long as there are potential occasions for ritual mobilization, there is the possibility for sudden and abrupt periods of change. Ritual can be repetitive and conservatizing, but it also provides the occasions on which changes break through.

In this respect IR theory mediates between postmodernist and similar theories that posit ubiquitous situational flux of meanings and identities, and a culturalist view that fixed scripts or repertoires are repeatedly called upon. The contrast is articulated by Lamont (2000, 243–44, 271), who provides evidence that there are "cultural and structural conditions that lead individuals to use some criteria of evaluation rather than others." The argument is parallel to my use of IR theory, which pushes the argument at a more micro-situational level: that the operative structural conditions are those that make up the ingredients of interaction ritual; and that cultural repertoires are created in particular kind of IRs, and fade out in others. To show the conditions under which ritual operates in one direction or the other is a principal topic of this book.

Intense moments of interaction ritual are high points not only for groups but also for individual lives. These are the events that we remember, that give meaning to our personal biographies, and sometimes to obsessive attempts to repeat them: whether participating in some great collective event such as a big political demonstration; or as spectator at some storied moment of popular entertainment or sports; or a personal encounter ranging from a sexual experience, to a strongly bonding friendly exchange, to a humiliating insult; the social atmosphere of an alcohol binge, a drug high, or a gambling victory; a bitter argument or an occasion of violence. Where these moments have a high degree of focused awareness and a peak of shared emotion, these personal experiences, too, can be crystalized in personal symbols, and kept alive in symbolic replays for greater or lesser expanses of one's life. These are the significant formative experiences that shape individuals; if the patterns endure, we are apt to call them personalities; if we disapprove of them we call them addictions. But this usage too easily reifies what is an ongoing flow of situations. The movement of individuals from one situation to another in what I call interaction ritual chains is an up-and-down of variation in the intensity of interaction rituals; shifts in behavior, in feeling and thought occur just as the situations shift. To be a constant personality is to be on an even keel where the kinds of interaction rituals flow constantly from one situation to the next. Here again, IR theory points up the dynamics of human lives, their possibility for dramatic shifts in direction.

IR theory provides a theory of individual motivation from one situation to the next. Emotional energy is what individuals seek; situations are attractive or unattractive to them to the extent that the interaction ritual is successful in providing emotional energy. This gives us a dynamic microsociology, in which we trace situations and their pull or push for individuals who come into them. Note the emphasis: the analytical starting point is the situation, and how it shapes individuals; situations generate and regenerate the emotions and the symbolism that charge up individuals and send them from one situation to another.

Interaction ritual is a full-scale social psychology, not only of emotions and situational behavior, but of cognition. Rituals generate symbols; experience in rituals inculcates those symbols in individual minds and memories. IR provides an explanation of variations in beliefs. Beliefs are not necessarily constant, but situationally fluctuate, as a number of theorists have argued and as researchers have demonstrated (Swidler 1986; Lamont 2000). What IR theory adds to contemporary cultural theory in this regard is that what people think they believe at a given moment is dependent upon the kind of interaction ritual taking place in that situation: people may genuinely and sincerely feel the beliefs they express at the moment they express them, especially when the conversational situation calls out a higher degree of emotional emphasis; but this does not mean that they act on these beliefs, or that they have a sincere feeling about them in other everyday interactions where the ritual focus is different. IR theory gives the conditions under which beliefs become salient, by rising and falling in emotional loading. Everyday life is the experience of moving through a chain of interaction rituals, charging up some symbols with emotional significance and leaving others to fade. IR theory leads us into a theory of the momentary flow of internal mental life, an explanation of subjectivity as well as intersubjectivity.

Durkheim held that the individual consciousness is a portion of the collective consciousness. This is tantamount to saying that the individual is socialized from the outside, by social experience carried within. This is surely true, as most social scientists would agree, as far as early childhood socialization is concerned. The argument of IR theory carries this further: we are constantly being socialized by our interactional experiences throughout our lives. But not in a unidirectional and homogeneous way; it is intense interaction rituals that generate the most powerful emotional energy and the most vivid symbols, and it is these that are internalized. Contrary to an implication of Freudian theory and others that stress early childhood experience, socialization once laid down does not endure forever; emotional energies and symbolic meanings fade if they are not renewed. IR theory is not a model of a wind-up doll, programmed early in life, which ever after walks through the pattern once laid down. It is a theory of moment-to-moment motivation, situation by situation. Thus it has high theoretical ambitions: to explain what any individual will do, at any moment in time; what he or she will feel, think, and say.

[…]

Chapter 2

AT THE CENTER OF AN INTERACTION RITUAL is the process in which participants develop a mutual focus of attention and become entrained in each other's bodily micro-rhythms and emotions. This chapter will present the details of this process in an explicit model of processes that take place in time: a fine-grained flow of micro-events that build up in patterns of split seconds and ebb away in longer periods of minutes, hours, and days. Rituals are constructed from a combination of

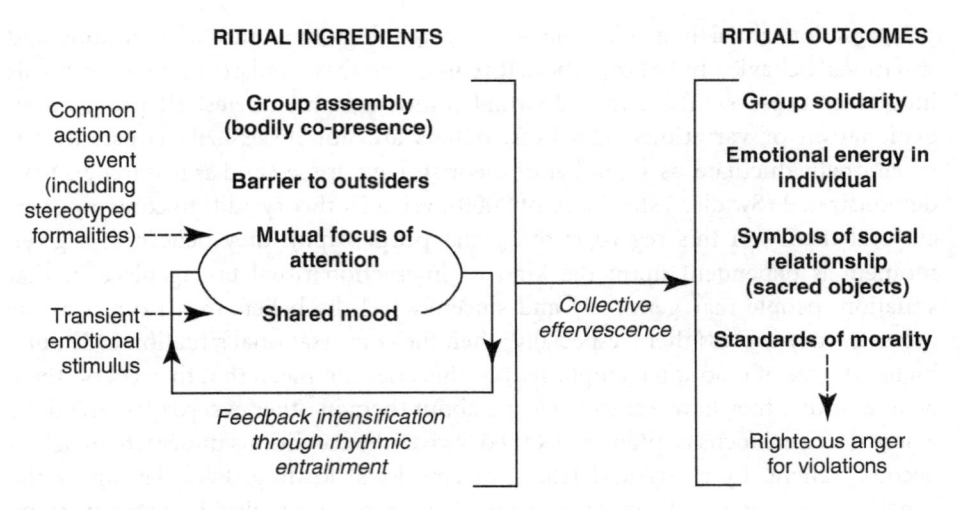

```
RITUAL INGREDIENTS                                RITUAL OUTCOMES

Common            Group assembly                    Group solidarity
action or         (bodily co-presence)
event                                                Emotional energy in
(including        Barrier to outsiders               individual
stereotyped
formalities) ---→ Mutual focus of                    Symbols of social
                  attention                          relationship
                                      Collective    (sacred objects)
Transient ---→    Shared mood         effervescence
emotional                                            Standards of morality
stimulus
                  Feedback intensification
                  through rhythmic                   Righteous anger
                  entrainment                        for violations
```

Figure 4.1 Interaction ritual.

ingredients that grow to differing levels of intensity, and result in the ritual outcomes of solidarity, symbolism, and individual emotional energy. This model enables us to examine carefully each part of the process. We will see what contingencies and variations can occur in each segment, and what effects these have on the outcomes. There are many different kinds of collective consciousness or intersubjectivity: different kinds of group membership, of symbolism, and of emotional tones of social experience. I will put forth a theory of how variations in interaction rituals generate the myriad varieties of human social life.

At a number of points, it is possible to bolster the theoretical model by empirical evidence from contemporary microsociology, notably studies of verbal conversation and studies in the sociology of emotions. As an illustration of what we can get from theoretical analysis of live video recordings of natural human interaction, I will present an analysis of a documentary film of firefighters and street crowds in the September 11, 2001 attack on New York City. This raw data brings out vividly how some IR conditions lead to merely momentary, others to long-term, effects.

Ritual ingredients, processes, and outcomes

Figure 4.1 depicts interaction ritual as a set of processes with causal connections and feedback loops among them. Everything in the model is a variable.

Interaction ritual (IR) has four main ingredients or initiating conditions:

1 Two or more people are physically assembled in the same place, so that they affect each other by their bodily presence, whether it is in the foreground of their conscious attention or not.
2 There are boundaries to outsiders so that participants have a sense of who is taking part and who is excluded.

3 People focus their attention upon a common object or activity, and by communicating this focus to each other become mutually aware of each other's focus of attention.
4 They share a common mood or emotional experience.

These ingredients feed back upon each other. Most importantly, number 3, the mutual focus of attention, and number 4, the common mood, reinforce each other. As the persons become more tightly focused on their common activity, more aware of what each other is doing and feeling, and more aware of each other's awareness, they experience their shared emotion more intensely, as it comes to dominate their awareness. Members of a cheering crowd become more enthusiastic, just as participants at a religious service become more respectful and solemn, or at a funeral become more sorrowful, than before they began. It is the same on the small-scale level of a conversation; as the interaction becomes more engrossing, participants get caught up in the rhythm and mood of the talk. We shall examine the micro-empirical evidence on this later. The key process is participants' mutual entrainment of emotion and attention, producing a shared emotional / cognitive experience. What Durkheim called collective consciousness is this micro-situational production of moments of intersubjectivity.

There are four main outcomes of interaction rituals. To the extent that the ingredients successfully combine and build up to high levels of mutually focused and emotionally shared attention, participants have the experience of

1 group solidarity, a feeling of membership;
2 emotional energy [EE] in the individual: a feeling of confidence, elation, strength, enthusiasm, and initiative in taking action;
3 symbols that represent the group: emblems or other representations (visual icons, words, gestures) that members feel are associated with themselves collectively; these are Durkheim's "sacred objects." Persons pumped up with feelings of group solidarity treat symbols with great respect and defend them against the disrespect of outsiders, and even more, of renegade insiders;
4 feelings of morality: the sense of rightness in adhering to the group, respecting its symbols, and defending both against transgressors. Along with this goes the sense of moral evil or impropriety in violating the group's solidarity and its symbolic representations.

These are the basic elements of the theory. In the following sections I will examine the evidence on how each of these operates.

Formal rituals and natural rituals

At first glance, what seems to be missing in this list are just those items that make up the usual definition of "ritual." In common parlance, a ritual is a formal ceremony, the going through of a set of stereotyped actions: reciting verbal formulas, singing, making traditional gestures, wearing traditional costumes. As we have seen from Durkheim's analysis of religious ritual, the formality and the stereotyped activity are not the crucial ingredients; they only contribute to the core process of intersubjectivity and shared emotion, which is to say to the experience of collective consciousness and collective effervescence, insofar as they contribute to a mutual focus of attention. This is indicated on the far left side of Figure 4.1, where a dashed arrow flows from "common action or event (including stereotyped formalities)" to "mutual focus of attention." Stereotyped formulas can generate a socially successful ritual, if indeed the participants also experience a shared emotion, and if they go on to heighten their sense of mutual participation by becoming strongly aware of each other's consciousness. Without this, the ritual is merely "formal," an empty going through of the forms, even a dead ceremonialism.

Mutual focus of attention is a crucial ingredient for a ritual to work; but this focus may come about spontaneously and without explicit concern that this is happening. Goffman's examples of the little interaction rituals of everyday sociability are generally of this sort. Whether you call people by their first names or not is usually not a matter of conscious attention, but it is a small-scale ritual nevertheless; and as we shall see, the difference between high-solidarity conversations and low-solidarity conversations happens on the level of rhythmic features that have no formally recognized rules attached to them. Goffman's examples come from the small scale of momentary social encounters, but spontaneously enacted rituals occur also on a larger scale of public groups, as in the examples Durkheim gives of political and military situations parallel to religious rituals. The crowds gathered during the French Revolution were often improvising new rituals. These were highly effective, even at their first moment without the resources of stereotyped activities, because they had a high degree of mutual focus and shared emotion. Out of such situations, as Durkheim was fond of noting, new symbols are created.

We may refer to those interactions as "natural rituals" that build up mutual focus and emotional entrainment without formally stereotyped procedures; and to those that are initiated by a commonly recognized apparatus of ceremonial procedures as "formal rituals." From the point of view of what makes an interaction ritual work, the core ingredients, processes, and outcomes are the same. Both natural ritual and formal rituals can generate symbols and feelings of membership, and both can reach high degrees of intensity. Beyond this commonality, not all symbolic memberships are of the same kind, and the details of how rituals are put together will affect the kind of membership categories that result. As we shall see, rituals initiated by formal procedures have a stronger effect on broadcasting and affirming a rigid sense of group boundaries than do rituals that begin spontaneously by a naturally occurring focus of attention and shared emotion. The latter give a more fluid sense of membership, unless they become crystallized and prolonged in symbols, which thereby tend to make subsequent IRs more formal. [...]

Failed rituals, empty rituals, forced rituals

Not all rituals are successful. Some fail dismally, even painfully; some mercifully fade away. Some are rebelled against as empty formalities, undergone under duress, gleefully discarded when possible. These variations are useful for refining our theory, and for testing the conditions that make rituals operate. Unsuccessful rituals are important substantively as well, for if every social encounter of everyday life from the most minor up to the major public gatherings is to be put before the scale and weighed against the standard of ritual intensity, we would not expect ritual intensity to be the same everywhere. Since I am going to argue that life is structured around the contrast between successful, socially magnetic ritual situations with their high degree of emotion, motivation, and symbolic charge, and situations of lesser ritualism, it is necessary to sharpen our eyes as to what makes the difference between rituals that are strong and those that are weak. Individuals are attracted to the most intense ritual charges they can get, indifferent to lesser rituals, and repelled by others; we see best what is doing the attracting if we look at what is causing the indifference and the repulsion.

Failed rituals are easiest to see in the case of formal rituals, since there is a public announcement and widespread understanding that a ritual is being attempted. Then we shall cast a glance at natural rituals that fail: political or other gatherings that don't click, demonstrations that don't come off; and at the little Goffmanian rituals of everyday life that don't work.

[...]

In this respect, natural rituals fail for much the same reasons that formal rituals can be empty: the political crowd that mills around aimlessly, its members' attention distracted to things happening outside the person making the speech or away from the enemy symbol to be confronted – individuals and little subgroups drifting away until those who are left are caught up in a deflationary emotion like rats leaving a sinking ship; the party that remains mired in little knots of perfunctory conversations and never builds up a collective effervescence. Here the missing ingredients are both a lack of shared attention – since duos are too fragmented from the larger group – and lack of a shared initial emotion that can be built up and transformed into a sense of collective participation. Low-intensity, perfunctory, or halting conversations exist in abundance, and in obvious contrast to those conversations that are engrossing. Although our normal form of attribution is to regard the conversations as indicators of the personalities one is encountering, these are situational outcomes that can be explained, as we shall later see in more detail, by the differing matchups of stocks of significant symbols to talk about, and by the level of synergy among the emotional energies of the parties to the conversational situation.

A nice contrast of successful and unsuccessful interaction rituals may be seen in the variety of New Year celebrations: some have a peak moment of genuine enthusiasm at the stroke of midnight (in this respect these celebrations are a mixture of traditional forms and natural, unscripted interactions) – while others consist in flat and perfunctory greetings for the new year. What makes the difference? My observation is that New Year celebrations that work are ones in which, in the hour or two before midnight, people in an assembled crowd start making noise – with the usual whistles, rattles, perhaps firecrackers – but above all making noises at each other, in their direction, better yet, in their face. This leads to entrainment; people start making noises and throwing streamers at each other, often breaking down barriers of acquaintanceship by drawing strangers into interaction. Notice that this interaction has no cognitive content; it is very much like small children running around and making noises at each other. In the context of the New Year celebration, this intruding noisily into someone else's personal space, sometimes even bodily in the mild and playful form of throwing streamers or confetti at them, is taken as friendly and not hostile or deviant. This mutual entrainment in noise-making builds up to a crescendo of noise as everyone is focused on counting down the seconds to midnight; when the anticipated focal point is reached, there is a burst of solidarity gestures, people hugging and kissing each other, even strangers. Compare the more staid New Year party: Individuals continue in normal conversations, saying intelligible things. This keeps them in distinctive little pockets of shared mentality, cutting them off from a larger intersubjectivity that might encompass the whole group. Interactions have not been reduced to the lowest common denominator, as in the mutual noise-making ties; shared emotion does not build up; and the climax of the stroke of midnight is given only perfunctory acknowledgment, immediately after which many participants say they are tired and want to go home. Successful rituals are exhilarating failed rituals are energy draining.

[...]

Is bodily presence necessary?

Ritual is essentially a bodily process. Human bodies moving into the same place starts off the ritual process. There is a buzz, an excitement, or at least a wariness when human bodies are near each other. Goffman (1981, 103) noted that even "when nothing eventful is occurring, sons in each other's presence are still nonetheless tracking one another and acting so as to make themselves trackable." From the point of view of evolutionary theory, humans as animals have evolved with nervous systems that pay attention to each other: there is always the possibility of fighting, or spreading an alarm; or, on the positive side, possible sexual contact and more generally sociable gestures. On the whole, the latter kind of evolved orientation toward positive interactions appears more central, since it helps explain why human bodies are so sensitive to each other, and so readily caught up in the shared attention and emotional entrainment that generates interaction rituals.

Yet isn't it possible to carry out a ritual without bodily presence? In modern times we have long-distance communications: by telephone, by video representations such as television, by computer screen. Is it not possible to generate mutual focus and emotional entrainment through these media of communication? In principle, these are empirical matters that can be studied experimentally: we could compare the amount of shared attention and emotion generated by these various interactional media, and their outcomes in level of solidarity, respect for symbolism, and individual EE. In lieu of systematic evidence, I suggest the following patterns.

[...]

Two further observations confirm the preference for bodily participation within an assembled group. After a particularly exciting or uplifting moment of vicarious participation, one wants to seek out someone else to tell about it. Thus, if one had been alone watching a game, a political election, or other engrossing public event, one wants to find someone else to share one's excitement with. If the excitement is strong enough, it isn't sufficient merely to tell the news, even in a loud, enthusiastic, repetitive voice. At peak moments of victory, or suspense followed by dramatic success, the excited viewer reaches out to touch, hug, or kiss someone. IR theory suggests testable details: the IR payoff should be highest in talking excitedly with someone who is also excited by the event; whereas viewers' own enthusiasm for their experienced drama ebbs away proportionately if the person they try to convey it to is less enthusiastic, passive, or remains uninvolved.

The same pattern is visible in sports celebrations and in other victory celebrations, as depicted in the famous photos of kissing and hugging on the street at the announcement of victory in World War II. Sports victory celebrations are events of predictable intensity, since there is a regular schedule leading up to championship games. At peak moments, built up emotionally in proportion to the amount of tension through the series of previous contests, there takes place an informal ritual in which the players touch each other repeatedly while repeating a few simple words or cries of victory. The bigger the victory and the more the suspense, the more body contact, and the more prolonged contact: the range goes from slapping hands, to body hugs, to piling onto a heap of bodies at the playing field. This is a stratified ritual, since the fans would also like to participate not only with their voices but by getting bodily as near to the players as possible. They are usually prevented from approaching them, thus leaving the high degree of bodily contact as a solidarity ritual reserved for the elite in the center of the ceremony; the fans can only watch, vocally participate, and engage in some bodily contact with each other.

Another observation supporting the preference for bodily present rituals is that attendance at sports events and other mass audience occasions has not declined with the availability of television. This is so even though, for many sports, television provides a better view of the action and the details of the athletes' performance. But people nevertheless prefer to go to the game, especially if it is a "big game" – that is a game in which the consequences are considered important and hence one can confidently expect to be part of an excited crowd. Watching on television is a second best if one cannot get tickets; and in that case, the preferred spectator experience – again, related to how much emotional intensity the game is expected to generate among its spectators – is to assemble a group of fans, a mini-crowd that provides its own resonance for building up shared excitement. Even for games that are routine – without important implications in the league standings, or other such significance – a large part of the pleasures of attending consists in just the moments when the crowd collectively builds up a sense of anticipation and its shared enthusiasm over the flow of events.

Games are rituals, contrived to produce situations of dramatic tension and victory; the rules of scoring and moving into position to score have been tinkered with over the years in order to make it "a better game" – which is to say, to provide moments of collective emotion. It is perfectly in keeping with such developments that sports emblems become sacred objects, venerated and treated with respect. Sports celebrities are themselves sacred objects, in just the same manner that Durkheim (1912/1965, 243–44) describes a political leader becoming an emblem for the crowd of which he is a center of attention [...]. The overt intent of the game – to win victories by following certain rules of competition, or to display athletic skill – is merely the surface content. What motivates people to witness games is primarily the experience of being at a highly successful ritual: successful because it has been contrived so that the ritual ingredients will all be present to a very high degree, especially the occurrence of strong emotion in a setting where it can be amplified by bodily interaction within the crowd focusing attention on the action of the game. The leisure time of modern societies – since the mid-nineteenth century when a sufficiently large group of spectators became available, free from the constraints of household and work – has become dominated by this species of deliberately invented ritual, designed to provide moments of ritual solidarity that previously would have been provided by religion, warfare, or political ceremony.

Sports events do not have the same recognized status as other formal rituals, but are generally regarded as a form of play, of the non-serious part of the world. Nevertheless, they are eminently successful in providing high points of ritual experience, and for many people they are preferred to participating in religious rituals (as evident when games compete with church services on Sundays). Games are natural rituals insofar as they unconsciously or nondeliberately bring about the ingredients for a successful ritual. But they are scheduled, predictable, and contrived (using a ritual technology to generate what might be considered an artificial ritual experience), and they bring together a community that has no other coherence, and no other purpose, than the experience of the peaks of ritual emotion itself.

The mechanism operates in the case of other forms of entertainment. Attending a concert has little advantage over listening to recordings as far as hearing the music is concerned; generally one hears it best on recordings. It is the experience of belonging to a focused crowd that provides the lure of a popular entertainment group; all the more so if the entertainers already have the status of being a sacred object, giving fans the additional excitement of being close to them – even if it is hundreds of feet away in a big arena. The main experience of the pop concert is the mood of the other fans; this is a textbook case of mutual buildup of emotion through bodily feedback in all its modalities. The same applies to a classical music performance, although the mood is more sedate, in keeping with the difference in social-class tone and atmosphere. Here, too, it is the experience of being at a special event – the hush of attention before the orchestra starts, the collective focus on the musicians – that makes the experience at the opera or the symphony a more significant experience than listening to the same music privately at home. This is not simply a matter of being seen by other people at a high-culture event – since under contemporary conditions these crowds are typically anonymous, in contrast to the more enclosed high-status communities in previous centuries who recognized each other at the opera – but comes from the subjective feelings of the ritual experience. The hypothesis is that participants have a stronger identification as persons attached to high culture if the crowd has been enthusiastic in response to the performance, than when the collective response is weaker; and that the effect of ritual intensity is stronger than the effect of being recognized by other people.

Televised and radio-broadcast concerts have such effects only weakly. The same holds for political and religious gatherings. Politicians' campaign speeches, nominating conventions, and important official addresses are televised and can be experienced at a distance. Nevertheless, persons who are strong partisans want to be physically present, confirming a reciprocal relation between identity and physical presence. The hypothesis is that attending political events in person increases partisanship, to the extent that the speech is a "good one" – in other words, that it involves the interplay of speaker and crowd that builds up shared enthusiasm; and reciprocally, those persons who already have an identification with the political leader or faction have a stronger desire to take part. The running off of these repetitive relationships is a self-reinforcing IR chain.

[...]

Religious services, like other collective experience of ritual, vary in their intensity. Distance media can provide some of the sense of shared attention and emotion, which give a feeling of attraction, membership, and respect. The strongest effects are reserved, however, for full bodily assembly. Conversion experiences – coming forward to be born again, or otherwise committing oneself to a life of religious dedication – happen primarily at big evangelical meetings (Johnson 1971). Personal presence in a crowd, worked up collectively to a strong shared emotion, gives the impetus for reshaping one's identity. The downside of religious conversion confirms the pattern as well. A considerable proportion of persons who are born again drop out of religious participation within a year; many persons are born again numerous times (Bromley 1988; Richardson 1978). It is the big, intense religious gatherings that bring forth the emotion and the shift in membership attachment; as one settles back into the routine of smaller and less collectively emotional church services, and then drifts away from attending, the identification and the emotional energy also fade.

[...]

On the whole, it appears that large-scale, relatively formal rituals come off better by remote communication than do small-scale natural rituals. This seems to be so because large-scale rituals are working with established symbols, already built up through previous iteration of an IR chain. Relatively impersonal rituals convey membership in large groups, only part of which ever assembles in one place; and thus distance communication gives a sense of something large that one belongs to. But this is effective only if there is at least intermittent personal contact with some other members, worshipers of the same symbols. And the remote broadcast must convey the audience's participation, not merely its leaders or performers.

How then do we assess recent forms of communication, including email and the Internet? For the most part, these lack the flow of interaction in real time; even if electronic communications happen within minutes, this is not the rhythm of immediate vocal participation, which as we shall see, is honed to tenths of seconds. There is little or no buildup of focus of attention in reading an email, no paralinguistic background signals of mutual engrossment. A written message may attempt to describe an emotion, or to cause one; but it seems rare that email is used for this purpose. A hypothesis is that the closer the flow of emails is to real conversational exchange, the more possibility of a sense of collective entrainment, as in a rapid exchange of emails in a period of minutes or seconds. But even here it is dubious that strong feelings of solidarity can be built up, or the charging up of a symbol with collective significance.

[...]

Solidarity prolonged and stored in symbols

High levels of emotional entrainment – collective effervescence – are ephemeral. How long will the solidarity and the emotional mood last? This depends on the transformation of short-term emotions into long-term emotions, which is to say, the extent to which they are stored in symbols that reinvoke them. Symbols, in turn, differ as to what kind of group solidarity they invoke, and thus what symbolic / emotional memories or meanings will do in affecting group interactions, and personal identities, in future situations.

Consider a range of situations where collective emotion is generated. At the lowest level are situations where a number of people are assembled, but with a very low focus of attention. Such would be people in a public waiting place like an airport departure lounge, or a queue lined up for tickets. Here there is little common mood, possibly even impatience and annoyance because the focus of different individuals and subclusters are at cross purposes. Nothing is prolonged from these situations except the fleeting desire to get it over with and get out of there.

At a higher intensity are situations with a buzz of excitement: being on a busy street in a city, in a crowded restaurant or bar. There is a palpable difference between being in an establishment where there are lots of people and one that is nearly empty. Unfocused crowds generate more tacit interaction than very sparse assemblies, and thus give a sense of social atmosphere. Even though there is no explicit interaction or focus of attention in such places, there is a form of social attraction to being there. Being in a crowd gives some sense of being "where the action is," even if you personally are not part of any well-defined action; the lure of the "bright lights of the city" is not so much the visual illumination but the minimal excitement of being within a mass of human bodies. As Durkheim indicates, the first step toward building up the "electricity" of collective effervescence is the move from sparse to dense bodily assembly. But in this alone there is little sense of solidarity with a recognizable group, and nothing that can prolong a sense of identification. What is lacking are symbols by means of which one could identify who was there, and that could reinvoke a sense of membership upon seeing them at another occasion.

A somewhat higher level of solidarity becomes possible in crowds that are focused by acting as an audience. Here the momentary sense of solidarity may become quite strong, insofar as the crowd takes part in a collective action – clapping, cheering, booing. These momentarily shared events, as we have seen, involve considerable micro-temporal coordination, a condition of collective entrainment that has very strong boundaries, intensely palpable when they are violated: one feels embarrassed when clapping at the wrong time or booing when others do not join in. The sense of collective solidarity and identity is stronger to just the extent that the crowd goes beyond being passive observers to actively taking part. This is an experience not only of responding to other people in the crowd (and to those on the stage, the playing field, or the podium) but of affecting them, thus becoming more of a part of the mutual entrainment by throwing oneself into it more fully. Thus applause is no mere passive response; the pleasure of the performance is to a considerable degree created in those moments when one has the opportunity to applaud, and from the audience's side the performer or the political speech-maker is being used to facilitate one's own feeling of collective action. Such effects are visible in a very high degree in collective experience where the crowd becomes very active, and especially in destructive or violent acts. Thus taking part in an ethnic riot (Horowitz 2001) is not simply a way of acting out a preexisting ethnic identity, but a way of strengthening it, re-creating or even creating it. The greater the entrainment, the greater the solidarity and identity consequences; and entrainment reaches much higher levels by activity than passivity.

Often these focused crowds acquire a symbol that can prolong the sense of the experience: usually this symbol is taken from whatever it was that the audience was consciously focused upon. For sports fans, this is the team itself, usually encapsulated in shorthand emblems; for entertainment fans, it is the performers, or possibly the music, play, or film itself that becomes the Durkheimian sacred object. But focused crowds nevertheless have rather weak long-term solidarity; their symbols, although charged up by the crowd's moment of collective effervescence, do not reinvoke the crowd itself, which on the whole is anonymous to most of its participants. There is no way for members of the group to recognize each other or identify with each other, except via what they clapped for. Those who happened to be together at an exciting moment at a sports stadium do not have much of a tie afterward. They may share some collective symbols, such as wearing the same team emblem, but their solidarity is rather situationally specific, reserved for those occasions when they happen to be at another sporting event, or in some area of conversation around just those symbols. These are examples of secondary group identities: groups whose members do not know each other personally. Benedict Anderson (1991) famously called them "imagined communities," but this is not quite accurate. What they imagine – what they have an image of – is the symbol that they focus upon, and the "community" is a volatile and episodic experience that comes out just at moments of high ritual intensity.

Focused crowds develop their collective effervescence in those moments when they are active rather than passive spectators. But since their feeling of solidarity is prolonged by symbols that are for the most part presented to them from outside, they do not have much opportunity to use those symbols in their own lives, as ingredients for constructing similarly engrossing IRs. These are passively received symbols that must wait to be recharged when there next occurs a performance of the concert, the game, or the political assembly. At best, they can recirculate the symbols in a second-order, conversational ritual, a reflexive meta-ritual referring to these primary rituals.

[...]

In sum, there are several distinctive ways in which symbols circulate and prolong group membership beyond ephemeral situations of emotional intensity. One is as objects that are in the focus of attention of emotionally entrained but otherwise anonymous crowds. The second is as symbols built up out of personal identities and narratives, in conversational rituals marking the tie between the conversationalists and the symbolic objects they are talking about. These symbols generally operate in two quite different circuits of social relationships; typically, the symbols of audiences, fans, partisans, and followers circulate from one mass gathering to another, and tend to fade in the interim; the symbols of personal identities and reputations are the small change of social relationships (and of business relationships), generally of lesser momentary intensity than audience symbols but used so frequently and in self-reinforcing networks so as to permeate their participants' sense of reality.

REFERENCES

Anderson, Benedict. 1991. *Imagined Communities: Reflections on the Origin and Spread of Nationalism*. London: Verso.

Bromley, Daniel G. 1988. *Falling from the Faith*. Newbury Park, CA: Sage.

Durkheim, Emile. 1965 (1912). *The Elementary Forms of the Religious Life*. New York: Free Press.

Goffman, Erving. 1981. *Forms of Talk*. Philadelphia, PA: University of Pennsylvania Press.

Horowitz, Donald J. 2001. *The Deadly Ethnic Riot*. Berkeley, CA: University of California Press.

Johnson, Weldon, T. 1971. "The Religious Crusade: Revival or Ritual?" *American Journal of Sociology*, 76: 873–80.

Lamont, Michele. 2000. *The Dignity of Working Men*. Cambridge, MA: Harvard University Press.

Richardson, James, T., ed. 1978. *Conversion Careers: In and Out of New Religions*. Beverly Hills, CA: Sage.

Swidler, Ann. 1986. "Culture in Action: Symbols and Strategies." *American Sociological Review*, 51: 273–86.

Part II

Exchange and Rationality

Introduction to Part II
5   Social Behavior as Exchange
6   Exchange and Power in Social Life
7   The Logic of Collective Action
8   A Theory of Group Solidarity
9   Cooperation without Law or Trust

Introduction to Part II

In *The Foundations of Social Theory*, James Coleman (1990) argued that the primary goal of social theory is to identify and explain the behavior of social systems, but that social systems are rarely observed as wholes. Instead, we observe the actions and interactions of actors (people, organizations) within the system. This distinction between what we want to explain and what we observe presents two theoretical challenges. First, theorists must account for how actors behave and second they must identify how the *interdependent* behavior of actors in the system combines to produce system behavior.

Social exchange and rational choice theories are primarily concerned with identifying the effects of interdependent action on social system behavior. Simplifying assumptions about how individuals behave allow theorists to set aside questions of individual motivation in favor of identifying how interdependent action relates to social system behavior. The basic behavioral assumption underlying these models, the rationality assumption, is that people are purposive actors who *optimize* (Coleman and Fararo, 1992: p. xi). Given a set of potential actions, actors choose the one that provides them the best outcome. The theoretical roots of optimization vary across theorists – with early accounts resting on Skinnerian behaviorism while more recent accounts rest strongly on ideas from microeconomics, and the extent of actors' ability or knowledge put in use to do the optimization varies widely by theorist – but the purposive, goal-oriented nature of individual action remains a key element of the work.

The basic postulate of optimization, seemingly benign when applied to normal situations such as finding the fastest route home from work, becomes sociologically interesting when other's optimization attempts intersect – when action becomes interdependent. Thus, the individually optimal route home transforms into a collective nightmare during rush hour, as each person's driving affects those around him or her.

Contemporary Sociological Theory, Third Edition. Edited by Craig Calhoun, Joseph Gerteis, James Moody, Steven Pfaff, and Indermohan Virk. Editorial material and organization © 2012 John Wiley & Sons, Ltd. Published 2012 by John Wiley & Sons, Ltd.

Moreover, when the "things" one optimizes are *social* (praise, esteem, or honor) instead of material, the quality of interaction might change. Since the value of social goods is hard to identify and can only be realized through interaction with others, the problem of optimization immediately becomes a problem of *social exchange*.

The strongest initial influence came from the behaviorist ideas of B.F. Skinner through the work of George Homans. For behaviorists, the primary determinant of individual action is the *operant conditioning* relationship between an actor and his or her environment. Operant conditioning states that any behavior elicits a response from the environment (which could be composed of other people). If the response is positive, actors are more likely to repeat the behavior, and when the response is negative they will be less likely to repeat the behavior. For example, the behavior "touching a hot stove" results in pain, which lessens the likelihood that one would touch the stove again. Based on what people have learned of the returns to past behaviors in their social environment, they modify their behavior in an attempt to maximize positive reactions and minimize negative reactions.

Homans' social version of operant conditioning posits that other people form the social environment that we react with. That each of us interacts as environment for another indicates a dual nature to interaction that can best be characterized as exchange. Simply put, "interaction between persons is an exchange of goods, material and non-material" (Homans, 1958: p. 597). For Homans, sociology consisted of explaining social behavior by identifying how people react to social situations, which in turn conditions the behavior of others, and thereby explains social facts. For example, norms in society work because, at their root, people want to avoid the social punishments meted out by others when a norm is violated. As each of us avoids disappointing others, and reprimanding those who disappoint us, norms are created. Homans later formalized his conception of social exchange theory into a set of basic propositions about individual behavior (Homans, 1961), which specified how people would be expected to act in the face of various types of rewards and punishments.

Homans' work was a direct response to functionalists such as Talcott Parsons. Homans argued that the elaborate theoretical schemes proposed by functionalists were unnecessary fictions that could not be observed and that were ineffective at explaining social behavior. Instead of grand structures, Homans wanted to focus more on local or "elementary" forms of social life. From these elementary building blocks, one could construct a more complete – and grounded – theory of social life. Parsons and Homans engaged in extended debates over which theoretical approach was most appropriate for sociology. The heart of the debate centers around what we can and can't know about society. Parsons argued that certain fundamental features of social systems were entirely social and could not be reduced to the individual level. Homans, on the other hand, felt that any property we could identify at the social system level must have its roots in the actions of individuals, and thus must ultimately be reducible to psychological factors. While each actively engaged the other, no resolution between the two approaches ever emerged. Instead, "We are left with an unresolved argument in which Parsons says that Homans has not explained structure and Homans says that Parsons has not explained structure." (Ritzer, 1992: p. 438)

In a second version of exchange theory, Peter Blau attempted to develop dyadic exchange theory without giving up the non-reducible character of social interaction (Blau, 1964). Blau's focus was on understanding collective outcomes, such as the distribution of power in a society. Instead of basing his work on operant conditioning, however, he worked more explicitly from an economic frame, arguing that social interaction has value and that people exchange these values. He argued that "To speak of social life is to speak of the associations between people" and that associations are, fundamentally, social exchanges (Blau, 2009: p. 12). Moreover, Blau differentiated himself from Homans by explicitly stating that some properties of social exchange are *emergent*, as the sum of social interaction could not be reduced to the psychological states of individuals. Building on Simmel's distinction between a triad and a dyad, Blau argued that extended patterns of exchange would give rise to organizational forms with qualities beyond those of the people in the organization.

The basis of social exchange for Blau rests on the anticipated rewards of association, with rewards being both intrinsic (the pleasure of being with someone) and extrinsic (a good or service that someone can provide). Social exchange, like economic exchange, occurs when association provides both parties with a good they could not get on their own. There are significant differences, however, between economic exchange and social exchange that hinge on the ambiguous nature of social exchange. First, because social goods (such as favors or giving advice) do not carry explicit values, one cannot be certain that an exchange is equal. Second, social exchanges usually occur over long periods (a favor one week for a favor weeks later), with no assurance that a "good" given will be returned. This results in two special features of social exchange. First, the ambiguity associated with social exchange requires trust for the exchange to function, a trust that is usually built slowly. Second, if the value of a good is ambiguous, and if people want to remain out of debt to others, then there is a tendency for social exchange to escalate. Social integration emerges from the individual desire for rewards. As Blau puts it, "An apparent 'altruism' pervades social life; people are anxious to benefit one another and to reciprocate for the benefits they receive. But beneath this seeming selflessness an underlying 'egoism' can be discovered; the tendency to help others is frequently motivated by the expectation that doing so will bring social rewards." (1964: 17). However, while the individual motivation to engage in social exchange has egoistic roots, Blau maintains that the emergent property of such action is greater social integration.

That people desire something others have is the basic element linking exchange to power. Power rests fundamentally on the ability to control access to a particular good. If one actor has exclusive access to something that other actors want, then they can extract greater rewards from them. While this is clear with a simple material commodity such as water, Blau argued that the same principle works for intrinsic social rewards. He illustrates this clearly with the example of the "principle of least interest" and romantic love. When one person in a relationship loves the other more (finds higher intrinsic value in the relationship) he or she will give up more to remain in the relationship, giving power to the one who loves the least.

If power comes from having something others want, then powerful people can extract social value from less powerful people through exchange. However, the only social commodity that *everyone* has access to is their own ability. As such, Blau argues that *subordination* is the one universal good that all can use for exchange. Those without access to a desired good can exchange with those who do have a desired good by subordinating themselves to the powerful. In so doing, an imbalance in exchange leads directly to a model of interpersonal power. By combining subordination with a process of legitimization (that people see some subordination as fair) Blau attempts (with limited success) to extend his dyadic model of power as a foundation for organizational power.

Recent developments from social exchange theory have tended in two directions. On the one hand, theorists have focused on how the organization of exchange modifies the distribution of power (Willer, 1999). Most of this work focuses on how restricting exchange to particular pairs in a wider network leads to differences in the distribution of power. The focus of this work is on *patterns* of exchange and the resulting system characteristics. A second approach has dealt less with exchange *per se* and more with the outcomes of interdependent action when actors are assumed individually rational. Unlike most current forms of exchange theory, much of this brand of rational choice theory is concerned with identifying population-level outcomes (such as the development of norms, the success of a political movement, the adoption of family planning practices, and so forth). The broad insight of this work is that there is often a marked distinction between what appears rational to an individual and what appears rational to a group.

The distinction between group and individual rationality is made most clearly by the economist Mancur Olson in his famous work on social movements. In *The Logic of Collective Action* (Olson, 1965), he shows that the existence of a large group with common interests is not sufficient to produce collective action for the good. When a good is indivisible – when all would benefit from it regardless of who contributed to producing it – rational individuals will not participate in producing the good. Since participation is a cost, people will free ride and let others produce the good. Of course, when everyone acts this way the good will not be produced. Identifying the conditions under which it is rational for people to participate in the production of collective goods has been one of the primary lines of research within this tradition (Oliver, Marwell, and Teixeira, 1985).

This line of reasoning forms the heart of Michael Hechter's *Principles of Group Solidarity*, where he attempts to provide an methodological individualist account for the classical problem of social order and group cohesion. Hechter argues that none of the classical approaches (norms, function, structure) can adequately account for variations in group solidarity (1987: p. 29), noting in particular the failure of such approaches to curtail free riding. For Hechter, "The challenge is to show how group obligations evolve and then how members are induced to honor them" without reference to black-box concepts such as "norms." Hechter reduces the problem of solidarity to the joint problem of the *extensiveness of group obligations* and the *probability of compliance with obligations*. Compliance is a complex problem with many variants, but ultimately rests on the control capacity of groups. This control capacity is also subject to free-riding issues (since it is a "second-order public good"), but they are often not as severe as general compliance. Interestingly, the strongest current theories of collective action suggest that interpersonal relations – or social exchanges of the type Blau identified – are important for producing collective actions (Kim and Bearman, 1997).

One of the most active theorists working in the rational choice field was James S. Coleman, who focused on basic questions of social origination, especially identifying how norms arise from a collection of self-interested actors. Norms – and regulative behavior more generally – require that individuals subordinate their interests to collective interests. Given the problems of free riding and the immediate returns to non-cooperation, even the well-recognized need for normative, regulative action is usually insufficient to produce such behavior. In *The Foundations of Social Theory* Coleman (1990) attempts to build a multi-level theory of social organization starting with individual actors, building through organizations, and on to society at large, based on the basic building blocks of individual self-interested action. The key to this work lies in the ability of people to control their own rights, with Coleman arguing that under certain circumstances it is individually rational for people to trade their rights in order to achieve collective ends.

Coming full circle to early exchange theorists and work on social networks, Coleman (1988) identifies networks of trust as an essential element in modern society (which sets up Cook, Hardin and Levi below). In his now classic treatment of social capital, Coleman describes how the relations actors have with others provides them with a generalized capacity for action – in much the same way as economic capital allows investors to build factories and start companies. While defining exactly what counts as "social capital" has sparked something of a minor industry in sociology, all agree that factors that contribute to the informal interactions among people contribute to a generalized capacity to act. For example, knowing many people increases your odds of knowing someone who can help you find a job, which provides a clear example of how social capital can generate economic capital. At the aggregate level, theorists have argued that social capital is key to understanding political participation and the ability of communities to cooperate for common good (Putnam, 2000). That relationships can provide an unspecified future resource changes the incentive structure implicit in much of the early work on social exchange, making decisions about who to exchange with and how power is distributed complex.

Much of the research on social capital and the importance of social ties for action and integration has focused on questions of trust. If we are to confidently interact with strangers, neighbors or even close friends, what level of trust do we need in each person? In each relation? Can trust serve as a mechanism for easing the sometimes self-defeating nature of otherwise self-interested actors? These types of questions have sparked a wide body of research on trust, ranging from the global economic implications of variance in trust to individual level social exchange experiments (Buchan *et al.*, 2002). Karen Cook has written a number of pieces that identify the social conditions that foster trust as well as the role of trust in building cooperation. But is trust necessary for *building* social institutions, or is trust a feature that while perhaps co-evolving with such institutions, nonetheless is absent at the moment of their formation? Cook, Hardin, and Levi tackle this question directly in the selection excerpted below, and they demonstrate that the ultimate success of these institutions rests on the chains of relations that compose social capital.

Critics of rational choice and exchange theory perspectives are many. First, many people argue that the basic behavioral assumptions of rational choice theory are incorrect. People simply do not optimize for their own self-interest, but instead act habitually, normatively or simply irrationally. While some rational choice theorists respond by changing the focus of rationality (a seemingly irrational act – such as throwing oneself on a grenade – is made rational by referencing one's perceived reputation as a hero afterward instead of focusing on death), such maneuvers quickly lead to tautology. Second, critics point out that the complex interdependencies implicit in interaction make predicting future outcomes impossible. As such, simple rational choice models that depend on people making judgments about the future are seen to be unrealistic. Eric Leifer (1988), for example, argues that so long as the meaning of a social event is not determined until it is long past, actors cannot base action on future expectations. Instead, successful actors behave locally – engaging others in a way that does not commit them to any particular exchange meaning. Finally, still other critics argue that sociology is best served by focusing on macro-level aspects of social organization directly, and that the search for a micro model of macro behavior is not productive. In an interesting biographical twist, Peter Blau has "recanted" his own social exchange theory in favor of a macro-level model of social interaction based on the distribution of types of people in the population (Blau, 1977: p. 994).

SELECTED BIBLIOGRAPHY

Blau, Peter. 1964. *Exchange and Power in Social Life*. New York: Wiley. (The major statement of Peter Blau's exchange theory. An excellent source for those seeking deeper understanding of his approach to social exchange theory.)

Blau, Peter. 1977. *Inequality and Heterogeneity: A Primitive Theory of Social Structure*. New York: Free Press. (The most complete presentation of Blau's macro-sociological work, which interestingly argues for a foundation of sociology at the macro level, recanting his own earlier work.)

Blau, Peter. 1994. *Structural Contexts of Opportunities*. Chicago, IL and London: University of Chicago Press. (A nice summary of all of Blau's work, that seeks to integrate the ideas of both exchange and power and inequality and heterogeneity by situating exchange within the macro-level.)

Buchan, Nancy R., Croson, Rachel T.A., and Dawes, Robyn M. 2002. "Swift Neighbors and Persistent Strangers: A Cross-Cultural Investigation of Trust and Reciprocity in Social Exchange." *American Journal of Sociology*, 108: 168–206.

Coleman, James. 1988. "Social Capital in the Creation of Human Capital." *American Journal of Sociology* 94: s95–s120. (While not the first introduction of the concept of social capital in sociology, one that has sparked much of the current works on social capital.)

Coleman, James. 1990. *Foundations of Social Theory*. Cambridge, MA: Belknap Press. (Arguably Coleman's magnum opus. A work that seeks to develop a complete theory of social organization from an methodological individualist standpoint. A difficult, though rewarding, work.)

Coleman, James and Fararo. Thomas J. 1992. *Rational Choice Theory: Advocacy and Critique*. Newbury Park, CA: Sage Publications. (An edited volume that contains some very good papers, both pro and con, on the value of rational choice theory in sociology.)

Hechter, Michael. 1987. *Principles of Group Solidarity*. Berkeley, CA: University of California Press. (Among the strongest statements of an individualist approach to social solidarity, that forms the foundation for much of the work that follows.)

Homans, George. 1958. "Social Behavior As Exchange." *American Journal of Sociology* 63: 597–606. (The first introduction of exchange from a behaviorist standpoint.)

Homans, George. 1961. *Social Behavior: Its Elementary Forms*. New York: Harcourt, Brace and World, Inc. (The full, expanded treatment of Homans' social exchange theory.)

Kim, Hyojung and Bearman, Peter S. 1997. "Who Counts in Collective Action? The Structure and Dynamics of Movement Participation." *American Sociological Review*: 70–93. (A nice example, though technically difficult, of how a methodologically individualist model of social movements incorporates social networks.)

Leifer, Eric. 1988. "Interaction Preludes to Role Setting: Exploratory Local Action." *American Sociological Review* 53: 865–78. (With the introduction of the concept of local action, Leifer shows the difficulty of actors attempting to follow a rational choice framework for action.)

Oliver, Pamela E., Marwell, Gerald, and Teixeira, Ruy. 1985. "A Theory of the Critical Mass. I. Interdependence, Group Heterogeneity, and the Production of Collective Action." *American Journal of Sociology* 91: 522–56. (A classic statement of the conditions under which rational actors will solve the collective action problem.)

Olson, Mancur. 1965. *The Logic of Collective Action: Public Goods and the Theory of Groups*. Cambridge, MA: Harvard University Press. (Olson's classic book provides a concise statement of why collective action among rational actors is rare.)

Putnam, Robert D. 2000. *Bowling Alone: The Collapse and Revival of American Community*. New York: Simon & Schuster. (Putnam describes trends and changes in the national distribution of social capital, conceived of as involvement in secondary associations.)

Ritzer, George. 1992. *Sociological Theory*. New York: McGraw-Hill. (An overview text, providing a nice discussion of exchange theory, as well as biographical information on Homans and Blau.)

Willer, David. 1999. *Network Exchange Theory*. Westport, CT: Praeger. (A nice overview book that summarizes the basic tenets of network exchange theory, the theoretical assumptions, and empirical findings of this field.)

Chapter 5

Social Behavior as Exchange [1958]
George C. Homans

An Exchange Paradigm

I start with the link to behavioral psychology and the kind of statement it makes about the behavior of an experimental animal such as the pigeon.[1] As a pigeon explores its cage in the laboratory, it happens to peck a target, whereupon the psychologist feeds it corn. The evidence is that it will peck the target again; it has learned the behavior, or, as my friend Skinner says, the behavior has been reinforced, and the pigeon has undergone *operant conditioning*. This kind of psychologist is not interested in how the behavior was learned: "learning theory" is a poor name for his field. Instead, he is interested in what determines changes in the rate of emission of learned behavior, whether pecks at a target or something else.

The more hungry the pigeon, the less corn or other food it has gotten in the recent past, the more often it will peck. By the same token, if the behavior is often reinforced, if the pigeon is given much corn every time it pecks, the rate of emission will fall off as the pigeon gets *satiated*. If, on the other hand, the behavior is not reinforced at all, then, too, its rate of emission will tend to fall off, though a long time may pass before it stops altogether, before it is *extinguished*. In the emission of many kinds of behavior the pigeon incurs *aversive stimulation*, or what I shall call "cost" for short, and this,

---

George C. Homans, "Social Behavior as Exchange," pp. 598–606 from George C. Homans, *American Journal of Sociology* 63: 6. Copyright © 1958 by American Journal of Sociology. Reprinted by permission of The University of Chicago Press.

Contemporary Sociological Theory, Third Edition. Edited by Craig Calhoun, Joseph Gerteis, James Moody, Steven Pfaff, and Indermohan Virk. Editorial material and organization © 2012 John Wiley & Sons, Ltd. Published 2012 by John Wiley & Sons, Ltd.

too, will lead in time to a decrease in the emission rate. Fatigue is an example of a "cost." Extinction, satiation, and cost, by decreasing the rate of emission of a particular kind of behavior, render more probable the emission of some other kind of behavior, including doing nothing. I shall only add that even a hard-boiled psychologist puts "emotional" behavior, as well as such things as pecking, among the unconditioned responses that may be reinforced in operant conditioning. As a statement of the propositions of behavioral psychology, the foregoing is, of course, inadequate for any purpose except my present one.

We may look on the pigeon as engaged in an exchange – pecks for corn – with the psychologist, but let us not dwell upon that, for the behavior of the pigeon hardly determines the behavior of the psychologist at all. Let us turn to a situation where the exchange is real, that is, where the determination is mutual. Suppose we are dealing with two men. Each is emitting behavior reinforced to some degree by the behavior of the other. How it was in the past that each learned the behavior he emits and how he learned to find the other's behavior reinforcing we are not concerned with. It is enough that each does find the other's behavior reinforcing, and I shall call the reinforcers – the equivalent of the pigeon's corn – *values*, for this, I think, is what we mean by this term. As he emits behavior, each man may incur costs, and each man has more than one course of behavior open to him.

This seems to me the paradigm of elementary social behavior, and the problem of the elementary sociologist is to state propositions relating the variations in the values and costs of each man to his frequency distribution of behavior among alternatives, where the values (in the mathematical sense) taken by these variables for one man determine in part their values for the other.[2]

I see no reason to believe that the propositions of behavioral psychology do not apply to this situation, though the complexity of their implications in the concrete case may be great indeed. In particular, we must suppose that, with men as with pigeons, an increase in extinction, satiation, or aversive stimulation of any one kind of behavior will increase the probability of emission of some other kind. The problem is not, as it is often stated, merely, what a man's values are, what he has learned in the past to find reinforcing, but how much of any one value his behavior is getting him now. The more he gets, the less valuable any further unit of that value is to him, and the less often he will emit behavior reinforced by it.

The Influence Process

We do not, I think, possess the kind of studies of two-person interaction that would either bear out these propositions or fail to do so. But we do have studies of larger numbers of persons that suggest that they may apply, notably the studies by Festinger, Schachter, Back, and their associates on the dynamics of influence. One of the variables they work with they call *cohesiveness*, defined as anything that attracts people to take part in a group. Cohesiveness is a value variable; it refers to the degree of reinforcement people find in the activities of the group. Festinger and his colleagues consider two kinds of reinforcing activity: the symbolic behavior we call "social approval" (sentiment) and activity valuable in other ways, such as doing something interesting.

The other variable they work with they call *communication* and others call *interaction*. This is a frequency variable; it is a measure of the frequency of emission of valuable and costly verbal behavior. We must bear in mind that, in general, the one kind of variable is a function of the other.

Festinger and his co-workers show that the more cohesive a group is, that is, the more valuable the sentiment or activity the members exchange with one another, the greater the average frequency of interaction of the members.[3] With men, as with pigeons, the greater the reinforcement, the more often is the reinforced behavior emitted. The more cohesive a group, too, the greater the change that members can produce in the behavior of other members in the direction of rendering these activities more valuable.[4] That is, the more valuable the activities that members get, the more valuable those that they must give. For if a person is emitting behavior of a certain kind, and other people do not find it particularly rewarding, these others will suffer their own production of sentiment and activity, in time, to fall off. But perhaps the first person has found their sentiment and activity rewarding, and, if he is to keep on getting them, he must make his own behavior more valuable to the others. In short, the propositions of behavioral psychology imply a tendency toward a certain proportionality between the value to others of the behavior a man gives them and the value to him of the behavior they give him.[5]

Schachter also studied the behavior of members of a group toward two kinds of other members, "conformers" and "deviates."[6] I assume that conformers are people whose activity the other members find valuable. For conformity is behavior that coincides to a degree with some group standard or norm, and the only meaning I can assign to *norm* is "a verbal description of behavior that many members find it valuable for the actual behavior of themselves and others to conform to." By the same token, a deviate is a member whose behavior is not particularly valuable. Now Schachter shows that, as the members of a group come to see another member as a deviate, their interaction with him – communication addressed to getting him to change his behavior – goes up, the faster, the more cohesive the group. The members need not talk to the other conformers so much; they are relatively satiated by the conformers' behavior: they have gotten what they want out of them. But if the deviate, by failing to change his behavior, fails to reinforce the members, they start to withhold social approval from him: the deviate gets low sociometric choice at the end of the experiment. And in the most cohesive groups – those Schachter calls "high cohesive-relevant" – interaction with the deviate also falls off in the end and is lowest among those members that rejected him most strongly, as if they had given him up as a bad job. But how plonking can we get? These findings are utterly in line with everyday experience.

Practical Equilibrium

At the beginning of this paper I suggested that one of the tasks of small-group research was to show the relation between the results of experimental work done under laboratory conditions and the results of field research on real-life small groups. Now the latter often appear to be in practical equilibrium, and by this I mean nothing fancy. I do not mean that all real-life groups are in equilibrium. I certainly do not mean that all groups must tend to equilibrium. I do not mean that groups have built-in antidotes to change: there is no homeostasis here. I do not mean that we assume equilibrium. I mean only that we sometimes *observe* it, that for the time we are with a group – and it is often short – there is no great change in the values of the variables we choose to measure. If, for instance, person A is interacting with B more than with C both at the beginning and at the end of the study, then at least by this crude measure the group is in equilibrium.

Many of the Festinger–Schachter studies are experimental, and their propositions about the process of influence seem to me to imply the kind of proposition that empirically holds good of real-life groups in practical equilibrium. For instance, Festinger et al. find that, the more cohesive a group is, the greater the change that members can produce in the behavior of other members. If the influence is exerted in the direction of conformity to group norms, then, when the process of influence has accomplished all the change of which it is capable, the proposition should hold good that, the more cohesive a group is, the larger the number of members that conform to its norms. And it does hold good.[7]

Again, Schachter found, in the experiment I summarized above, that in the most cohesive groups and at the end, when the effort to influence the deviate had failed, members interacted little with the deviate and gave him little in the way of sociometric choice. Now two of the propositions that hold good most often of real-life groups in practical equilibrium are precisely that the more closely a member's activity conforms to the norms the more interaction he receives from other members and the more liking choices he gets from them too. From these main propositions a number of others may be derived that also hold good.[8]

Yet we must ever remember that the truth of the proposition linking conformity to liking may on occasion be masked by the truth of other propositions. If, for instance, the man that conforms to the norms most closely also exerts some authority over the group, this may render liking for him somewhat less than it might otherwise have been.[9]

Be that as it may, I suggest that the laboratory experiments on influence imply propositions about the behavior of members of small groups, when the process of influence has worked itself out, that are identical with propositions that hold good of real-life groups in equilibrium. This is hardly surprising if all we mean by equilibrium is that all the change of which the system is, under present conditions, capable has been effected, so that no further change occurs. Nor would this be the first time that statics has turned out to be a special case of dynamics.

Profit and Social Control

Though I have treated equilibrium as an observed fact, it is a fact that cries for explanation. I shall not, as structural-functional sociologists do, use an assumed equilibrium as a means of explaining, or trying to explain, why the other features of a social system should be what they are. Rather, I shall take practical equilibrium as something that is itself to be explained by the other features of the system.

If every member of a group emits at the end of, and during, a period of time much the same kinds of behavior and in much the same frequencies as he did at the beginning, the group is for that period in equilibrium. Let us then ask why any one member's behavior should persist. Suppose he is emitting behavior of value A_1. Why does he not let his behavior get worse (less valuable or reinforcing to the others) until it stands at $A_1 - \Delta A$? True, the sentiments expressed by others toward him are apt to decline in value (become less reinforcing to him), so that what he gets from them may be $S_1 - \Delta S$. But it is conceivable that, since most activity carries cost, a decline in the value of what he emits will mean a reduction in cost to him that more than offsets his losses in sentiment. Where, then, does he stabilize his behavior? This is the problem of social control.[10]

Mankind has always assumed that a person stabilizes his behavior, at least in the short run, at the point where he is doing the best he can for himself under the circumstances, though his best may not be a "rational" best, and what he can do may not be at all easy to specify, except that he is not apt to think like one of the theoretical antagonists in the *Theory of Games*. Before a sociologist rejects this answer out of hand for its horrid profit-seeking implications, he will do well to ask himself if he can offer any other answer to the question posed. I think he will find that he cannot. Yet experiments designed to test the truth of the answer are extraordinarily rare.

I shall review one that seems to me to provide a little support for the theory, though it was not meant to do so. The experiment is reported by H. B. Gerard, a member of the Festinger–Schachter team, under the title "The Anchorage of Opinions in Face-to-Face Groups."[11] The experimenter formed artificial groups whose members met to discuss a case in industrial relations and to express their opinions about its probable outcome. The groups were of two kinds: high-attraction groups, whose members were told that they would like one another very much, and low-attraction groups, whose members were told that they would not find one another particularly likable.

At a later time the experimenter called the members in separately, asked them again to express their opinions on the outcome of the case, and counted the number that had changed their opinions to bring them into accord with those of other members of their groups. At the same time, a paid participant entered into a further discussion of the case with each member, always taking, on the probable outcome of the case, a position opposed to that taken by the bulk of the other members of the group to which the person belonged. The experimenter counted the number of persons shifting toward the opinion of the paid participant.

Table 5.1 Percentage of subjects changing toward someone in the group.

	Agreement	Mild disagreement	Strong disagreement
High attraction	0	12	44
Low attraction	0	15	9

Table 5.2 Percentage of subjects changing toward the paid participant.

	Agreement	Mild disagreement	Strong disagreement
High attraction	7	13	25
Low attraction	20	38	8

The experiment had many interesting results, from which I choose only those summed up in Tables 5.1 and 5.2. The three different agreement classes are made up of people who, at the original sessions, expressed different degrees of agreement with the opinions of other members of their groups. And the figure 44, for instance, means that, of all members of high-attraction groups whose initial opinions were strongly in disagreement with those of other members, 44 percent shifted their opinion later toward that of others.

In these results the experimenter seems to have been interested only in the differences in the sums of the rows, which show that there is more shifting toward the group, and less shifting toward the paid participant, in the high-attraction than in the low-attraction condition. This is in line with a proposition suggested earlier. If you think that the members of a group can give you much – in this case, liking – you are apt to give them much – in this case, a change to an opinion in accordance with their views – or you will not get the liking. And, by the same token, if the group can give you little of value, you will not be ready to give it much of value. Indeed, you may change your opinion so as to depart from agreement even further, to move, that is, toward the view held by the paid participant.

So far so good, but, when I first scanned these tables, I was less struck by the difference between them than by their similarity. The same classes of people in both tables showed much the same relative propensities to change their opinions, no matter whether the change was toward the group or toward the paid participant. We see, for instance, that those who change least are the high-attraction, agreement people and the low-attraction, strong-disagreement ones. And those who change most are the high-attraction, strong-disagreement people and the low-attraction, mild-disagreement ones.

How am I to interpret these particular results? Since the experimenter did not discuss them, I am free to offer my own explanation. The behavior emitted by the subjects is opinion and changes in opinion. For this behavior they have learned to expect two possible kinds of reinforcement. Agreement with the group gets the subject favorable sentiment (acceptance) from it, and the experiment was designed to give this reinforcement a higher value in the high-attraction condition than in the low-attraction one. The second kind of possible reinforcement is what I shall call the "maintenance of one's personal integrity," which a subject gets by sticking to his own opinion in the face of disagreement with the group. The experimenter does not mention this reward, but I cannot make sense of the results without something much like it. In different degrees for different subjects, depending on their initial positions, these rewards are in competition with one another: they are alternatives. They are not absolutely scarce goods, but some persons cannot get both at once.

Since the rewards are alternatives, let me introduce a familiar assumption from economics – that the cost of a particular course of action is the equivalent of the forgone value of an alternative[12] – and then add the definition: Profit = Reward – Cost.

Now consider the persons in the corresponding cells of the two tables. The behavior of the high-attraction, agreement people gets them much in the way of acceptance by the group, and for it they must give up little in the way of personal integrity, for their views are from the start in accord with those of the group. Their profit is high, and they are not prone to change their behavior. The low-attraction, strong-disagreement people are getting much in integrity, and they are not giving up for it much in valuable acceptance, for they are members of low-attraction groups. Reward less cost is high for them, too, and they change little. The high-attraction, strong-disagreement people are getting much in the way of integrity, but their costs in doing so are high, too, for they are in high-attraction groups and thus forgoing much valuable acceptance by the group. Their profit is low, and they are very apt to change, either toward the group or toward the paid participant, from whom they think, perhaps, they will get some acceptance while maintaining some integrity. The low-attraction, mild-disagreement people do not get much in the way of integrity, for they are only in mild disagreement with the group, but neither are they giving up much in acceptance, for they are members of low-attraction groups. Their rewards are low; their costs are low too, and their profit – the difference between the two – is also low. In their low profit they resemble the high-attraction, strong-disagreement people, and, like them, they are prone to change their opinions, in this case, more toward the paid participant. The subjects in the other two cells, who have medium profits, display medium propensities to change.

If we define profit as reward less cost, and if cost is value forgone, I suggest that we have here some evidence for the proposition that change in behavior is greatest when perceived profit is least. This constitutes no direct demonstration that change in behavior is least when profit is greatest, but if, whenever a man's behavior brought him a balance of reward and cost, he changed his behavior away from what got him, under the circumstances, the less profit, there might well come a time when his behavior would not change further. That is, his behavior would be stabilized, at least for the time being. And, so far as this were true for every member of a group, the group would have a social organization in equilibrium.

I do not say that a member would stabilize his behavior at the point of greatest conceivable profit to himself, because his profit is partly at the mercy of the behavior of others. It is a commonplace that the short-run pursuit of profit by several persons often lands them in positions where all are worse off than they might conceivably be. I do not say that the paths of behavioral change in which a member pursues his profit under the condition that others are pursuing theirs too are easy to describe or predict; and we can readily conceive that in jockeying for position they might never arrive at any equilibrium at all.

Distributive Justice

Yet practical equilibrium is often observed, and thus some further condition may make its attainment, under some circumstance, more probable than would the individual pursuit of profit left to itself. I can offer evidence for this further condition only in the behavior of subgroups and not in that of individuals. Suppose that there are two subgroups, working close together in a factory, the job of one being somewhat different from that of the other. And suppose that the members of the first complain and say: "We are getting the same pay as they are. We ought to get just a couple of dollars a week more to show that our work is more responsible." When you ask them what they mean by "more responsible," they say that, if they do their work wrong, more damage can result, and so they are under more pressure to take care.[13] Something like this is a common feature of industrial behavior. It is at the heart of disputes not over absolute wages but over wage differentials – indeed, at the heart of disputes over rewards other than wages.

In what kind of proposition may we express observations like these? We may say that wages and responsibility give status in the group, in the sense that a man who takes high responsibility and gets high wages is admired, other things equal. Then, if the members of one group score higher on responsibility than do the members of another, there is a felt need on the part of the first to score higher on pay too. There is a pressure, which shows itself in complaints, to bring the *status factors*, as I have called them, into line with one another. If they are in line, a condition of *status congruence* is said to exist. In this condition the workers may find their jobs dull or irksome, but they will not complain about the relative position of groups.

But there may be a more illuminating way of looking at the matter. In my example I have considered only responsibility and pay, but these may be enough, for they represent the two kinds of thing that come into the problem. Pay is clearly a reward; responsibility may be looked on, less clearly, as a cost. It means constraint and worry – or peace of mind forgone. Then the proposition about status congruence becomes this: If the costs of the members of one group are higher than those of another, distributive justice requires that their rewards should be higher too. But the thing works both ways: If the rewards are higher, the costs should be higher too. This last is the theory of *noblesse oblige*, which we all subscribe to, though we all laugh at it, perhaps because the *noblesse* often fails to *oblige*. To put the matter in terms of profit:

though the rewards and costs of two persons or the members of two groups may be different, yet the profits of the two – the excess of reward over cost – should tend to equality. And more than "should." The less-advantaged group will at least try to attain greater equality, as, in the example I have used, the first group tried to increase its profit by increasing its pay.

I have talked of distributive justice. Clearly, this is not the only condition determining the actual distribution of rewards and costs. At the same time, never tell me that notions of justice are not a strong influence on behavior, though we sociologists often neglect them. Distributive justice may be one of the conditions of group equilibrium.

Exchange and Social Structure

I shall end by reviewing almost the only study I am aware of that begins to show in detail how a stable and differentiated social structure in a real-life group might arise out of a process of exchange between members. This is Peter Blau's description of the behavior of sixteen agents in a federal law-enforcement agency.[14]

The agents had the duty of investigating firms and preparing reports on the firms' compliance with the law. Since the reports might lead to legal action against the firms, the agents had to prepare them carefully, in the proper form, and take strict account of the many regulations that might apply. The agents were often in doubt what they should do, and then they were supposed to take the question to their supervisor. This they were reluctant to do, for they naturally believed that thus confessing to him their inability to solve a problem would reflect on their competence, affect the official ratings he made of their work, and so hurt their chances for promotion. So agents often asked other agents for help and advice, and, though this was nominally forbidden, the supervisor usually let it pass.

Blau ascertained the ratings the supervisor made of the agents, and he also asked the agents to rate one another. The two opinions agreed closely. Fewer agents were regarded as highly competent than were regarded as of middle or low competence; competence, or the ability to solve technical problems, was a fairly scarce good. One or two of the more competent agents would not give help and advice when asked, and so received few interactions and little liking. A man that will not exchange, that will not give you what he has when you need it, will not get from you the only thing you are, in this case, able to give him in return, your regard.

But most of the more competent agents were willing to give help, and of them Blau says:

> A consultation can be considered an exchange of values: both participants gain something, and both have to pay a price. The questioning agent is enabled to perform better than he could otherwise have done, without exposing his difficulties to his supervisor. By asking for advice, he implicitly pays his respect to the superior proficiency of his colleague. This acknowledgment of inferiority is the cost of receiving assistance. The consultant gains prestige, in return for which he is willing to devote

some time to the consultation and permit it to disrupt his own work. The following remark of an agent illustrates this: "I like giving advice. It's flattering, I suppose, if you feel that others come to you for advice."[15]

Blau goes on to say: "All agents liked being consulted, but the value of any one of very many consultations became deflated for experts, and the price they paid in frequent interruptions became inflated."[16] This implies that, the more prestige an agent received, the less was the increment of value of that prestige; the more advice an agent gave, the greater was the increment of cost of that advice, the cost lying precisely in the forgone value of time to do his own work. Blau suggests that something of the same sort was true of an agent who went to a more competent colleague for advice: the more often he went, the more costly to him, in feelings of inferiority, became any further request. "The repeated admission of his inability to solve his own problems ... undermined the self-confidence of the worker and his standing in the group."[17]

The result was that the less competent agents went to the more competent ones for help less often than they might have done if the costs of repeated admissions of inferiority had been less high and that, while many agents sought out the few highly competent ones, no single agent sought out the latter much. Had they done so (to look at the exchange from the other side), the costs to the highly competent in interruptions to their own work would have become exorbitant. Yet the need of the less competent for help was still not fully satisfied. Under these circumstances they tended to turn for help to agents more nearly like themselves in competence. Though the help they got was not the most valuable, it was of a kind they could themselves return on occasion. With such agents they could exchange help and liking, without the exchange becoming on either side too great a confession of inferiority.

The highly competent agents tended to enter into exchanges, that is, to interact with many others. But, in the more equal exchanges I have just spoken of, less competent agents tended to pair off as partners. That is, they interacted with a smaller number of people, but interacted often with these few. I think I could show why pair relations in these more equal exchanges would be more economical for an agent than a wider distribution of favors. But perhaps I have gone far enough. The final pattern of this social structure was one in which a small number of highly competent agents exchanged advice for prestige with a large number of others less competent and in which the less competent agents exchanged, in pairs and in trios, both help and liking on more nearly equal terms.

Blau shows, then, that a social structure in equilibrium might be the result of a process of exchanging behavior rewarding and costly in different degrees, in which the increment of reward and cost varied with the frequency of the behavior, that is, with the frequency of interaction. Note that the behavior of the agents seems also to have satisfied my second condition of equilibrium: the more competent agents took more responsibility for the work, either their own or others', than did the less competent ones, but they also got more for it in the way of prestige. I suspect that the same kind of explanation could be given for the structure of many "informal" groups.

Summary

The current job of theory in small-group research is to make the connection between experimental and real-life studies, to consolidate the propositions that empirically hold good in the two fields, and to show how these propositions might be derived from a still more general set. One way of doing this job would be to revive and make more rigorous the oldest of theories of social behavior – social behavior as exchange.

Some of the statements of such a theory might be the following. Social behavior is an exchange of goods, material goods but also non-material ones, such as the symbols of approval or prestige. Persons that give much to others try to get much from them, and persons that get much from others are under pressure to give much to them. This process of influence tends to work out at equilibrium to a balance in the exchanges. For a person engaged in exchange, what he gives may be a cost to him, just as what he gets may be a reward, and his behavior changes less as profit, that is, reward less cost, tends to a maximum. Not only does he seek a maximum for himself, but he tries to see to it that no one in his group makes more profit than he does. The cost and the value of what he gives and of what he gets vary with the quantity of what he gives and gets. It is surprising how familiar these propositions are; it is surprising, too, how propositions about the dynamics of exchange can begin to generate the static thing we call "group structure" and, in so doing, generate also some of the propositions about group structure that students of real-life groups have stated.

In our unguarded moments we sociologists find words like "reward" and "cost" slipping into what we say. Human nature will break in upon even our most elaborate theories. But we seldom let it have its way with us and follow up systematically what these words imply.[18] Of all our many "approaches" to social behavior, the one that sees it as an economy is the most neglected, and yet it is the one we use every moment of our lives – except when we write sociology.

NOTES

1 B. F. Skinner, *Science and Human Behavior* (New York: Macmillan Co., 1953).
2 Ibid., pp. 297–329. The discussion of "double contingency" by T. Parsons and E. A. Shils could easily lead to a similar paradigm (see *Toward a General Theory of Action* [Cambridge, MA: Harvard University Press, 1951], pp. 14–16).
3 K. W. Back, "The Exertion of Influence through Social Communication," in L. Festinger, K. Back, S. Schachter, H. H. Kelley, and J. Thibaut (eds.), *Theory and Experiment in Social Communication* (Ann Arbor, MI: Research Center for Dynamics, University of Michigan, 1950), pp. 21–36.
4 S. Schachter, N. Ellertson, D. McBride, and D. Gregory, "An Experimental Study of Cohesiveness and Productivity," *Human Relations* 4 (1951): 229–38.
5 Skinner, *Science and Human Behavior*, p. 100.
6 S. Schachter, "Deviation, Rejection, and Communication," *Journal of Abnormal and Social Psychology* 46 (1951): 190–207.

7   L. Festinger, S. Schachter, and K. Back, *Social Pressures in Informal Groups* (New York: Harper & Bros., 1950), pp. 72–100.
8   For propositions holding good of groups in practical equilibrium see G. C. Homans, *The Human Group* (New York: Harcourt, Brace & Co., 1950), and H. W. Riecken and G. C. Homans, "Psychological Aspects of Social Structure," in G. Lindzey (ed.), *Handbook of Social Psychology* (Cambridge, MA: Addison-Wesley Publishing Co., 1954), 2, pp. 786–832.
9   See Homans, *The Human Group*, pp. 244–8, and R. F. Bales, "The Equilibrium Problem in Small Groups," in A. P. Hare, E. F. Borgatta, and R. F. Bales (eds.), *Small Groups* (New York: A. A. Knopf, 1953), pp. 450–6.
10 Homans, *The Human Group*, pp. 281–301.
11 *Human Relations* 7 (1954): 313–25.
12 G. J. Stigler, *The Theory of Price* (rev. ed.; New York: Macmillan Co., 1952), p. 99.
13 G. C. Homans, "Status among Clerical Workers," *Human Organization* 12 (1953): 5–10.
14 Peter M. Blau, *The Dynamics of Bureaucracy* (Chicago, IL: University of Chicago Press, 1955), pp. 99–116.
15 Ibid., p. 108.
16 Ibid., p. 108.
17 Ibid., p. 109.
18 Nancy C. Morse, *Satisfactions in The White-Collar Job* (Ann Arbor, MI: Survey Research Center, University of Michigan, 1953), pp. 115–27.

Chapter 6

Exchange and Power in Social Life [1964]

Peter M. Blau

Basic Processes

The basic social processes that govern associations among men have their roots in primitive psychological processes, such as those underlying the feelings of attraction between individuals and their desires for various kinds of rewards. These psychological tendencies are primitive only in respect to our subject matter, that is, they are taken as given without further inquiry into the motivating forces that produce them, for our concern is with the social forces that emanate from them.

The simpler social processes that can be observed in interpersonal associations and that rest directly on psychological dispositions give rise to the more complex social processes that govern structures of interconnected social associations, such as the social organization of a factory or the political relations in a community. New social forces emerge in the increasingly complex social structures that develop in societies, and these dynamic forces are quite removed from the ultimate psychological base of all social life. Although complex social systems have their foundation in simpler ones, they have their own dynamics with emergent properties. In this section, the basic processes of social associations will be presented in broad strokes, to be analyzed subsequently in greater detail, with special attention to their wider implications.

Peter M. Blau, "Exchange and Power in Social Life," pp. 19–31, 91–5 from Peter M. Blau, *Exchange and Power in Social Life*. New York: John Wiley and Sons, 1964. Copyright © 1964 by Peter M. Blau. Reprinted by permission of Judith Blau.

Contemporary Sociological Theory, Third Edition. Edited by Craig Calhoun, Joseph Gerteis, James Moody, Steven Pfaff, and Indermohan Virk. Editorial material and organization © 2012 John Wiley & Sons, Ltd. Published 2012 by John Wiley & Sons, Ltd.

Social attraction is the force that induces human beings to establish social associations on their own initiative and to expand the scope of their associations once they have been formed. Reference here is to social relations into which men enter of their own free will rather than to either those into which they are born (such as kinship groups) or those imposed on them by forces beyond their control (such as the combat teams to which soldiers are assigned), although even in these involuntary relations the extent and intensity of the association depend on the degree of mutual attraction. An individual is attracted to another if he expects associating with him to be in some way rewarding for himself, and his interest in the expected social rewards draws him to the other. The psychological needs and dispositions of individuals determine which rewards are particularly salient for them and thus to whom they will be attracted. Whatever the specific motives, there is an important difference between the expectation that the association will be an intrinsically rewarding experience and the expectation that it will furnish extrinsic benefits, for example, advice. This difference calls attention to two distinct meanings of the term "attraction" and its derivatives. In its narrower sense, social attraction refers to liking another person *intrinsically* and having positive feelings toward him; in the broader sense, in which the term is now used, social attraction refers to being drawn to another person for any reason whatsoever. The customer is attracted in this broader sense to the merchant who sells goods of a given quality at the lowest price, but he has no intrinsic feelings of attraction for him, unless they happen to be friends.

A person who is attracted to others is interested in proving himself attractive to them, for his ability to associate with them and reap the benefits expected from the association is contingent on their finding him an attractive associate and thus wanting to interact with him. Their attraction to him, just as his to them, depends on the anticipation that the association will be rewarding. To arouse this anticipation, a person tries to impress others. Attempts to appear impressive are pervasive in the early stages of acquaintance and group formation. Impressive qualities make a person attractive and promise that associating with him will be rewarding. Mutual attraction prompts people to establish an association, and the rewards they provide each other in the course of their social interaction, unless their expectations are disappointed, maintain their mutual attraction and the continuing association.

Processes of social attraction, therefore, lead to processes of social exchange. The nature of the exchange in an association experienced as intrinsically rewarding, such as a love relationship, differs from that between associates primarily concerned with extrinsic benefits, such as neighbors who help one another with various chores, but exchanges do occur in either case. A person who furnishes needed assistance to associates, often at some cost to himself, obligates them to reciprocate his kindness. Whether reference is to instrumental services or to such intangibles as social approval, the benefits each supplies to the others are rewards that serve as inducements to continue to supply benefits, and the integrative bonds created in the process fortify the social relationship.

A situation frequently arises, however, in which one person needs something another has to offer, for example, help from the other in his work, but has nothing the other needs to reciprocate for the help. While the other may be sufficiently rewarded by expressions of gratitude to help him a few times, he can hardly be expected regularly to devote time and effort to providing help without receiving any return to compensate him for his troubles. (In the case of intrinsic attraction, the only return expected is the willingness to continue the association.) The person in need of recurrent services from an associate to whom he has nothing to offer has several alternatives. First, he may force the other to give him help. Second, he may obtain the help he needs from another source. Third, he may find ways to get along without such help.[1] If he is unable or unwilling to choose any of these alternatives, however, there is only one other course of action left for him; he must subordinate himself to the other and comply with his wishes, thereby rewarding the other with power over himself as an inducement for furnishing the needed help. Willingness to comply with another's demands is a generic social reward, since the power it gives him is a generalized means, parallel to money, which can be used to attain a variety of ends. The power to command compliance is equivalent to credit, which a man can draw on in the future to obtain various benefits at the disposal of those obligated to him.[2] The unilateral supply of important services establishes this kind of credit and thus is a source of power.

Exchange processes, then, give rise to differentiation of power. A person who commands services others need, and who is independent of any at their command, attains power over others by making the satisfaction of their need contingent on their compliance. This principle is held to apply to the most intimate as well as the most distant social relations. The girl with whom a boy is in love has power over him, since his eagerness to spend much time with her prompts him to make their time together especially pleasant for her by acceding to her wishes. The employer can make workers comply with his directives because they are dependent on his wages. To be sure, the superior's power wanes if subordinates can resort to coercion, have equally good alternatives, or are able to do without the benefits at his disposal. But given these limiting conditions, unilateral services that meet basic needs are the penultimate source of power. Its ultimate source, of course, is physical coercion. While the power that rests on coercion is more absolute, however, it is also more limited in scope than the power that derives from met needs.

A person on whom others are dependent for vital benefits has the power to enforce his demands. He may make demands on them that they consider fair and just in relation to the benefits they receive for submitting to his power. On the other hand, he may lack such restraint and make demands that appear excessive to them, arousing feelings of exploitation for having to render more compliance than the rewards received justify. Social norms define the expectations of subordinates and their evaluations of the superior's demands. The fair exercise of power gives rise to approval of the superior, whereas unfair exploitation promotes disapproval. The greater the resources of a person on which his power rests, the easier it is for him to refrain from exploiting subordinates by making excessive demands, and consequently the better are the chances that subordinates will approve of the fairness of his rule rather than disapprove of its unfairness.

There are fundamental differences between the dynamics of power in a collective situation and the power of one individual over another. The weakness of the isolated subordinate limits the significance of his approval or disapproval of the superior. The agreement that emerges in a collectivity of subordinates concerning their judgment of the superior, on the other hand, has far-reaching implications for developments in the social structure.

Collective approval of power legitimates that power. People who consider that the advantages they gain from a superior's exercise of power outweigh the hardships that compliance with his demands imposes on them tend to communicate to each other their approval of the ruler and their feelings of obligation to him. The consensus that develops as the result of these communications finds expression in group pressures that promote compliance with the ruler's directives, thereby strengthening his power of control and legitimating his authority. "A feeling of obligation to obey the commands of the established public authority is found, varying in liveliness and effectiveness from one individual to another, among the members of any political society."[3] Legitimate authority is the basis of organization. It makes it possible to organize collective effort to further the achievement of various objectives, some of which could not be attained by individuals separately at all and others that can be attained more effectively by coordinating efforts. Although power that is not legitimated by the approval of subordinates can also be used to organize them, the stability of such an organization is highly precarious.

Collective disapproval of power engenders opposition. People who share the experience of being exploited by the unfair demands of those in positions of power, and by the insufficient rewards they receive for their contributions, are likely to communicate their feelings of anger, frustration, and aggression to each other. There tends to arise a wish to retaliate by striking down the existing powers. "As every man doth, so shall it be done to him, and retaliation seems to be the great law that is dictated to us by nature."[4] The social support the oppressed give each other in the course of discussing their common grievances and feelings of hostility justifies and reinforces their aggressive opposition against those in power. It is out of such shared discontent that opposition ideologies and movements develop – that men organize a union against their employer or a revolutionary party against their government.

In brief, differentiation of power in a collective situation evokes contrasting dynamic forces: legitimating processes that foster the organization of individuals and groups in common endeavors; and countervailing forces that deny legitimacy to existing powers and promote opposition and cleavage. Under the influence of these forces, the scope of legitimate organization expands to include ever larger collectivities, but opposition and conflict recurrently redivide these collectivities and stimulate reorganization along different lines.

The distinctive characteristic of complex social structures is that their constituent elements are also social structures. We may call these structures of interrelated groups "macrostructures" and those composed of interacting individuals "microstructures."

There are some parallels between the social processes in microstructures and macrostructures. Processes of social attraction create integrative bonds between associates, and integrative processes also unite various groups in a community. Exchange processes between individuals give rise to differentiation among them, and intergroup exchanges further differentiation among groups. Individuals become incorporated in legitimate organizations, and these in turn become part of broader bodies of legitimate authority. Opposition and conflict occur not only within collectivities but also between them. These parallels, however, must not conceal the fundamental differences between the processes that govern the interpersonal associations in microstructures and the forces characteristic of the wider and more complex social relations in macrostructures.

First, value consensus is of crucial significance for social processes that pervade complex social structures, because standards commonly agreed upon serve as mediating links for social transactions between individuals and groups without any direct contact. Sharing basic values creates integrative bonds and social solidarity among millions of people in a society, most of whom have never met, and serves as functional equivalent for the feelings of personal attraction that unite pairs of associates and small groups. Common standards of valuation produce media of exchange – money being the prototype but not the only one – which alone make it possible to transcend personal transactions and develop complex networks of indirect exchange. Legitimating values expand the scope of centralized control far beyond the reach of personal influence, as exemplified by the authority of a legitimate government. Opposition ideals serve as rallying points to draw together strangers from widely dispersed places and unite them in a common cause. The study of these problems requires an analysis of the significance of social values and norms that must complement the analysis of exchange transactions and power relations but must not become a substitute for it.

A second emergent property of macrostructures is the complex interplay between the internal forces within substructures and the forces that connect the diverse substructures, some of which may be microstructures composed of individuals while others may themselves be macrostructures composed of subgroups. The processes of integration, differentiation, organization, and opposition formation in the various substructures, which often vary greatly among the substructures, and the corresponding processes in the macrostructure all have repercussions for each other. A systematic analysis of these intricate patterns would have to constitute the core of a general theory of social structures.

Finally, enduring institutions typically develop in macrostructures. Established systems of legitimation raise the question of their perpetuation through time. The strong identification of men with the highest ideals and most sacred beliefs they share makes them desirous to preserve these basic values for succeeding generations. The investments made in establishing and expanding a legitimate organization create an interest in stabilizing it and assuring its survival in the face of opposition attacks. For this purpose, formalized procedures are instituted that make the organization independent of any individual member and permit it to persist beyond the life span or period of tenure of its members. Institutionalization refers to the emergence of social mechanisms through which social values and norms, organizing principles, and knowledge and skills are transmitted from generation to generation. A society's institutions constitute the social matrix in which individuals grow up and are socialized, with the result that some aspects of institutions are reflected in their own personalities, and others appear to them as the inevitable external conditions of human existence. Traditional institutions stabilize social life but also introduce rigidities that make adjustment to changing conditions difficult. Opposition movements may arise to promote such adjustment, yet these movements themselves tend to become institutionalized and rigid in the course of time, creating needs for fresh oppositions. [...]

There is a strain toward imbalance as well as toward reciprocity in social associations. The term "balance" itself is ambiguous inasmuch as we speak not only of balancing our books but also of a balance in our favor, which refers, of course, to a lack of equality between inputs and outputs. As a matter of fact, the balance of the accounting sheet merely rests, in the typical case, on an underlying imbalance between income and outlays, and so do apparent balances in social life. Individuals and groups are interested in, at least, maintaining a balance between inputs and outputs and staying out of debt in their social transactions; hence the strain toward reciprocity. Their aspirations, however, are to achieve a balance in their favor and accumulate credit that makes their status superior to that of others; hence the strain toward imbalance.

Arguments about equilibrium – that all scientific theories must be conceived in terms of equilibrium models or that any equilibrium model neglects the dynamics of real life – ignore the important point that the forces sustaining equilibrium on one level of social life constitute disequilibrating forces on other levels. For supply and demand to remain in equilibrium in a market, for example, forces must exist that continually disturb the established patterns of exchange. Similarly, the circulation of the elite, an equilibrium model, rests on the operation of forces that create imbalances and disturbances in the various segments of society. The principle suggested is that balanced social states depend on imbalances in other social states; forces that restore equilibrium in one respect do so by creating disequilibrium in others. The processes of association described illustrate this principle.

A person who is attracted to another will seek to prove himself attractive to the other. Thus a boy who is very much attracted to a girl, more so than she is to him, is anxious to make himself more attractive to her. To do so, he will try to impress her and, particularly, go out of his way to make associating with him an especially rewarding experience for her. He may devote a lot of thought to finding ways to please her, spend much money on her, and do the things she likes on their dates rather than those he would prefer. Let us assume that he is successful and she becomes as attracted to him as he is to her, that is, she finds associating with him as rewarding as he finds associating with her, as indicated by the fact that both are equally eager to spend time together.

Attraction is now reciprocal, but the reciprocity has been established by an imbalance in the exchange. To be sure, both obtain satisfactory rewards from the association at this stage, the boy as the result of her willingness to spend as much time with him as he wants, and the girl as the result of his readiness to make their dates enjoyable for her. These reciprocal rewards are the sources of their mutual attraction. The contributions made, however, are in imbalance. Both devote time to the association, which involves giving up alternative opportunities, but the boy contributes in addition special efforts to please her. Her company is sufficient reward by itself, while his is not, which makes her "the more useful or otherwise superior" in terms of their own evaluations, and he must furnish supplementary rewards to produce "equality in a sense between the parties." Although two lovers may, of course, be equally anxious to spend time together and to please one another, it is rare for a perfect balance of mutual affection to develop spontaneously. The reciprocal attraction in most intimate relations – marriages and lasting friendships as well as more temporary attachments – is the result of some imbalance of contributions that compensates for inequalities in spontaneous affection, notably in the form of one partner's greater willingness to defer to the other's wishes. [...]

The theoretical principle that has been advanced is that a given balance in social associations is produced by imbalances in the same associations in other respects. This principle, which has been illustrated with the imbalances that underlie reciprocal attraction, also applies to the process of social differentiation. A person who supplies services in demand to others obligates them to reciprocate. If some fail to reciprocate, he has strong inducements to withhold the needed assistance from them in order to supply it to others who do repay him for his troubles in some form. Those who have nothing else to offer him that would be a satisfactory return for his services, therefore, are under pressure to defer to his wishes and comply with his requests in repayment for his assistance. Their compliance with his demands gives him the power to utilize their resources at his discretion to further his own ends. By providing unilateral benefits to others, a person accumulates a capital of willing compliance on which he can draw whenever it is to his interest to impose his will upon others, within the limits of the significance the continuing supply of his benefits has for them. The general advantages of power enable men who cannot otherwise repay for services they need to obtain them in return for their compliance; although in the extreme case of the person who has much power and whose benefits are in great demand, even an offer of compliance may not suffice to obtain them.

Here, an imbalance of power establishes reciprocity in the exchange. Unilateral services give rise to a differentiation of power that equilibrates the exchange. The exchange balance, in fact, rests on two imbalances: unilateral services and unilateral power. Although these two imbalances make up a balance or equilibrium in terms of one perspective, in terms of another, which is equally valid, the exchange equilibrium reinforces and perpetuates the imbalances of dependence and power that sustain it. Power differences not only are an imbalance by definition but also are actually experienced as such, as indicated by the tendency of men to escape from domination if they can. Indeed, a major impetus for the eagerness of individuals to discharge their obligations and reciprocate for services they receive, by providing services in return, is the threat of becoming otherwise subject to the power of the supplier of the services. While reciprocal services create an interdependence that balances power, unilateral dependence on services maintains an imbalance of power.

Differentiation of power evidently constitutes an imbalance in the sense of an inequality of power; but the question must be raised whether differentiation of power also necessarily constitutes an imbalance in the sense of a strain toward change in the structure of social relations. Power differences as such, analytically conceived and abstracted from other considerations, create such a pressure toward change, because it can be assumed that men experience having to submit to power as a hardship from which they would prefer to escape. The advantages men derive from their ruler or government, however, may outweigh the hardships entailed in submitting to his or its power, with the result that the analytical imbalance or disturbance introduced by power differences is neutralized. The significance of power imbalances for social change depends, therefore, on the reactions of the governed to the exercise of power.

Social reactions to the exercise of power reflect once more the principle of reciprocity and imbalance, although in a new form. Power over others makes it possible to direct and organize their activities. Sufficient resources to command power over large numbers enable a person or group to establish a large organization. The members recruited to the organization receive benefits, such as financial remuneration, in exchange for complying with the directives of superiors and making various contributions to the organization. The leadership exercises power within the organization, and it derives power from the organization for use in relation with other organizations or groups. The clearest illustration of this double power of organizational leadership is the army commander's power over his own soldiers and, through the force of their arms, over the enemy. Another example is the power business management exercises over its own employees and, through the strength of the concern, in the market. The greater the external power of an organization, the greater are its chances of accumulating resources that put rewards at the disposal of the leadership for possible distribution among the members.

The normative expectations of those subject to the exercise of power, which are rooted in their social experience, govern their reactions to it. In terms of these standards, the benefits derived from being part of an organization or political society may outweigh the investments required to obtain them, or the demands made on members may exceed the returns they receive for fulfilling these demands. The exercise of power, therefore, may produce two different kinds of imbalance, a positive imbalance of benefits for subordinates or a negative imbalance of exploitation and oppression.

If the members of an organization, or generally those subject to a governing leadership, commonly agree that the demands made on them are only fair and just in view of the ample rewards the leadership delivers, joint feelings of obligation and loyalty to superiors will arise and bestow legitimating approval on their authority. A positive imbalance of benefits generates legitimate authority for the leadership and thereby strengthens and extends its controlling influence. By expressing legitimating approval of, and loyalty to, those who govern them subordinates reciprocate for the benefits their leadership provides, but they simultaneously fortify the imbalance of power in the social structure.

If the demands of the men who exercise power are experienced by those subject to it as exploitative and oppressive, and particularly if these subordinates have been unsuccessful in obtaining redress for their grievances, their frustrations tend to promote disapproval of existing powers and antagonism toward them. As the oppressed communicate their anger and aggression to each other, provided there are opportunities for doing so, their mutual support and approval socially justify and reinforce the negative orientation toward the oppressors, and their collective hostility may inspire them to organize an opposition. The exploitative use of coercive power that arouses active opposition is more prevalent in the relations between organizations and groups than within organizations. Two reasons for this are that the advantages of legitimating approval restrain organizational superiors and that the effectiveness of legitimate authority, once established, obviates the need for coercive measures. But the exploitative use of power also occurs within organizations, as unions organized in opposition to exploitative employers show. A negative imbalance for the subjects of power stimulates opposition. The opposition negatively reciprocates, or retaliates, for excessive demands in an attempt to even the score, but it simultaneously creates conflict, disequilibrium, and imbalance in the social structure.[5]

Even in the relatively simple structures of social association considered here, balances in one respect entail imbalances in others. The interplay between equilibrating and disequilibrating forces is still more evident, if less easy to unravel, in complex macrostructures with their cross-cutting substructures, where forces that sustain reciprocity and balance have disequilibrating and imbalancing repercussions not only on other levels of the same substructure but also on other substructures. As we shall see, disequilibrating and re-equilibrating forces generate a dialectical pattern of change in social structures.

Unspecified Obligations and Trust

The concept of exchange can be circumscribed by indicating two limiting cases. An individual may give another money because the other stands in front of him with a gun in a holdup. While this could be conceptualized as an exchange of his money for his life, it seems preferable to exclude the result of physical coercion from the range of social conduct encompassed by the term "exchange." An individual may also give away money because his conscience demands that he help support the underprivileged and without expecting any form of gratitude from them. While this could be conceptualized as an exchange of his money for the internal approval of his super-ego, here again it seems preferable to exclude conformity with internalized norms from the purview of the concept of social exchange. A social exchange is involved if an individual gives money to a poor man because he wants to receive the man's expressions of gratitude and deference and if he ceases to give alms to beggars who withhold such expressions.

"Social exchange," as the term is used here, refers to voluntary actions of individuals that are motivated by the returns they are expected to bring and typically do in fact bring from others. Action compelled by physical coercion is not voluntary, although compliance with other forms of power can be considered a voluntary service rendered in exchange for the benefits such compliance produces, as already indicated. Whereas conformity with internalized standards does not fall under the definition of exchange presented, conformity to social pressures tends to entail indirect exchanges. Men make charitable donations, not to earn the gratitude of the recipients, whom they never see, but to earn the approval of their peers who participate in the philanthropic campaign. Donations are exchanged for social approval, though the recipients of the donations and the suppliers of the approval are not identical, and the clarification of the connection between the two requires an analysis of the complex structures of indirect exchange. Our concern now is with the simpler direct exchanges.

The need to reciprocate for benefits received in order to continue receiving them serves as a "starting mechanism" of social interaction and group structure, as Gouldner has pointed out.[6] When people are thrown together, and before common norms or goals or role expectations have crystallized among them, the advantages to be gained from entering into exchange relations furnish incentives for social interaction, and the exchange processes serve as mechanisms for regulating social interaction, thus fostering the development of a network of social relations and a rudimentary group structure. Eventually, group norms to regulate and limit the exchange transactions emerge, including the fundamental and ubiquitous norm of reciprocity, which makes failure to discharge obligations subject to group sanctions. In contrast to Gouldner, however, it is held here that the norm of reciprocity merely reinforces and stabilizes tendencies inherent in the character of social exchange itself and that the fundamental starting mechanism of patterned social intercourse is found in the existential conditions of exchange, not in the norm of reciprocity. It is a necessary condition of exchange that individuals, in the interest of continuing to receive needed services, discharge their obligations for having received them in the past. Exchange processes utilize, as it were, the self-interests of individuals to produce a differentiated social structure within which norms tend to develop that require individuals to set aside some of their personal interests for the sake of those of the collectivity. Not all social constraints are normative constraints, and those imposed by the nature of social exchange are not, at least, not originally.

Social exchange differs in important ways from strictly economic exchange. The basic and most crucial distinction is that social exchange entails *unspecified* obligations. The prototype of an economic transaction rests on a formal contract that stipulates the exact quantities to be exchanged. The buyer pays $30,000 for a specific house, or he signs a contract to pay that sum plus interest over a period of years. Whether the entire transaction is consummated at a given time, in which case the contract may never be written, or not, all the transfers to be made now or in the future are agreed upon at the time of sale. Social exchange, in contrast, involves the principle that one person does another a favor, and while there is a general expectation of some future return, its exact nature is definitely *not* stipulated in advance. The distinctive implications of such unspecified obligations are brought into high relief by the institutionalized form they assume in the Kula discussed by Malinowski:

> The main principle underlying the regulations of actual exchange is that the Kula consists in the bestowing of a ceremonial gift, which has to be repaid by an equivalent counter-gift after a lapse of time.... But it can never be exchanged from hand to hand, with the equivalence between the two objects being discussed, bargained about and computed.... The second very important principle is that the equivalence of the counter-gift is left to the giver, and it cannot be enforced by any kind of coercion.... If the article given as a counter-gift is not equivalent, the recipient will be disappointed and angry, but he has no direct means of redress, no means of coercing his partner.[7]

Social exchange, whether it is in this ceremonial form or not, involves favors that create diffuse future obligations, not precisely specified ones, and the nature of the return cannot be bargained about but must be left to the discretion of the one who makes it. Thus, if a person gives a dinner party, he expects his guests to reciprocate at some future date. But he can hardly bargain with them about the kind of party to which they should invite him, although he expects them not simply to ask him for a quick lunch if he had invited them to a formal dinner. Similarly, if a person goes to some trouble on behalf of an acquaintance, he expects *some* expression of gratitude, but he can neither bargain with the other over how to reciprocate nor force him to reciprocate at all.

Since there is no way to assure an appropriate return for a favor, social exchange requires trusting others to discharge their obligations. While the banker who makes a loan to a man who buys a house does not have to trust him, although he hopes he will not have to foreclose the mortgage, the individual who gives another an expensive gift must trust him to reciprocate in proper fashion. Typically, however, exchange relations evolve in a slow process, starting with minor transactions in which little trust is required because little risk is involved. A worker may help a colleague a few times. If the colleague fails to reciprocate, the worker has lost little and can easily protect himself against further loss by ceasing to furnish assistance. If the colleague does reciprocate, perhaps excessively so out of gratitude for the volunteered help and in the hope of receiving more, he proves himself trustworthy of continued and extended favors. (Excessive reciprocation may be embarrassing, because it is a bid for a more extensive exchange relation than one may be willing to enter.) By discharging their obligations for services rendered, if only to provide inducements for the supply of more assistance, individuals demonstrate their trustworthiness, and the gradual expansion of mutual service is accompanied by a parallel growth of mutual trust. Hence, processes of social exchange, which may originate in pure self-interest, generate trust in social relations through their recurrent and gradually expanding character.

Only social exchange tends to engender feelings of personal obligation, gratitude, and trust; purely economic exchange as such does not. An individual is obligated to the banker who gives him a mortgage on his house merely in the technical sense of owing him money, but he does not feel personally obligated in the sense of experiencing a debt of gratitude to the banker, because all the banker's services, all costs and risks, are duly taken into account in and fully repaid by the interest on the loan he receives. A banker who grants a loan without adequate collateral, however, does make the recipient personally obligated for this favorable treatment, precisely because this act of trust entails a social exchange that is superimposed upon the strictly economic transaction.

In contrast to economic commodities, the benefits involved in social exchange do not have an exact price in terms of a single quantitative medium of exchange, which is another reason why social obligations are unspecific. It is essential to realize that this is a substantive fact, not simply a methodological problem. It is not just the social scientist who cannot exactly measure how much approval a given helpful action is worth; the actors themselves cannot precisely specify the worth of approval or of help in the absence of a money price. The obligations individuals incur in social exchange, therefore, are defined only in general, somewhat diffuse terms. Furthermore, the specific benefits exchanged are sometimes primarily valued as symbols of the supportiveness and friendliness they express, and it is the exchange of the underlying mutual support that is the main concern of the participants. Occasionally, a time-consuming service of great material benefit to the recipient might be properly repaid by mere verbal expressions of deep appreciation, since these are taken to signify as much supportiveness as the material benefits.[8] In the long run, however, the explicit efforts the associates in a peer relation make on one another's behalf tend to be in balance, if only because a persistent imbalance in these manifestations of good would raise questions about the reciprocity in the underlying orientations of support and congeniality.

NOTES

1. The last two of these alternatives are noted by Talcott Parsons (*The Structure of Social Action* (New York: McGraw-Hill, 1937), p. 252) in his discussion of a person's reactions to having his expectations frustrated by another.
2. See Talcott Parsons, "On the Concept of Influence," *Public Opinion Quarterly* 27 (1963): 37–62, esp. pp. 59–60.
3. Bertrand de Jouvenel, *Sovereignty* (University of Chicago Press, 1957), p. 87.
4. Adam Smith, *The Theory of Moral Sentiments*, 2nd edn. (London: A. Millar, 1761), p. 139.
5. Organized opposition gives expression to latent conflicts and makes them manifest.
6. Alvin W. Gouldner, "The Norm of Reciprocity," *American Sociological Review* 25 (1960): 161–78, esp. p. 176.
7. Bronislaw Malinowski, *Argonauts of the Western Pacific* (New York: Dutton, 1961), pp. 95–6.
8. See Erving Goffman, *Asylums* (Chicago, IL: Aldine, 1962), pp. 274–86.

Chapter 7

The Logic of Collective Action [1965]

Mancur Olson

The combination of individual interests and common interests in an organization suggests an analogy with a competitive market. The firms in a perfectly competitive industry, for example, have a common interest in a higher price for the industry's product. Since a uniform price must prevail in such a market, a firm cannot expect a higher price for itself unless all of the other firms in the industry also have this higher price. But a firm in a competitive market also has an interest in selling as much as it can, until the cost of producing another unit exceeds the price of that unit. In this there is no common interest; each firm's interest is directly opposed to that of every other firm, for the more other firms sell, the lower the price and income for any given firm. In short, while all firms have a common interest in a higher price, they have antagonistic interests where output is concerned. This can be illustrated with a simple supply-and-demand model. For the sake of a simple argument, assume that a perfectly competitive industry is momentarily in a disequilibrium position, with price exceeding marginal cost for all firms at their present output. Suppose, too, that all of the adjustments will be made by the firms already in the industry rather than by new entrants, and that the industry is on an inelastic portion of its demand curve. Since price exceeds marginal cost for all firms, output will increase. But as all firms increase production, the price falls; indeed, since the industry demand curve

Mancur Olson, "The Logic of Collective Action," pp. 9–16 from Mancur Olson, *The Logic of Collective Action: Public Goods and the Theory of Groups*. Cambridge, MA: Harvard University Press, 1965. Copyright © 1965, 1971 by the President and Fellows of Harvard College. Reprinted by permission of Harvard University Press.

Contemporary Sociological Theory, Third Edition. Edited by Craig Calhoun, Joseph Gerteis, James Moody, Steven Pfaff, and Indermohan Virk. Editorial material and organization © 2012 John Wiley & Sons, Ltd. Published 2012 by John Wiley & Sons, Ltd.

is by assumption inelastic, the total revenue of the industry will decline. Apparently each firm finds that with price exceeding marginal cost, it pays to increase its output, but the result is that each firm gets a smaller profit. Some economists in an earlier day may have questioned this result,[1] but the fact that profit-maximizing firms in a perfectly competitive industry can act contrary to their interests as a group is now widely understood and accepted.[2] A group of profit-maximizing firms can act to reduce their aggregate profits because in perfect competition each firm is, by definition, so small that it can ignore the effect of its output on price. Each firm finds it to its advantage to increase output to the point where marginal cost equals price and to ignore the effects of its extra output on the position of the industry. It is true that the net result is that all firms are worse off, but this does not mean that every firm has not maximized its profits. If a firm, foreseeing the fall in price resulting from the increase in industry output, were to restrict its own output, it would lose more than ever, for its price would fall quite as much in any case and it would have a smaller output as well. A firm in a perfectly competitive market gets only a small part of the benefit (or a small share of the industry's extra revenue) resulting from a reduction in that firm's output.

For these reasons it is now generally understood that if the firms in an industry are maximizing profits, the profits for the industry as a whole will be less than they might otherwise be. And almost everyone would agree that this theoretical conclusion fits the facts for markets characterized by pure competition. The important point is that this is true because, though all the firms have a common interest in a higher price for the industry's product, it is in the interest of each firm that the other firms pay the cost – in terms of the necessary reduction in output – needed to obtain a higher price.

About the only thing that keeps prices from falling in accordance with the process just described in perfectly competitive markets is outside intervention. Government price supports, tariffs, cartel agreements, and the like may keep the firms in a competitive market from acting contrary to their interests. Such aid or intervention is quite common. It is then important to ask how it comes about. How does a competitive industry obtain government assistance in maintaining the price of its product?

Consider a hypothetical, competitive industry, and suppose that most of the producers in that industry desire a tariff, a price-support program, or some other government intervention to increase the price for their product. To obtain any such assistance from the government, the producers in this industry will presumably have to organize a lobbying organization; they will have to become an active pressure group. This lobbying organization may have to conduct a considerable campaign. If significant resistance is encountered, a great amount of money will be required. Public relations experts will be needed to influence the newspapers, and some advertising may be necessary. Professional organizers will probably be needed to organize "spontaneous grass roots" meetings among the distressed producers in the industry, and to get those in the industry to write letters to their congressmen. The campaign for the government assistance will take the time of some of the producers in the industry, as well as their money.

There is a striking parallel between the problem the perfectly competitive industry faces as it strives to obtain government assistance, and the problem it faces in the marketplace when the firms increase output and bring about a fall in price. *Just as it was not rational for a particular producer to restrict his output in order that there might be a higher price for the product of his industry, so it would not be rational for him to sacrifice his time and money to support a lobbying organization to obtain government assistance for the industry. In neither case would it be in the interest of the individual producer to assume any of the costs himself. A lobbying organization, or indeed a labor union or any other organization, working in the interest of a large group of firms or workers in some industry, would get no assistance from the rational, self-interested individuals in that industry.* This would be true even if everyone in the industry were absolutely convinced that the proposed program was in their interest (though in fact some might think otherwise and make the organization's task yet more difficult).

Although the lobbying organization is only one example of the logical analogy between the organization and the market, it is of some practical importance. There are many powerful and well-financed lobbies with mass support in existence now, but these lobbying organizations do not get that support because of their legislative achievements. The most powerful lobbying organizations now obtain their funds and their following for other reasons, as later parts of this study will show.

Some critics may argue that the rational person will, indeed, support a large organization, like a lobbying organization, that works in his interest, because he knows that if he does not, others will not do so either, and then the organization will fail, and he will be without the benefit that the organization could have provided. This argument shows the need for the analogy with the perfectly competitive market. For it would be quite as reasonable to argue that prices will never fall below the levels a monopoly would have charged in a perfectly competitive market, because if one firm increased its output, other firms would also, and the price would fall; but each firm could foresee this, so it would not start a chain of price-destroying increases in output. In fact, it does not work out this way in a competitive market; nor in a large organization. When the number of firms involved is large, no one will notice the effect on price if one firm increases its output, and so no one will change his plans because of it. Similarly, in a large organization, the loss of one dues payer will not noticeably increase the burden for any other one dues payer, and so a rational person would not believe that if he were to withdraw from an organization he would drive others to do so.

The foregoing argument must at the least have some relevance to economic organizations that are mainly means through which individuals attempt to obtain the same things they obtain through their activities in the market. Labor unions, for example, are organizations through which workers strive to get the same things they get with their individual efforts in the market – higher wages, better working conditions, and the like. It would be strange indeed if the workers did not confront some of the same problems in the union that they meet in the market, since their efforts in both places have some of the same purposes.

However similar the purposes may be, critics may object that attitudes in organizations are not at all like those in markets. In organizations, an emotional or ideological element is often also involved. Does this make the argument offered here practically irrelevant?

A most important type of organization – the national state – will serve to test this objection. Patriotism is probably the strongest non-economic motive for organizational allegiance in modern times. This age is sometimes called the age of nationalism. Many nations draw additional strength and unity from some powerful ideology, such as democracy or communism, as well as from a common religion, language, or cultural inheritance. The state not only has many such powerful sources of support; it also is very important economically. Almost any government is economically beneficial to its citizens, in that the law and order it provides is a prerequisite of all civilized economic activity. But despite the force of patriotism, the appeal of the national ideology, the bond of a common culture, and the indispensability of the system of law and order, no major state in modern history has been able to support itself through voluntary dues or contributions. Philanthropic contributions are not even a significant source of revenue for most countries. Taxes, *compulsory* payments by definition, are needed. Indeed, as the old saying indicates, their necessity is as certain as death itself.

If the state, with all of the emotional resources at its command, cannot finance its most basic and vital activities without resort to compulsion, it would seem that large private organizations might also have difficulty in getting the individuals in the groups whose interests they attempt to advance to make the necessary contributions voluntarily.

The reason the state cannot survive on voluntary dues or payments, but must rely on taxation, is that the most fundamental services a nation-state provides are, in one important respect, like the higher price in a competitive market: they must be available to everyone if they are available to anyone. The basic and most elementary goods or services provided by government, like defense and police protection, and the system of law and order generally, are such that they go to everyone or practically everyone in the nation. It would obviously not be feasible, if indeed it were possible, to deny the protection provided by the military services, the police, and the courts to those who did not voluntarily pay their share of the costs of government, and taxation is accordingly necessary. The common or collective benefits provided by governments are usually called "public goods" by economists, and the concept of public goods is one of the oldest and most important ideas in the study of public finance. A common, collective, or public good is here defined as any good such that, if any person X_i in a group $X_1, \ldots, X_i, \ldots, X_n$ consumes it, it cannot feasibly be withheld from the others in that group. In other words, those who do not purchase or pay for any of the public or collective good cannot be excluded or kept from sharing in the consumption of the good, as they can where noncollective goods are concerned.

Students of public finance have, however, neglected the fact that *the achievement of any common goal or the satisfaction of any common interest means that a public or collective good has been provided for that group*. The very fact that a goal or purpose is *common* to a group means that no one in the group is excluded from the benefit or satisfaction brought about by its achievement. As the opening paragraphs of this chapter indicated, almost all groups and organizations have the purpose of serving the common interests of their members. As R. M. MacIver puts it, "Persons ... have common interests in the degree to which they participate in a cause ... which indivisibly embraces them all."[3] It is of the essence of an organization that it provides an inseparable, generalized benefit. It follows that the provision of public or collective goods is the fundamental function of organizations generally. A state is first of all an organization that provides public goods for its members, the citizens; and other types of organizations similarly provide collective goods for their members.

And just as a state cannot support itself by voluntary contributions, or by selling its basic services on the market, neither can other large organizations support themselves without providing some sanction, or some attraction distinct from the public good itself, that will lead individuals to help bear the burdens of maintaining the organization. The individual member of the typical large organization is in a position analogous to that of the firm in a perfectly competitive market, or the taxpayer in the state: his own efforts will not have a noticeable effect on the situation of his organization, and he can enjoy any improvements brought about by others whether or not he has worked in support of his organization.

There is no suggestion here that states or other organizations provide *only* public or collective goods. Governments often provide noncollective goods like electric power, for example, and they usually sell such goods on the market much as private firms would do. Moreover, as later parts of this study will argue, large organizations that are not able to make membership compulsory *must also* provide some noncollective goods in order to give potential members an incentive to join. Still, collective goods are the characteristic organizational goods, for ordinary noncollective goods can always be provided by individual action, and only where common purposes or collective goods are concerned is organization or group action ever indispensable.[4]

NOTES

1 See J. M. Clark, *The Economics of Overhead Costs* (Chicago: University of Chicago Press, 1923), p. 417, and Frank H. Knight, *Risk, Uncertainty and Profit* (Boston: Houghton Mifflin, 1921), p. 193.
2 Edward H. Chamberlin, *Monopolistic Competition*, 6th edn. (Cambridge, MA: Harvard University Press, 1950), p. 4.
3 R. M. MacIver in *Encyclopaedia of the Social Sciences*, 7th edn. (New York: Macmillan, 1932), p. 147.
4 It does not, however, follow that organized or coordinated group action is *always* necessary to obtain a collective good.

Chapter 8

A Theory of Group Solidarity [1987]

Michael Hechter

Consider the following situation. A large number of tent-dwellers live in an isolated and relatively unpopulated valley. Land is plentiful and free for the taking. Life is good, save for one recurring problem. The tent-dwellers are intermittently victimized by a roving band of outlaws who abscond with their crops and stored food. Each incident causes severe losses to a large number of households. To forestall this threatened loss, a majority of the tent-dwellers decides to form a protective association. The association determines that two measures must be taken to provide for the members' security. All the members' tents must be concentrated in one part of the valley. And members must participate in round-the-clock watches along the perimeter of the new settlement. Under this plan members alone will receive protection; those who choose not to join will remain unprotected.

Yet the ability to reach agreement on this set of rules does not guarantee adequate security. The security of these tent-dwellers is very much a joint good; its production is only assured when each member lives up to the obligation to stand watch. The member who neglects to do so in order to dally with the neighbor compromises the security of the whole encampment. Will the members comply with their obligation to stand watch? How solidary will the protective association be?

An adequate theory of group solidarity must be able to explain variation in the extensiveness of corporate obligations and in a group's capacity to induce its members to honor these obligations.

Michael Hechter, "A Theory of Group Solidarity," pp. 40–54 from Michael Hechter, *Principles of Group Solidarity*. Berkeley, CA: University of California Press, 1987. Reprinted with permission.

Contemporary Sociological Theory, Third Edition. Edited by Craig Calhoun, Joseph Gerteis, James Moody, Steven Pfaff, and Indermohan Virk. Editorial material and organization © 2012 John Wiley & Sons, Ltd. Published 2012 by John Wiley & Sons, Ltd.

The Extensiveness of Corporate Obligations

All rational choice explanations start with explicit behavioral assumptions; usually actors are considered to be rational egoists. Strangely, a similar assumption is smuggled into much classical sociological analysis, albeit implicitly. As the normativists observed, sanctions exist even in the most solidary of groups. Why? Because there is often a conflict of interest between the individual and the group.

True, at those times when groups encourage their members to pursue their private interests to the hilt, no such conflict need arise (Young 1979: 51–66). And not all compliance to norms need be costly to individuals (Coleman 1966; G. S. Becker 1974; Barry 1970: 44–46). Some norms – which are also called conventions (Lewis 1969) – enable individuals to make decisions about a host of matters that defy rational solution (Durkheim 1951 [1897]: 254–56). These are rules that designate appropriate standards of conduct in diverse situations ("one should always drive on the right side of the street"), and people may comply with them simply because it is not costly for them to do so (Stigler and Becker 1977: 82; Thibaut and Kelley 1959: 127–200). In the driving example, noncompliance is in fact the more costly choice. Yet even though conventional behavior imposes few costs, the violation of conventions always brings forth sanctions (Goffman 1959). Naturally, conflicts of interest between the individual and the group increase whenever group members seek predictable and consistent levels of normative compliance from one another, not just fitful compliance when it suits the member's fancy.

Whenever people are faced with two divergent courses of action – one in pursuit of some individual end, the other in pursuit of some collective end – I will assume that they will invariably choose the former. Since the obligations imposed by membership in a group generally interfere with and deflect from the members' pursuit of their own goals, they can be likened to a membership tax. Once a group's obligations are considered as if they were a tax, it is possible to predict how extensive, or costly, they will be in different circumstances.

The obligations of some groups can only be satisfied when members part with a rather large proportion of their private resources, whereas the obligations of others can be satisfied by substantially less onerous contributions. For example, the members of intentional communities like the Bruderhof (Zablocki 1971) face far more extensive obligations than the employees of General Motors. What accounts for variations in the extensiveness of obligations among different groups? The first answer has to do with the nature of the joint good that the group produces.

Recall that groups exist in order to supply their members with some desired joint good. This good can be attained only if members comply with various rules that are designed to assure its production. There are two alternative means of obtaining compliance with these production rules: it can be secured either through compensation or through obligation. In some group – for instance, firms – members are compensated (in wages) for the time that they spend complying with production rules. In general, members would always prefer to be compensated for complying with production rules, because this does not diminish their own assets. Since the wages that motivate compliance must themselves be produced, however, compensation is feasible only in groups that produce marketable goods (and services) for the consumption of nonmembers.[1] General Motors can largely rely on wages to fill its assembly line because revenue is generated from the sale of vehicles and other products; since the Bruderhof is not primarily interested in marketing some commodity, it cannot rely on wages to motivate compliance among its members.

In contrast to groups whose rationale is the marketing of commodities to nonmembers, those that are principally formed to consume joint goods must rely on obligation to secure compliance with production rules. The greater the extensiveness of obligation, the greater the tax that members must pay to consume the joint good. Yet (according to the law of demand), the greater the price of a given good, the lower the demand for it. Why then do we find groups whose members consent to highly extensive obligations?

Such groups must provide goods of great value to their members. A rational member will seek membership in a group only if the benefit derived from access to the joint good exceeds the cost of the obligations – that is, the member's share of the costs of producing that good. This reasoning has one immediate implication: the benefit derived from membership in obligatory groups must generally exceed that of membership in compensatory groups. Why must this be so? Because the members of obligatory groups are expected to bear a cost (compliance with production rules) without a corresponding compensation. This can be explained if, in contrast to firms and other compensatory groups, obligatory groups produce *immanent goods* – those that directly satisfy their members' utility (by increasing their sense pleasures, happiness, and so forth). General Motors workers do not join the firm because they like cars, any more than the people who work in Silicon Valley like silicon chips. Most workers join firms because of their interest in wages, not in the commodities that these firms produce. Since workers do not get to consume the goods that they jointly produce (like nonmembers, they must purchase the goods if they want them), they must be compensated for the time spent in complying with the firm's production rules.

The people who join a group that produces some immanent good for the consumption of members (entertainment, sense pleasures, enlightenment, and so forth), however, do have an interest in helping to provide it without compensation, for utility is its own reward. Hence, obligation is likely to play the predominant role only in groups whose rationale is the production of immanent joint goods.

Yet the extensiveness of obligations also varies among groups that supply immanent goods. After all, Orthodox Jews, Mormons, and members of the Communist Party face far more extensive obligations than Reform Jews, Unitarians, or members of the Republican Party. What accounts for systematic differences in the extensiveness of obligations across groups?

It is reasonable to suspect that the extensiveness of a group's obligations has something to do with the cost of producing a given immanent good – that is, with the sum of all the labor, capital, and other necessary inputs. If security is more costly to produce than the entertainment generated by a weekly poker game, then we would expect the obligations of the protective association to be far more extensive than those of the poker group. Thus, the extensiveness of group obligations ought to be determined in part by the cost of producing the good in question. Evidently, there must be some minimal level of obligation that is required to produce a good in groups of a certain size, but how can the members ever know what it is?

Suppose, for the sake of argument, that the good is produced under the frictionless market conditions specified in conventional neoclassical economic models. In this case competition among rival producers of the good enables members to determine the lowest cost of producing it and thereby to arrive at minimally extensive obligations in the long run. To the degree that there are many different sources of similar or comparable goods in the immediate environment; that members have perfect information about the availability, quality, and cost of all close substitutes; that they have complete freedom of mobility and face no barriers of exit or entry into alternative groups (implying zero moving costs between them); that exchanges between members of the group are impersonal; and that enforcement is costless, members will tend to adopt obligations that are just extensive enough, and no more than are necessary, to provide a given quantity of the good.

It is easy to show why this minimal level of obligations will be realized. Imagine the problems that the members of a protective association might have deciding how extensive their corporate obligations should be. Assume that all pastoralist members can receive an adequate amount of security from the protective association by contributing 10 percent of their total assets. This is a new venture, however, and the pastoralists have no idea how much it will ultimately cost to provide themselves with adequate security. Perhaps most are willing to contribute as much as 20 percent of their assets to attain it. Even if they initially agree to a 20 percent contribution, the rate will not remain at this high level for long. If they could obtain adequate security at less cost (say at 15 percent) by joining (or forming) a different protective association, then it would be rational for members to desert the first group and "vote with their feet." (Note that in this case the availability of free grazing land and portability of their tents mean that the nomads' moving costs are negligible.)

This out-migration will stop only when the initial group lowers its rate to that of its competition, namely 15 percent. Then suppose that another group offers security on the basis of a 10 percent contribution. (We happen to know that this is the lowest possible rate, but this information is unavailable to the pastoralists.) This leads either to wholesale migration or to a downward readjustment of the initial group's rate. What will stop the process? Suppose another protective association lowers its rate to 5 percent. A host of new members will join. But soon they will discover that the association is unable to live up to its promises, for a 5 percent contribution is too low to provide adequate security. In the wake of this group's failure, everyone will rush back to join the 10 percent group. In time, then, the competition between rival protective associations (or rate experimentation within one group caused by the threat from potential new producers) will induce all groups to offer the same quantity of security (for a membership of a given size) at roughly the same, or equilibrium, rate of contribution.[2] Whatever the immanent good may be, in this world of frictionless markets groups will provide it to their members at minimal cost – that is, with minimally extensive obligations (Brennan and Buchanan 1980: 172).

Since rational egoists always seek to minimize their costs, why can't minimally extensive obligations be arrived at in the absence of fully competitive markets? After all, members have an incentive to find ways either to reduce costs (if their initial estimate of the production cost was too high) or to increase costs (if their estimate was too low). Even though they seek to minimize their obligations, there are at least three reasons why members are unable to do so in the absence of frictionless market conditions. In the first place, each collective consideration of the level of obligations entails time and other costs of decision-making (Buchanan and Tullock 1962; Buchanan 1975), and these costs rise geometrically with the size of the membership. Rather than incurring such costs, members will settle for greater than minimal obligations. In the second place, to the degree that members place a high value on continued access to the immanent good, they may be reluctant to risk suboptimal provision of it (this may account for the sanctity of the defense budget in the eyes of American voters). Finally, if there are no alternative sources of the same good, then initial members may levy higher obligations on all subsequent ones and consume the resulting surplus themselves. This will create a two- (or multi-) tiered tax structure within the membership and raise the average extensiveness of obligations for the group as a whole.

The problem is that the assumption of frictionless markets is extremely stringent and unrealistic, and to the degree that it does not hold, the minimal production cost cannot be inferred. Hence, it is more reasonable to regard the dependence of members rather than the cost of production as the key determinant of the extensiveness of group obligations.

Rational egoists choose to belong to a group because they are *dependent* (Thibaut and Kelley 1959; Emerson 1962; and Blau 1964) on other members for access to some desired joint good. If they could attain this good without incurring the obligations of membership, they would always prefer to do so. Yet their degree of dependence varies widely. Our nomads may have only one source of security – their local protective association. But similar individuals living on the populated plain may have a multitude of security options; on this account they are likely to be less dependent on any one protective association. *The more dependent people are, the more tax they must pay for access to the same quantity of a given good*. This variable degree of dependence is indicated by the opportunity cost of leaving the group, or what may be termed (after Hirschman 1970) the members' cost of exit. This is the difference between the value received from membership in the group and the value that is gained from the member's best alternative, taking into account any costs incidental to the transfer.

To the degree that members face a high cost of exit, they are dependent on that group. As exit costs approach prohibitive levels, dependence on the group increases; ultimately, members may become beholden to it for their very survival. In this extreme situation (analogous to a monopoly) members will accept the most extensive obligations to gain access to a given immanent good. Correlatively, when the cost of exit decreases, members' dependence on the group diminishes. When the average dependence of members declines significantly, the extensiveness of obligations begins to approach the minimum as specified in the neoclassical analysis.

Ultimately, dependence is affected by environmental shifts, many of which are beyond the control of group members themselves. It is increased by limits on the supply of close substitutes available outside group boundaries, a lack of information about these alternatives, moving costs, and the existence of strong personal ties among members. Let us consider each of these factors separately.

1. *The supply of close substitutes.* If the number of distinct sources of substitutable goods in the environment is not large, the chance of finding a better alternative generally decreases. Groups may collude and levy the same tax for providing a given joint good to their members. If there are only a small number of groups, this collusion may be easy to organize and enforce. As the number of alternative sources increases, however, the costs of organizing and enforcing collusive agreements grow disproportionately.

2. *Lack of information about alternatives.* On the one hand, since groups are more or less exclusive, knowledge of their internal workings may be relatively difficult to obtain (Goffman 1959: 77–105). Uncertainty about the relative advantages of alternative groups breeds inertia. On the other hand, many groups are able to restrict information about available alternatives. To the degree that members are unaware of the existence of alternative sources of joint goods outside group boundaries, they will be willing to bear the cost of more extensive rules. If people are unaware of the existence of a better alternative, they can hardly choose to take advantage of it. And information is always costly to gather.

3. *Costs of moving.* Transfer costs, which must be taken into account in any decision to join or leave a group, are seldom zero. Since moving costs among the nomads are minimal, they can be very responsive to marginal differences in the cost of protection. It is not very costly to pack everything on your camels and move to another part of the valley where security is a better bargain. Were the nomads to opt for a sedentary lifestyle, however, then their moving costs would rise, thereby increasing their dependence on the initial protective association. It is far more costly to move a house than a tent. Beyond this, however, groups sometimes impose entry and exit costs. Entry to the most rudimentary rotating credit association requires character references, which are developed over a lifetime and thus are costly to obtain. Many intentional communities demand that exiting members leave some part of their personal assets with the group. Finally, groups vary widely in their exclusiveness; for example, younger groups are more likely to be open than older ones. To the degree that there are barriers to entry/exit (and to the degree that moving between groups entails costs), this increases the dependence of members.

4. *The strength of personal ties.* Sociability is one of the most important immanent goods that groups provide. Since personal ties tend to arise with repeated interaction– and thus only in the course of time – they are akin to an irredeemable investment (or sunk cost) in the group. The probability of repeated interaction increases with limitations of supply and with costly information and mobility, lowering the chance that close substitutes can be found outside group boundaries.

If these are some of the factors that create dependence, constitutional and legal arrangements have decisive implications for generating them. For most of human history the number and composition of voluntary associations has been regulated by political authorities. As Adam Smith (1961 [1789]) was at pains to emphasize, without effective constitutional guarantees of individual private property rights and the freedoms of mobility and association, dependence flourishes. It is also strengthened whenever rights are granted to groups, rather than to individuals. This occurs in western feudalism, but the Indian caste system provides perhaps the classic example (Weber 1946 [1916–17]; Bouglé 1971; Leach 1962; Dumont 1970; Barth 1962; Berreman 1972).

While there has been much disagreement about the precise definition of caste, nevertheless it is usually held that caste implies three things: hereditary occupational specialization, a hierarchical ranking of groups, and great social distance between them. Interaction between the members of different castes is governed by canons of purity and impurity. If an untouchable so much as gazes at the dinner of a Brahman, it will be considered impure. Exogamy is prohibited, and imbalanced sex ratios among the members of higher castes lead to hypergamy as well as female infanticide. The caste system restricts intergroup mobility and thereby limits the availability of benefits outside group boundaries. Less extreme instances follow from the distinctive legal status of groups such as Jews and Greeks under the Ottoman *millet* system, Indians in North America, or blacks in South African Bantustans. In each case the state makes individuals dependent on corporate membership by allocating resources to groups qua groups (Van Dyke 1977).

Just as laws that limit the individual's alternatives outside group boundaries promote dependence, those that provide new alternatives lessen it. Here the development of the welfare state takes pride of place. The welfare state provides citizens with a wide range of benefits, or entitlements, that were customarily supplied by mutual benefit associations, churches, trade unions, political parties, and other kinds of voluntary associations. Once these benefits are offered to all as public goods, the incentives to belong to these other kinds of organizations erode. In this way, the growth of government welfare is implicated in many significant social changes, from the decline of the American urban political boss to the rise of divorce and family instability.

Due to constitutional and legal arrangements, among other factors, the competition among providers of joint goods is often restricted. The less competitive the market for the joint good is, the greater the dependence of group members. This means that the obligations (taxes) that the members of different groups adopt for the production of the same joint good are likely to vary. As the cost of leaving a group rises, so does the net benefit of remaining in it. And the greater this benefit is, the greater the willingness to tolerate extensive obligations. Although the average dependence of group members may vary, it never disappears altogether, for the members of groups always depend upon the efforts of others for the production of joint goods. The solitary consumer of private goods, however, need not incur dependence.

Since it permits the initial members of a group to demand higher obligations of new members, dependence also has implications for the evolution of group hierarchy. The older members' ability to extract what in effect are rents from newer ones is, however, limited by the dependence of these new members. The less their dependence, the less extensive the obligations they will incur.

In summary, then, the greater the dependence of members, the greater the extensiveness of group obligations. The extensiveness of a group's obligations alone, however, has no necessary implications for group solidarity. What also matters is the probability that members will comply with these obligations. It is to this problem that I now turn.

The Probability of Compliance

Rational egoists may desire the benefits derived from group membership, but they hope to receive these unconditionally. If members value the joint good, they are willing to commit themselves (or to be obliged) to help produce it; yet they will still have an incentive to free ride. Even though all the members of the protective association place a high value on security, still they would prefer to receive it without honoring their full obligations (say, by understating their assets or – better yet – by refraining from making any contribution at all). This is precisely the difficulty encountered with the provision of public goods: since they can be consumed by anyone, then rational egoists will not help to produce them. Even though members may place a high value on some joint good, free riding can be curtailed only if there is some means of assuring compliance with corporate obligations. A group's ability to do this is a function of its control capacity. While extensive obligations arise only in groups that provide immanent joint goods, control is an issue in *all* groups – even in those producing marketable commodities.[3]

The relationship between control and compliance is intricate for two reasons. In the first place, the group must have sufficient resources at its disposal to effectively reward or punish its members contingent on their level of contribution or performance. This ability to provide what are essentially selective incentives can be called the group's *sanctioning* capacity.

By virtue of the fact that members are more or less dependent (by definition), all groups have at least one potential sanction – namely, exclusion from the group. Exclusion is the ultimate sanction in that it denies individuals access to the jointly produced good that they value. Yet some groups use this sanction more readily than others. For example, intentional communities are more likely to expel deviant members than are families. Though the effectiveness of the threat of expulsion varies with the member's dependence on the group, the group's willingness to employ it as a sanction is analytically distinct from the dependence of its members.

In any case, many groups employ additional sanctions that fall short of expulsion to motivate compliance with corporate obligations. Although these sanctions are collectively produced, *they are quite different from the benefits that lead people to join the group initially*. Like exclusion, many of these sanctions are negative and therefore cannot count as benefits at all: if members do not live up to their obligations, they will suffer the consequences. In further contrast to the good that motivates membership, the provision of sanctions need not be regular or guaranteed but can be intermittent and provisional. A union's strike pay, for example, can be an incentive for picketing, but it only comes into play during a strike.

In order to be effective, these sanctions must be distributed to members selectively. Whether these sanctions are material or nonmaterial, their supply is never unlimited. Thus, to attain maximum compliance, groups must not only devise means of producing or procuring stores of adequate sanctions, but they must also convince all members that they will receive the particular sanction that is appropriate to their past behavior. If compliant members are consistently punished while noncompliant ones are consistently rewarded, then the overall level of compliance will be at its nadir. And if there is too long a delay between behavior and subsequent sanctioning, the efficacy of a sanction declines.

The second reason for the intricacy of the relationship between control and compliance is that the group must be able to detect whether individuals comply with their obligations or not. This is its *monitoring* capacity. Monitoring is problematic because individual behavior is often difficult to observe, much less to measure. Some acts – those conducted in utter privacy – are intrinsically harder to monitor than others – those carried out in the full view of other members. When a group tries to attain attitudinal as against visible behavioral compliance, its monitoring task is all the more demanding.

True, not all members have an interest in concealing their behavior. Deviants alone have this incentive, but the compliant can usually be relied upon to publicize their virtue. Yet this does not mean that groups composed of the relatively virtuous can do without monitoring. Monitoring is required not only to ferret out the noncompliant but also to check on the allegedly compliant, for claims of virtuous behavior can never be taken at face value. In the absence of monitoring, deviants or shirkers are also likely to describe their past behavior as virtuous. Hence, all self-reports of compliance must be sifted to separate the wheat from the chaff, and this, in turn, requires monitoring.

Altogether, then, noncompliance with obligations (and with rules of any sort) can have at least two separate roots: it can be due to inadequate sanctioning or to impaired monitoring. Since each of these activities is costly, the total costs of control constitute a severe constraint on any group's ability to attain compliance.

What determines a group's control capacity? Many considerations come into play [...], and for illustrative purposes I shall only mention two of them here.

The first determinant is the measurability of the individual's contribution. Whenever an individual's contribution to the production of a joint good cannot be reliably indicated by an output – as is the case, for example, in teamwork – control is problematic. Since acts carried out in privacy are more difficult to monitor than public acts, another factor is the group's ability to limit the privacy of its members. It is in the interest of members to extend their privacy, just as it is in the interest of the collective to limit it.

A group's survival depends upon the adoption of effective techniques to control its members. Yet insofar as control enables group members to produce joint goods, it must be considered a second-order collective good (Laver 1981: 62–71). As such, the provision of control is itself subject to the free-rider dilemma. While each member may gain from the overall solidarity of the group (because solidarity is an enabling condition for the supply of the joint good), free riding remains each rational agent's best strategy. Members will not voluntarily assume the burden of control without sufficient compensation. It follows that all long-lived groups must include some individuals – sometimes called *agents* – who are compensated for providing control and are motivated to do it on this account. Without such agents groups cannot secure routine compliance. But agents come in varying sizes and shapes. In informal groups everyone is simultaneously an agent and a member; in more complex structures agents and members are differentiated and perform mutually exclusive roles. In some groups (American academic departments) members rotate into and out of the agency role; in others (capitalist firms) access to this role is more restricted. Different institutional arrangements – particularly those that affect the distribution of the joint good – determine the relations between agents and members in all groups.

Whereas dependence characterizes all voluntary groups, it is insufficient to solve the free-rider problem. Without control, group solidarity is, at best, a chimera. Large groups with relatively great control capacity are fundamentally different from those lacking this capacity. They are likely to have clear and consistent corporate goals, for these are necessary to precisely define the members' obligations. Control promotes the stability and exclusivity of groups.

To recapitulate, solidarity varies with the extensiveness of corporate obligation together with the probability that members fully comply with these obligations. The theory suggests three conclusions. (1) Since groups that produce goods for the marketplace can compensate their members with wages, solidarity will be confined to groups concerned with the production of joint, immanent goods for internal consumption. (2) Variations in the extensiveness of corporate obligations are due to the cost of producing the joint good (which sets the lower bound of extensiveness) and the dependence of its members (which sets the upper bound). Since the market for immanent joint goods is never the pure, frictionless market of the economists, dependence is crucial in determining the extensiveness of these obligations. Finally, (3) variations in compliance with corporate obligations are due to the control capacity of groups.

Thus the solidarity of any group increases to the degree that members are dependent on the group and their behavior is capable of being controlled by the group's agents. If agents have the means to fully control members' behavior, solidarity will be a function of their dependence on the group: the less the dependence, the less the solidarity, and vice versa. If agents do not have the means to control members' behavior, a group is unlikely to attain solidarity regardless of its members' level of dependence. More formally, dependence and the group's control capacity are both determinants of solidarity, but each is by itself insufficient. Solidarity can be achieved only by the combined effects of dependence and control.

Whereas members themselves tend to determine variations in control capacity, variations in dependence are often due to environmental factors that are beyond their control. For example, once a state enacts policies that limit its citizens' rights – to geographic mobility, education, information, association, suffrage, and the like – this raises the dependence of the affected members. Democratization therefore plays a vital role in making group boundaries permeable. In societies where persons have the right to join any group, individualism flourishes and people can become as distinctive as snowflakes. This very distinctiveness, in turn, tends to liberate them from having extensive obligations to any particular group (Simmel 1955 [1922]: 140). In this way an analysis of group solidarity that begins by considering the action of individuals inexorably leads to a conclusion emphasizing the primacy of institutional factors.

The theory holds that individuals comply with corporate obligations when they desire some good that is provided by membership in a given group. In practice, however, the situation is seldom this clear-cut. People can, and often do, belong to the same group for different kinds of reasons. And groups often produce more than one joint good. These points become critical when the analyst must specify the best existing alternative in an individual's environment. This alternative is identified by the fact that it provides access to the same joint good. But there is always some ambiguity here. If the individual's interest in joining a group is merely the attainment of fellowship, then this can be fulfilled by membership in nearly any kind of group. For such people the purpose and type of the group is irrelevant: to them a church group and a political party are viable alternatives.

Individuals who participate in a group to gain access to a highly specific good (the pleasure to be gained by playing chamber music) usually have fewer alternatives than people with more diffuse interests. In general, the more specific an individual's interest in a particular group, the greater that person's dependence. The specificity of goals is likely to vary across individuals, however, and, worse, it is not directly measurable. Thus there is a subjective element involved in specifying the individual's dependence.

Despite these qualifications, the theory proposes that the prospects for solidarity will be maximal in situations where individuals face limited sources of benefit, where their opportunities for multiple group affiliation are minimal, and where their social isolation is extreme. But even in these most favorable of circumstances, solidarity can be achieved only when groups have the capacity to monitor members' behavior so that sanctions can be dispensed to promote compliance.

[…]

NOTES

1 This definition includes all profit-making firms but is not limited to them: non-profit groups, like universities, also market goods, such as education, to given publics.
2 I ignore the fact that the nomads' productivity will increase under secure conditions, so that the cost of protection will in future consume a smaller proportion of their total resources. This might, of course, be offset by increased population.
3 If control is required in all groups, then what is the difference between compensation and obligation as means of assuring production? Compensation is based upon a strict quid pro quo, and the agent is paid for each compliant act. In obligatory groups, however, there is no quid pro quo: compliance is expected of members and, as such, merits no special attention or reward.

REFERENCES

Barry, Brian. 1970. *Sociologists, Economists, and Democracy*. Chicago, IL: University of Chicago Press.
Barth, Fredrik. 1962. "The System of Social Stratification in Swat, North Pakistan." In Edmund Leach, ed., *Aspects of Caste in South India, Ceylon, and North West Pakistan*, pp. 113–46. London: Cambridge University Press.
Becker, Gary S. 1974. "A Theory of Social Interactions." *Journal of Political Economy*, 82(6): 163–91.
Berreman, Gerald D. 1972. *Hindus of the Himalayas: Ethnography and Change*. Berkeley, CA: University of California Press.
Blau, Peter M. 1964. *Exchange and Power in Social Life*. New York: John Wiley.
Bouglé, Célestin. 1971. *Essays on the Caste System*. Cambridge, UK: Cambridge University Press.
Brennan, Geoffrey, and James M. Buchanan. 1980. *The Power to Tax: Analytical Foundations of a Fiscal Constitution*. Cambridge, UK: Cambridge University Press.
Buchanan, James N. 1975. *The Limits of Liberty*. Chicago, IL: University of Chicago Press.
Buchanan, James M., and Gordon Tullock. 1962. *The Calculus of Consent*. Ann Arbor, MI: University of Michigan Press.
Coleman, James S. 1966. "Individual Interests and Collective Action." *Papers on Non-Market Decision-Making*, (1): 49–62.
Dumont, Louis. 1970. *Homo Hierarchichus: The Caste System and Its Implications*. Chicago, IL: University of Chicago Press.
Durkheim, Emile. 1951. *Suicide*. New York: Free Press. [Originally published 1897.]
Emerson, Richard A. 1962. "Power-Dependence Relations." *American Sociological Review*, 27(1): 31–41.
Goffman, Erving. 1959. *The Presentation of Self in Everyday Life*. New York: Anchor.
Hirschman, Albert O. 1970. *Exit, Voice and Loyalty*. Cambridge, MA: Harvard University Press.
Laver, Michael. 1981. *The Politics of Private Desires*. Harmondsworth, England: Penguin.

Leach, Edmund. 1962. Introduction: "What Should We Mean by Caste?" In E. Leach, ed., *Aspects of Caste in South India, Ceylon and North West Pakistan*, pp. 1–10. London: Cambridge University Press.

Lewis, David. 1969. *Convention: A Philosophical Study*. Cambridge, MA: Harvard University Press.

Simmel, Georg. 1955. "The Web of Group Affiliations." Translated by Reinhard Bendix. In *Conflict and the Web of Group Affiliations*, pp. 125–95. New York: Free Press. [Originally published 1922.]

Smith, Adam. 1961. *The Wealth of Nations*, 2 volumes. London: University Paperbacks. [Originally published 1789.]

Stigler, George J., and Gary S. Becker. 1977. "De Gustibus Non Est Disputandum." *American Economic Review*, 67(2): 76–90.

Thibaut, John W., and Harold H. Kelley. 1959. *The Social Psychology of Groups*. New York: John Wiley.

Van Dyke, Vernon. 1977. "The Individual, the State, and Ethnic Communities in Political Theory." *World Politics*, 29(3): 342–69.

Weber, Max. 1946. "India: The Brahman and the Castes." In Hans Gerth and C. Wright Mills, eds., *From Max Weber: Essays in Sociology*, pp. 396–415. New York: Oxford University Press. [Originally published 1916–1917.]

Young, Oran. 1979. *Compliance and Public Authority*. Baltimore, CA: Johns Hopkins University Press.

Zablocki, Benjamin. 1971. *The Joyful Community*. Baltimore, CA: Penguin.

Zablocki. 1980. *Alienation and Charisma*. New York: Free Press.

Chapter 9

Cooperation without Law or Trust [2005]

Karen S. Cook, Russell Hardin, and Margaret Levi

Now we turn to the heart of our enterprise, which is to explain how people manage their lives in the absence of trust and largely in the absence of legal or state enforcement of cooperative arrangements, all despite sometime inequality of power and often solid grounds for distrust. As is prima facie evident, the existence of the state and a legal system to govern many relationships can substitute for trust and other spontaneous motivations for cooperation in joint ventures of various kinds. In the role of providing law and stability, the state does not generally provoke cooperation but only enables it. Indeed, this fact is the rationale of the Hobbesian vision of order under an all-powerful sovereign (Hobbes 1968[1651]).

The failure or limits of state regulation or legal devices often leads to the creative development of informal devices. For example, the informal economics of the Third World arise in the context of weak states. But such informal "contractual" dealings permeate First World contexts as well, in part because law is too imprecise and too costly to cover the details of ordinary commercial agreements (Macauley 1963; Portes and Sassen-Koob 1987). There is evidence that strong informal institutions can thrive locally when central government is weak. Contrary to the more nearly standard view, we might argue that, historically, commerce seems to have stimulated the growth of law and legal institutions, which were not necessary for the early

Karen S. Cook, Russell Hardin, and Margaret Levi, "Cooperation without Law or Trust," pp. 83–5, 86–7, 87–8, 89–94, 98–100, 101–3 from Karen S. Cook, Russell Hardin, and Margaret Levi, *Cooperation Without Trust?* New York: Russell Sage Foundation, 2005. Copyright © 2005 Russell Sage Foundation, 112 East 64th Street, New York, NY 10021. Reprinted with permission.

Contemporary Sociological Theory, Third Edition. Edited by Craig Calhoun, Joseph Gerteis, James Moody, Steven Pfaff, and Indermohan Virk. Editorial material and organization © 2012 John Wiley & Sons, Ltd. Published 2012 by John Wiley & Sons, Ltd.

development of commerce (Mueller 1999, 95–8). Adam Smith (1976 [1776]: 412), crediting David Hume with the original insight, remarks that with the rise of towns, "commerce and manufactures gradually introduced order and good government, and with them, the liberty and security of individuals." Robert Ellickson (1991, 1998) argues that, in the face of potentially prohibitive conflict more generally, local norms commonly handle many economic issues of cooperation that the law could not handle as efficiently or as well. In many of his cases, there is an ongoing relationship, which suggests the likelihood of developing a trust relationship that makes cooperation relatively easy. Ellickson's work and even the title of his 1991 book are forerunners to the present work, although he addresses cooperation without law and we are concerned with the supposedly even harder problem of cooperation with neither law nor trust. We may conclude that many activities are best regulated by norms and that the law itself requires norms to enable its own working (Hetcher 2004, ch. 2).

In analyzing cooperation without trust, we begin [...] at the individual level and with largely spontaneous interactions. Then we turn to relatively systematic patterns of interaction, but still at the level of individuals rather than of institutions. Many social practices can readily be seen de facto as devices for managing and motivating cooperative behavior in the absence of adequate trust, or even in the presence of substantial distrust. Often we need to be able to cooperate with some of those whom we do not trust. In fact, of course, we are in no position to trust the vast majority of people in our society, and possibly we cannot trust even the vast majority of those with whom we have to deal, both directly and indirectly. If we could handle these relationships through the law, we might not need to worry about the lack of trust. But many of the cooperative relations we would like to enter cannot be regulated by law. Even for many of those that could be brought under law, the costs of appealing to legal institutions might dwarf the benefits of the relationships. Ideally we might wish we could find people whom we could trust. In the large number of cases in which that is not possible, we would like to have some less formal social devices available to give potentially useful partners the incentive to be cooperative.

The state may lurk in the background for most of the interactions discussed here, but often the scale or the specificity (sometimes to the point of idiosyncrasy) of an interaction makes it not a good candidate for legal oversight. Even then, the general order that the state provides is usually the essential background on which all of these devices play out. If there were no stable order, we would not be so heavily engaged in cooperative interactions because we would be more focused on self-protection than on marginal improvements in our lives. All of the interactions discussed here are outside the law, although they are not necessarily illegal. They may sometimes even be pre-law. For example, communal norms must have worked even in many communities in which there was no powerful legal authority.

Many of the alternative devices rely on reputational effects, both of individual cooperators and of institutional agencies (short of government) and other formal institutions that back reputations with some degree of sanctioning for failure to live up to them. The force of reputation here is not that it carries information on past behavior (which would be of central importance for a dispositional theory of trustworthiness). Rather, the value of a reputation is that it can give others reason to believe one wishes to maintain the reputation *in order to enter into cooperative relations with others in the future*. Hence, when we refer to reputational effects here, we always mean their future-oriented effects. In this sense, the value of a reputation for trustworthiness is that it gives one incentive actually to be trustworthy, and it therefore gives others incentive to take the risk of assuming that one will be trustworthy, as in the encapsulated interest theory.

[…]

In this chapter, we address interactions that commonly have the form of A somehow inducing B to motivate C to do something A wants (or, in some cases, the shorter form of B motivating C to do something A wants or would value). For example, in Muhammad Yunus's Grameen Bank, it is groups of neighbors (usually women) who induce each other to repay their loans so that others in the group might also have access to loans. Yunus and his bank, A, do not need to be assiduous in chasing after repayment from a customer, C, because they have, in a sense, delegated the incentive for doing this to the neighbors, B. The loans from the Grameen Bank are too small for the bank to use legal devices to enforce repayment; in any case, in many of the societies in which such banks operate the legal system is not capable of enforcing repayment of any loans, large or small. In essence, the Grameen turns clusters of neighbors into network (social) capital.

[…]

This formula de facto captures the idea of social capital in one of its forms, as we argue later. In this particular form, *individuals can have access to social capital*. For you (A) to call on social capital is to have access to a facilitator (B) who can motivate the relevant provider (C) to act on your behalf. In an advanced society the relevant C is usually an institution of some kind, often government. B might also be an institution, but B is more likely to be a role holder in an institution. Social capital is a vague, not to say murky, concept that takes on many meanings. Many scholars include trust in the bag of many unrelated things that they say constitute social capital (for example, Putnam 1995a, 1995b, 2000; Brehm and Rahn 1997). As we conceive the idea of social capital that takes the form of individuals having access to it (Cook 2005), trust can play a small initiating role, but it does not have to do so.

It can happen that because a particular facilitator, B, trusts you, A, to some extent to reciprocate favors, B is induced to try to motivate a relevant C to act on your behalf. But the facilitator can do this even without trust because A and B can simply enter an exchange in which A pays for B's effort to motivate the provider C. As a crass but evidently very common example in American politics, you give money to B's campaign for political office, and B gets government agency C to do what you want. We spell out the implications of this general view later. Social capital enables us to get things done by people with whom we do not have a substantial trust relationship – indeed, people whom we need not even know. That is commonly why we want access to social capital – because it is the only form of access we might have to accomplish our purposes, although vernacular vocabulary would not put the case that way. Hence, although trust might be important in calling on social capital, social capital is not constituted by trust.

[…]

Social Capital

Although recent work on the social underpinnings of government often starts from claims about the nature or decline of social capital, the main role of social capital in our lives is in enabling us to accomplish things at the level of individuals and groups. There have been many different attempts to define social capital, but here we restrict the term to two forms. The first – and for present purposes the more important – of these takes the form of the various networks on which certain people can call to get things done. Again, many writers include trust in the category of social capital, although that is a mistake. Your trusting does not do much for you when you need to call on a network of associates to help you resolve some family or broader social problem, such as how to protect your child within the educational system. That there are people in your networks who trust you, however, may be very useful. Hence, as seems to be pervasive in discussions of trust, what – if anything – is really at stake here is trustworthiness rather than trust. The fact that you have found me trustworthy in some prior dealings makes it likely that you will now let me rely on you to get something done. If you have previously found me to be untrustworthy, you are likely to see no future in cooperating with me for my benefit because you would not expect me to reciprocate. Even to mention reciprocity here suggests the possibility of exchange, which need not be grounded in trust. Hence, our understanding of social capital is not yet complete.

The second form that social capital takes in the literature is the capacity of a group to act together in certain ways. Here we can meaningfully say that groups can have social capital. This capital inheres in the connections within groups. For example, if we all trust each other, we might all take the risk of investing in some collective enterprise at a cost to each of us as individuals, although we could not be a large group because we could not have thick enough relationships with a large number of people to be able meaningfully to trust them or judge their trustworthiness. Those who worry about declining social capital must have larger-scale issues in mind.

[…]

Very few writers are clear about the difference between individuals *having access to social capital* and groups *actually having social capital*. James Coleman (1988, 100–2; 1990, 302–4) makes the distinction (but sometimes blurs it) and gives examples of groups that have social capital that enables them to act collectively. We might similarly include many organizations in the list of "groups" that have social capital. Such group or organizational capital is explicitly the form of social capital that is of central interest to several writers (see, for example, Cohen and Prusak 2001). And it may be what is at issue in the recent literature about Tocqueville's claims for the import of group activity in the democratic politics of the early United States (as in Putnam 2000). He supposed that group organization was a laboratory for learning democracy. [...] Here we focus, however, on the first of these forms of social capital: individuals having access to social capital that can help them accomplish their goals. Again, individual access to social capital has the form of A getting B to motivate C to act on A's behalf.

Note that your individual access to social capital turns on the interaction between two things. First is the potential usefulness of some network in getting done what you want done. Second is the likely commitment of those in the network to be motivated to take actions on your behalf. In your ordinary life, there are probably many people in many networks with whom you deal, and those networks are much of the social capital that is, in some sense, available to you. Many of these people – but probably not all – would say they trust you in certain matters.

In this view of it, the social capital to which an individual might have access is analogous to physical capital, such as machinery. Any bit of physical capital enables you to do various things. It enables you more if you are especially talented at using it, so that the value of that capital to you is not identical to the value that same capital has to others. For example, you might be able to produce the sounds of a wonderful Mozart sonata from a violin while many others could produce only unpleasant screeches from it. Social capital is similar, but rather than a talent for making the violin or some machine do its tricks, you have relationships that enable you to get the network capital that is available to you to do its tricks. Your relationships might differ enough that you get different results from calling on the same networks for the same kind of issue. However, one could imagine using the same networks in a very different way. There might be professional enablers who can tap into the networks to get things done for those who pay for the service. This is essentially the story of how many contributors to politicians' election campaigns get things done. They have paid up front and can be expected to pay again at the next election, and they receive entrée to relevant networks to solve various problems. Similarly, some might be able to call on social capital because they reciprocate in some way; you can call on it because you have paid for access.

When we see social capital in this way, we can see two somewhat contrary effects. On the one hand, many of the problems of ordinary life can be resolved through its use, and this makes it sound like a generally beneficent thing. On the other hand, some people have access to networks – especially networks that connect with government – that far surpasses the access of the rest of us, although the government might formally be democratic and also supposedly egalitarian with respect to many policy implementations. These individuals' greater access to social capital distorts outcomes, because they have access to government personnel who might have substantial power to use public funds or political influence. This does not sound so clearly beneficent. But this general conclusion should come as no surprise because, in essence, social capital is merely a means to do things, and there is no reason to suppose that it can only be put to work to accomplish good or egalitarian things. It can also be put to work to accomplish generally bad or inegalitarian things.

The machine in a factory may be used to produce weapons or consumer goods. Similarly, social capital can produce both awful policies and good policies. The Ku Klux Klan can have access to social capital as great as that of the NAACP.

All of these networks depend on social order and technological access to people. In the past our networks were far more likely to have been face to face, although not exclusively. Now our networks cover far more ground, but perhaps they cover it more thinly (Leijonhufvud 1995; Hardin 1999). Yet Robert Putnam (1995a, 1995b, 2000) and many others argue that social capital in some advanced democracies is in decline. For Putnam, this is worrisome because he supposes that citizens' access to social capital makes government perform better. Differential access, as noted earlier, seems likely to make it perform especially well for some people and much less well for others.

In general, the claim in many recent discussions of declining social capital must be wrong. *Individual access to social capital in general is increasing for many people in modern societies, not decreasing.* People in advanced nations have many connections through their workplaces, their neighborhoods, their extended families, their fellow university alums, and numerous other groups. And they have various talents for figuring out which of these can best help them in various contexts. As evidence of how connected we are, every year many of us receive especially targeted solicitations for help of various kinds, usually for donations of money. These come through networks with which we have been long associated as well as from those we have joined very recently. It seems that every time we respond to one of these, we get several more, almost as though by return mail. For example, contributions to any police or hospital benefit, no matter how good the cause, are an invitation to be hassled incessantly by telephone solicitations, usually at dinnertime, for years to come. These are networks that commonly use us; we cannot so readily use them. But they are an indicator of our connectedness and our general level of access to varied networks. Changes in our degrees of connectedness over time are a worthy subject for investigation (see Watts 2003; for a relatively popular account of connectedness and its value, see Gladwell 1999).

Having individual access to social capital seems to be an important part of our lives for accomplishing many things at the personal or family level. Here we consider various social devices for accomplishing cooperative results even when there is little trust. In some of these cases, there might be some trust that gets things going, but the devices are not primarily exercises of trust and trustworthiness, and trust is not necessary for them to work. As usual, when there is trust, things may be easier, but trust is not a sine qua non. The devices considered here are exercises in applying individual pressure to individuals to get them to behave in certain ways. [...]

All of these spontaneous social devices, which take place outside the coverage of the law, regulate life when trust would be inadequate for the simple reason that there might not be much trust in many of these contexts because *there are conflicts of interest great enough to trump individual encapsulation of another's interests.* The greatest challenge to trust as encapsulated interest in many relationships is often such conflicts of interest. If law stood in the background for these interactions, trust between the relevant parties would also not be necessary. But these are cases in which law is not sufficient – because it is too poorly developed or because the stakes are too low to call on such heavy, expensive machinery. [...]

Communal Norms of Cooperativeness and Responsibility

There is virtually always a larger context in which trust relations play out. A somewhat stylized social history of trust relations is as follows (Cook and Hardin 2001). In relatively small-scale communal organization of life, trust is generally not at issue, and indeed there is no term for trust in English before about the twelfth century, and still none today in many languages of the world (Hardin 2002, 76). When everyone in a community knows everyone else and when everyone oversees everyone else's interactions, reliability can be enforced by norms that are backed by the sanctions the community would apply. Your default in an interaction with me commonly brings down sanctions from all of us, not merely from me. This fits the paradigm of social capital: A induces B to motivate C to do something for A. If C has been derelict in some dealing with A, A can induce the whole community, B, to motivate C to behave better toward A, or even to make some kind of restitution to A.

The stylized history of trust appears to be mirrored in systematic differences in the nature of helping and cooperative relations in contemporary small towns and large cities (Cook and Hardin 2001). Helping behavior in small towns is in fact not a matter of reciprocity but of helping or communal norms, whereas seemingly similar behavior in urban areas is typically a matter of reciprocity (Amato 1993). Moreover, in small communities behavior under communal norms is generalized to cover everyone in the community, whereas in cities the reciprocity governs behavior within particular networks. You reciprocate helping behavior toward those in your network who would help you in similar circumstances (and who may have helped you already). In small towns, the social networks are multiplex, membership is stable, and the norms for responsibility are relatively generalized. In urban settings, the networks tend to be more specialized, less multiplex, more sparsely connected (instead of almost wholly overlapping), and more numerous. They are multiple instead of multiplex (Fischer 1982), although there may be certain subcommunities within urban settings that approximate the character of small-town life.

An apparent implication of these differences in the nature of cooperation in small communities and in urban settings is that trust and trustworthiness help to ground, or grow out of, reciprocal exchange relations in cities. To examine this thesis we draw on theories of generalized exchange in networks and groups (Cook and Hardin 2001; Yamagishi and Cook 1993). Trustworthy behavior can be based on interests, on psychological dispositions, or on moral commitments. Trust must therefore be grounded in knowledge of the interests, the dispositional character, or the moral commitments of the trusted.

If helping behavior is based on norms, as in small communities, the relevant norms could have grown by socioevolution out of reciprocal exchange relations within groups. This could be a natural development for teaching a child, whom it might be much easier to teach a simple rule (as in a norm) than an understanding of the complexities of the interests of others and how these strategically relate to the child's own interests, especially long-run interests. Indeed, many adults appear to be unable to grasp even the logic of the interests embedded in iterated prisoner's dilemma (exchange) interactions (Hardin 1982a) or the logic of collective action (Hardin 1982b; Olson 1965). Communal norms can govern relatively little beyond some degree of cooperativeness, or they might be quite extensive, in which case they are likely to be imposed on some more heavily than on others. If they are grounded in strenuous religious principles, for instance, they can be very extensive and even draconian. We are concerned primarily with cooperativeness and how it is motivated in the absence of state power. Hence, we are not concerned with the full panoply of norms that might govern relations in some community, but only with norms of cooperativeness.

That a communal norm might commonly be enforced by interests could well help it to survive and to motivate people. A communal norm of helping or of trustworthiness might arise out of reciprocal exchange relations and then be transformed into a more generalized norm, albeit one that is still reinforced most strongly only as a within-group norm. The urban norms may be less normatively conceived and more openly grounded in reciprocal relations within ongoing networks, and they might almost never be generalized beyond their initial contexts. These differences have important implications for intergroup relations in both urban and small-community contexts.

Communal norms of cooperativeness and other positive matters are commonly backed by more onerous norms of exclusion. Such norms commonly work to keep members of various groups loyal to the group. They do this by using sanctions against those who are weakly committed or who violate expected practices within the group. The sanctions can range from mild reprimands to total exclusion from the group, with moderate shunning somewhere in between these extremes. There is often a supposition that efforts to control members of a group must be costly and therefore must commonly fail. For several reasons, this is often not true. Behavior that runs against a group's practices can actually be discomfiting to other members of the group, so that any costs of sanctioning can be offset with immediate gains. For example, some Indian tribes in the United States have recently revived the use of banishment of offensive members of the tribe from tribal lands. Banishment of some serves the interests of those who remain behind by protecting them from drug addiction and other offenses (Sarah Kershaw and Monica Davey, "Plagued by Drugs, Tribes Revive Ancient Penalty," *New York Times*, January 18, 2004, pp. 1, 26). Among the offenses for which a member can be banished from the Chippewa tribe of Grand Portage, Michigan, are "being in a gang, selling drugs, harming the [tribe's] cultural items, disrupting a religious ceremony, unauthorized hunting or fishing, and being banished from another reservation." The chair of the tribal council says, "We see ourselves here as kind of a big family, and so we needed to be part of the solution" (26).

In sum, small-community and urban contexts are strategically different in ways that lead to different modal ways of resolving the problem of mutual assistance. The small community commonly works through norms that are quasi-universal for the community and cover many aspects of potential cooperativeness. The urban society works through networks of ongoing relationships that are embedded within the much larger context. Any one of these networks is partial in that it covers only a particular realm of potential cooperation, so that each urbanite is involved in many quite different networks. In the urban setting, trust and trustworthiness might play a very large role in motivating behavior, while in the small community norms play the central role and trust might not even be cited.

Note that social capital takes two different forms in these two cases. In the communal norm of cooperativeness, the social capital on which you can call is that of mobilizing others in the community behind your sanctioning of a violator of your norm. Without a norm of exclusion, you could only renege from further co-operative ventures with the miscreant. That might be a real opportunity cost to the miscreant, but it would usually have a trivial effect in comparison to shunning by most of your fellow community members. Complete shunning or banishment could be devastating.

In the social networks of urban societies, we can affect your reputation among other participants in our network, and that might lead to your de facto exclusion from the network. That would, of course, affect only a small part of your social existence. Perversely, however, if your value to others is much higher than ours, our effort to degrade your reputation might lead to our own exclusion, even though it was you who violated our trust. Sadly, one can be excluded from a group or network for being injured by an especially important member of the group. Social networks are commonly valuable to their members only for what they can help provide to those members through enabling cooperation with others. Because the value of cooperation with one member can be substantially greater than that of cooperation with another member, network relations can be distorted by the problems of power inequality (see Cook and Emerson 1978; Farrell, 2004). But when the network works positively, broadcasting someone's violation of a network member's trust on a relevant matter (the matter for which the network is organized) can work well because the network provides or is a form of enabling capital to its members.

[...]

Communal Lending

Informal economic devices have been used to enable cooperative interactions in contexts that at first seem implausible: making loans that are unsecured to actors who have virtually no resources to use as collateral. Among the varied devices that have been used for securing such loans, two are especially noteworthy: practices that integrate new immigrants into an ethnic community through the work of those who have already succeeded and are no longer without resources; and organizations that are organized by sponsors or sponsoring institutions and that make small loans to poor entrepreneurs. With neither of these devices is there necessarily or even often any trust in the sense of encapsulated interest, because there is virtually no relationship between the lender and the recipient of the loan.

We begin the discussion with the seemingly similar practice of rotating credit associations. Such associations form among the poor and include no partner who is not also poor, and they seem to be governed by strong communal norms and therefore need not involve conscious trust. As we did in comparing multiplex communal norms and more focused networks earlier, we then turn to cases in which the relationships are more complex – for example, with third-party lenders in the cases of Cuban character loans and the Grameen Bank. The character loans are from established Cuban immigrants in Florida to newly arriving Cuban immigrants, who arrive with no resources other than their own human capital and perhaps some family connections. Both character loans and Grameen loans are made without collateral, and both are made plausible for the lending banks by the use of social capital to force repayment.

Rotating credit associations

Rotating credit associations typically have a small number of participants who all make regular contributions to a fund that is then given to one after another participant, in rotation. Although there are variations in the basis of associational membership (Ardener 1964; Light 1972; Velez-Ibanez 1983), these associations share some common features that distinguish them from other kinds of cooperative activity, including mutual benefit clubs. There is evidence of such associations throughout the centuries and in a wide variety of countries. They offer a solution to the lack of creditworthiness with banks and other formal institutions and to problems created by discrimination against even those who do possess some collateral. They exemplify a form of relational commitment that offers the promise of economic advancement.

Such associations also suffer from a very real threat of default and theft of funds (Besley, Coate, and Loury 1994; Hechter 1987), even by friends. In Kellee Tsai's (1998) study, Mrs. Chen, a middle-aged bean curd vendor, tells of the failure of her rotating credit association, which was organized by her friend. "Every month each of the ten members would contribute two hundred yuan to a collective pool and then one person would take the pot of two thousand yuan." Mrs. Chen wanted to rent a regular market stall rather than sell out of the back of her bicycle cart. Four months "after she joined the credit association, her friend did not show up to claim her usual space in the market place. 'I worried that she was sick,'" recalls Mrs. Chen. But in fact her friend had disappeared, and Mrs. Chen lost eight hundred yuan – the equivalent of one month's earnings (Tsai 1998). There is always a danger of default and always a problem of reliability, even among those who believe themselves to be friends, as Mrs. Chen's woeful story shows.

An irony of such an outcome is that the reason for creating this kind of association may be simply to help individuals overcome their own weakness of will in saving money for larger purposes. Each member requires of all other members that they contribute weekly or on some schedule. And each of them eventually gets a sum of money equal to what they contribute over time. As a matter of simple logic, each member could as easily save that much money individually. The joint effort offers them a bit of psychological trickery to get themselves to do the saving by invoking the power of communal sanction. As a Dominican says of his sociedade, "It forces us to save because we're committing ourselves to other people" (Sasha Abramsky, "Newcomers Savings and Loan," *New York Times*, October 22, 2000, Section 14, p. 4).

If we suffer from such weakness of will, we might wonder about how safe our money is when held by others like ourselves. It surely will not be very safe if ours is not an extremely stable, close society in which we can expect everyone to remain in it into the distant future. In such a close society, it is probably not so much trust that motivates us as communal norms. If you might soon leave the community, those norms are likely to have little sway over you. Rotating credit associations' members attempt to select out those who might be unreliable. This effort may be generally less successful than severe and effective penalties, generally enforced within a community (Hechter 1987, 107–11; Hardin 1995, ch. 4). These associations almost always form among those with little mobility and with strong ties to each other, such as exist among certain ethnic groups or within traditional societies.

In the rotating credit association, the form of incentives is that B, who are most of the rest of the members of the association and maybe other members of the society, motivate C to play fair with the communal holdings. B can do this only if there is a long enough future in which to sanction C effectively for default. Hence, such an association can work without trust among its members, although some of them might trust each other.

[…]

Microlending and the Grameen Bank

Another kind of lending when neither trust nor ordinary market incentives govern is the Grameen and similar banks. Like the Cuban banks in Florida, these banks make what are essentially business loans, often to start up new small businesses. Beginning in 1977, Muhammad Yunus (1999, 62–3) organized the Grameen Bank in Bangladesh. The way the Grameen Bank usually works today is that a collection of friends – typically five, and usually all women – come as a group to present their individual proposals for small loans to help them in their businesses. Typically two of the group are then picked to receive small loans (very small, maybe a few dollars). Others in the group are eligible to reapply after the initial recipients have at least seriously begun to repay their loans with weekly payments for at least six weeks. The periodic repayment is similar to mortgage loans but unlike many loans that require a lump-sum repayment at the end; Yunus thinks that the latter is a daunting and unreasonable expectation.

This system creates group responsibility that gives the others in the group strong incentive to make sure the first recipients are faithful in how they expend their funds, work to produce an income from those funds, and begin to make repayment. This is virtually holistic monitoring well beyond what would happen with ordinary bank loans. Not all of this was seen clearly at the outset of Yunus's program or noted fully by him in his account of how the system works. The use of what he calls support groups was a later discovery. But it is clear that the whole system offers a sophisticated set of incentives to enhance productivity through solidarity among those funded by Grameen and through competition between them in trying to succeed with their small businesses. As with Cuban character loans, there is no collateral to back these loans. But there is also not even law, because the smallness of the loans makes legal recourse too expensive to be worthwhile, whereas the Florida banks had law as a recourse against anyone whose business succeeded but who did not repay according to contract. The Grameen must rely entirely on social capital to induce repayment.

As noted at the beginning of this chapter, the Grameen Bank (A) does not need to be assiduous in chasing after repayment from a customer (C) because it has, in a sense, delegated the incentive for doing this to the group of neighborhood friends (B). Those friends become, by a bit of clever management, part of the bank's social capital, which it puts to work in the community to make life better for more or less all. The bank does this by relying on the social pressures within the neighborhood groups that apply for loans. Trust might play a role in some of these groups, but it need not, and it need not play any role in making the system work. In the end, however, the entrepreneurial successes among the recipients of Grameen loans might begin to develop trust relationships that enable them to enter into mutually beneficial but risky cooperative ventures. The result can be a thriving market economy that eventually displaces communal norms as the mobilizer of productive activities and exchange.

There is substantial disagreement on just how ideally the Grameen has worked. Yunus' account suggests that it has an astonishing repayment rate (Yunus 1998; 1999, 70; Holloway and Wallich 1992). Critics think it absorbs a lot of money from donors to cover for the defaults of many of its loan recipients (see, for example, some contributions to Bardhan 1999, especially Morduch 1999). There is also little compelling evidence that the social pressures from joint liability or "peer monitoring" are the main reason for what successes such banks have (for a general survey of the issues, see Ghatak and Guinnane 1999). Even if the Grameen's default rate is high, however, that does not mean it has failed. Some of the defaults must happen not because the incentive system for eliciting repayment fails to work but because some of the entrepreneurial activities fail, as is always true in all societies. The Grameen model may be brilliantly effective even though it cannot guarantee entrepreneurial success.

Incidentally, the Grameen Bank is itself the result of mobilizing social capital. As Yunus (1999, 117) says, "Though Bangladesh has a population of 120 million, it is run entirely by a handful of people, most of whom are college or university friends. Time and again, this unfortunate feature of Bangladesh society and politics has helped the Grameen overcome otherwise impossible bureaucratic hurdles." For the success of Grameen, Yunus is happily a member of this small club of people who can make things happen. He repeatedly tells of chance or deliberate meetings with people whom he has long known and who oversee national banking policy (89–91, 117). And repeatedly the result of his invoking their friendship is help for Grameen, either in the form of financial help or of easing cumbersome bureaucratic regulations that would make microloans expensive and unfeasible.

These devices [...] are spontaneously created in the face of the failure or limits of state regulation or legal devices for enabling people in straitened circumstances to obtain the funds to improve their lives. It is striking to see how well and how creatively people manage their lives in the absence of trust and largely in the absence of legal or state enforcement of cooperative arrangements, all despite sometime inequality of power and often solid grounds for distrust.

[...]

REFERENCES

Amato, Paul R. 1993. "Urban–Rural Differences in Helping Friends and Family Members." *Social Psychology Quarterly* 46: 249–62.

Ardener, Shirley. 1964. "The Comparative Study of Rotating Credit Associations." *Journal of the Royal Anthropolical Institute of Great Britain and Ireland* 94(2): 201–29.

Bardhan, Pranab (ed.). 1999. Special Issue on Group Lending. *Journal of Development Economics* 60(1).

Besley, Timothy, Stephen, Coate, and Glenn Loury. 1994. "Rotating Savings and Credit Associations, Credit Markets, and Efficiency." *Review of Economic Studies* 61(4): 701–19.

Brehm, John, and Wendy Rahn. 1997. "Individual-level Evidence of the Causes and Consequences of Social Capital." *American Journal of Political Science* 41(3): 999–1023.

Cohen, Don, and Laurence Prusak. 2001. *In Good Company: How Social Capital Makes Organizations Work*. Boston, MA: Harvard Business School Press.

Coleman, James S. 1988. "Social Capital in the Creation of Human Capital." *American Journal of Sociology* (supp.) 94: S95–120.

Coleman, James S. 1990. *Foundations of Social Theory*. Cambridge, MA: Harvard University Press.

Cook, Karen S. 2005. "Networks, Norms, and Trust: The Social Psychology of Social Capital." *Social Psychology Quarterly* 68(1): 4–14.

Cook, Karen S., and Richard M. Emerson. 1978. "Power Equity, and Commitment in Exchange Networks." *American Sociological Review* 43(5): 721–39.

Cook, Karen S., and Russell Hardin. 2001. "Norms of Cooperativeness and Networks of Trust." In Michael Hechter and Karl-Dieter Opp (eds.), *Social Norms*. New York: Russell Sage Foundation.

Ellickson, Robert C. 1991. *Order Without Law: How Neighbors Settle Disputes*. Cambridge, MA: Harvard University Press.

Ellickson, Robert C. 1998. "Law and Economics Discovers Social Norms." *Journal of Legal Studies* 27(2, pt. 2, June): 537–52.

Farrell, Henry. 2004. "Trust, Distrust and Power." In Russell Hardin (ed.), *Distrust*. New York: Russell Sage Foundation.

Fischer, Claude S. 1982. *To Dwell Among Friends: Personal Networks in Town and City*. Chicago, IL: University of Chicago Press.
Ghatak, Maitreesh and Timothy W. Guinnane. 1999. "The Economics of Lending with Joint Liability: Theory and Practice." *Journal of Development Economics* 60(1): 195–228.
Gladwell, Malcolm S. 1999. "Six Degrees of Lois Weisberg." *The New Yorker* (January 11): 52–63.
Hardin, Russell. 1982a. "Exchange Theory on Strategic Bases." *Social Science Information* 21(2): 251–72.
Hardin, Russell. 1982b. *Collective Action*. Baltimore, MD: Johns Hopkins University Press for Resources for the Future.
Hardin, Russell. 1995. *One for All: The Logic of Group Conflict*. Princeton, NJ: Princeton University Press.
Hardin, Russell. 1999. "From Bodo Ethics to Distributive Justice." *Ethical Theory and Moral Practice* 2(4): 337–63.
Hardin, Russell. 2002. *Trust and Trustworthiness*. New York: Russell Sage Foundation.
Hechter, Michael. 1987. *Principles of Group Solidarity*. Berkeley, CA: University of California Press.
Hetcher, Steven A. 2004. *Norms in a Wired World*. Cambridge, UK: Cambridge University Press.
Hobbes, Thomas. 1651/1968. *Leviathan*, ed. C. B. Macpherson. London: Penguin.
Holloway, Marguerite, and Paul Wallich. 1992. "A Risk Worth Taking." *Scientific American* (November): 126.
Leijonhufvud, Axel. 1995. "The Individual, the Market, and the Industrial Division of Labor." In Carlo Mongardini (ed.), *L'Individuo e il mercato*. Rome: Bulzoi.
Light, Ivan. 1972. *Ethnic Enterprise in America*. Berkeley, CA: University of California Press.
Macauley, Stewart. 1963. "Noncontractual Relations in Business: A Preliminary Study." *American Sociological Review* 28 (February): 55–67.
Morduch, Jonathan. 1999. "The Role of Subsidies in Microfinance: Evidence from the Grameen Bank." *Journal of Development Economics* 60(1): 228–48.
Mueller, John. 1999. *Capitalism, Democracy, and Ralph's Pretty Good Grocery Store*. Princeton, NJ: Princeton University Press.
Olson, Mancur, Jr. 1965. *The Logic of Collective Action*. Cambridge, MA: Harvard University Press.
Portes, Alejandro and Saskia Sassen-Koob. 1987. "Making It Underground: Comparative Material on the Informal Sector in Western Market Economies." *American Journal of Sociology* 93 (July): 30–61.
Putnam, Robert. 1995a. "Tuning In, Tuning Out: The Strange Disappearance of Social Capital in America." *PS: Political Science and Politics* 28(4): 664–83.
Putnam, Robert. 1995b. "Bowling Alone: America's Declining Social Capital." *Journal of Democracy* 6 (1, January): 65–78.
Putnam, Robert. 2000. *Bowling Alone: The Collapse and Revival of American Community*. New York: Simon & Schuster.
Smith, Adam. 1776/1976. *An Inquiry into the Nature and Causes of the Wealth of Nations*. Oxford: Oxford University Press; reprint, Indianapolis: Liberty Classics, 1981.
Tsai, Kellee S. 1998. "A Circle of Friends, a Web of Troubles: Rotating Credit Associations in China." *Harvard China Review* 1(1): 81–3.

Velez-Ibanez, Carlos G. 1983. *Bonds of Mutual Trust: The Cultural Systems of Rotating Credit Associations among Urban Mexicans and Chicanos*. New Brunswick, NJ: Rutgers University Press.

Watts, Duncan J. 2003. *Six Degrees: The Science of a Connected Age*. New York: Norton.

Yamagishi, Toshio, and Karen S. Cook. 1993. "Generalized Exchange and Social Dilemmas." *Social Psychology Quarterly* 56(4): 235–48.

Yunus, Muhammad. 1998. "Alleviating Poverty through Technology." *Science* (October 16): 409–10.

Yunus, Muhammad. 1999. *Banker to the Poor: Micro-Lending and the Battle Against World Poverty*. New York: Public Affairs.

Part III

Institutions and Networks

Introduction to Part III

10 Economic Embeddedness

11 The Iron Cage Revisited

12 Catnets

13 Structural Holes

Introduction to Part III

The concept of "institution" is one of the most enduring, and poorly defined, concepts in sociology. While this theoretical ambiguity has led some theorists to avoid the term, like "structure," "institution" seems to fill a rhetorical role that sociologists cannot do without (Sewell, 1992). In what follows, our institutional analysis focuses on the enduring social patterns that, ultimately, are embedded in social networks. DiMaggio and Powell's (1983) work on institutional isomorphism shows why certain organizational features dominate, even when they are not economically rational. Mark Granovetter similarly approaches individual economic action by asking how actions are conditioned by network contexts, providing a key insight into the problem of social embeddedness. The link between enduring social patterns and networks is made explicit in a classic piece by Harrison White that, while never published, had been in photocopy circulation for over 40 years. The turn toward networks is completed with a selection from Ronald Burt's classic *Structural Holes*; here we make a move back from large-scale enduring social institutions to a network mechanism for profit in economic settings. Given the breadth of literature on "institutions", we start next by briefly reviewing the history of institutions through Parsons, then introduce each author's wider work.

Most theories of social institutions are rooted in Durkheim's treatment of social facts, and in most work since Parsons institutions have been used as a foil for atomistic approaches to social life (DiMaggio and Powell, 1983). As with much of contemporary social theory, the shadow of Parsons falls heavily on current theories of institutions. Parsons based his subjective conception of institutions on individual action, arguing that institutions provide goal-oriented actors with means that are consistent with the overall value system of the society. That is, institutions reduce to "a set of regulatory norms that give rise to social structure or organization" (Coleman, 1990: 334).[1] Importantly, institutions for Parsons are *sets* of norms that go together; they are "a complex of institutionalized role integrates" (Parsons, 1951: p. 39) and are thus broader than norms.

As we would expect, Parsons argues that institutions are functional, contributing to the social order by ensuring that individual behavior conforms to societal interests. In addition, "the 'function' of institutions is not only to keep the means and ends of the intermediate chain in conformity with ultimate values, but also to endow the individual with the energy to live up to institutional norms" (Parsons, 1990 [1934]: 325). Institutions, however, are not legitimized solely because people have internalized the ultimate values implicit in the norm. Instead, institutions persist because "once really established, a system of institutional norms creates an interlocking of interests" that help keep it in place, even if individual devotion to the underlying values start to wane (Parsons, 1990 [1934]: 326), and this "interlocking" of interests is part of the natural affinity linking institutional questions to social networks.

According to Coleman (1990), Parsons' dual emphasis on the functional aspects of institutions and the subjective focus of institutional analysis was a fundamental flaw. By focusing on how individuals experience institutions, it is impossible to identify how they form, because the creation of norms rests on *interdependent* action. That is, showing that an institution is in an actor's long-term interest is not sufficient to explain the formation of the institution, since it might be in his or her short-term interest to violate the norm. Thus, "What [Parsons] failed to recognize was that the path from action to system lies in the relation between different actors' actions – it is there that the complexities arise and generate different kinds of systems of action" (p. 338).

Identifying the role of institutions in social life has had something of a renascence in the late 1980s and early 1990s, especially within economic sociology (see Powell and DiMaggio, 1991; Winship and Rosen, 1988). Much of this work has been a reaction to treatments of social life based on rational actor models, and are often "united by little but a common skepticism toward atomistic accounts of social processes and a common conviction that institutional arrangements and social processes matter" (Powell and DiMaggio, 1991: 3). This attack on individualism is made apparent in work by Williamson (1975; 1985) that identifies weaknesses with standard microeconomic assumptions. In Williamson's model, actors have limited cognitive capacity, poor information, often cannot monitor agreements and act opportunistically. Under these conditions, institutions develop to solve resulting organizational problems. For example, institutions reduce uncertainty and lower transaction costs, providing an efficient solution to bounded individual action. How institutions come to be, the extent to which they are economically efficient, and how they evolve, are all hotly debated topics within institutional theories of economic sociology.

Work on organizational behavior often starts with a process of rationalization based on Weber's famous prediction that organizations, through the dual engines of competition and rationalization, should become ever more bureaucratically rational. Empirical researchers, however, have had difficulty describing organizational behavior in such terms. Instead, inefficiency and non-productive ritual behavior is common (DiMaggio and Powell, 1983). Moreover, while organizations face many different challenges, the range of organizational responses is remarkably small, leading one to ask why organizations are so similar.

DiMaggio and Powell's answer rests on the process of isomorphism, which they define as "a constraining process that forces one unit in a population to resemble other units that face the same set of environmental conditions" (p. 149). They identify two types of isomorphism, competitive and institutional, and argue that rationalistic competition is not sufficient to explain most organizational similarity. Instead, competitive isomorphism must be supplemented by three non-competitive features of the organizational milieu: "1) Coercive isomorphism that stems from political influence and the problem of legitimacy; 2) mimetic isomorphism resulting from standard responses to uncertainty; and 3) normative isomorphism, associated with professionalization" (p. 150). This approach to understanding organizational behavior rests on a multi-level model of organizations; pressures at the organizational level (a search for legitimacy, standard conventions to control uncertainty) are combined with the socialization process of firm managers (professionalization). DiMaggio and Powell challenge theories that rest on elite control or simple population dynamics, arguing "that a theory of institutional isomorphism may help explain the observation that organizations are becoming more homogeneous, and that elites often get their way, while at the same time enabling us to understand the irrationality, the frustration of power, and the lack of innovation that are so commonplace in organizational life" (p. 157).

Granovetter's "Economic Action and Social Structure: The Problem of Embeddedness" (1985) is among the most-cited papers ever published in sociology and turns our discussion of institutions from the institutions themselves to the problem of action embedded in economic institutions. Granovetter asks how behavior and institutions are affected by social relations and directly challenges key questions in the "institutional economics" approach represented by DiMaggio and Powell. Granovetter, who is well-known for work on the power of seemingly unimportant "weak" social ties, draws a middle position for economic action between purely egoistic, autonomous, and economically rational actors ("undersocialized action") and deeply embedded, socially constrained and largely scripted normative behavior ("oversocialized action"). Instead, Granovetter posits an "embeddedness argument" that centers on "concrete personal relations and structures," arguing that social relations generate trust and discourage malfeasance. Since people's patterns of connections to others vary in strength and extent, this conception provides a clear mechanism to account for variability in observed trust.

If institutional analysis has, at its heart, the rejection of atomistic action theory as the starting point for sociology, theory and research on social networks represents this notion taken to full fruition. Harrison White is among the most well-known sociologists working in the area of social networks. His early work on the structural implications of kinship patterns (1963) formalized earlier ideas from structural anthropology and laid the foundation for his later work on abstracting relevant structural patterns from observed networks. Kinship systems provide a clear example of how primary relations (marriage and descent) can extend to other known roles (example: your mother's mother is your "grandmother," and your mother's mother's daughter's daughter is your cousin). The various concatenations of the two primary relations can be used to describe the full kinship system. White recognized that you can extend this argument to other kinds of relations and discover roles in systems by empirically tracing the most common patterns of extended network ties. Known as "blockmodeling," this approach founded a long tradition of research building on earlier role theories. The ultimate, abstract extension of these ideas takes White beyond individual actors to "identities" and from the specific analyses of particular network structures to the general strategies actors use to gain control (White, 1992; 2004).

White's second major contribution to social theory is a direct attack on classical economic market models. In a series of papers culminating in his book *Markets from Networks* (2004), White demonstrates that the basic competition model for commodities that is the foundation for most work on markets is really just a special case of the many possible ways markets can be organized. Instead of focusing on the supply and demand for commodities, White focuses on observable relations among product producers and how they negotiate a tradeoff between the quality of goods produced and the prices for those goods in comparison to similar other firms. In White's model, firms choose a position along a quality-price array to offer goods. For example, WalMart seeks to offer low-quality goods at the lowest prices, while Target offers slightly higher quality goods at higher prices. As you move up the quality-price curve, you would find retailers such as Macy's deliberately avoiding low prices in an effort to signal high quality. This insight has deep implications for market failures, prices and control.

The piece reprinted below existed as a mimeographed copy in circulation among White's students (and students of students of students) and has never been published before. While we are typically used to thinking of categories such as "race" or "sex" as essential fixed characteristics of people, White argues for a conception of categories that rests on the correspondence of network ties (Nets) with categories (Cats). A "catnet" is thus the correspondence between these two features of a population. Substantively, the idea reflects notions that we regularly observe: category membership (such as being "male" or "female") is only relevant to the degree that it shapes our relations with others.

We conclude this section with a chapter from Ronald Burt's book *Structural Holes*. Combining the insights of Georg Simmel and Granovetter's work on the strength of weak ties, Burt examines in detail the social-structural conditions of competition that lead to an ability to profit from networks. Seen as explicating the mechanism behind the weak-tie formulation, Burt focuses on the returns to linking others who are not otherwise connected. Filling a "structural hole" – creating a bridge between two people who are not connected – puts one in a unique position to profit from their activity. The profit is gained through both information (the efficiency of networks is built on having non-redundant contacts) and arbitrage – the ability to extract resources by mediating the interests of the two parties. A modern, formal representation of Simmel's classic *tertius gaudens*, Burt's work on structural holes has become a classic touchstone for modern network analysis.

NOTE

1   "This system of regulatory norms, of rules governing actions in pursuit of immediate ends in terms of their conformity with the ultimate common value-system of community, is what I call its institutions approached from the subjective point of view." (Parsons, 1990 [1934]: p. 324)

SELECTED BIBLIOGRAPHY

Burt, Ronald S. 2005. *Brokerage and Closure: An Introduction to Social Capital*. Oxford: Oxford University Press. (A nice introduction to the wider field of social capital research.)

Burt, Ronald S. 2010. *Neighbor Networks : Competitive Advantage Local and Personal*. Oxford: Oxford University Press. (A re-examination of the basic idea of structural hole theory, attempting to incorporate new evidence, building on the personal work actors have to do to make use of advantageous network positions.)

Coleman, James. 1990. "Commentary: Social Institutions and Social Theory." *American Sociological Review* 55: 333–9. (A discussion of Parsons' paper that includes Coleman's own understanding of what an institution is and how theory should approach the study of institutions.)

DiMaggio, Paul J. and Powell, Walter W. 1983. "The Iron Cage Revisited: Institutional Isomorphism and Collective Rationality in Organizational Fields." *American Sociological Review* 48: 147–60. (One of the foundational pieces in the application of institutional ideas in modern organizational theory.)

Form, William. 1990. "Institutional Analysis: An Organizational Approach." Pp. 257–71 in *Change in Societal Institutions*, Maureen T. Hallinan, David M. Klein, and Jennifer Glass. Plenum Publishing Corporation. (A nice review of the concept of institution, providing a new approach based on inter-organizational connections.)

Maclean, Alair and Olds Andy. 2001. "Interview with Harrison White" http://www.ssc.wisc.edu/theory@madison/papers/ivwWhite.pdf (a nice interview with Harrison White that describes his background and much of his work.)

Parsons, Talcott. 1951. *The Social System*. Glencoe, IL: Free Press.

Parsons, Talcott. 1990 [1934]. "Prolegomena to a Theory of Social Institutions." *American Sociological Review* 55: 319–33. (A recently discovered piece that outlines Parsons early thinking on institutions.)

Powell, Walter W. and DiMaggio, Paul J. 1991. *The New Institutionalism in Organizational Analysis*. Chicago, IL: University of Chicago Press. (The first chapter of this book provides a nice treatment of institutions as they relate to modern organizational theory.)

Sewell, William H. Jr. 1992. "A Theory of Structure: Duality, Agency, and Transformation." *American Journal of Sociology* 98: 1–29. (A good discussion of the meaning of "structure" in social theory. Insights here can readily be linked to the problems of various meanings of "institution.")

White, Harrison. 1963. *An Anatomy of Kinship: Mathematical Models for Structures of Cumulated Roles*. Englewood-Cliffs, NJ. (An early piece that sets the mathematical stage for much later work in social networks.)

White, Harrison. 1992. *Identity and Control: A Structural Theory of Social Action*. Princeton, NJ; Princeton University Press. (This book is known to be difficult going, but provides a theoretical model for linking networks to the key questions of institutions and action. The second edition (2010) is really a distinct book, and a major re-thinking of the ideas.)

White, Harrison. 2004. *Markets from Networks: Socioeconomic Models of Production*. Princeton, NJ: Princeton University Press. (White's ultimate statement of his model for markets. A key text to build a sociological extension of market models.)

Williamson, Oliver E. 1975. *Markets and Hierarchies*. New York: Free Press.

Williamson, Oliver E. 1985. *The Economic Institutions of Capitalism*. New York: Free Press. (These two books are classics in the application of institutional ideas to economic sociology.)

Winship, Christopher and Rosen, Sherwin. 1988. "Introduction: Sociological and Economic Approaches to the Analysis of Social Structure." *American Journal of Sociology* 94: s1–s16. (Contains a nice discussion of how sociological ideas of institutions contribute to understanding economic problems.)

Chapter 10

Economic Embeddedness [1985]

Mark Granovetter

Introduction: the Problem of Embeddedness

How behavior and institutions are affected by social relations is one of the classic questions of social theory. Since such relations are always present, the situation that would arise in their absence can be imagined only through a thought experiment like Thomas Hobbes's "state of nature" or John Rawls's "original position." Much of the utilitarian tradition, including classical and neoclassical economics, assumes rational, self-interested behavior affected minimally by social relations, thus invoking an idealized state not far from that of these thought experiments. At the other extreme lies what I call the argument of "embeddedness": the argument that the behavior and institutions to be analyzed are so constrained by ongoing social relations that to construe them as independent is a grievous misunderstanding.

[...]

My own view diverges from both schools of thought. I assert that the level of embeddedness of economic behavior is lower in nonmarket societies than is claimed by substantivists and development theorists, and it has changed less with "modernization" than they believe; but I argue also that this level has always been and continues to be more substantial than is allowed for by formalists and economists. [...]

Mark Granovetter, "Economic Embeddedness," pp. 481–2, 482–8, 488–9, 490–2, 492–3, 508–10 from Mark Granovetter "Economic Action and Social Structure: The Problem of Embeddedness," *American Journal of Sociology*, 91: 3 (November, 1985). Copyright © 1985 by American Journal of Sociology. Reprinted by permission of The University of Chicago Press.

Contemporary Sociological Theory, Third Edition. Edited by Craig Calhoun, Joseph Gerteis, James Moody, Steven Pfaff, and Indermohan Virk. Editorial material and organization © 2012 John Wiley & Sons, Ltd. Published 2012 by John Wiley & Sons, Ltd.

Over- and Undersocialized Conceptions of Human Action in Sociology and Economics

I begin by recalling Dennis Wrong's 1961 complaint about an "oversocialized conception of man in modern sociology" – a conception of people as overwhelmingly sensitive to the opinions of others and hence obedient to the dictates of consensually developed systems of norms and values, internalized through socialization, so that obedience is not perceived as a burden. [...]

Classical and neoclassical economics operates, in contrast, with an atomized, *undersocialized* conception of human action, continuing in the utilitarian tradition. The theoretical arguments disallow by hypothesis any impact of social structure and social relations on production, distribution, or consumption. In competitive markets, no producer or consumer noticeably influences aggregate supply or demand or, therefore, prices or other terms of trade. As Albert Hirschman has noted, such idealized markets, involving as they do "large numbers of price-taking anonymous buyers and sellers supplied with perfect information ... function without any prolonged human or social contact between the parties. Under perfect competition there is no room for bargaining, negotiation, remonstration or mutual adjustment and the various operators that contract together need not enter into recurrent or continuing relationships as a result of which they would get to know each other well" (1982: 1473).

It has long been recognized that the idealized markets of perfect competition have survived intellectual attack in part because self-regulating economic structures are politically attractive to many. Another reason for this survival, less clearly understood, is that the elimination of social relations from economic analysis removes the problem of order from the intellectual agenda, at least in the economic sphere. In Hobbes's argument, disorder arises because conflict-free social and economic transactions depend on trust and the absence of malfeasance. But these are unlikely when individuals are conceived to have neither social relationships nor institutional context – as in the "state of nature." Hobbes contains the difficulty by superimposing a structure of autocratic authority. The solution of classical liberalism, and correspondingly of classical economics, is antithetical: repressive political structures are rendered unnecessary by competitive markets that make force or fraud unavailing. Competition determines the terms of trade in a way that individual traders cannot manipulate. If traders encounter complex or difficult relationships, characterized by mistrust or malfeasance, they can simply move on to the legion of other traders willing to do business on market terms; social relations and their details thus become frictional matters.

In classical and neoclassical economics, therefore, the fact that actors may have social relations with one another has been treated, if at all, as a frictional drag that impedes competitive markets. In a much-quoted line, Adam Smith complained that "people of the same trade seldom meet together, even for merriment and diversion, but the conversation ends in a conspiracy against the public, or in some contrivance to raise prices." His laissez-faire politics allowed few solutions to this problem, but he did suggest repeal of regulations requiring all those in the same trade to sign a public register; the public existence of such information "connects individuals who might never otherwise be known to one another and gives every man of the trade a direction where to find every other man of it." Noteworthy here is not the rather lame policy prescription but the recognition that *social atomization is prerequisite to perfect competition* (Smith, 1979 [1776]: 232–3).

More recent comments by economists on "social influences" construe these as processes in which actors acquire customs, habits, or norms that are followed mechanically and automatically, irrespective of their bearing on rational choice. This view, close to Wrong's "oversocialized conception," is reflected in James Duesenberry's quip that "economics is all about how people make choices; sociology is all about how they don't have any choices to make" (1960: 233) and in E. H. Phelps Brown's description of the "sociologists' approach to pay determination" as deriving from the assumption that people act in "certain ways because to do so is customary, or an obligation, or the 'natural thing to do,' or right and proper, or just and fair" (1977, p. 17).

But despite the apparent contrast between under- and oversocialized views, we should note an irony of great theoretical importance: both have in common a conception of action and decision carried out by atomized actors. In the undersocialized account, atomization results from narrow utilitarian pursuit of self-interest; in the oversocialized one, from the fact that behavioral patterns have been internalized and ongoing social relations thus have only peripheral effects on behavior. That the internalized rules of behavior are social in origin does not differentiate this argument decisively from a utilitarian one, in which the source of utility functions is left open, leaving room for behavior guided entirely by consensually determined norms and values – as in the oversocialized view. Under- and oversocialized resolutions of the problem of order thus merge in their atomization of actors from immediate social context. This ironic merger is already visible in Hobbes's *Leviathan*, in which the unfortunate denizens of the state of nature, overwhelmed by the disorder consequent to their atomization, cheerfully surrender all their rights to an authoritarian power and subsequently behave in a docile and honorable manner; by the artifice of a social contract, they lurch directly from an undersocialized to an oversocialized state.

When modern economists do attempt to take account of social influences, they typically represent them in the oversocialized manner represented in the quotations above. In so doing, they reverse the judgment that social influences are frictional but sustain the conception of how such influences operate. In the theory of segmented labor markets, for example, Michael Piore has argued that members of each labor market segment are characterized by different styles of decision making and that the making of decisions by rational choice, custom, or command in upper-primary, lower-primary, and secondary labor markets respectively corresponds to the origins of workers in middle-, working-, and lower-class subcultures (Piore, 1975). Similarly, Samuel Bowles and Herbert Gintis, in their account of the consequences of American education, argue that different social classes display different cognitive processes because of differences in the education provided to each. Those destined for lower-level jobs are trained to be dependable followers of rules, while those who will be channeled into elite positions attend "elite four-year colleges" that "emphasize social relationships conformable with the higher levels in the production hierarchy. [...] As they 'master' one type of behavioral regulation they are either allowed to progress to the next or are channeled into the corresponding level in the hierarchy of production" (Bowles and Gintis, 1975: 132).

But these oversocialized conceptions of how society influences individual behavior are rather mechanical: once we know the individual's social class or labor market sector, everything else in behavior is automatic, since they are so well socialized. Social influence here is an external force that, like the deists' God, sets things in motion and has no further effects – a force that insinuates itself into the minds and bodies of individuals (as in the movie *Invasion of the Body Snatchers*), altering their way of making decisions. Once we know in just what way an individual has been affected, ongoing social relations and structures are irrelevant. Social influences are all contained inside an individual's head, so, in actual decision situations, he or she can be atomized as any *Homo economicus*, though perhaps with different rules for decisions. More sophisticated (and thus less oversocialized) analyses of cultural influences (e.g., Fine and Kleinman 1979; Cole 1979, chap. 1) make it clear that culture is not a once-for-all influence but an ongoing process, continuously constructed and reconstructed during interaction. It not only shapes its members but also is shaped by them, in part for their own strategic reasons.

Even when economists do take social relationships seriously, as do such diverse figures as Harvey Leibenstein (1976) and Gary Becker (1976), they invariably abstract away from the history of relations and their position with respect to other relations – what might be called the historical and structural embeddedness of relations. The interpersonal ties described in their arguments are extremely stylized, average, "typical" – devoid of specific content, history, or structural location. Actors' behavior results from their named role positions and role sets; thus we have arguments on how workers and supervisors, husbands and wives, or criminals and law enforcers will interact with one another, but these relations are not assumed to have individualized content beyond that given by the named roles. This procedure is exactly what structural sociologists have criticized in Parsonian sociology – the relegation of the specifics of individual relations to a minor role in the overall conceptual scheme, epiphenomenal in comparison with enduring structures of normative role prescriptions deriving from ultimate value orientations. In economic models, this treatment of social relations has the paradoxical effect of preserving atomized decision making even when decisions are seen to involve more than one individual. Because the analyzed set of individuals – usually dyads, occasionally larger groups – is abstracted out of social context, it is atomized in its behavior from that of other groups and from the history of its own relations. Atomization has not been eliminated, merely transferred to the dyadic or higher level of analysis. Note the use of an oversocialized conception – that of actors behaving exclusively in accord with their prescribed roles – to implement an atomized, undersocialized view.

A fruitful analysis of human action requires us to avoid the atomization implicit in the theoretical extremes of under- and oversocialized conceptions. Actors do not behave or decide as atoms outside a social context, nor do they adhere slavishly to a script written for them by the particular intersection of social categories that they happen to occupy. Their attempts at purposive action are instead embedded in concrete, ongoing systems of social relations. In the remainder of this article I illustrate how this view of embeddedness alters our theoretical and empirical approach to the study of economic behavior. I first narrow the focus to the question of trust and malfeasance in economic life and then use the "markets and hierarchies" problem to illustrate the use of embeddedness ideas in analyzing this question.

Embeddedness, Trust, and Malfeasance in Economic Life

Since about 1970, there has been a flurry of interest among economists in the previously neglected issues of trust and malfeasance. Oliver Williamson has noted that real economic actors engage not merely in the pursuit of self-interest but also in "opportunism" – "self-interest seeking with guile; agents who are skilled at dissembling realize transactional advantages. Economic man ... is thus a more subtle and devious creature than the usual self-interest seeking assumption reveals" (1975, p. 255).

But this points out a peculiar assumption of modern economic theory, that one's economic interest is pursued only by comparatively gentlemanly means. The Hobbesian question – how it can be that those who pursue their own interest do not do so mainly by force and fraud – is finessed by this conception. Yet, as Hobbes saw so clearly, there is nothing in the intrinsic meaning of "self-interest" that excludes force or fraud.

[...]

What has eroded this confidence in recent years has been increased attention to the micro-level details of imperfectly competitive markets, characterized by small numbers of participants with sunk costs and "specific human capital" investments. In such situations, the alleged discipline of competitive markets cannot be called on to mitigate deceit, so the classical problem of how it can be that daily economic life is not riddled with mistrust and malfeasance has resurfaced.

In the economic literature, I see two fundamental answers to this problem and argue that one is linked to an undersocialized, and the other to an oversocialized, conception of human action. The undersocialized account is found mainly in the new institutional economics – a loosely defined confederation of economists with an interest in explaining social institutions from a neoclassical viewpoint. (See, e.g., Furubotn and Pejovich 1972; Alchian and Demsetz 1973; Lazear 1979; Rosen 1982; Williamson 1975, 1979, 1981; Williamson and Ouchi 1981.) The general story told by members of this school is that social institutions and arrangements previously thought to be the adventitious result of legal, historical, social, or political forces are better viewed as the efficient solution to certain economic problems. The tone is similar to that of structural-functional sociology of the 1940s to the 1960s, and much of the argumentation fails the elementary tests of a sound functional explanation laid down by Robert Merton in 1947. Consider, for example, Schotter's view that to understand any observed economic institution requires only that we "infer the evolutionary problem that must have existed for the institution as we see it to have developed. Every evolutionary economic problem requires a social institution to solve it" (1981, p. 2).

Malfeasance is here seen to be averted because clever institutional arrangements make it too costly to engage in, and these arrangements – many previously interpreted as serving no economic function – are now seen as having evolved to discourage malfeasance. Note, however, that they do not produce trust but instead are a functional substitute for it. The main such arrangements are elaborate explicit and implicit contracts (Okun 1981), including deferred compensation plans and mandatory retirement – seen to reduce the incentives for "shirking" on the job or absconding with proprietary secrets (Lazear 1979; Pakes and Nitzan 1982) – and authority structures that deflect opportunism by making potentially divisive decisions by fiat (Williamson 1975). These conceptions are undersocialized in that they do not allow for the extent to which concrete personal relations and the obligations inherent in them discourage malfeasance, quite apart from institutional arrangements. *Substituting* these arrangements for trust results actually in a Hobbesian situation, in which any rational individual would be motivated to develop clever ways to evade them; it is then hard to imagine that everyday economic life would not be poisoned by ever more ingenious attempts at deceit.

Other economists have recognized that some degree of trust *must* be assumed to operate, since institutional arrangements alone could not entirely stem force or fraud. But it remains to explain the source of this trust, and appeal is sometimes made to the existence of a "generalized morality." Kenneth Arrow, for example, suggests that societies, "in their evolution have developed implicit agreements to certain kinds of regard for others, agreements which are essential to the survival of the society or at least contribute greatly to the efficiency of its working" (1974, p. 26; see also Akerlof [1983] on the origins of "honesty").

Now one can hardly doubt the existence of some such generalized morality; without it, you would be afraid to give the gas station attendant a 20-dollar bill when you had bought only five dollars' worth of gas. But this conception has the oversocialized characteristic of calling on a generalized and automatic response, even though moral action in economic life is hardly automatic or universal (as is well known at gas stations that demand exact change after dark).

[…]

The embeddedness argument stresses instead the role of concrete personal relations and structures (or "networks") of such relations in generating trust and discouraging malfeasance. The widespread preference for transacting with individuals of known reputation implies that few are actually content to rely on either generalized morality *or* institutional arrangements to guard against trouble. Economists *have* pointed out that one incentive not to cheat is the cost of damage to one's reputation; but this is an undersocialized conception of reputation as a generalized commodity, a ratio of cheating to opportunities for doing so. In practice, we settle for such generalized information when nothing better is available, but ordinarily we seek better information. Better than the statement that someone is known to be reliable is information from a trusted informant that he has dealt with that individual and found him so. Even better is information from one's own past dealings with that person. This is better information for four reasons: (1) it is cheap; (2) one trusts one's own information best – it is richer, more detailed, and known to be accurate; (3) individuals with whom one has a continuing relation have an economic motivation to be trustworthy, so as not to discourage future transactions; and (4) departing from pure economic motives, continuing economic relations often become overlaid with social content that carries strong expectations of trust and abstention from opportunism.

It would never occur to us to doubt this last point in more intimate relations, which make behavior more predictable and thus close off some of the fears that create difficulties among strangers. Consider, for example, why individuals in a burning theater panic and stampede to the door, leading to desperate results. Analysts of collective behavior long considered this to be prototypically irrational behavior, but Roger Brown (1965, chap. 14) points out that the situation is essentially an *n*-person Prisoner's Dilemma: each stampeder is actually being quite rational given the absence of a guarantee that anyone else will walk out calmly, even though all would be better off if everyone did so. Note, however, that in the case of the burning houses featured on the 11:00 P.M. news, we never hear that everyone stampeded out and that family members trampled one another. In the family, there is no Prisoner's Dilemma because each is confident that the others can be counted on.

In business relations the degree of confidence must be more variable, but Prisoner's Dilemmas are nevertheless often obviated by the strength of personal relations, and this strength is a property not of the transactors but of their concrete relations. Standard economic analysis neglects the identity and past relations of individual transactors, but rational individuals know better, relying on their knowledge of these relations. They are less interested in *general* reputations than in whether a particular other may be expected to deal honestly with *them* – mainly a function of whether they or their own contacts have had satisfactory past dealings with the other. One sees this pattern even in situations that appear, at first glance, to approximate the classic higgling of a competitive market, as in the Moroccan bazaar analyzed by Geertz (1979).

Up to this point, I have argued that social relations, rather than institutional arrangements or generalized morality, are mainly responsible for the production of trust in economic life. But I then risk rejecting one kind of optimistic functionalism for another, in which networks of relations, rather than morality or arrangements, are the structure that fulfills the function of sustaining order. There are two ways to reduce this risk. One is to recognize that as a solution to the problem of order, the embeddedness position is less sweeping than either alternative argument, since networks of social relations penetrate irregularly and in differing degrees in different sectors of economic life, thus allowing for what we already know: distrust, opportunism, and disorder are by no means absent.

The second is to insist that while social relations may indeed often be a necessary condition for trust and trustworthy behavior, they are not sufficient to guarantee these and may even provide occasion and means for malfeasance and conflict on a scale larger than in their absence. There are three reasons for this.

1. The trust engendered by personal relations presents, by its very existence, enhanced opportunity for malfeasance. In personal relations it is common knowledge that "you always hurt the one you love"; that person's trust in you results in a position far more vulnerable than that of a stranger. (In the Prisoner's Dilemma, knowledge that one's coconspirator is certain to deny the crime is all the more rational motive to confess, and personal relations that abrogate this dilemma may be less symmetrical than is believed by the party to be deceived.) This elementary fact of social life is the bread and butter of "confidence" rackets that simulate certain relationships, sometimes for long periods, for concealed purposes. In the business world, certain crimes, such as embezzling, are simply impossible for those who have not built up relationships of trust that permit the opportunity to manipulate accounts. The more complete the trust, the greater the potential gain from malfeasance. That such instances are statistically infrequent is a tribute to the force of personal relations and reputation; that they do occur with regularity, however infrequently, shows the limits of this force.

2. Force and fraud are most efficiently pursued by teams, and the structure of these teams requires a level of internal trust – "honor among thieves" – that usually follows preexisting lines of relationship. Elaborate schemes for kickbacks and bid rigging, for example, can hardly be executed by individuals working alone, and when such activity is exposed it is often remarkable that it could have been kept secret given the large numbers involved. Law-enforcement efforts consist of finding an entry point to the network of malfeasance – an individual whose confession implicates others who will, in snowball-sample fashion, "finger" still others until the entire picture is fitted together.

[…]

3. The extent of disorder resulting from force and fraud depends very much on how the network of social relations is structured. Hobbes exaggerated the extent of disorder likely in his atomized state of nature where, in the absence of sustained social relations, one could expect only desultory dyadic conflicts. More extended and large-scale disorder results from coalitions of combatants, impossible without prior relations. We do not generally speak of "war" unless actors have arranged themselves into two sides, as the end result of various coalitions. This occurs only if there are insufficient crosscutting ties, held by actors with enough links to both main potential combatants to have a strong interest in forestalling conflict. The same is

true in the business world, where conflicts are relatively tame unless each side can escalate by calling on substantial numbers of allies in other firms, as sometimes happens in attempts to implement or forestall takeovers.

Disorder and malfeasance do of course occur also when social relations are absent. This possibility is already entailed in my earlier claim that the presence of such relations inhibits malfeasance. But the *level* of malfeasance available in a truly atomized social situation is fairly low; instances can only be episodic, unconnected, small scale. The Hobbesian problem is truly a problem, but in transcending it by the smoothing effect of social structure, we also introduce the possibility of disruptions on a larger scale than those available in the "state of nature."

The embeddedness approach to the problem of trust and order in economic life, then, threads its way between the oversocialized approach of generalized morality and the undersocialized one of impersonal, institutional arrangements by following and analyzing concrete patterns of social relations. Unlike either alternative, or the Hobbesian position, it makes no sweeping (and thus unlikely) predictions of universal order or disorder but rather assumes that the details of social structure will determine which is found.

REFERENCES

Akerlof, George. 1983. "Loyalty Filters." *American Economic Review* 73 (1): 54–63.
Alchian, Armen, and Harold Demsetz. 1973. "The Property Rights Paradigm." *Journal of Economic History* 33 (March): 16–27.
Arrow, Kenneth. 1974. *The Limits of Organization*. New York: Norton.
Becker, Gary. 1976. *The Economic Approach to Human Behavior*. Chicago, IL: University of Chicago Press.
Bowles, Samuel, and Herbert Gintis. 1975. *Schooling in Capitalist America*. New York: Basic.
Brown, Roger. 1965. *Social Psychology*. New York: Free Press.
Cole, Robert. 1979. *Work, Mobility and Participation: A Comparative Study of American and Japanese Industry*. Berkeley and Los Angeles, CA: University of California Press.
Duesenberry, James. 1960. Comment on "An Economic Analysis of Fertility." In *Demographic and Economic Change in Developed Countries*, edited by the Universities–National Bureau Committee for Economic Research. Princeton, NJ: Princeton University Press.
Fine, Gary, and Sherryl Kleinman. 1979. "Rethinking Subculture: An Interactionist Analysis." *American Journal of Sociology* 85 (July): 1–20.
Furubotn, E., and S. Pejovich. 1972. "Property Rights and Economic Theory: A Survey of Recent Literature." *Journal of Economic Literature* 10 (3): 1137–62.
Geertz, Clifford. 1979. "Suq: The Bazaar Economy in Sefrou." Pp. 123–225 in *Meaning and Order in Moroccan Society*, edited by C. Geertz, H. Geertz, and L. Rosen. New York: Cambridge University Press.
Hirschman, Albert. 1982. "Rival Interpretations of Market Society: Civilizing, Destructive or Feeble?" *Journal of Economic Literature* 20 (4): 1463–84.
Lazear, Edward. 1979. "Why Is There Mandatory Retirement?" *Journal of Political Economy* 87 (6): 1261–84.
Leibenstein, Harvey. 1976. *Beyond Economic Man*. Cambridge, MA: Harvard University Press.

Merton, Robert. 1947. "Manifest and Latent Functions." pp. 19–84 in *Social Theory and Social Structure*. New York: Free Press.

Okun, Arthur. 1981. *Prices and Quantities*. Washington, D.C.: Brookings.

Pakes, Ariel, and Schmuel Nitzan. 1982. "Optimum Contracts for Research Personnel," NBER Working Paper no. 871. Cambridge, MA: National Bureau of Economic Research.

Phelps Brown, Ernest Henry. 1977. *The Inequality of Pay*. Berkeley, CA: University of California Press.

Piore, Michael. 1975. "Notes for a Theory of Labor Market Stratification." Pp. 125–50 in *Labor Market Segmentation*, edited by R. Edwards, M. Reich, and D. Gordon. Lexington, MA: Heath.

Rosen, Sherwin. 1982. "Authority, Control and the Distribution of Earnings." *Bell Journal of Economics* 13 (2): 311–23.

Schotter, Andrew. 1981. *The Economic Theory of Social Institutions*. New York: Cambridge University Press.

Smith, Adam. 1979[1776]. *The Wealth of Nations*, edited by Andrew Skinner. Baltimore: Penguin.

Williamson, Oliver. 1975. *Markets and Hierarchies*. New York: Free Press.

Williamson, Oliver. 1979. "Transaction-Cost Economics: The Governance of Contractual Relations." *Journal of Law and Economics* 22 (2): 233–61.

Williamson, Oliver. 1981. "The Economics of Organization: The Transaction Cost Approach." *American Journal of Sociology* 87 (November): 548–77.

Williamson, Oliver, and William Ouchi. 1981. "The Markets and Hierarchies and Visible Hand Perspectives." Pp. 347–70 in *Perspectives on Organizational Design and Behavior*, edited by Andrew Van de Ven and William Joyce. New York: Wiley.

Wrong, Dennis. 1961. "The Oversocialized Conception of Man in Modern Sociology." *American Sociological Review* 26 (2): 183–93.

Chapter 11

The Iron Cage Revisited: Institutional Isomorphism and Collective Rationality in Organizational Fields [1983]

Paul J. DiMaggio and Walter W. Powell

In *The Protestant Ethic and the Spirit of Capitalism*, Max Weber warned that the rationalist spirit ushered in by asceticism had achieved a momentum of its own and that, under capitalism, the rationalist order had become an iron cage in which humanity was, save for the possibility of prophetic revival, imprisoned "perhaps until the last ton of fossilized coal is burnt" (Weber, 1952: 181–2). In his essay on bureaucracy, Weber returned to this theme, contending that bureaucracy, the rational spirit's organizational manifestation, was so efficient and powerful a means of controlling men and women that, once established, the momentum of bureaucratization was irreversible (Weber, 1968).

The imagery of the iron cage has haunted students of society as the tempo of bureaucratization has quickened. But while bureaucracy has spread continuously in the eighty years since Weber wrote, we suggest that the engine of organizational rationalization has shifted. For Weber, bureaucratization resulted from three related causes: competition among capitalist firms in the marketplace; competition among states, increasing rulers' need to control their staff and citizenry; and bourgeois demands for equal protection under the law. Of these three, the most important was the competitive marketplace. "Today," Weber (1968: 974) wrote:

Paul J. DiMaggio and Walter W. Powell, "The Iron Cage Revisited," pp. 147–60 from Paul J. DiMaggio and Walter W. Powell, "The Iron Cage Revisited: Institutional Isomorphism and Collective Rationality in Organizational Fields," *American Sociological Review*, 48: 2 (1983). Copyright © 1983 by American Sociological Review. Reprinted by permission of the authors and the American Sociological Association.

Contemporary Sociological Theory, Third Edition. Edited by Craig Calhoun, Joseph Gerteis, James Moody, Steven Pfaff, and Indermohan Virk. Editorial material and organization © 2012 John Wiley & Sons, Ltd. Published 2012 by John Wiley & Sons, Ltd.

it is primarily the capitalist market economy which demands that the official business of administration be discharged precisely, unambiguously, continuously, and with as much speed as possible. Normally, the very large, modern capitalist enterprises are themselves unequalled models of strict bureaucratic organization.

We argue that the causes of bureaucratization and rationalization have changed. The bureaucratization of the corporation and the state have been achieved. Organizations are still becoming more homogeneous, and bureaucracy remains the common organizational form. Today, however, structural change in organizations seems less and less driven by competition or by the need for efficiency. Instead, we will contend, bureaucratization and other forms of organizational change occur as the result of processes that make organizations more similar without necessarily making them more efficient. Bureaucratization and other forms of homogenization emerge, we argue, out of the structuration (Giddens, 1979) of organizational fields. This process, in turn, is effected largely by the state and the professions, which have become the great rationalizers of the second half of the twentieth century. For reasons that we will explain, highly structured organizational fields provide a context in which individual efforts to deal rationally with uncertainty and constraint often lead, in the aggregate, to homogeneity in structure, culture, and output.

Organizational Theory and Organizational Diversity

Much of modern organizational theory posits a diverse and differentiated world of organizations and seeks to explain variation among organizations in structure and behavior (e.g., Woodward, 1965; Child and Kieser, 1981). Hannan and Freeman begin a major theoretical paper (1977) with the question, "Why are there so many kinds of organizations?" Even our investigatory technologies (for example, those based on least-squares techniques) are geared towards explaining variation rather than its absence.

We ask, instead, why there is such startling homogeneity of organizational forms and practices; and we seek to explain homogeneity, not variation. In the initial stages of their life cycle, organizational fields display considerable diversity in approach and form. Once a field becomes well established, however, there is an inexorable push towards homogenization.

Coser, Kadushin, and Powell (1982) describe the evolution of American college textbook publishing from a period of initial diversity to the current hegemony of only two models, the large bureaucratic generalist and the small specialist. Rothman (1980) describes the winnowing of several competing models of legal education into two dominant approaches. Starr (1980) provides evidence of mimicry in the development of the hospital field; Tyack (1974) and Katz (1975) show a similar process in public schools; Barnouw (1966–8) describes the development of dominant forms in the radio industry; and DiMaggio (1982) depicts the emergence of dominant organizational models for the provision of high culture in the late nineteenth century.

What we see in each of these cases is the emergence and structuration of an organizational field as a result of the activities of a diverse set of organizations; and, second, the homogenization of these organizations, and of new entrants as well, once the field is established.

By organizational field, we mean those organizations that, in the aggregate, constitute a recognized area of institutional life: key suppliers, resource and product consumers, regulatory agencies, and other organizations that produce similar services or products. The virtue of this unit of analysis is that it directs our attention not simply to competing firms, as does the population approach of Hannan and Freeman (1977), or to networks of organizations that actually interact, as does the interorganizational network approach of Laumann et al. (1978), but to the totality of relevant actors. In doing this, the field idea comprehends the importance of both *connectedness* (see Laumann et al., 1978) and *structural equivalence* (White et al., 1976).[1]

The structure of an organizational field cannot be determined a priori but must be defined on the basis of empirical investigation. Fields only exist to the extent that they are institutionally defined. The process of institutional definition, or "structuration," consists of four parts: an increase in the extent of interaction among organizations in the field; the emergence of sharply defined interorganizational structures of domination and patterns of coalition; an increase in the information load with which organizations in a field must contend; and the development of a mutual awareness among participants in a set of organizations that they are involved in a common enterprise (DiMaggio, 1982).

Once disparate organizations in the same line of business are structured into an actual field (as we shall argue, by competition, the state, or the professions), powerful forces emerge that lead them to become more similar to one another. Organizations may change their goals or develop new practices, and new organizations enter the field. But, in the long run, organizational actors making rational decisions construct around themselves an environment that constrains their ability to change further in later years. Early adopters of organizational innovations are commonly driven by a desire to improve performance. But new practices can become, in Selznick's words (1957: 17), "infused with value beyond the technical requirements of the task at hand." As an innovation spreads, a threshold is reached beyond which adoption provides legitimacy rather than improves performance (Meyer and Rowan, 1977). Strategies that are rational for individual organizations may not be rational if adopted by large numbers. Yet the very fact that they are normatively sanctioned increases the likelihood of their adoption. Thus organizations may try to change constantly; but, after a certain point in the structuration of an organizational field, the aggregate effect of individual change is to lessen the extent of diversity within the field.[2] Organizations in a structured field, to paraphrase Schelling (1978:14), respond to an environment that consists of other organizations responding to their environment, which consists of organizations responding to an environment of organizations' responses.

Zucker and Tolbert's (1981) work on the adoption of civil-service reform in the United States illustrates this process. Early adoption of civil-service reforms was related to internal governmental needs, and strongly predicted by such city characteristics as the size of immigrant population, political reform movements, socioeconomic composition, and city size. Later adoption, however, is not predicted by city characteristics, but is related to institutional definitions of the legitimate structural form for municipal administration. Marshall Meyer's (1981) study of the bureaucratization of urban fiscal agencies has yielded similar findings: strong relationships between city characteristics and organizational attributes at the turn of the century, null relationships in recent years. Carroll and Delacroix's (1982) findings on the birth and death rates of newspapers support the view that selection acts with great force only in the early years of an industry's existence. Freeman (1982:14) suggests that older, larger organizations reach a point where they can dominate their environments rather than adjust to them.

The concept that best captures the process of homogenization is *isomorphism*. In Hawley's (1968) description, isomorphism is a constraining process that forces one unit in a population to resemble other units that face the same set of environmental conditions. At the population level, such an approach suggests that organizational characteristics are modified in the direction of increasing compatibility with environmental characteristics; the number of organizations in a population is a function of environmental carrying capacity; and the diversity of organizational forms is isomorphic to environmental diversity. Hannan and Freeman (1977) have significantly extended Hawley's ideas. They argue that isomorphism can result because nonoptimal forms are selected out of a population of organizations *or* because organizational decision makers learn appropriate responses and adjust their behavior accordingly. Hannan and Freeman's focus is almost solely on the first process: selection.

Following Meyer (1979) and Fennell (1980), we maintain that there are two types of isomorphism: competitive and institutional. Hannan and Freeman's classic paper (1977), and much of their recent work, deals with competitive isomorphism, assuming a system rationality that emphasizes market competition, niche change, and fitness measures. Such a view, we suggest, is most relevant for those fields in which free and open competition exists. It explains parts of the process of bureaucratization that Weber observed, and may apply to early adoption of innovation, but it does not present a fully adequate picture of the modern world of organizations. For this purpose it must be supplemented by an institutional view of isomorphism of the sort introduced by Kanter (1972: 152–4) in her discussion of the forces pressing communes toward accommodation with the outside world. As Aldrich (1979: 265) has argued, "the major factors that organizations must take into account are other organizations." Organizations compete not just for resources and customers, but for political power and institutional legitimacy, for social as well as economic fitness. The concept of institutional isomorphism is a useful tool for understanding the politics and ceremony that pervade much modern organizational life.

Three mechanisms of institutional isomorphic change

We identify three mechanisms through which institutional isomorphic change occurs, each with its own antecedents: (1) *coercive* isomorphism that stems from political influence and the problem of legitimacy; (2) *mimetic* isomorphism resulting from standard responses to uncertainty; and (3) *normative* isomorphism, associated with professionalization. This typology is an analytic one: the types are not always empirically distinct. For example, external actors may induce an organization to conform to its peers by requiring it to perform a particular task and specifying the profession responsible for its performance. Or mimetic change may reflect environmentally constructed uncertainties.[3] Yet, while the three types intermingle in empirical setting, they tend to derive from different conditions and may lead to different outcomes.

Coercive isomorphism

Coercive isomorphism results from both formal and informal pressures exerted on organizations by other organizations upon which they are dependent and by cultural expectations in the society within which organizations function. Such pressures may be felt as force, as persuasion, or as invitations to join in collusion. In some circumstances, organizational change is a direct response to government mandate: manufacturers adopt new pollution control technologies to conform to environmental regulations; nonprofits maintain accounts, and hire accountants, in order to meet tax law requirements; and organizations employ affirmative-action officers to fend off allegations of discrimination. Schools mainstream special students and hire special education teachers, cultivate PTAs and administrators who get along with them, and promulgate curricula that conform with state standards (Meyer et al., 1981). The fact that these changes may be largely ceremonial does not mean that they are inconsequential. As Ritti and Goldner (1979) have argued, staff become involved in advocacy for their functions that can alter power relations within organizations over the long run.

The existence of a common legal environment affects many aspects of an organization's behavior and structure. Weber pointed out the profound impact of a complex, rationalized system of contract law that requires the necessary organizational controls to honor legal commitments. Other legal and technical requirements of the state – the vicissitudes of the budget cycle, the ubiquity of certain fiscal years, annual reports, and financial reporting requirements that ensure eligibility for the receipt of federal contracts or funds – also shape organizations in similar ways. Pfeffer and Salancik (1978: 188–224) have discussed how organizations faced with unmanageable interdependence seek to use the greater power of the larger social system and its government to eliminate difficulties or provide for needs. They observe that politically constructed environments have two characteristic features: political decisionmakers often do not experience directly the consequences of their actions; and political decisions are applied across the board to entire classes of organizations, thus making such decisions less adaptive and less flexible.

Meyer and Rowan (1977) have argued persuasively that as rationalized states and other large rational organizations expand their dominance over more arenas of social life, organizational structures increasingly come to reflect rules institutionalized and legitimated by and within the state (also see Meyer and Hannan, 1979). As a result, organizations are increasingly homogeneous within given domains and increasingly organized around rituals of conformity to wider institutions. At the same time, organizations are decreasingly structurally determined by the constraints posed by technical activities, and decreasingly held together by output controls. Under such circumstances, organizations employ ritualized controls of credentials and group solidarity.

Direct imposition of standard operating procedures and legitimated rules and structures also occurs outside the governmental arena. Michael Sedlak (1981) has documented the ways that United Charities in the 1930s altered and homogenized the structures, methods, and philosophies of the social service agencies that depended upon them for support. As conglomerate corporations increase in size and scope, standard performance criteria are not necessarily imposed on subsidiaries, but it is common for subsidiaries to be subject to standardized reporting mechanisms (Coser et al., 1982). Subsidiaries must adopt accounting practices, performance evaluations, and budgetary plans that are compatible with the policies of the parent corporation. A variety of service infrastructures, often provided by monopolistic firms – for example, telecommunications and transportation – exert common pressures over the organizations that use them. Thus, the expansion of the central state, the centralization of capital, and the coordination of philanthropy all support the homogenization of organizational models through direct authority relationships.

We have so far referred only to the direct and explicit imposition of organizational models on dependent organizations. Coercive isomorphism, however, may be more subtle and less explicit than these examples suggest. Milofsky (1981) has described the ways in which neighborhood organizations in urban communities, many of which are committed to participatory democracy, are driven to developing organizational hierarchies in order to gain support from more hierarchically organized donor organizations. Similarly, Swidler (1979) describes the tensions created in the free schools she studied by the need to have a "principal" to negotiate with the district superintendent and to represent the school to outside agencies. In general, the need to lodge responsibility and managerial authority at least ceremonially in a formally defined role in order to interact with hierarchical organizations is a constant obstacle to the maintenance of egalitarian or collectivist organizational forms (Kanter, 1972; Rothschild-Whitt, 1979).

Mimetic processes

Not all institutional isomorphism, however, derives from coercive authority. Uncertainty is also a powerful force that encourages imitation. When organizational technologies are poorly understood (March and Olsen, 1976), when goals are ambiguous, or when the environment creates symbolic uncertainty, organizations may model themselves on other organizations. The advantages of mimetic behavior in the economy of human action are considerable; when an organization faces a problem with ambiguous causes or unclear solutions, problemistic search may yield a viable solution with little expense (Cyert and March, 1963).

Modeling, as we use the term, is a response to uncertainty. The modeled organization may be unaware of the modeling or may have no desire to be copied; it merely serves as a convenient source of practices that the borrowing organization may use. Models may be diffused unintentionally, indirectly through employee transfer or turnover, or explicitly by organizations such as consulting firms or industry trade associations. Even innovation can be accounted for by organizational modeling. As Alchian (1950) has observed:

> While there certainly are those who consciously innovate, there are those who, in their imperfect attempts to imitate others, unconsciously innovate by unwittingly acquiring some unexpected or unsought unique attributes which under the prevailing circumstances prove partly responsible for the success. Others, in turn, will attempt to copy the uniqueness, and the innovation-imitation process continues.

One of the most dramatic instances of modeling was the effort of Japan's modernizers in the late nineteenth century to model new governmental initiatives on apparently successful western prototypes. Thus, the imperial government sent its officers to study the courts, Army, and police in France, the Navy and postal system in Great Britain, and banking and art education in the United States (see Westney, forthcoming). American corporations are now returning the compliment by implementing (their perceptions of) Japanese models to cope with thorny productivity and personnel problems in their own firms. The rapid proliferation of quality circles and quality-of-work-life issues in American firms is, at least in part, an attempt to model Japanese and European successes. These developments also have a ritual aspect; companies adopt these "innovations" to enhance their legitimacy, to demonstrate they are at least trying to improve working conditions. More generally, the wider the population of personnel employed by, or customers served by, an organization, the stronger the pressure felt by the organization to provide the programs and services offered by other organizations. Thus, either a skilled labor force or a broad customer base may encourage mimetic isomorphism.

Much homogeneity in organizational structures stems from the fact that despite considerable search for diversity there is relatively little variation to be selected from. New organizations are modeled upon old ones throughout the economy, and managers actively seek models upon which to build (Kimberly, 1980). Thus, in the arts one can find textbooks on how to organize a community arts council or how to start a symphony women's guild. Large organizations choose from a relatively small set of major consulting firms, which, like Johnny Appleseeds, spread a few organizational models throughout the land. Such models are powerful because structural changes are observable, whereas changes in policy and strategy are less easily noticed. With the advice of a major consulting firm, a large metropolitan public television station switched from a functional design to a multidivisional structure. The stations' executives were skeptical that the new structure was more efficient; in fact, some services were now duplicated across divisions. But they were convinced that the new design would carry a powerful message to the for-profit firms with whom the station regularly dealt. These firms, whether in the role of corporate underwriters or as potential partners in joint ventures, would view the reorganization as a sign that "the sleepy nonprofit station was becoming more business-minded" (Powell and Freidkin, 1986). The history of management reform in American government agencies, which are noted for their goal ambiguity, is almost a textbook case of isomorphic modeling, from the PPPB of the McNamara era to the zero-based budgeting of the Carter administration.

Organizations tend to model themselves after similar organizations in their field that they perceive to be more legitimate or successful. The ubiquity of certain kinds of structural arrangements can more likely be credited to the universality of mimetic processes than to any concrete evidence that the adopted models enhance efficiency. Marshall Meyer (1981) contends that it is easy to predict the organization of a newly emerging nation's administration without knowing anything about the nation itself, since "peripheral nations are far more isomorphic – in administrative form and economic pattern – than any theory of the world system of economic division of labor would lead one to expect."

Normative pressures

A third source of isomorphic organizational change is normative and stems primarily from professionalization. Following Larson (1977) and Collins (1979), we interpret professionalization as the collective struggle of members of an occupation to define the conditions and methods of their work, to control "the production of producers" (Larson, 1977: 49–52), and to establish a cognitive base and legitimation for their occupational autonomy. As Larson points out, the professional project is rarely achieved with complete success. Professionals must compromise with nonprofessional clients, bosses, or regulators. The major recent growth in the professions has been among organizational professionals, particularly managers and specialized staff of large organizations. The increased professionalization of workers whose futures are inextricably bound up with the fortunes of the organizations that employ them has rendered obsolescent (if not obsolete) the dichotomy between organizational commitment and professional allegiance that characterized traditional professionals in earlier organizations (Hall, 1968). Professions are subject to the same coercive and mimetic pressures as are organizations. Moreover, while various kinds of professionals within an organization may differ from one another, they exhibit much similarity to their professional counterparts in other organizations. In addition, in many cases, professional power is as much assigned by the state as it is created by the activities of the professions.

Two aspects of professionalization are important sources of isomorphism. One is the resting of formal education and of legitimation in a cognitive base produced by university specialists; the second is the growth and elaboration of professional networks that span organizations and across which new models diffuse rapidly.

Universities and professional training institutions are important centers for the development of organizational norms among professional managers and their staff. Professional and trace associations are another vehicle for the definition and promulgation of normative rules about organizational and professional behavior. Such mechanisms create a pool of almost interchangeable individuals who occupy similar positions across a range of organizations and possess a similarity of orientation and disposition that may override variations in tradition and control that might otherwise shape organizational behavior (Perrow, 1974).

One important mechanism for encouraging normative isomorphism is the filtering of personnel. Within many organizational fields filtering occurs through the hiring of individuals from firms within the same industry; through the recruitment of fast-track staff from a narrow range of training institutions; through common promotion practices, such as always hiring top executives from financial or legal departments; and from skill-level requirements for particular jobs. Many professional career tracks are so closely guarded, both at the entry level and throughout the career progression, that individuals who make it to the top are virtually indistinguishable. March and March (1977) found that individuals who attained the position of school superintendent in Wisconsin were so alike in background and orientation as to make further career advancement random and unpredictable. Hirsch and Whisler (1982) find a similar absence of variation among *Fortune* 500 board members. In addition, individuals in an organizational field undergo anticipatory socialization to common expectations about their personal behavior, appropriate style of dress, organizational vocabularies (Cicourel, 1970; Williamson, 1975) and standard methods of speaking, joking, or addressing others (Ouchi, 1980). Particularly in industries with a service or financial orientation (Collins, 1979, argues that the importance of credentials is strongest in these areas), the filtering of personnel approaches what Kanter (1977) refers to as the "homosexual reproduction of management." To the extent managers and key staff are drawn from the same universities and filtered on a common set of attributes, they will tend to view problems in a similar fashion, see the same policies, procedures and structures as normatively sanctioned and legitimated, and approach decisions in much the same way.

Entrants to professional career tracks who somehow escape the filtering process – for example, Jewish naval officers, woman stockbrokers, or Black insurance executives – are likely to be subjected to pervasive on-the-job socialization. To the extent that organizations in a field differ and primary socialization occurs on the job, socialization could reinforce, not erode, differences among organizations. But when organizations in a field are similar and occupational socialization is carried out in trade association workshops, in-service educational programs, consultant arrangements, employer-professional school networks, and in the pages of trade magazines, socialization acts as an isomorphic force.

The professionalization of management tends to proceed in tandem with the structuration of organizational fields. The exchange of information among professionals helps contribute to a commonly recognized hierarchy of status, of center and periphery, that becomes a matrix for information flows and personnel movement across organizations. This status ordering occurs through both formal and informal means. The designation of a few large firms in an industry as key bargaining agents in union – management negotiations may make these central firms pivotal in other respects as well. Government recognition of key firms or organizations through the grant or contract process may give these organizations legitimacy and visibility and lead competing firms to copy aspects of their structure or operating procedures in hope of obtaining similar rewards. Professional and trade associations provide other arenas in which center organizations are recognized and their personnel given positions of substantive or ceremonial influence. Managers in highly visible organizations may in turn have their stature reinforced by representation on the boards of other organizations, participation in industry-wide or inter-industry councils, and consultation by agencies of government (Useem, 1979). In the nonprofit sector, where legal barriers to collusion do not exist, structuration may proceed even more rapidly. Thus executive producers or artistic directors of leading theatres head trade or professional association committees, sit on government and foundation grant-award panels, or consult as government or foundation-financed management advisors to smaller theatres, or sit on smaller organizations' boards, even as their stature is reinforced and enlarged by the grants their theatres receive from government, corporate, and foundation funding sources (DiMaggio, 1982).

Such central organizations serve as both active and passive models; their policies and structures will be copied throughout their fields. Their centrality is reinforced as upwardly mobile managers and staff seek to secure positions in these central organizations in order to further their own careers. Aspiring managers may undergo anticipatory socialization into the norms and mores of the organizations they hope to join. Career paths may also involve movement from entry positions in the center organizations to middle-management positions in peripheral organizations. Personnel flows within an organizational field are further encouraged by structural homogenization, for example the existence of common career titles and paths (such as assistant, associate, and full professor) with meanings that are commonly understood.

It is important to note that each of the institutional isomorphic processes can be expected to proceed in the absence of evidence that they increase internal organizational efficiency. To the extent that organizational effectiveness is enhanced, the reason will often be that organizations are rewarded for being similar to other organizations in their fields. This similarity can make it easier for organizations to transact with other organizations, to attract career-minded staff, to be acknowledged as legitimate and reputable, and to fit into administrative categories that define eligibility for public and private grants and contracts. None of this, however, insures that conformist organizations do what they do more efficiently than do their more deviant peers.

Pressures for competitive efficiency are also mitigated in many fields because the number of organizations is limited and there are strong fiscal and legal barriers to entry and exit. Lee (1971: 51) maintains this is why hospital administrators are less concerned with the efficient use of resources and more concerned with status competition and parity in prestige. Fennell (1980) notes that hospitals are a poor market system because patients lack the needed knowledge of potential exchange partners and prices. She argues that physicians and hospital administrators are the actual consumers. Competition among hospitals is based on "attracting physicians, who, in turn, bring their patients to the hospital." Fennell (p. 505) concludes that:

> Hospitals operate according to a norm of social legitimation that frequently conflicts with market considerations of efficiency and system rationality. Apparently, hospitals can increase their range of services not because there is an actual need for a particular service or facility within the patient population, but because they will be defined as fit only if they can offer everything other hospitals in the area offer.

These results suggest a more general pattern. Organizational fields that include a large professionally trained labor force will be driven primarily by status competition. Organizational prestige and resources are key elements in attracting professionals. This process encourages homogenization as organizations seek to ensure that they can provide the same benefits and services as their competitors.

Predictors of Isomorphic Change

It follows from our discussion of the mechanism by which isomorphic change occurs that we should be able to predict empirically which organizational fields will be most homogeneous in structure, process, and behavior. While an empirical test of such predictions is beyond the scope of this paper, the ultimate value of our perspective will lie in its predictive utility. The hypotheses discussed below are not meant to exhaust the universe of predictors, but merely to suggest several hypotheses that may be pursued using data on the characteristics of organizations in a field, either cross-sectionally or, preferably, over time. The hypotheses are implicitly governed by *ceteris paribus* assumptions, particularly with regard to size, technology, and centralization of external resources.

A. Organizational-level predictors

There is variability in the extent to and rate at which organizations in a field change to become more like their peers. Some organizations respond to external pressures quickly; others change only after a long period of resistance. The first two hypotheses derive from our discussion of coercive isomorphism and constraint.

Hypothesis A-1: *The greater the dependence of an organization on another organization, the more similar it will become to that organization in structure, climate, and behavioral focus.* Following Thompson (1967) and Pfeffer and Salancik (1978), this proposition recognizes the greater ability of organizations to resist the demands of organizations on whom they are not dependent. A position of dependence leads to isomorphic change. Coercive pressures are built into exchange relationships. As Williamson (1979) has shown, exchanges are characterized by transaction-specific investments in both knowledge and equipment. Once an organization chooses a specific supplier or distributor for particular parts or services, the supplier or distributor develops expertise in the performance of the task as well as idiosyncratic knowledge about the exchange relationship. The organization comes to rely on the supplier or distributor and such transaction-specific investments give the supplier or distributor considerable advantages in any subsequent competition with other suppliers or distributors.

Hypothesis A-2: *The greater the centralization of organization A's resource supply, the greater the extent to which organization A will change isomorphically to resemble the organizations on which it depends for resources.* As Thompson (1967) notes, organizations that depend on the same sources for funding, personnel, and legitimacy will be more subject to the whims of resource suppliers than will organizations that can play one source of support off against another. In cases where alternative sources are either not readily available or require effort to locate, the stronger party to the transaction can coerce the weaker party to adopt its practices in order to accommodate the stronger party's needs (see Powell, 1983).

The third and fourth hypotheses derive from our discussion of mimetic isomorphism, modeling, and uncertainty.

Hypothesis A-3: *The more uncertain the relationship between means and ends the greater the extent to which an organization will model itself after organizations it perceives to be successful.* The mimetic thought process involved in the search for models is characteristic of change in organizations in which key technologies are only poorly understood (March and Cohen, 1974). Here our prediction diverges somewhat from Meyer and Rowan (1977) who argue, as we do, that organizations which lack well-defined technologies will import institutionalized rules and practices. Meyer and Rowan posit a loose coupling between legitimated external practices and internal organizational behavior. From an ecologist's point of view, loosely coupled organizations are more likely to vary internally. In contrast, we expect substantive internal changes in tandem with more ceremonial practices, thus greater homogeneity and less variation and change. Internal consistency of this sort is an important means of interorganizational coordination. It also increases organizational stability.

Hypothesis A-4: *The more ambiguous the goals of an organization, the greater the extent to which the organization will model itself after organizations that it perceives to be successful.* There are two reasons for this. First, organizations with ambiguous or disputed goals are likely to be highly dependent upon appearances for legitimacy. Such organizations may find it to their advantage to meet the expectations of important constituencies about how they should be designed and run. In contrast to our view, ecologists would argue that organizations that copy other organizations usually have no competitive advantage. We contend that, in most situations, reliance on established, legitimated procedures enhances organizational legitimacy and survival characteristics. A second reason for modeling behavior is found in situations where conflict over organizational goals is repressed in the interest of harmony; thus participants find it easier to mimic other organizations than to make decisions on the basis of systematic analyses of goals since such analyses would prove painful or disruptive.

The fifth and sixth hypotheses are based on our discussion of normative processes found in professional organizations.

Hypothesis A-5: *The greater the reliance on academic credentials in choosing managerial and staff personnel, the greater the extent to which an organization will become like other organizations in its field.* Applicants with academic credentials have already undergone a socialization process in university programs, and are thus more likely than others to have internalized reigning norms and dominant organizational models.

Hypothesis A-6: *The greater the participation of organizational managers in trade and professional associations, the more likely the organization will be, or will become, like other organizations in its field.* This hypothesis is parallel to the institutional view that the more elaborate the relational networks among organizations and their members, the greater the collective organization of the environment (Meyer and Rowan, 1977).

B. Field-level predictors

The following six hypotheses describe the expected effects of several characteristics of organizational fields on the extent of isomorphism in a particular field. Since the effect of institutional isomorphism is homogenization, the best indicator of isomorphic change is a decrease in variation and diversity, which could be measured by lower standard deviations of the values of selected indicators in a set of organizations. The key indicators would vary with the nature of the field and the interests of the investigator. In all cases, however, field-level measures are expected to affect organizations in a field regardless of each organization's scores on related organizational-level measures.

Hypothesis B-1: *The greater the extent to which an organizational field is dependent upon a single (or several similar) source(s) of support for vital resources, the higher the level of isomorphism.* The centralization of resources within a field both directly causes homogenization by placing organizations under similar pressures from resource suppliers, and interacts with uncertainty and goal ambiguity to increase their impact. This hypothesis is congruent with the ecologists' argument that the number of organizational forms is determined by the distribution of resources in the environment and the terms on which resources are available.

Hypothesis B-2: *The greater the extent to which the organizations in a field transact with agencies of the state, the greater the extent of isomorphism in the field as a whole.* This follows not just from the previous hypothesis, but from two elements of state/private-sector transactions: their rule-boundedness and formal rationality, and the emphasis of government actors on institutional rules. Moreover, the federal government routinely designates industry standards for an entire field which require adoption by all competing firms. John Meyer (1979) argues convincingly that the aspects of an organization which are affected by state transactions differ to the extent that state participation is unitary or fragmented among several public agencies.

The third and fourth hypotheses follow from our discussion of isomorphic change resulting from uncertainty and modeling.

Hypothesis B-3: *The fewer the number of visible alternative organizational models in a field, the faster the rate of isomorphism in that field.* The predictions of this hypothesis are less specific than those of others and require further refinement; but our argument is that for any relevant dimension of organizational strategies or structures in an organizational field there will be a threshold level, or a tipping point, beyond which adoption of the dominant form will proceed with increasing speed (Granovetter, 1978; Boorman and Levitt, 1979).

Hypothesis B-4: *The greater the extent to which technologies are uncertain or goals are ambiguous within a field, the greater the rate of isomorphic change.* Somewhat counterintuitively, abrupt increases in uncertainty and ambiguity should, after brief periods of ideologically motivated experimentation, lead to rapid isomorphic change. As in the case of A-4, ambiguity and uncertainty may be a function of environmental definition, and, in any case, interact both with centralization of resources (A-1, A-2, B-1, B-2) and with professionalization and structuration (A-5, A-6, B-5, B-6). Moreover, in fields characterized by a high degree of uncertainty, new entrants, which could serve as sources of innovation and variation, will seek to overcome the liability of newness by imitating established practices within the field.

The two final hypotheses in this section follow from our discussion of professional filtering, socialization, and structuration.

Hypothesis B-5: *The greater the extent of professionalization in a field, the greater the amount of institutional isomorphic change.* Professionalization may be measured by the universality of credential requirements, the robustness of graduate training programs, or the vitality of professional and trade associations.

Hypothesis B-6: *The greater the extent of structuration of a field, the greater the degree of isomorphics.* Fields that have stable and broadly acknowledged centers, peripheries, and status orders will be more homogeneous both because the diffusion structure for new models and norms is more routine and because the level of interaction among organizations in the field is higher. While structuration may not lend itself to easy measurement, it might be tapped crudely with the use of such familiar measures as concentration ratios, reputational interview studies, or data on network characteristics.

This rather schematic exposition of a dozen hypotheses relating the extent of isomorphism to selected attributes of organizations and of organizational fields does not constitute a complete agenda for empirical assessment of our perspective. We have not discussed the expected nonlinearities and ceiling effects in the relationships that we have posited. Nor have we addressed the issue of the indicators that one must use to measure homogeneity. Organizations in a field may be highly diverse on some dimensions, yet extremely homogeneous on others. While we suspect, in general, that the rate at which the standard deviations of structural or behavioral indicators approach zero will vary with the nature of an organizational field's technology and environment, we will not develop these ideas here. The point of this section is to suggest that the theoretical discussion is susceptible to empirical test, and to lay out a few testable propositions that may guide future analyses.

NOTES

1 By *connectedness* we mean the existence of transactions tying organizations to one another: A set of organizations that are strongly connected to one another and only weakly connected to other organizations constitutes a *clique*. By *structural equivalence* we refer to similarity of position in a network structure.
2 By organizational change, we refer to change in formal structure, organizational culture, and goals, program, or mission.
3 This point was suggested by John Meyer.

REFERENCES

Alchian, Armen (1950) "Uncertainty, evolution, and economic theory." *Journal of Political Economy* 58: 211–21.
Aldrich, Howard (1979) *Organizations and Environments*. Englewood Cliffs, NJ: Prentice-Hall.
Barnouw, Erik (1966–8) *A History of Broadcasting in the United States*, 3 volumes. New York: Oxford University Press.
Boorman, Scott A. and Paul R. Levitt (1979) "The cascade principle for general disequilibrium dynamics." Cambridge/New Haven: Harvard-Yale Preprints in Mathematical Sociology. Number 15.
Carroll, Glenn R. and Jacques Delacroix (1982) "Organizational mortality in the newspaper industries of Argentina and Ireland: an ecological approach." *Administrative Science Quarterly* 27: 169–98.
Child, John and Alfred Kieser (1981) "Development of organizations over time." Pp. 28–64 in Paul C. Nystrom and William H. Starbuck (eds.), *Handbook of Organizational Design*. New York: Oxford University Press.
Cicourel, Aaron (1970) "The acquisition of social structure: toward a developmental sociology of language." pp. 136–68 in Jack D. Douglas (ed.), *Understanding Everyday Life*. Chicago: Aldine.
Collins, Randall (1979) *The Credential Society*. New York: Academic Press.
Coser, Lewis, Charles Kadushin and Walter W. Powell (1982) *Books: The Culture and Commerce of Book Publishing*. New York: Basic Books.
Cyert, Richard M. and James G. March (1963) *A Behavioral Theory of the Firm*. Englewood Cliffs, NJ: Prentice-Hall.
DiMaggio, Paul (1982) "The structure of organizational fields: an analytical approach and policy implications." Paper prepared for SUNY-Albany Conference on Organizational Theory and Public Policy. April 1 and 2.
Fennell, Mary L. (1980) "The effects of environmental characteristics on the structure of hospital clusters." *Administrative Science Quarterly* 25: 484–510.

Freeman, John H. (1982) "Organizational life cycles and natural selection processes." pp. 1–32 in Barry Staw and Larry Cummings (eds.), *Research in Organizational Behavior*. Vol. 4. Greenwich, CT: JAI Press.

Giddens, Anthony (1979) *Central Problems in Social Theory: Action, Structure, and Contradiction in Social Analysis*. Berkeley, CA: University of California Press.

Granovetter, Mark (1978) "Threshold models of collective behavior." *American Journal of Sociology* 83: 1420–43.

Hall, Richard (1968) "Professionalization and bureaucratization." *American Sociological Review* 33: 92–104.

Hannan, Michael T. and John H. Freeman (1977) "The population ecology of organizations." *American Journal of Sociology* 82: 929–64.

Hawley, Amos (1968) "Human ecology." pp. 328–37 in David L. Sills (ed.), *International Encyclopedia of the Social Sciences*. New York: Macmillan.

Hirsch, Paul and Thomas Whisler (1982) "The view from the boardroom." Paper presented at Academy of Management Meetings, New York, NY.

Kanter, Rosabeth Moss (1972) *Commitment and Community*. Cambridge, MA: Harvard University Press.

Kanter, Rosabeth Moss (1977) *Men and Women of the Corporation*. New York: Basic Books.

Katz, Michael B. (1975) *Class, Bureaucracy, and Schools: The Illusion of Educational Change in America*. New York: Praeger.

Kimberley, John (1980) "Initiation, Innovation, and Institutionalization in the Creation Process." Pp. 18–43 in John Kimberley and Robert B. Miles (eds.), *The Organizational Life Cycle*. San Francisco, CA: Jossey-Bass.

Larson, Magali Sarfatti (1977) *The Rise of Professionalism: A Sociological Analysis*. Berkeley, CA: University of California Press.

Laumann, Edward O., Joseph Galaskiewicz and Peter Marsden (1978) "Community structure as interorganizational linkage." *Annual Review of Sociology* 4: 455–84.

Lee, M. L. (1971) "A conspicuous production theory of hospital behavior." *Southern Economic Journal* 38: 48–58.

March, James C. and James G. March (1977) "Almost random careers: the Wisconsin school superintendency, 1940–72." *Administrative Science Quarterly* 22: 378–409.

March, James G. and Michael Cohen (1974) *Leadership and Ambiguity: The American College President*. New York: McGraw-Hill.

March, James G. and Johan P. Olsen (1976) *Ambiguity and Choice in Organizations*. Bergen, Norway: Universitetsforlaget.

Meyer, John W. (1979) "The impact of the centralization of educational funding and control on state and local organizational governance." Stanford, CA: Institute for Research on Educational Finance and Governance, Stanford University, Program Report No. 79–B20.

Meyer, John W. and Michael Hannan (1979) *National Development and the World System: Educational, Economic, and Political Change*. Chicago, IL: University of Chicago Press.

Meyer, John W. and Brian Rowan (1977) "Institutionalized organizations: formal structure as myth and ceremony." *American Journal of Sociology* 83: 340–63.

Meyer, John W., W. Richard Scott and Terence C. Deal (1981) "Institutional and technical sources of organizational structure explaining the structure of educational organizations." In Herman Stein (ed.), *Organizations and the Human Services: Cross-Disciplinary Reflections*. Philadelphia, PA: Temple University Press.

Meyer, Marshall (1981) "Persistence and change in bureaucratic structures." Paper presented at the annual meeting of the American Sociological Association, Toronto, Canada.

Milofsky, Carl (1981) "Structure and process in community self-help organizations." New Haven: Yale Program on Non-Profit Organizations, Working Paper No. 17.

Ouchi, William G. (1980) "Markets, bureaucracies, and clans." *Administrative Science Quarterly* 25: 129–41.

Perrow, Charles (1974) "Is business really changing?" *Organizational Dynamics* Summer: 31–44.

Pfeffer, Jeffrey and Gerald Salancik (1978) *The External Control of Organizations: A Resource Dependence Perspective.* New York: Harper & Row.

Powell, Walter W. (1983) "New solutions to perennial problems of bookselling: whither the local bookstore?" *Daedalus*: Winter.

Powell, Walter W. and Rebecca Freidkin (1986) "Politics and Programs: Organizational Factors in Public Television Decision-making." pp. 245–69 in *Nonprofit Enterprise in the Arts*, ed. P. J. DiMaggio. New York: Oxford University Press.

Ritti, R. R. and Fred H. Goldner (1979) "Professional pluralism in an industrial organization." *Management Science* 16: 233–46.

Rothman, Mitchell (1980) "The evolution of forms of legal education." Unpublished manuscript. Department of Sociology, Yale University, New Haven, CT.

Rothschild-Whitt, Joyce (1979) "The collectivist organization: an alternative to rational bureaucratic models." *American Sociological Review* 44: 509–27.

Schelling, Thomas (1978) *Micromotives and Macrobehavior.* New York: W. W. Norton.

Sedlak, Michael W. (1981) "Youth policy and young women, 1950–1972: the impact of private-sector programs for pregnant and wayward girls on public policy." Paper presented at National Institute for Education Youth Policy Research Conference, Washington, D.C.

Selznick, Philip (1957) *Leadership in Administration.* New York: Harper & Row.

Starr, Paul (1980) "Medical care and the boundaries of capitalist organization." Unpublished manuscript. Program on Non-Profit Organizations, Yale University, New Haven, CT.

Swidler, Ann (1979) *Organization Without Authority: Dilemmas of Social Control of Free Schools.* Cambridge, MA: Harvard University Press.

Thompson, James (1967) *Organizations in Action.* New York: McGraw-Hill.

Tyack, David (1974) *The One Best System: A History of American Urban Education.* Cambridge, MA: Harvard University Press.

Useem, Michael (1979) "The social organization of the American business elite and participation of corporation directors in the governance of American institutions." *American Sociological Review* 44: 553–72.

Weber, Max (1952) *The Protestant Ethic and the Spirit of Capitalism.* New York: Scribner.

Weber, Max (1968) *Economy and Society: An Outline of Interpretive Sociology.* Three volumes. New York: Bedminster.

Westney, D. Eleanor (Forthcoming) *Organizational Development and Social Change in Meiji, Japan.*

White, Harrison C., Scott A. Boorman and Ronald L. Breiger (1976) "Social structure from multiple networks. I. Blockmodels of roles and positions." *American Journal of Sociology* 81: 730–80.

Williamson, Oliver E. (1975) *Markets and Hierarchies, Analysis and Antitrust Implications: A Study of the Economics of Internal Organization.* New York: Free Press.

Williamson, Oliver E. (1979) "Transaction-cost economics: the governance of contractual relations." *Journal of Law and Economics* 22:233–61.

Woodward, John (1965) *Industrial Organization, Theory and Practice*. London: Oxford University Press.

Zucker, Lynne G. and Pamela S. Tolbert (1981) "Institutional sources of change in the formal structure of organizations: the diffusion of civil service reform, 1880–1935." Paper presented at American Sociological Association annual meeting, Toronto, Canada.

Chapter 12

Catnets [1966]

Harrison White

Net

A "net" can be drawn as a set of points with straight lines connecting various pairs of points. In our usage the points represent persons or social parties and each line segment indicates a given kind of social relation between a pair of persons. If the line segment has an arrowhead, it represents an asymmetric relation. In any case, the relation must be familiar and clearly defined in the eyes of the people in the set so that it makes sense to say (1) each pair of people either is or is not in that relation and (2) the relation between one pair has about the same type of content and significance as the relation between another pair. This is the obvious part of our definition of a "net."

We sharpen this obvious definition of a net by adding further stipulations to make it more useful as a concept in sociology. The basic idea is that a net is more than an observer's recording of a set of relations between pairs of people, but yet is less than a map known and attended to by any or all of the people in the net. We stipulate:

(i) the persons in the net accept the idea that they have meaningful indirect relations with anyone paired with a person with whom they are paired (i.e., most of all persons, when considered as the ego viewing the net, accept "composition" as a meaningful "operator" on the net, to use mathematical language);
(ii) the relation diagramed implies sufficient familiarity with the other in a pair to have some idea of whom else he is related to;

Harrison White, "Catnets," from *Notes on the Constituents of Social Structure* (unpublished manuscript, 1966).

Contemporary Sociological Theory, Third Edition. Edited by Craig Calhoun, Joseph Gerteis, James Moody, Steven Pfaff, and Indermohan Virk. Editorial material and organization © 2012 John Wiley & Sons, Ltd. Published 2012 by John Wiley & Sons, Ltd.

(iii) yet the many possible indirect connections among people, at various removes (through various numbers and patterns of intermediary persons) are not recognized as falling into distinct new types of relations with their own definitions and contents, i.e., the indirect connections are not "institutionalized." (If they were, one would have really a superposition of nets, one for each kind of relation possible between a pair of people and it is better to give this more complex type of structure a different name, as we shall below.)

In other words, persons in a net recognize indirect connections implied by the set of pair relations, but these connections are recognized only in part, and over a limited number of removes, and they are reacted to in concrete terms rather than as well-defined new types of relations.

A second representation of nets helps in thinking about them and particularly in seeing their connection with category systems. Set up a table with one row for each person in the net and also one column. For visual clarity it helps to arrange the persons in the rows in the same order as the columns. Then the existence of an arrow from one person to another is indicated by a check or a one in the cell formed by the intersection of the row of the former with the column of the other. In this representation it is natural to think of making the concept of net more flexible by attaching a measure of strength to each arrow, just as the arrow is the more natural idea here than the undirected line – which can only be shown by two entries of unity in the table. The network can be regarded as formally similar to a cross-tabulation, defined below, with each person being regarded as a category and the relations being the items to be cross-tabulated.

Net Systems

A net continues indefinitely: its structure is essentially local, a matter of pair relations. Yet there must be a common culture to define a type of relations sharply and clearly, if there is to be a net defined by the presence or absence of that relation between pairs of persons. The implication of a common culture and the implication that a net is defined over some set of persons both lead one to define the population over which the net is perceived. Population is essentially a categorical concept; so the concept of net is not in fact independent of the concept of the cat. Once a concrete population is defined for the net the idea of other types of relation existing among the population requiring representation by other nets cannot be avoided.

Balanced net systems: If several types of relation are defined on a population, the obvious question is whether there are any limitations on the co-existence of different relations on the same pair. The next question in order of complexity is whether in any set of three people there are necessary connections between the relations of two pairs and the relation to be found between the third pair on the triangle.

One very simple set of propositions about the interconnections of relations on a triangle has gained wide currency, although it is not so much a law as a plausible suggestion confirmed with some regularity. Suppose one type of relation has positive connotations, as in friendship; then if one man is joined by it to each of two other men, they will tend to come into a friendly relation with each other too. Suppose a second type of relation has negative connotations of enmity, etc. Then the reasoning is that a man's enmity with each of two other men will be a force tending to generate a positive bond between them. More abstractly, in any triangle either none or two of the pair relations will tend to be negative, the other three or one of the relations (lines) being of positive quality.

This idea of balanced relations, directly parallel to the psychological ideas in consonance theory treated last term, can be extended to refer to larger clusters of points and longer circuits of relations in the graph. One prediction of such extended theories is the formation within the population of two opposed factions such that all positive relations are within the factions and all negative relations between them. The idea can also be extended to take into account the direct nature of the relation when the two parties perceive it differently. Furthermore, third types of relations, such as familiarity, can be introduced and propositions set forth about their impact on allowable configurations of the positive and negative qualities. No satisfactory theory of these complex interrelations has yet been proposed, and in particular no way of consistently introducing measures of the strengths of the relations has been devised. But this discussion can serve as a warning that our neglect hereafter of the existence and interaction of nets of different qualities is dangerous.

Limited systems

A question used commonly in sociometric work, for example the Coleman et al. study of drug diffusion, calls for the names of your three best friends or closest colleagues, etc. The implication is, and it seems to be confirmed in actual nets derived from direct observation, that there is an upper limit on the number of links a person has and should have in a net, and also a lower limit. When the population is large such constraints limit enormously the possible nets; in place of n(n-1) possible arrows in a population of n persons, there can be at most 3n. In abstract terms one can say that the set has a maximum "local degree."

The population for the net system and the requirements of balance among relations are also of course limits on net systems.

Cats

Concretely, a "cat" is a bunch of people alike in some respect, from someone's point of view.

Abstractly, a category is the respect in which persons may be grouped as similar – a "box" into which people do or do not fall. These "persons" can of course be any population of things or social parties.

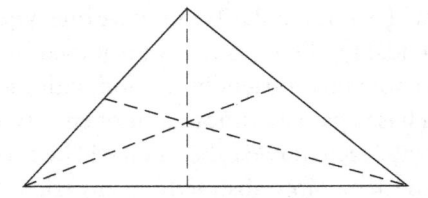

Figure 12.1 Relation between pairs in a triad.

"A single category" is therefore a meaningless idea: at a minimum there is at least the residual category or box into which fall "all others," those not alike in the given respect. To say category is to mean a system of categories.

The different aspects of the cat are emphasized by two different ways of formulating the cat in network terms, where we now use "network" in its formal sense.

Formally, a network is a collection of points in which some pairs are connected by lines.

1. Let one point be set apart from the others as the center and identified as the attribute or "respect" which the people, the other points, can have. Then those points connected to the center by lines form the cat. (The center need not be in a particular position since the confluence of lines on it is sufficient identification.)

Additional possible connotations of category are suggested by variations on this representation: Let the lines be directed by arrowheads. Arrows leading out from the center connote an attribute "received" by the points, say sex or citizenship. If all arrows run toward the center an "achieved" attribute, one "projected" by the persons, is implied, say political party or good health.

2. Let the subset of points which have the attribute be fully connected by lines: each line then represents the sharing of the attribute.

An implicit assumption has slipped in with representation (2) above that "sharing an attribute" is between pairs of people. Why not triplets? Then three persons in a category could be represented by where the dotted lines from each person to the "relation" between the other pair in the triad indicates that all three persons are bound up in each relation (see Figure 12.1). And so on through the quartet, the quintet, etc. as the fundamental unit of similarity. The point is that drawing a complete network of lines between pairs really indicates only one special, limited possible meaning of jointly belonging to a category. And the advantage of having tried to represent a cat in this network fashion is that it brings out complexities in the possible meanings of category.

Representation (1) can be seen as the limiting case of representation (2) in which not pairs, triads, etc. but the *total* group of persons in the cat is the smallest unit in which it is meaningful to speak of the sharing of the attribute which defines the category. Call this the *total* integration. Representation (1) can also be seen as the other extreme case of representation (2), wherein each person has the attribute as an individual with no connotation of sharing anything with others in the cat. Call this the isolate representation.

As in the definition of net so also here we are forced to introduce psychological and cultural elements in our very definitions of the elementary terms of social structure. The *total* representation of a cat is appropriate where there is an intense consciousness of joint categorical membership and/or clear recognition in the culture of common possession of the attribute. The *isolate* representation is most appropriate where the category is defined by some observer in a way not visible to the persons involved even though the category may in fact sharply describe their behavior. The distinction is an old and familiar one, of course, e.g., is "the proletariat" a self-conscious class of a construct of the observer?

Category Systems

Ad hoc

"Have attribute" versus "don't have it" is the simplest ad hoc "system" of categories. Any arbitrary set of categories such that any person in the population belongs to exactly one of them is an ad hoc system.

Generic

Mail addresses form a typical generic system of categories: a person is located within successively finer subdivisions of an initial large category. The first level of largest categories can be regarded as an ad hoc system, as can each level of subcategories within a next-larger category.

Cross-tabulation

A person is cross-tabulated by being placed simultaneously within two or more ad hoc category systems, each of which covers the entire population.

If he is placed first in his proper category within one system, and then in his proper category in the second system, and so on, the result looks like a generic category system. But here any one of the ad hoc systems can be applied first as the level of largest categories, and any other be applied next to refine the largest categories, and so on. Whereas in the generic system proper only one set of categories can be used as the first or highest level, and the breakdown into finer categories may be made in different ways within each of the biggest categories. Thus, location of an adult by the industry, company, division and title of his work affiliation is a generic system, whereas his specification by sex, age, religion, location, and income is a cross-tabulation.

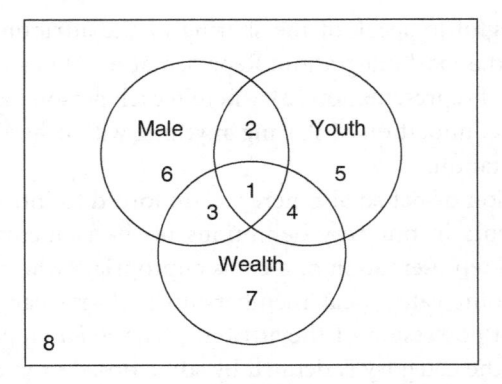

Figure 12.2 Venn diagram showing membership in three classes.

Two different representations of the "cells" or boxes in the cross-tabulation bring out different possible connotations. (The representations used for cats can also be used here, but are too clumsy to give much insight.)

1   The common procedure in social surveys is a "lay out" of the boxes as the intersections of rows for one ad hoc system with columns for the other. (Where three ad hoc systems are cross-tabulated one needs a cube, or on the printed page a series of such two-dimensional lay-outs.) The order of the rows, and the order of columns, and which system is laid out by rows and which by columns is immaterial.
2   A Venn diagram is the standard way to represent the overlapping memberships in different logical classes, which is just the special case of cross-tabulation with two classes (in vs. out) in each ad hoc system. The typical diagram for membership in three classes (say male sex, youth, and wealth) is shown in Figure 12.2.
    The eight numbered areas can equated to the eight cells in the cube for representation 1.

The distinctive thing in this representation is that one of the two categories of each ad hoc system (e.g., male in male vs. female above) is singled out by being shown as the inside of a circle. Thus the eight areas above are shown in distinctively different shapes, all centered around area 1 as the core of the classification system. Thus the Venn diagram is a relativistic or subjective way to present a cross-tabulation.

Note that representation 2 for cross-tabulations, using overlapping circles, breaks down if more than three classes are to be used. With four classes one needs 16 intersections (2∗2∗2∗2 = 16), 16 different combinations of the inside and outside areas of the four circles, and these cannot be found using circles on a plane. The contrast between representations 1 and 2 is made clearer by using rectangles in place of circles in the Venn diagram. Thus, the three-circle diagram in Figure 12.2 can be shown as a table (see Table 12.1) and a similar diagram for four overlapping rectangles (plus a corner as above for the residual category) can handle the core of

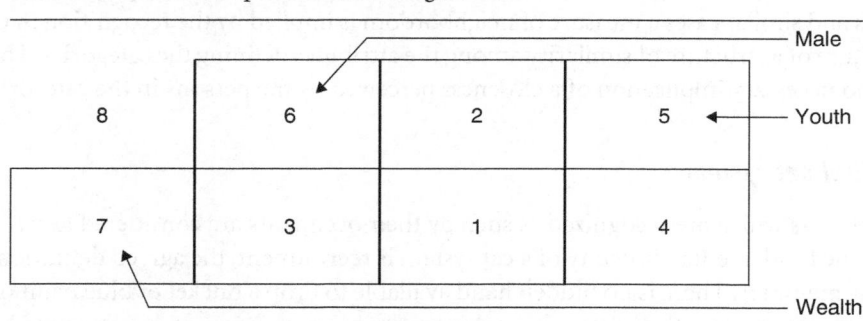

Table 12.1 Tabular representation of Figure 12.2.

8	6	2	5
7	3	1	4

Male — (upper row)
Youth — 5
Wealth — (lower row)

the four classes. You can see from this brief discussion that assumptions bootlegged in from our knowledge of two-dimensional spaces can bias our assumptions about such an elementary matter as the overlap of logical classes.

The first question one asks of a cross-tabulation is how much dependence it reveals between the category one belongs to in one ad hoc system and the category one belongs to in the other. Suppose there is no dependence at all: the two ad hoc systems are not only logically but also factually completely unrelated. Suppose 100 men of a tabulated population of 1,000 men belong to a given category in one ad hoc system, and 50 men belong to a certain category in the other ad hoc system. How many men would one expect to find who belonged to both categories? Clearly, 1/10 of the 50 men: but, equally clearly, 1/20 of the 100 men. Fortunately, there is no disagreement – one would expect to find five men belonging to both categories.

Contextual

Placement in a cat in this system is meaningful only within the context of the whole structure formed by the categories. A hierarchical system of social classes is an example. One is not upper class because of some intrinsic attribute but in contrast to being lower class. The actual criteria of upper class membership can change, and even become inverted in a given society over time, so that membership in the category is a matter of the context. In this simple case of two social classes one could just say membership is a relative matter, but the word context better conveys the complexity of assignment in more complex systems of categories which form structures. One example of a more complex system would be the schools and cliques in which artists are viewed as falling.

Both the generic and cross-category systems can be regarded as contextual in a primitive way.

Neighbordom is an aspect of each of these types of category systems: which categories are most akin? The answer is built into the definition of generic systems. It is usually clear in contextual systems.

Cities may be categorized in an ad hoc system by the size of their populations. In this and similar cases a measure of neighbordom is implied by the recognition in that culture of a structure of similarity among the attributes defining the categories. There is no necessary implication of a closeness perceived by the persons in the categories.

Initial cat system

Only cats which are recognized as such by their occupants are considered here.

The fundamental difficulty of a cat system is recruitment, the agreed definition of new members. There is no hidden hand available to drop a bucket of blue paint over a new person and thus define unambiguously his possession of the attribute blue and his membership in the blue cat. Instead new ties, representing the relation between sponsor and protégé, must continually be spun between people in the cats in a system, whether ad hoc or more complicated. Over time the ties between particular cats tend to become a tradition and one ends up with a network defined over the set of categories as nodes.

Wilensky has a concept of career systems as the backbone of our social structure. He describes career systems in terms of stages of advancement and thus presupposes as foundation a contextual system of categories. On the other hand, the idea of regularized paths of advancement suggests the spinning out of network ties among people in successive stages.

In a large society a catnet system tends to become perceived in a broader view as itself a category, one of an ad hoc system that grows links and evolves into a catnet system on a bigger scale. Lumpability is a simple term to use to describe the likelihood of a catnet system being lumped together as a single category in a broader system. As an example, we all repeatedly have the experience of leaving one life stage and moving on to another; as we do our previous highly refined and detailed perception of the internal social structure for the stage we have left is quickly drilled into a lumped representation as a category or stage.

Neighborhood systems

The idea of neighborhood has several connotations, all consistent with and sharpening the general idea of a catnet system evolved from an initial net. One neighborhood supplies others linked to it through some overlap in members and numerous relations between its members, and the others in turn have their neighboring neighborhoods. In the most common usage neighborhoods are residential areas spread out on the ground. Interconnections are implied by juxtaposition on a two-dimensional map. Yet we know from our own lives that the density of social relations between neighborhoods often has little to do with physical closeness.

The question is, what kind of space can best serve to map the relative closeness of a given system of neighborhoods? It is a very general question that we could also have asked about networks, except that the yes-or-no character of the relation between a pair of individuals hardly provides the basis for an elaborate discussion of

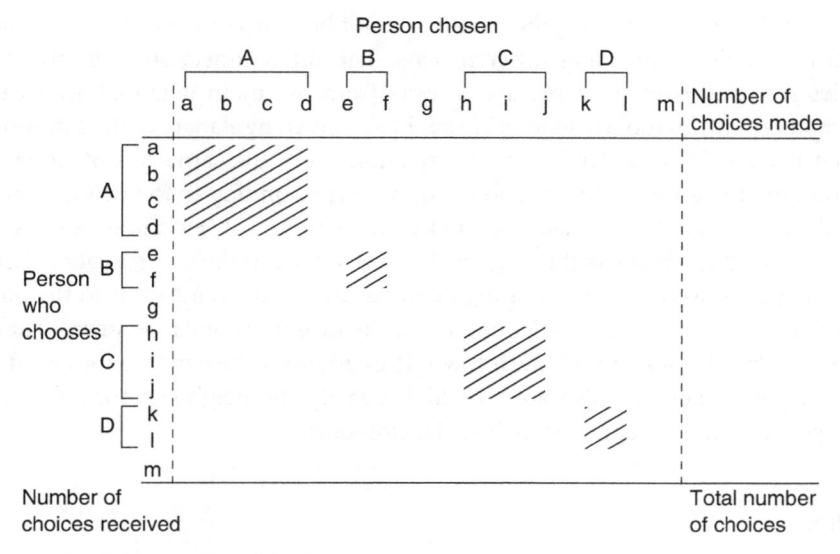

Figure 12.3 Mapping a neighborhood system.

the closeness of points on a net. Neighborhoods in one city may be best represented on a sphere with highest and lowest social status neighborhoods at the poles, and the broadest spectrum of distances between neighborhoods at the same class level being at the equator area representing the middle-class neighborhoods. In another city factors such as ethnicity, class and political views, which help set and summarize the distances among neighborhoods, may interact in such a complicated pattern that a doughnut (toroid) shape might be required for an accurate plot of neighborhoods.

The second representation of a net, as a cross-tabulation of each relation by the person making and the person receiving it, provides a basis for mapping a neighborhood system (see Figure 12.3). Let the rows for people thought to belong to each neighborhood be grouped together. Then if the columns are arranged in the same order a heavy clustering of entries in various-sized blocks along the diagonal should be apparent: Here small letters label individuals, capitals label the neighborhoods found, and the hatched areas indicate where an unusually high density of relations is found (in this case so few persons are concerned that it is hardly necessary to talk of a density of entries). In actually carrying out such a study a number of difficulties arise:

(i) Finding the best ordering of the individual rows to bring out the neighborhood clustering could take an enormous number of trials (note: $10! = 10*9*8*7*6*5*4*3*2*1$ is about 3 million, the number of ways just 10 people can be ordered).

(ii) Is it absolute or relative density of choice that should be the criterion? Suppose the individuals in a possible neighborhood make only one of the two "choices" apiece, but practically all of these choices are given to others in the small fraction of the total population. Is it a neighborhood?

The boundaries between neighborhoods will not be sharp of course: this is a catnet system with ties connecting different cats. The interconnections will appear as entries scattered over the table above away from the main diagonal. In a catnet system these entries too will tend to cluster in a few rectangular areas; the assumption is that persons in a cat tend to evolve relations with the same sets of others. By rearranging the groups of rows and columns corresponding to the neighborhoods found it is possible to make apparent the pattern of closeness among the neighborhoods, so to speak the neighborhood structure of the set of neighborhoods. If in the figure above the areas of high density are clustered adjacent to the blocks shown along the main diagonal, one can see the neighborhoods are strung out as if along a railroad track in a Western town. If in addition the extreme lower left and upper right corners are also areas of high density the neighborhoods should be arranged in a ring to represent their social closeness.

Frame

People develop culture in part to meet their needs to visualize, operate in and modify the social structure to which they belong. Some nets persist for a very long time. The pair relation on which the net is based remains stable and clearly defined. New persons are added to and leave the net, but according to clear-cut rules. In such a net it is natural for the simplest kinds of indirect relations to be "institutionalized," that is, recognized in that culture as a distinctive new kind of relation. Indeed, the rules of admission to the net regulate an indirect relation.

If the basic pair relation is any friendship, the man who is a friend of my friend may come to be defined as being in a definite relation to me, say acquaintance. Problems arise because of the enormous variety of types of indirect relations. For example, I also know of men who are friends with not just one but several friends of mine, who in turn may or may not be friends with one another. The natural step is to categorize many varieties together as a single new type of indirect relation: thus all the above types of friends at one remove can be lumped as acquaintances.

The end state of such an evolution of the cultural definition of a net is what we mean by a frame. The characteristics of a frame are:

(i) Indirect ties reckoned through at least one and possibly indefinitely many removes are grouped by a regular scheme into a smaller number of types.
(ii) Each type of indirect relation is recognized as a distinct and well-defined relation in its own right, with its own emotional quality and set of rights and duties. It is "institutionalized."
(iii) The types of indirect relations form a cumulative structure: just as the "sum" or composition of two direct relations may define a simplest type of indirect relation, so more complex types of indirect relations are regarded as the composition of simpler types.
(iv) The structure of indirect relations is a theory held in that culture. That is, it exists independent of any concrete net of relations existing in the society. In

particular, the structure is keyed to a central "person" which is really an abstract role; we call it ego. The structure is the same no matter who is assigned the role ego in a particular realization of it; a given person as ego will recognize every type of indirect relation even though no actual person in the existing population of the net is in that role to him.

(v) Since it is a theory, a frame tends to be used as an ideal type. Even in the abstract the frame may not be as fully developed and rationalized in a given culture as is implied by the preceding description. Certainly, many of the people who use it may have only a confused understanding of it. But even if it is fully developed, and fully understood by all users, the complexities and irregularities in the concrete net of relations may make it difficult to apply in a fully coherent way.

These "types" of indirect relations are categories, of course, and the frame can be seen as an extreme case of a contextual system of categories. But the frame is a floating system of categories which can be anchored on any person and applied from his point of view; in that sense it is subjective. Moreover, one type of indirect relation can be seen as the sum or composition of other types; in this sense the frame has the quality of a network as much as a category system.

Balanced net systems are also akin to frames. The latter can carry the process of cumulating indirect relations much further since they deal with a potential network of relations from the point of view of only one node in it at a time. For the same reason the frame does not deal with possible inconsistencies in the different types of relations which may coexist among a set of people; the frame is a statement about the structure of abstract types of relations, not about the combinations of different relations with ego or each other that are allowable for actual persons in the population.

A frame can be built using more than one basic type of relation. Indeed it is plausible to assert that a frame is more likely to develop when at least two distinct basic relations are present. The need for an ordering and simplification of indirect relations is more pressing then since the possible types that can result from combinations of two basic relations are much more numerous and intricate. And a culture rich enough to define two basic relations in an aspect of social life is more likely to be able to generate a frame.

Another way to search out patterns of neighbordom in an ad hoc system is through considering transitions of persons between the categories. Consider a cross-tabulation of the population in an ad hoc system by which category they are in at one time and which category they are in at a later time. There may be many more transitions between some than other pairs of categories; the relative frequency of transitions, with allowance made for the absolute sizes of categories, is a natural measure of neighbordom.

Catnets

The catnet evolves from a simpler system, either net or cat.

Chapter 13

Structural Holes [1992]

Ronald S. Burt

The Social Structure of Competition

[…]

Opportunity and Capital

A player brings at least three kinds of capital to the competitive arena. Other distinctions can be made, but three are sufficient here. First, the player has financial capital: cash in hand, reserves in the bank, investments coming due, lines of credit. Second, the player has human capital. Your natural qualities – charm, health, intelligence, and looks – combined with the skills you have acquired in formal education and job experience give you abilities to excel at certain tasks.

Third, the player has social capital: relationships with other players. You have friends, colleagues, and more general contacts through whom you receive opportunities to use your financial and human capital. I refer to opportunities in a broad sense, but I certainly mean to include the obvious examples of job promotions, participation in significant projects, influential access to important decisions, and so on. The social capital of people aggregates into the social capital of organizations. In a firm providing services – for example, advertising, brokerage, or consulting – there are people valued for their ability to deliver a quality product. Then there are "rainmakers," valued for their ability to deliver clients. Those who deliver the product do the work, and the rainmakers make it possible for all to profit from the work. The former represent the financial and human capital of the firm. The latter represent its social capital. More generally, property and human assets define the firm's production capabilities. Relations within and beyond the firm are social capital.

Distinguishing social capital

Financial and human capital are distinct in two ways from social capital. First, they are the property of individuals. They are owned in whole or in part by a single individual defined in law as capable of ownership, typically a person or corporation. Second, they concern the investment term in the market production equation. Whether held by a person or the fictive person of a firm, financial and human capital gets invested to create production capabilities. Investments in supplies, facilities, and people serve to build and operate a factory. Investments of money, time, and energy produce a skilled manager. Financial capital is needed for raw materials and production facilities. Human capital is needed to craft the raw materials into a competitive product.

Social capital is different on both counts. First, it is a thing owned jointly by the parties to a relationship. No one player has exclusive ownership rights to social capital. If you or your partner in a relationship withdraws, the connection, with whatever social capital it contained, dissolves. If a firm treats a cluster of customers poorly and they leave, the social capital represented by the firm-cluster relationship is lost. Second, social capital concerns rate of return in the market production equation. Through relations with colleagues, friends, and clients come the opportunities to transform financial and human capital into profit.

Social capital is the final arbiter of competitive success. The capital invested to bring your organization to the point of producing a superb product is as rewarding as the opportunities to sell the product at a profit. The investment to make you a skilled manager is as valuable as the opportunities – the leadership positions – you get to apply your managerial skills. The investment to make you a skilled scientist with state-of-the-art research facilities is as valuable as the opportunities – the projects – you get to apply those skills and facilities.

More accurately, social capital is as important as competition is imperfect and investment capital is abundant. Under perfect competition, social capital is a constant in the production equation. There is a single rate of return because capital moves freely from low-yield to high-yield investments until rates of return are homogeneous across alternative investments. When competition is imperfect, capital is less mobile and plays a more complex role in the production equation. There are financial, social, and legal impediments to moving cash between investments. There are impediments to reallocating human capital, both in terms of changing the people to whom you have a commitment and in terms of replacing them with new people. Rate of return depends on the relations in which capital is invested. Social capital is a critical variable. This is all the more true when financial and human capital are abundant – which in essence reduces the investment term in the production equation to an unproblematic constant.

These conditions are generic to the competitive arena, which makes social capital a factor as routinely critical as financial and human capital. Competition is never perfect. The rules of trade are ambiguous in the aggregate and everywhere negotiable in the particular. The allocation of opportunities is rarely made with respect to a single dimension of abilities needed for a task. Within an acceptable range of needed abilities, there are many people with financial and human capital comparable to your own. Whatever you bring to a production task, there are other people who could do the same job – perhaps not as well in every detail, but probably as well within the tolerances of the people for whom the job is done. Criteria other than financial and human capital are used to narrow the pool down to the individual who gets the opportunity. Those other criteria are social capital. New life is given to the proverb that says success is determined less by what you know than by whom you know. As a senior colleague once remarked (and Cole, 1992: chaps. 7–8, makes into an intriguing research program), "Publishing high-quality work is important for getting university resources, but friends are essential." Of those who are equally qualified, only a select few get the most rewarding opportunities. Of the products that are of comparably high quality, only some come to dominate their markets. The question is how.

[…]

Benefit-rich networks

A player with a network rich in information benefits has contacts: (a) established in the places where useful bits of information are likely to air, and (b) providing a reliable flow of information to and from those places.

Selecting contacts

The second criterion is as ambiguous as it is critical. It is a matter of trust, of confidence in the information passed and the care with which contacts look out for your interests. Trust is critical precisely because competition is imperfect. The question is not whether to trust, but whom to trust. In a perfectly competitive arena, you can trust the system to provide a fair return on your investments. In the imperfectly competitive arena, you have only your personal contacts. The matter comes down to a question of interpersonal debt. If I do for her, will she for me? There is no general answer. The answer lies in the match between specific people. If a contact feels that he is somehow better than you – a sexist male dealing with a woman, a racist white dealing with a black, an old-money matron dealing with an upwardly mobile ethnic – your investment in the relationship will be taken as proper obeisance to a superior. No debt is incurred. We use whatever cues can be found for a continuing evaluation of the trust in a relation, but we never know a debt is recognized until the trusted person helps us when we need it. With this kind

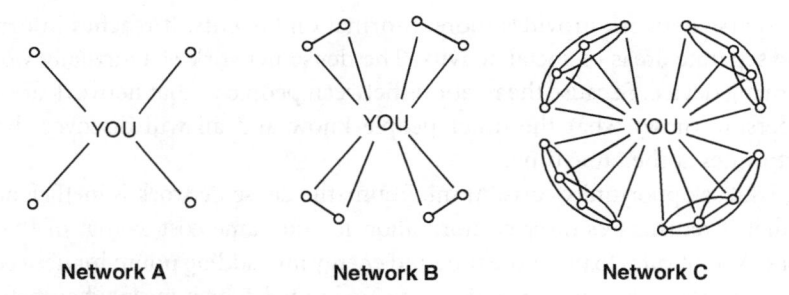

Figure 13.1 Network expansion.

of uncertainty, players are cautious about extending themselves for people whose reputation for honoring interpersonal debt is unknown. [...]

Siting contacts

[...] Everything else constant, a large, diverse network is the best guarantee of having a contact present where useful information is aired. This is not to say that benefits must increase linearly with size and diversity, a point to which I will return (Figure 13.5), but only that, other things held constant, the information benefits of a large, diverse network are more than the information benefits of a small, homogeneous network.

Size is the more familiar criterion. Bigger is better. Acting on this understanding, people can expand their networks by adding more and more contacts. They make more cold calls, affiliate with more clubs, attend more social functions. Numerous books and self-help groups can assist them in "networking" their way to success by putting them in contact with a large number of potentially useful, or helpful, or like-minded people. The process is illustrated by the networks in Figure 13.1. The four-contact network at the left expands to sixteen contacts at the right. Relations are developed with a friend of each contact in network A, doubling the contacts to eight in network B. Snowballing through friends of friends, there are sixteen contacts in network C, and so on.

Size is a mixed blessing. More contacts can mean more exposure to valuable information, more likely early exposure, and more referrals. But increasing network size without considering diversity can cripple a network in significant ways. What matters is the number of nonredundant contacts. Contacts are redundant to the extent that they lead to the same people, and so provide the same information benefits.

Consider two four-contact networks, one sparse, the other dense. There are no relations between the contacts in the sparse network, and strong relations between every contact in the dense network. Both networks cost whatever time and energy is required to maintain four relationships. The sparse network provides four nonredundant contacts, one for each relationship. No single one of the contacts gets the player to the same people reached by the other contacts. In the dense network, each relationship puts the player in contact with the same people reached through the other relationships. The dense network contains only one nonredundant contact. Any three are redundant with the fourth.

The sparse network provides more information benefits. It reaches information in four separate areas of social activity. The dense network is a virtually worthless monitoring device. Because the relations between people in that network are strong, each person knows what the other people know and all will discover the same opportunities at the same time.

The issue is opportunity costs. At minimum, the dense network is inefficient in the sense that it returns less diverse information for the same cost as that of the sparse network. A solution is to put more time and energy into adding nonredundant contacts to the dense network. But time and energy are limited, which means that inefficiency translates into opportunity costs. If I take four relationships as an illustrative limit on the number of strong relations that a player can maintain, the player in the dense network is cut off from three fourths of the information provided by the sparse network.

Structural Holes

I use the term structural hole for the separation between nonredundant contacts. Nonredundant contacts are connected by a structural hole. A structural hole is a relationship of nonredundancy between two contacts. The hole is a buffer, like an insulator in an electric circuit. As a result of the hole between them, the two contacts provide network benefits that are in some degree additive rather than overlapping.

Empirical indicators

Nonredundant contacts are disconnected in some way – either directly, in the sense that they have no direct contact with one another, or indirectly, in the sense that one has contacts that exclude the others. The respective empirical conditions that indicate a structural hole are cohesion and structural equivalence. Both conditions define holes by indicating where they are absent.

Under the cohesion criterion, two contacts are redundant to the extent that they are connected by a strong relationship. A strong relationship indicates the absence of a structural hole. Examples are father and son, brother and sister, husband and wife, close friends, people who have been partners for a long time, people who frequently get together for social occasions, and so on. You have easy access to both people if either is a contact. Redundancy by cohesion is illustrated at the top of Figure 13.2. The three contacts are connected to one another, and so provide the same network benefits. The presumption here – routine in network analysis since Festinger, Schachter, and Back's (1950) analysis of information flowing through personal relations and Homans's (1950) theory of social groups – is that the likelihood that information will move from one person to another is proportional to the strength of their relationship. Empirically, strength has two independent dimensions: frequent contact and emotional closeness (see Marsden and Hurlbert, 1988; Burt, 1990).

Structural equivalence is a useful second indicator for detecting structural holes. Two people are structurally equivalent to the extent that they have the same contacts.

Redundancy by Cohesion

Redundancy by Structural Equivalence

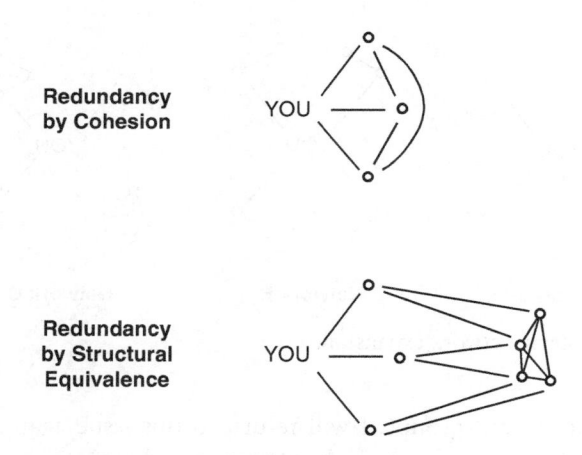

Figure 13.2 Structural indicators of redundancy.

Regardless of the relation between structurally equivalent people, they lead to the same sources of information and so are redundant. Cohesion concerns direct connection; structural equivalence concerns indirect connection by mutual contact. Redundancy by structural equivalence is illustrated at the bottom of Figure 13.2. The three contacts have no direct ties with one another. They are nonredundant by cohesion. But each leads you to the same cluster of more distant players. The information that comes to them, and the people to whom they send information, are redundant. Both networks in Figure 13.2 provide one nonredundant contact at a cost of maintaining three.

The indicators are neither absolute nor independent. Relations deemed strong are only strong relative to others. They are our strongest relations. Structural equivalence rarely reaches the extreme of complete equivalence. People are more or less structurally equivalent. In addition, the criteria are correlated. People who spend a lot of time with the same other people often get to know one another. The mutual contacts responsible for structural equivalence set a stage for the direct connection of cohesion. The empirical conditions between two players will be a messy combination of cohesion and structural equivalence, present to varying degrees, at varying levels of correlation.

Cohesion is the more certain indicator. If two people are connected with the same people in a player's network (making them redundant by structural equivalence), they can still be connected with different people beyond the network (making them nonredundant). But if they meet frequently and feel close to one another, then they are likely to communicate and probably have contacts in common. More generally, and especially for field work informed by attention to network benefits, the general guide is the definition of a structural hole. There is a structural hole between two people who provide nonredundant network benefits. If the cohesion and structural equivalence conditions are considered together, redundancy is most likely between structurally equivalent people connected by a strong relationship. Redundancy is unlikely, indicating a structural hole, between

Network A'   Network B'   Network C'

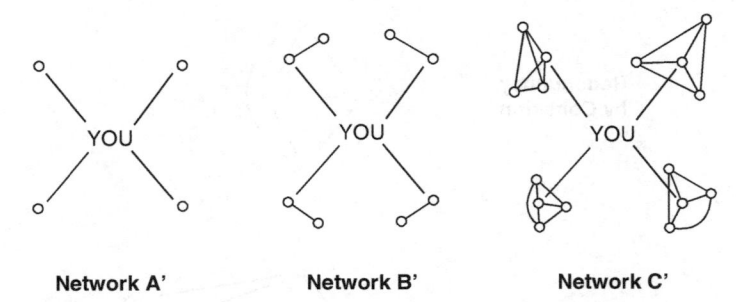

Figure 13.3 Strategic network expansion.

total strangers in distant groups. I will return to this issue again, to discuss the depth of a hole, after control benefits have been introduced.

The efficient-effective network

Balancing network size and diversity is a question of optimizing structural holes. The number of structural holes can be expected to increase with network size, but the holes are the key to information benefits. The optimized network has two design principles.

Efficiency

The first design principle of an optimized network concerns efficiency: Maximize the number of nonredundant contacts in the network to maximize the yield in structural holes per contact. Given two networks of equal size, the one with more nonredundant contacts provides more benefits. There is little gain from a new contact redundant with existing contacts. Time and energy would be better spent cultivating a new contact to unreached people. Maximizing the nonredundancy of contacts maximizes the structural holes obtained per contact.

Efficiency is illustrated by the networks in Figure 13.3. These reach the same people reached by the networks in Figure 13.1, but in a different way. What expands in Figure 13.1 is not the benefits, but the cost of maintaining the network. Network A provides four nonredundant contacts. Network B provides the same number. The information benefits provided by the initial four contacts are redundant with benefits provided by their close friends. All that has changed is the doubled number of relationships maintained in the network. The situation deteriorates even further with the sixteen contacts in network C. There are still only four nonredundant contacts in the network, but their benefits are now obtained at a cost of maintaining sixteen relationships.

With a little network surgery, the sixteen contacts can be maintained at a fourth of the cost. As illustrated in Figure 13.3, select one contact in each cluster to be a primary link to the cluster. Concentrate on maintaining the primary contact, and allow direct relationships with others in the cluster to weaken into indirect relations through the primary contact. These players reached indirectly are secondary contacts. Among the redundant contacts in a cluster, the primary contact should be the one most easily maintained and most likely to honor an interpersonal debt to you in particular. The secondary contacts are less easily maintained or less likely to work for you (even if they might work well for someone else). The critical decision obviously lies in selecting the right person to be a primary contact. The importance of trust has already been discussed. With a trustworthy primary contact, there is little loss in information benefits from the cluster and a gain in the reduced effort needed to maintain the cluster in the network.

Repeating this operation for each cluster in the network recovers effort that would otherwise be spent maintaining redundant contacts. By reinvesting that saved time and effort in developing primary contacts to new clusters, the network expands to include an exponentially larger number of contacts while expanding contact diversity. The sixteen contacts in network C of Figure 13.1, for example, are maintained at a cost of four primary contacts in network C' of Figure 13.3. Some portion of the time spent maintaining the redundant other twelve contacts can be reallocated to expanding the network to include new clusters.

Effectiveness

The second design principle of an optimized network requires a further shift in perspective: Distinguish primary from secondary contacts in order to focus resources on preserving the primary contacts. Here contacts are not people on the other end of your relations; they are ports of access to clusters of people beyond. Guided by the first principle, these ports should be nonredundant so as to reach separate, and therefore more diverse, social worlds of network benefits. Instead of maintaining relations with all contacts, the task of maintaining the total network is delegated to primary contacts. The player at the center of the network is then free to focus on properly supporting relations with primary contacts and expanding the network to include new clusters. The first principle concerns the average number of people reached with a primary contact; the second concerns the total number of people reached with all primary contacts. The first principle concerns the yield per primary contact. The second concerns the total yield of the network. More concretely, the first principle moves from the networks in Figure 13.1 to the corresponding networks in Figure 13.3. The second principle moves from left to right in Figure 13.3. The target is network C' in Figure 13.3: a network of few primary contacts, each a port of access to a cluster of many secondary contacts.

Figure 13.4 illustrates some complexities in unpacking a network to maximize structural holes. The "before" network contains five primary contacts and reaches a total of fifteen people. However, there are only two clusters of nonredundant contacts in the network. Contacts 2 and 3 are redundant in the sense of being connected with each other and reaching the same people (cohesion and structural equivalence criteria). The same is true of contacts 4 and 5. Contact 1 is not connected directly to contact 2, but he reaches the same secondary contacts; thus contacts 1 and 2 provide redundant network benefits (structural equivalence criterion). Illustrating the other

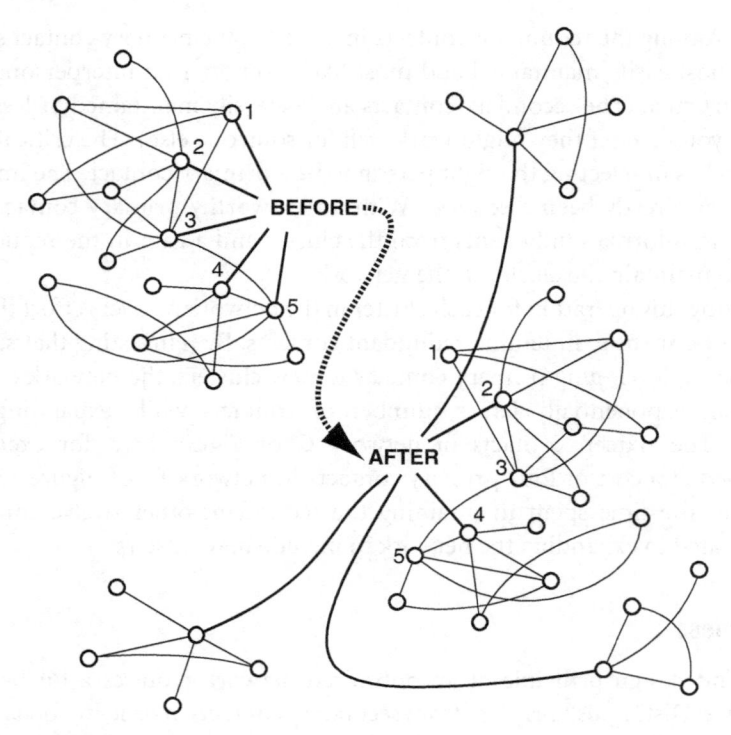

Figure 13.4 Optimizing for structural holes.

extreme, contacts 3 and 5 are connected directly, but they are nonredundant because they reach separate clusters of secondary contacts (structural equivalence criterion). In the "after" network, contact 2 is used to reach the first cluster in the "before" network and contact 4 is used to reach the second cluster. The time and energy saved by withdrawing from relations with the other three primary contacts is reallocated to primary contacts in new clusters. The "before" and "after" networks are both maintained at a cost of five primary relationships, but the "after" network is dramatically richer in structural holes, and so network benefits.

Network benefits are enhanced in several ways. There is a higher volume of benefits, because more contacts are included in the network. Beyond volume, diversity enhances the quality of benefits. Nonredundant contacts ensure exposure to diverse sources of information. Each cluster of contacts is an independent source of information. One cluster, no matter how numerous its members, is only one source of information, because people connected to one another tend to know about the same things at about the same time. The information screen provided by multiple clusters of contacts is broader, providing better assurance that you, the player, will be informed of opportunities and impending disasters. Further, because nonredundant contacts are only linked through the central player, you are assured of being the first to see new opportunities created by needs in one group that could be served by skills in another group. You become the person who first brings people together, which gives you the opportunity to coordinate their activities. These benefits are compounded by the fact that having a network that yields such benefits makes you even more attractive as a network contact to other people, thus easing your task of expanding the network to best serve your interests.

[…]

Control and the Tertius Gaudens

I have described how structural holes can determine who knows about opportunities, when they know, and who gets to participate in them. Players with a network optimized for structural holes, in addition to being exposed to more rewarding opportunities, are also more likely to secure favorable terms in the opportunities they choose to pursue. The structural holes that generate information benefits also generate control benefits, giving certain players an advantage in negotiating their relationships. To describe how this is so, I break the negotiation into structural, motivational, and outcome components (corresponding to the textbook distinction between market structure, market conduct, and market performance; for example, Caves, 1982). The social structure of the competitive arena defines opportunities, a player decides to pursue an opportunity, and is sometimes successful. I will begin with the outcome.

Tertius gaudens

Sometimes you will emerge successful from negotiation as the *tertius gaudens*. Taken from the work of Georg Simmel, the *tertius* role is useful here because it defines successful negotiation in terms of the social structure of the situation in which negotiation is successful. The role is the heart of Simmel's (1922) later analysis of the freedom an individual derives from conflicting group affiliations (see Coser, 1975, for elaboration). The *tertius gaudens* is "the third who benefits" (Simmel, 1923:154, 232). The phrase survives in an Italian proverb, *Far i due litiganti, il terzo gode* (Between two fighters, the third benefits), and, to the north, in a more jovial Dutch wording, *de lachende derde* (the laughing third). *Tertius, terzo,* or *derde*, the phrase describes an individual who profits from the disunion of others.

There are two *tertius* strategies: being the third between two or more players after the same relationship, and being the third between players in two or more relations with conflicting demands. The first, and simpler, strategy is the familiar one that occurs in economic bargaining between buyer and seller. When two or more players want to buy something, the seller can play their bids against one another to get a higher price. The strategy extends directly: a woman with multiple suitors or a professor with simultaneous offers of positions in rival institutions.

The control benefits of having a choice between players after the same relationship extends directly to choice between the simultaneous demands of players in separate relationships. The strategy can be seen between hierarchical statuses in the enterprising subordinate under the authority of two or more superiors: for example, the student who strikes her own balance between the simultaneous demands of imperious faculty advisors. The bargaining is not limited to situations of explicit competition. In some situations, emerging as the *tertius* depends on creating competition. In proposing the concept of a role-set, for example, Merton (1957:393–394) identifies this as a strategy to resolve conflicting role demands. Make simultaneous, contradictory demands explicit to the people posing them, and ask them to resolve their – now explicit – conflict. Even where it doesn't exist, competition can be produced by defining issues such that contact demands become contradictory and must be resolved before you can meet their requests. Failure is possible. You might provide too little incentive for the contacts to resolve their differences. Contacts drawn from different social strata need not perceive one another's demands as carrying equal weight. Or you might provide too much incentive. Now aware of one another, the contacts could discover sufficient reason to cooperate in forcing you to meet their mutually agreed-upon demands (Simmel, 1902:176, 180–181, calls attention to such failures). But if the strategy is successful, the pressure on you is alleviated and is replaced with an element of control over the negotiation. Merton (1957:430) states the situation succinctly: the player at the center of the network, "originally at the focus of the conflict, virtually becomes a more or less influential bystander whose function it is to highlight the conflicting demands by members of his role-set and to make it a problem for them, rather than for him, to resolve *their* contradictory demands."

The strategy holds equally well with large groups. Under the rubric "divide and rule," Simmel (1902:185–186) describes institutional mechanisms through which the Incan and Venetian governments obtained advantage by creating conflict between subjects. The same point is illustrated more richly in Barkey's (1991) comparative description of state control in early seventeenth-century France and Turkey. After establishing the similar conditions in the two states at the time, Barkey asks why peasant-noble alliances developed in France against the central state while no analogous or substitutable alliances developed in Turkey. The two empires were comparable with respect to many factors that scholars have cited to account for peasant revolt. They differed in one significant factor correlated with revolt – not in the structure of centralized state control, but in control strategy. In France, the king sent trusted representatives as agents to collect taxes and to carry out military decisions in provincial populations. These outside agents, *intendants*, affected fundamental local decisions and their intrusion was resented by the established local nobility. Local nobility formed alliances with the peasantry against the central state. In Turkey, the sultan capitalized on conflict among leaders in the provinces. When a bandit became a serious threat to the recognized governor, a deal was struck with the bandit to make him the legitimate governor. Barkey (1991:710) writes: "At its extreme, the state could render a dangerous rebel legitimate overnight by striking a bargain that ensured new sources of revenue for the rebel and momentary relief from internal warfare and, perhaps, an army or two for the state." The two empires differed in their use of structural holes. The French king, assuming he had absolute authority, ignored them. The Turkish sultan, promoting competition between alternative leaders, strategically exploited them. Conflict within the Turkish empire remained in the province, rather than being directed against the central state. As is characteristic of the control obtained via structural holes, the resulting Turkish control was more negotiated than was the absolute control exercised in France. It was also more effective.

The essential tension

There is a presumption of tension here. Control emerges from *tertius* brokering tension between other players. No tension, no *tertius*.
  […]
  The tension essential to the *tertius* is merely uncertainty. Separate the uncertainty of control from its consequences. The consequences can be life or death, in the extreme, or merely a question of embarrassment. Everyone knows you made an effort to get that job, but it went to someone else. The *tertius* strategies can be applied to control with severe consequences or to control of little consequence. What is essential is that control is uncertain, that no one can act as if he or she has absolute authority. Where there is any uncertainty about whose preferences should dominate a relationship, there is an opportunity for the *tertius* to broker the negotiation for control by playing demands against one another. There is no long-term contract that keeps a relationship strong, no legal binding that can secure the trust necessary to a productive relationship. Your network is a pulsing swirl of mixed, conflicting demands. Each contact wants your exclusive attention, your immediate response when a concern arises. All, to warrant their continued confidence in you, want to see you measure up to the values against which they judge themselves. Within this preference webwork, where no demands have absolute authority, the *tertius* negotiates for favorable terms.

The connection with information benefits

Structural holes are the setting for *tertius* strategies. Information is the substance. Accurate, ambiguous, or distorted information is moved between contacts by the *tertius*. One bidder is informed of a competitive offer in the first *tertius* strategy. A player in one relationship is informed of demands from other relationships in the second *tertius* strategy.
  The two kinds of benefits augment and depend on one another. Application of the *tertius* strategies elicits additional information from contacts interested in resolving the negotiation in favor of their own preferences. The information benefits of access, timing, and referrals enhance the application of strategy. Successful application of the *tertius* strategies involves bringing together players who are willing to negotiate, have sufficiently comparable resources to view one another's preferences as valid, but won't negotiate with one another directly to the exclusion of the *tertius*. Having access to information means being able to identify where there will be an advantage in bringing contacts together and is the key to understanding the resources and preferences being played against one another. Having that information early is

the difference between being the one who brings together contacts versus being just another person who hears about the negotiation. Referrals further enhance strategy. It is one thing to distribute information between two contacts during negotiation. It is another thing to have people close to each contact endorsing the legitimacy of the information you distribute.

[…]

Secondary Holes

[…] I have linked opportunity to structural holes, but not with respect to the whole domain of relevant holes. Thus far, a network optimized for entrepreneurial opportunity has a vine-and-cluster structure. As illustrated in Figures 13.3 and 13.4, a player has direct relations with primary contacts, each a port of access to a cluster of redundant secondary contacts. Structural holes between the primary contacts, primary structural holes, provide information and control benefits. But the benefits they provide are affected by structural holes just beyond the border of the network. Structural holes among the secondary contacts within the cluster around each primary contact play a role in the *tertius* strategies. These are secondary structural holes.

Control benefits and secondary structural holes

The ultimate threat in negotiating a relationship is withdrawal: either severing your link to a former contact's cluster or transferring the primary relationship to a new person in the cluster. This threat depends on two things. First, there must be alternatives, secondary contacts who are redundant with your primary contact and capable of replacing the primary contact in your network. Examples include an alternative spouse in the case of negotiating a conjugal relationship, an alternative job in the case of negotiating with a truculent supervisor, or an alternative supplier in the case of a firm renewing a contract with a past supplier. Second, there must be structural holes among the secondary contacts. If there are no contacts substitutable for your current primary contact, he or she is free to impose demands – up to the limit of structural holes between primary contacts. If your current primary contact is in collusion with whatever substitutes exist, which eliminates structural holes you might exploit, he or she is free to impose demands – again, up to the limit of structural holes between primary contacts.

Consider Figure 13.5. You are negotiating with a primary contact in a cluster of redundant contacts indicated by dots enclosed by a gray circle. Situation A illustrates the familiar negotiation between buyer and seller. You use the offer from one buyer to raise the other's offer.

Situation B illustrates the exact opposite condition. Here the redundant contacts are all connected by strong relations. This is the situation of negotiating with a member of a social clique or cult. In the absence of holes over which you can broker

A. Market

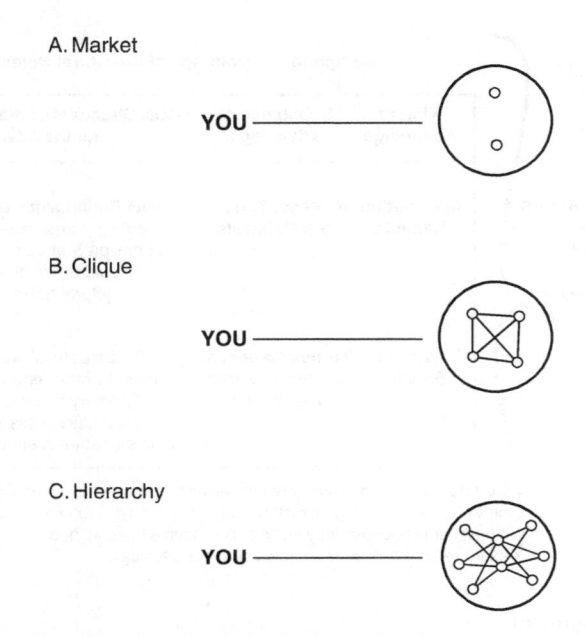

YOU ———————

B. Clique

YOU ———————

C. Hierarchy

YOU ———————

Figure 13.5 Contact clusters with and without secondary structural holes.

the connection between redundant contacts, your only recourse is to live with your contact's demands, dominate the cluster, or cut the cluster from your network.

Network density is not the issue here. Situation C is a relatively low density cluster (43% of the 28 relations within the cluster are marked with a line as strong), but contacts within the cluster are coordinated through their joint ties to two leaders in the center. It doesn't make sense to negotiate the price of a purchase in a department store by playing one sales clerk against another. They both answer to a higher authority. You have to make a purchase sufficiently large that it allows you to deal with someone higher in the organization. Then, as in Situation C, you can develop the structural hole between the two leaders at the center of the circle and play one leader against the other.

[…]

Structural Autonomy

The argument can now be summarized with a concept defining the extent to which a player's network is rich in structural holes, and thus rich in entrepreneurial opportunity, and thus rich in information and control benefits. The concept is structural autonomy and the general argument is sketched in Figure 13.6. […]

The argument began with a generic production equation. Profit equals an investment multiplied by a rate of return. The benefits of a relationship can be expressed in an analogous form: time and energy invested to reach a contact

Competitive Advantage of Structural Holes

A Question of Production ⎫
Profit = Investment · Rate of Return
A Question of Opportunity ⎭

Kind of Advantage	Substance of Advantage	Social Structural Condition Responsible for the Advantage
Information Benefits	Access, Timing and Referrals	Contact Redundancy & Structural Holes network trust, size & diversity, cohesion & structural equivalence efficient-effective networks structural holes & weak ties
Control Benefits	Tertius Gaudens, Entrepreneurial Motivation	Structural Autonomy holes & entrepreneurial opportunity primary holes & constraint secondary holes & constraint hole signature & structural autonomy

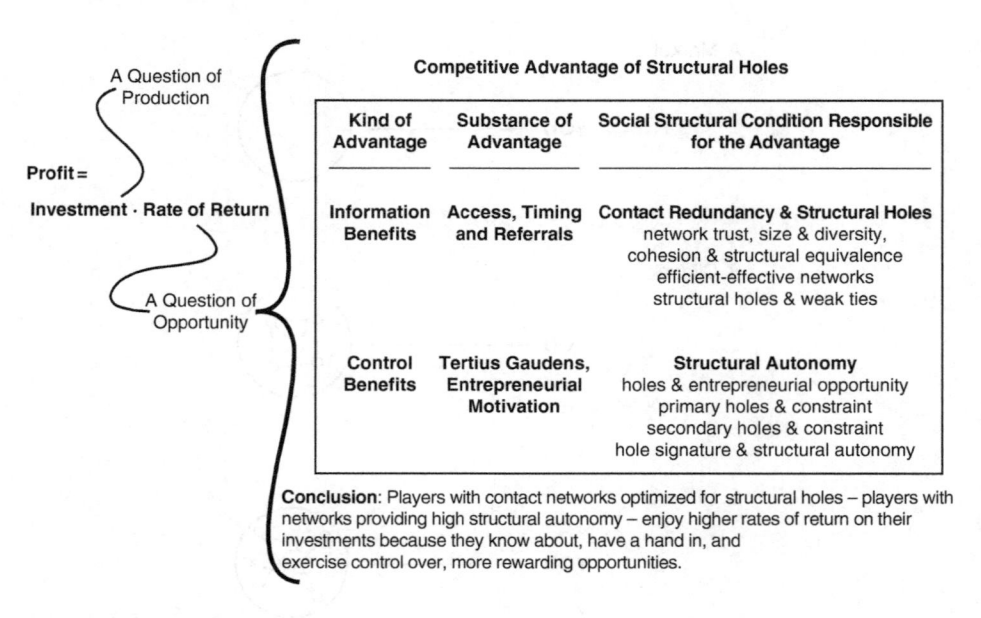

Conclusion: Players with contact networks optimized for structural holes – players with networks providing high structural autonomy – enjoy higher rates of return on their investments because they know about, have a hand in, and exercise control over, more rewarding opportunities.

Figure 13.6 Argument.

multiplied by a rate of return. A player's entrepreneurial opportunities are enhanced by a relationship to the extent that: (a) the player has invested substantial time and energy to secure a connection with the contact, and (b) there are many structural holes around the contact ensuring a high rate of return on the investment. More specifically, rate of return concerns how and whom you reach with the relationship. Time and energy invested to reach a player with more resources generates more social capital. For the sake of argument, as explained in the discussion of social capital, I assume that a player with a network optimized for structural holes can identify suitably endowed contacts. My concern is the how of a relationship, defined by the structure of a network and its connection with the social structure of the competitive arena. Thus the rate of return keyed to structural holes is a product of the extent to which there are: (a) many primary structural holes between the contact and others in the player's network, and (b) many secondary structural holes between the contact and others outside the network who could replace the contact.

There is also the issue of structural holes around the player. As the holes around contacts provide information and control benefits to the player, holes around the player can be developed by contacts for their benefit. [...] Your contacts have the option of replacing you with one of your colleagues who provides the same network benefits that you do. To manage this uncertainty, you might develop relationships with your colleagues so that it would be difficult to play them off against you (an oligopoly strategy), or you might specialize in some way so that they no longer provide network benefits redundant with your own (a differentiation strategy). [...] The point here is that your negotiating position is weaker than expected from the distribution of structural holes around contacts. Developing entrepreneurial opportunities depends on having numerous structural holes around your contacts and none attached to yourself.

These considerations come together in the concept of structural autonomy. Players with relationships free of structural holes at their own end and rich in structural holes at the other end are structurally autonomous. These are the players best positioned for the information and control benefits that a network can provide. [...] Structural autonomy summarizes the action potential of the *tertius*'s network. The budget equation for optimizing structural autonomy has an upper limit set by the time and energy of the *tertius*, and a trade-off between the structural holes a new contact provides versus the time and energy required to maintain a productive relationship with the contact.

[...]

REFERENCES

Barkey, Karen. 1991. Rebellious alliances: the state and peasant unrest in early seventeenth century France and the Ottoman empire. *American Sociological Review* 56: 699–715.

Burt, Ronald S. 1990. Kinds of relations in American discussion networks. pp. 411–451 in *Structures of Power and Constraint*, ed. C. Calhoun, M. W. Meyer, and W. R. Scott. New York: Cambridge University Press.

Caves, Richard E. 1982. *American Industry: Structure, Conduct, Performance*. Englewood Cliffs, N.J.: Prentice-Hall.

Cole, Stephen. 1992. *Making Science*. Cambridge, MA: Harvard University Press.

Coser, Rose Laub. 1975. The complexity of roles as a seedbed of individual autonomy. Pp. 237–263 in *The Idea of Social Structure*, ed. L. A. Coser. New York: Harcourt, Brace, Jovanovich.

Festinger, Leon, Stanley Schachter, and Kurt W. Back. 1950. *Social Pressures in Informal Groups*. Stanford, CA: Stanford University Press.

Homans, George C. 1950. *The Human Group*. New York: Harcourt, Brace and World.

Marsden, Peter V. and Jeanne S. Hurlbert. 1988. Social resources and mobility outcomes: application and extension. *Social Forces* 67: 1038–1059.

Merton, Robert K. (1957) 1968. Continuities in the theory of reference group behavior. pp. 335–440 in *Social Theory and Social Structure*. New York: Free Press.

Simmel, Georg. 1902. The number of members as determining the sociological form of the group, II. Trans. A. Small. *American Journal of Sociology* 8: 158–96.

Simmel, Georg. (1922) 1955. *Conflict and Web of Group Affiliations*. Trans. K. H. Wolff and R. Bendix. New York: Free Press.

Simmel, Georg. (1923) 1950. *The Sociology of Georg Simmel*. Trans. K. H. Wolff. New York: Free Press.

Part IV

Power and Inequality

Introduction to Part IV

14   The Power Elite

15   On Hegemony

16   Coercion, Capital and European States

17   Power: A Radical View

18   State, Society and Modern History

Introduction to Part IV

Power and inequality are two of the most central concepts in sociology. At the heart of any inquiry into social organization lies an examination of social stratification, the positioning of social groups and individuals within social structures that leads to unequal opportunities and constraints. Different forms of social stratification—economic, political, racial, gendered, sexual—occur within specific historical and cultural contexts. In effect, the ranking of social groups and individuals in society does not occur in random ways, but is shaped by larger, enduring structural forces.

Sociologists pay so much attention to social stratification because it has real and systematic consequences for people's social relationships and the quality of their lived experiences. Those occupying higher positions in the hierarchy existing in any particular society have greater access to the resources of that society and the ability to influence decisions in their favor. Needless to say, disadvantaged social groups and individuals lack this influence.

The roots of the concepts of power and inequality in sociology are very deep and widespread. Most of the theorists comprising the early traditions of formal sociology, notably Marx and Weber, addressed this subject. In *Classical Sociological Theory*, volume 1 of this series, for instance, we read Marx's thoughts on the structural contradictions underlying modern, capitalist societies. Elaborating his materialist theory of history, he argues that capitalism as an economic system is based on the division of society into the bourgeoisie, the owners of the means of production, and the proletariat, the owners of labor-power. The latter merely have their labor-power (ability to work) to sell in order to make a living. The success of capitalism—the accumulation of capital through increased production—then is inherently based on the exploitation of workers by capitalists. In this analysis of modern, capitalist societies, Marx goes on to suggest that capitalists, by virtue of the power they possess in the economic realm, also possess the ability to influence other social

Contemporary Sociological Theory, Third Edition. Edited by Craig Calhoun, Joseph Gerteis, James Moody, Steven Pfaff, and Indermohan Virk. Editorial material and organization © 2012 John Wiley & Sons, Ltd. Published 2012 by John Wiley & Sons, Ltd.

institutions— political, cultural, religious, etc.—in their favor. So, in addition to providing a solid theory of social class, he also offers a more general theory of power.

Max Weber (again, in volume 1) elaborates and further refines Marx's theory. In his analysis of the distribution of power and influence, he adds to the discussion of social class (market position) the concepts of status (social honor) and party (political power). In this way, he provides us with a more multidimensional analysis of power and inequality in society. According to him, while class is an important determinant of power, it is not the only one. In his writings, Weber also explicitly outlines the concept of power: non-legitimate domination (coercion) and legitimate domination (authority). Domination does not always result from economic sources; in some cases, it could be the result of legal, charismatic, or traditional factors.

Different Approaches to Study of Power and Inequality

One of the most influential approaches in the study of power and inequality in sociology has been the Marxian approach. Marx's ideas have been elaborated by others following in that tradition. Marxist sociologists in general focus on property and authority relations as the basis of people's inequitable access to power. In *Class and Class Conflict in Industrial Society* (1959), Ralf Dahrendorf argues that capitalism has undergone significant changes since the time Marx developed his theory. In "post-capitalist" societies that provide workers with opportunities to negotiate work conditions through trade unions and wider franchise, classes should be seen not so much in economic terms but as groups having differential access to authority—the "command class" and the "obey class."

Others like Eric Olin Wright, for instance, have outlined more elaborate models of class. In their view, while the position of capitalists in modern societies remains largely unchallenged, technological and structural changes have reconfigured the class composition. Wright proposes that people's positions in the labor market and their relationship to property ownership shapes their class positions. He claims that these positions are in many cases "contradictory" class positions as they don't fit neatly into any one classification, for example, managers and supervisors and small employers. In *Class Counts: Comparative Studies in Class Analysis* (1997), Wright presents a 12-class structure in modern, advanced industrial societies, in which labor market position strongly shapes people's income levels.

The Marxist perspective also laid the grounds for what has widely come to be called the conflict approach in sociology. This approach developed as a reaction against the functionalist approach (see *Classical Sociological Theory*). To recapitulate, the functionalist approach that arose in the early twentieth century assumes that people fulfill different roles in the occupational structure of any society on the basis of specific rewards and incentives. Each role fulfills a certain function in society, and the fulfillment of these different functions serves to maintain stability and consensus in society.

The conflict approach arose as a challenge to the ideas expressed by functionalism. It questions the assumption that the inequitable distribution of scarce resources in society is addressed in a harmonious fashion. On the contrary, theorists of this approach suggest that conflict is the inevitable consequence of different forms of inequality present in most societies. They would go so far as to say that it is, in fact, necessary in order to bring about social change. Dahrendorf, for instance, argues that it is utopian to think of societies without conflict. As a matter of fact, conflict is a natural outcome of social inequality; in post-capitalist societies, for instance, different classes will compete for access to authority.

Others focused more specifically on elites. Elite theorists focused on the ruling classes, specifically, those wielding political power in society. Vilfredo Pareto and Gaetano Mosca, for instance, argue, in various ways, that a small group of people holds social and political power over the masses on the basis of some personal qualities. This group makes every attempt to consolidate its power, only to be replaced by another group. In this way, there is a continual circulation of elites. Who comprises the elite will change, not the fact of elite control of power. Proposing his "iron law of oligarchy," Robert Michels suggests that all forms of social organization are likely to develop oligarchic tendencies; in other words, the accumulation of power by a small group.

Even though Marx envisioned that after a socialist revolution the abolition of private property would lead to the establishment of a classless society, the reality has proved to be otherwise. Inequality did not disappear in socialist societies (Djilas, 1957; Szelényi, 2010). Rather, a new class of officials occupied positions of power, both in socialist and postsocialist societies.

Although these approaches differ in their foci, they share in common their singular interest in the distribution of power and inequality in society.

Theorizing Power and Inequality

We have selected the work of some leading theorists of power in this section. In his work, C. Wright Mills (1916–62) focused largely on questions of social and political power. As a career sociologist, he taught at Columbia University for most of his academic life. In *White Collar* (1951), he examines the emergence of the salaried middle classes. He argues that modern corporations and the government are increasingly managed by occupational groups selected for their technical and administrative skills. Mills argues that in the highly centralized, rational society of his time, power is vested in the hands of the managerial classes. In the absence of any autonomy and creative outlet in their rational, bureaucratic jobs, white collar workers are alienated from their work and become susceptible to manipulation by their superiors.

Building on this work, Mills goes on to outline in *The Power Elite* (1956) a more elaborate description of those in power. The power elite, who tend to be a small group, occupy key bureaucratic positions in industrial societies. Mills argues that these positions tend to be in three of the most important realms—the financial, government, and military realms. While bureaucracies become larger and more centralized, the power elite become smaller and more exclusive. As a group, they share similar socioeconomic backgrounds. There is considerable fluidity between the top positions in all three realms, with people moving from corporations to the government, from the military to corporations. In this sense, power lies quite exclusively in the hands of the privileged few, who move easily between the interlocking directorates of the three most important realms of society.

Antonio Gramsci (1891–1937) comes from a different background from C. Wright Mills. An Italian thinker and activist, Gramsci was involved with the foundation of the Communist Party in Italy in 1921. His political activities led to his imprisonment from 1926 to 1937 by Mussolini's Fascist government, during which time he wrote his *Prison Notebooks* (1947). Gramsci is best known for his theory of hegemony. Gramsci proposes this concept as an explanation for the control exercised by capitalists over the working class. His concept of hegemony builds on Marx's argument that the ruling economic class also dominates the cultural and ideological realms. In Gramsci's theory, hegemony plays just as crucial a role as domination in the economic realm. It should also not be underestimated in relation to actual coercion. Hegemony is the ideological process by which the working classes consent to their own domination by the ruling class. This process occurs through the subtle diffusion of ideas supportive of the ruling classes in the institutions of civil society—education, religion, media—such that they become embedded in the everyday practices and the "common sense" of the working classes. Implanted in the common sense of the working classes in this way, hegemony obfuscates the source and power of these ideas.

In his work, Gramsci also discusses the role of intellectuals in the production of hegemonic ideologies. He believes that each class has its own set of intellectuals, and it is possible for the working class to produce its own. Its intellectuals must, however, arise organically from within its own ranks and develop their own revolutionary ideology.

Steven Lukes (1941–) is a political and social theorist who has taught at several prestigious European and North American universities, most recently at New York University. Lukes is known primarily as a scholar of Durkheim's work, but has also written about subjects such as individualism and morality. In *Power: A Radical View* ([1974] 2005), Lukes interrogates the concept of power. His main argument is that we need to pay attention to those aspects of power that are least accessible to observation. Power is inevitably value-dependent; in other words, it is related to interests that are based in normative moral and political judgments. As such, it is more veiled and more insidious.

In making this argument, Lukes sketches three types of power: 1) the one-dimensional view of power that focuses on observable behavior in decision-making in situations where subjective interests are seen through policy preferences; 2) the two-dimensional view of power that comprises a critique of the first type, proposing observation of both decision-making and non decision-making in current and potential cases; and 3) the three-dimensional view of power offered by Lukes as a critique of the behavioral model of power.

The three-dimensional view is conceptualized as a critique of the behavioral focus of the first two views, which Lukes claims tend to be too individualistic. The radical view proposed instead allows for consideration of the different ways in which potential issues are made invisible by the operation of social and institutional forces. This view makes possible the identification of latent conflicts between the interests of those exercising power and the real interests of those excluded.

In his book, *Coercion, Capital and European States, AD 990–1990* (1990), Charles Tilly discusses the role of states as powerful organizations. He defines states as organizations that have the ability to use force and coercion in the advancement of their interests. His argument is that those in control of coercive authority try to extend the range of populations and regions over which they exert power. Where they do not encounter someone with a comparable control of coercion, they conquer that territory. Where they do encounter comparable rivals, they make war. He suggests that these impulses were major factors behind state-formation in European history.

Charles Tilly (1929–2008) was a sociologist whose work was has been most closely associated with historical sociology. During his successful academic career, Tilly studied closely the social and political development of European societies from the Middle Ages to the present. He focused in particular on the nation state as a political entity.

In the reading selected here, Tilly explores the relationship between military coercion and capital in the different forms of state development in Europe. In the words of the author, "Where capital defines a realm of exploitation, coercion defines a realm of domination." State-formation took three different routes in early modern Europe: capital-intensive, coercion-intensive, and capitalized-coercion. The latter route, witnessed, notably, in England and France, dominated due to its mobilization of both capital and coercion and became the model of modern state formation.

In *Nation State and Violence* (1987), Anthony Giddens tells a related story of industrialism, capitalism, and the nation-state. Giddens (1938–), a British sociologist, has written extensively on subjects such as modernity, capitalism, and globalization. Our selection addresses some of these subjects.

Giddens argues that the state in modern societies wields an expanded ability to control the most intimate aspects of daily life. This power is exercised by administrative organizations, such as business firms, hospitals, universities, which are the repositories of the state's resources. In more class-divided traditional societies, on the other hand, power was vested in castles, manors, cities. Elites in such societies were in positions of using coercive power, including waging wars, to appropriate resources for their own benefit. While violence is not so much a part of the daily lives of citizens in modern societies, the administrative rationalization customary in such societies makes possible a thorough surveillance of its citizens. In modern societies, war is the exclusive domain of professional militaries.

The readings selected here are located within the larger sociological discourse about class, capitalism, and the state. Needless to say, they do not address specifically other sources of power and inequality, such as race, gender, ethnicity, and sexual orientation. Much theoretical and empirical work in sociology has noted in recent years the role of such identities in social stratification, often in complex interplay with more standard sociological factors, such as class, status, and political power.

SELECTED BIBLIOGRAPHY

Dahrendorf, Ralf. 1959. *Class and Class Conflict in Industrial Society*. Stanford: Stanford University Press. (One of the classics that builds on Marx's work by examining inequality in capitalist societies.)

Djilas, Milovan. 1957. *The New Class*. New York: Praeger. (A classic examination of inequality in socialist societies.)

Grusky, David. (editor, in collaboration with Manwai C. Ku and Szonja Szelényi). 2008. *Social Stratification: Class, Race, and Gender in Sociological Perspective*. 3rd edn. Boulder, CO: Westview Press. (A rigorous anthology of the literature on stratification.)

Lenski, Gerhard. 1966. *Power and Privilege*. New York: McGraw-Hill. (Another classic—an examination of the causes and consequences of inequality.)

Moore, Barrington. 1966. *Social Origins of Dictatorship and Democracy: Lord and Peasant in the Making of the Modern World*. Boston, MA: Beacon Press. (A classic examination of the conditions contributing to different political forms.)

Schumpeter, Joseph. 1951. *Imperialism and Social Classes*. New York: Augustus M. Kelley. (A powerful analysis of class.)

Szelényi, Ivan. 2010. *Essays on Socialism, Post-communism and the New Class* Beijing: Academy Press. (A collection of essays about class and power in socialist societies.)

Tilly, Charles. 1998. *Durable Inequality*. Los Angeles, CA: University of California Press. (A recent theoretical examination of the enduring causes of inequality.)

Wright, Erik Olin. 1997. *Class Counts: Comparative Studies in Class Analysis*. Cambridge: Cambridge University Press. (An empirical analysis of class, drawing on Marx's ideas.)

Chapter 14

The Power Elite [1956]

C. Wright Mills

The Higher Circles

The powers of ordinary men are circumscribed by the everyday worlds in which they live, yet even in these rounds of job, family, and neighborhood they often seem driven by forces they can neither understand nor govern. 'Great changes' are beyond their control, but affect their conduct and outlook none the less. The very framework of modern society confines them to projects not their own, but from every side, such changes now press upon the men and women of the mass society, who accordingly feel that they are without purpose in an epoch in which they are without power.

But not all men are in this sense ordinary. As the means of information and of power are centralized, some men come to occupy positions in American society from which they can look down upon, so to speak, and by their decisions mightily affect, the everyday worlds of ordinary men and women. They are not made by their jobs; they set up and break down jobs for thousands of others; they are not confined by simple family responsibilities; they can escape. They may live in many hotels and houses, but they are bound by no one community. They need not merely 'meet the demands of the day and hour'; in some part, they create these demands, and cause others to meet them. Whether or not they profess their power, their technical and political experience of it far transcends that of the underlying population. What Jacob Burckhardt said of 'great men,' most Americans might well say of their elite: 'They are all that we are not.'

C. Wright Mills, "The Power Elite," pp. 3–4, 6, 7–11, 287–9, 296 from C. Wright Mills, *The Power Elite*. Oxford: Oxford University Press, 1956. © 1956 Oxford University Press Inc. Reprinted with permission of Oxford University Press.

Contemporary Sociological Theory, Third Edition. Edited by Craig Calhoun, Joseph Gerteis, James Moody, Steven Pfaff, and Indermohan Virk. Editorial material and organization © 2012 John Wiley & Sons, Ltd. Published 2012 by John Wiley & Sons, Ltd.

The power elite is composed of men whose positions enable them to transcend the ordinary environments of ordinary men and women; they are in positions to make decisions having major consequences. Whether they do or do not make such decisions is less important than the fact that they do occupy such pivotal positions: their failure to act, their failure to make decisions, is itself an act that is often of greater consequence than the decisions they do make. For they are in command of the major hierarchies and organizations of modern society. They rule the big corporations. They run the machinery of the state and claim its prerogatives. They direct the military establishment. They occupy the strategic command posts of the social structure, in which are now centered the effective means of the power and the wealth and the celebrity which they enjoy.

The power elite are not solitary rulers. Advisers and consultants, spokesmen and opinion-makers are often the captains of their higher thought and decision. Immediately below the elite are the professional politicians of the middle levels of power, in the Congress and in the pressure groups, as well as among the new and old upper classes of town and city and region. Mingling with them, in curious ways which we shall explore, are those professional celebrities who live by being continually displayed but are never, so long as they remain celebrities, displayed enough. If such celebrities are not at the head of any dominating hierarchy, they do often have the power to distract the attention of the public or afford sensations to the masses, or, more directly, to gain the ear of those who do occupy positions of direct power. More or less unattached, as critics of morality and technicians of power, as spokesmen of God and creators of mass sensibility, such celebrities and consultants are part of the immediate scene in which the drama of the elite is enacted. But that drama itself is centered in the command posts of the major institutional hierarchies.

1

[…]

Within American society, major national power now resides in the economic, the political, and the military domains. Other institutions seem off to the side of modern history, and, on occasion, duly subordinated to these. No family is as directly powerful in national affairs as any major corporation; no church is as directly powerful in the external biographies of young men in America today as the military establishment; no college is as powerful in the shaping of momentous events as the National Security Council. Religious, educational, and family institutions are not autonomous centers of national power; on the contrary, these decentralized areas are increasingly shaped by the big three, in which developments of decisive and immediate consequence now occur.

[…]

Within each of the big three, the typical institutional unit has become enlarged, has become administrative, and, in the power of its decisions, has become centralized. Behind these developments there is a fabulous technology, for as institutions, they have incorporated this technology and guide it, even as it shapes and paces their developments.

The economy – once a great scatter of small productive units in autonomous balance – has become dominated by two or three hundred giant corporations, administratively and politically interrelated, which together hold the keys to economic decisions.

The political order, once a decentralized set of several dozen states with a weak spinal cord, has become a centralized, executive establishment which has taken up into itself many powers previously scattered, and now enters into each and every crany of the social structure.

The military order, once a slim establishment in a context of distrust fed by state militia, has become the largest and most expensive feature of government, and, although well versed in smiling public relations, now has all the grim and clumsy efficiency of a sprawling bureaucratic domain.

In each of these institutional areas, the means of power at the disposal of decision makers have increased enormously; their central executive powers have been enhanced; within each of them modern administrative routines have been elaborated and tightened up.

As each of these domains becomes enlarged and centralized, the consequences of its activities become greater, and its traffic with the others increases. The decisions of a handful of corporations bear upon military and political as well as upon economic developments around the world. The decisions of the military establishment rest upon and grievously affect political life as well as the very level of economic activity. The decisions made within the political domain determine economic activities and military programs. There is no longer, on the one hand, an economy, and, on the other hand, a political order containing a military establishment unimportant to politics and to money-making. There is a political economy linked, in a thousand ways, with military institutions and decisions. On each side of the world-split running through central Europe and around the Asiatic rimlands, there is an ever-increasing interlocking of economic, military, and political structures. If there is government intervention in the corporate economy, so is there corporate intervention in the governmental process. In the structural sense, this triangle of power is the source of the interlocking directorate that is most important for the historical structure of the present.

The fact of the interlocking is clearly revealed at each of the points of crisis of modern capitalist society – slump, war, and boom. In each, men of decision are led to an awareness of the interdependence of the major institutional orders. In the nineteenth century, when the scale of all institutions was smaller, their liberal integration was achieved in the automatic economy, by an autonomous play of market forces, and in the automatic political domain, by the bargain and the vote. It was then assumed that out of the imbalance and friction that followed the limited decisions then possible a new equilibrium would in due course emerge. That can no longer be assumed, and it is not assumed by the men at the top of each of the three dominant hierarchies.

For given the scope of their consequences, decisions – and indecisions – in any one of these ramify into the others, and hence top decisions tend either to become co-ordinated or to lead to a commanding indecision. It has not always been like this. When numerous small entrepreneurs made up the economy, for example, many of them could fail and the consequences still remain local; political and military authorities did not intervene. But now, given political expectations and military commitments, can they afford to allow key units of the private corporate economy to break down in slump? Increasingly, they do intervene in economic affairs, and as they do so, the controlling decisions in each order are inspected by agents of the other two, and economic, military, and political structures are interlocked.

At the pinnacle of each of the three enlarged and centralized domains, there have arisen those higher circles which make up the economic, the political, and the military elites. At the top of the economy, among the corporate rich, there are the chief executives; at the top of the political order, the members of the political directorate; at the top of the military establishment, the elite of soldier-statesmen clustered in and around the Joint Chiefs of Staff and the upper echelon. As each of these domains has coincided with the others, as decisions tend to become total in their consequence, the leading men in each of the three domains of power – the warlords, the corporation chieftains, the political directorate – tend to come together, to form the power elite of America.

2

The higher circles in and around these command posts are often thought of in terms of what their members possess: they have a greater share than other people of the things and experiences that are most highly valued. From this point of view, the elite are simply those who have the most of what there is to have, which is generally held to include money, power, and prestige – as well as all the ways of life to which these lead. But the elite are not simply those who have the most, for they could not 'have the most' were it not for their positions in the great institutions. For such institutions are the necessary bases of power, of wealth, and of prestige, and at the same time, the chief means of exercising power, of acquiring and retaining wealth, and of cashing in the higher claims for prestige.

By the powerful we mean, of course, those who are able to realize their will, even if others resist it. No one, accordingly, can be truly powerful unless he has access to the command of major institutions, for it is over these institutional means of power that the truly powerful are, in the first instance, powerful. Higher politicians and key officials of government command such institutional power; so do admirals and generals, and so do the major owners and executives of the larger corporations. Not all power, it is true, is anchored in and exercised by means of such institutions, but only within and through them can power be more or less continuous and important.

Wealth also is acquired and held in and through institutions. The pyramid of wealth cannot be understood merely in terms of the very rich; for the great inheriting families, as we shall see, are now supplemented by the corporate institutions of modern society: every one of the very rich families has been and is closely connected – always legally and frequently managerially as well – with one of the multi-million dollar corporations.

The modern corporation is the prime source of wealth, but, in latter-day capitalism, the political apparatus also opens and closes many avenues to wealth. The amount as well as the source of income, the power over consumer's goods as well as over productive capital, are determined by position within the political economy. If our interest in the very rich goes beyond their lavish or their miserly consumption, we must examine their relations to modern forms of corporate property as well as to the state; for such relations now determine the chances of men to secure big property and to receive high income.

Great prestige increasingly follows the major institutional units of the social structure. It is obvious that prestige depends, often quite decisively, upon access to the publicity machines that are now a central and normal feature of all the big institutions of modern America. Moreover, one feature of these hierarchies of corporation, state, and military establishment is that their top positions are increasingly interchangeable. One result of this is the accumulative nature of prestige. Claims for prestige, for example, may be initially based on military roles, then expressed in and augmented by an educational institution run by corporate executives, and cashed in, finally, in the political order, where, for General Eisenhower and those he represents, power and prestige finally meet at the very peak. Like wealth and power, prestige tends to be cumulative: the more of it you have, the more you can get. These values also tend to be translatable into one another: the wealthy find it easier than the poor to gain power; those with status find it easier than those without it to control opportunities for wealth.

If we took the one hundred most powerful men in America, the one hundred wealthiest, and the one hundred most celebrated away from the institutional positions they now occupy, away from their resources of men and women and money, away from the media of mass communication that are now focused upon them – then they would be powerless and poor and uncelebrated. For power is not of a man. Wealth does not center in the person of the wealthy. Celebrity is not inherent in any personality. To be celebrated, to be wealthy, to have power requires access to major institutions, for the institutional positions men occupy determine in large part their chances to have and to hold these valued experiences.

[...]

3

Despite their social similarity and psychological affinities, the members of the power elite do not constitute a club having a permanent membership with fixed and formal boundaries. It is of the nature of the power elite that within it there is a good deal of shifting about, and that it thus does not consist of one small set of the same men in the same positions in the same hierarchies. Because men know each other personally does not mean that among them there is a unity of policy; and because they do not know each other personally does not mean that among them there is a disunity. The conception of the power elite does not rest, as I have repeatedly said, primarily upon personal friendship.

As the requirements of the top places in each of the major hierarchies become similar, the types of men occupying these roles at the top – by selection and by training in the jobs – become similar. This is no mere deduction from structure to personnel. That it is a fact is revealed by the heavy traffic that has been going on between the three structures, often in very intricate patterns. The chief executives, the warlords, and selected politicians came into contact with one another in an intimate, working way during World War II; after that war ended, they continued their associations, out of common beliefs, social congeniality, and coinciding interests. Noticeable proportions of top men from the military, the economic, and the political worlds have during the last fifteen years occupied positions in one or both of the other worlds: between these higher circles there is an interchangeability of position, based formally upon the supposed transferability of 'executive ability,' based in substance upon the co-optation by cliques of insiders. As members of a power elite, many of those busy in this traffic have come to look upon 'the government' as an umbrella under whose authority they do their work.

As the business between the big three increases in volume and importance, so does the traffic in personnel. The very criteria for selecting men who will rise come to embody this fact. The corporate commissar, dealing with the state and its military, is wiser to choose a young man who has experienced the state and its military than one who has not. The political director, often dependent for his own political success upon corporate decisions and corporations, is also wiser to choose a man with corporate experience. Thus, by virtue of the very criterion of success, the interchange of personnel and the unity of the power elite is increased.

Given the formal similarity of the three hierarchies in which the several members of the elite spend their working lives, given the ramifications of the decisions made in each upon the others, given the coincidence of interest that prevails among them at many points, and given the administrative vacuum of the American civilian state along with its enlargement of tasks – given these trends of structure, and adding to them the psychological affinities we have noted – we should indeed be surprised were we to find that men said to be skilled in administrative contacts and full of organizing ability would fail to do more than get in touch with one another. They have, of course, done much more than that: increasingly, they assume positions in one another's domains.

The unity revealed by the interchangeability of top roles rests upon the parallel development of the top jobs in each of the big three domains. The interchange occurs most frequently at the points of their coinciding interest, as between regulatory agency and the regulated industry; contracting agency and contractor. And, as we shall see, it leads to co-ordinations that are more explicit, and even formal.

The inner core of the power elite consists, first, of those who interchange commanding roles at the top of one dominant institutional order with those in another: the admiral who is also a banker and a lawyer and who heads up an important federal commission; the corporation executive whose company was one of the two or three leading war materiel producers who is now the Secretary of Defense; the wartime general who dons civilian clothes to sit on the political directorate and then becomes a member of the board of directors of a leading economic corporation.

Although the executive who becomes a general, the general who becomes a statesman, the statesman who becomes a banker, see much more than ordinary men in their ordinary environments, still the perspectives of even such men often remain tied to their dominant locales. In their very career, however, they interchange roles within the big three and thus readily transcend the particularity of interest in any one of these institutional milieux. By their very careers and activities, they lace the three types of milieux together. They are, accordingly, the core members of the power elite.

These men are not necessarily familiar with every major arena of power. We refer to one man who moves in and between perhaps two circles – say the industrial and the military – and to another man who moves in the military and the political, and to a third who moves in the political as well as among opinion-makers. These in-between types most closely display our image of the power elite's structure and operation, even of behind-the-scenes operations. To the extent that there is any 'invisible elite,' these advisory and liaison types are its core. Even if – as I believe to be very likely – many of them are, at least in the first part of their careers, 'agents' of the various elites rather than themselves elite, it is they who are most active in organizing the several top milieux into a structure of power and maintaining it.

The inner core of the power elite also includes men of the higher legal and financial type from the great law factories and investment firms, who are almost professional go-betweens of economic, political and military affairs, and who thus act to unify the power elite. The corporation lawyer and the investment banker perform the functions of the 'go-between' effectively and powerfully. By the nature of their work, they transcend the narrower milieu of any one industry, and accordingly are in a position to speak and act for the corporate world or at least sizable sectors of it. The corporation lawyer is a key link between the economic and military and political areas; the investment banker is a key organizer and unifier of the corporate world and a person well versed in spending the huge amounts of money the American military establishment now ponders. When you get a lawyer who handles the legal work of investment bankers you get a key member of the power elite.

[…]

4

The idea of the power elite rests upon and enables us to make sense of (1) the decisive institutional trends that characterize the structure of our epoch, in particular, the military ascendancy in a privately incorporated economy, and more broadly, the several coincidences of objective interests between economic, military, and political institutions; (2) the social similarities and the psychological affinities of the men who occupy the command posts of these structures, in particular the increased interchangeability of the top positions in each of them and the increased traffic between these orders in the careers of men of power; (3) the ramifications, to the point of virtual totality, of the kind of decisions that are made at the top, and the rise to power of a set of men who, by training and bent, are professional organizers of considerable force and who are unrestrained by democratic party training.

Negatively, the formation of the power elite rests upon (1) the relegation of the professional party politician to the middle levels of power, (2) the semi-organized stalemate of the interests of sovereign localities into which the legislative function has fallen, (3) the virtually complete absence of a civil service that constitutes a politically neutral, but politically relevant, depository of brainpower and executive skill, and (4) the increased official secrecy behind which great decisions are made without benefit of public or even Congressional debate.

As a result, the political directorate, the corporate rich, and the ascendant military have come together as the power elite, and the expanded and centralized hierarchies which they head have encroached upon the old balances and have now relegated them to the middle levels of power. Now the balancing society is a conception that pertains accurately to the middle levels, and on that level the balance has become more often an affair of intrenched provincial and nationally irresponsible forces and demands than a center of power and national decision.

Chapter 15

On Hegemony [1971]

Antonio Gramsci

Relation Between Science, Religion and Common Sense

Religion and common sense cannot constitute an intellectual order, because they cannot be reduced to unity and coherence even within an individual consciousness, let alone collective consciousness. Or rather they cannot be so reduced "freely" – for this may be done by "authoritarian" means, and indeed within limits this has been done in the past.

Note the problem of religion taken not in the confessional sense but in the secular sense of a unity of faith between a conception of the world and a corresponding norm of conduct. But why call this unity of faith "religion" and not "ideology", or even frankly "politics"?[1]

Philosophy in general does not in fact exist. Various philosophies or conceptions of the world exist, and one always makes a choice between them. How is this choice made? Is it merely an intellectual event, or is it something more complex? And is it not frequently the case that there is a contradiction between one's intellectual choice and one's mode of conduct? Which therefore would be the real conception of the world: that logically affirmed as an intellectual choice? or that which emerges from the real activity of each man, which is implicit in his mode of action? And since all action is political, can one not say that the real philosophy of each man is contained in its entirety in his political action?

Antonio Gramsci, "On Hegemony," pp. 326–31, 333–5, 338–43, 348–51 from Antonio Gramsci, *Selections from the Prison Notebooks of Antonio Gramsci*, edited and translated by Quentin Hoare and Geoffrey Nowell-Smith. New York: International Publishers, 1971. Reprinted with permission of International Publishers.

Contemporary Sociological Theory, Third Edition. Edited by Craig Calhoun, Joseph Gerteis, James Moody, Steven Pfaff, and Indermohan Virk. Editorial material and organization © 2012 John Wiley & Sons, Ltd. Published 2012 by John Wiley & Sons, Ltd.

This contrast between thought and action, i.e. the co-existence of two conceptions of the world, one affirmed in words and the other displayed in effective action, is not simply a product of self-deception [*malafede*]. Self-deception can be an adequate explanation for a few individuals taken separately, or even for groups of a certain size, but it is not adequate when the contrast occurs in the life of great masses. In these cases the contrast between thought and action cannot but be the expression of profounder contrasts of a social historical order. It signifies that the social group in question may indeed have its own conception of the world, even if only embryonic; a conception which manifests itself in action, but occasionally and in flashes – when, that is, the group is acting as an organic totality. But this same group has, for reasons of submission and intellectual subordination, adopted a conception which is not its own but is borrowed from another group; and it affirms this conception verbally and believes itself to be following it, because this is the conception which it follows in "normal times"[2] – that is when its conduct is not independent and autonomous, but submissive and subordinate. Hence the reason why philosophy cannot be divorced from politics. And one can show furthermore that the choice and the criticism of a conception of the world is also a political matter.

What must next be explained is how it happens that in all periods there co-exist many systems and currents of philosophical thought, how these currents are born, how they are diffused, and why in the process of diffusion they fracture along certain lines and in certain directions. The fact of this process goes to show how necessary it is to order in a systematic, coherent and critical fashion one's own intuitions of life and the world, and to determine exactly what is to be understood by the word "systematic", so that it is not taken in the pedantic and academic sense. But this elaboration must be, and can only be, performed in the context of the history of philosophy, for it is this history which shows how thought has been elaborated over the centuries and what a collective effort has gone into the creation of our present method of thought which has subsumed and absorbed all this past history, including all its follies and mistakes. Nor should these mistakes themselves be neglected, for, although made in the past and since corrected, one cannot be sure that they will not be reproduced in the present and once again require correcting.

What is the popular image of philosophy? It can be reconstructed by looking at expressions in common usage. One of the most usual is "being philosophical about it", which, if you consider it, is not to be entirely rejected as a phrase. It is true that it contains an implicit invitation to resignation and patience, but it seems to me that the most important point is rather the invitation to people to reflect and to realise fully that whatever happens is basically rational and must be confronted as such, and that one should apply one's power of rational concentration and not let oneself be carried away by instinctive and violent impulses. These popular turns of phrase could be compared with similar expressions used by writers of a popular stamp – examples being drawn from a large dictionary – which contain the terms "philosophy" or "philosophically". One can see from these examples that the terms have a quite precise meaning: that of overcoming bestial and elemental passions through a conception of necessity which gives a conscious direction to one's activity. This is the healthy nucleus that exists in "common sense", the part of it which can be called "good sense" and which deserves to be made more unitary and coherent. So it appears that here again it is not possible to separate what is known as "scientific" philosophy from the common and popular philosophy which is only a fragmentary collection of ideas and opinions.

But at this point we reach the fundamental problem facing any conception of the world, any philosophy which has become a cultural movement, a "religion", a "faith", any that has produced a form of practical activity or will in which the philosophy is contained as an implicit theoretical "premiss". One might say "ideology" here, but on condition that the word is used in its highest sense of a conception of the world that is implicitly manifest in art, in law, in economic activity and in all manifestations of individual and collective life. This problem is that of preserving the ideological unity of the entire social bloc which that ideology serves to cement and to unify. The strength of religions, and of the Catholic church in particular, has lain, and still lies, in the fact that they feel very strongly the need for the doctrinal unity of the whole mass of the faithful and strive to ensure that the higher intellectual stratum does not get separated from the lower. The Roman church has always been the most vigorous in the struggle to prevent the "official" formation of two religions, one for the "intellectuals" and the other for the "simple souls". This struggle has not been without serious disadvantages for the Church itself, but these disadvantages are connected with the historical process which is transforming the whole of civil society and which contains overall a corrosive critique of all religion, and they only serve to emphasise the organisational capacity of the clergy in the cultural sphere and the abstractly rational and just relationship which the Church has been able to establish in its own sphere between the intellectuals and the simple. The Jesuits have undoubtedly been the major architects of this equilibrium, and in order to preserve it they have given the Church a progressive forward movement which has tended to allow the demands of science and philosophy to be to a certain extent satisfied. But the rhythm of the movement has been so slow and methodical that the changes have passed unobserved by the mass of the simple, although they appear "revolutionary" and demagogic to the "integralists".

One of the greatest weaknesses of immanentist[3] philosophies in general consists precisely in the fact that they have not been able to create an ideological unity between the bottom and the top, between the "simple" and the intellectuals. In the history of Western civilisation the fact is exemplified on a European scale, with the rapid collapse of the Renaissance and to a certain extent also the Reformation faced with the Roman church. Their weakness is demonstrated in the educational field, in that the immanentist philosophies have not even attempted to construct a conception which could take the place of religion in the education of children. Hence the pseudo-historicist sophism whereby non-religious, non-confessional, and in reality atheist, educationalists justify allowing the teaching of religion on the grounds that religion is the philosophy of the infancy of mankind renewed in every non-metaphorical infancy. Idealism has also shown itself opposed to cultural movements which "go out to the people", as happened with the so-called "Popular

Universities"⁴ and similar institutions. Nor was the objection solely to the worst aspects of the institutions, because in that case they could simply have tried to improve them. And yet these movements were worthy of attention, and deserved study. They enjoyed a certain success, in the sense that they demonstrated on the part of the "simple" a genuine enthusiasm and a strong determination to attain a higher cultural level and a higher conception of the world. What was lacking, however, was any organic quality either of philosophical thought or of organisational stability and central cultural direction. One got the impression that it was all rather like the first contacts of English merchants and the negroes of Africa: trashy baubles were handed out in exchange for nuggets of gold. In any case one could only have had cultural stability and an organic quality of thought if there had existed the same unity between the intellectuals and the simple as there should be between theory and practice. That is, if the intellectuals had been organically the intellectuals of those masses, and if they had worked out and made coherent the principles and the problems raised by the masses in their practical activity, thus constituting a cultural and social bloc. The question posed here was the one we have already referred to, namely this: is a philosophical movement properly so called when it is devoted to creating a specialised culture among restricted intellectual groups, or rather when, and only when, in the process of elaborating a form of thought superior to "common sense" and coherent on a scientific plane, it never forgets to remain in contact with the "simple" and indeed finds in this contact the source of the problems it sets out to study and to resolve? Only by this contact does a philosophy become "historical", purify itself of intellectualistic elements of an individual character and become "life".[5]

   A philosophy of praxis[6] cannot but present itself at the outset in a polemical and critical guise, as superseding the existing mode of thinking and existing concrete thought (the existing cultural world). First of all, therefore, it must be a criticism of "common sense", basing itself initially, however, on common sense in order to demonstrate that "everyone" is a philosopher and that it is not a question of introducing from scratch a scientific form of thought into everyone's individual life, but of renovating and making "critical" an already existing activity. It must then be a criticism of the philosophy of the intellectuals out of which the history of philosophy developed and which, in so far as it is a phenomenon of individuals (in fact it develops essentially in the activity of single particularly gifted individuals) can be considered as marking the "high points" of the progress made by common sense, or at least the common sense of the more educated strata of society but through them also of the people. Thus an introduction to the study of philosophy must expound in synthetic form the problems that have grown up in the process of the development of culture as a whole and which are only partially reflected in the history of philosophy. (Nevertheless it is the history of philosophy which, in the absence of a history of common sense, impossible to reconstruct for lack of documentary material, must remain the main source of reference.) The purpose of the synthesis must be to criticise the problems, to demonstrate their real value, if any, and the significance they have had as superseded links of an intellectual chain, and to determine what the new contemporary problems are and how the old problems should now be analysed.

[…]

The active man-in-the-mass has a practical activity, but has no clear theoretical consciousness of his practical activity, which nonetheless involves understanding the world in so far as it transforms it.[7] His theoretical consciousness can indeed be historically in opposition to his activity. One might almost say that he has two theoretical consciousnesses (or one contradictory consciousness): one which is implicit in his activity and which in reality unites him with all his fellow-workers in the practical transformation of the real world; and one, superficially explicit or verbal, which he has inherited from the past and uncritically absorbed. But this verbal conception is not without consequences. It holds together a specific social group, it influences moral conduct and the direction of will, with varying efficacity but often powerfully enough to produce a situation in which the contradictory state of consciousness does not permit of any action, any decision or any choice, and produces a condition of moral and political passivity. Critical understanding of self takes place therefore through a struggle of political "hegemonies" and of opposing directions, first in the ethical field and then in that of politics proper, in order to arrive at the working out at a higher level of one's own conception of reality. Consciousness of being part of a particular hegemonic force (that is to say, political consciousness) is the first stage towards a further progressive self-consciousness in which theory and practice will finally be one. Thus the unity of theory and practice is not just a matter of mechanical fact, but a part of the historical process, whose elementary and primitive phase is to be found in the sense of being "different" and "apart", in an instinctive feeling of independence, and which progresses to the level of real possession of a single and coherent conception of the world. This is why it must be stressed that the political development of the concept of hegemony represents a great philosophical advance as well as a politico-practical one.[8] For it necessarily supposes an intellectual unity and an ethic in conformity with a conception of reality that has gone beyond common sense and has become, if only within narrow limits, a critical conception.

However, in the most recent developments of the philosophy of praxis the exploration and refinement of the concept of the unity of theory and practice is still only at an early stage. There still remain residues of mechanism, since people speak about theory as a "complement" or an "accessory" of practice, or as the handmaid of practice.[9] It would seem right for this question too to be considered historically, as an aspect of the political question of the intellectuals. Critical self-consciousness means, historically and politically, the creation of an *élite*[10] of intellectuals. A human mass does not "distinguish" itself, does not become independent in its own right without, in the widest sense, organising itself; and there is no organisation without intellectuals, that is without organisers and leaders, in other words, without the theoretical aspect of the theory-practice nexus being distinguished concretely by the existence of a group of people "specialised" in conceptual and philosophical elaboration of ideas. But the process of creating intellectuals is long, difficult, full of contradictions, advances and retreats, dispersals and regroupings, in which the loyalty of the masses is often sorely tried. (And one must not forget that at this early stage loyalty and discipline are the ways in which the masses participate and collaborate in the development of the cultural movement as a whole.)

The process of development is tied to a dialectic between the intellectuals and the masses. The intellectual stratum develops both quantitatively and qualitatively, but every leap forward towards a new breadth and complexity of the intellectual stratum is tied to an analogous movement on the part of the mass of the "simple", who raise themselves to higher levels of culture and at the same time extend their circle of influence towards the stratum of specialised intellectuals, producing outstanding individuals and groups of greater or less importance. In the process, however, there continually recur moments in which a gap develops between the mass and the intellectuals (at any rate between some of them, or a group of them), a loss of contact, and thus the impression that theory is an "accessory", a "complement" and something subordinate. Insistence on the practical element of the theory-practice nexus, after having not only distinguished but separated and split the two elements (an operation which in itself is merely mechanical and conventional), means that one is going through a relatively primitive historical phase, one which is still economic-corporate, in which the general "structural" framework is being quantitatively transformed and the appropriate quality-superstructure is in the process of emerging, but is not yet organically formed. One should stress the importance and significance which, in the modern world, political parties have in the elaboration and diffusion of conceptions of the world, because essentially what they do is to work out the ethics and the politics corresponding to these conceptions and act as it were as their historical "laboratory". The parties recruit individuals out of the working mass, and the selection is made on practical and theoretical criteria at the same time. The relation between theory and practice becomes even closer the more the conception is vitally and radically innovatory and opposed to old ways of thinking. For this reason one can say that the parties are the elaborators of new integral and totalitarian intelligentsias[11] and the crucibles where the unification of theory and practice, understood as a real historical process, takes place. It is clear from this that the parties should be formed by individual memberships and not on the pattern of the British Labour Party, because, if it is a question of providing an organic leadership for the entire economically active mass, this leadership should not follow old schemas but should innovate. But innovation cannot come from the mass, at least at the beginning, except through the mediation of an *élite* for whom the conception implicit in human activity has already become to a certain degree a coherent and systematic ever-present awareness and a precise and decisive will.

[...]

What are the influential factors in the process of diffusion (which is also one of a substitution of the old conception, and, very often, of combining old and new), how do they act, and to what extent? Is it the rational form in which the new conception is expounded and presented? Or is it the authority (in so far as this is recognised and appreciated, if only generically) of the expositor and the thinkers and experts whom the expositor calls in in his support? Or the fact of belonging to the same organisation as the man who upholds the new conception (assuming, that is, that one has entered the organisation for other reasons than that of already sharing the new conception)?

In reality these elements will vary according to social groups and the cultural level of the groups in question. But the enquiry has a particular interest in relation to the popular masses, who are slower to change their conceptions, or who never change them in the sense of accepting them in their "pure" form, but always and only as a more or less heterogeneous and bizarre combination. The rational and logically coherent form, the exhaustive reasoning which neglects no argument, positive or negative, of any significance, has a certain importance, but is far from being decisive. It can be decisive, but in a secondary way, when the person in question is already in a state of intellectual crisis, wavering between the old and the new, when he has lost his faith in the old and has not yet come down in favour of the new, etc.

One could say this about the authority of thinkers and experts: it is very important among the people, but the fact remains that every conception has its thinkers and experts to put forward, and authority does not belong to one side; further, with every thinker it is possible to make distinctions, to cast doubt on whether he really said such and such a thing, etc.

One can conclude that the process of diffusion of new conceptions takes place for political (that is, in the last analysis, social) reasons; but that the formal element, that of logical coherence, the element of authority and the organisational element have a very important function in this process immediately after the general orientation has been reached, whether by single individuals or groups of a certain size. From this we must conclude, however, that in the masses *as such*, philosophy can only be experienced as a faith.

Imagine the intellectual position of the man of the people: he has formed his own opinions, convictions, criteria of discrimination, standards of conduct. Anyone with a superior intellectual formation with a point of view opposed to his can put forward arguments better than he and really tear him to pieces logically and so on. But should the man of the people change his opinions just because of this? Just because he cannot impose himself in a bout of argument? In that case he might find himself having to change every day, or every time he meets an ideological adversary who is his intellectual superior. On what elements, therefore, can his philosophy be founded? and in particular his philosophy in the form which has the greatest importance for his standards of conduct?

The most important element is undoubtedly one whose character is determined not by reason but by faith. But faith in whom, or in what? In particular in the social group to which he belongs, in so far as in a diffuse way it thinks as he does. The man of the people thinks that so many like-thinking people can't be wrong, not so radically, as the man he is arguing against would like him to believe; he thinks that, while he himself, admittedly, is not able to uphold and develop his arguments as well as the opponent, in his group there is someone who could do this and could certainly argue better than the particular man he has against him; and he remembers, indeed, hearing expounded, discursively, coherently, in a way that left him convinced, the reasons behind his faith. He has no concrete memory of the reasons and could not repeat them, but he knows that reasons exist, because he has heard them expounded, and was convinced by them. The fact of having once suddenly seen the light and been convinced is the permanent reason for his reasons persisting, even if the arguments in its favour cannot be readily produced.

These considerations lead, however, to the conclusion that new conceptions have an extremely unstable position among the popular classes; particularly when they are in contrast with orthodox convictions (which can themselves be new) conforming socially to the general interests of the ruling classes. This can be seen if one considers the fortunes of religions and churches. Religion, or a particular church, maintains its community of faithful (within the limits imposed by the necessities of general historical development in so far as it nourishes its faith permanently and in an organised fashion, indefatigably repeating its apologetics, struggling at all times and always with the same kind of arguments, and maintaining a hierarchy of intellectuals who give to the faith, in appearance atleast, the dignity of thought. Whenever the continuity of relations between the Church and the faithful has been violently interrupted for political reasons, as happened during the French Revolution the losses suffered by the Church have been incalculable. If the conditions had persisted for a long time in which it was difficult to carry on practising one's own religion, it is quite possible that these losses would have been definitive, and a new religion would have emerged, as indeed one did emerge in France in combination with the old Catholicism. Specific necessities can be deduced from this for any cultural movement which aimed to replace common sense and old conceptions of the world in general:

1. Never to tire of repeating its own arguments (though offering literary variation of form): repetition is the best didactic means for working on the popular mentality.

2. To work incessantly to raise the intellectual level of ever-growing strata of the populace, in other words, to give a personality to the amorphous mass element. This means working to produce *élites* of intellectuals of a new type which arise directly out of the masses, but remain in contact with them to become, as it were, the whalebone in the corset.[12]

This second necessity, if satisfied, is what really modifies the "ideological panorama" of the age. But these *élites* cannot be formed or developed without a hierarchy of authority and intellectual competence growing up within them. The culmination of this process can be a great individual philosopher. But he must be capable of re-living concretely the demands of the massive ideological community and of understanding that this cannot have the flexibility of movement proper to an individual brain, and must succeed in giving formal elaboration to the collective doctrine in the most relevant fashion, and the one most suited to the modes of thought of a collective thinker.

It is evident that this kind of mass creation cannot just happen "arbitrarily", around any ideology, simply because of the formally constructive will of a personality or a group which puts it foward solely on the basis of its own fanatical philosophical or religious convictions. Mass adhesion or non-adhesion to an ideology is the real critical test of the rationality and historicity of modes of thinking. Any arbitrary constructions are pretty rapidly eliminated by historical competition, even if sometimes, through a combination of immediately favourable circumstances, they manage to enjoy popularity of a kind; whereas constructions which respond to the demands of a complex organic period of history always impose themselves and prevail in the end, even though they may pass through several intermediary phases during which they manage to affirm themselves only in more or less bizarre and heterogeneous combinations.

These developments pose many problems, the most important of which can be subsumed in the form and the quality of the relations between the various intellectually qualified strata; that is, the importance and the function which the creative contribution of superior groups must and can have in connection with the organic capacity of the intellectually subordinate strata to discuss and develop new critical concepts. It is a question, in other words, of fixing the limits of freedom of discussion and propaganda, a freedom which should not be conceived of in the administrative and police sense, but in the sense of a self-limitation which the leaders impose on their own activity, or, more strictly, in the sense of fixing the direction of cultural policy. In other words – who is to fix the "rights of knowledge" and the limits of the pursuit of knowledge? And can these rights and limits indeed be fixed? It seems necessary to leave the task of researching after new truths and better, more coherent, clearer formulations of the truths themselves to the free initiative of individual specialists, even though they may continually question the very principles that seem most essential. And it will in any case not be difficult to expose the fact whenever such proposals for discussion arise because of interested and not scientific motives. Nor is it inconceivable that individual initiatives should be disciplined and subject to an ordered procedure, so that they have to pass through the sieve of academies or cultural institutes of various kinds and only become public after undergoing a process of selection.

It would be interesting to study concretely the forms of cultural organisation which keep the ideological world in movement within a given country, and to examine how they function in practice. A study of the numerical relationship between the section of the population professionally engaged in active cultural work in the country in question and the population as a whole, would also be useful, together with an approximate calculation of the unattached forces. The school, at all levels, and the Church, are the biggest cultural organisations in every country, in terms of the number of people they employ. Then there are newspapers, magazines and the book trade and private educational institutions, either those which are complementary to the state system, or cultural institutions like the Popular Universities. Other professions include among their specialised activities a fair proportion of cultural activity. For example, doctors, army officers, the legal profession. But it should be noted that in all countries, though in differing degrees, there is a great gap between the popular masses and the intellectual groups, even the largest ones, and those nearest to the peripheries of national life, like priests and school teachers. The reason for this is that, however much the ruling class may affirm to the contrary, the State, as such, does not have a unitary, coherent and homogeneous conception, with the result that intellectual groups are scattered between one stratum and the next, or even within a single stratum. The Universities, except in a few countries, do not exercise any unifying influence: often an independent thinker he has more influence than the whole of university institutions, etc.

With regard to the historical role played by the fatalistic conception of the philosophy of praxis one might perhaps prepare a funeral oration, emphasising its usefulness for a certain period of history, but precisely for this reason underlining the need to buy it with all due honours. Its role could really be compared with that of the theory of predestination and grace for the beginnings of the modern world, a theory which found its culmination in classical German philosophy and in its conception of freedom as the consciousness of necessity. It has been a replacement in the popular consciousness for the cry of "'tis God's will", although even on this primitive, elementary plane it was the beginnings of a new modern and fertile conception than that contained in the expression "'tis God's will" or in the theory of grace. Is it possible that a "formally" new conception can present itself in a guise other than the crude, unsophisticated version of the populace? And yet the historian, with the benefit of all necessary perspective, manages to establish and to understand the fact that the beginnings of a new world, rough and jagged though they always are, are better than the passing away of the world in its death-throes and the swansong that it produces.[13]

[...]

"Language", Languages and Common Sense

In what exactly does the merit of what is normally termed "common sense" or "good sense" consist? Not just in the fact that, if only implicitly, common sense applies the principle of causality, but in the much more limited fact that in a whole range of judgments common sense identifies the exact cause, simple and to hand, and does not let itself be distracted by fancy quibbles and pseudo-profound, pseudo-scientific metaphysical mumbo-jumbo. It was natural that "common sense" should have been exalted in the seventeenth and eighteenth centuries, when there was a reaction against the principle of authority represented by Aristotle and the Bible. It was discovered indeed that in "common sense" there was a certain measure of "experimentalism" and direct observation of reality, though empirical and limited. Even today, when a similar state of affairs exists, we find the same favourable judgment on common sense, although the situation has in fact changed and the "common sense" of today has a much more limited intrinsic merit.

We have established that philosophy is a conception of the world and that philosophical activity is not to be conceived solely as the "individual" elaboration of systematically coherent concepts, but also and above all as a cultural battle to transform the popular "mentality" and to diffuse the philosophical innovations which will demonstrate themselves to be "historically true" to the extent that they become concretely – i.e. historically and socially – universal. Given all this, the question of language in general and of languages in the technical sense[15] must be put in the forefront of our enquiry. What the pragmatists[16] wrote about this question merits re-examination.

In the case of the pragmatists, as generally with any attempt to systematise philosophy in an organic fashion, it is not made clear whether the reference is to the system in its entirety or just to its essential nucleus. It seems to me safe to say that the conception of language held by Vailati and other pragmatists is not acceptable. But it also seems that they felt real needs and "described" them with an exactness that was not far off the mark, even if they did not succeed in posing the problems fully or in providing a solution. It seems that one can say that "language" is essentially a collective term which does not presuppose any single thing existing in time and space. Language also means culture and philosophy (if only at the level of common sense) and therefore the fact of "language" is in reality a multiplicity of facts more or less organically coherent and co-ordinated. At the limit it could be said that every speaking being has a personal language of his own, that is his own particular way of thinking and feeling. Culture, at its various levels, unifies in a series of strata, to the extent that they come into contact with each other, a greater or lesser number of individuals who understand each other's mode of expression in differing degrees, etc. It is these historico-social distinctions and differences which are reflected in common language and produce those "obstacles" and "sources of error" which the pragmatists have talked about.

From this one can deduce the importance of the "cultural aspect", even in practical (collective) activity. An historical act can only be performed by "collective man", and this presupposes the attainment of a "cultural-social" unity through which a multiplicity of dispersed wills, with heterogeneous aims, are welded together with a single aim, on the basis of an equal and common conception of the world, both general and particular, operating in transitory bursts (in emotional ways) or permanently (where the intellectual base is so well rooted, assimilated and experienced that it becomes passion.[17] Since this is the way things happen, great importance is assumed by the general question of language, that is, the question of collectively attaining a single cultural "climate".

This problem can and must be related to the modern way of considering educational doctrine and practice, according to which the relationship between teacher and pupil is active and reciprocal so that every teacher is always a pupil and every pupil a teacher.[18] But the educational relationship should not be restricted to the field of the strictly "scholastic" relationships by means of which the new generation comes into contact with the old and absorbs its experiences and its historically necessary values and "matures" and develops a personality of its own which is historically and culturally superior. This form of relationship exists throughout society as a whole and for every individual relative to other individuals. It exists between intellectual and non-intellectual sections of the population, between the rulers and the ruled, *élites* and their followers, leaders [*dirigenti*] and led, the vanguard and the body of the army. Every relationship of "hegemony" is necessarily an educational relationship and occurs not only within a nation, between the various forces of which the nation is composed, but in the international and world-wide field, between complexes of national and continental civilisations.

One could say therefore that the historical personality of an individual philosopher is also given by the active relationship which exists between him and the cultural environment he is proposing to modify. The environment reacts back on the philosopher and imposes on him a continual process of self-criticism. It is his "teacher". This is why one of the most important demands that the modern intelligentsias have made in the political field has been that of the so-called "freedom of thought and of the expression of thought" ("freedom of the press", "freedom of association"). For the relationship between master and disciple in the general sense referred to above is only realised where this political condition exists, and only then do we get the "historical" realisation of a new type of philosopher, whom we could call a "democratic philosopher" in the sense that he is a philosopher convinced that his personality is not limited to himself as a physical individual but is an active social relationship of modification of the cultural environment. When the "thinker" is content with his own thought, when he is "subjectively", that is abstractly, free, that is when he nowadays becomes a joke. The unity of science and life is precisely an active unity, in which alone liberty of thought can be realised; it is a master-pupil relationship, one between the philosopher and the cultural environment in which he has to work and from which he can draw the necessary problems for formulation and resolution. In other words, it is the relationship between philosophy and history.

[...]

NOTES

1 [...] By "politics" Gramsci means conscious action (praxis) in pursuit of a common social goal.
2 "normal times": as opposed to the exceptional (and hence potentially revolutionary) moments in history in which a class or group discovers its objective and subjective unity in action.
3 By "immanentist philosophies" Gramsci normally means Italian idealism of the beginning of the century (Croce, Gentile, etc.), one of whose features was its rejection of Catholic transcendentalism; but he uses the term here also to characterise much of the philosophical thought of, for example, the Renaissance, which was in a similar way hermetic and incapable of extending its influence beyond elite circles. It should be noted however that Gramsci also describes the philosophy of praxis as in a different sense "immanentist", in that it offers the most consistent rejection of any form of transcendence.
4 "Popular Universities" – *Università Popolari*. Independent institutes of adult education, more or less equivalent in scope, though not in extension, to the English W.E.A.
5 Perhaps it is useful to make a "practical" distinction between philosophy and common sense in order to indicate more clearly the passage from one moment to the other. In philosophy the features of individual elaboration of thought are the most salient: in

common sense on the other hand it is the diffuse, unco-ordinate features of a generic form of thought common to a particular period and a particular popular environment. But every philosophy has a tendency to because the common sense of a fairly limited environment (that of all the intellectuals). It is a matter therefore of starting with a philosophy which already enjoys, or could enjoy, a certain diffusion, because it is connected to and implicit in practical life, and elaborating it so that it becomes a renewed common sense possessing the coherence and the sinew of individual philosophies. But this can only happen if the demands of cultural contact with the "simple" are continually felt.

6 "philosophy of praxis."
7 A reference to the 11th of Marx's *Theses on Feuerbach*, which Gramsci interprets as meaning that philosophy (and, in particular, the philosophy of praxis) is a socio-practical activity, in which thought and action are reciprocally determined.
8 The reference here is not only to Marx's argument about "ideas becoming a material force", but also to Lenin and the achievement of proletarian hegemony through the Soviet revolution [. . .].
9 The notion of the subservience of theory to practice, neatly summed up in this adaptation of the mediaeval adage *philosophia ancilla theologiae* (philosophy the handmaid of theology) has been widespread in the Marxist movement, in forms as diverse as Stalin's formulation "theory must serve practice" (Works, Vol. VI p. 88) and Rosa Luxemburg's argument (in *Stillstand und Fortschritt im Marxismus*) that theory only develops to the extent that the need for it is created by the practice of the movement.
10 "*élite*." As is made clear later in the text, Gramsci uses this word (in French in the original) in a sense very different from that of the reactionary post-Pareto theorists of "political *élites*". The *élite* in Gramsci is the revolutionary vanguard of a social class in constant contact with its political and intellectual base.
11 "*intellettualità totalitarie*." It seems certain that *intellettualità* here is a concrete noun meaning "intelligentsia" rather than the abstract "intellectual conception". "Totalitarian" is to be understood not in its modern sense, but as meaning simultaneously "unified" and "all-absorbing".
12 For Gramsci's theory of the "organic" intellectuals see the essay "The Formation of the Intellectuals", pp. 5–14. [in the original]
13 The fading away of "fatalism" and "mechanicism" marks a great historical turning-point: hence the great impression of Mirsky's résumé. Memories that it has raised: I remember in Florence in November 1917, a discussion with Mario Trozzi, and the first mention of Bergsonism, voluntarism, etc.[14] One could make a semi-serious sketch of how this conception presented itself in reality. I also remember a discussion with Professor Presutti in Rome in June 1924. Comparison with Capt. Giulietti made by G. M. Serrati, which was for him decisive and conferred a death sentence. For Serrati, Giulietti was like the Confucian to the Taoist, like the southern Chinese, the busy and active merchant, in the eyes of the mandarin scholar from the North, who looks down with the supreme contempt of the enlightened sage for whom life holds no more mysteries, on the southern mannikins who hope, with their busy, ant-like movements, to capture "the way". Speech by Claudio Treves on expiation. This speech had something of the spirit of an Old Testament prophet. Those who had wanted and had made the war, who had torn the world from its hinges and were therefore responsible for post-war disorder, had to expiate their sins and bear the responsibility for the disorder; they were guilty of "voluntarism" and had to be punished for their sin, etc.

There was a certain priestly grandeur about this speech, a crescendo of maledictions which should have petrified us with terror but were instead a great consolation, because they showed that the undertaker was not yet ready and that Lazarus could still rise again.

14   The meeting in question took place between various leaders and adherents of the "intransigent" current of the Socialist Party on the night of 18 November 1917. It was mainly concerned with preparing a document criticising the reformist wing of the Party for its attitude to the war. In the course of the discussion Trozzi appears to have taken Gramsci to task for Bergsonian voluntarism. That Gramsci's views at the time were decidedly unorthodox by the standards of the Second International, is shown by his famous article saluting the Soviet revolution, *La Rivoluzione contro il 'Capitale'*, published in *Avanti!* a week after the meeting with Trozzi and others, which was subsequently widely criticised for apparently counterposing "Leninist" revolutionism to "Marxist" passivity and determinism. Gramsci, in fact, as he makes clear here in the *Quaderni*, did not know Bergson's writing at the time. Bergson had, however, influenced Sorel, who in turn had influenced Gramsci in an early period. The result of Trozzi's charge was to lead Gramsci to a re-examination and criticism of idealistic and Bergsonian influences in Sorel's work.

15   The English word language does the work of two Italian words here: *lingua* ("languages in the technical sense"), meaning a particular system of verbal signs, as it were the English or Italian language; and *linguaggio* ("language in general"), in the generic sense of the faculty to transmit messages, verbal or otherwise, by means of a common code. In modern linguistics (and Gramsci studied linguistics at the very beginning of the modern period) *lingua* ("la langue") usually means the code, and *linguaggio* ("le langage"), besides its generic sense, also refers to the set of messages transmitted, i.e. the concretisation of the abstract rules of a *lingua*.

16   "pragmatists": adherents of the philosophical theory of pragmatism, which originated in America and is connected with the names of William James and C. S. Peirce. Pragmatism enjoyed a certain vogue in Italy as an off-shoot and partial reaction against the positivist movement. Its most noteworthy exponent was Giovanni Vailati (1863–1909), also a distinguished mathematician and logician. The sociologist Pareto was also influenced by pragmatism.

17   "passion:" a Crocean term, denoting active as well as passive subjective emotionality. Croce generally uses the term disparagingly, arguing for example that politics is mere "passion", and not, as Gramsci was to maintain, the active centre of human life. Gramsci tends to follow the Crocean usage and devotes a lot of space to arguing (see, for example, pp. 138–40) that politics is precisely not passion in the Crocean sense. Here, however, the word has an approving sense of a strongly-felt internalised commitment to an objective goal.

18   This point is also made elsewhere by Gramsci, and further extended to cover the whole relationship of man to his environment in the sense of Marx's Theses on Feuerbach ("the educator must be educated.").

Chapter 16

Coercion, Capital, and European States [1990]

Charles Tilly

Cities and States in World History

States in history

Some 3,800 years ago, the ruler of a small Mesopotamian city-state conquered all the region's other city-states, and made them subject to Marduk, his own city's god. Hammurabi, ruler of Babylon, became the supreme king of Mesopotamia. By conquering, he gained the right and obligation to establish laws for all the people. In the introduction to his famous laws, Hammurabi claimed instruction from the great gods Anu and Enlil:

> then did Anu and Enlil call me to afford well-being to the people,
> me, Hammurabi, the obedient, godfearing prince, to cause righteousness
>   to appear in the land
> to destroy the evil and the wicked, that the strong harm not the weak
> and that I rise like the sun over the black-headed people,
>   lighting up the land.
>
> (Frankfort 1946: 193)

Wrapped in a divine calling, Hammurabi could confidently call those who opposed his rule "evil" and "wicked." Vilifying victims, annihilating allies, and razing rival

Charles Tilly, "Coercion, Capital, and European States," pp. 1–5, 16–23, 96–9 from Charles Tilly, *Coercion, Capital and European States, AD 990–1990*. Oxford: Basil Blackwell Ltd., 1990. Reprinted with permission of Wiley-Blackwell.

Contemporary Sociological Theory, Third Edition. Edited by Craig Calhoun, Joseph Gerteis, James Moody, Steven Pfaff, and Indermohan Virk. Editorial material and organization © 2012 John Wiley & Sons, Ltd. Published 2012 by John Wiley & Sons, Ltd.

cities, he claimed that divine justice stood behind him. Hammurabi was building the power of his city, and founding a state; his gods and their particular vision of justice would prevail.

States have been the world's largest and most powerful organizations for more than five thousand years. Let us define states as coercion-wielding organizations that are distinct from households and kinship groups and exercise clear priority in some respects over all other organizations within substantial territories. The term therefore includes city-states, empires, theocracies, and many other forms of government, but excludes tribes, lineages, firms, and churches as such. Such a definition is, alas, controversial; while many students of politics use the term in this organizational way, some extend it to whatever structure of power exists in a large, contiguous population, and others restrict it to relatively powerful, centralized, and differentiated sovereign organizations – roughly to what I will call a national state. I will, furthermore, eventually compromise the definition by including such entities as today's Monaco and San Marino, despite their lack of "substantial" territories, on the ground that other unambiguous states treat them as fellow-states.

For the moment, let us stick with the organizational definition. By such a standard, archaeological remains first signal the existence of states as of 6000 BC, and written or pictorial records testify to their presence two millennia later. Through most of the last eight millennia, states have only occupied a minority of the earth's inhabited space. But with the passage of millennia their dominance has grown.

Cities originated in the same era. Some time between 8000 and 7600 BC, the settlement later called Jericho contained a temple and stone houses; within the next thousand years, it acquired a thick wall and differentiated buildings. By that time, one could reasonably call Jericho a city, and other Middle Eastern settlements were beginning to acquire the signs of urbanization as well. In Anatolia, Çatal Hüyük's remains include rich houses, shrines, and works of art dating to well before 6000 BC. Full-fledged cities and recognizable states, then, appeared at roughly the same point in world history, a moment of great expansion in human capacity for creativity and for destruction. For a few millennia, indeed, the states in question were essentially city-states, often consisting of a priest-ruled capital surrounded by a tribute-paying hinterland. By 2500 BC, however, some Mesopotamian cities, including Ur and Lagash, were building empires ruled by warriors and held together by force and tribute; Hammurabi's unification of southern Mesopotamia came seven centuries after the first empires formed there. From that point on, the coexistence of substantial states and numerous cities has marked the great civilizations, from Mesopotamia, Egypt, and China to Europe.

Over the eight or ten millennia since the couple first appeared, cities and states have oscillated between love and hate. Armed conquerors have often razed cities and slaughtered their inhabitants, only to raise new capitals in their place. City people have bolstered their independence and railed against royal interference in urban affairs, only to seek their king's protection against bandits, pirates, and rival groups of merchants. Over the long run and at a distance, cities and states have proved indispensable to each other.

Through most of history, *national* states – states governing multiple contiguous regions and their cities by means of centralized, differentiated, and autonomous structures – have appeared only rarely. Most states have been *non*-national: empires, city-states, or something else. The term national state, regrettably, does not necessarily mean *nation*-state, a state whose people share a strong linguistic, religious, and symbolic identity. Although states such as Sweden and Ireland now approximate that ideal, very few European national states have ever qualified as nation-states. Great Britain, Germany, and France – quintessential national states – certainly have never met the test. With militant nationalities in Estonia, Armenia, and elsewhere, the Soviet Union now lives the distinction painfully every single day. China, with nearly three thousand years' experience of successive national states (but, given its multiple languages and nationalities, not one year as a nation-state), constitutes an extraordinary exception. Only during the last few centuries have national states mapped most of the world into their own mutually exclusive territories, including colonies. Only since World War II has almost the entire world come to be occupied by nominally independent states whose rulers recognize, more or less, each other's existence and right to exist.

As this final partitioning of the world into substantial states has proceeded, two important counter-currents have begun to flow. First, speakers for many populations that do not form distinct states have made claims to independent statehood. Not only the inhabitants of former colonies, but also minorities within old, established Western states, have demanded their own states with surprising frequency. While I write, groups of Armenians, Basques, Eritreans, Kanaks, Kurds, Palestinians, Sikhs, Tamils, Tibetans, Western Saharans, and many more stateless peoples are demanding the right to separate states; thousands have died for claiming that right. Within a Soviet Union that long seemed an unbreakable monolith, Lithuanians, Estonians, Azerbaijanis, Ukrainians, Armenians, Jews, and numerous other "nationalities" are pressing for varying degrees of distinctness – and even, sometimes, independence.

In the recent past, Bretons, Flemings, French Canadians, Montenegrins, Scots, and Welsh have also made bids for separate power, either inside or outside the states that now control them. Minorities claiming their own states have, furthermore, regularly received sympathetic hearings from third parties, if not from the states currently governing the territories they have claimed. If all the peoples on behalf of whom someone has recently made a claim to separate statehood were actually to acquire their own territories, the world would splinter from its present 160-odd recognized states to thousands of statelike entities, most of them tiny and economically unviable.

The second counter-current also runs strong: powerful rivals to states – blocs of states such as NATO, the European Economic Community or the Warsaw Pact, world-wide networks of traders in expensive, illicit commodities such as drugs and arms, and financial organizations such as giant international oil companies – have emerged to challenge their sovereignty. In 1992, members of the European Economic Community will dissolve economic barriers to a degree that will significantly limit their ability to pursue independent policies in respect of money, prices, and employment. These signs show that states as we know them will not last forever, and may soon lose their incredible hegemony.

In one of his sardonic "laws" of organizational behavior, C. Northcote Parkinson revealed that "a perfection of planned layout is achieved only by institutions on the point of collapse" (Parkinson 1957: 60). Cases in point include St Peter's basilica, and the Vatican Palace (completed during the sixteenth and seventeenth centuries, after the popes had lost most of their temporal power), the peacemaking Palace of the League of Nations (completed in 1937, just in time for the preliminaries to World War II), and the planning of colonial New Delhi, where "each phase of the [British] retreat was exactly paralleled with the completion of another triumph in civic design" (Parkinson 1957: 68). Perhaps a similar principle applies here. States may be following the old routine by which an institution falls into ruin just as it becomes complete. In the meantime, nevertheless, states remain so dominant that anyone who dreams of a stateless world seems a heedless visionary.

States form *systems* to the extent that they interact, and to the degree that their interaction significantly affects each party's fate. Since states always grow out of competition for control of territory and population, they invariably appear in clusters, and usually form systems. The system of states that now prevails almost everywhere on earth took shape in Europe after AD 990, then began extending its control far outside the continent five centuries later. It eventually absorbed, eclipsed, or extinguished all its rivals, including the systems of states that then centered on China, India, Persia, and Turkey. At the Millennium, however, Europe as such had no coherent existence; it consisted of the territory north of the Mediterranean once occupied by the Roman Empire, plus a large northeastern frontier never conquered by Rome, but largely penetrated by missionaries of the Christian churches which a disintegrating empire left as its souvenirs. At the same time Muslim empires controlled a significant part of southern Europe.

The continent we recognize today did have some potential bases of unity. An uneven network of trading cities connected much of the territory, and provided links to the more prosperous systems of production and commerce that extended from the Mediterranean to East Asia. The bulk of the region's population were peasants rather than hunters, pastoralists, or mercantile city-dwellers. Even in areas of urban concentration such as northern Italy, landlords ruled most of the population, and agriculture predominated among economic activities. Religion, language, and the residues of Roman occupation probably made the European population more culturally homogeneous than any other comparable world area outside of China. Within the area previously conquered by Rome, furthermore, traces of Roman law and political organization remained amid the splinters of sovereignty.

These features would eventually have a significant impact on Europe's history. Let us take AD 990 as an arbitrary point of reference. On the world stage the Europe of a thousand years ago was not a well-defined, unitary, independent actor. For that reason, any attempt to explain the continent's subsequent transformation in terms of its distinctive ethos or social structure runs a great risk of reasoning backwards.

What is more, individual countries such as Germany, Russia and Spain simply did not exist as coherent entities; they took shape over succeeding centuries as a result of processes this book traces. Arguments that begin with the distinctive, enduring characteristics of "Germany" or "Russia" misrepresent the troubled, contingent history of European states.

So natural do the rise of national states, the growth of national armies, and the long European hegemony appear, indeed, that scholars rarely ask why plausible alternatives to them – such as the systems of loosely-articulated regional empires that thrived in Asia, Africa, and the Americas well past AD 990 – did not prevail in Europe. Surely part of the answer lies in the dialectic of cities and states that developed within a few hundred years after 990. For the coincidence of a dense, uneven urban network with a division into numerous well-defined and more or less independent states eventually set apart Europe from the rest of the world. Behind the changing geography of cities and states operated the dynamics of capital (whose preferred sphere was cities) and of coercion (which crystallized especially in states). Inquiries into the interplay between cities and states rapidly become investigations of capital and coercion.

A surprising range of combinations between coercion and capital appeared at one point or another in European history. Empires, city-states, federations of cities, networks of landlords, churches, religious orders, leagues of pirates, warrior bands, and many other forms of governance prevailed in some parts of Europe at various times over the last thousand years. Most of them qualified as states of one kind or another: they were organizations that controlled the principal concentrated means of coercion within delimited territories, and exercised priority in some respects over all other organizations acting within the territories. But only late and slowly did the national state become the predominant form. Hence the critical double question: *What accounts for the great variation over time and space in the kinds of states that have prevailed in Europe since AD 990, and why did European states eventually converge on different variants of the national state?* Why were the directions of change so similar and the paths so different? This book aims to clarify that problem, if not to resolve it entirely.

[…]

Logics of capital and coercion

The story concerns capital and coercion. It recounts the ways that wielders of coercion, who played the major part in the creation of national states, drew for their own purposes on manipulators of capital, whose activities generated cities. Of course the two interacted; Figure 16.1 represents the general condition. Although states strongly reflect the organization of coercion, they actually show the effects of capital as well; as the rest of this book will demonstrate, various combinations of capital and coercion produced very different kinds of states. Again, cities respond especially to changes in capital, but the organization of coercion affects their character as well; Lewis Mumford's baroque city lived on capital like its cousins, but

```
     Capital              Coercion

        ↓  ╲            ╱  ↓
            ╲        ╱
             ╲    ╱
              ╳
             ╱    ╲
            ╱        ╲
        ↓  ╱            ╲  ↓
     Cities               States
```

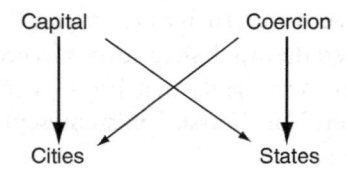

Figure 16.1 How capital and coercion generate cities and states.

showed a clearer imprint of princely power – in palaces, parade grounds, and barracks – than they did. Over time, furthermore, the place of capital in the form of states grew ever larger, while the influence of coercion (in the guise of policing and state intervention) expanded as well.

Capital – cities – exploitation

Before entering into these complexities, however, it will help to explore the capital–cities and coercion–states relationships separately. Let us think of *capital* generously, including any tangible mobile resources, and enforceable claims on such resources. Capitalists, then, are people who specialize in the accumulation, purchase, and sale of capital. They occupy the realm of *exploitation*, where the relations of production and exchange themselves yield surpluses, and capitalists capture them. Capitalists have often existed in the absence of capitalism, the system in which wage-workers produce goods by means of materials owned by capitalists. Through most of history, indeed, capitalists have worked chiefly as merchants, entrepreneurs, and financiers, rather than as the direct organizers of production. The system of capitalism itself arrived late in the history of capital. It grew up in Europe after 1500, as capitalists seized control of production. It reached its apex – or, depending on your perspective, its nadir – after 1750, when capital-concentrated manufacturing became the basis of prosperity in many countries. For millennia before then, capitalists had flourished without much intervening in production.

The processes that accumulate and concentrate capital also produce cities. Cities figure prominently in this book's analyses, both as favored sites of capitalists and as organizational forces in their own right. To the extent that the survival of households depends on the presence of capital through employment, investment, redistribution or any other strong link, the distribution of population follows that of capital. (Capital, however, sometimes follows cheap labor; the relationship is reciprocal.) Trade, warehousing, banking, and production that depends closely on any of them all benefit from proximity to each other. Within limits set by the productivity of agriculture, that proximity promotes the formation of dense, differentiated populations having extensive outside connections – cities. When capital both accumulates and concentrates within a territory, urban growth tends to occur throughout the same territory – more intensely at the greatest point of concentration, and secondarily elsewhere (see Figure 16.2). The form of urban growth, however, depends on the balance between concentration and accumulation. Where capital

```
           Capital concentration
                    ↑
                    |         ↗ Urban growth
           Capital accumulation
```

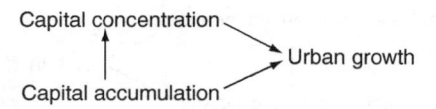

Figure 16.2 How capital generates urban growth.

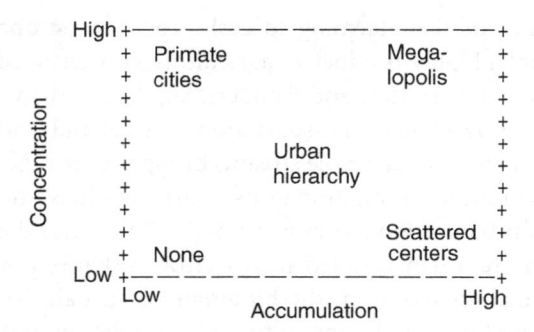

```
          High +-------------------+
               +  Primate    Mega- +
               +  cities     lopolis +
               +                   +
   Concentration +                 +
               +        Urban      +
               +     hierarchy     +
               +                   +
               +                   +
               +           Scattered +
               +  None      centers +
          Low  +-------------------+
               Low                High
                    Accumulation
```

Figure 16.3 Alternative forms of urban growth as functions of capital accumulation and concentration.

accumulation occurs quite generally, but concentration remains relatively low, many smaller centers develop. Where a single concentration of capital emerges, urban population concentrates around that center.

Properly speaking, then, cities represent regional economies; around every city or urban cluster lies a zone of agriculture and trade (and sometimes of manufacturing as well) that interacts closely with it. Where accumulation and concentration occur in tandem, a hierarchy from small centers to large tends to take shape (see Figure 16.3). These tendencies have always operated within important limits. City people normally depend on others to raise most or all of their food and fuel; the transportation and preservation of these requisites for large cities consumes a great deal of energy. Until very recently, most of the world's agricultural areas, including those of Europe, were too unproductive to permit much more than a tenth of the nearby population to live off the land. Cities that could not reach agricultural areas conveniently by means of low-cost water transportation, furthermore, faced prohibitively high food costs. Berlin and Madrid provide good examples: except as their rulers force-fed them, they did not grow.

Health mattered as well. Through almost all of the last thousand years, despite their disproportionate recruitment of vigorous migrants of working age, cities have had significantly higher death rates than their hinterlands. Only after 1850, with improvements in urban sanitation and nutrition, did the balance shift in favor of city-dwellers. As a result, cities have only grown rapidly when agriculture and transportation were becoming relatively efficient or when powerful pressures were driving people off the land.

The sheer growth of cities, however, produced a spiral of change in all these regards. In the vicinity of active cities, people farmed more intensively and devoted

```
Concentration of coercive means ─┐
                ↑                 ╲
                │                  ➤ Growth of states
                │                 ╱
Accumulation of coercive means ──┘
```

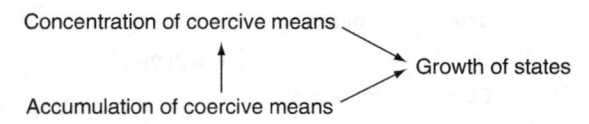

Figure 16.4 How coercion generates the growth of states.

a higher proportion of their farming to cash crops; in Europe of the sixteenth century, for example, highly productive agriculture concentrated in the two most urbanized regions, northern Italy and Flanders. Similarly, urban growth stimulated the creation and improvement of transportation by water and land; the Netherlands' superb system of canals and navigable streams brought down the cost, and brought up the speed, of communication among its swarm of cities, thus serving as both cause and effect of urbanization (de Vries 1978). The pressures that drove people off the land, furthermore, often resulted in part from urbanization, as when urban landlords drove smallholders from the hinterland or urban demand fostered the capitalization of the hinterland's agriculture. Accumulation and concentration of capital fostered urban growth, while transforming the regions surrounding new clusters of cities.

Coercion – states – domination

What of coercion? Coercion includes all concerted application, threatened or actual, of action that commonly causes loss or damage to the persons or possessions of individuals or groups who are aware of both the action and the potential damage. (The cumbersome definition excludes inadvertent, indirect, and secret damage.) Where capital defines a realm of exploitation, coercion defines a realm of domination. The means of coercion center on armed force, but extend to facilities for incarceration, expropriation, humiliation, and publication of threats. Europe created two major overlapping groups of specialists in coercion: soldiers and great landlords; where they merged and received ratification from states in the form of titles and privileges they crystallized into nobilities, who in turn supplied the principal European rulers for many centuries. Coercive means, like capital, can both accumulate and concentrate: some groups (such as monastic orders) have few coercive means, but those few are concentrated in a small number of hands; others (such as armed frontiersmen) have many coercive means that are widely dispersed. Coercive means and capital merge where the same objects (e.g. workhouses) serve exploitation and domination. For the most part, however, they remain sufficiently distinct to allow us to analyze them separately.

When the accumulation and concentration of coercive means grow together, they produce states; they produce distinct organizations that control the chief concentrated means of coercion within well-defined territories, and exercise priority in some respects over all other organizations operating within those territories (see Figure 16.4). Efforts to subordinate neighbors and fight off more distant rivals create state structures in the form not only of armies but also of civilian staffs that gather the means to sustain armies and that organize the ruler's day-to-day control over the rest of the civilian population.

War drives state formation and transformation

The deployment of coercive means in war and domestic control presents warriors with two dilemmas. First, to the extent that they are successful in subduing their rivals outside or inside the territory they claim, the wielders of coercion find themselves obliged to administer the lands, goods, and people they acquire; they become involved in extraction of resources, distribution of goods, services, and income, and adjudication of disputes. But administration diverts them from war, and creates interests that sometimes tell against war. We can see the dilemma in the five-century conquest of Muslim Spain by Christian warriors. Starting with the taking of Coimbra in 1064, standard siege practice ran like this:

> Residents of a town under siege who surrendered promptly could remain with full freedoms after the conquest. If the Muslims surrendered after having been under siege for some time, they could leave with only those goods they could carry. If they waited for the town to fall by force, they faced death or enslavement.
>
> (Powers 1988: 18)

Any of the three responses set a problem for conquerors. The first imposed the obligation – at least temporarily – to establish a system of parallel rule. The second called for a redistribution of property as well as the settlement and administration of a depopulated town. The third left slaves in the hands of the victors, and posed even more sharply the challenge of reestablishing production and population. In one way or another, conquest entailed administration. On a larger scale, these problems dogged the whole reconquest of Iberia. In different forms, they marked the history of conquest throughout Europe.

The second dilemma parallels the first. Preparation for war, especially on a large scale, involves rulers ineluctably in extraction. It builds up an infrastructure of taxation, supply, and administration that requires maintenance of itself and often grows faster than the armies and navies that it serves; those who run the infrastructure acquire power and interests of their own; their interests and power limit significantly the character and intensity of warfare any particular state can carry on. Europe's Mongol and Tatar states resolved the dilemmas by raiding and looting without building much durable administration, but their strategy put inherent limits on their power, and eventually made them vulnerable to well-financed mass armies. In contrast highly commercial states such as Genoa resolved the dilemmas by borrowing or contracting out the structure necessary to extract the means of war. Between the two extremes, European states found a number of other ways of reconciling the demands of warmaking, extraction, and other major activities.

European states differed significantly, indeed, with respect to their salient activities and organizations. Three different types of state have all proliferated in various parts of Europe during major segments of the period since 990: tribute-taking empires; systems of fragmented sovereignty such as city-states and urban federations, and national states. The first built a large military and extractive apparatus, but left most local administration to regional powerholders who retained great autonomy. In systems of fragmented sovereignty, temporary coalitions and consultative institutions played significant parts in war and extraction, but little durable state apparatus emerged on a national scale. National states unite substantial military, extractive, administrative, and sometimes even distributive and productive organizations in a relatively coordinated central structure. The long survival and coexistence of all three types tells against any notion of European state formation as a single, unilinear process, or of the national state – which did, indeed, eventually prevail – as an inherently superior form of government.

Over the centuries, tribute-taking empires have dominated the world history of states. Empires appeared mainly under conditions of relatively low accumulation of coercive means with high concentration of the available means. When anyone other than the emperor accumulated important coercive means, or the emperor lost the ability to deploy massive coercion, empires often disintegrated. For all its appearance of massive durability, the Chinese Empire suffered incessantly from rebellions, invasions, and movements for autonomy, and long spent a major part of its budget on tribute to Mongols and other nomadic predators. Nor did Europe's empires enjoy greater stability. Napoleon's 1808 invasion of the Iberian peninsula, for instance, shattered much of the Spanish overseas empire. Within months, movements for independence formed in most of Spanish Latin America, and within ten years practically all of the region had broken into independent states.

Federations, city-states, and other arrangements of fragmented sovereignty differed from empires in almost every respect. They depended on relatively high accumulations, and relatively low concentrations, of coercion; the widespread urban militias of fourteenth-century western Europe typify that combination. In such states, a relatively small coalition of nominal subjects could equal the ruler's forces, while individuals, groups, and whole populations had abundant opportunities for defection to competing jurisdictions.

Fourteenth-century Prussia and Pomerania offer a telling contrast: in Prussia, then dominated by the Teutonic Knights, no great princes rivalled the Knights' Grand Master, and towns wielded little power. But the landlords installed by the Knights had wide discretion within their own extensive domains, just so long as revenues flowed to the Knights. In nearby Pomerania, a duchy established simultaneously by smaller-scale German conquests and alliances, many armed rivals to the duke arose, and smaller lords took to outright banditry, as towns dominated the duchy's Estates and provided major military forces in time of war.

During the 1326–8 war between the dukes of Pomerania and Mecklenburg, Pomerania's towns generally sided with their duke while nobles aligned themselves with Mecklenburg. When the Pomeranian house won, the Estates, in which the cities had much say, "were granted far-reaching privileges: the guardianship over minor dukes, the decision whether new ducal castles should be built or pulled down, the right to choose a new master if ever the duke broke his promises or wronged his subjects" (Carsten 1954: 90). The cities' ability to give or withhold support afforded them great bargaining power.

In between tribute-taking empires and city-states stand national states – built around war, statemaking, and extraction like other states, but compelled by bargaining over the subject population's cession of coercive means to invest heavily in protection, adjudication, and sometimes even production and distribution. The later history of Prussia illustrates the process by which national states formed. During the fourteenth century, as we have seen, the Teutonic Knights established a centralized empire there. During the fifteenth century, the Knights, shaken by plague, out-migration of peasants, and military defeat, began to disintegrate, and the regional magnates they had previously controlled became Prussian political powers in their own right. They used their power to impose greater and greater restrictions on the peasants who remained on their estates; with coerced labor the increasingly powerful landlords shifted toward demesne farming and the export of grain to western Europe.

At the same time, the rulers of Brandenburg and Pomerania, previously weakened by alliances of their dukes with prosperous burghers, began to win their incessant struggles with the towns, as the towns' position in international trade declined and the ability of the Hanseatic League to intercede on their behalf weakened. The rulers then had to bargain with noble-dominated Estates, which acquired the fundamental power to grant – or deny – royal revenues for war and dynastic aggrandizement. Over the next few centuries the Hohenzollern margraves of Brandenburg fought their way to pre-eminence in what became Brandenburg-Prussia, absorbing much of old Pomerania in the process; they contracted marriage and diplomatic alliances that eventually expanded their domains into adjacent areas and into the capital-rich areas of the lower Rhine; and they negotiated agreements with their nobility that ceded privileges and powers to the lords within their own regions, but gave the monarch access to regular revenues.

Out of battles, negotiations, treaties, and inheritances emerged a national state in which the great landlords of Prussia, Brandenburg, and Pomerania had great power within domains the crown had never wrested from them. During the eighteenth century, such monarchs as Frederick the Great locked the last pieces of the structure into place by incorporating peasants and lords alike into the army, the one under the command of the other. Prussia's army mimicked the countryside, with nobles serving as officers, free peasants as sergeants, and serfs as ordinary soldiers. Peasants and serfs paid the price: many peasants fell into serfdom, and "In war and peace Old Prussia's military obligations weakened the social position, the legal rights, and the property holding of serfs vis à vis the noble estate" (Busch 1962: 68). In this respect, Prussia followed a different path from Great Britain (where peasants became rural wage-workers) and France (where peasants survived with a fair amount of property into the nineteenth century). But Prussia, Great Britain, and France all trembled with struggles between monarch and major classes over the means of war, and felt the consequent creation of durable state structure.

```
              High +————————————+
                   +                            +
                   +  Empires        Super-     +
                   +                 states     +
   c               +                            +
   o               +                            +
   i               +       Systems of           +
   t               +       national states      +
   a               +                            +
   r               +                            +
   t               +                            +
   n               +  No             Fragmented +
   e               +  state          sovereignty+
   c               +                            +
   n               +                            +
   o          Low  +————————————+
   C                Low                     High
                          Accumulation
```

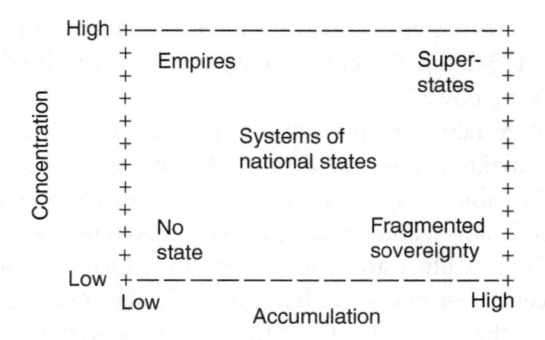

Figure 16.5 Alternative conditions of state growth as functions of accumulation and concentration of coercion.

As military allies and rivals, Prussia, Great Britain, and France also shaped each other's destinies. In the nature of the case, national states always appear in competition with each other, and gain their identities by contrast with rival states; they belong to *systems* of states. The broad differences among major types of state structure are schematized in Figure 16.5. Well developed examples of all four kinds of state existed in different parts of Europe well after AD 990. Full-fledged empires flourished into the seventeenth century, and the last major zones of fragmented sovereignty only consolidated into national states late in the nineteenth.

[…]

States and Their Citizens

From wasps to locomotives

Over the last thousand years, European states have undergone a peculiar evolution: from wasps to locomotives. Long they concentrated on war, leaving most activities to other organizations, just so long as those organizations yielded tribute at appropriate intervals. Tribute-taking states remained fierce but light in weight by comparison with their bulky successors; they stung, but they didn't suck dry. As time went on, states – even the capital-intensive varieties – took on activities, powers and commitments whose very support constrained them. These locomotives ran on the rails of sustenance from the civilian population and maintenance by a civilian staff. Off the rails, the warlike engines could not run at all.

A state's essential minimum activities form a trio:

statemaking: attacking and checking competitors and challengers within the territory claimed by the state;

warmaking: attacking rivals outside the territory already claimed by the state;

protection: attacking and checking rivals of the rulers' principal allies, whether inside or outside the state's claimed territory.

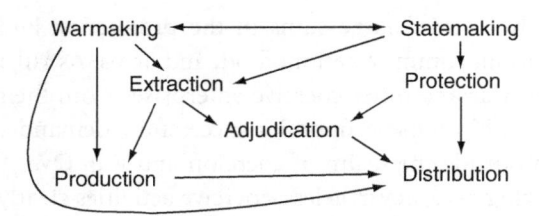

Figure 16.6 Relations among major activities of states.

No state lasts long, however, that neglects a crucial fourth activity:

extraction: drawing from its subject population the means of statemaking, warmaking, and protection.

At the minimum, tribute-taking states stayed close to this indispensable set of four activities, intervening in the lives of their nominal subjects chiefly to impose ruling-class power and to extract revenues. Beyond a certain scale, however, all states found themselves venturing into three other risky terrains:

adjudication: authoritative settlement of disputes among members of the subject population;
distribution: intervention in the allocation of goods among members of the subject population;
production: control of the creation and transformation of goods and services by members of the subject population.

The major connections among these activities run roughly as shown in Figure 16.6. Warmaking and statemaking reinforced each other, indeed remained practically indistinguishable until states began to form secure, recognized boundaries around substantial contiguous territories. Both led to extraction of resources from the local population. The play of alliances and the attempt to draw resources from relatively powerful or mobile actors promoted the state's involvement in protection, checking the competitors and enemies of selected clients. As extraction and protection expanded, they created demands for adjudication of disputes within the subject population, including the legal regularization of both extraction and protection themselves.

Over time, the weight and impact of state activities standing lower in the diagram – adjudication, production, and distribution – grew faster than those at the top: warmaking, statemaking, extraction, and protection. The sheer volume most European states invested in warmaking (attacking rivals outside the territory claimed by the state) or statemaking (attacking and checking competitors and challengers within the territory) continued to increase irregularly into the twentieth century; but adjudication, production, and distribution went from trivial to tremendous. Even those non-socialist states that maintained wide private ownership, for example, eventually invested large sums in the production and/or regulation of energy, transportation, communication, food, and arms. As rulers drew more and more resources for war and other coercive enterprises from their local economies, the major classes within those economies successfully demanded more and more state intervention outside the realm of coercion and war. Over the thousand-year span we are surveying here, nevertheless, coercive activities clearly predominated.

Warmaking frequently involved European states in the production of arms, and extraction in the production of goods (e.g. salt, matches, and tobacco) whose monopolies fed state coffers. Later, all states intervened more generally in production as demands from workers and intellectuals for the checking of capitalist excesses became effective; socialist states merely represent the extreme of a general tendency. Extraction, protection, and adjudication intertwined, finally, to draw states into control of distribution – first as a way of assuring state revenues from the flow of goods, then as a response to popular demands for correction of inequities and local shortages. Again socialist states mark but the extreme version of a very general expansion in state activity outside the military realm.

In the course of extracting resources and pacifying the population, every European state eventually created new administrative structure at the local and regional levels as well as on a national scale. The treaty of Cateau-Cambrésis (1559), for example, created the kingdom of Savoy-Piedmont, and placed Emmanuel-Philibert on its throne. Soon the quest for funds drove the new king to innovate: first a profitable forced sale of salt, second a census to determine who was taxable, then a tax based on each community's productive area. The tax forced adjacent communities to delineate their boundaries precisely, which drew them into preparing cadasters and creating officials to administer them (Rambaud and Vincienne 1964: 11). Everywhere extractive efforts not only withdrew valuable resources from their customary uses but also created new forms of political organization.

State activities therefore had profound implications for the interests of the general population, for collective action, and for the rights of citizens. As rulers and agents of states pursued the work of warmaking, statemaking, protection, extraction, adjudication, distribution, and production, they impinged on well-defined interests of people who lived within their range of control; the impact was often negative, since states repeatedly seized for their own use land, capital, goods, and services that had previously served other commitments. Most of the resources that kings and ministers used to build armed might came ultimately from the labor and accumulation of ordinary people, and represented a diversion of valuable means from pursuits to which ordinary people attached much higher priority. Although capitalists sometimes invested gladly in state finances and in the protection that state power gave to their business, and although regional magnates sometimes allied themselves with kings in order to hold off their own enemies, most people who had an investment in the resources that monarchs sought to seize resisted royal demands tenaciously.

The labor, goods, money, and other resources demanded by states were, after all, typically embedded in webs of obligation and committed to ends that households and communities prized. From the short-run perspectives of ordinary people, what we in blithe retrospect call "state formation" included the setting of ruthless tax farmers against poor peasants and artisans, the forced sale for taxes of animals that would have paid for dowries, the imprisoning of local leaders as hostages to the local community's payment of overdue taxes, the hanging of others who dared to protest, the loosing of brutal soldiers on a hapless civilian population, the conscription of young men who were their parents' main hope for comfort in old age, the forced purchase of tainted salt, the elevation of already arrogant local propertyholders into officers of the state, and the imposition of religious conformity in the name of public order and morality. Small wonder that powerless Europeans so often accepted the legend of the "good tsar" who had been misled, or even held captive, by bad advisors.

Both the character and the weight of state activity varied systematically as a function of the economy that prevailed within a state's boundaries. In *coercion-intensive* regions, rulers commonly drew resources for warmaking and other activities in kind, through direct requisition and conscription. Customs and excise yielded small returns in relatively uncommercialized economies, but the institution of head taxes and land taxes created ponderous fiscal machines, and put extensive power into the hands of landlords, village heads, and others who exercised intermediate control over essential resources. In *capital-intensive* regions, the presence of capitalists, commercial exchange, and substantial municipal organizations set serious limits on the state's direct exertion of control over individuals and households, but facilitated the use of relatively efficient and painless taxes on commerce as sources of state revenue. The ready availability of credit, furthermore, allowed rulers to spread the costs of military activity over substantial periods rather than extracting in quick, calamitous bursts. As a result, states in those regions generally created slight, segmented central apparatuses. In regions of *capitalized coercion*, an intermediate situation prevailed: however uneasily, rulers relied on acquiescence from both landlords and merchants, drew revenues from both land and trade, and thus created dual state structures in which nobles confronted – but also finally collaborated with – financiers.

REFERENCES

Busch, Otto, 1962. *Militarsystem und Sozialleben im alten Preussen 1713–1807: Die Anfänge der sozialen Militarisierung der perussisch-deutschen Gesellschaft*. Berlin: de Gruyter.
Carsten, F.L., 1954. *The Origins of Prussia*. Oxford: Clarendon Press.
Frankfort, Henrie et al., 1946. *The Intellectual Adventure of Ancient Man. An Essay on Speculative Thought in the Ancient Near East*. Chicago: University of Chicago Press.
Parkinson, C. Northcote, 1957. *Parkinson's Law and Other Studies in Administration*. Boston, MA: Houghton Mifflin.
Powers, J.F., 1988. *A Society Organized for War: The Iberian Municipal Militias in the Central Middle Ages, 1000–1284*. Berkeley: University of California Press.
Rambaud, Placide and Vincienne, Monique, 1964. *Les transformations d'une société rurale. La Maurienne (1561–1962)*. Paris: Armand Colin.
Vries, Jan de, 1978. "Barges and Capitalism. Passenger Transportation in the Dutch Economy 1632–1839," *A. A. G. Bijdragen* 21: 33–398.

Chapter 17

Power: A Radical View [2005]

Steven Lukes

[...]

The One-Dimensional View

This is often called the 'pluralist' view of power, but that label is already misleading, since it is the aim of Dahl, Polsby, Wolfinger and others to demonstrate that power (as they identify it) is, in fact, distributed pluralistically in, for instance, New Haven and, more generally, in the United States' political system as a whole. To speak, as these writers do, of a 'pluralist view' of, or 'pluralist approach' to, power, or of a 'pluralist methodology', is to imply that the pluralists' conclusions are already built into their concepts, approach and method. I do not, in fact, think that this is so. I think that these are capable of generating non-pluralist conclusions in certain cases. Their view yields elitist conclusions when applied to elitist decision-making structures, and pluralist conclusions when applied to pluralist decision-making structures (and also, as I shall argue, pluralist conclusions when applied to structures which it identifies as pluralist, but other views of power do not). So, in attempting to characterize it, I shall identify its distinguishing features independently of the pluralist conclusions it has been used to reach.

Steven Lukes, "Power: A Radical View," pp. 16–17, 19–21, 25–30, 34–8, 58–9 from Steven Lukes, *Power: A Radical View*, 2nd Edition. Basingstoke: Palgrave Macmillan, 2005. Reprinted with permission of Palgrave Macmillan.

Contemporary Sociological Theory, Third Edition. Edited by Craig Calhoun, Joseph Gerteis, James Moody, Steven Pfaff, and Indermohan Virk. Editorial material and organization © 2012 John Wiley & Sons, Ltd. Published 2012 by John Wiley & Sons, Ltd.

In his early article 'The Concept of Power', Dahl describes his 'intuitive idea of power' as 'something like this: *A* has power over *B* to the extent that he can get *B* to do something that *B* would not otherwise do' (Dahl 1957, in Bell, Edwards and Harrison Wagner (eds) 1969: 80). A little later in the same article he describes his 'intuitive view of the power relation' slightly differently: it seemed, he writes, 'to involve a successful attempt by *A* to get *a* to do something he would not otherwise do' (ibid., p. 82). Note that the first statement refers to *A*'s capacity ('... to the extent that he can get *B* to do something ...'), while the second specifies a successful attempt – this, of course, being the difference between potential and actual power, between its possession and its exercise. It is the latter – the exercise of power – which is central to this view of power (in reaction to the so-called 'elitists' focus on power reputations). Dahl's central method in *Who Governs?* is to 'determine for each decision which participants had initiated alternatives that were finally adopted, had vetoed alternatives initiated by others, or had proposed alternatives that were turned down. These actions were then tabulated as individual "successes" or "defeats". The participants with the greatest proportion of successes out of the total number of successes were then considered to be the most influential' (Dahl 1961: 336). In short, as Polsby writes, 'In the pluralist approach ... an attempt is made to study specific outcomes in order to determine who actually prevails in community decision-making' (Polsby 1963: 113). The stress here is on the study of concrete, observable *behaviour*. The researcher, according to Polsby, 'should study actual behavior, either at first hand or by reconstructing behavior from documents, informants, newspapers, and other appropriate sources' (ibid., p. 121). Thus the pluralist methodology, in Merelman's words, 'studied actual behavior, stressed operational definitions, and turned up evidence. Most important, it seemed to produce reliable conclusions which met the canons of science' (Merelman 1968: 451).

[...]

The Two-Dimensional View

In their critique of this view, Bachrach and Baratz argue that it is restrictive and, in virtue of that fact, gives a misleadingly sanguine pluralist picture of American politics. Power, they claim, has two faces. The first face is that already considered, according to which 'power is totally embodied and fully reflected in "concrete decisions" or in activity bearing directly upon their making' (1970: 7). As they write

> Of course power is exercised when *A* participates in the making of decisions that affect *B*. Power is also exercised when *A* devotes his energies to creating or reinforcing social and political values and institutional practices that limit the scope of the political process to public consideration of only those issues which are comparatively innocuous to *A*. To the extent that *A* succeeds in doing this, *B* is prevented, for all practical purposes, from bringing to the fore any issues that might in their resolution be seriously detrimental to *A*'s set of preferences. (p. 7)

Their 'central point' is this: 'to the extent that a person or group – consciously or unconsciously – creates or reinforces barriers to the public airing of policy conflicts, that person or group has power' (p. 8), and they cite Schattschneider's famous and often-quoted words:

> All forms of political organization have a bias in favour of the exploitation of some kinds of conflict and the suppression of others, because *organization is the mobilization of bias*. Some issues are organized into politics while others are organized out. (Schattschneider 1960: 71)

The importance of Bachrach and Baratz's work is that they bring this crucially important idea of the 'mobilization of bias' into the discussion of power. It is, in their words,

> a set of predominant values, beliefs, rituals, and institutional procedures ('rules of the game') that operate systematically and consistently to the benefit of certain persons and groups at the expense of others. Those who benefit are placed in a preferred position to defend and promote their vested interests. More often than not, the 'status quo defenders' are a minority or elite group within the population in question. Elitism, however, is neither foreordained nor omnipresent: as opponents of the war in Viet Nam can readily attest, the mobilization of bias can and frequently does benefit a clear majority. (1970: 43–4)

[...]

The Three-Dimensional View

There is no doubt that the two-dimensional view of power represents a major advance over the one-dimensional view: it incorporates into the analysis of power relations the question of the control over the agenda of politics and of the ways in which potential issues are kept out of the political process. None the less, it is, in my view, inadequate on three counts.

In the first place, its critique of behaviourism is too qualified, or, to put it another way, it is still too committed to behaviourism – that is, to the study of overt, 'actual behaviour', of which 'concrete decisions' in situations of conflict are seen as paradigmatic. In trying to assimilate all cases of exclusion of potential issues from the political agenda to the paradigm of a decision, it gives a misleading picture of the ways in which individuals and, above all, groups and institutions succeed in excluding potential issues from the political process. Decisions are choices consciously and intentionally made by individuals between alternatives, whereas the bias of the system can be mobilized, recreated and reinforced in ways that are neither consciously chosen nor the intended result of particular individuals' choices. As Bachrach and Baratz themselves maintain, the domination of defenders of the status quo may be so secure and pervasive that they are unaware of any potential challengers to their position and thus of any alternatives to the existing political process, whose bias they work to maintain. As 'students of power and its consequences', they write, 'our main concern is not whether the defenders of the status quo use their power consciously, but rather if and how they exercise it and what effects it has on the political process and other actors within the system' (Bachrach and Baratz 1970: 50).

Moreover, the bias of the system is not sustained simply by a series of individually chosen acts, but also, most importantly, by the socially structured and culturally patterned behaviour of groups, and practices of institutions, which may indeed be manifested by individuals' inaction. Bachrach and Baratz follow the pluralists in adopting too methodologically individualist a view of power. In this both parties follow in the steps of Max Weber, for whom power was the probability of *individuals realizing their wills* despite the resistance of others, whereas the power to control the agenda of politics and exclude potential issues cannot be adequately analysed unless it is seen as a function of collective forces and social arrangements. There are, in fact, two separable cases here. First, there is the phenomenon of collective action, where the policy or action of a collectivity (whether a group, e.g. a class, or an institution, e.g. a political party or an industrial corporation) is manifest, but not attributable to particular individuals' decisions or behaviour. Second, there is the phenomenon of 'systemic' or organizational effects, where the mobilization of bias results, as Schattschneider put it, from the form of organization. Of course, such collectivities and organizations are made up of individuals – but the power they exercise cannot be simply conceptualized in terms of individuals' decisions or behaviour. As Marx succinctly put it, 'Men make their own history but they do not make it just as they please; they do not make it under circumstances chosen by themselves, but under circumstances directly encountered, given and transmitted from the past.'

The second count on which the two-dimensional view of power is inadequate is in its association of power with actual, observable conflict. In this respect also the pluralists' critics follow their adversaries too closely (and both in turn again follow Weber, who, as we have seen, stressed the realization of one's will, *despite the resistance of others*). This insistence on actual conflict as essential to power will not do, for at least two reasons.

The first is that, on Bachrach and Baratz's own analysis, two of the types of power may not involve such conflict: namely, manipulation and authority – which they conceive as 'agreement based upon reason' (Bachrach and Baratz 1970: 20), though elsewhere they speak of it as involving a 'possible conflict of values' (p. 37).

The second reason why the insistence on actual and observable conflict will not do is simply that it is highly unsatisfactory to suppose that power is only exercised in situations of such conflict. To put the matter sharply, *A* may exercise power over *B* by getting him to do what he does not want to do, but he also exercises power over him by influencing, shaping or determining his very wants. Indeed, is it not the supreme exercise of power to get, another or others to have the desires you want them to have – that is, to secure their compliance by controlling their thoughts and desires? One does not have to go to the lengths of talking about *Brave New World*, or the world of B. F. Skinner, to see this: thought control takes many less total and more mundane forms, through the control of information, through the mass media and through the processes of socialization. Indeed, ironically, there are some excellent descriptions of this phenomenon in *Who Governs?* Consider the picture of the rule of the 'patricians' in the early nineteenth century: 'The elite seems to have possessed that most indispensable of all characteristics in a dominant group – the sense, shared not only by themselves but by the populace, that their claim to govern was legitimate' (Dahl 1961: 17). And Dahl also sees this phenomenon at work under modern 'pluralist' conditions: leaders, he says, 'do not merely *respond* to the preferences of constituents; leaders also *shape* preferences' (p. 164), and, again, 'almost the entire adult population has been subjected to *some* degree of indoctrination through the schools' (p. 317), etc. The trouble seems to be that both Bachrach and Baratz and the pluralists suppose that because power, as they conceptualize it, only shows up in cases of actual conflict, it follows that actual conflict is necessary to power. But this is to ignore the crucial point that the most effective and insidious use of power is to prevent such conflict from arising in the first place.

The third count on which the two-dimensional view of power is inadequate is closely linked to the second: namely, its insistence that nondecision-making power only exists where there are grievances which are denied entry into the political process in the form of issues. If the observer can uncover no grievances, then he must assume there is a 'genuine' consensus on the prevailing allocation of values. To put this another way, it is here assumed that if people feel no grievances, then they have no interests that are harmed by the use of power. But this is also highly unsatisfactory. In the first place, what, in any case, is a grievance – an articulated demand, based on political knowledge, an undirected complaint arising out of everyday experience, a vague feeling of unease or sense of deprivation? (See Lipsitz 1970.) Second, and more important, is it not the supreme and most insidious exercise of power to prevent people, to whatever degree, from having grievances by shaping their perceptions, cognitions and preferences in such a way that they accept their role in the existing order of things, either because they can see or imagine no alternative to it, or because they see it as natural and unchangeable, or because they value it as divinely ordained and beneficial? To assume that the absence of grievance equals genuine consensus is simply to rule out the possibility of false or manipulated consensus by definitional fiat.

In summary, the three-dimensional view of power involves a *thoroughgoing critique of the behavioural focus* of the first two views as too individualistic and allows for consideration of the many ways in which *potential issues* are kept out of politics, whether through the operation of social forces and institutional practices or through individuals' decisions. This, moreover, can occur in the absence of actual, observable conflict, which may have been successfully averted – though there remains here an implicit reference to potential conflict. This potential, however, may never in fact be actualized. What one may have here is a *latent conflict*, which consists in a contradiction between the interests of those exercising power and the *real interests* of those they exclude. These latter may not express or even be conscious of their interests, but, as I shall argue, the identification of those interests ultimately always rests on empirically supportable and refutable hypotheses.

The distinctive features of the three views of power presented above are summarized below.

One-Dimensional View of Power

Focus on (a) behaviour
(b) decision-making
(c) (key) issues
(d) observable (overt) conflict
(e) (subjective) interests, seen as policy preferences revealed by political participation

Two-Dimensional View of Power

(Qualified) critique of behavioural focus
Focus on (a) decision-making and nondecision-making
(b) issues and potential issues
(c) observable (overt or covert) conflict
(d) (subjective) interests, seen as policy preferences or grievances

Three-Dimensional View of Power

Critique of behavioural focus
Focus on (a) decision-making and control over political agenda (not necessarily through decisions)
(b) issues and potential issues
(c) observable (overt or covert), and latent conflict
(d) subjective and real interests

The Underlying Concept of Power

One feature which these three views of power share is their evaluative character: each arises out of and operates within a particular moral and political perspective. Indeed, I maintain that power is one of those concepts which is ineradicably value-dependent. By this I mean that both its very definition and any given use of it, once defined, are inextricably tied to a given set of (probably unacknowledged) value-assumptions which predetermine the range of its empirical application – and I shall maintain below that some such uses permit that range to extend further and deeper than others. Moreover, the concept of power is, in consequence, what has been called an 'essentially contested concept' – one of those concepts which 'inevitably involve endless disputes about their proper uses on the part of their users' (Gallie 1955–6: 169). Indeed, to engage in such disputes is itself to engage in politics.

The absolutely basic common core to, or primitive notion lying behind, all talk of power is the notion that A in some way affects B. But, in applying that primitive (causal) notion to the analysis of social life, something further is needed – namely, the notion that A does so in a non-trivial or significant manner (see White 1972).

Clearly, we all affect each other in countless ways all the time: the concept of power, and the related concepts of coercion, influence, authority, etc., pick out ranges of such affecting as being significant in specific ways. A way of conceiving power (or a way of defining the concept of power) that will be useful in the analysis of social relationships must imply an answer to the question: 'what counts as a significant manner?', 'what makes A's affecting B significant?' Now, the *concept* of power, thus defined, when interpreted and put to work, yields one or more *views* of power – that is, ways of identifying cases of power in the real world. The three views we have been considering can be seen as alternative interpretations and applications of one and the same underlying concept of power, according to which A exercises power over B when A affects B in a manner contrary to B's interests. There are, however, alternative (no less contestable) ways of conceptualizing power, involving alternative criteria of significance.

[...]

These conceptualizations of power are rationally defensible. It is, however, the contention of this book that they are of less value than that advanced here for two reasons.

In the first place, they are revisionary persuasive redefinitions of power which are out of line with the central meanings of 'power' as traditionally understood and with the concerns that have always centrally preoccupied students of power. They focus on the locution 'power to', ignoring 'power over'. Thus power indicates a 'capacity', a 'facility', an 'ability', not a relationship. Accordingly, the conflictual aspect of power – the fact that it is exercised *over* people – disappears altogether from view. And along with it there disappears the central interest of studying power relations in the first place – an interest in the (attempted or successful) securing of people's compliance by overcoming or averting their opposition.

In the second place, the point of these definitions is, as we have seen, to reinforce certain theoretical positions; but everything that can be said by their means can be said with greater clarity by means of the conceptual scheme here proposed, without thereby concealing from view the (central) aspects of power which they define out of existence. Thus, for instance, Parsons objects to seeing power as a 'zero-sum' phenomenon and appeals to the analogy of credit creation in the economy, arguing that the use of power, as when the ruled have justified confidence in their rulers, may achieve objectives which all desire and from which all benefit. It has been argued in defence of this view that 'in any type of group, the existence of defined "leadership" positions does "generate" power which may be used to achieve aims desired by the majority of the members of the group' (Giddens 1968: 263). Similarly, Arendt wants to say that members of a group acting in concert are exercising power. According to the conceptual scheme here advanced, all such cases of co-operative activity, where individuals or groups significantly affect one another in the absence of a conflict of interests between them, will be identifiable, as cases of 'influence' but not of 'power'. All that Parsons and Arendt wish to say about consensual behaviour remains sayable, but so also does all that they wish to remove from the language of power.

```
                CONFLICT OF INTERESTS    NO CONFLICT OF INTERESTS

            Observable  |  Latent
            (overt or   |
            covert)     |
```

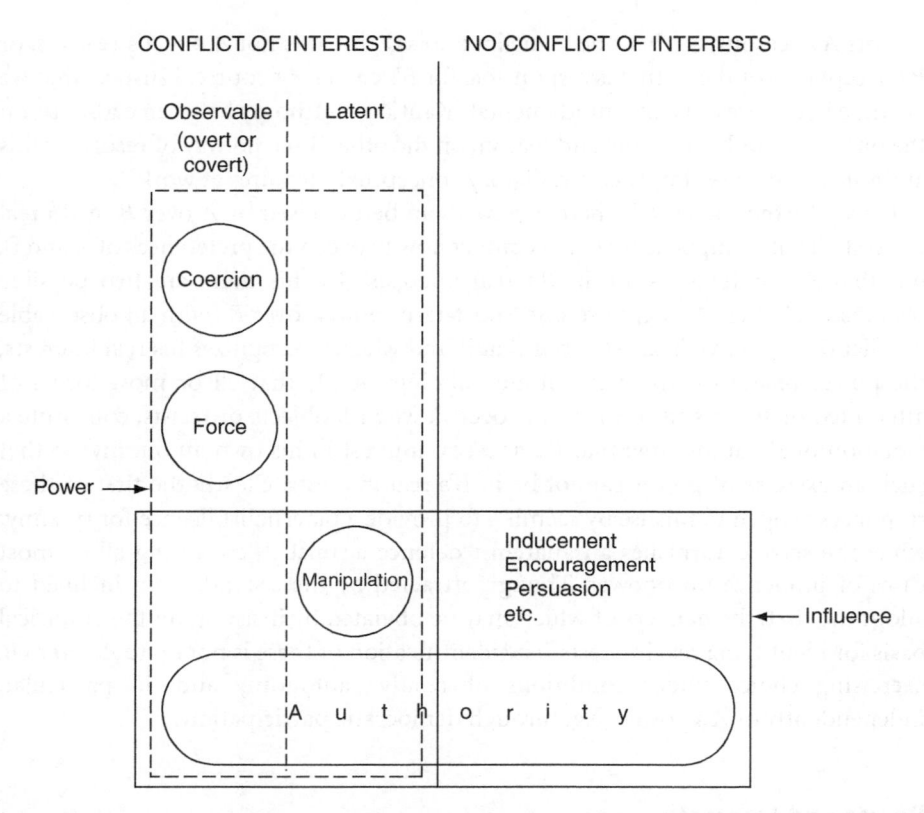

Figure 17.1 A conceptual map of Power and its Cognates.

It may be useful if at this point I set out a conceptual map (Figure 17.1) of power and its cognates (all modes of 'significant affecting') – a map which broadly follows Bachrach and Baratz's typology, [...]. Needless to say, this map is itself essentially contestable – and, in particular, although it is meant to analyse and situate the concept of power which underlies the one-, two- and three-dimensional views of power, I do not claim that it would necessarily be acceptable to all the proponents of those respective views. One reason for that, of course, is that it is developed from the perspective of the three-dimensional view, which incorporates and therefore goes further than the other two.

It will be seen that in this scheme power may or may not be a form of influence – depending on whether sanctions are involved; while influence and authority may or may not be a form of power – depending on whether a conflict of interests is involved. Consensual authority, with no conflict of interests, is not, therefore, a form of power.

The question of whether rational persuasion is a form of power and influence cannot be adequately treated here. For what it is worth, my inclination is to say both yes and no. Yes, because it is a form of significant affecting: *A* gets (causes) *B* to do or think what he would not otherwise do or think. No, because *B* autonomously accepts A's reasons, so that one is inclined to say that it is not A but A's reasons, or B's acceptance of them, that is responsible for B's change of course. I suspect that we are here in the presence of a fundamental (Kantian) antinomy between causality, on the one hand, and autonomy and reason, on the other. I see no way of resolving this antinomy: there are simply contradictory conceptual pressures at work.

It may further be asked whether power can be exercised by A over B in B's real interests. That is, suppose there is a conflict now between the preferences of A and B, but that A's preferences are in B's real interests. To this there are two possible responses: (1) that A might exercise 'short-term power' over B (with an observable conflict of subjective interests), but that if and when B recognizes his real interests, the power relation ends: it is self-annihilating; or (2) that all or most forms of attempted or successful control by A over B, when B objects or resists, constitute a violation of B's autonomy; that B has a real interest in his own autonomy; so that such an exercise of power cannot be in B's real interests. Clearly the first of these responses is open to misuse by seeming to provide a paternalist licence for tyranny; while the second furnishes an anarchist defence against it, collapsing all or most cases of influence into power. Though attracted by the second, I am inclined to adopt the first, the dangers of which may be obviated by insisting on the empirical basis for identifying real interests. The identification of these is not up to A, *but to B*, exercising choice under conditions of relative autonomy and, in particular, independently of A's power (e.g. through democratic participation).

Power and Interests

I have defined the concept of power by saying that A exercises power over B when A affects B in a manner contrary to B's interests. Now the notion of 'interests' is an irreducibly evaluative notion (Balbus 1971, Connolly 1972): if I say that something is in your interests, I imply that you have a prima facie claim to it, and if I say that 'policy x is in A's interest' this constitutes a prima facie justification for that policy. In general, talk of interests provides a licence for the making of normative judgments of a moral and political character. So it is not surprising that different conceptions of what interests *are* are associated with different moral and political positions. Extremely crudely, one might say that the liberal takes people as they are and applies want-regarding principles to them, relating their interests to what they actually want or prefer, to their policy preferences as manifested by their political participation. The reformist, seeing and deploring that not everyone's wants are given equal weight by the political system, also relates their interests to what they want or prefer, but allows that this may be revealed in more indirect and sub-political ways – in the form of deflected, submerged or concealed wants and preferences. The radical, however, maintains that people's wants may themselves be a product of a system which works against their interests, and, in such cases, relates the latter to what they would want and prefer, were they able to make the choice. Each of these three picks out a certain range of the entire class of actual and potential wants as the relevant object of moral appraisal. In brief, my suggestion is that the one-dimensional view of power presupposes a liberal conception of interests, the two-dimensional view a reformist conception, and the three-dimensional view a radical conception. (And I would maintain that any view of power rests on some normatively specific conception of interests.)

[...]

Conclusion

The one-dimensional view of power offers a clear-cut paradigm for the behavioural study of decision-making power by political actors, but it inevitably takes over the bias of the political system under observation and is blind to the ways in which its political agenda is controlled. The two-dimensional view points the way to examining that bias and control, but conceives of them too narrowly: in a word, it lacks a sociological perspective within which to examine, not only decision-making and nondecision-making power, but also the various ways of suppressing latent conflicts within society. Such an examination poses a number of serious difficulties.

These difficulties are serious but not overwhelming. They certainly do not require us to consign the three-dimensional view of power to the realm of the merely metaphysical or the merely ideological. My conclusion, in short, is that a deeper analysis of power relations is possible – an analysis that is at once value-laden, theoretical and empirical. A pessimistic attitude towards the possibility of such an analysis is unjustified. As Frey has written (1971: 1095), such pessimism amounts to saying: 'Why let things be difficult when, with just a little more effort, we can make them seem impossible?'

REFERENCES

Bachrach, P. and Baratz, M. S. (1970) *Power and Poverty: Theory and Practice*. New York: Oxford University Press.

Balbus, I. D. (1971) 'The Concept of Interest in Pluralist and Marxist Analysis', *Politics and Society*, 1: 151–77.

Bell, R., Edwards, D. V. and Harrison Wagner, R. (1969) *Political Power: A Reader in Theory and Research*. New York: Free Press.

Connolly, W. E. (1972) 'On "Interests" in Politics', *Politics and Society*, 2: 459–77; reprinted in Connolly 1983.

Dahl, R. A. (1957) 'The Concept of Power', *Behavioral Science*, 2: 201–15; reprinted in Scott (ed.) 1994.

Dahl, R. A. (1961) *Who Governs? Democracy and Power in an American City*. New Haven, CT: Yale University Press.

Frey, F. W. (1971) 'Comment: On Issues and Nonissues in the Study of Power', *American Political Science Review* 65: 1081–1101.

Gallie, W. B. (1955–6) 'Essentially Contested Concepts', *Proceedings of the Aristotelian Society*, 56: 167–98.

Giddens, A. (1968) '"Power" in the Recent Writings of Talcott Parsons', *Sociology*, 2: 257–72.
Lipsitz, L. (1970) 'On Political Belief: the Grievances of the Poor', in P. Green and S. Levinson (eds), *Power and Community: Dissenting Essays in Political Science*. New York: Random House, Vintage Books.
Merelman, R. (1968) 'On the Neo-elitist Critique of Community Power', *American Political Science Review*, 62: 451–60.
Polsby, N. W. (1963) *Community Power and Political Theory*, 2nd edn 1980. New Haven, CT: Yale University Press.
Schattschneider, E. E. (1960) *The Semi-Sovereign People: A Realist's View of Democracy in America*. New York: Holt, Rinehart & Winston.
White, D. M. (1972) 'The Problem of Power', *British Journal of Political Science*, 2(4): 479–90.

Chapter 18

State, Society and Modern History [1987]

Anthony Giddens

Power and Domination

In this opening section I outline some general notions connected with the concept of power, which will help construct basic underlying themes of the book as a whole. 'Power', along with 'agency' and 'structure', is an elementary concept in social science.[1] To be a human being is to be an agent – although not all agents are human beings – and to be an agent is to have power. 'Power' in this highly generalized sense means 'transformative capacity', the capability to intervene in a given set of events so as in some way to alter them. The logical connection between agency and power is of the first importance for social theory, but the 'universal' sense of power thus implied needs considerable conceptual refinement if it is to be put to work in the interests of substantive social research.

Such conceptual refinement needs to be of two principal sorts. On the one hand, power must be related to the resources that agents employ in the course of their activities in order to accomplish whatever they do. Resources implicated in the reproduction of social systems that have some degree of continuity – and thus 'existence' – across space and time form aspects of the structural properties of those social systems. Two types of resource can be distinguished – the allocative and the authoritative. By the first of these I refer to dominion over material facilities, including material goods and the natural forces that may be harnessed in their production. The second concerns the means of dominion over the activities of

Anthony Giddens, "State Society and Modern History," pp. 7–17 from Anthony Giddens, *The Nation-State and Violence*, Volume Two of *A Contemporary Critique of Historical Materialism*. Palgrave Macmillan 1987. Reprinted with permission of Palgrave Macmillan.

Contemporary Sociological Theory, Third Edition. Edited by Craig Calhoun, Joseph Gerteis, James Moody, Steven Pfaff, and Indermohan Virk. Editorial material and organization © 2012 John Wiley & Sons, Ltd. Published 2012 by John Wiley & Sons, Ltd.

human beings themselves.² Both sources of power depend in large degree upon the management of time-space relations.

In the sociological and anthropological literature, both Marxist and non-Marxist, primacy has often been given to allocative resources in the constitution of society and in the explication of social change. Such a view is given full and direct expression, of course, in historical materialism, if that term be taken to refer to the interpretation of history that Marx outlines in the 'Preface' to *A Contribution to the Critique of Political Economy*.³ 'History' there is understood in terms of the expansion of the forces of production, underlying both the institutional organization of different types of society and their processes of change. But it is by no means only in historical materialism that this sort of emphasis appears. It is characteristic of virtually all those theories that can be classified under the rubrics of 'cultural' or 'social evolutionism'. Such theories attempt to understand social change in terms of the differential adaptation of forms of society to their 'environment'. I have criticized this view extensively elsewhere, and there is no point in recapitulating that critique here.⁴ Suffice it to say that, according to the standpoint informing this book, no account of history that gives to allocative resources some sort of determining role in either social organization or social change can be defended.

To say this does not mean moving to the other extreme – placing the whole weight of the emphasis upon authoritative resources. If there are no prime movers in human history (even in the last instance) the problem for social analysis becomes that of examining a variety of relations between allocative and authoritative resources in the constitution of social systems and in the dynamics of social change.⁵

Resources do not in any sense 'automatically' enter into the reproduction of social systems, but operate only in so far as they are drawn upon by contextually located actors in the conduct of their day-to-day lives. All social systems, in other words, can be studied as incorporating or expressing modes of *domination* and it is this concept more than any other that provides the focal point for the investigation of power. Social systems that have some regularized existence across time-space are always 'power systems', or exhibit forms of domination, in the sense that they are comprised of relations of autonomy and dependence between actors or collectivities of actors.⁶ As has been exhaustively discussed in controversies over the nature of power, forms of domination thus portrayed cannot be reduced to acts or decisions taken, or policies forged, by individual agents. Power as the capability to effectively decide about courses of events, even where others might contest such decisions, is undeniably important. But 'decisions', and 'contested policies', represent only one aspect of domination. The term 'non-decision-making' is an unhappy one to refer to the other aspect of power, but it has become quite firmly established in some sectors of political science. What matters is not just that certain decisions are not made, but that they are not even considered. Non-decision-making, in other words, is not accurately seen just as the obverse of decision-making, but as influencing the circumstances in which certain courses of action are open to 'choice' in any way at all. Power may be at its most alarming, and quite often its most horrifying, when applied as a sanction of force. But it is typically at its most intense and durable when running silently through the repetition of institutionalized practices.[7] As I use it, therefore, 'domination' is not a concept that carries an intrinsically negative connotation.[8]

All social systems of any duration involve an 'institutional mediation of power'.[9] That is to say, domination is expressed in and through the institutions that represent the most deeply embedded continuities of social life. But in the context of any collectivity, association or organization,[10] domination is expressed as modes of *control*, whereby some agents seek to achieve and maintain the compliance of others. I shall refer to relatively stable forms of control as types of *rule*. Forms of rule are (more or less) stable relations of autonomy and dependence in social systems and are sustained by the routine practices that those in superordinate positions employ to influence the activities of others. As such they are to be analytically separated from the institutional mediation of power.[11] Thus, for example, a given type of bureaucratic organization may generate a high level of power in the sense of transformative capacity. This is true, for example, of the modern, large industrial corporation, as judged in terms of both the allocative and authoritative resources it commands. However, the capability of any individual, or group of individuals, to control what goes on in the organization is not a direct extension of the 'amount' of power generated. An individual may be in a 'powerful' position in the sense that he or she has the capability to deploy a range of resources. But how far these can be used to secure specific outcomes depends upon securing whatever compliance is necessary from others.[12] The frequently stated experience of those in positions of 'high power' that what they can accomplish is hedged with very defined limits is not wholly disingenuous.

We should distinguish the 'scope' of rule from its 'intensity'.[13] The former refers to how far actors in superordinate positions are able to control large areas of the activities of those subject to their rule. The scope of control of a managerial executive over those in lower echelons of the labour force may be quite extensive, although usually confined to whatever goes on in the sphere of 'work' only. By the intensity of control I refer to the sanctions that can be invoked to secure compliance, the most extreme being the command over the means of violence, of life and death. A variety of possible relations exist between the scope and intensity of control – a matter of great significance for the themes of this book. Thus, many traditional rulers have possessed 'complete' power over their subjects, in the sense that those subjects are supposed to obey their every command 'under pain of death'. But such power by no means yields a wide scope of actual mastery over the conduct of the subject population. Ruling groups in traditional states, as I shall argue in some detail later, lack the means of regularly influencing the day-to-day lives of their subject populations. One of the major characteristics of the modern state, by contrast, is a vast expansion of the capability of state administrators to influence even the most intimate features of daily activity.

All types of rule, then, rest upon the institutional mediation of power, but channel this through the use of definite strategies of control. Strategies of control naturally always depend in substantial degree upon the form of domination within which they are invoked. In a modern industrial setting, for instance, strategies used by managers to achieve compliance from workers operate within a framework in which the direct threat of violence or the use of force cannot be brought to bear. Much of what 'management' means in modern industry derives from this fact. Nonetheless, the resources that managers are able to draw upon to sustain control over the workforce can be focused and applied in a range of different ways. All strategies of control employed by superordinate individuals or groups call forth counter-strategies on the part of subordinates. This phenomenon represents what I call the *dialectic of control* in social systems, something that connects back directly to the theme of human agency with which I opened this discussion. To be an agent is to be able to make a difference to the world, and to be able to make a difference is to have power (where power means transformative capacity). No matter how great the scope or intensity of control superordinates possess, since their power presumes the active compliance of others, those others can bring to bear strategies of their own, and apply specific types of sanctions. 'Self-consciousness', Hegel says, 'attains its satisfaction only in another self-consciousness',[14] speaking of the master-slave dialectic. Hegel makes of this a teleological philosophy of history but, stripped of such grandiose pretensions, what is at issue is the capability even of the most dependent, weak and the most oppressed to have the ability to carve out spheres of autonomy of their own.

All forms of rule have their 'openings' that can be utilized by those in subordinate positions to influence the activities of those who hold power over them. One consequence of this is that technologies of power – in other words, formalized procedures of rule – rarely if ever work with the 'fixity' which on the face of things they might seem to possess. The more a social system is one in which the control exercised by superordinates depends upon a considerable scope of power over subordinates, the more shifting and potentially volatile its organization is likely to be. The literature on prisons or asylums, for example, is replete with descriptions of the 'effort-bargains' which those who administer such organizations are forced to conclude with inmates in order to make their rule effective.

All social reproduction and, therefore, all systems of power, are grounded in the 'predictability' of day-to-day routines. The predictable – that is to say, regularized – character of day-to-day activity is not something that just 'happens', it is in substantial part 'made to happen' by actors in the diverse settings of social life. Of course, actors do not do this 'consciously' in the ordinary sense of the term, although they do often discursively reflect upon the nature of the activities in which they engage. Many of the characteristics of social life that actors 'make happen' are accomplished via non-discursive 'practical consciousness'.[15] That is to say, actors routinely monitor reflexively what they do in the light of their complex knowledge of social conventions, sustaining or reproducing those conventions in the process. Since agents in all societies are 'social theorists', whose discursively articulated accounts are in some part constitutive of the social forms they reproduce in their conduct, it is never the case that they blindly enact and re-enact the routines of daily life. Even in the most traditional of cultures 'tradition' is reflexively appropriated and in some sense 'discursively understood'.

In traditional societies, however, especially in small oral cultures, 'tradition' is not known as such, because there is nothing that escapes its influence and, therefore, nothing with which to contrast it. 'History' is not understood as the use of the past to mobilize change in the future, but as the repetitiveness of 'reversible time'.[16] A significant alteration in the conditions of human social existence comes about with the invention of 'history'. From then on the circumstances of social reproduction are themselves reflexively monitored in an effort to influence the form institutions assume. I take this to be the main feature that separates *organizations* from other types of collectivity. The term 'organization' will crop up a great deal in this study. An organization is a collectivity in which knowledge about the conditions of system reproduction is reflexively used to influence, shape or modify that system reproduction. All forms of state administrative bodies are organizations in this sense, for reasons I shall document at some length in what follows. In modern nation-states, however, the reflexive monitoring of system reproduction is much more highly accentuated than in any pre-existing form of state and, in addition, 'organization' characterizes many other aspects of social life.

I have earlier linked domination with the mastery of time-space. Elaborating the implications of this means giving some conceptual attention to the timing and spacing of human social activities.[17] It is particularly important to emphasize the association between power and *locales*, which will also be one of the leading themes of the book. I use 'locale' in deliberate preference to the notion of 'place' as ordinarily employed by geographers, because 'place' is often only a vaguely formulated notion and because it does not usually mean the co-ordination of time as well as space. Locales refer to the settings of interaction, including the physical aspects of setting – their 'architecture' – within which systemic aspects of interaction and social relations are concentrated. The proximate aspects of settings are chronically employed by social actors in the constitution of interaction, a matter of quite fundamental significance to its 'meaningful' qualities.[18] But settings also are everywhere involved in the reproduction of institutionalized activities across wide spans of time and space. Thus, a dwelling is a locale displaying specific architectural features: these are socially relevant in so far as they are bound up with the distribution and the character of behaviour in time-space. A dwelling which has several rooms is 'regionalized', not just in the sense that there are various distinct 'places' which it thereby contains, but in the sense that the rooms are habitually used for different types of pursuit, distributed differentially in the routines of day-to-day life. I do not mean by 'locale', however, just settings of a fairly confined nature. Locales include internally regionalized settings of very wide time-space extension, from cities to nation-states and beyond.

The importance of locales to the theory of power can be spelled out as follows. Certain types of locale form 'power containers' – circumscribed arenas for the generation of administrative power. A locale is a power container in so far as it permits a concentration of allocative and authoritative resources. In what I shall call class-divided societies, castles, manorial estates – but above all cities – are containers for the generation of power. In the modern world, the administrative settings of organizations – business firms, schools, universities, hospitals, prisons, etc. – are centres for the concentration of resources. But the modern state, as nation-state, becomes in many respects the pre-eminent form of power container, as a territorially bounded (although internally highly regionalized) administrative unity.

It is possible to give some general indication of how power is generated by the 'containment' of resources, although naturally there are many specific differences between settings within different types of society. Power containers generate power, as has been mentioned, first and foremost through the concentration of allocative and administrative resources. The generation of allocative resources is, of course, influenced directly by forms of available technology in any society, but the level of their concentration depends primarily upon factors creating authoritative resources. These are of the following kinds.

1   The possibilities of surveillance that settings of various kinds allow. 'Surveillance' refers to two related sorts of phenomena. One is the accumulation of 'coded information', which can be used to administer the activities of individuals about whom it is gathered. It is not just the collection of information, but its storage that is important here. Human memory is a storage device, but the storage of information is enhanced vastly by various other kinds of marks or traces that can be used as modes of recording. If writing is in all cultures the main phenomenon involved, in modern states electronic storage – tapes, records, discs, etc. – considerably expands the range of available storage mechanisms. All modes of information storage are simultaneously forms of communication, cutting across the face-to-face communication that is exhaustive of human interaction in oral cultures. The 'externalized' character of information traces inevitably severs communication from its intrinsic connection with the body and the face. But electronic communication for the first time in history separates 'immediate' communication from presence, thereby initiating developments in modern culture that I shall later argue are basic to the emergence and consolidation of the nation-state.

The other sense of surveillance is that of the direct supervision of the activities of some individuals by others in positions of authority over them. The concentration of activities within clearly bounded settings greatly enlarges the degree to which those activities can be 'watched over', and thus controlled, by superordinates. In most types of non-modern society, the possibilities of surveillance in this second sense (as in the first) are relatively limited. There are many examples of large aggregates of people being brought together in the construction of public projects, for example, the building of temples, monuments or roads. But these groupings usually only exist for a limited duration and are relatively marginal to the activities and involvements of the majority of the population. Within fairly confined areas, such as small rural communities, certain kinds of surveillance procedures can be sustained in class-divided societies and these can be linked to larger networks with varying degrees of success. Examples can be found in the role of local priests in medieval Catholicism, or in the use of informers by the traditional Chinese state. But only in cities could direct and regular surveillance be maintained by the central agencies of the state, and then with a low degree of success compared with modern organizations. In modern organizations, either large segments of the daily lives of social actors (as in factories or offices), or substantial periods of their lives in a more 'total' setting (as in prisons, or asylums) can be subject to more-or-less continuous surveillance.

The two senses of surveillance belong quite closely together, since the collection of information about social activities can, and very often is, directly integrated with styles of supervision – something which again tends to be maximized in modern types of organization.

2   The possibilities of assembling, within definite settings, large numbers of individuals who do not spend most of their daily activity involved in direct material production. The formation of organizations, and of any substantial level of disciplinary power, depends upon the existence of specialized administrative officials of some kind. In orthodox versions of historical materialism, the early emergence of such administrative specialism is 'explained' in terms of the prior development of surplus production. But the way this explanation is often presented makes it neither plausible nor even a valid empirical description. It is hardly an explanation at all, even in the most general sense of that term, because surplus production has to be co-ordinated in some way if it is to become a resource for the generation of administrative power. However, it is also empirically wanting. If 'surplus production' means anything specific, the term must refer to material production which develops beyond what, for a given population of producers, are traditional or pre-established needs. Thus defined, surplus production is not even the necessary condition for the formation of specialized administrative apparatuses. Such organizations have very often come into being in circumstances of acute deprivation for many of the subjects of their rule – the appropriation of the 'surplus' perhaps being at the origin of that deprivation.[19]

As Max Weber emphasizes, the regularized 'containing' of assemblages of individuals within the settings of organizations can only be extensively achieved in a society given various other conditions in addition to the expansion of 'surplus production'. Some of these conditions are peculiar to the modern West. They include, particularly, the disappearance of 'prebendal' forms of renumeration and the associated development of a full-blown money economy. The purely 'vocational' official is one with a salaried income, whose sources of renumeration have become wholly cut off from the use of the official position to gather material resources put to private use.

3   The facilitating of the scope and intensity of sanctions, above all the development of military power. There are two locales of overwhelming significance here, or so I shall argue – the city in class-divided societies and, in modern societies, the nation-state. The relation between military power and sanctions of law is always important. Organizations of all types develop legal rules of some sort. All forms of law, in turn, involve sanctions administered in one way or another via officials. Such

administration is backed, in a direct or a more indirect manner, by the threat of the use of violence.[20] It will be part of my main thesis later in this book, however, that in many modern organizations – in contradistinction to what was the case in class-divided societies – the sanction of the use of violence is quite indirect and attenuated. Moreover, military power on the whole tends to become rather clearly distinct from policing power, the one turned 'externally', the other pointed 'internally'.

The first formation of permanent armed forces injects something substantially new into world history. But in all class-divided societies, no matter how strong the military forces commanded by the state, there are significant sources of armed opposition that escape the control of the central apparatus. The prominence of local war-lords, the existence of marauding nomadic groups, and all kinds of pirates and brigands, express the segmental character that class-divided societies display.

4   The creation of certain conditions that influence the formation of ideology. The system integration of class-divided societies does not depend in a significant way upon the overall acceptance of particular symbolic orders by the majority of the population within those societies. What matters is the hegemony achieved through such acceptance on the part of the members of dominant groups or classes. Concentration of activities within city *milieux* plays an important part here in more than one way. Through the expansion of surveillance, especially for example as pressed into the service of some kind of formal education, even if this is confined to a small stratum of the literate, the influence of ideology can be considerably sharpened. But probably also the sheer physical lay-out of many traditional cities has ideological effects. In such urban forms, the city is frequently dominated architecturally by state and religious edifices, giving a visual representation of power that no doubt makes an impress upon the minds of those who move in the vicinity of them.[21]

[...]

NOTES

The following books by the author are referred to in abbreviated form throughout the notes:

> *Central Problems in Social Theory* (London: Hutchinson, 1977) – *CPST*.
> *New Rules of Sociological Method* (London: Hutchinson, 1976) – *NRSM*.
> *The Class Structure of the Advanced Societies* (London: Hutchinson, 1979; revised edition, 1981) – *CSAS*.
> *A Contemporary Critique of Historical Materialism* (London: Macmillan, 1981), vol. I – *CCHM*, vol. I.
> *The Constitution of Society* (Cambridge: Polity Press, 1984) – *CS*.

State, Society and Modern History

1. cf. *CPST*, ch. 2; *CS, passim*.
2. For a fuller exposition, see *CPST*, ch. 3.
3. K. Marx, 'Preface' to 'A Contribution to the Critique of Political Economy', in K. Marx and F. Engels, *Selected Works in One Volume* (London: Lawrence and Wishart, 1968); cf. *CPST*, ch. 3.
4. *CS*, ch. 5.
5. See especially *CCHM*, vol. 1, chs 3, 4 and 5; *CS*, chs 4 and 5.
6. *NRSM*, ch. 3.
7. Talcott Parsons, 'On the concept of political power', *Proceedings of the American Philosophical Society*, 107, 1963.
8. *CPST*, p. 91ff.
9. *CSAS*, pp. 156–62.
10. *CS*, ch. 5.
11. Ibid., p. 14ff.
12. *CPST*, pp. 88–94.
13. Ibid.
14. G. W. F. Hegel, *The Phenomenology of Spirit* (Oxford: Clarendon Press, 1977). p. 126.
15. *CPST*, chapter 2; *CS*, ch. 1 and *passim*.
16. On this matter see the celebrated debate between Lévi-Strauss and Sartre about the nature of history. For a summary version, cf. Claude Lévi-Strauss: 'Réponses à quelques questions', *Esprit*. 31, 1963.
17. *CS* ch. 3 and *passim*. Simmel's remarks on such matters can still be read with profit. See 'Der Raum und die raumlichen Ordnungen der Gesellschaft', in his *Soziologie* (Leipzig: Duncker and Humbolt, 1908).
18. *CPST*, pp. 84–5.
19. *CCHM*, vol. I, pp. 97–100. The work of Jane Jacobs, however it might be criticized in some respects, is particularly important here.
20. In this book I use 'violence' in a straightforward sense, not in the much wider meaning attributed to it by Bourdieu and others. I mean by 'control of the means of violence' control over the capabilities of doing physical harm to the human body by the use of force.
21. *CCHM*, pp. 140–56.

Part V

The Sociological Theory of Michel Foucault

Introduction to Part V

19 The History of Sexuality

20 Truth and Power

21 Discipline and Punish

Part V

Introduction to Part V

The work of Michel Foucault (1926–84) has had a tremendous impact on a number of disciplines. Although not a sociologist by training, he worked on deeply sociological issues and other had significant influence on the work of other sociologists. Foucault did not attempt to construct a systematic theory. Rather, as Cousins and Hussain (1984: p. 1) put it, one encounters certain "habitual features of Foucault's analyses." These features are both substantive and methodological in nature. Substantively, Foucault explores issues of power through his historical examination of different "discourses" such as madness, medicine, prisons, and sexuality. Methodologically, Foucault creatively employs archaeology and genealogy as tools to investigate the history of culture and ideas. While some scholars consider Foucault to be a neostructuralist (Wuthnow et al., 1984), he has been most closely associated with the intellectual movement known as "poststructuralism." Others (most notably, Dreyfus and Rabinow, 1983) oppose such categorizations of Foucault's work. They suggest that he employs a unique interpretation of different intellectual traditions.

Foucault's Life and Intellectual Context

Foucault was born in Poitiers, France in 1926. He received his early education at local state schools, and then transferred to a Catholic school where he attained his *baccalauréat* with distinction. Foucault went on to study philosophy and psychology at the prestigious École Normale Supérieure, and also obtained a diploma in psychopathology. At the École, Foucault became acquainted with Louis Althusser, who introduced him to Marxist structuralism. Foucault later also acknowledged an intellectual debt to Jean Hyppolite, whose work focused on Hegel's philosophy; to Georges Canguilhem, an historian of ideas; and to Georges Dumezil, whose

Contemporary Sociological Theory, Third Edition. Edited by Craig Calhoun, Joseph Gerteis, James Moody, Steven Pfaff, and Indermohan Virk. Editorial material and organization © 2012 John Wiley & Sons, Ltd. Published 2012 by John Wiley & Sons, Ltd.

interests included the history of myth, art, and religion. After receiving his diploma, Foucault worked as an intern at a mental hospital in Paris and taught courses in psychopathology at the Sorbonne. In 1954, Foucault left France to teach French at Uppsala University in Sweden, then at the University of Warsaw and the University of Hamburg. During this period, Foucault began a study of the history of psychiatry. This resulted in the *Histoire de la folie à l'âge classique* (later translated in abridged form as *Madness and Civilization*), which was accepted as his doctoral thesis in the history of science in 1960.

Foucault returned to France the same year to head the philosophy department at the University of Clermont-Ferrand. While the *Madness and Civilization* and his next book, *The Birth of the Clinic*, did not initially receive significant interest, the publication of *The Order of Things* in 1966 was enthusiastically received, as was *The Archaeology of Knowledge* in 1969. After a brief tenure at the University of Vincennes and a teaching stint in Tunisia, Foucault was appointed professor of the History of Systems of Thought at the prestigious Collège de France in 1970.

Following the tumultuous political climate of 1968, Foucault's interests took a more political turn. Along with other intellectuals, he participated in committees against racism, and for patients' rights and reforms in the field of health. The most prominent of these committees was the Groupe d'Information sur les Prisons (GIP), whose aim was to provide a forum for prisoners to address their concerns during a period of prison unrest. Foucault's overall political turn manifested itself in his work in a focus on the institutional representation of power. This theme is explored in some of his major works from this period, such as *Discipline and Punish* and *The History of Sexuality*. In the course of his intellectual career, Foucault also pursued his literary interest through works on writers and artists such as Raymond Roussel, Georges Bataille, Maurice Blanchot, Hölderlin, and René Magritte. Foucault died in 1984.

Before specifically addressing his work, it may be useful to situate Foucault within the political and intellectual climate in France. Intellectuals in postwar France were greatly persuaded by the subject-centered theories of existential phenomenology in understanding the events surrounding the Second World War. As a student at the École, Foucault was particularly familiar with the ideas of Sartre and Merleau-Ponty. During this period, a large number of intellectuals also turned to the Communist Party in their desire to become politically engaged. A number of political events beginning in the mid-1950s, however, led to a reversal of this political trend. O'Farrell (1989) notes that Communist Party support of the center-left government's "pacification" measures in Algeria, the condemnation of the Stalinist regime by the Khrushchev report, and the suppression of the Hungarian Revolution led to disillusionment and depoliticization among intellectuals. It also resulted in a turn away from literature and the humanities toward more "scientific" disciplines, such as epistemology, ethnology, psychoanalysis, linguistics, and the social sciences. This period was also marked by the rise of structuralism.

In their attempt to "decenter" the subject, structuralists wanted to study human activity scientifically by looking for basic elements of their behavior and the rules or laws by which they are combined. Structuralism owed an intellectual debt to the work of Durkheim (see *Classical Sociological Theory*) and to the linguist Ferdinand de Saussure. Saussure proposed that language must be considered as a self-contained relational structure in which words have linguistic value only in relation to other words, thus shifting the emphasis from the signified to the signifier. Inspired by Saussure, the anthropologist Claude Lévi-Strauss applied structural linguistics to the study of society. In particular, he studied the structural aspects of kinship systems and mythological representations. In his commitment to scientism, Lévi-Strauss shifted the focus away from human subjectivity and epistemology to the formal study of social and cultural life as symbolic systems. For instance, in his analysis of myth in *The Raw and the Cooked*, Lévi-Strauss claimed to reveal the underlying structure of the cultural system in the basic oppositions between the raw, the cooked, and the rotten.

Using a structuralist approach to analyze everyday life, Roland Barthes analyzed ordinary experiences, such as films, advertisements, and propaganda to reveal the semiological structure underlying communications in advanced capitalist societies. Although most structuralists tended to identify themselves as Marxists, it was Louis Althusser (among others, such as Godelier and Sebag) who provided a structuralist reading of Marx. Rejecting the focus on class subjectivity and humanist Marxism, structural Marxists sought to redefine dialectical materialism and historical materialism. In doing so, Althusser dismissed empiricism as a form of ideology because it conflated theoretical objects with real objects. In other words, he argued that the "real" world exists only as a product of the ideological representations we make of it. Taking inspiration from the later Marx, Althusser shifted attention instead to a more "scientific" analysis of the structures of society.

Structuralism began to lose favor in France in the 1980s. Poststructuralism arose out of, and in response to, structuralism. Incorporating Nietzschean and psychoanalytic concepts, poststructuralists emphasize the importance of language. For instance, Derrida, whose name has been closely associated with poststructuralism, argues that all claims of originary speech are misleading. Opposing a systemic approach to language, Derrida suggests instead that it is "*différance*" that marks writing. In other words, this term suggest both a differing and deferring of the presence of meaning for language. Like structuralists in general, poststructuralists seek to decenter the subject, but they propose that subjects are created by the discourse in which they are embedded.

Foucault's work reflects this intellectual context in France. He has, for instance, been labeled both a structuralist and a poststructuralist. However, as Dreyfus and Rabinow (1983: p. xxiiiff.) point out, Foucault constantly sought to move beyond the existing alternatives available for the study of human beings. He avoided the structuralist analysis which eliminates notions of meaning altogether; avoided the phenomenological project of tracing all meaning back to the autonomous, transcendental subject; and finally avoided hermeneutic approaches to hidden meanings of which social actors are unaware to bring greater attention to everyday understanding as it shapes social life. This made Foucault's work an inspiration to a new generation of intellectuals seeking to break out of traditional intellectual approaches and examine social change not just through the idea of progress but with attention to more radical shifts in perspective (Eribon, 2011).

Foucault's Work

In his work, Foucault sought to conduct a "genealogy of the modern subject as a historical and cultural reality" (Smart, 1985: p. 18). His first major work was on madness. In *Madness and Civilization*, Foucault examines the historical conditions of the confinement and exclusion of different groups of people: lepers in the Middle Ages; the mad during the Renaissance; and the poor, the mad, and the homeless during the Classical Age. This story of spatial exclusion is one of the classification of different categories of people as a technology of power. Providing a history of the birth of the asylum at the end of the eighteenth century, Foucault traces the historical conditions of the emergence of modern medical, psychiatric, and human sciences. He unravels the Enlightenment privileging of reason to reveal the connection between power and knowledge. In his next book, *The Birth of the Clinic*, Foucault conducts an archaeology of medicine. He reinterprets the standard explanation provided by the medical profession about its shift in the eighteenth century from superstition to objective truth about the body and disease. In a structuralist mode, Foucault demonstrates how the medical theories of the Classical Age were as much governed by structural "codes of knowledge" as are those of modern medicine. In this book, Foucault traces how the gaze of modern medicine has increasingly come to be directed on the constitution of "man" as an object of knowledge.

Foucault next shifted his attention from an archaeology of institutions to that of discourse. Specifically, he extended his investigation to the human sciences. In *The Order of Things*, Foucault attempts to study the structure of the discourses of various disciplines regarding society, individuals, and language. He identifies the epistemic systems (or approaches to knowledge) that underlie three major epochs in Western thought: Renaissance, the Classical Age, and Modernity. Whereas there was no place for the representation of the activity of human beings in the classical episteme, Modernity is characterized as the Age of Man, in which "man" is the subject and object of his own knowledge. In *The Archaeology of Knowledge*, Foucault presents his method in the analysis of human sciences in greater detail. In the analysis of knowledge, he specifies the difference between his conceptual framework and those of conventional historical accounts in the history of ideas and the history of science. Discounting the standard conceptualization of history in terms of continuity, development, and progress, Foucault emphasizes discontinuity, rupture, and transformation in the analysis of discursive formations.

This analysis of how new forms of discipline and knowledge made the modern individual led Foucault to focus on power. In *Discipline and Punish* and *The History of Sexuality*, Foucault explores the relations between power, knowledge, and the body in modern society. In *Discipline and Punish*, he conducts a genealogy of modern disciplinary technology. He analyzes the transformation of punishment from torture in medieval times to the representation of crime in the Classical Age to the role of the prison and a normative social science in producing the modern individual. Power is increasingly exercised in the form of surveillance by a large array of apparatuses; through the classification and documentation of individuals; and the turning of subjects into objects of knowledge. Foucault extended his analysis of power relations to the area of sexuality in *The History of Sexuality*. His argument is that during the eighteenth and nineteenth centuries, sexuality became an object of scientific investigation and social concern. This was the result of a spread of bio-power, which was deployed in the case of sexuality through the practice of the confessional. In his writings on power in general, Foucault makes the case that power is not restricted to political institutions. Rather, it is multidirectional, operating from above and from below.

Foucault's Legacy

Until English translations of Foucault's work began to appear in the 1970s, he was little known in the English-speaking world. By the time of his death in 1984, however, Foucault's influence was so great that it was reported in newspapers around the world. This influence is also evident in the large body of literature that has been produced on Foucault's work during his life and since. In particular, as O'Farrell (1989: pp. 20–30) notes, many English-speaking critics have expressed an overwhelming interest in classifying Foucault's work. It is more helpful instead to emphasize the connections his work created between different inquiries. He was at once a sociologist, historian, and philosopher. He was a pioneer in the study of sexuality and the body, and connected this to the study of medical and other systems of knowledge and to modern social institutions from clinics to prisons. He integrated the analysis of subjective self-understanding with the analysis of social and cultural structure. He showed how power and discipline lead not only to restraint but to creative and sometimes disruptive responses. Across several disciplines he focused attention on the way basic shifts in the structure of knowledge and culture are associated with basic reorganizations of social life.

BIBLIOGRAPHY

Dreyfus, Hubert and Paul Rabinow. 1983. *Beyond Structuralism and Hermeneutics*. 2nd edition. Chicago, IL: University of Chicago Press. (An excellent interpretation of Foucault's work by two of the leading scholars on Foucault.)
Eribon, Didier. 2011. *Michel Foucault*. Cambridge, MA: Harvard University Press, 1991; rev.ed. 2011.
Habermas, Jürgen. 1981. "Modernity versus Postmodernity." *New German Critique* 22: 3–14. (An important essay on Foucault's treatment of the Enlightenment by a leading critical theorist.)

Hoy, David (ed.). 1986. *Foucault: A Critical Reader*. Oxford: Basil Blackwell. (A collection of serious essays by leading theorists.)

Lemert, Charles. 1990. "The Uses of French Structuralisms in Sociology." In George Ritzer (ed.), *Frontiers of Social Theory: The New Syntheses*. New York: Columbia University Press. (A good essay for an intellectual context of Foucault's writings.)

Lemert, Charles and Garth Gillan. 1982. *Michel Foucault: Social Theory and Transgressions*. New York: Columbia University Press. (A useful source for a sociological discussion of the major themes in Foucault's work.)

O'Farrell, Clare. 1989. *Foucault: Historian or Philosopher?* New York: St. Martin's Press. (A solid introduction to Foucault's work.)

Poster, Mark. 1975. *Existential Marxism in Postwar France: From Sartre to Althusser*. Princeton, NJ: Princeton University Press. (An excellent intellectual history of postwar France.)

Poster, Mark. 1984. *Foucault, Marxism and History*. Cambridge: Polity Press. (An analysis of Foucault's work in relation to Marxist theory.)

Rabinow, Paul. 1984. "Introduction." In Paul Rabinow (ed.), *The Foucault Reader*. New York: Pantheon Books. (A good essay on the major themes underlying Foucault's work.)

Sheridan, Alan. 1980. *Michel Foucault: The Will to Truth*. London: Tavistock Publications. (An authoritative commentary on Foucault's work by a leading scholar.)

Shumway, David. 1989. *Michel Foucault*. Boston, MA: Twayne Publishers. (A helpful survey of Foucault's major writings and themes.)

Smart, Barry. 1983. *Foucault, Marxism, and Critique*. London: Routledge & Kegan Paul. (A discussion of Foucault in relation to Marxist theory.)

Smart, Barry. 1985. *Michel Foucault*. London: Tavistock Publications. (A concise summary of Foucault's major works.)

Wuthnow, Robert et al. 1984. *Cultural Analysis: The Work of Peter Berger, Mary Douglas, Michel Foucault, and Jürgen Habermas*. London: Routledge & Kegan Paul. (A discussion of Foucault as a neostructuralist from a sociological perspective.)

Chapter 19

The History of Sexuality [1976]

Michel Foucault

For a long time, one of the characteristic privileges of sovereign power was the right to decide life and death. In a formal sense, it derived no doubt from the ancient *patria potestas* that granted the father of the Roman family the right to "dispose" of the life of his children and his slaves; just as he had given them life, so he could take it away. By the time the right of life and death was framed by the classical theoreticians, it was in a considerably diminished form. It was no longer considered that this power of the sovereign over his subjects could be exercised in an absolute and unconditional way, but only in cases where the sovereign's very existence was in jeopardy: a sort of right of rejoinder. If he were threatened by external enemies who sought to overthrow him or contest his rights, he could then legitimately wage war, and require his subjects to take part in the defense of the state; without "directly proposing their death," he was empowered to "expose their life": in this sense, he wielded an "indirect" power over them of life and death.[1] But if someone dared to rise up against him and transgress his laws, then he could exercise a direct power over the offender's life: as punishment, the latter would be put to death. Viewed in this way, the power of life and death was not an absolute privilege: it was conditioned by the defense of the sovereign, and his own survival. Must we follow Hobbes in

Michel Foucault, "The History of Sexuality," pp. 135–50 from Michel Foucault, *The History of Sexuality*, vol. I: *An Introduction*, translated from French by Robert Hurley. New York: Random House, Vintage Books, 1980. Copyright © 1978 by Random House, Inc., New York. Originally published in France as *La Volenté de Savoir*. Copyright © 1976 by Éditions Gallimard. Translation copyright © 1978 by Random House, Inc. Reprinted by permission of Georges Borchardt, Inc., for Éditions Gallimard, and Penguin Books Ltd.

seeing it as the transfer to the prince of the natural right possessed by every individual to defend his life even if this meant the death of others? Or should it be regarded as a specific right that was manifested with the formation of that new juridical being, the sovereign?[2] In any case, in its modern form – relative and limited – as in its ancient and absolute form, the right of life and death is a dissymmetrical one. The sovereign exercised his right of life only by exercising his right to kill, or by refraining from killing; he evidenced his power over life only through the death he was capable of requiring. The right which was formulated as the "power of life and death" was in reality the right to *take* life or *let* live. Its symbol, after all, was the sword. Perhaps this juridical form must be referred to a historical type of society in which power was exercised mainly as a means of deduction (*prélèvement*), a subtraction mechanism, a right to appropriate a portion of the wealth, a tax of products, goods and services, labor and blood, levied on the subjects. Power in this instance was essentially a right of seizure: of things, time, bodies, and ultimately life itself; it culminated in the privilege to seize hold of life in order to suppress it.

Since the classical age the West has undergone a very profound transformation of these mechanisms of power. "Deduction" has tended to be no longer the major form of power but merely one element among others, working to incite, reinforce, control, monitor, optimize, and organize the forces under it: a power bent on generating forces, making them grow, and ordering them, rather than one dedicated to impeding them, making them submit, or destroying them. There has been a parallel shift in the right of death, or at least a tendency to align itself with the exigencies of a life-administering power and to define itself accordingly. This death that was based on the right of the sovereign is now manifested as simply the reverse of the right of the social body to ensure, maintain, or develop its life. Yet wars were never as bloody as they have been since the nineteenth century, and all things being equal, never before did regimes visit such holocausts on their own populations. But this formidable power of death – and this is perhaps what accounts for part of its force and the cynicism with which it has so greatly expanded its limits – now presents itself as the counterpart of a power that exerts a positive influence on life, that endeavors to administer, optimize, and multiply it, subjecting it to precise controls and comprehensive regulations. Wars are no longer waged in the name of a sovereign who must be defended; they are waged on behalf of the existence of everyone; entire populations are mobilized for the purpose of wholesale slaughter in the name of life necessity: massacres have become vital. It is as managers of life and survival, of bodies and the race, that so many regimes have been able to wage so many wars, causing so many men to be killed. And through a turn that closes the circle, as the technology of wars has caused them to tend increasingly toward all-out destruction, the decision that initiates them and the one that terminates them are in fact increasingly informed by the naked question of survival. The atomic situation is now at the end point of this process: the power to expose a whole population to death is the underside of the power to guarantee an individual's continued existence. The principle underlying the tactics of battle – that one has to be capable of killing in order to go on living – has become the principle that defines the strategy of states.

But the existence in question is no longer the juridical existence of sovereignty; at stake is the biological existence of a population. If genocide is indeed the dream of modern powers, this is not because of a recent return of the ancient right to kill; it is because power is situated and exercised at the level of life, the species, the race, and the large-scale phenomena of population.

On another level, I might have taken up the example of the death penalty. Together with war, it was for a long time the other form of the right of the sword; it constituted the reply of the sovereign to those who attacked his will, his law, or his person. Those who died on the scaffold became fewer and fewer, in contrast to those who died in wars. But it was for the same reasons that the latter became more numerous and the former more and more rare. As soon as power gave itself the function of administering life, its reason for being and the logic of its exercise – and not the awakening of humanitarian feelings – made it more and more difficult to apply the death penalty. How could power exercise its highest prerogatives by putting people to death, when its main role was to ensure, sustain, and multiply life, to put this life in order? For such a power, execution was at the same time a limit, a scandal, and a contradiction. Hence capital punishment could not be maintained except by invoking less the enormity of the crime itself than the monstrosity of the criminal, his incorrigibility, and the safeguard of society. One had the right to kill those who represented a kind of biological danger to others.

One might say that the ancient right to *take* life or *let* live was replaced by a power to *foster* life or *disallow* it to the point of death. This is perhaps what explains that disqualification of death which marks the recent wane of the rituals that accompanied it. That death is so carefully evaded is linked less to a new anxiety which makes death unbearable for our societies than to the fact that the procedures of power have not ceased to turn away from death. In the passage from this world to the other, death was the manner in which a terrestrial sovereignty was relieved by another, singularly more powerful sovereignty; the pageantry that surrounded it was in the category of political ceremony. Now it is over life, throughout its unfolding, that power establishes its dominion; death is power's limit, the moment that escapes it; death becomes the most secret aspect of existence, the most "private." It is not surprising that suicide – once a crime, since it was a way to usurp the power of death which the sovereign alone, whether the one here below or the Lord above, had the right to exercise – became, in the course of the nineteenth century, one of the first conducts to enter into the sphere of sociological analysis; it testified to the individual and private right to die, at the borders and in the interstices of power that was exercised over life. This determination to die, strange and yet so persistent and constant in its manifestations, and consequently so difficult to explain as being due to particular circumstances or individual accidents, was one of the first astonishments of a society in which political power had assigned itself the task of administering life.

In concrete terms, starting in the seventeenth century, this power over life evolved in two basic forms; these forms were not antithetical, however; they constituted rather two poles of development linked together by a whole intermediary cluster of relations. One of these poles – the first to be formed, it seems – centered on the body as a machine: its disciplining, the optimization of its capabilities, the extortion of its forces, the parallel increase of its usefulness and its docility, its integration into systems of efficient and economic controls, all this was ensured by the procedures of power that characterized the *disciplines*: an *anatomo-politics of the human body*. The second, formed somewhat later, focused on the species body, the body imbued with the mechanics of life and serving as the basis of the biological processes: propagation, births and mortality, the level of health, life expectancy and longevity, with all the conditions that can cause these to vary. Their supervision was effected through an entire series of interventions and *regulatory controls: a bio-politics of the population*. The disciplines of the body and the regulations of the population constituted the two poles around which the organization of power over life was deployed. The setting up, in the course of the classical age, of this great bipolar technology – anatomic and biological, individualizing and specifying, directed toward the performances of the body, with attention to the processes of life – characterized a power whose highest function was perhaps no longer to kill, but to invest life through and through.

The old power of death that symbolized sovereign power was now carefully supplanted by the administration of bodies and the calculated management of life. During the classical period, there was a rapid development of various disciplines – universities, secondary schools, barracks, workshops; there was also the emergence, in the field of political practices and economic observation, of the problems of birthrate, longevity, public health, housing, and migration. Hence there was an explosion of numerous and diverse techniques for achieving the subjugation of bodies and the control of populations, marking the beginning of an era of "bio-power." The two directions taken by its development still appeared to be clearly separate in the eighteenth century. With regard to discipline, this development was embodied in institutions such as the army and the schools, and in reflections on tactics, apprenticeship, education, and the nature of societies, ranging from the strictly military analyses of Marshal de Saxe to the political reveries of Guibert of Servan. As for population controls, one notes the emergence of demography, the evaluation of the relationship between resources and inhabitants, the constructing of tables analyzing wealth and its circulation: the work of Quesnay, Moheau, and Süssmilch. The philosophy of the "Ideologists," as a theory of ideas, signs, and the individual genesis of sensations, but also a theory of the social composition of interests – Ideology being a doctrine of apprenticeship, but also a doctrine of contracts and the regulated formation of the social body – no doubt constituted the abstract discourse in which one sought to coordinate these two techniques of power in order to construct a general theory of it. In point of fact, however, they were not to be joined at the level of a speculative discourse, but in the form of concrete arrangements (*agencements concrets*) that would go to make up the great technology of power in the nineteenth century: the deployment of sexuality would be one of them, and one of the most important.

This bio-power was without question an indispensable element in the development of capitalism; the latter would not have been possible without the controlled insertion of bodies into the machinery of production and the adjustment of the phenomena of population to economic processes. But this was not all it required; it also needed the growth of both these factors, their reinforcement as well as their availability and docility; it had to have methods of power capable of optimizing forces, aptitudes, and life in general without at the same time making them more difficult to govern. If the development of the great instruments of the state, as *institutions* of power, ensured the maintenance of production relations, the rudiments of anatomo- and bio-politics, created in the eighteenth century as *techniques* of power present at every level of the social body and utilized by very diverse institutions (the family and the army, schools and the police, individual medicine and the administration of collective bodies), operated in the sphere of economic processes, their development, and the forces working to sustain them. They also acted as factors of segregation and social hierarchization, exerting their influence on the respective forces of both these movements, guaranteeing relations of domination and effects of hegemony. The adjustment of the accumulation of men to that of capital, the joining of the growth of human groups to the expansion of productive forces and the differential allocation of profit, were made possible in part by the exercise of bio-power in its many forms and modes of application. The investment of the body, its valorization, and the distributive management of its forces were at the time indispensable.

One knows how many times the question has been raised concerning the role of an ascetic morality in the first formation of capitalism; but what occurred in the eighteenth century in some Western countries, an event bound up with the development of capitalism, was a different phenomenon having perhaps a wider impact than the new morality; this was nothing less than the entry of life into history, that is, the entry of phenomena peculiar to the life of the human species into the order of knowledge and power, into the sphere of political techniques. It is not a question of claiming that this was the moment when the first contact between life and history was brought about. On the contrary, the pressure exerted by the biological on the historical had remained very strong for thousands of years; epidemics and famine were the two great dramatic forms of this relationship that was always dominated by the menace of death. But through a circular process, the economic – and primarily agricultural – development of the eighteenth century, and an increase in productivity and resources even more rapid than the demographic growth it encouraged, allowed a measure of relief from these profound threats: despite some renewed outbreaks, the period of great ravages from starvation and plague had come to a close before the French Revolution; death was ceasing to torment life so directly. But at the same time, the development of the different fields of knowledge concerned with life in general, the improvement of agricultural techniques, and the observations and measures relative to man's life and survival contributed to this relaxation: a relative control over life averted some of the imminent risks of death. In the space for movement thus conquered, and broadening and organizing that space, methods of power and knowledge assumed responsibility for the life processes and undertook to control and modify them. Western man was gradually learning what it meant to be a living species in a living world, to have a body, conditions of existence, probabilities of life, an individual and collective welfare, forces that could be modified, and a space in which they could be distributed in an optimal manner. For the first time in history, no doubt, biological existence was reflected in political existence; the fact of living was no longer an inaccessible substrate that only emerged from time to time, amid the randomness of death and its fatality; part of it passed into knowledge's field of control and power's sphere of intervention. Power would no longer be dealing simply with legal subjects over whom the ultimate dominion was death, but with living beings, and the mastery it would be able to exercise over them would have to be applied at the level of life itself; it was the taking charge of life, more than the threat of death, that gave power its access even to the body. If one can apply the term *bio-history* to the pressures through which the movements of life and the processes of history interfere with one another, one would have to speak of *bio-power* to designate what brought life and its mechanisms into the realm of explicit calculations and made knowledge-power an agent of transformation of human life. It is not that life has been totally integrated into techniques that govern and administer it; it constantly escapes them. Outside the Western world, famine exists, on a greater scale than ever; and the biological risks confronting the species are perhaps greater, and certainly more serious, than before the birth of microbiology. But what might be called a society's "threshold of modernity" has been reached when the life of the species is wagered on its own political strategies. For millennia, man remained what he was for Aristotle: a living animal with the additional capacity for a political existence; modern man is an animal whose politics places his existence as a living being in question.

This transformation had considerable consequences. It would serve no purpose here to dwell on the rupture that occurred then in the pattern of scientific discourse and on the manner in which the twofold problematic of life and man disrupted and redistributed the order of the classical episteme. If the question of man was raised – insofar as he was a specific living being, and specifically related to other living beings – the reason for this is to be sought in the new mode of relation between history and life: in this dual position of life that placed it at the same time outside history, in its biological environment, and inside human historicity, penetrated by the latter's techniques of knowledge and power. There is no need either to lay further stress on the proliferation of political technologies that ensued, investing the body, health, modes of subsistence and habitation, living conditions, the whole space of existence.

Another consequence of this development of bio-power was the growing importance assumed by the action of the norm, at the expense of the juridical system of the law. Law cannot help but be armed, and its arm, *par excellence*, is death; to those who transgress it, it replies, at least as a last resort, with that absolute menace. The law always refers to the sword. But a power whose task is to take charge of life needs continuous regulatory and corrective mechanisms. It is no longer a matter of bringing death into play in the field of sovereignty, but of distributing the living in the domain of value and utility. Such a power has to qualify, measure, appraise, and hierarchize, rather than display itself in its murderous splendor; it does not have to draw the line that separates the enemies of the sovereign from his obedient subjects;

it effects distributions around the norm. I do not mean to say that the law fades into the background or that the institutions of justice tend to disappear, but rather that the law operates more and more as a norm, and that the judicial institution is increasingly incorporated into a continuum of apparatuses (medical, administrative, and so on) whose functions are for the most part regulatory. A normalizing society is the historical outcome of a technology of power centered on life. We have entered a phase of juridical regression in comparison with the pre-seventeenth-century societies we are acquainted with; we should not be deceived by all the Constitutions framed throughout the world since the French Revolution, the Codes written and revised, a whole continual and clamorous legislative activity: these were the forms that made an essentially normalizing power acceptable.

Moreover, against this power that was still new in the nineteenth century, the forces that resisted relied for support on the very thing it invested, that is, on life and man as a living being. Since the last century, the great struggles that have challenged the general system of power were not guided by the belief in a return to former rights, or by the age-old dream of a cycle of time or a Golden Age. One no longer aspired toward the coming of the emperor of the poor, or the kingdom of the latter days, or even the restoration of our imagined ancestral rights; what was demanded and what served as an objective was life, understood as the basic needs, man's concrete essence, the realization of his potential, a plenitude of the possible. Whether or not it was Utopia that was wanted is of little importance; what we have seen has been a very real process of struggle; life as a political object was in a sense taken at face value and turned back against the system that was bent on controlling it. It was life more than the law that became the issue of political struggles, even if the latter were formulated through affirmations concerning rights. The "right" to life, to one's body, to health, to happiness, to the satisfaction of needs, and beyond all the oppressions or "alienations," the "right" to rediscover what one is and all that one can be, this "right" – which the classical juridical system was utterly incapable of comprehending – was the political response to all these new procedures of power which did not derive, either, from the traditional right of sovereignty.

This is the background that enables us to understand the importance assumed by sex as a political issue. It was at the pivot of the two axes along which developed the entire political technology of life. On the one hand it was tied to the disciplines of the body: the harnessing, intensification, and distribution of forces, the adjustment and economy of energies. On the other hand, it was applied to the regulation of populations, through all the far-reaching effects of its activity. It fitted in both categories at once, giving rise to infinitesimal surveillances, permanent controls, extremely meticulous orderings of space, indeterminate medical or psychological examinations, to an entire micro-power concerned with the body. But it gave rise as well to comprehensive measures, statistical assessments, and interventions aimed at the entire social body or at groups taken as a whole. Sex was a means of access both to the life of the body and the life of the species. It was employed as a standard for the disciplines and as a basis for regulations. This is why in the nineteenth century sexuality was sought out in the smallest details of individual existences; it was tracked down in behavior, pursued in dreams; it was suspected of underlying the least follies, it was traced back into the earliest years of childhood; it became the stamp of individuality – at the same time what enabled one to analyze the latter and what made it possible to master it. But one also sees it becoming the theme of political operations, economic interventions (through incitements to or curbs on procreation), and ideological campaigns for raising standards of morality and responsibility: it was put forward as the index of a society's strength, revealing of both its political energy and its biological vigor. Spread out from one pole to the other of this technology of sex was a whole series of different tactics that combined in varying proportions the objective of disciplining the body and that of regulating populations.

Whence the importance of the four great lines of attack along which the politics of sex advanced for two centuries. Each one was a way of combining disciplinary techniques with regulative methods. The first two rested on the requirements of regulation, on a whole thematic of the species, descent, and collective welfare, in order to obtain results at the level of discipline; the sexualization of children was accomplished in the form of a campaign for the health of the race (precocious sexuality was presented from the eighteenth century to the end of the nineteenth as an epidemic menace that risked compromising not only the future health of adults but the future of the entire society and species); the hysterization of women, which involved a thorough medicalization of their bodies and their sex, was carried out in the name of the responsibility they owed to the health of their children, the solidity of the family institution, and the safeguarding of society. It was the reverse relationship that applied in the case of birth controls and the psychiatrization of perversions: here the intervention was regulatory in nature, but it had to rely on the demand for individual disciplines and constraints (*dressages*). Broadly speaking, at the juncture of the "body" and the "population," sex became a crucial target of a power organized around the management of life rather than the menace of death.

The blood relation long remained an important element in the mechanisms of power, its manifestations, and its rituals. For a society in which the systems of alliance, the political form of the sovereign, the differentiation into orders and castes, and the value of descent lines were predominant; for a society in which famine, epidemics, and violence made death imminent, blood constituted one of the fundamental values. It owed its high value at the same time to its instrumental role (the ability to shed blood), to the way it functioned in the order of signs (to have a certain blood, to be of the same blood, to be prepared to risk one's blood), and also to its precariousness (easily spilled, subject to drying up, too readily mixed, capable of being quickly corrupted). A society of blood – I was tempted to say, of "sanguinity" – where power spoke *through* blood: the honor of war, the fear of famine, the triumph of death, the sovereign with his sword, executioners, and tortures; blood was *a reality with a symbolic function*. We, on the other hand, are in a society of "sex," or rather a society "with a sexuality": the mechanisms of power are addressed to the body, to life, to what causes it to proliferate, to what reinforces the species, its stamina, its ability to dominate, or its capacity for being used. Through the themes of health, progeny, race, the future of the species, the vitality of the social body, power spoke *of* sexuality and *to* sexuality; the latter was not a mark or a symbol, it was an object and a target. Moreover, its importance was due less to its rarity or its precariousness than to its insistence, its insidious presence, the fact that it was everywhere an object of excitement and fear at the same time. Power delineated it, aroused it, and employed it as the proliferating meaning that had always to be taken control of again lest it escape; it was *an effect with a meaning-value*. I do not mean to say that a substitution of sex for blood was by itself responsible for all the transformations that marked the threshold of our modernity. It is not the soul of two civilizations or the organizing principle of two cultural forms that I am attempting to express; I am looking for the reasons for which sexuality, far from being repressed in the society of that period, on the contrary was constantly aroused. The new procedures of power that were devised during the classical age and employed in the nineteenth century were what caused our societies to go from *a symbolics of blood* to *an analytics of sexuality*. Clearly, nothing was more on the side of the law, death, transgression, the symbolic, and sovereignty than blood; just as sexuality was on the side of the norm, knowledge, life, meaning, the disciplines, and regulations.

Sade and the first eugenists were contemporary with this transition from "sanguinity" to "sexuality." But whereas the first dreams of the perfecting of the species inclined the whole problem toward an extremely exacting administration of sex (the art of determining good marriages, of inducing the desired fertilities, of ensuring the health and longevity of children), and while the new concept of race tended to obliterate the aristocratic particularities of blood, retaining only the controllable effects of sex, Sade carried the exhaustive analysis of sex over into the mechanisms of the old power of sovereignty and endowed it with the ancient but fully maintained prestige of blood; the latter flowed through the whole dimension of pleasure – the blood of torture and absolute power, the blood of the caste which was respected in itself and which nonetheless was made to flow in the major rituals of parricide and incest, the blood of the people, which was shed unreservedly since the sort that flowed in its veins was not even deserving of a name. In Sade, sex is without any norm or intrinsic rule that might be formulated from its own nature; but it is subject to the unrestricted law of a power which itself knows no other law but its own; if by chance it is at times forced to accept the order of progressions carefully disciplined into successive days, this exercise carries it to a point where it is no longer anything but a unique and naked sovereignty: an unlimited right of all-powerful monstrosity.

While it is true that the analytics of sexuality and the symbolics of blood were grounded at first in two very distinct regimes of power, in actual fact the passage from one to the other did not come about (any more than did these powers themselves) without overlappings, interactions, and echoes. In different ways, the preoccupation with blood and the law has for nearly two centuries haunted the administration of sexuality. Two of these interferences are noteworthy, the one for its historical importance, the other for the problems it poses. Beginning in the second half of the nineteenth century, the thematics of blood was sometimes called on to lend its entire historical weight toward revitalizing the type of political power that was exercised through the devices of sexuality. Racism took shape at this point (racism in its modern, "biologizing," statist form): it was then that a whole politics of settlement (*peuplement*), family, marriage, education, social hierarchization, and property, accompanied by a long series of permanent interventions at the level of the body, conduct, health, and everyday life, received their color and their justification from the mythical concern with protecting the purity of the blood and ensuring the triumph of the race. Nazism was doubtless the most cunning and the most naïve (and the former because of the latter) combination of the fantasies of blood and the paroxysms of a disciplinary power. A eugenic ordering of society, with all that implied in the way of extension and intensification of micro-powers, in the guise of an unrestricted state control (*étatisation*), was accompanied by the oneiric exaltation of a superior blood; the latter implied both the systematic genocide of others and the risk of exposing oneself to a total sacrifice. It is an irony of history that the Hitlerite politics of sex remained an insignificant practice while the blood myth was transformed into the greatest bloodbath in recent memory.

At the opposite extreme, starting from this same end of the nineteenth century, we can trace the theoretical effort to reinscribe the thematic of sexuality in the system of law, the symbolic order, and sovereignty. It is to the political credit of psychoanalysis – or at least, of what was most coherent in it – that regarded with suspicion (and this from its inception, that is, from the moment it broke away from the neuropsychiatry of degenerescence) the irrevocably proliferating aspects which might be contained in these power mechanisms aimed at controlling and administering the everyday life of sexuality: whence the Freudian endeavor (out of reaction no doubt to the great surge of racism that was contemporary with it) to ground sexuality in the law – the law of alliance, tabooed consanguinity, and the Sovereign-Father, in short, to surround desire with all the trappings of the old order of power. It was owing to this that psychoanalysis was – in the main, with a few exceptions – in theoretical and practical opposition to fascism. But this position of psychoanalysis was tied to a specific historical conjuncture. And yet, to conceive the category of the sexual in terms of the law, death, blood, and sovereignty – whatever the references to Sade and Bataille, and however one might gauge their "subversive" influence – is in the last analysis a historical "retro-version." We must conceptualize the deployment of sexuality on the basis of the techniques of power that are contemporary with it.

NOTES

1 Samuel von Pufendorf, *Le Droit de la nature* (French trans., 1734), p. 445.
2 "Just as a composite body can have properties not found in any of the simple bodies of which the mixture consists, so a moral body, by virtue of the very union of persons of which it is composed, can have certain rights which none of the individuals could expressly claim and whose exercise is the proper function of leaders alone." Pufendorf, *Le Droit de la nature*, p. 452.

Chapter 20

Truth and Power* [1977]

Michel Foucault

I think one can be confident in saying that you were the first person to pose the question of power regarding discourse, and that at a time when analyses in terms of the concept or object of the "text," along with the accompanying methodology of semiology, structuralism, etc., were the prevailing fashion. Posing for discourse the question of power means basically to ask whom does discourse serve? ... Could you briefly situate within your work this question you have posed – if indeed it's true that you have posed it?

I don't think I was the first to pose the question. On the contrary, I'm struck by the difficulty I had in formulating it. When I think back now, I ask myself what else it was that I was talking about, in *Madness and Civilisation* or *The Birth of the Clinic*, but power? Yet I'm perfectly aware that I scarcely ever used the word and never had such a field of analyses at my disposal. I can say that this was an incapacity linked undoubtedly with the political situation we found ourselves in. It is hard to see where, either on the Right or the Left, this problem of power could then have been

---

* Originally translated by Colin Gordon, Leo Marshall, John Mepham, and Kate Soper. Interviewers: Alessandro Fontana and Pasquale Pasquino.

Michel Foucault, "Truth and Power," pp. 113, 115–17, 118–26, 131–3 from Michel Foucault, *Power/Knowledge: Selected Interviews and Other Writings, 1972–1977*, edited by Colin Gordon. New York: Random House, Pantheon Books, 1972. Copyright © 1972, 1975, 1976, 1977 by Michel Foucault. Preface and Afterword © 1980 by Colin Gordon. Bibliography © 1980 by Colin Gordon. This collection © 1980 by The Harvester Press. Used by permission of Pantheon Books, a division of Random House, Inc.

Contemporary Sociological Theory, Third Edition. Edited by Craig Calhoun, Joseph Gerteis, James Moody, Steven Pfaff, and Indermohan Virk. Editorial material and organization © 2012 John Wiley & Sons, Ltd. Published 2012 by John Wiley & Sons, Ltd.

posed. On the Right, it was posed only in terms of constitution, sovereignty, etc., that is, in juridical terms; on the Marxist side, it was posed only in terms of the State apparatus. The way power was exercised – concretely and in detail – with its specificity, its techniques and tactics, was something that no one attempted to ascertain; they contented themselves with denouncing it in a polemical and global fashion as it existed among the "others," in the adversary camp. Where Soviet socialist power was in question, its opponents called it totalitarianism; power in Western capitalism was denounced by the Marxists as class domination; but the mechanics of power in themselves were never analysed. This task could only begin after 1968, that is to say on the basis of daily struggles at grass roots level, among those whose fight was located in the fine meshes of the web of power. This was where the concrete nature of power became visible, along with the prospect that these analyses of power would prove fruitful in accounting for all that had hitherto remained outside the field of political analysis. To put it very simply, psychiatric internment, the mental normalisation of individuals, and penal institutions have no doubt a fairly limited importance if one is only looking for their economic significance. On the other hand, they are undoubtedly essential to the general functioning of the wheels of power. So long as the posing of the question of power was kept subordinate to the economic instance and the system of interests which this served, there was a tendency to regard these problems as of small importance.

> So a certain kind of Marxism and a certain kind of phenomenology constituted an objective obstacle to the formulation of this problematic?

Yes, if you like, to the extent that it's true that, in our student days, people of my generation were brought up on these two forms of analysis, one in terms of the constituent subject, the other in terms of the economic in the last instance, ideology and the play of superstructures and infrastructures.

> Still within this methodological context, how would you situate the genealogical approach? As a questioning of the conditions of possibility, modalities and constitution of the "objects" and domains you have successively analysed, what makes it necessary?

I wanted to see how these problems of constitution could be resolved within a historical framework, instead of referring them back to a constituent object (madness, criminality or whatever). But this historical contextualisation needed to be something more than the simple relativisation of the phenomenological subject. I don't believe the problem can be solved by historicising the subject as posited by the phenomenologists, fabricating a subject that evolves through the course of history. One has to dispense with the constituent subject, to get rid of the subject itself, that's to say, to arrive at an analysis which can account for the constitution of the subject within a historical framework. And this is what I would call genealogy, that is, a form of history which can account for the constitution of knowledges, discourses, domains of objects etc., without having to make reference to a subject which is either transcendental in relation to the field of events or runs in its empty sameness throughout the course of history.

> Marxist phenomenology and a certain kind of Marxism have clearly acted as a screen and an obstacle; there are two further concepts which continue today to act as a screen and an obstacle, ideology on the one hand and repression on the other ... Could you perhaps use this occasion to specify more explicitly your thoughts on these matters? ...

The notion of ideology appears to me to be difficult to make use of, for three reasons. The first is that, like it or not, it always stands in virtual opposition to something else which is supposed to count as truth. Now I believe that the problem does not consist in drawing the line between that in a discourse which falls under the category of scientificity or truth, and that which comes under some other category, but in seeing historically how effects of truth are produced within discourses which in themselves are neither true nor false. The second drawback is that the concept of ideology refers, I think necessarily, to something of the order of a subject. Thirdly, ideology stands in a secondary position relative to something which functions as its infrastructure, as its material, economic determinant, etc. For these three reasons, I think that this is a notion that cannot be used without circumspection.

The notion of repression is a more insidious one, or at all events I myself have had much more trouble in freeing myself of it, in so far as it does indeed appear to correspond so well with a whole range of phenomena which belong among the effects of power. When I wrote *Madness and Civilisation*, I made at least an implicit use of this notion of repression. I think indeed that I was positing the existence of a sort of living, voluble and anxious madness which the mechanisms of power and psychiatry were supposed to have come to repress and reduce to silence. But it seems to me now that the notion of repression is quite inadequate for capturing what is precisely the productive aspect of power. In defining the effects of power as repression, one adopts a purely juridical conception of such power, one identifies power with a law which says no, power is taken above all as carrying the force of a prohibition. Now I believe that this is a wholly negative, narrow, skeletal conception of power, one which has been curiously widespread. If power were never anything but repressive, if it never did anything but to say no, do you really think one would be brought to obey it? What makes power hold good, what makes it accepted, is simply the fact that it doesn't only weigh on us as a force that says no, but that it traverses and produces things, it induces pleasure, forms knowledge, produces discourse. It needs to be considered as a productive network which runs through the whole social body, much more than as a negative instance whose function is repression. In *Discipline and Punish* what I wanted to show was how, from the seventeenth and eighteenth centuries onwards, there was a veritable technological take-off in the productivity of power. Not only did the monarchies of the Classical period develop great state apparatuses (the army, the police and fiscal administration), but above all there was established at this period what one might call a new "economy" of power, that is to say procedures which allowed the effects of power to circulate in a manner at once continuous, uninterrupted, adapted and "individualised" throughout the entire social body. These new techniques are both much more efficient and much less wasteful (less costly economically, less risky in their results, less open to loopholes and resistances) than the techniques previously employed which were based on a mixture of more or less forced tolerances (from recognised privileges to endemic criminality) and costly ostentation (spectacular and discontinuous interventions of power, the most violent form of which was the "exemplary," because exceptional, punishment).

> Repression is a concept used above all in relation to sexuality. It was held that bourgeois society represses sexuality, stifles sexual desire, and so forth. And when one considers for example the campaign launched against masturbation in the eighteenth century, or the medical discourse on homosexuality in the second half of the nineteenth century, or discourse on sexuality in general, one does seem to be faced with a discourse of repression. ...

Certainly. It is customary to say that bourgeois society repressed infantile sexuality to the point where it refused even to speak of it or acknowledge its existence. It was necessary to wait until Freud for the discovery at last to be made that children have a sexuality. Now if you read all the books on pedagogy and child medicine – all the manuals for parents that were published in the eighteenth century – you find that children's sex is spoken of constantly and in every possible context. One might argue that the purpose of these discourses was precisely to prevent children from having a sexuality. But their *effect* was to din it into parents' heads that their children's sex constituted a fundamental problem in terms of their parental educational responsibilities, and to din it into children's heads that their relationship with their own body and their own sex was to be a fundamental problem as far as *they* were concerned; and this had the consequence of sexually exciting the bodies of children while at the same time fixing the parental gaze and vigilance on the peril of infantile sexuality. The result was a sexualising of the infantile body, a sexualising of the bodily relationship between parent and child, a sexualising of the familial domain. "Sexuality" is far more of a positive product of power than power was ever repression of sexuality. I believe that it is precisely these positive mechanisms that need to be investigated, and here one must free oneself of the juridical schematism of all previous characterisations of the nature of power. Hence a historical problem arises, namely that of discovering why the West has insisted for so long on seeing the power it exercises as juridical and negative rather than as technical and positive.

> Perhaps this is because it has always been thought that power is mediated through the forms prescribed in the great juridical and philosophical theories, and that there is a fundamental, immutable gulf between those who exercise power and those who undergo it.

I wonder if this isn't bound up with the institution of monarchy. This developed during the Middle Ages against the backdrop of the previously endemic struggles between feudal power agencies. The monarchy presented itself as a referee, a power capable of putting an end to war, violence and pillage and saying no to these struggles and private feuds. It made itself acceptable by allocating itself a juridical and negative function, albeit one whose limits it naturally began at once to overstep. Sovereign, law and prohibition formed a system of representation of power which was extended during the subsequent era by the theories of right: political theory has never ceased to be obsessed with the person of the sovereign. Such theories still continue today to busy themselves with the problem of sovereignty. What we need, however, is a political philosophy that isn't erected around the problem of sovereignty, nor therefore around the problems of law and prohibition. We need to cut off the King's head: in political theory that has still to be done.

> The King's head still hasn't been cut off, yet already people are trying to replace it by discipline, that vast system instituted in the seventeenth century comprising the functions of surveillance, normalisation and control and, a little later, those of punishment, correction, education and so on. One wonders where this system comes from, why it emerges and what its use is. ...

To pose the problem in terms of the State means to continue posing it in terms of sovereign and sovereignty, that is to say in terms of law. If one describes all these phenomena of power as dependent on the State apparatus, this means grasping them as essentially repressive: the Army as a power of death, police and justice as punitive instances, etc. I don't want to say that the State isn't important; what I want to say is that relations of power, and hence the analysis that must be made of them, necessarily extend beyond the limits of the State. In two senses: first of all because the State, for all the omnipotence of its apparatuses, is far from being able to occupy the whole field of actual power relations, and further because the State can only operate on the basis of other, already existing power relations. The State is superstructural in relation to a whole series of power networks that invest the body, sexuality, the family, kinship, knowledge, technology and so forth. True, these networks stand in a conditioning–conditioned relationship to a kind of "meta-power" which is structured essentially round a certain number of great prohibition functions; but this meta-power with its prohibitions can only take hold and secure its footing where it is rooted in a whole series of multiple and indefinite power relations that supply the necessary basis for the great negative forms of power. That is just what I was trying to make apparent in my book.

> Doesn't this open up the possibility of overcoming the dualism of political struggles that eternally feed on the opposition between the State on the one hand and Revolution on the other? Doesn't it indicate a wider field of conflicts than that of those where the adversary is the State?

I would say that the State consists in the codification of a whole number of power relations which render its functioning possible, and that Revolution is a different type of codification of the same relations. This implies that there are many different kinds of revolution, roughly speaking as many kinds as there are possible subversive recodifications of power relations, and further that one can perfectly well conceive of revolutions which leave essentially untouched the power relations which form the basis for the functioning of the State.

> You have said about power as an object of research that one has to invert Clausewitz's formula so as to arrive at the idea that politics is the continuation of war by other means. Does the military model seem to you on the basis of your most recent researches to be the best one for describing power; is war here simply a metaphorical model, or is it the literal, regular, everyday mode of operation of power?

This is the problem I now find myself confronting. As soon as one endeavours to detach power with its techniques and procedures from the form of law within which it has been theoretically confined up until now, one is driven to ask this basic question: isn't power simply a form of warlike domination? Shouldn't one therefore conceive all problems of power in terms of relations of war? Isn't power a sort of generalised war which assumes at particular moments the forms of peace and the State? Peace would then be a form of war, and the State a means of waging it.

A whole range of problems emerge here. Who wages war against whom? Is it between two classes, or more? Is it a war of all against all? What is the role of the army and military institutions in this civil society where permanent war is waged? What is the relevance of concepts of tactics and strategy for analysing structures and political processes? What is the essence and mode of transformation of power relations? All these questions need to be explored. In any case it's astonishing to see how easily and self-evidently people talk of war-like relations of power or of class struggle without ever making it clear whether some form of war is meant, and if so what form.

> We have already talked about this disciplinary power whose effects, rules and mode of constitution you describe in *Discipline and Punish*. One might ask here, why surveillance? What is the use of surveillance? ... Even if you are only perhaps at the beginning of your researches here, could you say how you see the nature of the relationships (if any) which are engendered between these different bodies: the molar body of the population and the micro-bodies of individuals?

Your question is exactly on target. I find it difficult to reply because I am working on this problem right now. I believe one must keep in view the fact that along with all the fundamental technical inventions and discoveries of the seventeenth and eighteenth centuries, a new technology of the exercise of power also emerged which was probably even more important than the constitutional reforms and new forms of government established at the end of the eighteenth century. In the camp of the Left, one often hears people saying that power is that which abstracts, which negates the body, represses, suppresses, and so forth. I would say instead that what

I find most striking about these new technologies of power introduced since the seventeenth and eighteenth centuries is their concrete and precise character, their grasp of a multiple and differentiated reality. In feudal societies power functioned essentially through signs and levies. Signs of loyalty to the feudal lords, rituals, ceremonies and so forth, and levies in the form of taxes, pillage, hunting, war etc. In the seventeenth and eighteenth centuries a form of power comes into being that begins to exercise itself through social production and social service. It becomes a matter of obtaining productive service from individuals in their concrete lives. And in consequence, a real and effective "incorporation" of power was necessary, in the sense that power had to be able to gain access to the bodies of individuals, to their acts, attitudes and modes of everyday behaviour. Hence the significance of methods like school discipline, which succeeded in making children's bodies the object of highly complex systems of manipulation and conditioning. But at the same time, these new techniques of power needed to grapple with the phenomena of population, in short to undertake the administration, control and direction of the accumulation of men (the economic system that promotes the accumulation of capital and the system of power that ordains the accumulation of men are, from the seventeenth century on, correlated and inseparable phenomena): hence there arise the problems of demography, public health, hygiene, housing conditions, longevity and fertility. And I believe that the political significance of the problem of sex is due to the fact that sex is located at the point of intersection of the discipline of the body and the control of the population.

> Finally, a question you have been asked before: the work you do, these preoccupations of yours, the results you arrive at, what use can one finally make of all this in everyday political struggles? ... If one isn't an "organic" intellectual acting as the spokesman for a global organisation, if one doesn't purport to function as the bringer, the master of truth, what position is the intellectual to assume?

The important thing here, I believe, is that truth isn't outside power, or lacking in power: contrary to a myth whose history and functions would repay further study, truth isn't the reward of free spirits, the child of protracted solitude, nor the privilege of those who have succeeded in liberating themselves. Truth is a thing of this world: it is produced only by virtue of multiple forms of constraint. And it induces regular effects of power. Each society has its régime of truth, its "general politics" of truth: that is, the types of discourse which it accepts and makes function as true; the mechanisms and instances which enable one to distinguish true and false statements, the means by which each is sanctioned; the techniques and procedures accorded value in the acquisition of truth; the status of those who are charged with saying what counts as true.

In societies like ours, the "political economy" of truth is characterised by five important traits. "Truth" is centred on the form of scientific discourse and the institutions which produce it; it is subject to constant economic and political incitement (the demand for truth, as much for economic production as for political power); it is the object, under diverse forms, of immense diffusion and consumption (circulating through apparatuses of education and information whose extent is relatively broad in the social body, not withstanding certain strict limitations); it is produced and transmitted under the control, dominant if not exclusive, of a few great political and economic apparatuses (university, army, writing, media); lastly, it is the issue of a whole political debate and social confrontation ("ideological" struggles).

It seems to me that what must now be taken into account in the intellectual is not the "bearer of universal values." Rather, it's the person occupying a specific position – but whose specificity is linked, in a society like ours, to the general functioning of an apparatus of truth. In other words, the intellectual has a three-fold specificity: that of his class position (whether as petty-bourgeois in the service of capitalism or "organic" intellectual of the proletariat); that of his conditions of life and work, linked to his condition as an intellectual (his field of research, his place in a laboratory, the political and economic demands to which he submits or against which he rebels, in the university, the hospital, etc.); lastly, the specificity of the politics of truth in our societies. And it's with this last factor that his position can take on a general significance and that his local, specific struggle can have effects and implications which are not simply professional or sectoral. The intellectual can operate and struggle at the general level of that régime of truth which is so essential to the structure and functioning of our society. There is a battle "for truth," or at least "around truth" – it being understood once again that by truth I do not mean "the ensemble of truths which are to be discovered and accepted," but rather "the ensemble of rules according to which the true and the false are separated and specific effects of power attached to the true," it being understood also that it's not a matter of a battle "on behalf" of the truth, but of a battle about the status of truth and the economic and political role it plays. It is necessary to think of the political problems of intellectuals not in terms of "science" and "ideology," but in terms of "truth" and "power." And thus the question of the professionalisation of intellectuals and the division between intellectual and manual labour can be envisaged in a new way.

All this must seem very confused and uncertain. Uncertain indeed, and what I am saying here is above all to be taken as a hypothesis. In order for it to be a little less confused, however, I would like to put forward a few "propositions" – not firm assertions, but simply suggestions to be further tested and evaluated.

"Truth" is to be understood as a system of ordered procedures for the production, regulation, distribution, circulation and operation of statements.

"Truth" is linked in a circular relation with systems of power which produce and sustain it, and to effects of power which it induces and which extend it. A "régime" of truth.

This régime is not merely ideological or superstructural; it was a condition of the formation and development of capitalism. And it's this same régime which, subject to certain modifications, operates in the socialist countries (I leave open here the question of China, about which I know little).

The essential political problem for the intellectual is not to criticise the ideological contents supposedly linked to science, or to ensure that his own scientific practice is accompanied by a correct ideology, but that of ascertaining the possibility of constituting a new politics of truth. The problem is not changing people's consciousnesses – or what's in their heads – but the political, economic, institutional régime of the production of truth.

It's not a matter of emancipating truth from every system of power (which would be a chimera, for truth is already power) but of detaching the power of truth from the forms of hegemony, social, economic and cultural, within which it operates at the present time.

The political question, to sum up, is not error, illusion, alienated consciousness or ideology; it is truth itself. Hence the importance of Nietzsche.

Chapter 21

Discipline and Punish* [1975]

Michel Foucault

Bentham's *Panopticon* is the architectural figure of this composition. We know the principle on which it was based: at the periphery, an annular building; at the centre, a tower; this tower is pierced with wide windows that open onto the inner side of the ring; the peripheric building is divided into cells, each of which extends the whole width of the building; they have two windows, one on the inside, corresponding to the windows of the tower; the other, on the outside, allows the light to cross the cell from one end to the other. All that is needed, then, is to place a supervisor in a central tower and to shut up in each cell a madman, a patient, a condemned man, a worker or a schoolboy. By the effect of backlighting, one can observe from the tower, standing out precisely against the light, the small captive shadows in the cells of the periphery. They are like so many cages, so many small theatres, in which each actor is alone, perfectly individualized and constantly visible. The panoptic mechanism arranges spatial unities that make it possible to see constantly and to recognize immediately. In short, it reverses the principle of the dungeon; or rather of its three

---

* Originally translated from the French by Alan Sheridan.

Michel Foucault, "Discipline and Punish," pp. 200–2, 215–16, 218–24 from Michel Foucault, *Discipline and Punish: The Birth of the Prison*. New York: Penguin Books, 1975. English translation copyright © 1977 by Alan Sheridan (New York: Pantheon). Originally published in French as *Surveiller et Punir: Naissance de la prison* (by Éditions Gallimard 1975, Allen Lane 1975). Copyright © 1975 by Éditions Gallimard. Reprinted by permission of Georges Borchardt, Inc., for Éditions Gallimard, and Penguin Books Ltd.

Classical Sociological Theory, Third Edition. Edited by Craig Calhoun, Joseph Gerteis, James Moody, Steven Pfaff, and Indermohan Virk. Editorial material and organization © 2012 John Wiley & Sons, Ltd. Published 2012 by John Wiley & Sons, Ltd.

functions – to enclose, to deprive of light and to hide – it preserves only the first and eliminates the other two. Full lighting and the eye of a supervisor capture better than darkness, which ultimately protected. Visibility is a trap.

To begin with, this made it possible – as a negative effect – to avoid those compact, swarming, howling masses that were to be found in places of confinement, those painted by Goya or described by Howard. Each individual, in his place, is securely confined to a cell from which he is seen from the front by the supervisor; but the side walls prevent him from coming into contact with his companions. He is seen, but he does not see; he is the object of information, never a subject in communication. The arrangement of his room, opposite the central tower, imposes on him an axial visibility; but the divisions of the ring, those separated cells, imply a lateral invisibility. And this invisibility is a guarantee of order. If the inmates are convicts, there is no danger of a plot, an attempt at collective escape, the planning of new crimes for the future, bad reciprocal influences; if they are patients, there is no danger of contagion; if they are madmen there is no risk of their committing violence upon one another; if they are school children, there is no copying, no noise, no chatter, no waste of time; if they are workers, there are no disorders, no theft, no coalitions, none of those distractions that slow down the rate of work, make it less perfect or cause accidents. The crowd, a compact mass, a locus of multiple exchanges, individualities merging together, a collective effect, is abolished and replaced by a collection of separated individualities. From the point of view of the guardian, it is replaced by a multiplicity that can be numbered and supervised; from the point of view of the inmates, by a sequestered and observed solitude (Bentham, 60–4).

Hence the major effect of the Panopticon: to induce in the inmate a state of conscious and permanent visibility that assures the automatic functioning of power. So to arrange things that the surveillance is permanent in its effects, even if it is discontinuous in its action; that the perfection of power should tend to render its actual exercise unnecessary; that this architectural apparatus should be a machine for creating and sustaining a power relation independent of the person who exercises it; in short, that the inmates should be caught up in a power situation of which they are themselves the bearers. To achieve this, it is at once too much and too little that the prisoner should be constantly observed by an inspector: too little, for what matters is that he knows himself to be observed; too much, because he has no need in fact of being so. In view of this, Bentham laid down the principle that power should be visible and unverifiable. Visible: the inmate will constantly have before his eyes the tall outline of the central tower from which he is spied upon. Unverifiable: the inmate must never know whether he is being looked at at any one moment; but he must be sure that he may always be so. In order to make the presence or absence of the inspector unverifiable, so that the prisoners, in their cells, cannot even see a shadow, Bentham envisaged not only venetian blinds on the windows of the central observation hall, but, on the inside, partitions that intersected the hall at right angles and, in order to pass from one quarter to the other, not doors but zig-zag openings; for the slightest noise, a gleam of light, a brightness in a half-opened door would betray the presence of the guardian. The Panopticon is a machine for dissociating the see/being seen dyad: in the peripheric ring, one is totally seen, without ever seeing; in the central tower, one sees everything without ever being seen.

It is an important mechanism, for it automatizes and disindividualizes power. Power has its principle not so much in a person as in a certain concerted distribution of bodies, surfaces, lights, gazes; in an arrangement whose internal mechanisms produce the relation in which individuals are caught up. The ceremonies, the rituals, the marks by which the sovereign's surplus power was manifested are useless. There is a machinery that assures dissymmetry, disequilibrium, difference. Consequently, it does not matter who exercises power. Any individual, taken almost at random, can operate the machine: in the absence of the director, his family, his friends, his visitors, even his servants (Bentham, 45). Similarly, it does not matter what motive animates him: the curiosity of the indiscreet, the malice of a child, the thirst for knowledge of a philosopher who wishes to visit this museum of human nature, or the perversity of those who take pleasure in spying and punishing. The more numerous those anonymous and temporary observers are, the greater the risk for the inmate of being surprised and the greater his anxious awareness of being observed. The Panopticon is a marvellous machine which, whatever use one may wish to put it to, produces homogeneous effects of power. […]

"Discipline" may be identified neither with an institution nor with an apparatus; it is a type of power, a modality for its exercise, comprising a whole set of instruments, techniques, procedures, levels of application, targets; it is a "physics" or an "anatomy" of power, a technology. And it may be taken over either by "specialized" institutions (the penitentiaries or "houses of correction" of the nineteenth century), or by institutions that use it as an essential instrument for a particular end (schools, hospitals), or by pre-existing authorities that find in it a means of reinforcing or reorganizing their internal mechanisms of power (one day we should show how intra-familial relations, essentially in the parents–children cell, have become "disciplined", absorbing since the classical age external schemata, first educational and military, then medical, psychiatric, psychological, which have made the family the privileged locus of emergence for the disciplinary question of the normal and the abnormal); or by apparatuses that have made discipline their principle of internal functioning (the disciplinarization of the administrative apparatus from the Napoleonic period), or finally by state apparatuses whose major, if not exclusive, function is to assure that discipline reigns over society as a whole (the police).

On the whole, therefore, one can speak of the formation of a disciplinary society in this movement that stretches from the enclosed disciplines, a sort of social "quarantine", to an indefinitely generalizable mechanism of "panopticism". Not because the disciplinary modality of power has replaced all the others; but because it has infiltrated the others, sometimes undermining them, but serving as an intermediary between them, linking them together, extending them and above all making it possible to bring the effects of power to the most minute and distant elements. It assures an infinitesimal distribution of the power relations.

A few years after Bentham, Julius gave this society its birth certificate (Julius, 384–6). Speaking of the panoptic principle, he said that there was much more there than architectural ingenuity: it was an event in the "history of the human mind". In appearance, it is merely the solution of a technical problem; but, through it, a whole type of society emerges. [...]

The formation of the disciplinary society is connected with a number of broad historical processes – economic, juridico-political and, lastly, scientific – of which it forms part.

1. Generally speaking, it might be said that the disciplines are techniques for assuring the ordering of human multiplicities. It is true that there is nothing exceptional or even characteristic in this: every system of power is presented with the same problem. But the peculiarity of the disciplines is that they try to define in relation to the multiplicities a tactics of power that fulfils three criteria: firstly, to obtain the exercise of power at the lowest possible cost (economically, by the low expenditure it involves; politically, by its discretion, its low exteriorization, its relative invisibility, the little resistance it arouses); secondly, to bring the effects of this social power to their maximum intensity and to extend them as far as possible, without either failure or interval; thirdly, to link this "economic" growth of power with the output of the apparatuses (educational, military, industrial or medical) within which it is exercised; in short, to increase both the docility and the utility of all the elements of the system. This triple objective of the disciplines corresponds to a well-known historical conjuncture. One aspect of this conjuncture was the large demographic thrust of the eighteenth century; an increase in the floating population (one of the primary objects of discipline is to fix; it is an anti-nomadic technique); a change of quantitative scale in the groups to be supervised or manipulated (from the beginning of the seventeenth century to the eve of the French Revolution, the school population had been increasing rapidly, as had no doubt the hospital population; by the end of the eighteenth century, the peace-time army exceeded 200,000 men). The other aspect of the conjuncture was the growth in the apparatus of production, which was becoming more and more extended and complex; it was also becoming more costly and its profitability had to be increased. The development of the disciplinary methods corresponded to these two processes, or rather, no doubt, to the new need to adjust their correlation. Neither the residual forms of feudal power nor the structures of the administrative monarchy, nor the local mechanisms of supervision, nor the unstable, tangled mass they all formed together could carry out this role: they were hindered from doing so by the irregular and inadequate extension of their network, by their often conflicting functioning, but above all by the "costly" nature of the power that was exercised in them. It was costly in several senses: because directly it cost a great deal to the Treasury; because the system of corrupt offices and farmed-out taxes weighed indirectly, but very heavily, on the population; because the resistance it encountered forced it into a cycle of perpetual reinforcement; because it proceeded essentially by levying (levying on money or products by royal, seigniorial, ecclesiastical taxation; levying on men or time by *corvées* of press-ganging, by locking up or banishing vagabonds). The development of the disciplines marks the appearance of elementary techniques belonging to a quite different economy: mechanisms of power which, instead of

proceeding by deduction, are integrated into the productive efficiency of the apparatuses from within, into the growth of this efficiency and into the use of what it produces. For the old principle of "levying-violence", which governed the economy of power, the disciplines substitute the principle of "mildness-production-profit". These are the techniques that make it possible to adjust the multiplicity of men and the multiplication of the apparatuses of production (and this means not only "production" in the strict sense, but also the production of knowledge and skills in the school, the production of health in the hospitals, the production of destructive force in the army).

In this task of adjustment, discipline had to solve a number of problems for which the old economy of power was not sufficiently equipped. It could reduce the inefficiency of mass phenomena: reduce what, in a multiplicity, makes it much less manageable than a unity; reduce what is opposed to the use of each of its elements and of their sum; reduce everything that may counter the advantages of number. That is why discipline fixes; it arrests or regulates movements; it clears up confusion; it dissipates compact groupings of individuals wandering about the country in unpredictable ways; it establishes calculated distributions. It must also master all the forces that are formed from the very constitution of an organized multiplicity; it must neutralize the effects of counter-power that spring from them and which form a resistance to the power that wishes to dominate it: agitations, revolts, spontaneous organizations, coalitions – anything that may establish horizontal conjunctions. Hence the fact that the disciplines use procedures of partitioning and verticality, that they introduce, between the different elements at the same level, as solid separations as possible, that they define compact hierarchical networks, in short, that they oppose to the intrinsic, adverse force of multiplicity the technique of the continuous, individualizing pyramid. They must also increase the particular utility of each element of the multiplicity, but by means that are the most rapid and the least costly, that is to say, by using the multiplicity itself as an instrument of this growth. Hence, in order to extract from bodies the maximum time and force, the use of those overall methods known as timetables, collective training, exercises, total and detailed surveillance. Furthermore, the disciplines must increase the effect of utility proper to the multiplicities, so that each is made more useful than the simple sum of its elements: it is in order to increase the utilizable effects of the multiple that the disciplines define tactics of distribution, reciprocal adjustment of bodies, gestures and rhythms, differentiation of capacities, reciprocal coordination in relation to apparatuses or tasks. Lastly, the disciplines have to bring into play the power relations, not above but inside the very texture of the multiplicity, as discreetly as possible, as well articulated on the other functions of these multiplicities and also in the least expensive way possible: to this correspond anonymous instruments of power, coextensive with the multiplicity that they regiment, such as hierarchical surveillance, continuous registration, perpetual assessment and classification. In short, to substitute for a power that is manifested through the brilliance of those who exercise it, a power that insidiously objectifies those on whom it is applied; to form a body of knowledge about these individuals, rather than to deploy the ostentatious signs of sovereignty. In a word, the disciplines are the ensemble of minute technical inventions that made it possible to increase the useful size of multiplicities by decreasing the inconveniences of the power which, in order to make them useful, must control them. A multiplicity, whether in a workshop or a nation, an army or a school, reaches the threshold of a discipline when the relation of the one to the other becomes favourable.

If the economic take-off of the West began with the techniques that made possible the accumulation of capital, it might perhaps be said that the methods for administering the accumulation of men made possible a political take-off in relation to the traditional, ritual, costly, violent forms of power, which soon fell into disuse and were superseded by a subtle, calculated technology of subjection. In fact, the two processes – the accumulation of men and the accumulation of capital – cannot be separated; it would not have been possible to solve the problem of the accumulation of men without the growth of an apparatus of production capable of both sustaining them and using them; conversely, the techniques that made the cumulative multiplicity of men useful accelerated the accumulation of capital. At a less general level, the technological mutations of the apparatus of production, the division of labour and the elaboration of the disciplinary techniques sustained an ensemble of very close relations (cf. Marx, *Capital*, vol. I, chapter XIII and the very interesting analysis in Guerry and Deleule). Each makes the other possible and necessary; each provides a model for the other. The disciplinary pyramid constituted the small cell of power within which the separation, coordination and supervision of tasks was imposed and made efficient; and analytical partitioning of time, gestures and bodily forces constituted an operational schema that could easily be transferred from the groups to be subjected to the mechanisms of production; the massive projection of military methods onto industrial organization was an example of this modelling of the division of labour following the model laid down by the schemata of power. But, on the other hand, the technical analysis of the process of production, its "mechanical" breaking-down, were projected onto the labour force whose task it was to implement it: the constitution of those disciplinary machines in which the individual forces that they bring together are composed into a whole and therefore increased is the effect of this projection. Let us say that discipline is the unitary technique by which the body is reduced as a "political" force at the least cost and maximized as a useful force. The growth of a capitalist economy gave rise to the specific modality of disciplinary power, whose general formulas, techniques of submitting forces and bodies, in short, "political anatomy", could be operated in the most diverse political régimes, apparatuses or institutions.

2. The panoptic modality of power – at the elementary, technical, merely physical level at which it is situated – is not under the immediate dependence or a direct extension of the great juridico-political structures of a society; it is nonetheless not absolutely independent. Historically, the process by which the bourgeoisie became in the course of the eighteenth century the politically dominant class was masked by the establishment of an explicit, coded and formally egalitarian juridical framework, made possible by the organization of a parliamentary, representative régime. But the

development and generalization of disciplinary mechanisms constituted the other, dark side of these processes. The general juridical form that guaranteed a system of rights that were egalitarian in principle was supported by these tiny, everyday, physical mechanisms, by all those systems of micro-power that are essentially non-egalitarian and asymmetrical that we call the disciplines. And although, in a formal way, the representative régime makes it possible, directly or indirectly, with or without relays, for the will of all to form the fundamental authority of sovereignty, the disciplines provide, at the base, a guarantee of the submission of forces and bodies. The real, corporal disciplines constituted the foundation of the formal, juridical liberties. The contract may have been regarded as the ideal foundation of law and political power; panopticism constituted the technique, universally widespread, of coercion. It continued to work in depth on the juridical structures of society, in order to make the effective mechanisms of power function in opposition to the formal framework that it had acquired. The "Enlightenment", which discovered the liberties, also invented the disciplines.

In appearance, the disciplines constitute nothing more than an infra-law. They seem to extend the general forms defined by law to the infinitesimal level of individual lives; or they appear as methods of training that enable individuals to become integrated into these general demands. They seem to constitute the same type of law on a different scale, thereby making it more meticulous and more indulgent. The disciplines should be regarded as a sort of counter-law. They have the precise role of introducing insuperable asymmetries and excluding reciprocities. First, because discipline creates between individuals a "private" link, which is a relation of constraints entirely different from contractual obligation; the acceptance of a discipline may be underwritten by contract; the way in which it is imposed, the mechanisms it brings into play, the non-reversible subordination of one group of people by another, the "surplus" power that is always fixed on the same side, the inequality of position of the different "partners" in relation to the common regulation, all these distinguish the disciplinary link from the contractual link, and make it possible to distort the contractual link systematically from the moment it has as its content a mechanism of discipline. We know, for example, how many real procedures undermine the legal fiction of the work contract: workshop discipline is not the least important. Moreover, whereas the juridical systems define juridical subjects according to universal norms, the disciplines characterize, classify, specialize; they distribute along a scale, around a norm, hierarchize individuals in relation to one another and, if necessary, disqualify and invalidate. In any case, in the space and during the time in which they exercise their control and bring into play the asymmetries of their power, they effect a suspension of the law that is never total, but is never annulled either. Regular and institutional as it may be, the discipline, in its mechanism, is a "counter-law". And, although the universal juridicism of modern society seems to fix limits on the exercise of power, its universally widespread panopticism enables it to operate, on the underside of the law, a machinery that is both immense and minute, which supports, reinforces, multiplies the asymmetry of power and undermines the limits that are traced around the law. The minute disciplines, the panopticisms of every day may well be below the level of emergence of the great apparatuses and the great political struggles. But, in the genealogy of modern society, they have been, with the class domination that traverses it, the political counterpart of the juridical norms according to which power was redistributed. Hence, no doubt, the importance that has been given for so long to the small techniques of discipline, to those apparently insignificant tricks that it has invented, and even to those "sciences" that give it a respectable face; hence the fear of abandoning them if one cannot find any substitute; hence the affirmation that they are at the very foundation of society, and an element in its equilibrium, whereas they are a series of mechanisms for unbalancing power relations definitively and everywhere; hence the persistence in regarding them as the humble, but concrete form of every morality, whereas they are a set of physico-political techniques.

To return to the problem of legal punishments, the prison with all the corrective technology at its disposal is to be resituated at the point where the codified power to punish turns into a disciplinary power to observe; at the point where the universal punishments of the law are applied selectively to certain individuals and always the same ones; at the point where the redefinition of the juridical subject by the penalty becomes a useful training of the criminal; at the point where the law is inverted and passes outside itself, and where the counter-law becomes the effective and institutionalized content of the juridical forms. What generalizes the power to punish, then, is not the universal consciousness of the law in each juridical subject; it is the regular extension, the infinitely minute web of panoptic techniques.

3. Taken one by one, most of these techniques have a long history behind them. But what was new, in the eighteenth century, was that, by being combined and generalized, they attained a level at which the formation of knowledge and the increase of power regularly reinforce one another in a circular process. At this point, the disciplines crossed the "technological" threshold. First the hospital, then the school, then, later, the workshop were not simply "reordered" by the disciplines; they became, thanks to them, apparatuses such that any mechanism of objectification could be used in them as an instrument of subjection, and any growth of power could give rise in them to possible branches of knowledge; it was this link, proper to the technological systems, that made possible within the disciplinary element the formation of clinical medicine, psychiatry, child psychology, educational psychology, the rationalization of labour. It is a double process, then: an epistemological "thaw" through a refinement of power relations; a multiplication of the effects of power through the formation and accumulation of new forms of knowledge.

REFERENCES

Bentham, J., *Works*, ed. Bowring, IV, 1843.
Guéry, F. and Deleule, D., *Le Corps productif*, 1973.
Julius, N. H., *Leçons sur les prisons*, I, 1831 (Fr. trans.).

Part VI

The Sociological Theory of Pierre Bourdieu

Introduction to Part VI

22 Social Space and Symbolic Space

23 Structures, *Habitus*, Practices

24 The Field of Cultural Production, or: The Economic World Reversed

25 Rethinking the State: Genesis and Structure of the Bureaucratic Field

Introduction to Part VI

The most influential and original French sociologist since Durkheim, Pierre Bourdieu (1930– 2002) was at once a leading theorist and an empirical researcher of extraordinarily broad interests and distinctive style. In fact, Bourdieu strongly criticized what he called "theoretical theory" – that is, work that is more concerned with building abstract systems of categories and concepts than with using them to understand the world.

Bourdieu's approach was to rethink major philosophical themes and issues by means of empirical observation and analyses rooted in "a practical sense of theoretical things" rather than through purely theoretical disquisition (see *Pascalian Meditations* [2001]). In other words, it is important to know theory and address theoretical challenges, but knowledge advances by putting theory to use in doing sociological analyses, and requires continual innovation. In the course of this practical work of understanding and explanation, the researcher is driven to refine his concepts and think in deeper ways about questions like the nature of human action or the social systems that constrain and organize it.

In keeping with this view, Bourdieu developed his theory through a wide array of empirical investigations. His work began in Algeria, during the last years of French colonial rule. He looked at the country as a whole, but also especially at the people of Kabylia who were regarded as tribal and traditional by both urban, Arab Algerians and the French. The Kabyle were undergoing rapid social change with urbanization, the introduction of money, and markets that brought labor migration and transformed agricultural society (*Algeria 1960* [1979]; *The Uprooted* (with Sayad, 1964); *Work and Workers in Algeria* (with Darbel, Rivet, and Seibel, 1963).

Bourdieu developed the core of his theory as an effort to understand the clash between enduring ways of life and larger systems of power and capital, the ways in which cultural and social structures are reproduced even amid dramatic change, and the ways in which action and structure are not simply opposed but depend on each

Contemporary Sociological Theory, Third Edition. Edited by Craig Calhoun, Joseph Gerteis, James Moody, Steven Pfaff, and Indermohan Virk. Editorial material and organization © 2012 John Wiley & Sons, Ltd. Published 2012 by John Wiley & Sons, Ltd.

other. Bourdieu presented this in his 1976 *Outline of a Theory of Practice*, a book which he revised twice, eventually producing the longer synthesis, *The Logic of Practice* (1990). In these works, Bourdieu draws together theoretical influences from Max Weber, Emile Durkheim, Marcel Mauss, Karl Marx, phenomenological philosophers like Maurice Merleau-Ponty, the structuralist anthropologist Claude Lévi-Strauss, the philosopher Ludwig Wittgenstein and other more empirical linguists, and his own teachers including the philosopher of science Gaston Bachelard.

Bourdieu wove these many different intellectual sources together in an original and powerful perspective. In *Pascalian Meditations* (2001), he reflected on the way these sources influenced his work. But for the most part, he undertook empirical analyses, putting his theory to work seeking to understand class and cultural hierarchies in France (*Distinction* [1984], *The Love of Art*, with Darbel, 1969), *Photography* as a hobby and an art form (with Boltanski, Castel, Chamboredon, and Schnapper, 1965), the role of schools in reproducing inequality (*The Inheritors*, with Passeron, 1963, *Reproduction in Education, Culture, and Society*, with Passeron, 1967), the university and the field of scholarship (*Homo Academicus* [1988]), the way literature and especially novels emerged as a distinctive field from other kinds of writing (*The Rules of Art* [1996]), and the ways people experience and respond to poverty and social inequality (*The Weight of the World: Social Suffering in Contemporary Society*, 1993).

Throughout this extraordinary body of research, Bourdieu's central concerns remained the ways in which action and structure were joined in an always incomplete but powerful process of structuration, the way in which inequality was reproduced even amid economic growth, the reasons people misrecognize social conditions and sometimes participate in imposing limits on themselves, and the ways in which different kinds of value – say on art or on education or on money – were organized in relation to each other. Shortly before his death, he also examined the ways that globalization threatens the achievements of past social struggles by undermining social institutions. This connected his early work on Algeria under colonialism to the contemporary predicament of France amid European integration and capitalist globalization:

> As I was able to observe in Algeria, the unification of the economic field tends, especially through monetary unification and the generalization of monetary exchanges that follow, to hurl all social agents into an economic game for which they are not equally prepared and equipped, culturally and economically. It tends by the same token to submit them to standards objectively imposed by competition from more efficient productive forces and modes of production, as can readily be seen with small rural producers who are more and more completely torn away from self-sufficiency. In short, *unification benefits the dominant*.[1]

Bourdieu came by these concerns biographically. Born in the Béarne region of southwestern France, Bourdieu was the son of a village postman and the grandson of a share-cropper. By means of scholarships, he went on to study at France's elite Ecole Normale Superieure and eventually became the most famous intellectual in the country, awarded a chair at the prestigious Collège de France. His work was always aimed at shining critical light on social processes that maintained inequality and kept the playing field of social struggles from being level. In addition to his individual research and writing, he organized several collaborative research projects, founded the journal *Actes de la recherche en sciences sociales*, and led a major research center. He was the subject of a feature-length documentary, "La sociologie est un sport de combat" ("Sociology is a Combat Sport").

Structure and Action: False Dichotomies

Bourdieu described one of his central motivations as a determination to transcend the closely related but misleading dichotomies of objectivism/subjectivism and of structure/action.[2] Taken together, these dichotomies have marked relatively stable poles in the social sciences, with structural explanation tending to see social life as completely external and objective, and action-oriented sociology looking at social life through subjective experience. Bourdieu suggested that it is crucial not just to see both sides of the issue, but also to see how they are inseparably related.

In recent French social theory, the structuralist anthropology of Claude Lévi-Strauss has been the dominant representative of objectivist thinking. Structuralism is in many ways the descendent of Durkheim's work, especially his later examinations of culture. Bourdieu was heavily influenced by structuralism – a good example is his continued interest in explaining the stable cultural oppositions that appear in language, physical space, and social space. But structuralism attempted to understand the meaning of such oppositions by taking up an objective, "scientific" point of view from outside of the action. It thus tended to explain the structuring of action only as the result of external forces that either push us in one direction or constrain us from going in another. Bourdieu, by contrast, argued for a social science based on the study of actors who always have some practical knowledge about their world, even if they cannot articulate that knowledge. In other words, social structure is internalized by each of us because we have learned from the experience of previous actions a practical mastery of how to do things that takes objective constraints into account.

Bourdieu's stress on the presence of social structure inside the actor is not only a challenge to objectivism, but also to most forms of subjectivism. In subjectivist accounts, the observer takes the individuals' own motivations as the source of the action. The major representative of this approach in France was the existentialism of Jean-Paul Sartre. Bourdieu criticized this way of thinking because it tends to miss the cultural or material constraints that shape people's actions, making each action appear to be "a kind of antecedent-less confrontation between the subject and the world."[3] In other words, subjectivism neglects the extent to which people's very abilities to understand and choose and act have been shaped by processes of learning which are themselves objectively structured and socially produced. As a result, subjectivist approaches commonly present social life as much less structured, much more contingent, than it really is.

In short, objective accounts can help us understand structure, and subjective accounts can help us understand action. But both are one-sided in that they divorce action from structure. Bourdieu's effort has been to develop a "genetic structuralism," that is, a sociology that uses the intellectual resources of structural analysis, but approaches structures in terms of the ways in which they are produced and reproduced in action. Understood in this way, structures are "structuring" in the sense that they guide and constrain action. But they are also "structured" in the sense that they are generated and reproduced by actors. Bourdieu thus insisted on a dialectic of structure and action, but he also made clear that he thinks the crucial first step for social science comes with the discovery of objective structure, and the break with everyday knowledge that this entails. The "objective truth" is not simply the sum total of the facts that happen to exist (as a purely empiricist view might suggest). Rather, what is "objectively" the deepest "reality" in social life is not the surface phenomena that we see all around us, but the underlying structural features that make these surface phenomena possible. The "objectivist" task of sociology is to grasp these underlying structural features. This is hard, because it demands that we call into question our taken-for-granted, preconscious understandings of the world and our place in it.

Habitus and Misrecognition

The way to get an empirical handle on the dynamic relationship between structure and action, Bourdieu contended, is through what he termed a relational analysis of social tastes and practices. By "relational," Bourdieu meant that tastes and practices are organized by actors' relative locations in social space. This relational analysis is organized by three central concepts – positions, dispositions ("*habitus*") and position-taking (or "practices").

Actors occupy positions in social space relative to one another. Such positions may be defined by occupation, education, or proximity to power. What matters is not exactly how such positions are measured, but that people stake their claims to social status on them, and therefore use them to understand their place in the world. Positions are maintained and signaled to others through a process of position-taking (translations sometimes retain the French term "*prises de position*"). For example, certain social positions are signaled by styles of dress, leisure activities, or consumer choices. Bourdieu stressed that there is no direct, mechanical connection between positions in the social structure and the practices that attach to them. In different times and different places, different sets of practices work just as well to signal a given position. In one of the readings included below, Bourdieu used the example of names that businesses chose for themselves – high-status shops in New York often have French names, while similar ones in Paris often have English names. In other cases, practices can either gain or lose prestige over time.

If there is no direct connection between practices and positions (Bourdieu called this the "substantialist" position), then what ties the two together? Bourdieu argued that *habitus* is the site of the interplay between structure and practice. *Habitus* refers to embodied knowledge, especially the ways people learn to generate improvisations – to say new things (even using old words), to create new business deals, or to play new music interactively with others. We improvise on the basis of what we have learned from practical experience, not from following conscious rules. It is on the basis of *habitus* that Bourdieu defines social groups (including social classes), since those who occupy similar positions in the social structure will have the same *habitus*. *Habitus* refers to the relatively stable dispositions that are shaped by the experiences of actors in particular positions in the social structure, which "generate and organize practices and representations."[4] The *habitus* is thus the site of our understanding of the world. In order for us to live in the social world, we require the kind of orientation to action and awareness that *habitus* gives.

In this sense, the *habitus* is not only constraining, it is also enabling. It does not operate as a set of strict rules about what to do or not to do, what to like or not to like. Instead, it works as a set of loose guidelines of which actors are not necessarily aware. Because they are loose guidelines, these dispositions are flexible, even though they are deeply rooted. They leave a great deal of room for improvisation and are easily applied to new settings, but in a way shaped by rules and social learning. As the word suggests, *habitus* is acquired through repetition, like a habit; we know it in our bodies not just our minds. A former rugby player, Bourdieu often used the metaphor of games to convey his sense of social life. But by "game" he doesn't mean mere diversions or entertainments. Rather, he meant the experience of being passionately involved in a kind of activity in which the physical and mental are merged in action. In a game there are formal rules but also a constant need to improvise strategy according to unarticulated but deeply ingrained "sense" of the game. Out of what meets with approval or doesn't, what works, or does not, we develop a characteristic way of generating new actions, of improvising the moves of the game of our lives. The resistance we confront in struggling to do well teaches us to accept inequality in our societies. Although it often reflects class or other aspects of social structure, it comes to feel natural. We learn and incorporate into our *habitus* a sense of what we can "reasonably" expect. This shapes how we choose careers, how we decide which people are "right" for us to date or marry, and how we raise our children.

These taken-for-granted dispositions of the *habitus* also imply misrecognitions, partial and distorted understandings. The idea of misrecognition allows Bourdieu a subtle approach to issues commonly addressed through the concept of ideology. Marxist and other analysts have pointed to the ways in which people's beliefs conform to either power structures or the requirements of the social order as a whole. "Ideology" is commonly understood as a set of partial and distorted beliefs that serves some specific set of social interests. Common use of the notion of ideology, however, tends to imply that it is possible to be without ideology, to have an objectively correct or undistorted understanding of the social world. Bourdieu rejects this. One can shake the effects of specific ideologies, but one cannot live without taken-for-granted assumptions that come with *habitus*. Misrecognition is built into the very practical mastery that makes our actions effective.

Because of this, sociology is itself a "combat sport" (like a martial art) according to Bourdieu. Sociologists must struggle against the tendency everyone has to accept the products of social history as though they were natural. This means also that we should not accept people's everyday accounts of their action as fully explaining it. We may say, for example, that holiday gifts are given without expectation of return, but in fact where there is no reciprocation we tend to stop giving. More generally, participation in any set of social practices embeds us in characteristic misrecognitions. Bourdieu saw this starkly in his early research in Algeria. The French colonists understood themselves as part of a civilizing mission in which modern France would help traditional Algeria. But they systematically misrecognized the power and exploitation that were basic to the French presence. These sparked the Algerian struggle for independence and became manifest in the bloody French effort to repress it.

Fields and Capital

One of the ways in which Bourdieu uses the metaphor of "games" is to describe the different fields on which distinct games are played. Like a soccer field or a rugby field, a social field is simply the terrain upon which the game is played. Broadly speaking, a field is a domain of social life that has its own rules of organization, generates a set of positions, and supports the practices associated with them. Like players in a game, participants in social fields have different positions. For example, a small town lawyer and a Supreme Court Justice are both participants in the legal field. But their different positions open different sets of opportunities for them, and different sets of strategies that they may take. Bourdieu sees action in a field not simply as a static reflection of established positions, but as the result of many contending projects of position-taking.

The possession of different forms of "capital" provides the basic structure for the organization of fields, and thus the generation of the various *habitus* and practices associated with them. "A capital does not exist and function except in relation to a field," Bourdieu claims.[5] Yet successful lawyers and successful authors both, for example, seek to convert their own successes into improved standards of living and chances for their children. To do so, they must convert the capital specific to their field of endeavor into other forms. In addition to material property (economic capital), families may accumulate networks of connections (social capital) and prestige (cultural capital) by the way in which they raise children and plan their marriages. By conceptualizing capital as taking many different forms, Bourdieu stresses (a) that there are many different kinds of goods that people pursue and resources that they accumulate, (b) that these are inextricably social, because they derive their meaning from the social relationships that constitute different fields (rather than simply from some sort of material things being valuable in and of themselves), and (c) that the struggle to accumulate capital is hardly the whole story;

the struggle to reproduce capital is equally basic and often depends on the ways in which it can be converted across fields.

Bourdieu's analysis of the differences in forms of capital and dynamics of conversion between them is one of the most original and important features of his theory (though it builds on Weber's distinction between class and status). There are two senses in which capital is converted from one form to another. One is as part of the intergenerational reproduction of capital. Wealthy people try to make sure that their children go to good colleges. In America at least, this often involves the use of significant economic capital, since good colleges are often expensive colleges. But it also involves cultural capital, for example in knowing which expensive schools are "good" – that is, prestigious – and which are not. The second sense of conversion of capital is more immediate. By attending a prestigious college, and gaining lots of social connections among the people there, a person may then attempt to turn social and cultural capital into economic capital by landing a highly paid job.

In his empirical investigations, Bourdieu generally discusses two ways in which capital orders the social space. The most basic is what he calls "capital volume," which distinguishes between positions with a great deal of capital overall (and the practices associated with them) and those without much capital of any kind. Of course, this contrast between high and low is so obvious to most members of society that not much energy has to go into maintaining the social distance that goes along with it. Much more energy goes into maintaining the second dimension, which might be called the capital mix. This distinguishes between positions that are high on one dimension (for example, cultural capital) and those that are high on another (such as economic capital). Those positions with relatively high capital volume are most invested in maintaining this opposition. This is interesting, because it shifts attention from the opposition between the elites and the masses to the struggle *between* different privileged groups over the control of symbolic goods. As Bourdieu claims, "minimum objective difference in social space can coincide with maximum subjective distance. This is partly because what is 'closest' presents the greatest threat to social identity."[6]

Bourdieu situates his logic of multiple fields and specific forms of capital in relation to a more general notion of power. The field of art, thus, has its own internal struggles for recognition, power, and capital, but it also has a specific relationship to the overall field of power. Even highly rewarded artists generally cannot convert their professional prestige into power in other institutional domains. By contrast, businesspeople and lawyers are more able to do this. The question is not just who is higher or lower in terms of overall capital, but also how different groups relate to each other based on the kind of capital they control. This is true at all levels of the social hierarchy, as for example holders of a "white collar" job may feel superior to "blue collar" workers even if they are paid no more. This is based on a claim to cultural capital and its prestige. It also reflects a general tendency to make social classifications tools of domination. More generally, Bourdieu draws attention to "symbolic violence," the ways in which people may be harmed by the ways they are labeled or categorized socially.

Structure and Practice in Social Life

Bourdieu's key concepts, like *habitus*, symbolic violence, cultural capital, and field are useful in themselves, but derive their greatest theoretical significance from their interrelationships. These are best seen not mechanistically, in the abstract, but at work in sociological analysis. Indeed, Bourdieu is virtually unique among major theorists in the extent to which he has focused on and been influential through empirical research.

Bourdieu's theory is thus often embedded in empirical analyses, but he constantly tried to signal his theoretical positions to his readers. He did this not only in his arguments, but also in his writing style. This can make it difficult to read his work for the first time. Understanding what Bourdieu is doing and why he is doing it can help, however. There are two stylistic elements that are most baffling to new readers. The first is the self-conscious circularity of the sentences. English-language readers who are used to a more linear writing style are often bothered by this, though the style will seem more familiar to those who have some practice reading French social theory. By writing in this manner, Bourdieu hoped to show where his argument might diverge from the reader's assumptions. The second element that causes some confusion is the use of what Bourdieu calls a "hierarchy of text." The main text is broken by passages that are offset or printed in a smaller font. This was meant to break the formal facade of scientific argument with less formal asides and examples that show the development of the ideas. It was also intended to bridge the distance between author and reader by making the text more like a conversation.

The four readings that follow are not meant to cover the entire range of Bourdieu's writing. Instead, they illustrate key points of his theoretical arguments, particularly regarding *habitus*, capital and field. The first selection, "Social Space and Symbolic Space" is an argument for the importance of relational analysis. It is the most plainly-written of the four essays, since it was originally presented as a lecture to introduce his work on French society to a Japanese audience. The second reading, "Structures, *Habitus*, Practices," from *The Logic of Practice*, is a more theoretical treatment of the concept of *habitus* and the way it mediates between the social space of positions and the symbolic space of position-taking. The stress is on the way that the *habitus* is oriented to concrete practices. It is only by studying practices, Bourdieu tells us, that we can see the connection between structure and action. Bourdieu also stresses the social nature of the *habitus*. Even when we are speaking of the *habitus* of an individual rather than a group, we are talking about a set of internalized dispositions that is a result of social interaction. The *habitus* is therefore social in the same way as the concept of "self" in the writing of George Herbert Mead. The next reading, "The Field of Cultural Production, Or: The Economic World Reversed," discusses the way different forms of capital structure a particular field. The case in question is the literary field, which Bourdieu uses as an example of artistic production more generally. Bourdieu shows that while the literary field has its own organizing logic, it is not completely separate from considerations of power. Oppositions between different sets of positions are structured simultaneously by relation to the economic market and by claims to artistic purity. High status in the field demanded not just talent, or vision, but also a commitment to "art for art's sake." This meant producing works specifically designed for the field of art, rather than the market. The final reading considers the state as a "bureaucratic field" which generates both relations of power and its own *habitus* in ingrained habits of thought and action.

NOTES

1 Pierre Bourdieu, "Unifying to Better Dominate," *Items and Issues,* winter 2001; orig. 2000 (forthcoming in *Firing Back*, New York: New Press, 2002.
2 See Bourdieu and Wacquant (1992), p. 7.
3 Bourdieu (1990), p. 42.
4 Bourdieu (1990), p. 53.
5 Bourdieu and Wacquant (1992), p. 101.
6 Bourdieu (1990), p. 137.

SELECTED BIBLIOGRAPHY

Bourdieu, Pierre. 1984. *Distinction: A Social Critique of the Judgment of Taste.* Translated by Richard Nice. Cambridge MA: Harvard University Press. (An analysis of the place of cultural hierarchy in the French class structure: e.g., why do intellectuals like jazz and modernist art, why do elites collect uncomfortable antiques while workers prefer solid, body-friendly furniture?)

Bourdieu, Pierre. 1990. *The Logic of Practice.* Translated by Richard Nice. Stanford CA: Stanford University Press. (Bourdieu's most systematic statement of the core his theory of embodied practice; partially a revision of the more famous *Outline of a Theory of Practice.*)

Bourdieu, Pierre. 1996. *The Rules of Art.* (A study of the origins of the French literary field in the work of Flaubert and Baudelaire which is also Bourdieu's most sustained development of his concept of field and analysis of what 'art for art's sake' means and why cultural capital is opposed to economic.)

Bourdieu, Pierre. 1998. *Practical Reason.* Stanford: Stanford University Press. (Speeches and essays for relatively general audiences that constitute one of the most accessible introductions to (and clarifications of) Bourdieu's sociological theory.)

Bourdieu, Pierre. 1998. *Acts of Resistance: Against the Tyranny of Markets.* New York: New Press. (A collection of Bourdieu's analyses of the threats neoliberal globalization poses to culture and intellectuals and the importance of an alternative form of internationalism.)

Bourdieu, Pierre 1998/2001. Pascalian Meditations. Stanford: Stanford University Press. (Bourdieu's reflections, late in his life, on the intellectual sources and significance of his distinctive approach to sociology – including doing philosophy by means of empirical sociology.)

Bourdieu, Pierre and Loic Wacquant. 1992. *An Invitation to Reflexive Sociology.* Chicago, IL: University of Chicago Press. (A clarification of various questions about Bourdieu's work, structured as questions from one of his leading students and answers from Bourdieu.)

Calhoun, Craig. 2011. "Pierre Bourdieu," pp. 696–730 in George Ritzer, ed.: *The Blackwell Companion to the Major Social Theorists*, 3rd edn. Cambridge, MA: Blackwell. (An introduction to and overview of Bourdieu's sociology.)

Calhoun, Craig. 2012. "For the Social History of the Present: Pierre Bourdieu as Historical Sociologist," in P. Gorski, ed.: *Bourdieusian Theory and Historical Sociology*. Durham, NC: Duke University Press. (An account of the way Bourdieu's work addressed specific historical contexts: colonial Algeria, the postwar boom in France, the formation of cultural fields in the modern era, and the undermining of institutional fields by neoliberalism in the late 1990s.)

Calhoun, Craig, Edward LiPuma, and Moishe Postone (eds.). 1993. *Bourdieu: Critical Perspectives*. Chicago: The University of Chicago Press. (Critical essays on Bourdieu from leading theorists in anthropology, philosophy, linguistics, and sociology.)

Fowler, Bridget 1997 *Pierre Bourdieu and Cultural Theory: Critical Investigations*. London: Sage. (Explicates Bourdieu's theory in relation to Anglo-American cultural studies and sociology of culture.)

Grenfell, Michael 2004. *Pierre Bourdieu: Agent Provocateur*. New York: Continuum.

Lane, Jeremy. 2000. Pierre Bourdieu: A Critical Introduction. London: Pluto. (The best book on Bourdieu and his intellectual background and context.)

Robbins, Derrick. 2000. *Bourdieu and Culture*. (A very sympathetic but idiosyncratic introduction emphasizing Bourdieu's cultural analyses of the 1980s and 1990s.)

Swartz, David. 1997. *Culture and Power: The Sociology of Pierre Bourdieu*. Chicago: University of Chicago Press. (An accessible introduction to Bourdieu's work and its development; the best one-volume introduction.)

Chapter 22

Social Space and Symbolic Space [1994]

Pierre Bourdieu

I think that if I were Japanese I would dislike most of the things that non-Japanese people write about Japan. Over twenty years ago, at the time when I began to do research on French society, I recognized my irritation at American ethnologies of France in the criticism that Japanese sociologists, notably Hiroshi Miami and Tetsuro Watsuji, had levied against Ruth Benedict's famous book, *The Chrysanthemum and the Sword*. Thus, I shall not talk to you about the "Japanese sensibility," nor about the Japanese "mystery" or "miracle." I shall talk about France, a country I know fairly well, not because I was born there and speak its language, but because I have studied it a great deal. Does this mean that I shall confine myself to the particularity of a single society and shall not talk in any way about Japan? I do not think so. I think, on the contrary, that by presenting the model of social space and symbolic space that I constructed for the particular case of France, I shall still be speaking to you about Japan (just as, in other contexts, I would be speaking about Germany or the United States). For you to understand fully this discourse which concerns you and which might seem to you full of personal allusions when I speak about the French *homo academicus*, I would like to encourage you to go beyond a particularizing reading which, besides being an excellent defense mechanism against analysis, is the precise equivalent, on the reception side, of the curiosity for exotic particularism that has inspired so many works on Japan.

Pierre Bourdieu, "Social Space and Symbolic Space," pp. 627–38 from Pierre Bourdieu, "Social Space and Symbolic Space: Introduction to a Japanese Reading of Distinction," *Poetics Today*, 12: 4 (1991). Copyright © 1991 by the Porter Institute for Poetics and Semiotics, Tel Aviv University. All rights reserved. Used by permission of the publisher, Duke University Press.

Contemporary Sociological Theory, Third Edition. Edited by Craig Calhoun, Joseph Gerteis, James Moody, Steven Pfaff, and Indermohan Virk. Editorial material and organization © 2012 John Wiley & Sons, Ltd. Published 2012 by John Wiley & Sons, Ltd.

My work, and especially *Distinction*, is particularly exposed to such a reading. Its theoretical model is not embellished with all the marks by which one usually recognizes "grand theory," such as lack of any reference to some empirical reality. The notions of social space, symbolic space, or social class are never studied in and for themselves; rather, they are tested through research in which the theoretical and the empirical are inseparable and which mobilizes numerous methods of observation and measurement – quantitative and qualitative, statistical and ethnographic, macrosociological and microsociological (all of which are meaningless oppositions) – for the purpose of studying an object well defined in space and time, that is, French society in the 1970s. The report of this research does not appear in the language to which certain sociologists, especially Americans, have accustomed us and whose appearance of universality is due only to the imprecision of a vocabulary hardly distinguishable from everyday usage (I shall mention only one example, the notion of "profession"). Thanks to a discursive montage which facilitates the juxtaposition of statistical tables, photographs, excerpts from interviews, facsimiles of documents, and the abstract language of analysis, this report makes the most abstract coexist with the most concrete, a photograph of the president of the Republic playing tennis or an interview with a baker with the most formal analysis of the generative and unifying power of the habitus.

My entire scientific enterprise is indeed based on the belief that the deepest logic of the social world can be grasped only if one plunges into the particularity of an empirical reality, historically located and dated, but with the objective of constructing it as a "special case of what is possible," as Bachelard puts it, that is, as an exemplary case in a finite world of possible configurations. Concretely, this means that an analysis of French social space in the 1970s is comparative history, which takes the present as its object, or comparative anthropology, which focuses on a particular cultural area: in both cases, the aim is to try to grasp the invariant, the structure in each variable observed.

I am convinced that, although it has all the appearance of ethnocentrism, an approach consisting of applying a model constructed according to this logic to another social world is without doubt more respectful of historical realities (and of people) and above all more fruitful in scientific terms than the interest in superficial features of the lover of exoticism who gives priority to picturesque differences (I am thinking, for instance, of what has been said and written, in the case of Japan, about the "culture of pleasure"). The researcher, both more modest and more ambitious than the collector of curiosities, seeks to apprehend the structures and mechanisms that are overlooked – although for different reasons – by the native and the foreigner alike, such as the principles of construction of social space or the mechanisms of reproduction of that space, and that the researcher seeks to represent in a model aspiring to a *universal validity*. In that way it is possible to register the real differences that separate both structures and dispositions (habitus), the principle of which must be sought not in the peculiarities of some national character – or "soul" – but in the particularities of different *collective histories*.

The Real is Relational

In this spirit I will present the model I constructed in *Distinction*, first cautioning against a "substantialist" reading of analyses which intend to be structural or, better, relational (I refer here, without being able to go into detail, to the opposition suggested by Ernst Cassirer between "substantial concepts" and "functional or relational concepts"). The "substantialist" and naively realist reading considers each practice (playing golf, for example) or pattern of consumption (Chinese food, for instance) in and for itself, independently of the universe of substitutable practices, and conceives of the correspondence between social positions (or classes, thought of as substantial sets) and tastes or practices as a mechanical and direct relation. According to this logic, naive readers could consider as a refutation of the model the fact that, to take a perhaps facile example, Japanese or American intellectuals pretend to like French food, whereas French intellectuals like to go to Chinese or Japanese restaurants; or that the fancy shops of Tokyo or Fifth Avenue often have French names, whereas the fancy shops of the Faubourg Saint-Honoré display English names, such as "hairdresser." Another example which is, I believe, even more striking: in Japan, the rate of participation in general elections is highest among the least educated women of rural districts, whereas in France, as I demonstrated in an analysis of nonresponse to opinion polls, the rate of nonresponse – and of indifference to politics – is especially high among women and among the least educated and the most economically and socially dispossessed. This is an example of a false difference that conceals a real one: the apathy associated with dispossession of the means of production of political opinions, which is expressed in France as simple absenteeism, translates, in the case of Japan, as a sort of apolitical participation. We should ask further what historical conditions (and here we should invoke the whole political history of Japan) have resulted in the fact that conservative parties in Japan have been able, through quite particular forms of clientelism, to benefit from the inclination toward unconditional delegation deriving from the conviction of not being in possession of the *statutory* and *technical* competence which is necessary for participation.

The substantialist mode of thought, which characterizes common sense – and racism – and which is inclined to treat the activities and preferences specific to certain individuals or groups in a society at a certain moment as if they were substantial properties, inscribed once and for all in a sort of biological or cultural *essence*, leads to the same kind of error, whether one is comparing different societies or successive periods in the same society. Some would thus consider the fact that, for example, tennis or even golf is not nowadays as exclusively associated with dominant positions as in the past, or that the noble sports, such as riding or fencing (or, in Japan, the martial arts), are no longer specific to nobility as they originally were, as a refutation of the proposed model, which Figure 22.1, presenting the correspondence between the space of constructed classes and the space of practices, captures in a visual and synoptic way. An initially aristocratic practice can be given up by the aristocracy – and this occurs quite frequently – when it is adopted by a growing

CAPITAL VOLUME +
(combining all forms of capital)

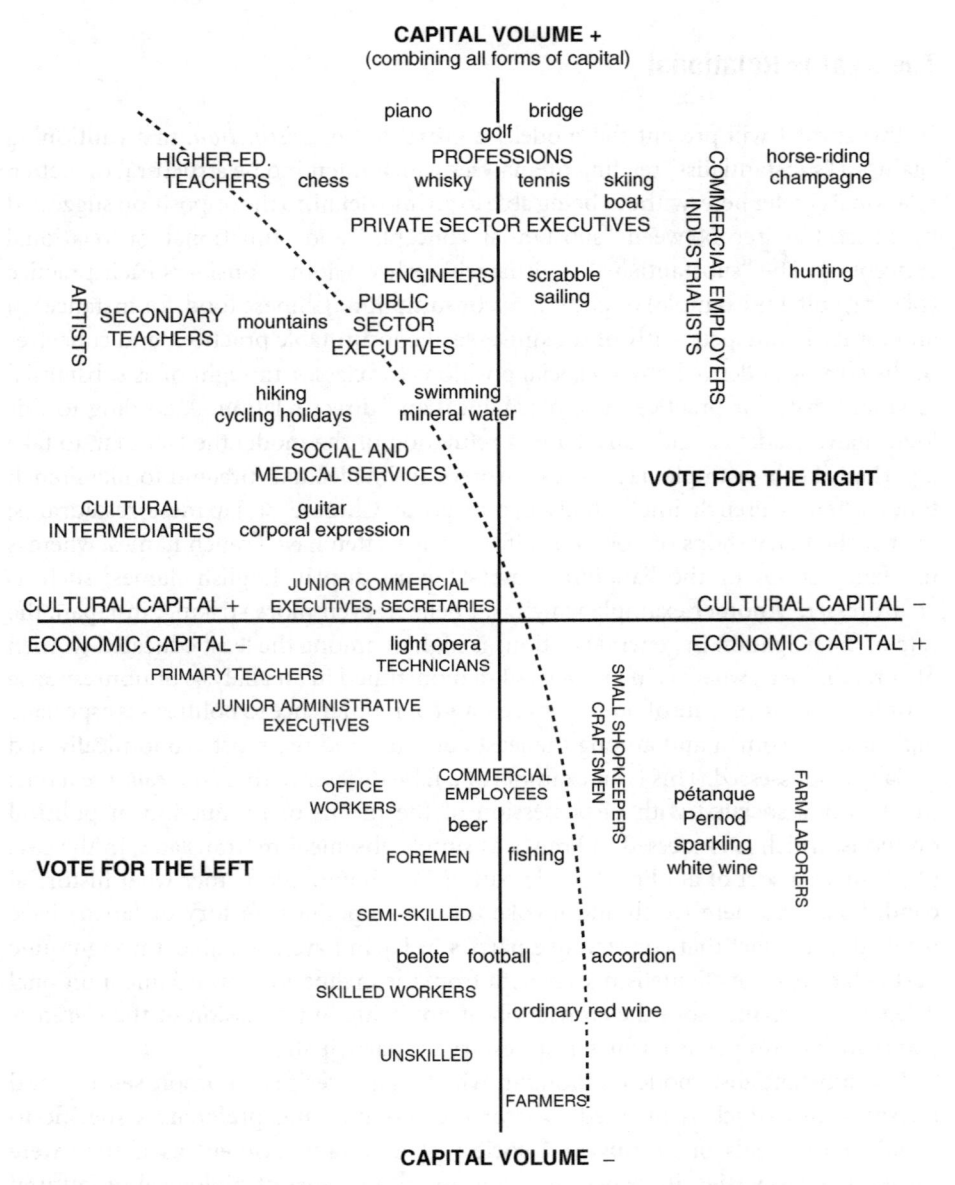

```
                    piano     bridge
                         golf
   HIGHER-ED.         PROFESSIONS              horse-riding
    TEACHERS   chess  whisky  tennis  skiing    champagne
                                        boat
               PRIVATE SECTOR EXECUTIVES

                  ENGINEERS   scrabble           hunting
                  PUBLIC       sailing
  SECONDARY       SECTOR
   TEACHERS   mountains EXECUTIVES

                       swimming
            hiking     mineral water
         cycling holidays
                  SOCIAL AND
                  MEDICAL SERVICES          VOTE FOR THE RIGHT

    CULTURAL         guitar
 INTERMEDIARIES   corporal expression

               JUNIOR COMMERCIAL
CULTURAL CAPITAL +  EXECUTIVES, SECRETARIES    CULTURAL CAPITAL –

ECONOMIC CAPITAL –    light opera              ECONOMIC CAPITAL +
          PRIMARY TEACHERS  TECHNICIANS
            JUNIOR ADMINISTRATIVE
                EXECUTIVES
                      COMMERCIAL
              OFFICE   EMPLOYEES                pétanque
             WORKERS                             Pernod
                        beer                    sparkling
                     FOREMEN   fishing         white wine     FARM LABORERS

                    SEMI-SKILLED
VOTE FOR THE LEFT
                     belote  football    accordion
                   SKILLED WORKERS
                                       ordinary red wine
                     UNSKILLED
                                    FARMERS
```

(axis labels on right: COMMERCIAL EMPLOYERS / INDUSTRIALISTS; ARTISTS on left; SMALL SHOPKEEPERS CRAFTSMEN)

CAPITAL VOLUME –

Figure 22.1 The space of social positions and the space of lifestyles (the dotted line indicates probable orientation toward the right or left).

fraction of the bourgeoisie or petit-bourgeoisie, or even the lower classes (this is what happened in France to boxing, which was enthusiastically practiced by aristocrats at the end of the nineteenth century). Conversely, an initially lower-class practice can sometimes be taken up by nobles. In short, one has to avoid turning into necessary and intrinsic properties of some group (nobility, samurai, as well as workers or employees) the properties which belong to this group at a given moment in time because of its position in a determinate social space and in a determinate state of the *supply* of possible goods and practices. Thus, at every moment of each society, one has to deal with a set of social positions which is bound by a relation of homology to a set of activities (the practice of golf or piano) or of goods (a second home or an old master painting) that are themselves characterized relationally.

This formula, which might seem abstract and obscure, states the first conditions for an adequate reading of the analysis of the relation between *social positions* (a relational concept), *dispositions* (or habitus), and *position-takings* (*prises de position*), that is, the "choices" made by the social agents in the most diverse domains of practice, in food or sport, music or politics, and so forth. It is a reminder that comparison is possible only from *system to system*, and that the search for direct equivalences between features grasped in isolation, whether, appearing at first sight different, they prove to be "functionally" or technically equivalent (like Pernod and *shôchû* or saké) or nominally identical (the practice of golf in France and Japan, for instance), risks unduly identifying structurally different properties or wrongly distinguishing structurally identical properties. The very title *Distinction* serves as a reminder that what is commonly called distinction, that is, a certain quality of bearing and manners, most often considered innate (one speaks of *distinction naturelle*, "natural refinement"), is nothing other than *difference*, a gap, a distinctive feature, in short, a *relational* property existing only in and through its relation with other properties.

This idea of difference, or a gap, is at the basis of the very notion of *space*, that is, a set of distinct and coexisting positions which are exterior to one another and which are defined in relation to one another through their *mutual exteriority* and their relations of proximity, vicinity, or distance, as well as through relations of order, such as above, below, and *between*. Certain properties of members of the petit-bourgeoisie can, for example, be deduced from the fact that they occupy an intermediate position between two extreme positions, without being objectively identifiable and subjectively identified either with one or the other position.

Social space is constructed in such a way that agents or groups are distributed in it according to their position in statistical distributions based on the *two principles of differentiation* which, in the most advanced societies, such as the United States, Japan, or France, are undoubtedly the most efficient: economic capital and cultural capital. It follows that all agents are located in this space in such a way that the closer they are to one another in those two dimensions, the more they have in common; and the more remote they are from one another, the less they have in common. Spatial distances on paper are equivalent to social distances. More precisely, as expressed in the diagram in *Distinction* in which I tried to represent social space (Figure 22.1), agents are distributed in the first dimension according to the overall volume of the different kinds of capital they possess, and in the second dimension according to the structure of their capital, that is, according to the relative weight of the different kinds of capital, economic and cultural, in the total volume of their capital.

Thus, in the first dimension, which is undoubtedly the most important, the holders of a great volume of overall capital, such as industrial employers, members of liberal professions, and university professors are opposed, in the mass, to those who are most deprived of economic and cultural capital, such as unskilled workers. But from another point of view, that is, from the point of view of the relative weight of economic capital and cultural capital in their patrimony, professors (relatively wealthier in cultural capital than in economic capital) are strongly opposed to industrial employers (relatively wealthier in economic capital than in cultural capital), and this is no doubt as true in Japan as in France (although it remains to be verified).

The second opposition, like the first, is the source of differences in dispositions and, therefore, in position-takings. This is the case of the opposition between intellectuals and industrial employers or, on a lower level of the social hierarchy, between primary school teachers and small merchants, which, in postwar France and Japan alike, translates, in politics, into an opposition between left and right (as is suggested in the diagram, the probability of leaning politically toward the right or the left depends at least as much on the position in the horizontal dimension as on the position in the vertical dimension, that is, on the relative weight of cultural capital and economic capital in the volume of capital possessed at least as much as on the volume itself).

In a more general sense, the space of social positions is retranslated into a space of position-takings through the mediation of the space of dispositions (or habitus). In other words, the system of differential deviations which defines the different positions in the two major dimensions of social space corresponds to the system of differential deviations in agents' properties (or in the properties of constructed classes of agents), that is, in their practices and in the goods they possess. To each class of positions there corresponds a class of habitus (or *tastes*) produced by the social conditioning associated with the corresponding condition and, through the mediation of the habitus and its generative capability, a systematic set of goods and properties, which are united by an affinity of style.

One of the functions of the notion of habitus is to account for the unity of style, which unites the practices and goods of a single agent or a class of agents (this is what writers such as Balzac or Flaubert have so finely expressed through their descriptions of settings – such as the Pension Vauquer in *Le Père Goriot* or the elegant dishes and drinks consumed in the homes of different protagonists of *L'Éducation sentimentale* – which are at the same time descriptions of the characters who live in them). The habitus is this generative and unifying principle which retranslates the intrinsic and relational characteristics of a position into a unitary lifestyle, that is, a unitary set of choices of persons, goods, practices.

Like the positions of which they are the product, habitus are differentiated, but they are also differentiating. Being distinct and distinguished, they are also distinction operators, implementing different principles of differentiation or using differently the common principles of differentiation.

Habitus are generative principles of distinct and distinctive practices – what the worker eats, and especially the way he eats it, the sport he practices and the way he practices it, his political opinions and the way he expresses them are systematically different from the industrial owner's corresponding activities. But habitus are also classificatory schemes, principles of classification, principles of vision and division, different tastes. They make distinctions between what is good and what is bad, between what is right and what is wrong, between what is distinguished and what is vulgar, and so forth, but the distinctions are not identical. Thus, for instance, the same behavior or even the same good can appear distinguished to one person, pretentious to someone else, and cheap or showy to yet another.

But the essential point is that, when perceived through these social categories of perception, these principles of vision and division, the differences in practices, in the goods possessed, or in the opinions expressed become symbolic differences and constitute a veritable *language*. Differences associated with different positions, that is, goods, practices, and especially *manners*, function, in each society, in the same way as differences which constitute symbolic systems, such as the set of phonemes of a language or the set of distinctive features and of differential "*écarts*" that constitute a mythical system, that is, as *distinctive signs*.

Here I open a parenthesis in order to dispel a frequent, yet disastrous, misunderstanding about the title *Distinction*, which has led some to believe that the entire book was limited to saying that the driving force of all human behavior was the search for distinction. This does not make sense and, moreover, it would not be anything new if one thinks, for example, of Veblen and his notion of conspicuous consumption. In fact, the main idea is that to exist within a social space, to occupy a point or to be an individual within a social space, is to differ, to be different. According to Benveniste's formula regarding language, "to be distinctive, to be significant, is the same thing," significant being opposed to insignificant, or to different meanings. More precisely – Benveniste's formulation is a little too quick [...] – a difference, a distinctive property, white or black skin, slenderness or stoutness, Volvo or VW Beetle, red wine or champagne, Pernod or scotch, golf or soccer, piano or accordion, bridge or *belote* (I proceed with oppositions, because things tend to operate in this fashion most of the time, although the situation is more complicated than this), only becomes a visible, perceptible, non-indifferent, socially *pertinent* difference if it is perceived by someone who is capable of *making the distinction* – because, being inscribed in the space in question, he or she is not *indifferent* and is endowed with categories of perception, with classificatory schemata, with certain *taste*, which permits her to make differences, to discern, to distinguish – between a color print and a painting or between Van Gogh and Gauguin. Difference becomes a sign and a sign of distinction (or vulgarity) only if a principle of vision and division is applied to it which, being the product of the incorporation of the structure of objective differences (for example, the structure of the distribution in the social space of the piano or the accordion or those who prefer one or the other), is present among all the agents, piano owners or accordion lovers, and structures the perceptions of owners or lovers of pianos or accordions (there was a need to spell out this analysis of the logic – that of symbolic violence – according to which dominated lifestyles are almost always perceived, even by those who live them, from the destructive and reductive point of view of the dominant aesthetic).

The Logic of Classes

To construct social space, this invisible reality that cannot be shown but which organizes agents' practices and representations, is at the same time to create the possibility of constructing *theoretical classes* that are as homogeneous as possible from the point of view of the two major determinants of practices and of all their attendant properties. The principle of classification thus put into play is genuinely *explanatory*. It is not content with describing the set of classified realities, but rather, like the good taxonomies of the natural sciences, it fixes on determinant properties which, unlike the apparent differences of bad classifications, allow for the prediction of the other properties and which distinguish and bring together agents who are as similar to each other as possible and as different as possible from members of other classes, whether adjacent or remote.

But the very validity of the classification risks encouraging a perception of theoretical classes, which are fictitious regroupings existing only *on paper*, through an intellectual decision by the researcher, as *real* classes, real groups, that are constituted as such in reality. The danger is all the greater as the research makes it appear that the divisions drawn in *Distinction* do indeed correspond to real differences in the most different, and even the most unexpected, domains of practice. Thus, to take the example of a curious property, the distribution of the dog and cat owners is organized according to the model: commercial employers (on the right in Figure 22.1) tend to prefer dogs, intellectuals (on the left in Figure 22.1) tend to prefer cats.

The model thus defines distances that are *predictive* of encounters, affinities, sympathies, or even desires. Concretely, this means that people located at the top of the space have little chance of marrying people located toward the bottom, first because they have little chance of physically meeting them (except in what are called "bad places," that is, at the cost of a transgression of the social limits which reflect spatial distances); secondly because, if they do accidentally meet them on some occasion, they will not get on together, will not really understand each other, will not appeal to one another. On the other hand, proximity in social space predisposes to closer relations: people who are inscribed in a restricted sector of the space will be both closer (in their properties and in their dispositions, *their tastes*) and more disposed to get closer, as well as being easier to bring together, to mobilize. But this does not mean that they constitute a class in Marx's sense, that is, a group which is mobilized for common purposes, and especially against another class.

The theoretical classes that I construct are, more than any other theoretical divisions (more, for example, than divisions according to sex, ethnicity, and so on), predisposed to become classes in the Marxist sense of the term. If I am a political leader and I propose creating one big party bringing together both industrial employers and workers, I have little chance of success, since these groups are very distant in social space; in a certain conjuncture, in a national crisis, on the bases of nationalism or chauvinism, it will be possible for them to draw closer, but this solidarity will still be rather superficial and very provisional. This does not mean that, inversely, proximity in social space automatically engenders unity. It defines an objective potentiality of unity or, to speak like Leibniz, a "claim to exist" as a group, a *probable class*. Marxist theory makes a mistake quite similar to the one Kant denounced in the ontological argument or to the one for which Marx criticized Hegel: it makes a "death-defying leap" from existence in theory to existence in practice, or, as Marx puts it, "from the things of logic to the logic of things."

Marx, who more than any other theoretician exerted the *theory effect* – the properly political effect that consists in making tangible (*theorein*) a "reality" that cannot entirely exist insofar as it remains unknown and unrecognized – paradoxically failed to take this effect into account in his own theory [...] One moves from class-on-paper to the "real" class only at the price of a political work of mobilization. The "real" class, if it has ever "really" existed, is nothing but the realized class, that is, the mobilized class, a result of the *struggle of classifications*, which is a properly symbolic (and political) struggle to impose a vision of the social world, or, better, a way to construct that world, in perception and in reality, and to construct classes in accordance with which this social world can be divided.

The very existence of classes, as everyone knows from his or her own experience, is a stake in a struggle. And this fact undoubtedly constitutes the major obstacle to a scientific knowledge of the social world and to the resolution (for *there is one* [...]) of the problem of social classes. Denying the existence of classes, as the conservative tradition has persisted in doing for reasons not all of which are absurd (and all research done in good faith encounters them along the way), means in the final analysis denying the existence of differences and of principles of differentiation. This is just what those who pretend that nowadays the American, Japanese, and French societies are each nothing but an enormous "middle class" do, although in a more paradoxical way, since those who believe this nevertheless preserve the term "class" (according to a survey, 80 percent of the Japanese say they belong to the "middle class"). This position is, of course, unsustainable. All my work shows that in a country said to be on the way to becoming homogenized, democratized, and so on, difference is everywhere. And in the United States, every day some new piece of research appears showing diversity where one *expected to see* homogeneity, conflict where one expected to see consensus, reproduction and conservation where one expected to see mobility. Thus, *difference* (which I express in describing social *space*) exists and persists. But does this mean that we must accept or affirm the existence of classes? No. Social classes do not exist (even if political work, armed with Marx's theory, had in some cases contributed to making them at least exist through instances of mobilization and proxies). What exists is a social space, a space of differences, in which classes exist in some sense in a state of virtuality, not as something given but as *something to be done*.

Nevertheless, if the social world, with its divisions, is something that social agents have to do, to construct, individually and especially *collectively*, in cooperation and conflict, these constructions still do not take place in a social void, as certain ethnomethodologists seem to believe. The position occupied in social space, that is, in the structure of the distribution of different kinds of capital, which are also weapons, commands the representations of this space and the position-takings in the struggles to conserve or transform it.

To summarize the intricate relation between objective structures and subjective constructions, which is located beyond the usual alternatives of objectivism and subjectivism, of structuralism and constructivism, and even of materialism and idealism, I usually quote, with a little distortion, a famous formula of Pascal's: "The world comprehends me and swallows me like a point, but I comprehend it." The social world embraces me like a point. But this point is a *point of view*, the principle of a view adopted from a point located in social space, a *perspective* which is defined, in its form and contents, by the objective position from which it is adopted. The social space is indeed the first and last reality, since it still commands the representations that the social agents can have of it.

I am coming to the end of what has been a kind of introduction to the reading of *Distinction*, in which I have undertaken to state the principles of a relational, structural reading that is capable of developing the full import of the model I propose. A relational but also a *generative* reading. By this I mean that I hope my readers will try to apply the model in this other "particular case of the possible," that is, Japanese society, that they will try to construct the Japanese social space and symbolic space, to define the basic principles of objective differentiation (I think they are the same, but one should verify whether, for instance, they do not have different relative weights – I do not think so, given the exceptional importance which is traditionally attributed to education in Japan) and especially the principles of distinction, the specific distinctive signs in the domains of sport, food, drink, and so on, the relevant features which make significant differences in the different symbolic subspaces. This is, in my opinion, the condition for a *comparativism of the essential* that I called for at the beginning and, at the same time, for the universal knowledge of the invariants and variations that sociology can and must produce.

As for me, I shall undertake in my next lecture to say what the mechanisms are which, in France as in Japan and all other advanced countries, guarantee the reproduction of social space and symbolic space, without ignoring the contradictions and conflicts that can be at the basis of their transformation.

Chapter 23

Structures, *Habitus*, Practices* [1994]

Pierre Bourdieu

Objectivism constitutes the social world as a spectacle offered to an observer who takes up a "point of view" on the action and who, putting into the object the principles of his relation to the object, proceeds as if it were intended solely for knowledge and as if all the interactions within it were purely symbolic exchanges. This viewpoint is the one taken from high positions in the social structure, from which the social world is seen as a representation (as the word is used in idealist philosophy, but also as in painting) or a performance (in the theatrical or musical sense), and practices are seen as no more than the acting-out of roles, the playing of scores or the implementation of plans. The theory of practice as practice insists, contrary to positivist materialism, that the objects of knowledge are constructed, not passively recorded, and, contrary to intellectualist idealism, that the principle of this construction is the system of structured, structuring dispositions, the *habitus*, which is constituted in practice and is always oriented towards practical functions. It is possible to step down from the sovereign viewpoint from which objectivist idealism orders the world, as Marx demands in the *Theses on Feuerbach*, but without having to abandon to it the "active aspect" of apprehension of the world by reducing knowledge to a mere recording. To do this, one has to situate oneself within "real

---

*Originally translated by Richard Nice.

Pierre Bourdieu, "Structures, *Habitus*, Practice," from Pierre Bourdieu, *The Logic of Practice*. Cambridge: Polity Press, in association with Blackwell Publishers, 1990. English translation copyright © 1990 by Polity Press. Originally published in French as *Le Sens Pratique* by Les Éditions des Minuit. Original French text copyright © 1980 Les Éditions des Minuit. Reprinted by permission of Stanford University Press and Georges Borchardt.

Contemporary Sociological Theory, Third Edition. Edited by Craig Calhoun, Joseph Gerteis, James Moody, Steven Pfaff, and Indermohan Virk. Editorial material and organization © 2012 John Wiley & Sons, Ltd. Published 2012 by John Wiley & Sons, Ltd.

activity as such", that is, in the practical relation to the world, the preoccupied, active presence in the world through which the world imposes its presence, with its urgencies, its things to be done and said, things made to be said, which directly govern words and deeds without ever unfolding as a spectacle. One has to escape from the realism of the structure, to which objectivism, a necessary stage in breaking with primary experience and constructing the objective relationships, necessarily leads when it hypostatizes these relations by treating them as realities already constituted outside of the history of the group – without falling back into subjectivism, which is quite incapable of giving an account of the necessity of the social world. To do this, one has to return to practice, the site of the dialectic of the *opus operatum* and the *modus operandi*; of the objectified products and the incorporated products of historical practice; of structures and *habitus*.

> The bringing to light of the presuppositions inherent in objectivist construction has paradoxically been delayed by the efforts of all those who, in linguistics as in anthropology, have sought to "correct" the structuralist model by appealing to "context" or "situation" to account for variations, exceptions and accidents (instead of making them simple variants, absorbed into the structure, as the structuralists do). They have thus avoided a radical questioning of the objectivist mode of thought, when, that is, they have not simply fallen back on to the free choice of a rootless, unattached, pure subject. Thus, the method known as "situational analysis", which consists of "observing people in a variety of social situations" in order to determine "the way in which individuals are able to exercise choices within the limits of a specified social structure",[1] remains locked within the framework of the rule and the exception, which Edmund Leach (often invoked by the exponents of this method) spells out explicitly: "I postulate that structural systems in which all avenues of social action are narrowly institutionalized are impossible. In all viable systems, there must be an area where the individual is free to make choices so as to manipulate the system to his advantage".[2]

The conditionings associated with a particular class of conditions of existence produce *habitus*, systems of durable, transposable dispositions, structured structures predisposed to function as structuring structures, that is, as principles which generate and organize practices and representations that can be objectively adapted to their outcomes without presupposing a conscious aiming at ends or an express mastery of the operations necessary in order to attain them. Objectively "regulated" and "regular" without being in any way the product of obedience to rules, they can be collectively orchestrated without being the product of the organizing action of a conductor.

It is, of course, never ruled out that the responses of the *habitus* may be accompanied by a strategic calculation tending to perform in a conscious mode the operation that the *habitus* performs quite differently, namely an estimation of chances presupposing transformation of the past effect into an expected objective. But these responses are first defined, without any calculation, in relation to objective potentialities, immediately inscribed in the present, things to do or not to do, things to say or not to say, in relation to a probable, "upcoming" future (*un à venir*), which –

in contrast to the future seen as "absolute possibility" (*absolute Möglichkeit*) in Hegel's (or Sartre's) sense, projected by the pure project of a "negative freedom" – puts itself forward with an urgency and a claim to existence that excludes all deliberation. Stimuli do not exist for practice in their objective truth, as conditional, conventional triggers, acting only on condition that they encounter agents conditioned to recognize them. The practical world that is constituted in the relationship with the *habitus*, acting as a system of cognitive and motivating structures, is a world of already realized ends – procedures to follow, paths to take – and of objects endowed with a "permanent teleological character", in Husserl's phrase, tools or institutions. This is because the regularities inherent in an arbitrary condition ("arbitrary" in Saussure's and Mauss's sense) tend to appear as necessary, even natural, since they are the basis of the schemes of perception and appreciation through which they are apprehended.

If a very close correlation is regularly observed between the scientifically constructed objective probabilities (for example, the chances of access to a particular good) and agents' subjective aspirations ("motivations" and "needs"), this is not because agents consciously adjust their aspirations to an exact evaluation of their chances of success, like a gambler organizing his stakes on the basis of perfect information about his chances of winning. In reality, the dispositions durably inculcated by the possibilities and impossibilities, freedoms and necessities, opportunities and prohibitions inscribed in the objective conditions (which science apprehends through statistical regularities such as the probabilities objectively attached to a group or class) generate dispositions objectively compatible with these conditions and in a sense pre-adapted to their demands. The most improbable practices are therefore excluded, as unthinkable, by a kind of immediate submission to order that inclines agents to make a virtue of necessity, that is, to refuse what is anyway denied and to will the inevitable. The very conditions of production of the *habitus*, a virtue made of necessity, mean that the anticipations it generates tend to ignore the restriction to which the validity of calculation of probabilities is subordinated, namely that the experimental conditions should not have been modified. Unlike scientific estimations, which are corrected after each experiment according to rigorous rules of calculation, the anticipations of the *habitus*, practical hypotheses based on past experience, give disproportionate weight to early experiences. Through the economic and social necessity that they bring to bear on the relatively autonomous world of the domestic economy and family relations, or more precisely, through the specifically familial manifestations of this external necessity (forms of the division of labour between the sexes, household objects, modes of consumption, parent – child relations, etc.), the structures characterizing a determinate class of conditions of existence produce the structures of the *habitus*, which in their turn are the basis of the perception and appreciation of all subsequent experiences.

The *habitus*, a product of history, produces individual and collective practices – more history – in accordance with the schemes generated by history. It ensures the active presence of past experiences, which, deposited in each organism in the form of schemes of perception, thought and action, tend to guarantee the "correctness" of practices and their constancy over time, more reliably than all formal rules and explicit norms. This system of dispositions – a present past that tends to perpetuate itself into the future by reactivation in similarly structured practices, an internal law through which the law of external necessities, irreducible to immediate constraints, is constantly exerted – is the principle of the continuity and regularity which objectivism sees in social practices without being able to account for it; and also of the regulated transformations that cannot be explained either by the extrinsic, instantaneous determinisms of mechanistic sociologism or by the purely internal but equally instantaneous determination of spontaneist subjectivism. Overriding the spurious opposition between the forces inscribed in an earlier state of the system, outside the body, and the internal forces arising instantaneously as motivations springing from free will, the internal dispositions – the internalization of externality – enable the external forces to exert themselves, but in accordance with the specific logic of the organisms in which they are incorporated, i.e. in a durable, systematic and non-mechanical way. As an acquired system of generative schemes, the *habitus* makes possible the free production of all the thoughts, perceptions and actions inherent in the particular conditions of its production – and only those. Through the *habitus*, the structure of which it is the product governs practice, not along the paths of a mechanical determinism, but within the constraints and limits initially set on its inventions. This infinite yet strictly limited generative capacity is difficult to understand only so long as one remains locked in the usual antinomies – which the concept of the *habitus* aims to transcend – of determinism and freedom, conditioning and creativity, consciousness and the unconscious, or the individual and society. Because the *habitus* is an infinite capacity for generating products – thoughts, perceptions, expressions and actions – whose limits are set by the historically and socially situated conditions of its production, the conditioned and conditional freedom it provides is as remote from creation of unpredictable novelty as it is from simple mechanical reproduction of the original conditioning.

    Nothing is more misleading than the illusion created by hindsight in which all the traces of a life, such as the works of an artist or the events at a biography, appear as the realization of an essence that seems to pre-exist them. Just as a mature artistic style is not contained, like a seed, in an original inspiration but is continuously defined and redefined in the dialectic between the objectifying intention and the already objectified intention, so too the unity of meaning which, after the event, may seem to have preceded the acts and works announcing the final significance, retrospectively transforming the various stages of the temporal series into mere preparatory sketches, is constituted through the confrontation between questions that only exist in and for a mind armed with a particular type of schemes and the solutions obtained through application of these same schemes. The genesis of a system of works or practices generated by the same *habitus* (or homologous *habitus*, such as those that underlie the unity of the life-style of a group or a class) cannot be described either as the autonomous development of a unique and always self-identical essence, or as a continuous creation of novelty, because it arises from the necessary yet unpredictable confrontation between the *habitus* and an event that can exercise a pertinent incitement on the *habitus* only if the latter snatches it from the contingency of the accidental and constitutes it as a problem by applying to it the very principles of its solution; and also because the *habitus*, like every "art of inventing", is what makes it possible to produce an infinite number of practices that are relatively unpredictable (like the corresponding situations) but also limited in their diversity. In short, being the product of a particular class of objective regularities, the *habitus* tends to generate all the "reasonable", "common-sense", behaviours (and only these) which are possible within the limits of these regularities, and which are likely to be positively sanctioned because they are objectively adjusted to the logic characteristic of a particular field, whose objective future they anticipate. At the same time, "without violence, art or argument", it tends to exclude all "extravagances" ("not for the likes of us"), that is, all the behaviours that would be negatively sanctioned because they are incompatible with the objective conditions.

Because they tend to reproduce the regularities immanent in the conditions in which their generative principle was produced while adjusting to the demands inscribed as objective potentialities in the situation as defined by the cognitive and motivating structures that constitute the *habitus*, practices cannot be deduced either from the present conditions which may seem to have provoked them or from the past conditions which have produced the *habitus*, the durable principle of their production. They can therefore only be accounted for by relating the social conditions in which the *habitus* that generated them was constituted, to the social conditions in which it is implemented, that is, through the scientific work of performing the interrelationship of these two states of the social world that the *habitus* performs, while concealing it, in and through practice. The "unconscious", which enables one to dispense with this interrelating, is never anything other than the forgetting of history which history itself produces by realizing the objective structures that it generates in the quasi-natures of *habitus*. As Durkheim[3] puts it:

> In each one of us, in differing degrees, is contained the person we were yesterday, and indeed, in the nature of things it is even true that our past *personae* predominate in us, since the present is necessarily insignificant when compared with the long period of the past because of which we have emerged in the form we have today. It is just that we don't directly feel the influence of these past selves precisely because they are so deeply rooted within us. They constitute the unconscious part of ourselves. Consequently we have a strong tendency not to recognize their existence and to ignore their legitimate demands. By contrast, with the most recent acquisitions of civilization we are vividly aware of them just because they are recent and consequently have not had time to be assimilated into our collective unconscious.

The *habitus* – embodied history, internalized as a second nature and so forgotten as history – is the active presence of the whole past of which it is the product. As such, it is what gives practices their relative autonomy with respect to external determinations of the immediate present. This autonomy is that of the past, enacted and acting, which, functioning as accumulated capital, produces history on the basis of history and so ensures the permanence in change that makes the individual agent a world within the world. The *habitus* is a spontaneity without consciousness or will, opposed as much to the mechanical necessity of things without history in mechanistic theories as it is to the reflexive freedom of subjects "without inertia" in rationalist theories.

Thus the dualistic vision that recognizes only the self-transparent act of consciousness or the externally determined thing has to give way to the real logic of action, which brings together two objectifications of history, objectification in bodies and objectification in institutions or, which amounts to the same thing, two states of capital, objectified and incorporated, through which a distance is set up from necessity and its urgencies. This logic is seen in paradigmatic form in the dialectic of expressive dispositions and instituted means of expression (morphological, syntactic and lexical instruments, literary genres, etc.) which is observed in the intentionless invention of regulated improvisation. Endlessly overtaken by his own words, with which he maintains a relation of "carry and be carried", as Nicolai Hartmann put it, the virtuoso finds in his discourse the triggers for his discourse, which goes along like a train laying its own rails.[4] In other words, being produced by a *modus operandi* which is not consciously mastered, the discourse contains an "objective intention", as the Scholastics put it, which outruns the conscious intentions of its apparent author and constantly offers new pertinent stimuli to the *modus operandi* of which it is the product and which functions as a kind of "spiritual automaton". If witticisms strike as much by their unpredictability as by their retrospective necessity, the reason is that the *trouvaille* that brings to light long buried resources presupposes a *habitus* that so perfectly possesses the objectively available means of expression that it is possessed by them, so much so that it asserts its freedom from them by realizing the rarest of the possibilities that they necessarily imply. The dialectic of the meaning of the language and the "sayings of the tribe" is a particular and particularly significant case of the dialectic between *habitus* and institutions, that is, between two modes of objectification of past history, in which there is constantly created a history that inevitably appears, like witticisms, as both original and inevitable.

This durably installed generative principle of regulated improvisations is a practical sense which reactivates the sense objectified in institutions. Produced by the work of inculcation and appropriation that is needed in order for objective structures, the products of collective history, to be reproduced in the form of the durable, adjusted dispositions that are the condition of their functioning, the *habitus*, which is constituted in the course of an individual history, imposing its particular logic on incorporation, and through which agents partake of the history objectified in institutions, is what makes it possible to inhabit institutions, to appropriate them practically, and so to keep them in activity, continuously pulling them from the state of dead letters, reviving the sense deposited in them, but at the same time imposing the revisions and transformations that reactivation entails. Or rather, the *habitus* is what enables the institution to attain full realization: it is through the capacity for incorporation, which exploits the body's readiness to take seriously the performative magic of the social, that the king, the banker or the priest are hereditary monarchy, financial capitalism or the Church made flesh. Property appropriates its owner, embodying itself in the form of a structure generating practices perfectly conforming with its logic and its demands. If one is justified in saying, with Marx, that "the lord of an entailed estate, the first-born son, belongs to the land", that "it inherits him", or that the "persons" of capitalists are the "personification" of capital, this is because the purely social and quasimagical process of socialization, which is inaugurated by the act of marking that institutes an individual as an eldest son, an heir, a successor, a Christian, or simply as a man (as opposed to a woman), with all the corresponding privileges and obligations, and which is prolonged, strengthened and confirmed by social treatments that tend to transform instituted difference into natural distinction, produces quite real effects, durably inscribed in the body and in belief. An institution, even an economy, is complete and fully viable only if it is durably objectified not only in things, that is, in the logic, transcending individual agents, of a particular field, but also in bodies, in durable dispositions to recognize and comply with the demands immanent in the field.

In so far – and only in so far – as *habitus* are the incorporation of the same history, or more concretely, of the same history objectified in *habitus* and structures, the practices they generate are mutually intelligible and immediately adjusted to the structures, and also objectively concerted and endowed with an objective meaning that is at once unitary and systematic, transcending subjective intentions and conscious projects, whether individual or collective. One of the fundamental effects of the harmony between practical sense and objectified meaning (*sens*) is the production of a common-sense world, whose immediate self-evidence is accompanied by the objectivity provided by consensus on the meaning of practices and the world, in other words the harmonization of the agents' experiences and the constant reinforcement each of them receives from expression – individual or collective (in festivals, for example), improvised or programmed (commonplaces, sayings) – of similar or identical experiences.

> The homogeneity of *habitus* that is observed within the limits of a class of conditions of existence and social conditionings is what causes practices and works to be immediately intelligible and foreseeable, and hence taken for granted. The *habitus* makes questions of intention superfluous, not only in the production but also in the deciphering of practices and works. Automatic and impersonal, significant without a signifying intention, ordinary practices lend themselves to an understanding that is no less automatic and impersonal. The picking up of the objective intention they express requires neither "reactivation" of the "lived" intention of their originator, nor the "intentional transfer into the Other" cherished by the phenomenologists and all advocates of a "participationist" conception of history or sociology, nor tacit or explicit inquiry ("What do you *mean*?") as to other people's intentions. "Communication of consciousnesses" presupposes community of "unconsciouses" (that is, of linguistic and cultural competences). Deciphering the objective intention of practices and works has nothing to do with "reproduction" (*Nachbildung*, as the early Dilthey puts it) of lived experiences and the unnecessary and uncertain reconstitution of an "intention" which is not their real origin.

The objective homogenizing of group or class *habitus* that results from homogeneity of conditions of existence is what enables practices to be objectively harmonized without any calculation or conscious reference to a norm and mutually adjusted in the absence of any direct interaction or, *a fortiori*, explicit co-ordination. The interaction itself owes its form to the objective structures that have produced the dispositions of the interacting agents, which continue to assign them their relative positions in the interaction and elsewhere. "Imagine", Leibniz suggests,[5] "two clocks or watches in perfect agreement as to the time. This may occur in one of three ways. The first consists in mutual influence; the second is to appoint a skilful workman to correct them and synchronize constantly; the third is to construct these two clocks with such art and precision that one can be assured of their subsequent agreement." So long as one ignores the true principle of the conductorless orchestration which gives regularity, unity and systematicity to practices even in the absence of any spontaneous or imposed organization of individual projects, one is condemned to the naive artificialism that recognizes no other unifying principle than conscious co-ordination. The practices of the members of the same group or, in a differentiated society, the same class, are always more and better harmonized than the agents know or wish, because, as Leibniz again says, "following only (his) own laws", each "nonetheless agrees with the other". The *habitus* is precisely this immanent law, *lex insita*, inscribed in bodies by identical histories, which is the precondition not only for the co-ordination of practices but also for practices of co-ordination. The corrections and adjustments the agents themselves consciously carry out presuppose mastery of a common code; and undertakings of collective mobilization cannot succeed without a minimum of concordance between the *habitus* of the mobilizing agents (prophet, leader, etc.) and the dispositions of those who recognize themselves in their practices or words, and, above all, without the inclination towards grouping that springs from the spontaneous orchestration of dispositions.

> It is certain that every effort at mobilization aimed at organizing collective action has to reckon with the dialectic of dispositions and occasions that takes place in every agent, whether he mobilizes or is mobilized (the hysteresis of *habitus* is doubtless one explanation of the structural lag between opportunities and the dispositions to grasp them which is the cause of missed opportunities and, in particular, of the frequently observed incapacity to think historical crises in categories of perception and thought other than those of the past, however revolutionary). It is also certain that it must take account of the objective orchestration established among dispositions that are objectively co-ordinated because they are ordered by more or less identical objective necessities. It is, however, extremely dangerous to conceive collective action by analogy with individual action, ignoring all that the former owes to the relatively autonomous logic of the institutions of mobilization (with their own history, their specific organization, etc.) and to the situations, institutionalized or not, in which it occurs.

Sociology treats as identical all biological individuals who, being the products of the same objective conditions, have the same *habitus*. A social class (in-itself) – a class of identical or similar conditions of existence and conditionings – is at the same time a class of biological individuals having the same *habitus*, understood as a system of dispositions common to all products of the same conditionings. Though it is impossible for all (or even two) members of the same class to have had the same experiences, in the same order, it is certain that each member of the same class is more likely than any member of another class to have been confronted with the situations most frequent for members of that class. Through the always convergent experiences that give a social environment its physiognomy, with its "closed doors", "dead ends" and "limited prospects", the objective structures that sociology apprehends in the form of probabilities of access to goods, services and powers, inculcate the "art of assessing likelihoods", as Leibniz put it, of anticipating the objective future, in short, the "sense of reality", or realities, which is perhaps the best-concealed principle of their efficacy.

To define the relationship between class *habitus* and individual *habitus* (which is inseparable from the organic individuality that is immediately given to immediate perception – *intuitus personae* – and socially designated and recognized – name, legal identity, etc.), class (or group) *habitus*, that is, the individual habitus in so far as it expresses or reflects the class (or group), could be regarded as a subjective but non-individual system of internalized structures, common schemes of perception, conception and action, which are the precondition of all objectification and apperception; and the objective co-ordination of practices and the sharing of a world-view could be founded on the perfect impersonality and interchangability of singular practices and views. But this would amount to regarding all the practices or representations produced in accordance with identical schemes as impersonal and interchangeable, like individual intuitions of space which, according to Kant, reflect none of the particularities of the empirical ego. In fact, the singular *habitus* of members of the same class are united in a relationship of homology, that is, of diversity within homogeneity reflecting the diversity within homogeneity characteristic of their social conditions of production. Each individual system of dispositions is a structural variant of the others, expressing the singularity of its position within the class and its trajectory. "Personal" style, the particular stamp marking all the products of the same *habitus*, whether practices or works, is never more than a deviation in relation to the style of a period or class, so that it relates back to the common style not only by its conformity – like Phidias, who, for Hegel, had no "manner" – but also by the difference that makes the "manner".

The principle of the differences between individual *habitus* lies in the singularity of their social trajectories, to which there correspond series of chronologically ordered determinations that are mutually irreducible to one another. The *habitus* which, at every moment, structures new experiences in accordance with the structures produced by past experiences, which are modified by the new experiences within the limits defined by their power of selection, brings about a unique integration, dominated by the earliest experiences, of the experiences statistically common to members of the same class. Early experiences have particular weight because the *habitus* tends to ensure its own constancy and its defence against change through the selection it makes within new information by rejecting information capable of calling into question its accumulated information, if exposed to it accidentally or by force, and especially by avoiding exposure to such information. One only has to think, for example, of homogamy, the paradigm of all the "choices" through which the *habitus* tends to favour experiences likely to reinforce it (or the empirically confirmed fact that people tend to talk about politics with those who have the same opinions). Through the systematic "choices" it makes among the places, events and people that might be frequented, the *habitus* tends to protect itself from crises and critical challenges by providing itself with a milieu to which it is as pre-adapted as possible, that is, a relatively constant universe of situations tending to reinforce its dispositions by offering the market most favourable to its products. And once again it is the most paradoxical property of the *habitus*, the unchosen principle of all "choices", that yields the solution to the paradox of the information needed in order to avoid information. The schemes of perception and appreciation of the *habitus* which are the basis of all the avoidance strategies are largely the product of a non-conscious, unwilled avoidance, whether it results automatically from the conditions of existence (for example, spatial segregation) or has been produced by a strategic intention (such as avoidance of "bad company" or "unsuitable books") originating from adults themselves formed in the same conditions.

Even when they look like the realization of explicit ends, the strategies produced by the *habitus* and enabling agents to cope with unforeseen and constantly changing situations are only apparently determined by the future. If they seem to be oriented by anticipation of their own consequences, thereby encouraging the finalist illusion, this is because, always tending to reproduce the objective structures that produced them, they are determined by the past conditions of production of their principle of production, that is, by the already realized outcome of identical or interchangeable past practices, which coincides with their own outcome only to the extent that the structures within which they function are identical to or homologous with the objective structures of which they are the product. Thus, for example, in the interaction between two agents or groups of agents endowed with the same *habitus* (say A and B), everything takes place as if the actions of each of them (say a_1 for A) were organized by reference to the reactions which they call forth from any agent possessing the same *habitus* (say b_1 for B). They therefore objectively imply anticipation of the reaction which these reactions in turn call forth (a_2, A's reaction to b_1). But the teleological description, the only one appropriate to a "rational actor" possessing perfect information as to the preferences and competences of the other actors, in which each action has the purpose of making possible the reaction to the reaction it induces (individual A performs an action a_1, a gift for example, in order to make individual B produce action b_1, so that he can then perform action a_1, a stepped-up gift), is quite as naive as the mechanistic description that presents the action and the riposte as so many steps in a sequence of programmed actions produced by a mechanical apparatus.

To have an idea of the difficulties that would be encountered by a mechanistic theory of practice as mechanical reaction, directly determined by the antecedent conditions and entirely reducible to the mechanical functioning of pre-established devices – which would have to be assumed to exist in infinite number, like the chance configurations of stimuli capable of triggering them from outside – one only has to mention the grandiose, desperate undertaking of the anthropologist, fired with positivist ardour, who recorded 480 elementary units of behaviour in 20 minutes' observation of his wife in the kitchen: "Here we confront the distressing fact that the sample episode chain under analysis is a fragment of a larger segment of behavior which in the complete record contains some 480 separate episodes. Moreover, it took only twenty minutes for these 480 behavior stream events to occur. If my wife's rate of behavior is roughly representative of that of other actors, we must be prepared to deal with an inventory of episodes produced at the rate of some 20,000 per sixteen-hour day per actor ... In a population consisting of several hundred actor-types, the number of different episodes in the total repertory must amount to many millions in the course of an annual cycle".[6]

The *habitus* contains the solution to the paradoxes of objective meaning without subjective intention. It is the source of these strings of "moves" which are objectively organized as strategies without being the product of a genuine strategic intention – which would presuppose at least that they be apprehended as one among other possible strategies. If each stage in the sequence of ordered and oriented actions that constitute objective strategies can appear to be determined by anticipation of the future, and in particular, of its own consequences (which is what justifies the use of the concept of strategy), it is because the practices that are generated by the *habitus* and are governed by the past conditions of production of their generative principle are adapted in advance to the objective conditions whenever the conditions in which the *habitus* functions have remained identical, or similar, to the conditions in which it was constituted. Perfectly and immediately successful adjustment to the objective conditions provides the most complete illusion of finality, or – which amounts to the same thing – of self-regulating mechanism.

The presence of the past in this kind of false anticipation of the future performed by the *habitus* is, paradoxically, most clearly seen when the sense of the probable future is belied and when dispositions ill-adjusted to the objective chances because of a hysteresis effect (Marx's favourite example of this was Don Quixote) are negatively sanctioned because the environment they actually encounter is too different from the one to which they are objectively adjusted. In fact the persistence of the effects of primary conditioning, in the form of the *habitus*, accounts equally well for cases in which dispositions function out of phase and practices are objectively ill-adapted to the present conditions because they are objectively adjusted to conditions that no longer obtain. The tendency of groups to persist in their ways, due *inter alia* to the fact that they are composed of individuals with durable dispositions that can outlive the economic and social conditions in which they were produced, can be the source of misadaptation as well as adaptation, revolt as well as resignation.

One only has to consider other possible forms of the relationship between dispositions and conditions to see that the pre-adjustment of the *habitus* to the objective conditions is a "particular case of the possible" and so avoid unconsciously universalizing the model of the near-circular relationship of near-perfect reproduction, which is completely valid only when the conditions of production of the *habitus* and the conditions of its functioning are identical or homothetic. In this particular case, the dispositions durably inculcated by the objective conditions and by a pedagogic action that is tendentially adjusted to these conditions, tend to generate practices objectively compatible with these conditions and expectations pre-adapted to their objective demands (*amor fati*).[7] As a consequence, they tend, without any rational calculation or conscious estimation of the chances of success, to ensure immediate correspondence between the *a priori* or *ex ante* probability conferred on an event (whether or not accompanied by subjective experiences such as hopes, expectation, fears, etc.) and the *a posteriori* or *ex post* probability that can be established on the basis of past experience. They thus make it possible to understand why economic models based on the (tacit) premise of a "relationship of intelligible causality", as Max Weber[8] calls it, between generic ("typical") chances "objectively existing as an average" and "subjective expectations", or, for example, between investment or the propensity to invest and the rate of return expected or really obtained in the past, fairly exactly account for practices which do not arise from knowledge of the objective chances.

By pointing out that rational action, "judiciously" oriented according to what is "objectively valid",[9] is what "would have happened if the actors had had knowledge of all the circumstances and all the participants' intentions",[10] that is, of what is "valid in the eyes of the scientist", who alone is able to calculate the system of objective chances to which perfectly informed action would have to be adjusted, Weber shows clearly that the pure model of rational action cannot be regarded as an anthropological description of practice. This is not only because real agents only very exceptionally possess the complete information, and the skill to appreciate it, that rational action would presuppose. Apart from rare cases which bring together the economic and cultural conditions for rational action oriented by knowledge of the profits that can be obtained in the different markets, practices depend not on the average chances of profit, an abstract and unreal notion, but on the specific chances that a singular agent or class of agents possesses by virtue of its capital, this being understood, in this respect, as a means of appropriation of the chances theoretically available to all.

> Economic theory which acknowledges only the rational "responses" of an indeterminate, interchangeable agent to "potential opportunities", or more precisely to average chances (like the "average rates of profit" offered by the different markets), converts the immanent law of the economy into a universal norm of proper economic behaviour. In so doing, it conceals the fact that the "rational" *habitus* which is the precondition for appropriate economic behaviour is the product of particular economic condition, the one defined by possession of the economic and cultural capital required in order to seize the "potential opportunities" theoretically available to all; and also that the same

dispositions, by adapting the economically most deprived to the specific condition of which they are the product and thereby helping to make their adaptation to the generic demands of the economic cosmos (as regards calculation, forecasting, etc.) lead them to accept the negative sanctions resulting from this lack of adaptation, that is, their deprivation. In short, the art of estimating and seizing chances, the capacity to anticipate the future by a kind of practical induction or even to take a calculated gamble on the possible against the probable, are dispositions that can only be acquired in certain social conditions, that is, certain social conditions. Like the entrepreneurial spirit or the propensity to invest, economic information is a function of one's power over the economy. This is, on the one hand, because the propensity to acquire it depends on the chances of using it successfully, and the chances of acquiring it depend on the chances of successfully using it; and also because economic competence, like all competence (linguistic, political, etc.), far from being a simple technical capacity acquired in certain conditions, is a power tacitly conferred on those who have power over the economy or (as the very ambiguity of the word "competence" indicates) an attribute of status.

Only in imaginary experience (in the folk tale, for example), which neutralizes the sense of social realities, does the social world take the form of a universe of possibles equally possible for any possible subject. Agents shape their aspirations according to concrete indices of the accessible and the inaccessible, of what is and is not "for us", a division as fundamental and as fundamentally recognized as that between the sacred and the profane. The pre-emptive rights on the future that are defined by law and by the monopolistic right to certain possibles that it confers are merely the explicitly guaranteed form of the whole set of appropriated chances through which the power relations of the present project themselves into the future, from where they govern present dispositions, especially those towards the future. In fact, a given agent's practical relation to the future, which governs his present practice, is defined in the relationship between, on the one hand, his *habitus* with its temporal structures and dispositions towards the future, constituted in the course of a particular relationship to a particular universe of probabilities, and on the other hand a certain state of the chances objectively offered to him by the social world. The relation to what is possible is a relation to power; and the sense of the probable future is constituted in the prolonged relationship with a world structured according to the categories of the possible (for us) and the impossible (for us), of what is appropriated in advance by and for others and what one can reasonably expect for oneself. The *habitus* is the principle of a selective perception of the indices tending to confirm and reinforce it rather than transform it, a matrix generating responses adapted in advance to all objective conditions identical to or homologous with the (past) conditions of its production; it adjusts itself to a probable future which it anticipates and helps to bring about because it reads it directly in the present of the presumed world, the only one it can ever know. It is thus the basis of what Marx[11] calls "effective demand" (as opposed to "demand without effect", based on need and desire), a realistic relation to what is possible, founded on and therefore limited by power. This disposition, always marked by its (social) conditions of acquisition and realization, tends to adjust to the objective chances of satisfying need or desire, inclining agents to "cut their coats according to their cloth", and so to become the accomplices of the processes that tend to make the probable a reality.

NOTES

1 M. Gluckman, "Ethnographic Data in British Social Anthropology." *Sociological Review*, 9 (1961) 5–17; cf. also J. Van Velson, *The Politics of Kinship: A Study in Social Manipulation among the Lakeside Tonga* (Manchester: Manchester University Press, 1964).
2 E. Leach, "On Certain Unconsidered Aspects of Double Descent Systems." *Man* 62 (1962) 133.
3 E. Durkheim, *The Evolution of Educational Thought* (London: Routledge & Kegan Paul, 1977), p. 11.
4 R. Ruyer, *Paradoxes de la conscience et limites de l'automatisme* (Paris: Albin Michel 1966).
5 G. W. Leibniz, *Second éclaircissement du système de la communication des substances* (first pub. 1696). In *Œuvres philosophiques*, ed. P. Janet (Paris: Ladrange, 1866).
6 M. Harris, *The Nature of Cultural Things* (New York: Random House, 1964).
7 For some psychologists' attempts at direct verification of this relationship, see E. Brunswik, "Systematic and Representative Design of Psychological Experiments." In J. Neyman (ed.), *Proceedings of the Berkeley Symposium on Mathematical Statistics and Probability* (Berkeley, Calif: University of California Press 1949); M. G. Preston, and P. Baratta, "An Experimental Study of the Action-value of an Uncertain Income." *American Journal of Psychology*, 61 (1948) 183–93; F. Attneave, 1953: "Psychological Probability as a Function of Experienced Frequency." *Journal of Experimental Psychology*, 46 (1953) 81–6.
8 M. Weber, *Gesammelte Aufsätze zur Wissenschaftslehre* (Tübingen: J. C. Mohr, 1922).
9 Ibid.
10 M. Weber, *Economy and Society*, vol. I (New York: Bedminster, 1968) p. 6.
11 K. Marx, *Economic and Philosophic Manuscripts of 1844*. In K. Marx, *Early Writings* (Harmondsworth: Penguin, 1956).

Chapter 24

The Field of Cultural Production, or: The Economic World Reversed* [1993]

Pierre Bourdieu

Preliminaries

Few areas more clearly demonstrate the heuristic efficacy of *relational* thinking than that of art and literature. Constructing an object such as the literary field[1] requires and enables us to make a radical break with the substantialist mode of thought (as Ernst Cassirer calls it) which tends to foreground the individual, or the visible interactions between individuals, at the expense of the structural relations – invisible, or visible only through their effects – between social positions that are both occupied and manipulated by social agents, which may be isolated individuals, groups or institutions. There are in fact very few other areas in which the glorification of "great men", unique creators irreducible to any condition or conditioning, is more common or uncontroversial – as one can see, for example, in the fact that most analysts uncritically accept the division of the corpus that is imposed on them by the names of authors ("the work of Racine") or the titles of works (*Phèdre* or *Bérénice*).

To take as one's object of study the literary or artistic field of a given period and society (the field of Florentine painting in the Quattrocento or the field of French literature in the Second Empire) is to set the history of art and literature a task which it never completely performs, because it fails to take it on explicitly, even when it does break out of the routine of monographs which, however interminable, are

---

* Originally translated from French by Richard Nice.

Pierre Bourdieu, "The Field of Cultural Production, or: The Economic World Reversed," pp. 312–13, 315–16, 319–26, 341–6, 349–50, 353–6 from Pierre Bourdieu, *Poetics*, 12. Elsevier Science Publishers, B.V. (1983). Copyright © 1983 by Poetics. Reprinted by permission of Elsevier.

Contemporary Sociological Theory, Third Edition. Edited by Craig Calhoun, Joseph Gerteis, James Moody, Steven Pfaff, and Indermohan Virk. Editorial material and organization © 2012 John Wiley & Sons, Ltd. Published 2012 by John Wiley & Sons, Ltd.

necessarily inadequate (since the essential explanation of each work lies outside each of them, in the objective relations which constitute this field). The task is that of constructing the space of positions and the space of the position-takings (*prises de position*) in which they are expressed. The science of the literary field is a form of *analysis situs* which establishes that each position – e.g. the one which corresponds to a genre such as the novel or, within this, to a sub-category such as the "society novel" (*roman mondain*) or the "popular" novel – is objectively defined by the system of distinctive properties by which it can be situated relative to other positions; that every position, even the dominant one, depends for its very existence, and for the determinations it imposes on its occupants, on the other positions constituting the field; and that the structure of the field, i.e. of the space of positions, is nothing other than the structure of the distribution of the capital of specific properties which governs success in the field and the winning of the external or specific profits (such as literary prestige) which are at stake in the field.

The *space of literary or artistic position-takings*, i.e. the structured set of the manifestations of the social agents involved in the field – literary or artistic works, of course, but also political acts or pronouncements, manifestoes or polemics, etc. – is inseparable from the *space of literary or artistic positions* defined by possession of a determinate quantity of specific capital (recognition) and, at the same time, by occupation of a determinate position in the structure of the distribution of this specific capital. The literary or artistic field is a *field of forces*, but it is also a *field of struggles* tending to transform or conserve this field of forces. The network of objective relations between positions subtends and orients the strategies which the occupants of the different positions implement in their struggles to defend or improve their positions (i.e. their position-takings), strategies which depend for their force and form on the position each agent occupies in the power relations (*rapports de force*).

Every position-taking is defined in relation to the *space of possibles* which is objectively realized as a *problematic* in the form of the actual or potential position-taking corresponding to the different positions; and it receives its distinctive *value* from its negative relationship with the coexistent position-takings to which it is objectively related and which determine it by delimiting it. It follows from this, for example, that a *prise de position* changes, even when it remains identical, whenever there is change in the universe of options that are simultaneously offered for producers and consumers to choose from. The meaning of a work (artistic, literary, philosophical, etc.) changes automatically with each change in the field within which it is situated for the spectator or reader.

This effect is most immediate in the case of so-called classic works, which change constantly as the universe of coexistent works changes. This is seen clearly when the simple *repetition* of a work from the past in a radically transformed field of compossibles produces an entirely automatic *effect of parody* (in the theatre, for example, this effect requires the performers to signal a slight distance from a text impossible to defend as it stands; it can also arise in the presentation of a work corresponding to one extremity of the field before an audience corresponding structurally to the other extremity – e.g. when an avant-garde play is performed to a bourgeois audience, or the contrary, as more often happens). It is significant that breaks with the most orthodox works of the past, i.e. with the *belief* they impose on the newcomers, often takes the form of *parody* (intentional, this time), which presupposes and confirms *emancipation*. In this case, the newcomers "get beyond" (*"dépassent"*) the dominant mode of thought and expression not by explicitly denouncing it but by repeating and reproducing it in a sociologically non-congruent context, which has the effect of rendering it incongruous or even absurd, simply by making it perceptible as the arbitrary convention which it is. This form of heretical break is particularly favoured by ex-believers, who use pastiche or parody as the indispensable means of objectifying, and thereby appropriating, the form of thought and expression by which they were formerly possessed.

> This explains why writers' efforts to control the reception of their own works are always partially doomed to failure (one thinks of Marx's "I am not a Marxist"); if only because the very effect of their work may transform the conditions of its reception and because they would not have had to write many things they did write and write them as they did – e.g. resorting to rhetorical strategies intended to "twist the stick in the other direction" – if they had been granted from the outset what they are granted retrospectively.

[...]

When we speak of a *field* of *prises de position*, we are insisting that what can be constituted as a *system* for the sake of analysis is not the product of a coherence-seeking intention or an objective consensus (even if it presupposes unconscious agreement on common principles) but the product and prize of a permanent conflict; or, to put it another way, that the generative, unifying principle of this "system" is the struggle, with all the contradictions it engenders (so that participation in the struggle – which may be indicated objectively by, for example, the attacks that are suffered – can be used as the criterion establishing that a work belongs to the field of *prises de position* and its author to the field of positions).[2]

In defining the literary and artistic field as, inseparably, a field of positions and a field of *prises de position*, we also escape from the usual dilemma of internal ("tautegorical") reading of the work (taken in isolation or within the system of works to which it belongs) and external (or "allegorical") analysis, i.e. analysis of the social conditions of production of the producers and consumers which is based on the – generally tacit – hypothesis of the spontaneous correspondence or deliberate matching of production to demand or commissions. And by the same token we escape from the correlative dilemma of the charismatic image of artistic activity as pure, disinterested creation by an isolated artist, and the reductionist vision which claims to explain the act of production and its product in terms of their conscious or unconscious external functions, by referring them, for example, to the interests of the dominant class or, more subtly, to the ethical or aesthetic values of one or another of its fractions, from which the patrons or audience are drawn.

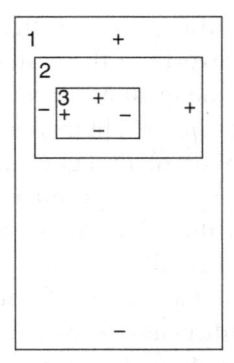

Figure 24.1 Diagram of the artistic field (3), contained within the field of power (2) which is itself situated within the field of class relations (1). "+" = positive pole, implying a dominant position; "−" = negative pole (dominated).

The Field of Cultural Production and the Field of Power

In Figure 24.1, the literary and artistic field (3) is contained within the field of power (2), while possessing a relative autonomy with respect to it, especially as regards its economic and political principles of hierarchization. It occupies a *dominated position* (at the negative pole) in this field, which is itself situated at the dominant pole of the field of class relations (1). It is thus the site of a double hierarchy: the *heteronomous* principle of hierarchization, which would reign unchallenged if, losing all autonomy, the literary and artistic field were to disappear as such (so that writers and artists became subject to the ordinary law prevailing in the field of power, and more generally in the economic field), is *success*, as measured by indices such as book sales, number of theatrical performances, etc. or honours, appointments, etc. The *autonomous* principle of hierarchization, which would reign unchallenged if the field of production were to achieve total autonomy with respect to the laws of the market, is *degree of specific consecration* (literary or artistic prestige), i.e. the degree of recognition accorded by those who recognize no other criterion of legitimacy than recognition by those whom they recognize. In other words, the specificity of the literary and artistic field is defined by the fact that the more autonomous it is, i.e. the more completely it fulfils its own logic as a field, the more it tends to suspend or reverse the dominant principle of hierarchization; but also that, whatever its degree of independence, it continues to be affected by the laws of the field which encompasses it, those of economic and political profit. The more autonomous the field becomes, the more favourable the symbolic power balance is to the most autonomous producers and the more clearcut is the division between the field of restricted production, in which the producers produce for other producers, and the field of "mass-audience" production (*la grande production*), which is *symbolically* excluded and discredited (this symbolically dominant definition is the one that the historians of art and literature *unconsciously* adopt when they exclude from their object of study, writers and artists who produced for the market and have often fallen into oblivion). Because it is a good measure of the degree of autonomy, and therefore of presumed adherence to the disinterested values which constitute the specific law of the field, the degree of public success is no doubt the main differentiating factor. But lack of success is not in itself a sign and guarantee of election, and "*poètes maudits*", like "successful playwrights", must take account of a secondary differentiating factor whereby some "*poètes maudits*" may also be "failed writers" (even if exclusive reference to the first criterion can help them to avoid realizing it), whilst some box-office successes may be recognized, at least in some sectors of the field, as genuine art.

Thus, at least in the most perfectly autonomous sector of the field of cultural production, where the only audience aimed at is other producers (e.g. Symbolist poetry), the economy of practices is based, as in a generalized game of "loser wins", on a systematic inversion of the fundamental principles of all ordinary economies, that of business (it excludes the pursuit of profit and does not guarantee any sort of correspondence between investments and monetary gains), that of power (it condemns honours and temporal greatness), and even that of institutionalized cultural authority (the absence of any academic training or consecration may be considered a virtue).

> One would have to analyse in these terms the relations between writers or artists and publishers or gallery directors. The latter are equivocal figures, through whom the logic of the economy is brought to the heart of the sub-field of production-for-fellow-producers; they need to possess, simultaneously, economic dispositions which, in some sectors of the fields, are totally alien to the producers and also properties close to those of the producers whose work they valorize and exploit. The logic of the structural homologies between the field of publishers or gallery directors and the field of the corresponding artists or writers does indeed mean that the former present properties close to those of the latter, and this favours the relationship of trust and belief which is the basis of an exploitation presupposing a high degree of misrecognition on each site. These "merchants in the temple" make their living by tricking the artist or writer into taking the consequences of his statutory professions of disinterestedness.

This explains the inability of all forms of economism, which seek to grasp this anti-economy in economic terms, to understand this upside-down economic world. The literary and artistic world is so ordered that those who enter it have an interest in disinterestedness. And indeed, like prophecy, especially the prophecy of misfortune, which according to Weber (1952), demonstrates its authenticity by the fact that it brings in no income, a heretical break with the prevailing artistic traditions proves its claim to authenticity by its disinterestedness. As we shall see, this does not mean that there is not an economic logic to this charismatic economy based on the social miracle of an act devoid of any determination other than the specifically aesthetic intention. There are economic conditions for the indifference to economy which induces a pursuit of the riskiest positions in the intellectual and artistic avant-garde, and also for the capacity to remain there over a long period without any economic compensation.

The struggle for the dominant principle of hierarchization

The literary or artistic field is at all times the site of a struggle between the two principles of hierarchization: the heteronomous principle, favourable to those who dominate the field economically and politically (e.g. "bourgeois art") and the autonomous principle (e.g. "art for art's sake"), which those of its advocates who are least endowed with specific capital tend to identify with degree of independence from the economy, seeing temporal failure as a sign of election and success as a sign of compromise.[3] The state of the power relations in this struggle depends on the overall degree of autonomy possessed by the field, i.e. the extent to which it manages to impose its own norms and sanctions on the whole set of producers, including those who are closest to the dominant pole of the field of power and therefore most responsive to external demands (i.e. the most heteronomous); this degree of autonomy varies considerably from one period and one national tradition to another, and affects the whole structure of the field. Everything seems to indicate that it depends on the value which the specific capital of writers and artists represents for the dominant fractions, on the one hand in the struggle to conserve the established order and, perhaps especially, in the struggle between the fractions aspiring to domination within the field of power (bourgeoisie and aristocracy, old bourgeoisie and new bourgeoisie, etc.), and on the other hand in the production and reproduction of economic capital (with the aid of experts and cadres).[4] All the evidence suggests that, at a given level of overall autonomy, intellectuals are, other things being equal, proportionately more responsive to the seduction of the powers that be, the less well-endowed they are with specific capital.[5]

The struggle in the field of cultural production over the imposition of the legitimate mode of cultural production is inseparable from the struggle within the dominant class (with the opposition between "artists" and "bourgeois") to impose the dominant principle of domination (i.e., ultimately, the definition of human accomplishment). In this struggle, the artists and writers who are richest in specific capital and most concerned for their autonomy are considerably weakened by the fact that some of their competitors identify their interests with the dominant principles of hierarchization and seek to impose them even within the field, with the support of the temporal powers. The most heteronomous cultural producers (i.e. those with least symbolic capital) can offer the least resistance to external demands, of whatever sort. To defend their own position, they have to produce weapons, which the dominant agents (within the field of power) can immediately turn against the cultural producers most attached to their autonomy. In endeavouring to discredit every attempt to impose an autonomous principle of hierarchization, and thus serving their own interests, they serve the interests of the dominant fractions of the dominant class, who obviously have an interest in there being only one hierarchy. In the struggle to impose the legitimate definition of art and literature, the most autonomous producers naturally tend to exclude "bourgeois" writers and artists, whom they see as "enemy agents". This means, incidentally, that sampling problems cannot be resolved by one of those arbitrary decisions of positivist ignorance which are dignified by the term "operational definition": these amount to blindly arbitrating on debates which are inscribed in reality itself, such as the question as to whether such and such a group ("bourgeois" theatre, the "popular" novel, etc.) or such and such an individual claiming the title of writer or artist (or philosopher, or intellectual, etc.) belongs to the population of writers or artists or, more precisely, as to who is legitimately entitled to designate legitimate writers or artists.

The preliminary reflexions on the definition of the object and the boundaries of the population, which studies of writers, artists, and especially intellectuals, often indulge in as to give themselves an air of scientificity, ignore the fact, which is more than scientifically attested, that the definition of the writer (or artist, etc.) is an issue at stake in struggles in every literary (or artistic, etc.) field.[6] In other words, the field of cultural production is the site of struggles in which what is at stake is the power to impose the dominant definition of the writer and therefore to delimit the population of those entitled to take part in the struggle to define the writer. The established definition of the writer may be radically transformed by an enlargement of the set of people who have a legitimate voice in literary matters. It follows from this that every survey aimed at establishing the hierarchy of writers predetermines the hierarchy by determining the population deemed worthy of helping to establish it. In short, the fundamental stake in literary struggles is the monopoly of literary legitimacy, i.e., *inter alia*, the monopoly of the power to say with authority who is authorized to call himself a writer; or, to put it another way, it is the monopoly of the power to consecrate producers or products (we are dealing with a world of belief and the consecrated writer is the one who has the power to consecrate and to win assent when he consecrates an author or a work – with a preface, a favourable review, a prize, etc.). While it is true that every literary field is the site of a struggle over the definition of the writer (a universal proposition), the fact remains if he is not to make the mistake of universalizing the particular case, the scientific analyst needs to know that he will only ever encounter historical definitions of the writer, corresponding to a particular state of the struggle to impose the legitimate definition of the writer. There is no other criterion of membership of a field than the objective fact of producing effects within it. One of the difficulties of orthodox defence against heretical transformation of the field by a redefinition of the tacit or explicit terms of entry is the fact that polemics imply a form of recognition; an adversary whom one would prefer to destroy by ignoring him cannot be combated without consecrating him. The *Théâtre Libre* effectively entered the sub-field of drama once it came under attack from the accredited advocates of bourgeois theatre, who thus helped to produce the recognition they sought to prevent. The "*nouveaux philosophes*" came into existence as active elements in the philosophical field – and no longer just that of journalism – as soon as consecrated philosophers felt called upon to take issue with them.

The *boundary* of the field is a stake of struggles, and the social scientist's task is not to draw a dividing-line between the agents involved in it, by imposing a so-called operational definition, which is most likely to be imposed on him by his own prejudices or presuppositions, but to describe a *state* (long-lasting or temporary) of these struggles and therefore of the frontier delimiting the territory held by the competing agents. One could thus examine the characteristics of this boundary, which may or may not be institutionalized, i.e. protected by conditions of entry that are tacitly and practically required (such as a certain cultural capital) or explicitly codified and legally guaranteed (e.g. all the forms of entrance examination aimed at ensuring a *numerus clausus*). It would be found that one of the most significant properties of the field of cultural production, explaining its extreme dispersion and the conflicts between rival principles of legitimacy, is the extreme permeability of its frontiers and, consequently, the extreme diversity of the "posts" it offers, which defy any unilinear hierarchization. It is clear from comparison that the field of cultural production neither demands as much inherited economic capital as the economic field nor as much educational capital as the university sub-field or even sectors of the field of power such as the top civil service, or even the field of the "liberal professions".[7] However, precisely because it represents one of the *indeterminate sites* in the social structure, which offer ill-defined posts, waiting to be made rather than ready-made, and therefore extremely elastic and undemanding, and career-paths which are themselves full of uncertainty and extremely dispersed (unlike bureaucratic careers, such as those offered by the university system), they attract agents who differ greatly in their properties and dispositions but the most favoured of whom are sufficiently secure to be able to disdain a university career and to take on the risks of an occupation which is not a "job" (since it is almost always combined with a private income or a "bread-and-butter" occupation).

> The "profession" of writer or artist is one of the least professionalized there are, despite all the efforts of "writers' associations", "Pen Clubs", etc. This is shown clearly by (*inter alia*) the problems which arise in classifying these agents, who are able to exercise what they regard as their main occupation only on condition that they have a secondary occupation which provides their main income (problems very similar to those encountered in classifying students).

The most disputed frontier of all is the one which separates the field of cultural production and the field of power. It may be more or less clearly marked in different periods, positions occupied in each field may be more or less totally incompatible, moves from one universe to the other more or less frequent, and the overall distance between the corresponding populations more or less great (e.g. in terms of social origin, educational background, etc.).

The effect of the homologies

The field of cultural production produces its most important effects through the play of the *homologies* between the fundamental opposition which gives the field its structure and the oppositions structuring the field of power and the field of class relations. These homologies may give rise to ideological effects which are produced automatically whenever oppositions at different levels are superimposed or merged. They are also the basis of partial alliances: the struggles within the field of power are never entirely independent of the struggle between the dominated classes and the dominant class; and the logic of the homologies between the two spaces means that the struggles going on within the inner field are always overdetermined and always tend to aim at two birds with one stone. The cultural producers, who occupy the economically dominated and symbolically dominant position within the field of cultural production, tend to feel solidarity with the occupants of the economically and culturally dominated positions within the field of class relations. Such alliances, based on homologies of position combined with profound differences in condition, are not exempt from misunderstandings and even bad faith. The structural affinity between the literary avant-garde and the political vanguard is the basis of rapprochements, between intellectual anarchism and the Symbolist movement for example, in which convergences are flaunted (e.g. Mallarmé referring to a book as an "*attentat*" – an act of terrorist violence) but distances prudently maintained. The fact remains that the cultural producers are able to use the power conferred on them, especially in periods of crisis, by their capacity to put forward a critical definition of the social world, to mobilize the potential strength of the dominated classes and subvert the order prevailing in the field of power.

> The effects of homology are not all and always automatically granted. Thus whereas the dominant fractions, in their relationship with the dominant fractions, are on the side of nature, common sense, practice, instinct, the upright and the male, and also order, reason, etc., they can no longer bring certain aspects of this representation into play in their relationship with the dominated classes, to whom they are opposed as culture to nature, reason to instinct. They need to draw on what they are offered by the dominated fractions, in order to justify their class domination, to themselves as well. The cult of art and the artist (rather than of the intellectual) is one of the necessary component of the bourgeois "art of living", to which it brings a "*supplément d'âme*", its spiritualistic point of honour.

Even in the case of the seemingly most heteronomous forms of cultural production, such as journalism, adjustment to demand is not the product of a conscious arrangement between producers and consumers. It results from the correspondence between the space of the producers, and therefore of the products offered, and the space of the consumers, which is brought about, on the basis of the homology between the two spaces, only through the competition between the producers and through the strategies imposed by the correspondence between the space of possible *prises de position* and the space of positions. In other words, by obeying the logic of the objective competition between mutually exclusive positions within the field, the various categories of producers tend to supply products adjusted to the expectations of the various positions in the field of power, but without any conscious striving for such adjustment.

> If the various positions in the field of cultural production can be so easily characterized in terms of the audience which corresponds to them, this is because the encounter between a work and its audience (which may be an absence of immediate audience) is,

strictly speaking, a *coincidence* which is not explained either by conscious, even cynical adjustment (though there are exceptions), or by the constraints of commission and demand. Rather, it results from the homology between positions occupied in the space of production, with the correlative *prises de position*, and positions in the space of consumption, i.e. in this case, in the field of power, with the opposition between the dominant and the dominated fractions, or in the field of class relations, with the opposition between the dominant and the dominated classes. In the case of the relation between the field of cultural production and the field of power, we are dealing with an almost perfect homology between two chiastic structures. Just as, in the dominant class, economic capital increases as one moves from the dominated to the dominant fractions, whereas cultural capital varies in the opposite way, so too in the field of cultural production economic profits increase as one moves from the "autonomous" pole to the "heteronomous" pole, whereas specific profits increase in the opposite direction. Similarly, the secondary opposition which divides the most heteronomous sector into "bourgeois art" and "industrial" art clearly corresponds to the opposition between the dominant and the dominated classes (cf. Bourdieu, 1979: 463–541).

[...]

Positions and Dispositions

The meeting of two histories

To understand the practices of writers and artists, and not least their products, entails understanding that they are the result of the meeting of two histories: the history of the positions they occupy and the history of their dispositions. Although position helps to shape dispositions, the latter, insofar as they are the product of independent conditions, have an existence and efficacy of their own and can help to shape positions. In no field is the confrontation between positions and dispositions more continuous or uncertain than in the literary and artistic field. Offering positions that are relatively uninstitutionalized, never legally guaranteed, therefore open to symbolic challenge, and non-hereditary (although there are specific forms of transmission), it is the arena *par excellence* of struggles over job definition. In fact, however great the effect of position – and we have seen many examples of it – it never operates mechanically, and the relationship between positions and *prises de position* is mediated by the dispositions of the agents.

[...]

The "post" of poet as it presents itself to the young aspirant in the 1880s is the crystallized product of the whole previous history. It is a position in the hierarchy of literary crafts, which, by a sort of effect of *caste*, gives its occupants, subjectively at least, the assurance of an essential superiority over all other writers; the lowest of the poets (Symbolist, at this time) sees himself as superior to the highest of the (Naturalist) novelists. It is a set of "exemplary figures" – Hugo, Gautier, etc. – who have composed the character and assigned roles, such as, for intellectuals (after Zola), that of the intellectual as the champion of great causes. It is a cluster of representations – that of the "pure" artist, for example, indifferent to success and to the verdicts of the market – and mechanisms which, through their sanctions, support them and give them real efficacy, etc. In short, one would need to work out the full social history of the *long, collective* labour which leads to the progressive invention of the crafts of writing, and in particular to *awareness* of the *fundamental law* of the field, i.e. the theory of art for art's sake, which is to the field of cultural production what the axiom "business is business" (and "in business there's no room for feelings") is to the economic field.[8] Nor, of course, must one forget the role of the mechanism which, here as elsewhere, leads people to make a virtue of necessity, in the constitution of the field of cultural production as a space radically independent of the economy and of politics and, as such, amenable to a sort of pure theory. The work of real emancipation, of which the "post" of artist or poet is the culmination, can be performed and pursued only if the post encounters the appropriate dispositions, such as disinterestedness and daring, and the (external) conditions of these virtues, such as a private income. In this sense, the collective invention which results in the post of writer or artist endlessly has to be repeated, even if the objectification of past discoveries and the recognition ever more widely accorded to an activity of cultural production that is an end in itself, and the will to emancipation that it implies, tend constantly to reduce the cost of this permanent reinvention. The more the autonomizing process advances, the more possible it becomes to occupy the position of producer without having the properties – or not all of them, or not to the same degree – that had to be possessed to produce the position; the more, in other words, the newcomers who head for the most "autonomous" positions can dispense with the more or less heroic sacrifices and breaks of the past.

The position of "pure" writer or artist, like that of intellectual, is an institution of freedom, constructed against the "bourgeoisie" (in the artists' sense) and against institutions – in particular against the State bureaucracies, Academies, Salons, etc. – by a series of breaks, partly cumulative, but sometimes followed by regressions, which have often been made possible by diverting the resources of the market – and therefore the "bourgeoisie" – and even the State bureaucracies.[9] Owing to its objectively contradictory intention, it only exists at the lowest degree of institutionalization, in the form of words ("avant-garde", for example) or models (the avant-garde writer and his exemplary deeds) which constitute a tradition of freedom and criticism, and also, but above all, in the form of a field of competition, equipped with its own institutions (the paradigm of which might be the "*Salon des refusés*" or the little avant-garde review) and articulated by mechanisms of competition capable of providing incentives and gratification for emancipatory endeavours. For example, the acts of prophetic denunciation of which *J'accuse* is the paradigm have become, since Zola, and perhaps especially since Sartre, so intrinsic to the personage of the intellectual that anyone who aspires to a position (especially a dominant one) in the intellectual field has to perform such exemplary acts.[10] This explains why it is that the producers most freed from external constraints – Mallarmé, Proust, Joyce or Virginia Woolf – are also those who have taken most advantage of a historical heritage accumulated through collective labour against external constraints.

Having established, in spite of the illusion of the constancy of the things designated, which is encouraged by the constancy of the words, artist, writer, bohemian, academy, etc., what each of the positions is at each moment, one still has to understand how those who occupy them have been formed and, more precisely, the shaping of the dispositions which help to lead them to these positions and to define their way of operating within them and staying in them. The field, as a field of possible forces, presents itself to each agent as *a space of possibles* which is defined in the relationship between the structure of average chances of access to the different positions (measured by the "difficulty" of attaining them and, more precisely, by the relationship between the number of positions and the number of competitors) and the dispositions of each agent, the subjective basis of the perception and appreciation of the objective chances. In other words, the objective probabilities (of economic or symbolic profit, for example) inscribed in the field at a given moment only become operative and active through "vocations", "aspirations" and "expectations", i.e. insofar as they are perceived and appreciated through the schemes of perception and appreciation which constitute a habitus. These schemes, which reproduce in their own logic the fundamental divisions of the field of positions – "pure art"/"commercial art", "bohemian"/"bourgeois", "left bank"/"right bank", etc. – are one of the mediations through which dispositions are adjusted to positions. Writers and artists, particularly newcomers, do not react to an "objective reality" functioning as a sort of stimulus valid for every possible subject, but to a "problem-raising situation", as Popper puts it; they help to create its intellectual and affective "physiognomy" (horror, seduction, etc.) and therefore even the symbolic force it exerts on them. A position as it appears to the (more or less adequate) "sense of investment" which each agent applies to it presents itself either as a sort of necessary locus which beckons those who are made for it ("vocation") or, by contrast, as an impossible destination, an unacceptable destiny or one that is acceptable only as temporary refuge or a secondary, accessory position. This sense of social direction which orients agents, according to their modesty or daring, their disinterestedness or thirst for profit, towards the risky, long-term investments of journalism, serials or the theatre, is the basis of the astonishingly close correspondence that is found between positions and dispositions, between the social characteristics of "posts" and the social characteristics of the agents who fill them. The correspondence is such that in all cases of coincidence and concordance in which the position is in a sense materialized in the dispositions of its occupants, it would be equally wrong to impute everything solely to position or solely to dispositions.

> The mechanistic model that is, more or less consciously, put into operation when social origin, or any other variable, is made the principle of a linear series of determinations – e.g. father's occupation, more or less crudely defined, determining position, e.g. occupational position, which in turn determines opinions – totally ignores the effects of the field, in particular those which result from the way in which the influx of newcomers is quantitatively and qualitatively regulated.[11] Thus the absence of statistical relation between the agents' social origin and their *prises de position* may result from an unobserved transformation of the field and of the

relationship between social origin and *prise de position*, such that, for two successive generations, the same dispositions will lead to different *prises de position*, or even opposing ones (which will tend to cancel each other out).

There is nothing mechanical about the relationship between the field and the habitus. The space of available positions does indeed help to determine the properties expected and even demanded of possible candidates, and therefore the categories of agents they can attract and above all *retain*; but the perception of the space of possible positions and trajectories and the appreciation of the value each of them derives from its location in the space depend on these dispositions. It follows as a point of method that one cannot give a full account of the relationship obtaining at a given moment between the space of positions and the space of dispositions, and, therefore, of the set of *social trajectories* (or constructed biographies), unless one establishes the configuration, at that moment, and at the various critical turning-points in each career, of the space of available possibilities – in particular, the economic and symbolic hierarchy of the genres, schools, styles, manners, subjects, etc. – the social value attached to each of them, and also the meaning and value they received for the difference agents or classes of agents in terms of the socially constituted categories of perception and appreciation they applied to them.
[…]

The habitus and the possibles

The propensity to move towards the economically most risky positions, and above all the capacity to persist in them (a condition for all avant-garde undertakings which precede the demands of the market), even when they secure no short-term economic profit, seem to depend to a large extent on possession of substantial economic and social capital. This is firstly because economic capital provides the conditions for freedom from economic necessity, a private income (*la rente*) being one of the best substitutes for sales (*la vente*), as Théophile Gautier said to Feydeau: "Flaubert was smarter than us. […] He had the wit to come into the world with money, something which is indispensable for anyone who wants to get anywhere in art" (quoted by Cassagne, 1979: 218).

> Those who do manage to stay in the risky positions long enough to receive the symbolic profit they can bring are indeed mainly drawn from the most privileged categories, who have also had the advantage of not having to devote time and energy to secondary, "bread-and-butter" activities. Thus, as Ponton shows (1977: 69–70), some of the Parnassians, all from the *petite bourgeoisie*, either had to abandon poetry at some stage and turn to better-paid literary activities, such as the "novel of manners", or, from the outset, devoted part of their time to complementary activities such as plays or novels (e.g. François Coppée, Catulle Mendès, Jean Aicard), whereas the wealthier Parnassians could concentrate almost exclusively on their art (and when they did change to another genre, it was only after a long poetic career). We also find that the least well-off writers resign themselves more readily to "industrial literature", in which writing becomes a job like any other.

It is also because economic capital provides the guarantees (*assurances*) which can be the basis of self-assurance, audacity and indifference to profit – dispositions which, together with the flair associated with possession of a large social capital and the corresponding familiarity with the field, i.e. the art of sensing the new hierarchies and the new structures of the chances of profit, point towards the outposts, the most exposed positions of the avant-garde, and towards the riskiest investments, which are also, however, very often the most profitable symbolically, and in the long run, at least for the earliest investors.

> The sense of investment seems to be one of the dispositions most closely linked to social and geographical origin, and, consequently, through the associated social capital, one of the mediations through which the effects of the opposition between Parisian and provincial origin make themselves felt in the logic of the field.[12] Thus we find that as a rule those richest in economic, cultural and social capital are the first to move into the new positions (and this seems to be true in all fields, economic, scientific, etc.). This is the case with the writers who, around Paul Bourget, abandon Symbolist poetry for a new form of novel which breaks with Naturalism and is better adjusted to the expectations of the cultivated audience. By contrast, a faulty sense of investment, linked to social distance (among writers from the working class or the petite bourgeoisie) or geographical distance (among provincials and foreigners) inclines beginners to aim for the dominant positions at a time when, precisely because of their attractiveness (due, for example, to the economic profits they secure, in the case of the Naturalist novel, or the symbolic profits they promise, in the case of Symbolist poetry) and the intensified competition for them, the profits are tending to decline. It may also make them persist in declining or threatened positions when the best-informed agents are abandoning them. ...

Finally, we must ask explicitly a question which is bound to be asked: what is the degree of conscious strategy, cynical calculation, in the objective strategies which observation brings to light and which ensure the correspondence between positions and dispositions? One only has to read literary testimonies, correspondence, diaries, and especially perhaps, explicit *prises de position* on the literary world as such (like those collected by Huret) to see that there is no simple answer to these questions and that lucidity is always partial and is, once again, a matter of position and trajectory within the field, so that it varies from one agent and one moment to another. As for awareness of the logic of the game as such, and of the *illusio* on which it is based, I had been inclined to think that it was excluded by membership of the field, which presupposes (and induces) belief in everything which depends on the existence of the field, i.e. literature, the writer, etc., because such lucidity would make the literary or artistic undertaking itself a cynical mystification, a conscious trickery. So I thought, until I came across a text by Mallarmé which provides both the programme and the balance-sheet of a rigorous science of the literary field and the recognized fictions that are engendered within it:

> We know, captives of an absolute formula that, indeed, there is only that which is. Forthwith to dismiss the cheat, however, on a pretext, would indict our inconsequence, denying the pleasure we want to take: for that *beyond* is its agent, and the engine I

might say were I not loath to perform, in public, the impious dismantling of the fiction and consequently of the literary mechanism, to display the principal part or nothing. But I venerate how, by a trick, we project to a height forfended – and with thunder! – the conscious lack in us of what shines up there.
What is it for?
A game. (Mallarmé, 1945: 647)

This quasi-Feuerbachian theory reduces beauty, which is sometimes thought of as a Platonic Idea, endowed with an objective, transcendent existence, to no more than the projection into a metaphysical beyond of what is lacking in the here-and-now of literary life. But is that how it is to be taken? Hermeticism, in this case, perfectly fulfils its function: to utter "in public" the true nature of the field, and of its mechanisms, is sacrilege *par excellence*, the unforgivable sin which all the censorships constituting the field seek to repress. These are things that can only be said in such a way that they are not said. If Mallarmé can, without excluding himself from the field, utter the truth about a field which excludes the *publishing* of its own truth, this is because he says it in a language which is designed to be *recognized* within the field because everything, in its very *form*, that of euphemism and *Verneinung*, affirms that he *recognizes* its censorships. Marcel Duchamp was to do exactly the same thing when he made artistic acts out of his bluffs, demystificatory mystifications which denounce fiction as mere fiction, and with it the collective belief which is the basis of this "legitimate" imposture (as Austin would have put it). But Mallarmé's hermeticism, which bespeaks his concern not to destroy the *illusio*, has another basis too: if the Platonic illusion is the "agent" of a pleasure which we take only because "we *want* to take it", if the pleasure of the love of art has its source in unawareness of producing the source of what produces it, then it is understandable that one might, by another willing suspension of disbelief, choose to "venerate" the authorless trickery which places the fragile fetish beyond the reach of critical lucidity.

NOTES

1 Or any other kind of field; art and literature being one area among others for application of the method of object-construction designated by the concept of the field.
2 In this (and only this) respect, the theory of the field could be regarded as a generalized Marxism, freed from the realist mechanism implied in the theory of "instances".
3 The status of "social art" is, in this respect, thoroughly ambiguous. Although it relates artistic or literary production to external functions (which is what the advocates of "art for art's sake" object to about it), it shares with "art for art's sake" a radical rejection of the dominant principle of hierarchy and of the "bourgeois" art which recognizes it.
4 The specific, and therefore autonomous, power which writers and artists possess *qua* writers and artists must be distinguished from the alienated, heteronomous power they wield *qua* experts or cadres – a share in domination, but with the status of dominated mandatories, granted to them by the dominant.
5 Thus, writers and artists who are "second-rank" in terms of the specific criteria may invoke populism and social art to impose their reign on the "leading intellectuals" who, as has happened in China and elsewhere, will protest against the disparity between the revolutionary ideal and the reality, i.e., the reign of functionaries devoted to the Party (see Godman, 1967).

6   Throughout this passage, "writer" can be replaced by "artist", "philosopher", "intellectual", etc. The intensity of the struggle, and the degree to which it takes visible, and therefore conscious, forms, no doubt vary according to the genre and according to the rarity of the specific competence each genre requires in different periods, i.e., according to the probability of "unfair competition" or "illegal exercise of the profession". (This no doubt explains why the intellectual field, with the permanent threat of casual essayism, is one of the key areas in which to grasp the logic of the struggles which pervade all fields.)

7   Only just over a third of the writers in the sample studied by Rémy Ponton had had any higher education, whether or not it led to a degree (Ponton, 1977: 43). (For the comparison between the literary field and other fields, see Charle, 1981.)

8   The painters still had to win their autonomy with respect to the writers, without whom they would perhaps not have succeeded in freeing themselves from the constraints of the bureaucracies and academicism.

9   To those who seek to trace a direct relationship between any producers and the group from which they draw their economic support, it has to be pointed out that the logic of a relatively autonomous field means that one can use the resources provided by a group or institution to produce products deliberately or unconsciously directed against the interests or values of that group or institutions.

10 It goes without saying that freedom with respect to institutions can never be truly institutionalized. This contradiction, which every attempt to institutionalize heresy comes up against (it is the antinomy of the Reformed Church), is seen clearly in the ambivalent image of institutional acts of consecration, and not only those performed by the most heteronomous institutions, such as academies (one thinks of Sartre's refusal of the Nobel Prize).

11 Although I realize that theoretical warnings count for little against the social drives which induce simplistic, apologetic or terroristic use of more-or-less scientific-seeming reference to "father's occupation", it seems useful to condemn the inclination – in which the worst adversaries and acolytes too easily find common ground – to reduce the model that is proposed, to the mechanical and mechanistic mode of thinking in which inherited capital (internalized in habitus, or objectified) determines the position occupied, which in turn directly determines *prises de position*.

12 An example of this is the case of Anatole France, whose father's unusual position (a Paris bookseller) enabled him to acquire a social capital and a familiarity with the world of letters which compensated for his low economic and cultural capital.

REFERENCES

Bourdieu, P. (1979). *La distinction*. Paris: Ed. de Minuit.
Cassagne, A. (1979). *La théorie de l'art pour l'art en France chez les derniers romantiques et les premiers réalistes*. Geneva: Slatkine Reprints. (Originally published Paris, 1906.)
Charle, C. (1981). *Situation du champ littéraire*. Littérature 44: 8–20.
Godman, M. (1967). *Literary Dissent in Communist China*. Cambridge, MA: Harvard University Press.
Mallarmé, Stéphane (1945). "La musique et les lettres". In: *Oeuvres complètes*. Paris: Gallimard (Pléiade).
Ponton, Rémy (1977). *Le champ littéraire de 1865 à 1905*. Paris: EHESS.
Weber, Max (1952). *Ancient Judaism*. Glencoe, IL: Free Press.

Chapter 25

Rethinking the State: Genesis and Structure of the Bureaucratic Field [1994]

Pierre Bourdieu

To endeavor to think the state is to take the risk of taking over (or being taken over by) a thought of the state, i.e. of applying to the state categories of thought produced and guaranteed by the state and hence to misrecognize its most profound truth.[1] This proposition, which may seem both abstract and preemptory, will be more readily accepted if, at the close of the argument, one agrees to return to this point of departure, but armed this time with the knowledge that one of the major powers of the state is to produce and impose (especially through the school system) categories of thought that we spontaneously apply to all things of the social world – including the state itself.

However, to give a first and more intuitive grasp of this analysis and to expose the danger of always being thought by a state that we believe we are thinking, I would like to cite a passage from *Alte Meister Komödie* by Thomas Bernhard:

> School is the state school where young people are turned into state persons and thus into nothing other than henchmen of the state. Walking to school, I was walking into the state and, since the state destroys people, into the institution for the destruction of people … The state forced me, like everyone else, into myself, and made me compliant

Translation by: Loïc J.D. Wacquant and Samar Farage

Pierre Bourdieu, "Rethinking the State: Genesis and Structure of the Bureaucratic Field," pp. 1–5, 12–18 from Pierre Bourdieu, "Rethinking the State: Genesis and Structure of the Bureaucratic Field," translated by Loïc J. D. Wacquant and Samar Farage. *Sociological Theory*, vol. 12, no. 1 (Mar., 1994). Reprinted with permission of the American Sociological Association.

Contemporary Sociological Theory, Third Edition. Edited by Craig Calhoun, Joseph Gerteis, James Moody, Steven Pfaff, and Indermohan Virk. Editorial material and organization © 2012 John Wiley & Sons, Ltd. Published 2012 by John Wiley & Sons, Ltd.

towards it, the state, and turned me into a state person, regulated and registered and trained and finished and perverted and dejected, like everyone else. When we see people, we only see state people, the state servants, as we quite rightly say, who serve the state all their lives and thus serve unnature all their lives.[2]

The idiosyncratic rhetoric of T. Bernhard, one of excess and of hyperbole in anathema, is well suited to my intention, which is to subject the state and the thought of the state to a sort of *hyperbolic doubt*. For, when it comes to the state, one never doubts enough. And, though literary exaggeration always risks self-effacement by de-realizing itself in its very excess, one should take what Thomas Bernhard says seriously: to have any chance of thinking a state that still thinks itself through those who attempt to think it (as in the case of Hegel or Durkheim), one must strive to question all the presuppositions and preconstructions inscribed in the reality under analysis as well as in the very thoughts of the analyst.

To show both the difficulty and the necessity of a rupture with the thought of the state, present in the most intimate of our thoughts, one could analyze the battle recently declared – in the midst of the Gulf War – in France about a seemingly insignificant topic: orthography. Correct spelling, designated and guaranteed as normal by law, i.e., by the state, is a social artifact only imperfectly founded upon logical or even linguistic reason; it is the product of a work of normalization and codification, quite analogous to that which the state effects concurrently in other realms of social life.[3] Now, when, at a particular moment, the state or any of its representatives undertakes a reform of orthography (as was done, with similar effects, a century ago), i.e., to undo by decree what the state had ordered by decree, this immediately triggers the indignation protest of a good number of those whose status depends on "writing," in its most common sense but also in the sense given to it by writers. And remarkably, all those defenders of orthographic orthodoxy mobilize in the name of *natural* spelling and of the satisfaction, experienced as intrinsically aesthetic, given by the perfect agreement between mental structures and objective structures – between the mental forms socially instituted in minds through the teaching of correct spelling and the reality designated by words rightfully spelled. For those who possess spelling to the point where they are possessed by it, the perfectly arbitrary "ph" of the word "*nénuphar*" has become so evidently inextricable from the flower it designates that they can, in all good faith, invoke nature and the *natural* to denounce an intervention of the state aimed at reducing the arbitrariness of a spelling which itself is, in all evidence, the product of an earlier arbitrary intervention of the same.

One could offer countless similar instances in which the effects of choices made by the state have so completely impressed themselves in reality and in minds that possibilities initially discarded have become totally unthinkable (e.g., a system of domestic production of electricity analogous to that of home heating). Thus, if the mildest attempt to modify school programs, and especially time tables for the different disciplines, almost always and everywhere encounters great resistance, it is not only because powerful occupational interests (such as those of the teaching staff) are attached to the established academic order. It is also because matters of culture, and in particular the social divisions and hierarchies associated with them, are constituted as such by the actions of the state which, by instituting them both in things and in minds, confers upon the cultural arbitrary all the appearances of the natural.

A Radical Doubt

To have a chance to really think a state which still thinks itself through those who attempt to think it, then, it is imperative to submit to radical questioning all the presuppositions inscribed in the reality to be thought and in the very thought of the analyst.

It is in the realm of symbolic production that the grip of the state is felt most powerfully. State bureaucracies and their representatives are great producers of "social problems" that social science does little more than ratify whenever it takes them over as "sociological" problems. (It would suffice to demonstrate this, to plot the amount of research, varying across countries and periods, devoted to problems of the state, such as poverty, immigration, educational failure, more or less rephrased in scientific language.)

Yet the best proof of the fact that the thought of the bureaucratic thinker (*penseur fonctionnaire*) is pervaded by the official representation of the official, is no doubt the power of seduction wielded by those representations of the state (as in Hegel) that portray bureaucracy as a "universal group" endowed with the intuition of, and a will to, universal interest; or as an "organ of reflection" and a rational instrument in charge of realizing the general interest (as with Durkheim, in spite of his great prudence on the matter).[4]

The specific difficulty that shrouds this question lies in the fact that, behind the appearance of thinking it, most of the writings devoted to the state partake, more or less efficaciously and directly, of the *construction* of the state, i.e., of its very existence. This is particularly true of all juridical writings which, especially during the phase of construction and consolidation, take their full meaning not only as theoretical contributions to the knowledge of the state but also as political strategies aimed at imposing a particular vision of the state, a vision in agreement with the interests and values associated with the particular position of those who produce them in the emerging bureaucratic universe (this is often forgotten by the best historical works, such as those of the Cambridge school).

From its inception, social science itself has been part and parcel of this work of construction of the representation of the state which makes up part of the reality of the state itself. All the issues raised about bureaucracy, such as those of neutrality and disinterestedness, are posed also about sociology itself – only at a higher degree of difficulty since there arises in addition the question of the latter's autonomy from the state. It is therefore the task of the history of the social sciences to uncover all the unconscious ties to the social world that the social sciences owe to the history which has produced them (and which are recorded in their problematics, theories, methods, concepts, etc.) Thus one discovers, in particular, that social science in the modern sense of the term (in opposition to the political philosophy of the counselors of the Prince) is intimately linked to social struggles and socialism, but less as a direct expression of these movements and of their theoretical ramifications than as an answer to the problems that these struggles formulated and brought forth. Social science finds its first advocates among the philanthropists and the reformers, that is, in the enlightened avant-garde of the dominant who expect that "social economics" (as an auxiliary science to political science) will provide them with a solution to "social problems" and particularly to those posed by individuals and groups "with problems."

A comparative survey of the development of the social sciences suggests that a model designed to explain the historical and cross-national variations of these disciplines should take into account two fundamental factors. The first is the form assumed by the social demand for knowledge of the social world, which itself depends, among other things, on the philosophy dominant within state bureaucracies (e.g., liberalism of Keynesianism). Thus a powerful state demand may ensure conditions propitious to the development of a social science relatively independent from economic forces (and of the direct claims of the dominant) – but strongly dependent upon the state. The second factor is the degree of autonomy both of the educational system and of the scientific field from the dominant political and economic forces, an autonomy that no doubt requires both a strong outgrowth of social movements and of the social critique of established powers as well as a high degree of independence of social scientists from these movements.

History attests that the social sciences can increase their independence from the pressures of social demand – which is a major precondition of their progress towards scientificity – only by increasing their reliance upon the state. And thus they run the risk of losing their autonomy *from* the state, unless they are prepared to use *against* the state the (relative) freedom that it grants them.

The Genesis of the State: A Process of Concentration

To sum up the results of the analysis by way of anticipation, I would say, using a variation around Max Weber's famous formula, that the state is an X (to be determined) which successfully claims the monopoly of the legitimate use of physical and *symbolic* violence over a definite territory and over the totality of the corresponding population. If the state is able to exert symbolic violence, it is because it incarnates itself simultaneously in objectivity, in the form of specific organizational structures and mechanisms, and in subjectivity in the form of mental structures and categories of perception and thought. By realizing itself in social structures and in the mental structures adapted to them, the instituted institution makes us forget that it issues out of a long series of acts of *institution* (in the active sense) and hence has all the appearances of the *natural*.

This is why there is no more potent tool for rupture than the reconstruction of genesis: by bringing back into view the conflicts and confrontations of the early beginnings and therefore all the discarded possibles, it retrieves the possibility that things could have been (and still could be) otherwise. And, through such a practical utopia, it questions the "possible" which, among all others, was actualized. Breaking with the temptation of the analysis of essence, but without renouncing for that the intention of uncovering invariants, I would like to outline *a model of the emergence of the state* designed to offer a systematic account of the properly historical logic of the processes which have led to the institution of this "X" we call the state. Such a project is most difficult, impossible indeed, for it demands joining the rigor and coherence of theoretical construction with submission to the almost boundless data accumulated by historical research. To suggest the complexity of such a task, I will simply cite one historian, who, because he stays within the limits of his specialty, evokes it only partially himself:

> The most neglected zones of history have been border zones, as for instance the borders between specialties. Thus, the study of government requires knowledge of the theory of government (i.e., of the history of political thought), knowledge of the practice of government (i.e., of the history of institutions) and finally knowledge of governmental personnel (i.e., of social history). Now, few historians are capable of moving across these specialties with equal ease ... There are other border zones of history that would also require study, such as warfare technology at the beginning of the modern period. Without a better knowledge of such problems, it is difficult to measure the importance of the logistical effort undertaken by such government in a given campaign. However, these technical problems should not be investigated solely from the standpoint of the military historian as traditionally defined. The military historian must also be a historian of government. In the history of public finances and taxation, too, many unknowns remain. Here again the specialist must be more than a narrow historian of finances, in the old meaning of the word; he must be a historian of government and an economist. Unfortunately, such a task has not been helped by the fragmentation of history into sub-fields, each with its monopoly of specialists, and by the feeling that certain aspects of history are fashionable while others are not.[5]

The state is the *culmination of a process of concentration of different species of capital*: capital of physical force or instruments of coercion (army, police), economic capital, cultural or (better) informational capital, and symbolic capital. It is this concentration as such which constitutes the state as the holder of a sort of meta-capital granting power over other species of capital and over their holders. Concentration of the different species of capital (which proceeds hand in hand with the construction of the corresponding fields) leads indeed to the *emergence* of a specific, properly statist capital (*capital étatique*) which enables the state to exercise power over the different fields and over the different particular species of capital, and especially over the rates of conversion between them (and thereby over the relations of force between their respective holders). It follows that the construction of the state proceeds apace with the construction of a *field of power*, defined as the space of play within which the holders of capital (of different species) struggle *in particular* for power over the state, i.e., over the statist capital granting power over the different species of capital and over their reproduction (particularly through the school system).

[...] The different dimensions of this process of concentration (armed forces, taxation, law, etc.) are *interdependent*.
[...]

Minds of State

In order truly to understand the power of the state in its full specificity, i.e., the particular symbolic efficacy it wields, one must, as I suggested long ago in another article,[6] integrate into one and the same explanatory model intellectual traditions customarily perceived as incompatible. It is necessary, first, to overcome the opposition between a physicalist vision of the social world that conceives of social relations as relations of physical force and a "cybernetic" or semiological vision which portrays them as relations of symbolic force, as relations of meaning or relations of communication. The most brutal relations of force are always simultaneously symbolic relations. And acts of submission and obedience are cognitive acts which as such involve cognitive structures, forms and categories of perception, principles of vision and division. Social agents construct the social world through cognitive structures that may be applied to all things of the world and in particular to social structures (Cassirer called these principles of vision of division "symbolic forms" and Durkheim "forms of classification": these are so many ways of saying the same thing in more or less separate theoretical traditions).

These *structuring structures* are historically constituted forms and therefore arbitrary in the Saussurian sense, conventional, "*ex instituto*" as Leibniz said, which means that we can trace their social genesis. Generalizing the Durkheimian hypothesis according to which the "forms of classification" that the "primitives" apply to the world are the product of the embodiment of their group structures, we may seek the basis of these cognitive structures in the actions of the state. Indeed, we may posit that, in differentiated societies, the state has the ability to impose and inculcate in a universal manner, within a given territorial expanse, a *nomos* (from *nemo*: to share, divide, constitute separate parts), a shared principle of vision and division, identical or similar cognitive and evaluative structures. And that the state is therefore the foundation of a "logical conformism" and of a "moral conformism" (these are Durkheim's expressions),[7] of a tacit, pre-reflexive agreement over the meaning of the world which itself lies at the basis of the experience the world as "commonsense world." (Neither the phenomenologists, who brought this experience to light, nor the ethnomethodologists who assign themselves the task of describing it, have the means of accounting for this experience because they fail to raise the question of the social construction of the principles of construction of the social reality that they strive to explicate and to question the contribution of the state to the constitution of the principles of constitution that agents apply to the social order.)

In less differentiated societies, the common principles of vision and division – the paradigm of which is the opposition masculine/feminine – are instituted in minds (or in bodies) through the whole spatial and temporal organization of social life, and especially through *rites of institution* that establish definite differences between those who submitted to the rite and those who did not.[8] In our societies, the state makes a decisive contribution to the production and reproduction of the instruments of construction of social reality. As organizational structure and regulator of practices, the state exerts an ongoing action formative of durable dispositions through the whole range of constraints and through the corporeal and mental discipline it uniformly imposes upon all agents. Furthermore, it imposes and inculcates all the fundamental principles of classification, based to sex, age, "skill," etc. And it lies at the basis of the symbolic efficacy of all rites of institution, such as those underlying the family for example, or those that operate through the routine functioning of the school system as the site of *consecration* where lasting and often irrevocable differences are instituted between the chosen and the excluded, in the manner of the medieval ritual of the dubbing of knights.

The construction of the state is accompanied by the construction of a sort of common historical transcendental, immanent to all its "subjects." Through the framing it imposes upon practices, the state establishes and inculcates common forms and categories of perception and appreciation, social frameworks of perceptions, of understanding or of memory, in short *state forms of classification*. It thereby creates the conditions for a kind of immediate orchestration of habituses which is itself the foundation of a consensus over this set of shared evidences constitutive of (national) common sense. Thus, for example, the great rhythms of the societal calendar (think of the schedule of school or patriotic vacations that determine the great "seasonal migrations" of many contemporary societies) provide both shared objective referents and compatible subjective principles of division which underlie internal experiences of time sufficiently concordant to make social life possible.[9]

But in order fully to understand the immediate submission that the state order elicits, it is necessary to break with the intellectualism of the neo-Kantian tradition to acknowledge that cognitive structures are not forms of consciousness but *dispositions of the body*. That the obedience we grant to the injunctions of the state cannot be understood either as mechanical submission to an external force or as conscious consent to an order (in the double sense of the term). The social world is riddled with *calls to order* that function as such only for those who are predisposed to heeding them as they *awaken* deeply buried corporeal dispositions, outside the channels of consciousness and calculation. It is this doxic submission of the dominated to the structures of a social order of which their mental structures are the product that Marxism cannot understand insofar as it remains trapped in the intellectualist tradition of the philosophies of consciousness. In the notion of false consciousness that it invokes to account for effects of symbolic domination, that superfluous term is "consciousness." And to speak of "ideologies" is to locate in the realm of *representations* – liable to be transformed through this intellectual conversion called "awakening of consciousness" (*prise de conscience*) – what in fact belongs to the order of *belief*, i.e., to the level of the most profound corporeal dispositions. Submission to the established order is the product of the agreement between, on the one hand, the cognitive structures inscribed in bodies by both collective history (phylogenesis) and individual history (ontogenesis) and, on the other, the objective structures of the world to which these cognitive structures are applied. State injunctions owe their obviousness, and thus their potency, to the fact that the state has imposed the very cognitive structures through which it is perceived (one should rethink along those lines the conditions that make possible the supreme sacrifice: *pro patria mori*).

But we need to go beyond the Neo-Kantian tradition, even in its Durkheimian form, on yet another count. Because it focuses on the *opus operatum*, symbolic structuralism à la Lévi-Strauss (or the Foucault of *The Order of Things*) is bound to neglect the active dimension of symbolic production (as, for example, with mythologies), the question of the *modus operandi*, of "generative grammar" (in Chomsky's sense). It does have the advantage of seeking to uncover the internal coherence of symbolic systems *qua* systems, that is, one of the major basis of their efficacy – as can be clearly seen in the case of the law in which coherence is deliberately sought, but also in myth and religion. Symbolic order rests on the imposition upon all agents of structuring structures that owe part of their consistency and resilience to the fact that they are coherent and systematic (at least in appearance) and that they are objectively in agreement with the objective structures of the social world. It is this immediate and tacit agreement, in every respect opposed to an explicit contract, that founds the relation of *doxic submission* which attaches us to the established order with all the ties of the unconscious. The recognition of legitimacy is not, as Weber believed, a free act of clear conscience. It is rooted in the immediate, pre-reflexive, agreement between objective structures and embodied structures, now turned unconscious (such as those that organize temporal rhythms: viz. the quite arbitrary divisions of school schedules into periods).

It is this pre-reflexive agreement that explains the ease, rather stunning when we think of it, with which the dominant impose their domination:

> Nothing is as astonishing for those who consider human affairs with a philosophic eye than to see the ease with which the *many* will be governed by the *few* and to observe the implicit submission with which men revoke their own sentiments and passions in favor of their leaders. When we inquire about the means through which such an astonishing thing is accomplished, we find that force being always on the side of the governed, only opinion can sustain the governors. It is thus solely on opinion that government is founded, and such maxim applies to the most despotic and military government as well as to the freest and most popular.[10]

Hume's astonishment brings forth the fundamental question of all political philosophy, which one occults, paradoxically, by posing a problem that is not really posed as such in ordinary existence: the problem of legitimacy. Indeed, essentially, what is problematic is the fact that the established order is *not* problematic; and that the question of the legitimacy of the state, and of the order it institutes, does not arise except in crisis situations. The state does not necessarily have to give orders or to exercise physical coercion in order to produce an ordered social world, as long as it is capable of producing embodied cognitive structures that accord with objective structures and thus of ensuring the belief of which Hume spoke – namely, doxic submission to the established order.

This being said, it should not be forgotten that such primordial political belief, this doxa, is an orthodoxy, a right, correct, dominant vision which has more often than not been imposed through struggles against competing visions. This means that the "natural attitude" mentioned by the phenomenologists, i.e., the primary experience of the world of common sense, is a politically produced relation, as are the categories of perception that sustain it. What appears to us today as self-evident, as beneath consciousness and choice, has quite often been the stake of struggles and instituted only as the result of dogged confrontations between dominant and dominated groups. The major effect of historical evolution is to abolish history by relegating to the past, i.e., to the unconscious, the lateral possibles that it eliminated. The analysis of the genesis of the state as the foundation of the principles of vision and division operative within its territorial expanse enables us to understand at once the doxic adherence to the order established by the state as well as the properly political foundations of such apparently natural adherence. Doxa is a particular point of view, the point of view of the dominant, when it presents and imposes itself as a universal point of view – the point of view of those who dominate by dominating the state and who have constituted their point of view as universal by constituting the state.

Thus, to account fully for the properly symbolic dimension of the power of the state, we may build on Max Weber's decisive contribution (in his writings on religion) to the theory of symbolic systems by reintroducing specialized agents and their specific interests. Indeed, if he shares with Marx an interest in the function – rather than the structure – of symbolic systems, Weber nonetheless has the merit of calling attention to the producers of these particular products (religious agents, in the case that concerns him) and to their *interactions* (conflict, competition, etc.).[11] In opposition to the Marxists, who have overlooked the existence of specialized agents of production (notwithstanding a famous text of Engels which states that to understand law one needs to focus on the corporation of the jurists), Weber reminds us that, to understand religion, it does not suffice to study symbolic forms of the religious type, as Cassirer or Durkheim did, nor even the immanent structure of the religious message or of the mythological corpus, as with the structuralists. Weber focuses specifically on the producers of the religious message, on the specific interests that move them and on the strategies they use in their struggle (e.g., excommunication). In order to grasp these symbolic systems simultaneously in their function, structure and genesis, it suffices, thence, to apply the structuralist mode of thinking (completely alien to Weber) not solely to the symbolic systems or, better, to the space of *position takings* or stances adopted in a determinate domain of practice (e.g., religious messages), but to the system of agents who produce them as well or, to be more precise, to the space of *positions* they occupy (what I call the religious field) in the competition that opposes them.[12]

The same holds for the state. To understand the symbolic dimension of the effect of the state, and in particular what we may call the *effect of universality*, it is necessary to understand the specific functioning of the bureaucratic microcosm and thus to analyze the genesis and structure of this universe of agents of the state who have constituted themselves into a state nobility by instituting the state,[13] and in particular, by producing the performative discourse on the state which, under the guise of saying what the state is, caused the state to come into being by stating what it should be – i.e., what should be the position of the producers of this discourse in the division of labor of domination. One must focus in particular on the structure of the juridical field and uncover both the generic interests of the holders of that particular form of cultural capital, predisposed to function as symbolic capital, that is juridical competence, as well as the specific interests imposed on each of them by virtue of their position in a still weakly autonomous juridical field (that is, essentially in relation to royal power). And to account for those effects of universality and rationality I just evoked, it is necessary to understand why these agents had an interest in giving a universal form to the expression of their vested interests, to elaborate a theory of public service and of public order, and thus to work to autonomize the *reason of state* from dynastic reason, from the "house of the king," and to invent thereby the *Res publica* and later the republic as an instance transcendent to the agents (the King included) who are its temporary incarnations. One must understand how, by virtue and because of their specific capital and particular interests, they were led to produce a discourse of state which, by providing justifications for their own positions, constituted the state – this *fictio juris* which slowly stopped being a mere fiction of jurists to become an autonomous order capable of imposing ever more widely the submission to its functions and to its functioning and the recognition of its principles.

The Monopolization of Monopoly and the State Nobility

The construction of the state monopoly over physical and symbolic violence is inseparable from the construction of the field of struggles for the monopoly over the advantages attached to this monopoly. The relative unification and universalization associated with the emergence of the state has for counterpart the monopolization by the few of the universal resources that it produces and procures (Weber, and Elias after him, ignored the process of constitution of a statist capital and the process of monopolization of this capital by the state nobility which has contributed to its production or, better, which has produced itself as such by producing it). However, this *monopoly of the universal* can only be obtained at the cost of a submission (if only in appearance) to the universal and of a universal recognition of the universalist representation of domination presented as legitimate and disinterested. Those who – like Marx – invert the official image that the bureaucracy likes to give of itself, and describe bureaucrats as usurpators of the universal who act as private proprietors of public resources, ignore the very real effects of the obligatory reference to the values of neutrality and disinterested loyalty to the public good. Such values impose themselves with increasing force upon the functionaries of the state as the history of the long work of symbolic construction unfolds whereby the official representation of the state as the site of universality and of service of the general interest is invented and imposed.

The monopolization of the universal is the result of a work of universalization which is accomplished within the bureaucratic field itself. As would be revealed by the analysis of the functioning of this strange institution called *commission*, i.e., a set of individuals vested with a mission of general interest and invited to transcend their particular interests in order to produce universal propositions, officials constantly have to labor, if not to sacrifice their particular point of view on behalf of the "point of view of society," at least to constitute their point of view into a legitimate one, i.e., as universal, especially through use of the rhetoric of the official.

The universal is the object of universal recognition and the sacrifice of selfish (especially economic) interests is universally recognized as legitimate. (In the effect to rise from the singular and selfish point of view of the individual to the point of view of the group, collective judgement cannot but perceive, and approve, an expression of recognition of the value of the group and of the group itself as the fount of all value, and thus a passage from "is" to "ought".) This means that all social universes tend to offer, to varying degrees, material or symbolic profits of universalization (those very profits pursued by strategies seeking to "play by the rule"). It also implies that the universes which, like the bureaucratic field, demand with utmost insistence that one submits to the universal, are particularly favorable to obtaining such profits. It is significant that administrative law which, being aimed at establishing a universe of dedication to the general interest, has the obligation of neutrality as its fundamental law the obligation of neutrality, should institute as a practical principle of evaluation the suspicion of generosity: "the government does not make gifts"; any action by a public bureaucracy which individually benefits a private person is suspect if not illegal.

The profit of universalization is no doubt one of the historical engines of the progress of the universal. This is because it favors the creation of universes where universal values (reason, virtue, etc.) are at least verbally recognized and wherein operates a circular process of mutual reinforcement of the strategies of universalization seeking to obtain the profits (if only negative) associated with conformity to universal rules and to the structures of those universes officially devoted to the universal. The sociological vision cannot ignore the discrepancy between the official norm as stipulated in administrative law and the reality of bureaucratic practice, with all its violations of the obligation of disinterestedness, all the cases of "private use of public services" (from the diversion of public goods and functions to graft to corruption). Nor can it ignore the more perverse abuses of law and the administrative tolerances, exemptions, bartering of favors, that result from the faulty implementation or from the transgression of the law. Yet sociology cannot for all that remain blind to the effects of this norm which demands that agents sacrifice their private interests for the obligations inscribed in their function ("the agent should devote himself fully to his function"), nor, in a more realistic manner, to the effects of the interest to disinterestedness and of all those forms of "pious hypocrisy" that the paradoxical logic of the bureaucratic field can promote.

NOTES

1. This text is the partial and revised transcription of a lecture delivered in Amsterdam on June 29, 1991.
2. Bernhard, Thomas, *The Old Masters*, trans. Ewald Osers, Quartet Books, London, 1989, p. 27.
3. Pierre Bourdieu, *Language and Symbolic Power*, Cambridge, Polity Press, 1991, ch. 2.
4. Emile Durkheim, *Leçons de sociologie*, Paris, Presses Universitaires de France, 1922, esp. pp. 84–90.
5. Richard Bonney, "Guerre, fiscalité et activité d'Etat en France (1500–1660): some preliminary remarks on possibilities of research," in Ph. Genet and M. Le Mené, eds., *Genèse del'Etat moderne. Prélèvement et redistribution*, Paris, Ed. du CNRS, 1987, pp. 193–201, citation p. 193.
6. P. Bourdieu, "On Symbolic Power," in *Language and Symbolic Power*, op. cit., pp. 163–170 (originally in *Annales*, 3 June 1977, pp. 405–411).
7. E. Durhkeim, *The Elementary Forms of the Religious Life*, New York, Free Press, 1965 (orig. 1912).
8. P. Bourdieu, "Rites of Institution," in *Language and Symbolic Power, op. cit.*, pp. 117–126 (orig. pub. 1982).
9. Another example would be the division of the academic and scientific worlds into disciplines, which is inscribed in the minds in the form of disciplinary habituses generating distorted relations between the representatives of different disciplines as well as limitations and mutilations in the representations and practices of each of them.
10. David Hume, "On the first Principles of Government," in *Essays and Treatises on Several Subjects*, 1758.
11. For a fuller discussion, see P. Bourdieu, "Legitimation and Structured Interests in Weber's Sociology of Religion," pp. 119–136 in *Max Weber, Rationality and Modernity*, edited by Sam Whimster and Scott Lash, London, Allen and Unwin, 1987.
12. For a fuller demonstration of this point, see P. Bourdieu, "Genesis and Structure of the Religious Field," *Comparative Social Research*, 13, 1991, pp. 1–43 (first pub. 1971).
13. Pierre Bourdieu, *La noblesse d'Etat*, Paris, Editions du Seuil, 1989, especially part V.

Part VII

Race, Gender, Difference

Introduction to Part VII

26 The Conceptual Practices of Power

27 Black Feminist Epistemology

28 Black Skin, White Masks

29 The Paradoxes of Integration

Part VII

Race, Gender, Difference

Introduction to Part VII

This section examines work that speaks in various ways to a central issue for contemporary theory: the challenge of difference. Although the question of difference is basic to all social experience, the work included here is focused on race and gender as key dimensions of difference. Race and gender have been important themes in sociology since its inception, and yet the theoretical implications of these classifications were by no means always taken seriously. In the past several decades – especially since the 1960s – sociological theorists have begun to revisit the issue of difference, and to deal with it in increasingly prominent and sophisticated ways.

Many factors were behind the re-emergence of questions about identity and difference in contemporary theory. Probably chief among them was the impact of several powerful social movements. Anti-colonial revolutions throughout Africa, civil-rights struggles in America, the continuing development of feminism worldwide, and gay liberation movements all provided a voice to previously marginalized groups. In doing so, they accomplished two things. First, they publicly tied social categories to meaningful identities. Second, the movements made claims for political and cultural recognition based on those identities. The same demands for recognition that motivated these movements also began to appear in sociological theory, and for many of the same reasons. As these movements emerged, and as the discipline of sociology itself became more diverse, sociological attempts to think seriously about difference also developed.

Theorizing Difference

Recent work has emphasized that gender and race – and other dimensions of difference, such as sexual orientation and nationality – are not simply variables that need to be included in sociological explanations; they are also fundamental categories

Contemporary Sociological Theory, Third Edition. Edited by Craig Calhoun, Joseph Gerteis, James Moody, Steven Pfaff, and Indermohan Virk. Editorial material and organization © 2012 John Wiley & Sons, Ltd. Published 2012 by John Wiley & Sons, Ltd.

of experience that need to be analyzed. Theorizing difference has meant at least three things.

First, it has meant simply correcting for the false generalizations implicit in much classic thought about social life. Such generalizations did not always go unchallenged, but they were pervasive. For example, in the eighteenth century, almost as soon as Patrick Henry wrote his "Essay on the Rights of Man," Mary Wolstonecraft answered with her "Vindication of the Rights of Women." Wolstonecraft supported Henry's vision of liberty, but not the exclusion of women from it. When Henry wrote of the rights of "Man" he implied that he was writing about people in general, but in fact wrote – and was read – as describing rights that pertained to men only. In this sense, theorizing difference has meant bringing gender, race, and other dimensions of difference back into our thinking about social life, and being clear about the limits of established theory and research.

Second, it has involved questioning whether the categories of gender and race, which we often take for granted, really have objective and stable meanings. This includes inquiry into how the concepts are produced historically, how they are applied in practice, and what ambiguities are ignored to make the distinctions appear natural. It extends into explorations of how gender and race categories are renewed in response to social change. For example, American racial formation has generally – but arbitrarily – categorized the children of Black/White marriages as Black.[1] Recently, however, many such "mixed race" people have demanded distinctive racial categorizations that recognize their "both/and" status. This challenges the typically "either/or" way that race has been constructed in the English-speaking world, a construction influenced by the legacy of slavery in the USA, European colonialism, and the rise of evolutionary thought in biology.[2] What was new in this was not simply making group distinctions nor even looking down on members of other groups, especially dominated groups. These are both old and nearly universal human habits. The novelty was the production of elaborate systems of alleged (though often pseudoscientific) biological classifications of races. Recent sociological theory recognizes that racial distinctions are not simply reflections of biology, since even the selection of which characteristics count in identifying racial groups is basically cultural.

A similar point may be made in relation to sex and gender. Obviously biology plays a role in gender distinctions, but here too most sociologists emphasize the role of culture and power relations. It is common to distinguish between "sex," the physical differences relevant to reproduction, and "gender," the social and cultural identifications that we attach to sex. Many sociologists have pointed out the fact that gender is a social construction that varies over time and across cultures. Though this is clarifying, we should also note that there is an intrusion of cultural values into the very linkage of "sex" to reproduction. Historically, this is what has made homosexuality seem a transgression not just of gender roles but also of sexual classification more generally. Such views are changing, in large part because of struggles over gay rights. Increasingly, one can be seen, for example, as both a lesbian and a woman without contradiction.

Third, theorizing difference has involved thinking about the role of ideas of gender and race in structuring society itself. This is perhaps especially important in the case of gender – or at least, it applies everywhere in the case of gender and in varying degree in different settings in the case of race. Dealing with this question in part means understanding the social implications of the associations that people apply to categories such as gender. For example, feminist theory has pointed out that the understanding of women as emotional and men as rational has profoundly influenced the distinction between public and private spheres of social life – a distinction which structures the way we conceive of the state, among other things. The issue goes deeper than associations, though, since gender categories are among the most basic used to conceptualize the nature of society itself and of basic social institutions like family. In other words, although building social organization by means of such assumed differences creates certain sorts of problems, it is also basic to some senses of solidarity – as the examples of class and nation show as much as those of race and gender. It is one of the ways social organization is accomplished, for good or ill. Theoretically, this is perhaps the deepest challenge of difference.

Identity and Difference

While critical theoretical attention to race has been increasingly prominent and sophisticated in recent decades, this should not be taken to indicate that the problem of difference has somehow been solved. The issue of difference is still problematic, and one of the major reasons is that people are so deeply invested in social boundaries. There are two sorts of questions that are still very active in the theoretical literature. The first has to do with the nature of identity, and whether categories such as "Black" or "woman" point to something that is essential, or whether such categories are constructed in social life. The second question has to do with whether knowledge is necessarily based on the experiences of actors in particular social positions, or whether objective knowledge is possible.

Gender and race are especially important examples of the more general phenomena of differentiating people on the basis of "categorical identities." They are often used in ways that suggest that the internal similarities of the members of any such category outweigh their differences from each other, and conversely that all members share the same sort of differences from other people. The issue here is not just sexism or racism. It also arises in the struggles for recognition that seek to oppose such domination. The struggles over such claims for recognition are often termed "identity politics." In many social movements, legitimating claims to identity was a crucial goal as well as a condition of struggle. Thus the slogan "black is beautiful" challenged the tendency of white-dominated culture to treat Black identity as less valuable. The women's movement sought to establish that women were legitimate presences and that women's concerns were legitimately important in public as well as private life. In each case, these claims to identity involved an adoption of the very categories of gender and race that are so theoretically problematic. But this left a crucial theoretical issue unresolved. Did identity exist first, even if it was sometimes hidden or distorted? This was often called the "essentialist" position. Or did the movements together with other dimensions of social action and cultural creativity make the identities, giving them their definition and meaning? This was called the "constructionist" position.

Most sociologists and other social scientists have accepted the constructionist perspective; they regard gender, race, and most other sorts of identities as largely socially and culturally created. At the same time, few argue that such identities are merely matters of choice. First, there may be some aspects of inheritance or biology involved, even if what these mean is shaped by cultural interpretation. Second, culture and social relations are powerful; one cannot throw off the identities one has developed by growing up in a specific social setting simply at will. Moreover, as the American feminist Judith Butler has argued, when people confront shared injustice they may find it strategically valuable to accept the resulting common identities as though they were essential – at least in the context of struggle against injustice.

A closely related issue concerns the ways in which identities and social locations shape the production of knowledge. Since the seventeenth century it has been common to try to achieve a perfectly neutral perspective for the production of scientific knowledge (or for that matter, judicial fairness). This suggested that humans could step outside of their own subjective positions and see the world objectively. Critics argued that this position simply missed the degree to which all social actors – including jurists and sociologists – are bounded, at least to some degree, by their own positions and experiences in society. Following Hegel, Marx, and others, they claimed that knowledge must be shaped by the standpoint of observation. A truly objective position (or, more pejoratively, a "view from nowhere") is not possible, they maintain. The question then arises whether some standpoints are better than others. The argument for privileging the standpoint of those in subordinate positions has a rather long history, as it turns out. Hegel, writing about the archetypal characters of "the master" and "the slave," claimed that those in subordinate positions may be able to develop a more complete knowledge, since they must take account of the conditions of their own knowledge as well as those of the dominant. Simmel, writing about the position of "the stranger," later made the same claim. Marx and his follower Georg Lukacs argued for taking the standpoint of the proletariat, partly of the Hegelian basis and partly because it represented the majority of members of modern societies and, they thought, the direction of social progress. Later, a number of feminist theorists argued that it was important to create knowledge from the standpoint of women. For some, this meant merely balancing the previous dominance of male standpoints. For others, it suggested a certain superiority, precisely because women's knowledge was clearly privileged with regard to much of social life. While it was relatively straightforward for women to gain access to the dominant forms of male knowledge, it was harder for men to gain access to the kind of knowledge that was based on women's distinctive experience. Somewhat similar arguments have been made concerning race in place of gender.

Relatively few sociologists believe that there is one social standpoint that is clearly superior for all forms of knowledge. They differ on whether they think that it is best to try to overcome the particular standpoints in favor of objectivity, or whether they think that this is an impossible goal and that what is needed instead is (a) an ability to analyze clearly one's own standpoint and its implications, and (b) a theory of knowledge that addresses the ways it is produced. Either way, the ongoing debate shows the connection between issues of gender and racial difference and very basic questions of epistemology and theory.

Race, Gender, and Sociological Theory

The first reading is by Dorothy Smith (b. 1926), excerpted from her book, *The Conceptual Practices of Power: A Feminist Sociology of Knowledge* (1990). Sociological research on gender and race has both contributed to and been shaped by its profoundly interdisciplinary context. Smith, a Canadian researcher, is perhaps the most influential interdisciplinary sociologist in the field of feminist theory. Although she has studied social health and survey methods as well as gender, she is best known as a pioneer in feminist standpoint theory. Her theoretical innovations grow from her reading of existing theory as well as from her own experiences. Smith developed standpoint theory by asking how the social world would look different when seen from the standpoint of women. Among the dimensions this opened up to Smith was a new sense of the everyday world as problematic – a thing to be explained.[3] In exploring this, Smith drew on insights from both ethnomethodology and Marxism, and her work is significant for making important links between "macro" and "micro" dimensions usually left too separate.

Her concern in the reading included here is with the ways that sociological knowledge is produced. She suggests that one major problem is that much of what is touted as "objective" knowledge implicitly has been based a "male social universe, even when women have participated in its doing." Because of this, she argues, it is not enough for sociology to simply study women. Sociologists must begin to recognize their own position in the social world. Recognizing the standpoint of the researcher, and building into our accounts the standpoint of women, challenges the discipline's claim to scientific objectivity, and Smith thinks this is an important starting point for an alternative vision of what sociology should be.

This challenge to social theory is continued in the reading by Patricia Hill Collins (b. 1948), drawn from her book *Black Feminist Thought: Knowledge, Consciousness, and the Politics of Empowerment*, second edition (2000). She embraces Smith's approach to experience as the basis for knowledge – an epistemology, or theory of knowledge, rooted in practical, everyday life rather than in an attempt at scientific distancing. While she appropriates the general idea of standpoint theory, she also introduces a major critique by suggesting that taking the standpoint of women – implicitly, mainly white women – obscures the more specific standpoint or experience of Black women. Collins draws on diverse sources in sociological research, psychology, literature, and other fields to demonstrate the distinctive perspective afforded Black women (mainly Black American women) by their experience. At the same time, she seeks to show that achieving an understanding of their own experience as a legitimate basis for knowledge is important to Black women's subjectivity.

Collins came to sociology from a prior career as a schoolteacher and remains concerned with the educational dimensions of sociological theory. This refers not only to the extent to which sociology can inform better pedagogical practices, but also to the extent to which good sociological theory grows out of educational activity. She draws on her experience as a teacher, and that of her students, to show how social knowledge develops. She also argues that we should not see theory as being developed only in abstract scientific writings, but as being created as part of narratives that carry their own lessons about how the social world works. Indeed, narrative may be especially important to women, racial minorities, and others seeking to establish and share the legitimacy of views rooted in their own experience, precisely because this experience is obscured or ignored by dominant ways of thinking.

Collins's work broadens standpoint theory, and shows that it can be adapted to more specific perspectives. Collins envisions a threefold matrix of domination comprised of class, race, and gender. She argues that Black women occupy subordinate positions on all three dimensions, and therefore share a particular subjectivity. This of course raises another question of whether race, class, and gender is enough. Collins recognizes this at least implicitly by mentioning sexuality and nationality as other salient dimensions of experience. But how much specificity is enough? Her own theory could be challenged in the same way she challenged Smith's – by pointing to neglected subcategories, such as Black immigrant women. Within this category, one could introduce further distinctions, for example between Somali and Caribbean immigrant women. It remains an open question whether we can decide, either theoretically or empirically, how many dimensions we must consider before we arrive at a social experience unified enough to be treated as an autonomous subjectivity.

Frantz Fanon also engages the question of difference, but from a different perspective. Fanon (1925–61) was born in the French Caribbean colony of Martinique, and trained as a psychiatrist in France. He became one of the most influential Marxist intellectuals of the twentieth century and an advocate of anti-colonial revolution. His book *The Wretched of the Earth* (1963) was among the most widely read accounts of the struggles of the colonized poor. In it, Fanon develops his controversial theory that violence is a necessary (or almost necessary) element of revolutionary struggle not only because it helps to defeat governments and others in power but because it provides an occasion for self-transformation. While many would reject Fanon's argument on moral grounds, there is support for some of the social psychology underpinning it. Fanon draws on psychoanalysis, Marxism, and existentialism to make the case that colonialism involves both external domination and psychological repression. Together, these not only challenge individuals but also make it difficult for the people of a country to forge a national identity that empowers them to make their own future.

The selection here is from his first book, *Black Skin, White Masks* (1967 [1952]), a theoretical reflection on his experiences as a Black professional in the West Indies. More focused on social psychology and less on political struggle, this book emphasizes how the experience of growing up under colonial rule (or other sorts of domination) may produce a kind of psychological internalization of the power of the oppressor. As a French-speaking intellectual, Fanon's theoretical framework was influenced by the existentialist philosophy of Sartre and others. As a result, while Smith and Collins emphasize epistemology, or a study of knowing, Fanon's emphasis is on ontology, the study of being. Fanon draws on Hegel's notion of "being for others" to argue that for Black people in a white-controlled world, one's self is not framed just by being Black, but by "being black for the White man." Culture plays a crucial role in this. For Fanon, adopting the French language, for example, meant taking on the "whole weight of a civilization," including how that civilization understood the descendents of former slaves in its colonies. Fanon relies on the notion of a potential authentic identity to make clear why the alienation he describes is damaging, but at the same time argues that a strong identity is something people have to achieve, whether as individuals or as collectivities, not something that can be taken for granted on the basis of biology or even culture.

The final reading in this section is by Orlando Patterson (b. 1940). Patterson is also Caribbean, but from the Anglophone West Indies. He attained prominence in Jamaica before continuing his career as a sociology professor at Harvard University. In the 1980s and early 1990s, Patterson published a distinctive series of books on slavery and freedom. In *Slavery and Social Death* (1982), he traced the ways that the institution of slavery reflected a conception of society in which some people could suffer a kind of civic death even while alive and working. Slavery was not merely a matter of domination and oppression, thus, but distinctively an institution that revealed the socially constructed nature of civil rights, citizenship and indeed freedom. Patterson developed this argument in a larger work on the nature of freedom itself, drawing on ancient Greek as well as more recent American examples to show the extent to which the development of the very specific notion of freedom that is basic to philosophy and much of the discourse of human rights reflected roots in the opposition between slavery and freedom.

These reflections provided a philosophical and historical background for Patterson's analysis of how issues of difference connect with democracy, especially in the United States. The selection included here is from his book, *The Ordeal of Integration: Progress and Resentment in America's "Racial" Crisis* (1997). The central issue is how ideas about difference get incorporated into the civil society and the polity. Addressing the legacy of slavery in the USA, Patterson focuses attention on its ironic centrality to the history of the idea of freedom so basic to American political culture. In the post-slavery legacy of troubled tolerance and integration, he considers a number of paradoxical legacies that we are left with, including that of having to recognize race in order to overcome its effects, and the danger that this might lead to a kind of reification of the racial divide. Ironically, as Patterson has noted, some Black activists – and theorists – have sought to keep considerations of race within the kind of either/or categorization that was created by racist ideology. Some worry, for example, that the popularity of mixed-race identity will dilute the solidarity needed for the struggle against racism. Where Fanon's theory poses the question of whether this might reflect a psychological desire to escape from a stigmatized racial identity, Patterson's asks whether there is a way to preserve the struggle for freedom while moving beyond race. Both are possible – but, as Patterson's sociology suggests, the answer may be specific to social and historical context.

NOTES

1 On the concept of "racial formation" and the ways that racial categories have been applied in American society, see Omi and Winant (1994).
2 For an interesting review of the ways that "race" has been conceptualized within scientific discourse, see Banton (1998). On the connection between racial images and genetic science, see Duster (2003).
3 Dorothy Smith, *The Everyday World as Problematic: A Feminist Sociology* (Boston, MA: Northeastern University Press, 1987).

BIBLIOGRAPHY

Banton, Michael. 1998. *Racial Theories*, second edition. Cambridge: Cambridge University Press. (A very interesting review of the history of the concept of "race" in scientific discourse. The book covers both the early biological theories and recent social scientific conceptions.)

Calhoun, Craig (ed.). 1994. *Social Theory and the Politics of Identity*. Oxford: Blackwell Publishers. (A volume of essays dealing with the question of identity and identity struggles in social theory. The introductory essay provides a good overview of the theoretical debates outlined above.)

Calhoun, Craig. 1995. *Critical Social Theory*. Oxford: Blackwell Publishers. (The last three chapters in particular take up the question of difference in social theory, dealing with stand-point epistemology, the broader politics of identity, and the question of nationalism.)

Collins, Patricia Hill. 1991. *Black Feminist Thought: Knowledge, Consciousness, and the Politics of Empowerment*. New York: Routledge. (A pioneering synthesis of analyses that try to deal with race and gender together, noteworthy for its integration of literature written by African-American women with sociological theory and for its advocacy of a "matrix" concept of identity – allowing for "both/and" rather than "either/or" constructions.)

Collins, Patricia Hill. 1997. *Fighting Words*. Minneapolis, MN: University of Minnesota Press. (Collins's second major book, which takes up not only the question of hate speech but the relationship of education to sociology and the importance of narrative as an alternative to the conventional abstract presentation of theory.)

Duster, Troy. 2003. *Backdoor to Eugenics*. Second edition. New York: Routledge. (An examination of the ways that latent assumptions about racial difference shape scientific debates and modern genetic science, as well as the consequences of those assumptions.)

Fanon, Frantz. [1963]1968. *The Wretched of the Earth*. New York: Grove Press. (Fanon's most famous book, one of the major calls to action on behalf of those suffering during and after colonialism and also an influential analysis of the social psychology of domination and resistance.)

Fanon, Frantz. 1967 (1952). *Black Skins, White Masks*. (Fanon's combination of psychological and sociological analysis in examining the ways in which the legacy of colonialism and racial domination can become internalized by those whose lives have been shaped by it, and how they can struggle to overcome this.)

Gilman, Sander L. 1985. *Difference and Pathology: Stereotypes of Sexuality, Race, and Madness*. Ithaca, NY: Cornell University Press. (A brilliant account of the ways in which biology, medicine, and behavioral science joined in developing racialized accounts of pathology, especially in nineteenth-century Europe, and an examination of the question of why race and sexuality have such entangled modern histories.)

Gilroy, Paul. 1993. *The Black Atlantic*. Cambridge, MA: Harvard University Press. (A pioneering examination of the extent to which the development of post-slavery black identities combine elements from North American, Caribbean, and European experience – an analysis that could be extended to other contexts as well.)

Gilroy, Paul. 2000. *Against Race: Imagining Political Culture Beyond the Color Line*. Cambridge, MA: Harvard University Press. (A somewhat unwieldy but important analysis of the difficulties of simultaneously resisting racism and resisting the reification of racial categories or their mobilization in favor of unsavory cultural politics.)

Omi, Michael and Howard Winant. 1994. *Racial Formation in the United States: From the 1960s to the 1990s*. New York: Routledge. (The most important sociological examination of the ways in which "race" is reproduced and mobilized recurrently in the United States.)

Patterson, Orlando. 1997. *The Ordeal of Integration: Progress and Resentment in America's "Racial" Crisis*. Washington DC: Civitas/Counterpoint. (An engaging work and part of a series of race in America that also includes the recent *Rituals of Blood* [2000].)

Smith, Dorothy. 1987. *The Everyday World as Problematic: A Feminist Sociology*. Boston, MA: Northeastern University Press. (Smith's pioneering study in feminist sociology, still the theoretical classic in the field. A remarkable combination of insights from ethnomethodology, feminism, Marxism, and practical research experience to show how the gendered nature of the world of everyday lived experience was obscured by much previous sociology and how research from the standpoint of women can illuminate everyday life.)

Smith, Dorothy E. 1990. *The Conceptual Practices of Power*. Boston, MA: Northeastern University Press. (Smith's examination of the ways in which the making of conceptual schemes both serves as a tool of the powerful and obscures uncomfortable reality from the privileged. Contributes to the sociology of knowledge – and of sociology – drawing on a Marxist-feminist and ethnomethodological heritage; in some ways similar to Foucault, but with much more explicit attention to gender.)

Wallace, Michele. 1976. *Black Macho and the Myth of the Superwoman*. New York: Verso, 2nd edn 1999. (A remarkable early work by a leading Black feminist scholar of literature and culture. Wallace shows both the heritage of slavery and racist institutions and the extent to which certain forms of Black popular identity exacerbate rather than mitigate their effects.)

Chapter 26

The Conceptual Practices of Power [1990]

Dorothy E. Smith

It is not enough to supplement an established sociology by addressing ourselves to what has been left out or overlooked, or by making women's issues into sociological issues. That does not change the standpoint built into existing sociological procedures, but merely makes the sociology of women an addendum to the body of objectified knowledge.

The first difficulty is that how sociology is thought – its methods, conceptual schemes, and theories – has been based on and built up within the male social universe, even when women have participated in its doing. This sociology has taken for granted not only an itemized inventory of issues or subject matters (industrial sociology, political sociology, social stratification, and so forth) but the fundamental social and political structures under which these become relevant and are ordered. There is thus a disjunction between how women experience the world and the concepts and theoretical schemes by which society's self-consciousness is inscribed. […]

A second difficulty is that the worlds opened up by speaking from the standpoint of women have not been and are not on a basis of equality with the objectified bodies of knowledge that have constituted and expressed the standpoint of men. The worlds of men have had, and still have, an authority over the worlds that are traditionally women's and still are predominantly women's – the worlds of household, children, and neighborhood. And though women do not inhabit only these worlds, for the vast majority of women they are the primary ground of our

Dorothy E. Smith, "The Conceptual Practices of Power," pp. 12–19, 21–7 from Dorothy E. Smith, *The Conceptual Practices of Power: A Feminist Sociology of Knowledge*. Boston, MA: Northeastern University Press, 1990. Copyright © 1990 by Dorothy E. Smith. Reprinted by permission of University Press of New England, Hanover, NH.

Contemporary Sociological Theory, Third Edition. Edited by Craig Calhoun, Joseph Gerteis, James Moody, Steven Pfaff, and Indermohan Virk. Editorial material and organization © 2012 John Wiley & Sons, Ltd. Published 2012 by John Wiley & Sons, Ltd.

lives, shaping the course of our lives and our participation in other relations. Furthermore, objectified knowledges are part of the world from which our kind of society is governed. The domestic world stands in a dependent relation to that other, and its whole character is subordinate to it.

The two difficulties are related to each other in a special way. The effect of the second interacting with the first is to compel women to think their world in the concepts and terms in which men think theirs. Hence the established social forms of consciousness alienate women from their own experience.

The profession of sociology has been predicated on a universe grounded in men's experience and relationships and still largely appropriated by men as their "territory." Sociology is part of the practice by which we are all governed; that practice establishes its relevances. Thus the institutions that lock sociology into the structures occupied by men are the same institutions that lock women into the situations in which we have found ourselves oppressed. To unlock the latter leads logically to an unlocking of the former. What follows, then, or rather what then becomes possible – for it is of course by no means inevitable – is less a shift in the subject matter than a different conception of how sociology might become a means of understanding our experience and the conditions of our experience (both women's and men's) in contemporary capitalist society.

Relations of Ruling and Objectified Knowledge

When I speak here of governing or ruling I mean something more general than the notion of government as political organization. I refer rather to that total complex of activities, differentiated into many spheres, by which our kind of society is ruled, managed, and administered. It includes what the business world calls *management*, it includes the professions, it includes government and the activities of those who are selecting, training, and indoctrinating those who will be its governors. The last includes those who provide and elaborate the procedures by which it is governed and develop methods for accounting for how it is done – namely, the business schools, the sociologists, the economists. These are the institutions through which we are ruled and through which we, and I emphasize this *we*, participate in ruling.

Sociology, then, I conceive as much more than a gloss on the enterprise that justifies and rationalizes it, and at the same time as much less than "science." The governing of our kind of society is done in abstract concepts and symbols, and sociology helps create them by transposing the actualities of people's lives and experience into the conceptual currency with which they can be governed.

Thus the relevances of sociology are organized in terms of a perspective on the world, a view from the top that takes for granted the pragmatic procedures of governing as those that frame and identify its subject matter. Issues are formulated because they are administratively relevant, not because they are significant first in the experience of those who live them. The kinds of facts and events that matter to sociologists have already been shaped and given their character and substance by the methods and practice of governing. […]

Sociologists, when they go to work, enter into the conceptually ordered society they are investigating. They observe, analyze, explain, and examine that world as if there were no problem in how it becomes observable to them. They move among the doings of organizations, governmental processes, and bureaucracies as people who are at home in that medium. The nature of that world itself, how it is known to them, the conditions of its existence, and their relation to it are not called into question. Their methods of observation and inquiry extend into it as procedures that are essentially of the same order as those that bring about the phenomena they are concerned with. Their perspectives and interests may differ, but the substance is the same. They work with facts and information that have been worked up from actualities and appear in the form of documents that are themselves the product of organizational processes, whether their own or those of some other agency. They fit that information back into a framework of entities and organizational processes which they take for granted as known, without asking how it is that they know them or by what social processes the actual events – what people do or utter – are construed as the phenomena known.

Where a traditional gender division of labor prevails, men enter the conceptually organized world of governing without a sense of transition. The male sociologist in these circumstances passes beyond his particular and immediate setting (the office he writes in, the libraries he consults, the streets he travels, the home he returns to) without attending to the shift in consciousness. He works in the very medium he studies.

But, of course, like everyone else, he also exists in the body in the place in which it is. This is also then the place of his sensory organization of immediate experience; the place where his coordinates of here and now, before and after, are organized around himself as center; the place where he confronts people face to face in the physical mode in which he expresses himself to them and they to him as more and other than either can speak. This is the place where things smell, where the irrelevant birds fly away in front of the window, where he has indigestion, where he dies. Into this space must come as actual material events – whether as sounds of speech, scratchings on the surface of paper, which he constitutes as text, or directly – anything he knows of the world. It has to happen here somehow if he is to experience it at all.

Entering the governing mode of our kind of society lifts actors out of the immediate, local, and particular place in which we are in the body. What becomes present to us in the governing mode is a means of passing beyond the local into the conceptual order. This mode of governing creates, at least potentially, a bifurcation of consciousness. It establishes two modes of knowing and experiencing and doing, one located in the body and in the space it occupies and moves in, the other passing beyond it. Sociology is written in and aims at the latter mode of action. Robert Bierstedt writes, "Sociology can liberate the mind from time and space themselves and remove it to a new and transcendental realm where it no longer depends upon these Aristotelian categories." Even observational work aims at description in the categories and hence conceptual forms of the "transcendental realm." Yet the local and particular site of knowing that is the other side of the bifurcated consciousness has not been a site for the development of systematic knowledge.

Women's Exclusion from the Governing Conceptual Mode

The suppression of the local and particular as a site of knowledge has been and remains gender organized. The domestic sites of women's work, traditionally identified with women, are outside and subservient to this structure. Men have functioned as subjects in the mode of governing; women have been anchored in the local and particular phase of the bifurcated world. It has been a condition of a man's being able to enter and become absorbed in the conceptual mode, and to forget the dependence of his being in that mode upon his bodily existence, that he does not have to focus his activities and interests upon his bodily existence. Full participation in the abstract mode of action requires liberation from attending to needs in the concrete and particular. The organization of work in managerial and professional circles depends upon the alienation of subjects from their bodily and local existence. The structure of work and the structure of career take for granted that these matters have been provided for in such a way that they will not interfere with a man's action and participation in that world. Under the traditional gender regime, providing for a man's liberation from Bierstedt's Aristotelian categories is a woman who keeps house for him, bears and cares for his children, washes his clothes, looks after him when he is sick, and generally provides for the logistics of his bodily existence.

Women's work in and around professional and managerial settings performs analogous functions. Women's work mediates between the abstracted and conceptual and the material form in which it must travel to communicate. Women do the clerical work, the word processing, the interviewing for the survey; they take messages, handle the mail, make appointments, and care for patients. At almost every point women mediate for men at work the relationship between the conceptual mode of action and the actual concrete forms in which it is and must be realized, and the actual material conditions upon which it depends.

Marx's concept of alienation is applicable here in a modified form. The simplest formulation of alienation posits a relation between the work individuals do and an external order oppressing them in which their work contributes to the strength of the order that oppresses them. This is the situation of women in this relation. The more successful women are in mediating the world of concrete particulars so that men do not have to become engaged with (and therefore conscious of) that world as a condition to their abstract activities, the more complete men's absorption in it and the more effective its authority. The dichotomy between the two worlds organized on the basis of gender separates the dual forms of consciousness; the governing consciousness dominates the primary world of a locally situated consciousness but cannot cancel it; the latter is a subordinated, suppressed, absent, but absolutely essential ground of the governing consciousness. The gendered organization of subjectivity dichotomizes the two worlds, estranges them, and silences the locally situated consciousness by silencing women.

Knowing a Society from Within: A Woman's Perspective

An alternative sociological approach must somehow transcend this contradiction without reentering Bierstedt's "transcendental realm." Women's standpoint, as I am analyzing it here, discredits sociology's claim to constitute an objective knowledge independent of the sociologist's situation. Sociology's conceptual procedures, methods, and relevances organize its subject matter from a determinate position in society. This critical disclosure is the basis of an alternative way of thinking sociology. If sociology cannot avoid being situated, then it should take that as its beginning and build it into its methodological and theoretical strategies. As it is now, these strategies separate a sociologically constructed world from that of direct experience; it is precisely that separation that must be undone.

I am not proposing an immediate and radical transformation of the subject matter and methods of the discipline nor the junking of everything that has gone before. What I am suggesting is more in the nature of a reorganization of the relationship of sociologists to the object of our knowledge and of our problematic. This reorganization involves first placing sociologists where we are actually situated, namely, at the beginning of those acts by which we know or will come to know, and second, making our direct embodied experience of the everyday world the primary ground of our knowledge.

A sociology worked on in this way would not have as its objective a body of knowledge subsisting in and of itself; inquiry would not be justified by its contribution to the heaping up of such a body. We would reject a sociology aimed primarily at itself. We would not be interested in contributing to a body of knowledge whose uses are articulated to relations of ruling in which women participate only marginally, if at all. The professional sociologist is trained to think in the objectified modes of sociological discourse, to think sociology as it has been and is thought; that training and practice has to be discarded. Rather, as sociologists we would be constrained by the actualities of how things come about in people's direct experience, including our own. A sociology for women would offer a knowledge of the social organization and determinations of the properties and events of our directly experienced world. Its analyses would become part of our ordinary interpretations of the experienced world, just as our experience of the sun's sinking below the horizon is transformed by our knowledge that the world turns away from a sun that seems to sink.

The only way of knowing a socially constructed world is knowing it from within. We can never stand outside it. A relation in which sociological phenomena are objectified and presented as external to and independent of the observer is itself a special social practice also known from within. The relation of observer and object of observation, of sociologist to "subject," is a specialized social relationship. Even to be a stranger is to enter a world constituted from within as strange. The strangeness itself is the mode in which it is experienced.

When Jean Briggs made her ethnographic study of the ways in which an Eskimo people structure and express emotion, what she learned emerged for her in the context of the actual developing relations between her and the family with whom she lived and other members of the group. Her account situates her knowledge in the context of those relationships and in the actual sites in which the work of family subsistence was done. Affections, tensions, and quarrels, in some of which she was implicated, were the living texture in which she learned what she describes. She makes it clear how this context structured her learning and how what she learned and can speak of became observable to her.

Briggs tells us what is normally discarded in the anthropological or sociological telling. Although sociological inquiry is necessarily a social relation, we have learned to dissociate our own part in it. We recover only the object of our knowledge as if it stood all by itself. Sociology does not provide for seeing that there are always two terms to this relation. An alternative sociology must preserve in it the presence, concerns, and experience of the sociologist as knower and discoverer.

To begin from direct experience and to return to it as a constraint or "test" of the adequacy of a systematic knowledge is to begin from where we are located bodily. The actualities of our everyday world are already socially organized. Settings, equipment, environment, schedules, occasions, and so forth, as well as our enterprises and routines, are socially produced and concretely and symbolically organized prior to the moment at which we enter and at which inquiry begins. By taking up a standpoint in our original and immediate knowledge of the world, sociologists can make their discipline's socially organized properties first observable and then problematic.

When I speak of *experience* I do not use the term as a synonym for *perspective*. Nor in proposing a sociology grounded in the sociologist's actual experience am I recommending the self-indulgence of inner exploration or any other enterprise with self as sole focus and object. Such subjectivist interpretations of *experience* are themselves an aspect of that organization of consciousness that suppresses the locally situated side of the bifurcated consciousness and transports us straight into mind country, stashing away the concrete conditions and practices upon which it depends. We can never escape the circles of our own heads if we accept that as our territory. Rather, sociologists' investigation of our directly experienced world as a problem is a mode of discovering or rediscovering the society from within. We begin from our own original but tacit knowledge and from within the acts by which we bring it into our grasp in making it observable and in understanding how it works. We aim not at a reiteration of what we already (tacitly) know, but at an exploration of what passes beyond that knowledge and is deeply implicated in how it is.

Sociology as Structuring Relations between Subject and Object

Our knowledge of the world is given to us in the modes by which we enter into relations with the object of knowledge. But in this case the object of our knowledge is or originates in the co-ordering of activities among "subjects." The constitution of an objective sociology as an authoritative version of how things are is done from a position in and as part of the practices of ruling in our kind of society. Our training as sociologists teaches us to ignore the uneasiness at the junctures where multiple and diverse experiences are transformed into objectified forms. That juncture shows in the ordinary problems respondents have of fitting their experience of the world to the questions in the interview schedule. The sociologist who is a woman finds it hard to preserve this exclusion, for she discovers, if she will, precisely that uneasiness in her relation to her discipline as a whole. The persistence of the privileged sociological version (or versions) relies upon a substructure that has already discredited and deprived of authority to speak the voices of those who know the society differently. The objectivity of a sociological version depends upon a special relationship with others that makes it easy for sociologists to remain outside the others' experience and does not require them to recognize that experience as a valid contention.

Riding a train not long ago in Ontario I saw a family of Indians – woman, man, and three children – standing together on a spur above a river watching the train go by. I realized that I could tell this incident – the train, those five people seen on the other side of the glass – as it was, but that my description was built on my position and my interpretations. I have called them "Indians" and a family; I have said they were watching the train. My understanding has already subsumed theirs. Everything may have been quite different for them. My description is privileged to stand as what actually happened because theirs is not heard in the contexts in which I may speak. If we begin from the world as we actually experience it, it is at least possible to see that we are indeed located and that what we know of the other is conditional upon that location. There are and must be different experiences of the world and different bases of experience. We must not do away with them by taking advantage of our privileged speaking to construct a sociological version that we then impose upon them as their reality. We may not rewrite the other's world or impose upon it a conceptual framework that extracts from it what fits with ours. Their reality, their varieties of experience, must be an unconditional datum. It is the place from which inquiry begins.

A Bifurcation of Consciousness

My experience in the train epitomizes a sociological relation. I am already separated from the world as it is experienced by those I observe. That separation is fundamental to the character of that experience. Once I become aware of how my world is put together as a practical everyday matter and of how my relations are shaped by its concrete conditions (even in so simple a matter as that I am sitting in the train and it travels, but those people standing on the spur do not), I am led into the discovery that I cannot understand the nature of my experienced world by staying within its ordinary boundaries of assumption and knowledge. To account for that moment on the train and for the relation between the two experiences (or more) and the two positions from which those experiences begin I must posit a larger socioeconomic order in back of that moment. The coming together that makes the observation possible as well as how we were separated and drawn apart as well as how I now make use of that here – these properties are determined elsewhere than in that relation itself.

Furthermore, how our knowledge of the world is mediated to us becomes a problem of knowing how that world is organized for us prior to our participation in it. As intellectuals we ordinarily receive it as a media world, a world of texts, images, journals, books, talk, and other symbolic modes. We discard as an essential focus of our practice other ways of knowing. Accounting for that mode of knowing and the social organization that sets it up for us again leads us back into an analysis of the total socioeconomic order of which it is part. Inquiry remaining within the circumscriptions of the directly experienced cannot explore and explicate the relations organizing the everyday matrices of direct experience.

If we address the problem of the conditions as well as the perceived forms and organization of immediate experience, we should include in it the events as they actually happen and the ordinary material world we encounter as a matter of fact: the urban renewal project that uproots four hundred families; how it is to live on welfare as an ordinary daily practice; cities as the actual physical structures in which we move; the organization of academic occasions such as that in which this chapter originated. When we examine them, we find that there are many aspects of how these things come about of which we, as sociologists, have little to say. We have a sense that the events entering our experience originate somewhere in a human intention, but we are unable to track back to find it and to find out how it got from there to here.

Or take this room in which I work or that room in which you are reading and treat that as a problem. If we think about the conditions of our activity here, we can trace how these chairs, this table, the walls, our clothing, our presence come to be here; how these places (yours and mine) are cleaned and maintained; and so forth. There are human activities, intentions, and relations that are not apparent as such in the actual material conditions of our work. The social organization of the setting is not wholly available to us in its appearance. We bypass in the immediacy of the specific practical activity a complex division of labor that is an essential precondition to it. Such preconditions are fundamentally mysterious to us and present us with problems in grasping social relations with which sociology is ill equipped to deal. We experience the world as largely incomprehensible beyond the limits of what we know in a common sense. No amount of observation of face-to-face relations, no amount of commonsense knowledge of everyday life, will take us beyond our essential ignorance of how it is put together. Our direct experience of it makes it (if we will) a problem, but it does not offer any answers. We experience a world of "appearances," the determinations of which lie beyond it.

We might think of the appearances of our direct experience as a multiplicity of surfaces, the properties and relations among which are generated by social organizations not observable in their effects. The relations underlying and generating the characteristics of our own directly experienced world bring us into unseen relations with others. Their experience is necessarily different from ours. If we would begin from our experienced world and attempt to analyze and account for how it is, we must posit others whose experience is not the same as ours.

Women's situation in sociology discloses to us a typical bifurcate structure with the abstracted, conceptual practices on the one hand and the concrete realizations, the maintenance routines, and so forth, on the other. Taking each for granted depends upon being fully situated in one or the other so that the other does not appear in contradiction to it. Women's direct experience places us a step back, where we can recognize the uneasiness that comes from sociology's claim to be about the world we live in, and, at the same time, its failure to account for or even describe the actual features we experience. Yet we cannot find the inner principle of our own activity through exploring what is directly experienced. We do not see how it is put together because it is determined elsewhere. The very organization of the world that has been assigned to us as the primary locus of our being, shaping other projects and desires, is determined by and subordinate to the relations of society founded in a capitalist mode of production. The aim of an alternative sociology would be to explore and unfold the relations beyond our direct experience that shape and determine it. An alternative sociology would be a means to anyone of understanding how the world comes about for us and how it is organized so that it happens to us as it does in our experience. An alternative sociology, from the standpoint of women, makes the everyday world its problematic.

Chapter 27

Black Feminist Epistemology [1990]

Patricia Hill Collins

As critical social theory, US Black feminist thought reflects the interests and standpoint of its creators. Tracing the origin and diffusion of Black feminist thought or any comparable body of specialized knowledge reveals its affinity to the power of the group that created it (Mannheim, 1936). Because elite White men control Western structures of knowledge validation, their interests pervade the themes, paradigms, and epistemologies of traditional scholarship. As a result, US Black women's experiences as well as those of women of African descent transnationally have been routinely distorted within or excluded from what counts as knowledge.

US Black feminist thought as specialized thought reflects the distinctive themes of African-American women's experiences. Black feminist thought's core themes of work, family, sexual politics, motherhood, and political activism rely on paradigms that emphasize the importance of intersecting oppressions in shaping the US matrix of domination. But expressing these themes and paradigms has not been easy because Black women have had to struggle against White male interpretations of the world.

In this context, Black feminist thought can best be viewed as subjugated knowledge. Traditionally, the suppression of Black women's ideas within White-male-controlled social institutions led African-American women to use music, literature, daily conversations, and everyday behavior as important locations for constructing a Black feminist consciousness. More recently, higher education and the news media

Patricia Hill Collins, "Black Feminist Epistemology," pp. 251–6, 266–71 from Patricia Hill Collins, *Black Feminist Thought: Knowledge, Consciousness, and the Politics of Empowerment*, 2nd edn. New York: Routledge, Taylor & Francis, 2000. Copyright © 2000. Reproduced by permission of the author and Routledge/Taylor & Francis Group, LLC.

Contemporary Sociological Theory, Third Edition. Edited by Craig Calhoun, Joseph Gerteis, James Moody, Steven Pfaff, and Indermohan Virk. Editorial material and organization © 2012 John Wiley & Sons, Ltd. Published 2012 by John Wiley & Sons, Ltd.

have emerged as increasingly important sites for Black feminist intellectual activity. Within these new social locations, Black feminist thought has often become highly visible, yet curiously, despite this visibility, it has become differently subjugated.

Investigating the subjugated knowledge of subordinate groups – in this case a Black women's standpoint and Black feminist thought – requires more ingenuity than that needed to examine the standpoints and thought of dominant groups. I found my training as a social scientist inadequate to the task of studying the subjugated knowledge of a Black women's standpoint. This is because subordinate groups have long had to use alternative ways to create independent self-definitions and self-valuations and to rearticulate them through our own specialists. Like other subordinate groups, African-American women not only have developed a distinctive Black women's standpoint, but have done so by using alternative ways of producing and validating knowledge.

Epistemology constitutes an overarching theory of knowledge (Harding, 1987). It investigates the standards used to assess knowledge or *why* we believe what we believe to be true. Far from being the apolitical study of truth, epistemology points to the ways in which power relations shape who is believed and why. For example, various descendants of Sally Hemmings, a Black woman owned by Thomas Jefferson, claimed repeatedly that Jefferson fathered her children. These accounts forwarded by Jefferson's African-American descendants were ignored in favor of accounts advanced by his White progeny. Hemmings's descendants were routinely disbelieved until their knowledge claims were validated by DNA testing.

Distinguishing among epistemologies, paradigms, and methodologies can prove to be useful in understanding the significance of competing epistemologies (Harding 1987). In contrast to epistemologies, *paradigms* encompass interpretive frameworks such as intersectionality that are used to explain social phenomena. *Methodology* refers to the broad principles of how to conduct research and how interpretive paradigms are to be applied. The level of epistemology is important because it determines which questions merit investigation, which interpretive frameworks will be used to analyze findings, and to what use any ensuing knowledge will be put.

In producing the specialized knowledge of US Black feminist thought, Black women intellectuals often encounter two distinct epistemologies: one representing elite White male interests and the other expressing Black feminist concerns. Whereas many variations of these epistemologies exist, it is possible to distill some of their distinguishing features that transcend differences among the paradigms within them. Epistemological choices about whom to trust, what to believe, and why something is true are not benign academic issues. Instead, these concerns tap the fundamental question of which versions of truth will prevail.

Eurocentric Knowledge Validation Processes and US Power Relations

In the United States, the social institutions that legitimate knowledge as well as the Western or Eurocentric epistemologies that they uphold constitute two interrelated parts of the dominant knowledge validation processes. In general, scholars, publishers, and other experts represent specific interests and credentialing processes, and their knowledge claims must satisfy the political and epistemological criteria of the contexts in which they reside (Kuhn, 1962; Mulkay, 1979). Because this enterprise is controlled by elite White men, knowledge validation processes reflect this group's interests. Although designed to represent and protect the interests of powerful White men, neither schools, government, the media and other social institutions that house these processes nor the actual epistemologies that they promote need be managed by White men themselves. White women, African-American men and women, and other people of color may be enlisted to enforce these connections between power relations and what counts as truth. Moreover, not all White men accept these power relations that privilege Eurocentrism. Some have revolted and subverted social institutions and the ideas they promote.

Two political criteria influence knowledge validation processes. First, knowledge claims are evaluated by a group of experts whose members bring with them a host of sedimented experiences that reflect their group location in intersecting oppressions. No scholar can avoid cultural ideas and his or her placement in intersecting oppressions of race, gender, class, sexuality, and nation. In the United States, this means that a scholar making a knowledge claim typically must convince a scholarly community controlled by elite White avowedly heterosexual men holding US citizenship that a given claim is justified. Second, each community of experts must maintain its credibility as defined by the larger population in which it is situated and from which it draws its basic, taken-for-granted knowledge. This means that scholarly communities that challenge basic beliefs held in US culture at large will be deemed less credible than those that support popular ideas. For example, if scholarly communities stray too far from widely held beliefs about Black womanhood, they run the risk of being discredited.

When elite White men or any other overly homogeneous group dominates knowledge validation processes, both of these political criteria can work to suppress Black feminist thought. Given that the general US culture shaping the taken-for-granted knowledge of the community of experts is permeated by widespread notions of Black female inferiority, new knowledge claims that seem to violate this fundamental assumption are likely to be viewed as anomalies (Kuhn, 1962). Moreover, specialized thought challenging notions of Black female inferiority is unlikely to be generated from within White-male-controlled academic settings because both the kinds of questions asked and the answers to them would necessarily reflect a basic lack of familiarity with Black women's realities. Even those who think they are familiar can reproduce stereotypes. Believing that they are already knowledgeable, many scholars staunchly defend controlling images of US Black women as mammies, matriarchs, and jezebels, and allow these commonsense beliefs to permeate their scholarship.

The experiences of African-American women scholars illustrate how individuals who wish to rearticulate a Black women's standpoint through Black feminist thought can be suppressed by prevailing knowledge validation processes. Exclusion from basic literacy, quality educational experiences, and faculty and administrative positions has limited US Black women's access to influential academic positions. Black women have long produced knowledge claims that contested those advanced by elite White men. But because Black women have been denied positions of authority, they often relied on alternative knowledge validation processes to generate competing knowledge claims. As a consequence, academic disciplines typically rejected such claims. Moreover, any credentials controlled by White male academicians could then be denied to Black women who used alternative standards on the grounds that Black women's work did not constitute credible research.

Black women with academic credentials who seek to exert the authority that our status grants us to propose new knowledge claims about African-American women face pressures to use our authority to help legitimate a system that devalues and excludes the majority of Black women. When an outsider group – in this case, African-American women – recognizes that the insider group – namely, elite White men – requires special privileges from the larger society, those in power must find ways of keeping the outsiders out and at the same time having them acknowledge the legitimacy of this procedure. Accepting a few "safe" outsiders addresses this legitimation problem (Berger and Luckmann, 1966). One way of excluding the majority of Black women from the knowledge validation process is to permit a few Black women to acquire positions of authority in institutions that legitimate knowledge, and to encourage us to work within the taken-for-granted assumptions of Black female inferiority shared by the scholarly community and the culture at large. Those Black women who accept these assumptions are likely to be rewarded by their institutions. Those challenging the assumptions can be placed under surveillance and run the risk of being ostracized.

African-American women academicians who persist in trying to rearticulate a Black women's standpoint also face potential rejection of our knowledge claims on epistemological grounds. Just as the material realities of powerful and dominated groups produce separate standpoints, these groups may also deploy distinctive epistemologies or theories of knowledge. Black women scholars may know that something is true – at least, by standards widely accepted among African-American women – but be unwilling or unable to legitimate our claims using prevailing scholarly norms. For any discourse, new knowledge claims must be consistent with an existing body of knowledge that the group controlling the interpretive context accepts as true. [...]

Criteria for methodological adequacy associated with positivism illustrate the standards that Black women scholars, especially those in the social sciences, would have to satisfy in legitimating Black feminist thought. Though I describe Western or Eurocentric epistemologies as a single cluster, many interpretive frameworks or paradigms are subsumed under this category. Moreover, my focus on positivism should be interpreted neither to mean that all dimensions of positivism are inherently problematic for Black women nor that nonpositivist frameworks are better.

Positivist approaches aim to create scientific descriptions of reality by producing objective generalizations. Because researchers have widely differing values, experiences, and emotions, genuine science is thought to be unattainable unless all human characteristics except rationality are eliminated from the research process. By following strict methodological rules, scientists aim to distance themselves from the values, vested interests, and emotions generated by their class, race, sex, or unique situation. By decontextualizing themselves, they allegedly become detached observers and manipulators of nature (Jaggar, 1983; Harding, 1986).

Several requirements typify positivist methodological approaches. First, research methods generally require a distancing of the researcher from her or his "object" of study by defining the researcher as a "subject" with full human subjectivity and by objectifying the "object" of study (Keller, 1985; Asante, 1987). A second requirement is the absence of emotions from the research process (Jaggar, 1983). Third, ethics and values are deemed inappropriate in the research process, either as the reason for scientific inquiry or as part of the research process itself (Richards, 1980). Finally, adversarial debates, whether written or oral, become the preferred method of ascertaining truth: The arguments that can withstand the greatest assault and survive intact become the strongest truths (Moulton, 1983).

Such criteria ask African-American women to objectify ourselves, devalue our emotional life, displace our motivations for furthering knowledge about Black women, and confront in an adversarial relationship those with more social, economic, and professional power. On the one hand, it seems unlikely that Black women would rely exclusively on positivist paradigms in rearticulating a Black women's standpoint. For example, Black women's experiences in sociology illustrate diverse responses to encountering an entrenched positivism. Given Black women's long-standing exclusion from sociology prior to 1970, the sociological knowledge about race and gender produced during their absence, and the symbolic importance of Black women's absence to sociological self-definitions as a science, African-American women acting as agents of knowledge faced a complex situation. In order to refute the history of Black women's unsuitability for science, they had to invoke the tools of sociology by using positivistic frameworks to demonstrate their capability as scientists. However, they simultaneously needed to challenge the same structure that granted them legitimacy. Their responses to this dilemma reflect the strategic use of the tools of positivism when needed, coupled with overt challenges to positivism when that seemed feasible.

On the other hand, many Black women have had access to another epistemology that encompasses standards for assessing truth that are widely accepted among African-American women. An experiential, material base underlies a Black feminist epistemology, namely, collective experiences and accompanying worldviews that US Black women sustained based on our particular history. The historical conditions of Black women's work, both in Black civil society and in paid employment, fostered a series of experiences that when shared and passed on become the collective wisdom of a Black women's standpoint. Moreover, a set of principles for assessing knowledge claims may be available to those having these shared experiences. These principles pass into a more general Black women's wisdom and, further, into what I call here a Black feminist epistemology.

This alternative epistemology uses different standards that are consistent with Black women's criteria for substantiated knowledge and with our criteria for methodological adequacy. Certainly this alternative Black feminist epistemology has been devalued by dominant knowledge validation processes and may not be claimed by many African-American women. But if such an epistemology exists, what are its contours? Moreover, what are its actual and potential contributions to Black feminist thought?

[…]

Black Women as Agents of Knowledge

Social movements of the 1950s, 1960s, and 1970s stimulated a greatly changed intellectual and political climate in the United States. Compared to the past, many more US Black women became legitimated agents of knowledge. No longer passive objects of knowledge manipulated within prevailing knowledge validation processes, African-American women aimed to speak for ourselves.

African-American women in the academy and other positions of authority who aim to advance Black feminist thought now encounter the often conflicting epistemological standards of three key groups. First, Black feminist thought must be validated by ordinary African-American women who, in the words of Hannah Nelson, grow to womanhood "in a world where the saner you are, the madder you are made to appear" (Gwaltney, 1980: 7). To be credible in the eyes of this group, Black feminist intellectuals must be personal advocates for their material, be accountable for the consequences of their work, have lived or experienced their material in some fashion, and be willing to engage in dialogues about their findings with ordinary, everyday people.

Historically, living life as an African-American woman facilitated this endeavor because knowledge validation processes controlled in part or in full by Black women occurred in particular organizational settings. When Black women were in charge of our own self-definitions, these four dimensions of Black feminist epistemology – lived experience as a criterion of meaning, the use of dialogue, the ethic of personal accountability, and the ethic of caring – came to the forefront. When the core themes and interpretive frameworks of Black women's knowledge were informed by Black feminist epistemology, a rich tradition of Black feminist thought ensued.

Traditionally women engaged in this overarching intellectual and political project were blues singers, poets, autobiographers, storytellers, and orators. They became Black feminist intellectuals both by doing intellectual work and by being validated as such by everyday Black women. Black women in academia could not openly join their ranks without incurring a serious penalty. [...]

The community of Black women scholars constitutes a second constituency whose epistemological standards must be met. As the number of Black women academics grows, this heterogeneous collectivity shares a similar social location in higher education, yet finds a new challenge in building group solidarities across differences. African-American women scholars place varying amounts of importance on furthering Black feminist scholarship. However, despite this new-found diversity, since more African-American women earn advanced degrees, the range of Black feminist scholarship has expanded. Historically, African-American women may have brought sensibilities gained from Black feminist epistemology to their scholarship. But gaining legitimacy often came with the cost of rejecting such an epistemology. Studying Black women's lives at all placed many careers at risk. More recently, increasing numbers of African-American women scholars have chosen to study Black women's experiences, and to do so by relying on elements of Black feminist epistemology in framing their work. [...]

A third group whose epistemological standards must be met consists of dominant groups who still control schools, graduate programs, tenure processes, publication outlets, and other mechanisms that legitimate knowledge. African-American women academics who aim to advance Black feminist thought typically must use dominant Eurocentric epistemologies for this group. The difficulties these Black women now face lie less in demonstrating that they could master White male epistemologies than in resisting the hegemonic nature of these patterns of thought in order to see, value, and use existing alternative Black feminist ways of knowing. For Black women who are agents of knowledge within academia, the marginality that accompanies outsider-within status can be the source of both frustration and creativity. In an attempt to minimize the differences between the cultural context of African-American communities and the expectations of mainstream social institutions, some women dichotomize their behavior and become two different people. Over time, the strain of doing this can be enormous. Others reject Black women's accumulated wisdom and work against their own best interests by enforcing the dominant group's specialized thought. Still others manage to inhabit both contexts but do so critically, using perspectives gained from their outsider-within social locations as a source of insights and ideas. But while such women can make substantial contributions as agents of knowledge, they rarely do so without substantial personal cost. "Eventually it comes to you," observes Lorraine Hansberry, "the thing that makes you exceptional, if you are at all, is inevitably that which must also make you lonely" (1969: 148).

Just as migrating between Black and White families raised special issues for Black women domestic workers, moving among different and competing interpretive communities raises similar epistemological concerns for Black feminist thinkers. The dilemma facing Black women scholars, in particular, engaged in creating Black feminist thought illustrates difficulties that can accompany grappling with multiple interpretive communities. A knowledge claim that meets the criteria of adequacy for one group and thus is judged to be acceptable may not be translatable into the terms of a different group. [...]

Once Black women scholars face the notion that on certain dimensions of a Black women's standpoint, it may be fruitless to try to translate into other frameworks truths validated by Black feminist epistemology, then other choices emerge. Rather than trying to uncover universal knowledge claims that can withstand the translation from one epistemology to another (initially, at least), Black women intellectuals might find efforts to rearticulate a Black women's standpoint especially fruitful. Rearticulating a Black women's standpoint refashions the particular and reveals the more universal human dimensions of Black women's everyday lives. [...]

Toward Truth

The existence of Black feminist thought suggests another path to the universal truths that might accompany the "truthful identity of what is." In this volume I place Black women's subjectivity in the center of analysis and examine the interdependence of the everyday, taken-for-granted knowledge shared by African-American women as a group, the more specialized knowledge produced by Black women intellectuals, and the social conditions shaping both types of thought. This approach allows me to describe the creative tension linking how social conditions influenced a Black women's standpoint and how the power of the ideas themselves gave many African-American women the strength to shape those same social conditions. I approach Black feminist thought as situated in a context of domination and not as a system of ideas divorced from political and economic reality. Moreover, I present Black feminist thought as subjugated knowledge in that African-American women have long struggled to find alternative locations and epistemologies for validating our own self-definitions. In brief, I examined the situated, subjugated standpoint of African-American women in order to understand Black feminist thought as a partial perspective on domination.

Because US Black women have access to the experiences that accrue to being both Black and female, an alternative epistemology used to rearticulate a Black women's standpoint should reflect the convergence of both sets of experiences. Race and gender may be analytically distinct, but in Black women's everyday lives, they work together. The search for the distinguishing features of an alternative epistemology used by African-American women reveals that some ideas that Africanist scholars identify as characteristically "Black" often bear remarkable resemblance to similar ideas claimed by feminist scholars as characteristically "female." This similarity suggests that the actual contours of intersecting oppressions can vary dramatically and yet generate some uniformity in the epistemologies used by subordinate groups. Just as US Black women and African women encountered diverse patterns of intersecting oppressions yet generated similar agendas concerning what mattered in their feminisms, a similar process may be at work regarding the epistemologies of oppressed groups. Thus the significance of a Black feminist epistemology may lie in its ability to enrich our understanding of how subordinate groups create knowledge that fosters both their empowerment and social justice.

This approach to Black feminist thought allows African-American women to explore the epistemological implications of transversal politics. Eventually this approach may get us to a point at which, claims Elsa Barkley Brown, "all people can learn to center in another experience, validate it, and judge it by its own standards without need of comparison or need to adopt that framework as their own" (1989: 922). In such politics, "one has no need to 'decenter' anyone in order to center someone else; one has only to constantly, appropriately, 'pivot the center'" (p. 922).

Rather than emphasizing how a Black women's standpoint and its accompanying epistemology differ from those of White women, Black men, and other collectivities, Black women's experiences serve as one specific social location for examining points of connection among multiple epistemologies. Viewing Black feminist epistemology in this way challenges additive analyses of oppression claiming that Black women have a more accurate view of oppression than do other groups. Such approaches suggest that oppression can be quantified and compared and that adding layers of oppression produces a potentially clearer standpoint (Spelman, 1988). One implication of some uses of standpoint theory is that the more subordinated the group, the purer the vision available to them. This is an outcome of the origins of standpoint approaches in Marxist social theory, itself reflecting the binary thinking of its Western origins. Ironically, by quantifying and ranking human oppressions, standpoint theorists invoke criteria for methodological adequacy that resemble those of positivism. Although it is tempting to claim that Black women are more oppressed than everyone else and therefore have the best standpoint from which to understand the mechanisms, processes, and effects of oppression, this is not the case.

Instead, those ideas that are validated as true by African-American women, African-American men, Latina lesbians, Asian-American women, Puerto Rican men, and other groups with distinctive standpoints, with each group using the epistemological approaches growing from its unique standpoint, become the most "objective" truths. Each group speaks from its own standpoint and shares its own partial, situated knowledge. But because each group perceives its own truth as partial, its knowledge is unfinished. Each group becomes better able to consider other groups' standpoints without relinquishing the uniqueness of its own standpoint or suppressing other groups' partial perspectives. "What is always needed in the appreciation of art, or life," maintains Alice Walker, "is the larger perspective. Connections made, or at least attempted, where none existed before, the straining to encompass in one's glance at the varied world the common thread, the unifying theme through immense diversity" (1983: 5). Partiality, and not universality, is the condition of being heard; individuals and groups forwarding knowledge claims without owning their position are deemed less credible than those who do.

Alternative knowledge claims in and of themselves are rarely threatening to conventional knowledge. Such claims are routinely ignored, discredited, or simply absorbed and marginalized in existing paradigms. Much more threatening is the challenge that alternative epistemologies offer to the basic process used by the powerful to legitimate knowledge claims that in turn justify their right to rule. If the epistemology used to validate knowledge comes into question, then all prior knowledge claims validated under the dominant model become suspect. Alternative epistemologies challenge all certified knowledge and open up the question of whether what has been taken to be true can stand the test of alternative ways of validating truth. The existence of a self-defined Black women's standpoint using Black feminist epistemology calls into question the content of what currently passes as truth and simultaneously challenges the process of arriving at that truth.

REFERENCES

Asante, Molefi Kete. 1987. *The Afrocentric Idea*. Philadelphia: Temple University Press.
Berger, Peter L., and Thomas Luckmann. 1966. *The Social Construction of Reality*. New York: Doubleday.
Brown, Elsa Barkley. 1989. "African-American Women's Quilting: A Framework for Conceptualizing and Teaching African-American Women's History." *Signs* 14 (4): 921–9.
Gwaltney, John Langston. 1980. *Drylongso, A Self-Portrait of Black America*. New York: Vintage.
Hansberry, Lorraine. 1969. *To Be Young, Gifted and Black*. New York: Signet.
Harding, Sandra. 1986. *The Science Question in Feminism*. Ithaca, NY: Cornell University Press.

Harding, Sandra. 1987. "Introduction: Is There a Feminist Method?" In *Feminism and Methodology*, ed. Sandra Harding, pp. 1–14. Bloomington: Indiana University Press.
Jaggar, Alison M. 1983. *Feminist Politics and Human Nature*. Totawa, NJ: Rowman & Allanheld.
Keller, Evelyn Fox. 1985. *Reflections on Gender and Science*. New Haven, CT: Yale University Press.
Kuhn, Thomas. 1962. *The Structure of Scientific Revolution*. Second edition. Chicago, IL: University of Chicago Press.
Mannheim, Karl. 1936. *Ideology and Utopia*. New York: Harcourt, Brace & World.
Moulton, Janice. 1983. "A Paradigm of Philosophy: The Adversary Method." In *Discovering Reality*, ed. Sandra Harding and Merrill B. Hintikka, pp. 149–64. Boston, MA: D. Reidel.
Mulkay, Michael. 1979. *Science and the Sociology of Knowledge*. Boston, MA: Unwin Hyman.
Richards, Dona. 1980. "European Mythology: The Ideology of 'Progress.'" In *Contemporary Black Thought*, ed. Molefi Kete Asante and Abdulai S. Vandi, pp. 59–79. Beverly Hills, CA: Sage.
Spelman, Elizabeth V. 1988. *Inessential Woman: Problems of Exclusion in Feminist Thought*. Boston, MA: Beacon.
Walker, Alice. 1983. *In Search of Our Mothers' Gardens*. New York: Harcourt Brace Jovanovich.

Chapter 28

Black Skin, White Masks [1952]

Frantz Fanon

The Negro and Language

I ascribe a basic importance to the phenomenon of language. That is why I find it necessary to begin with this subject, which should provide us with one of the elements in the colored man's comprehension of the dimension of *the other*. For it is implicit that to speak is to exist absolutely for the other.

The black man has two dimensions. One with his fellows, the other with the white man. A Negro behaves differently with a white man and with another Negro. That this self-division is a direct result of colonialist subjugation is beyond question. … No one would dream of doubting that its major artery is fed from the heart of those various theories that have tried to prove that the Negro is a stage in the slow evolution of monkey into man. Here is objective evidence that expresses reality.

But when one has taken cognizance of this situation, when one has understood it, one considers the job completed. How can one then be deaf to that voice rolling down the stages of history: "What matters is not to know the world but to change it."

This matters appallingly in our lifetime.

To speak means to be in a position to use a certain syntax, to grasp the morphology of this or that language, but it means above all to assume a culture, to support the weight of a civilization. Since the situation is not one-way only, the statement of it should reflect the fact. Here the reader is asked to concede certain

---

Frantz Fanon, "Black Skin, White Masks," pp. 17–8, 109–16, 216–22 from Frantz Fanon, *Black Skin, White Masks*. New York: Grove Press, 1967. Translated from the French by Charles Lam Markmann. Copyright © 1967. Reprinted by permission of Grove Press, Inc.

Contemporary Sociological Theory, Third Edition. Edited by Craig Calhoun, Joseph Gerteis, James Moody, Steven Pfaff, and Indermohan Virk. Editorial material and organization © 2012 John Wiley & Sons, Ltd. Published 2012 by John Wiley & Sons, Ltd.

points that, however unacceptable they may seem in the beginning, will find the measure of their validity in the facts.

The problem that we confront in this chapter is this: The Negro of the Antilles will be proportionately whiter – that is, he will come closer to being a real human being – in direct ratio to his mastery of the French language. I am not unaware that this is one of man's attitudes face to face with Being. A man who has a language consequently possesses the world expressed and implied by that language. What we are getting at becomes plain: Mastery of language affords remarkable power. Paul Valéry knew this, for he called language "the god gone astray in the flesh."[1]

In a work now in preparation I propose to investigate this phenomenon.[2] For the moment I want to show why the Negro of the Antilles, whoever he is, has always to face the problem of language. Furthermore, I will broaden the field of this description and through the Negro of the Antilles include every colonized man.

Every colonized people – in other words, every people in whose soul an inferiority complex has been created by the death and burial of its local cultural originality – finds itself face to face with the language of the civilizing nation; that is, with the culture of the mother country. The colonized is elevated above his jungle status in proportion to his adoption of the mother country's cultural standards. He becomes whiter as he renounces his blackness, his jungle. [...]

The Fact of Blackness

"Dirty nigger!" Or simply, "Look, a Negro!"

I came into the world imbued with the will to find a meaning in things, my spirit filled with the desire to attain to the source of the world, and then I found that I was an object in the midst of other objects.

Sealed into that crushing objecthood, I turned beseechingly to others. Their attention was a liberation, running over my body suddenly abraded into nonbeing, endowing me once more with an agility that I had thought lost, and by taking me out of the world, restoring me to it. But just as I reached the other side, I stumbled, and the movements, the attitudes, the glances of the other fixed me there, in the sense in which a chemical solution is fixed by a dye. I was indignant; I demanded an explanation. Nothing happened. I burst apart. Now the fragments have been put together again by another self.

As long as the black man is among his own, he will have no occasion, except in minor internal conflicts, to experience his being through others. There is of course the moment of "being for others," of which Hegel speaks, but every ontology is made unattainable in a colonized and civilized society. It would seem that this fact has not been given sufficient attention by those who have discussed the question. In the *Weltanschauung* of a colonized people there is an impurity, a flaw that outlaws any ontological explanation. Someone may object that this is the case with every individual, but such an objection merely conceals a basic problem. Ontology – once it is finally admitted as leaving existence by the wayside – does not permit us to understand the being of the black man. For not only must the black man be black; he must be black in relation to the white man. Some critics will take it on themselves to remind us that this proposition has a converse. I say that this is false. The black man has no ontological resistance in the eyes of the white man. Overnight the Negro has been given two frames of reference within which he has had to place himself. His metaphysics, or, less pretentiously, his customs and the sources on which they were based, were wiped out because they were in conflict with a civilization that he did not know and that imposed itself on him.

The black man among his own in the twentieth century does not know at what moment his inferiority comes into being through the other. Of course I have talked about the black problem with friends, or, more rarely, with American Negroes. Together we protested, we asserted the equality of all men in the world. In the Antilles there was also that little gulf that exists among the almost-white, the mulatto, and the nigger. But I was satisfied with an intellectual understanding of these differences. It was not really dramatic. And then. ...

And then the occasion arose when I had to meet the white man's eyes. An unfamiliar weight burdened me. The real world challenged my claims. In the white world the man of color encounters difficulties in the development of his bodily schema. Consciousness of the body is solely a negating activity. It is a third-person consciousness. The body is surrounded by an atmosphere of certain uncertainty. I know that if I want to smoke, I shall have to reach out my right arm and take the pack of cigarettes lying at the other end of the table. The matches, however, are in the drawer on the left, and I shall have to lean back slightly. And all these movements are made not out of habit but out of implicit knowledge. A slow composition of my *self* as a body in the middle of a spatial and temporal world – such seems to be the schema. It does not impose itself on me; it is, rather, a definitive structuring of the self and of the world – definitive because it creates a real dialectic between my body and the world.

For several years certain laboratories have been trying to produce a serum for "denegrification"; with all the earnestness in the world, laboratories have sterilized their test tubes, checked their scales, and embarked on researches that might make it possible for the miserable Negro to whiten himself and thus to throw off the burden of that corporeal malediction. Below the corporeal schema I had sketched a historico-racial schema. The elements that I used had been provided for me not by "residual sensations and perceptions primarily of a tactile, vestibular, kinesthetic, and visual character,"[3] but by the other, the white man, who had woven me out of a thousand details, anecdotes, stories. I thought that what I had in hand was to construct a physiological self, to balance space, to localize sensations, and here I was called on for more.

"Look, a Negro!" It was an external stimulus that flicked over me as I passed by. I made a tight smile.

"Look, a Negro!" It was true. It amused me.

"Look, a Negro!" The circle was drawing a bit tighter. I made no secret of my amusement.

"Mama, see the Negro! I'm frightened!" Frightened! Frightened! Now they were beginning to be afraid of me. I made up my mind to laugh myself to tears, but laughter had become impossible.

I could no longer laugh, because I already knew that there were legends, stories, history, and above all *historicity*, which I had learned about from Jaspers. Then, assailed at various points, the corporeal schema crumbled, its place taken by a racial epidermal schema. In the train it was no longer a question of being aware of my body in the third person but in a triple person. In the train I was given not one but two, three places. I had already stopped being amused. It was not that I was finding febrile coordinates in the world. I existed triply: I occupied space. I moved toward the other ... and the evanescent other, hostile but not opaque, transparent, not there, disappeared. Nausea. ...

I was responsible at the same time for my body, for my race, for my ancestors. I subjected myself to an objective examination, I discovered my blackness, my ethnic characteristics; and I was battered down by tom-toms, cannibalism, intellectual deficiency, fetishism, racial defects, slave-ships, and above all else, above all: "Sho' good eatin'."

On that day, completely dislocated, unable to be abroad with the other, the white man, who unmercifully imprisoned me, I took myself far off from my own presence, far indeed, and made myself an object. What else could it be for me but an amputation, an excision, a hemorrhage that spattered my whole body with black blood? But I did not want this revision, this thematization. All I wanted was to be a man among other men. I wanted to come lithe and young into a world that was ours and to help to build it together.

But I rejected all immunization of the emotions. I wanted to be a man, nothing but a man. Some identified me with ancestors of mine who had been enslaved or lynched: I decided to accept this. It was on the universal level of the intellect that I understood this inner kinship – I was the grandson of slaves in exactly the same way in which President Lebrun was the grandson of tax-paying, hard-working peasants. In the main, the panic soon vanished.

In America, Negroes are segregated. In South America, Negroes are whipped in the streets, and Negro strikers are cut down by machine-guns. In West Africa, the Negro is an animal. And there beside me, my neighbor in the university, who was born in Algeria, told me: "As long as the Arab is treated like a man, no solution is possible."

"Understand, my dear boy, color prejudice is something I find utterly foreign. ... But of course, come in, sir, there is no color prejudice among us. ... Quite, the Negro is a man like ourselves. ... It is not because he is black that he is less intelligent than we are. ... I had a Senegalese buddy in the army who was really clever. ..."

Where am I to be classified? Or, if you prefer, tucked away?

"A Martinican, a native of 'our' old colonies."

Where shall I hide?

"Look at the nigger! ... Mama, a Negro! ... Hell, he's getting mad. ... Take no notice, sir, he does not know that you are as civilized as we. ..."

My body was given back to me sprawled out, distorted, recolored, clad in mourning in that white winter day. The Negro is an animal, the Negro is bad, the Negro is mean, the Negro is ugly; look, a nigger, it's cold, the nigger is shivering, the nigger is shivering because he is cold, the little boy is trembling because he is afraid of the nigger, the nigger is shivering with cold, that cold that goes through your bones, the handsome little boy is trembling because he thinks that the nigger is quivering with rage, the little white boy throws himself into his mother's arms: Mama, the nigger's going to eat me up.

All round me the white man, above the sky tears at its navel, the earth rasps under my feet, and there is a white song, a white song. All this whiteness that burns me. . . .

I sit down at the fire and I become aware of my uniform. I had not seen it. It is indeed ugly. I stop there, for who can tell me what beauty is?

Where shall I find shelter from now on? I felt an easily identifiable flood mounting out of the countless facets of my being. I was about to be angry. The fire was long since out, and once more the nigger was trembling.

"Look how handsome that Negro is! . . ."

"Kiss the handsome Negro's ass, madame!"

Shame flooded her face. At last I was set free from my rumination. At the same time I accomplished two things: I identified my enemies and I made a scene. A grand slam. Now one would be able to laugh.

The field of battle having been marked out, I entered the lists.

What? While I was forgetting, forgiving, and wanting only to love, my message was flung back in my face like a slap. The white world, the only honorable one, barred me from all participation. A man was expected to behave like a man. I was expected to behave like a black man – or at least like a nigger. I shouted a greeting to the world and the world slashed away my joy. I was told to stay within bounds, to go back where I belonged.

They would see, then! I had warned them, anyway. Slavery? It was no longer even mentioned, that unpleasant memory. My supposed inferiority? A hoax that it was better to laugh at. I forgot it all, but only on condition that the world not protect itself against me any longer. I had incisors to test. I was sure they were strong. And besides. . . .

What! When it was I who had every reason to hate, to despise, I was rejected? When I should have been begged, implored, I was denied the slightest recognition? I resolved, since it was impossible for me to get away from an *inborn complex*, to assert myself as a BLACK MAN. Since the other hesitated to recognize me, there remained only one solution: to make myself known.

In *Anti-Semite and Jew* (p. 95), Sartre says: "They [the Jews] have allowed themselves to be poisoned by the stereotype that others have of them, and they live in fear that their acts will correspond to this stereotype. . . . We may say that their conduct is perpetually overdetermined from the inside."

All the same, the Jew can be unknown in his Jewishness. He is not wholly what he is. One hopes, one waits. His actions, his behavior are the final determinant. He is a white man, and, apart from some rather debatable characteristics, he can sometimes go unnoticed. He belongs to the race of those who since the beginning of time have never known cannibalism. What an idea, to eat one's father! Simple enough, one has only not to be a nigger. Granted, the Jews are harassed – what am I thinking of? They are hunted down, exterminated, cremated. But these are little family quarrels. The Jew is disliked from the moment he is tracked down. But in my case everything takes on a *new* guise. I am given no chance. I am overdetermined from without. I am the slave not of the "idea" that others have of me but of my own appearance.

I move slowly in the world, accustomed now to seek no longer for upheaval. I progress by crawling. And already I am being dissected under white eyes, the only real eyes. I am *fixed*. Having adjusted their microtomes, they objectively cut away slices of my reality. I am laid bare. I feel, I see in those white faces that it is not a new man who has come in, but a new kind of man, a new genus. Why, it's a Negro!

[…]

The Negro and Recognition

> Self-consciousness exists in itself and for itself, in that and by the fact that it exists for another self-consciousness; that is to say, it is only by being acknowledged or recognized.
>
> Hegel, *The Phenomenology of Mind*

Man is human only to the extent to which he tries to impose his existence on another man in order to be recognized by him. As long as he has not been effectively recognized by the other, that other will remain the theme of his actions. It is on that other being, on recognition by that other being, that his own human worth and reality depend. It is that other being in whom the meaning of his life is condensed.

There is not an open conflict between white and black. One day the White Master, *without conflict*, recognized the Negro slave.

But the former slave wants to *make himself recognized*.

At the foundation of Hegelian dialectic there is an absolute reciprocity which must be emphasized. It is in the degree to which I go beyond my own immediate being that I apprehend the existence of the other as a natural and more than natural reality. If I close the circuit, if I prevent the accomplishment of movement in two directions, I keep the other within himself. Ultimately, I deprive him even of this being-for-itself.

The only means of breaking this vicious circle that throws me back on myself is to restore to the other, through mediation and recognition, his human reality, which is different from natural reality. The other has to perform the same operation. "Action from one side only would be useless, because what is to happen can only be brought about by means of both. …"; "*they recognize themselves as mutually recognizing each other.*"[4]

In its immediacy, consciousness of self is simple being-for-itself. In order to win the certainty of oneself, the incorporation of the concept of recognition is essential.

Similarly, the other is waiting for recognition by us, in order to burgeon into the universal consciousness of self. Each consciousness of self is in quest of absoluteness. It wants to be recognized as a primal value without reference to life, as a transformation of subjective certainty (*Gewissheit*) into objective truth (*Wahrheit*).

When it encounters resistance from the other, self-consciousness undergoes the experience of *desire* – the first milestone on the road that leads to the dignity of the spirit. Self-consciousness accepts the risk of its life, and consequently it threatens the other in his physical being. "It is solely by risking life that freedom is obtained; only thus is it tried and proved that the essential nature of self-consciousness is not *bare existence*, is not the merely immediate form in which it at first makes its appearance, is not its mere absorption in the expanse of life."[5]

Thus human reality in-itself-for-itself can be achieved only through conflict and through the risk that conflict implies. This risk means that I go beyond life toward a supreme good that is the transformation of subjective certainty of my own worth into a universally valid objective truth.

As soon as I *desire* I am asking to be considered. I am not merely here-and-now, sealed into thingness. I am for somewhere else and for something else. I demand that notice be taken of my negating activity insofar as I pursue something other than life; insofar as I do battle for the creation of a human world – that is, of a world of reciprocal recognitions.

He who is reluctant to recognize me opposes me. In a savage struggle I am willing to accept convulsions of death, invincible dissolution, but also the possibility of the impossible.

The other, however, can recognize me without struggle: "The individual, who has not staked his life, may, no doubt, be recognized as a *person*, but he has not attained the truth of this recognition as an independent self-consciousness."[6]

Historically, the Negro steeped in the inessentiality of servitude was set free by his master. He did not fight for his freedom.

Out of slavery the Negro burst into the lists where his masters stood. Like those servants who are allowed once every year to dance in the drawing room, the Negro is looking for a prop. The Negro has not become a master. When there are no longer slaves, there are no longer masters.

The Negro is a slave who has been allowed to assume the attitude of a master.

The white man is a master who has allowed his slaves to eat at his table.

One day a good white master who had influence said to his friends, "Let's be nice to the niggers. ..."

The other masters argued, for after all it was not an easy thing, but then they decided to promote the machine-animal-men to the supreme rank of *men*.

Slavery shall no longer exist on French soil.

The upheaval reached the Negroes from without. The black man was acted upon. Values that had not been created by his actions, values that had not been born of the systolic tide of his blood, danced in a hued whirl round him. The upheaval did not make a difference in the Negro. He went from one way of life to another, but not from one life to another. Just as when one tells a much improved patient that in a few days he will be discharged from the hospital, he thereupon suffers a relapse, so the announcement of the liberation of the black slaves produced psychoses and sudden deaths.

It is not an announcement that one hears twice in a lifetime. The black man contented himself with thanking the white man, and the most forceful proof of the fact is the impressive number of statues erected all over France and the colonies to show white France stroking the kinky hair of this nice Negro whose chains had just been broken.

"Say thank you to the nice man," the mother tells her little boy ... but we know that often the little boy is dying to scream some other, more resounding expression. ...

The white man, in the capacity of master,[7] said to the Negro, "From now on you are free."

But the Negro knows nothing of the cost of freedom, for he has not fought for it. From time to time he has fought for Liberty and Justice, but these were always white liberty and white justice; that is, values secreted by his masters. The former slave, who can find in his memory no trace of the struggle for liberty or of that anguish of liberty of which Kierkegaard speaks, sits unmoved before the young white man singing and dancing on the tightrope of existence.

When it does happen that the Negro looks fiercely at the white man, the white man tells him: "Brother, there is no difference between us." And yet the Negro *knows* that there is a difference. He *wants* it. He wants the white man to turn on him and shout: "Damn nigger." Then he would have that unique chance – to "show them. ..."

But most often there is nothing – nothing but indifference, or a paternalistic curiosity.

The former slave needs a challenge to his humanity, he wants a conflict, a riot. But it is too late: The French Negro is doomed to bite himself and just to bite. I say "the French Negro," for the American Negro is cast in a different play. In the United States, the Negro battles and is battled. There are laws that, little by little, are invalidated under the Constitution. There are other laws that forbid certain forms of discrimination. And we can be sure that nothing is going to be given free.

There is war, there are defeats, truces, victories.

"The twelve million black voices" howled against the curtain of the sky. Torn from end to end, marked with the gashes of teeth biting into the belly of interdiction, the curtain fell like a burst balloon.

On the field of battle, its four corners marked by the scores of Negroes hanged by their testicles, a monument is slowly being built that promises to be majestic.

And, at the top of this monument, I can already see a white man and a black man *hand in hand*.

For the French Negro the situation is unbearable. Unable ever to be sure whether the white man considers him consciousness in-itself-for-itself, he must forever absorb himself in uncovering resistance, opposition, challenge.

This is what emerges from some of the passages of the book that Mounier has devoted to Africa.[8] The young Negroes whom he knew there sought to maintain their alterity. Alterity of rupture, of conflict, of battle.

The self takes its place by opposing itself, Fichte said. Yes and no.

I said in my introduction that man is a *yes*. I will never stop reiterating that.

Yes to life. *Yes* to love. *Yes* to generosity.

But man is also a *no*. *No* to scorn of man. *No* to degradation of man. *No* to exploitation of man. *No* to the butchery of what is most human in man: freedom.

Man's behavior is not only reactional. And there is always resentment in a *reaction*. Nietzsche had already pointed that out in *The Will to Power*.

To educate man to be *actional*, preserving in all his relations his respect for the basic values that constitute a human world, is the prime task of him who, having taken thought, prepares to act.

NOTES

1 *Charmes* (Paris: Gallimard, 1952).
2 *Le langage et l'agressivité*.
3 Jean Lhermitte, *L'Image de notre corps* (Paris: Nouvelle Revue critique, 1939), p. 17.
4 G. W. F. Hegel, *The Phenomenology of Mind*, trans. by J. B. Baillie, 2nd rev. edn. (London: Allen & Unwin, 1949), pp. 230, 231.
5 Ibid., p. 233.
6 Hegel, *Phenomenology of Mind*, p. 233.
7 I hope I have shown that here the master differs basically from the master described by Hegel. For Hegel there is reciprocity; here the master laughs at the consciousness of the slave. What he wants from the slave is not recognition but work.

   In the same way, the slave here is in no way identifiable with the slave who loses himself in the object and finds in his work the source of his liberation.

   The Negro wants to be like the master.

   Therefore he is less independent than the Hegelian slave.

   In Hegel the slave turns away from the master and turns toward the object.

   Here the slave turns toward the master and abandons the object.
8 Emmanuel Mounier, *L'éveil de l'Afrique noire* (Paris: Éditions du Seuil, 1948).

Chapter 29

The Paradoxes of Integration [1997]

Orlando Patterson

After two and a half centuries of slavery, followed by a century of rural semiserfdom and violently imposed segregation, wanton economic discrimination, and outright exclusion of Afro-Americans from the middle and upper echelons of the nation's economy, it was inevitable that when the nation finally committed itself to the goal of ethnic justice and integration the transition would be painful, if not traumatic. The prejudices of centuries die hard, and even when they wane, the institutional frameworks that sustained them are bound to linger.

What is more, Afro-Americans, like once-oppressed peoples and classes everywhere, were bound to develop strategies of survival and patterns of adaptation to their centuries of discrimination and exclusion that were to become dysfunctional under newer, less constrained circumstances. Only supermen remain unimpaired by sustained systemic and personal assault. Centuries of public dishonor and ritualized humiliation by Euro-Americans were also certain to engender deep distrust, not only of those who actively humiliated and exploited them, but of all those who passively benefited from their oppression, which is to say, all persons of European ancestry.

In light of all this, the achievements of the American people over the past half century in reducing racial prejudice and discrimination and in improving the socio-economic and political condition of Afro-Americans are nothing short of astonishing. Viewed from the perspective of comparative history and sociology, it

Orlando Patterson, "The Paradoxes of Integration," pp. 15–6, 64–6, 68–74, 76–7 from Orlando Patterson, *The Ordeal of Integration: Progress and Resentment in America's "Racial" Crisis.* Washington, DC: Perseus Books, LLC, Counterpoint Press, 1997. Copyright © 1997 by Orlando Patterson. Reprinted by permission of Basic Civitas Books, a member of The Perseus Books Group.

can be said, unconditionally, that the changes that have taken place in the United States over the past fifty years are unparalleled in the history of minority-majority relations. With the possible exception of the Netherlands – which is really too small to be meaningfully compared to America – there does not exist a single case in modern or earlier history that comes anywhere near the record of America in changing majority attitudes, in guaranteeing legal and political rights, and in expanding socio-economic opportunities for its disadvantaged minorities. […]

In what follows I attempt to make sense of the sociological knot of "race" in America, fraught with paradox at almost every turn. I argue that the present condition of Afro-Americans is itself paradoxical, and the perceptions of this condition and the attempts to understand it are further riddled with paradoxes and contradictions. Observing this is like watching the foreplay of two octopuses through the distorting window of a glass-bottom boat. They appear to be consuming each other when, in fact, they are really trying to connect. […]

The experiential and perceptual mismatch I have just described is exacerbated further by yet another paradox of changing ethnic relations, what I call the outrage of liberation. A formerly oppressed group's sense of outrage at what has been done to them increases the more equal they become with their former oppressors. This is, in part, simply a case of relative deprivation. It is also partly a result of having a greater voice – more literate and vocal leadership, more access to the media, and so on.

But it also reflects the formerly deprived group's increased sense of dignity and, ironically, its embrace of the formerly oppressive Other within its moral universe. The slave, the sharecropping serf, the Afro-American person living under Jim Crow laws administered by vicious Euro-American policemen and prejudiced judges – all were obliged, for reasons of sheer survival, to accommodate somehow to the system. One form of accommodation was to expect and demand less from the discriminating group. To do so was in no way to diminish one's contempt, even hatred and loathing, for the racist oppressors. Indeed, one's lowered expectations may even have been a sign of contempt.

In the discourse on racism, it has often been observed that one of its worst consequences is the denial of the Afro-American person's humanity. What often goes unnoticed is the other side of this twisted coin: that racism left most Afro-Americans persuaded that Euro-Americans were less than human. Technically clever, yes; powerful, well armed, and prolific, to be sure; but without an ounce of basic human decency. No one whose community of memory was etched with the vision of lynched, barbecued ancestors, no Afro-American person who has seen the flash of greedy, obsessive hatred in the fish-blue stare of a cracker's cocked eyes could help but question his inherent humanness. Most Afro-Americans, whatever their outward style of interaction with Euro-Americans, genuinely believed, as did the mother of Henry Louis Gates, that most Euro-Americans were inherently filthy and evil, or that, as the poet Sterling Brown once wrote, there was no place in heaven for "Whuffolks … being so onery," that indeed, for most of them "hell would be good enough – if big enough."

Integration, however partially, began to change all that. By disalienating the Other, the members of each group came, however reluctantly, to accept each other's humanness. But that acceptance comes at a price: for Euro-Americans, it is the growing sense of disbelief at what the nightly news brings in relentless detail from the inner cities. For Afro-Americans, it is the sense of outrage that someone truly human could have done what the evidence of over three and a half centuries makes painfully clear. Like a woman chased and held down in a pitch dark night who discovers, first to her relief, then to her disbelief, that the stranger recoiling from her in the horror of recognition had been her own brother, the moral embrace of integration is a liberation with a doubletake of outrage verging on incomprehension.

The Paradoxes of Ideology and Interpretation

The paradox of antiracist racism

A good part of the present turmoil in American ethnic relations – both the problem itself and the attempt to explain it – springs from the failure of Afro-American leaders to recognize the limits of one important, but risky and necessarily transitional, strategy in the struggle for ethnic equality. That strategy is itself a paradox, first described by Jean-Paul Sartre with the gripping phrase "anti-racist racism."

What Sartre was getting at is the fact that any group that has experienced centuries of racial hatred and oppression has, of necessity, to go through a period of self-liberation in which it draws attention to, and even celebrates, the very thing that was used against it. Afro-Americans had no choice but to emphasize their Afro-Americanness in mobilizing against the iniquities of a system that discriminated against them because they were Afro-American. And after centuries of being brainwashed by every symbol and medium of the dominant culture into a sense of their own inferiority and unattractiveness, it was inevitable that Afro-Americans go through a process of psychological liberation that entailed not just the denial of their worthlessness but some emphasis on the positive worth of being Afro-American.

What was true on the psychological level held equally on the economic and political fronts. Some recognition of "race" had to inform policies aimed at alleviating centuries of racial injuries. It is disingenuous in the extreme to argue – as Euro-American and Afro-American conservatives do – that because the ideal of the civil rights movement, and of all persons of ethnic good will, is a color-blind world, any policy that takes account of African ancestry betrays this ideal.

Fire, as the old saying goes, can sometimes only be fought with fire. The Afro-American identity movements and some form of affirmative action were the inevitable social fires that had to be ignited in the fight against the centuries-long holocaust of Euro-American racism.

We are approaching the limits of the antiracist strategy in politics, but, tragically, Afro-American leaders now seem trapped by the fire they started. The results are disastrous for the mass of Afro-American people. Afro-American identity rhetoric and race-conscious politics not only have negative educational consequences but play straight into the hands of the most reactionary political forces in society. [...]

The paradox of the "one-drop" rule

Commitment to the risky strategy of antiracist racism partly explains another ethnic paradox, although sheer cultural and political inertia and elite self-interest may be as important in understanding it. This is the persistence of what once went by the name of the "one-drop" rule. America is unusual among Western Hemisphere societies in its traditional commitment to a binary conception of race. Despite the fact that the vast majority of non-Euro-American persons of African ancestry are mixed, all persons with the proverbial "one drop" of African ancestry are classified as "black."

This unusual mode of racial classification has a vicious ideological history rooted in the notion of "racial" purity and in the racist horror of miscegenation. Traditionally, it was used as a major ideological bulwark of legalized segregation, and was at the heart of the "white" supremacist opposition to any form of integration. There is no gainsaying the fact that this conception of "race" historically rationalized the most pernicious legal, social, and political injustices against Afro-Americans.

An important aspect of contemporary ethnic change is the fact that this binary conception of "race" is under siege, for reasons I will mention shortly. The paradox is that the two groups of Americans now most committed to its survival are "white" supremacists and most Afro-American intellectual and political leaders!

First, we should note the social factors undermining the one-drop rule. One was the integrationist ideal of the early phase of the civil rights movement. By definition, this struggle called into question the one-drop "purist" rule. Integrating schools meant accepting the prospect of mixed dating, the ultimate anathema of "white" supremacists. The direct assault on antimiscegenation laws, culminating in their prohibition by the Supreme Court, implicitly attacked the one-drop rule.

Of even greater importance, however, have been the demographic and cultural changes resulting from the current wave of immigration with the inflow of mainly brown-skinned Latin Americans and Asians. Previous immigrants played by the binary rule as soon as they landed on these shores: those who were visibly brown, such as West Indians, were assimilated into the Afro-American population whether they wished to be or not (and most did not, coming from societies in which minute, socially meaningful distinctions of color were the norm). Those who were visibly or vaguely "white" eagerly sought membership within the Caucasian chalk circle and were usually welcomed as long as they could prove no trace of African "blood." Indeed, "whiteness," or rather non-"blackness," became a powerful unifying force in the integration of immigrants who previously never imagined that they had anything so important in common. Swarthy Sicilians and Arabs now found themselves one with blond Northern Europeans, Irish Catholics with English Protestants, formerly persecuted Jews with Gentiles, refugees from Communist Eastern Europe and Cuba with Western Europeans – all were united in the great "white republic" of America by virtue simply of not being tainted by one drop of the despised Afro-American blood. The demonization of blackness in the one-drop rule not only served the interests of "white" supremacists but was a major unifying force in the rise of this great democracy of the non-blacks.

This pernicious system of racial ideology worked only as long as there were no ambiguous third "races" to muddy the binary construction. Native Americans were not only too small in numbers but also, cut off on reservations, out of sight and out of mind. All this was to change with the massive inflow of brown people. The sheer strength of their numbers was enough to bring the binary conception of "race" into question. In addition, the new wave of immigrants refused to play by the binary game. Unlike previous Latin immigrants, recently arrived Latinos insist that they are neither "white" nor "black." And Asians not only look different but are usually sufficiently proud of their distinctive somatic type not to want to play the binary game either. East Indians are the main exceptions.

In recent years, there has also been a significant increase in children of mixed Afro-American and Euro-American parentage. Although still small proportionately, their absolute numbers have been growing phenomenally. The census found 1.5 million mixed marriages in 1990, with 2 million children claiming mixed ancestry. They are also disproportionately middle and upper class and are concentrated in the major metropolitan centers. They have recently broken ranks with the established Afro-American leadership in insisting on being classified for what they are: mixed. In July 1996 they held a Multiracial Solidarity March in Washington to register their demand for a census category recognizing their mixed heritage.

All these developments have had a profound impact on the nation's traditional conception of ethnic norms and ideals. The traditionally staid Census Bureau has now become what one report calls a "political hotbed" as numerous groups challenge the five official racial and ethnic categories in use since 1977. The most cursory review of recent media images and of intermarriage rates clearly indicates that the nation's traditional Western European somatic norm is being replaced by a mixed or "morphed" type that is a blend of darker-skinned and lighter-skinned peoples. Shadowing this development has been a similar change in the physical-beauty ideal from its traditional Nordic image to one that reflects a mix. Euro-Americans increasingly risk skin cancer and the plastic surgeon's knife to acquire darker skin and larger, more trans-Saharan lips. And whatever Afrocentrists or multiculturalists may say, the huge proportion of their incomes that Afro-Americans devote to processing and lengthening their hair indicates an appearance ideal that is neither European nor African but something in-between, more like Tiger Woods, the ultimate hybrid prodigy in whom America sees its somatic future.

In the face of all this, it is odd that the orthodox line among Afro-American leaders is now a firm commitment to the one-drop rule. The extent to which Afro-American leaders will go to defend what was once a cardinal principle of "white" supremacy is best illustrated by the position of the National Association of Black Social Workers on "transracial" adoption. Not only is the group adamantly opposed to such adoption on the grounds that it constitutes what the social workers claim to be a form of "genocide," but many of their spokespeople imply that it is better for an Afro-American child to suffer the hardship and impoverishment of multiple foster families and state wardship than to be subjected to adoption by Euro-American middle-class parents. Astonishingly, both the Congressional Black

Caucus and a number of liberal Euro-American politicians have been intimidated into accepting this blatantly racist and cruel dogma. It is one of the many ironies and paradoxes of modern American ethnic politics that it took a Republican-controlled Congress to legislate against it.

Afro-Americans offer two main reasons in defense of the one-drop rule. One is the Afrocentrist position that it is good to preserve the Africanness of the Afro-American population. "Blackness" is to be celebrated as a virtue in itself. While Afrocentrists are at least honest enough to openly acknowledge this, many more established Afro-Americans are uncomfortable with the idea for the simple reason that it is merely the Afro-American version of the Euro-American purist position.

More commonly heard is the political defense of the one-drop rule: the fact that a recognition of the mixed segment of the Afro-American population will dilute the demographic and political base of Afro-Americans. There is something amiss, even circular, in this argument. If mixed persons choose to identify with other non-Euro-Americans politically – as many of them insist they do – there is nothing to fear, since they will continue to join forces with all such non-Euro-Americans. But if their insistence on a separate identification entails separate political interests, it is undemocratic and possibly illegal to force them to continue doing so. I strongly suspect that most ordinary Afro-Americans would just as soon say "good riddance" to any group of light-skinned non-Euro-Americans wishing to dissociate themselves from an "Afro-American" identity, a point made with some emphasis in Spike Lee's *School Daze*.

Ironically, a study conducted by the Census Bureau in 1995 on this subject indicated that, should the "multiracial" category be included, Afro-American leadership has nothing to fear concerning the dilution of their political base. While 1.5 percent of the surveyed population identified themselves as "multiracial," the proportion identifying themselves as Afro-American was not affected by the introduction of the multiracial option in the list of "racial" categories.

The paradox of liberal racialization in academic and public discourse

A strange contradiction has emerged in liberal discourse and studies of "race" in America. It is somewhat related to the one-drop paradox, but is more insidious and pervades all scholarship and popular writings on intergroup relations. Having demolished and condemned as racist the idea that observed group differences have any objective, biological foundation, the liberal intellectual community has revived the "race" concept as an essential category of human experience with as much ontological validity as the discarded racist notion of biologically distinct groups.

The paradox lies hidden in the seemingly innocent distinction between "race" and ethnicity. Almost all social scientists, social commentators, and journalists, not to mention ordinary Americans, now routinely use the terms *race* and *ethnicity* as if they referred to different, if related, social things. My question is, why do we need the term *race* at all? What explains its nonredundancy in the phrase "race and ethnic relations"? Trying to understand why social scientists, in particular, insist on making this distinction leads us into a Pandora's box of liberal contradictions and unwitting racism.

The standard liberal explanation is that "race," while not meaningful biologically, is nonetheless important because people believe it to be important, and this has severe consequences in "multiracial" societies such as our own. The problem with this explanation is that the same holds true for "ethnic" differences and prejudices. Why then distinguish between the terms *racial* and *ethnic*? The conventional response is that ethnic distinctions and prejudices, while admittedly similar in their believed-in and self-fulfilling nature, nonetheless differ from "racial" distinctions and beliefs because they refer not to observed and believed-in "physical" differences, but to observed and believed-in cultural ones. The object of a false belief, then, is what justifies the distinction even among speakers who recognize and reject its falseness. "Racial" beliefs, the argument goes, are based on observed differences that, while not biologically salient, are outwardly real and somehow immutable, and this differentiates interactions and beliefs pertaining to racial differences from those pertaining to ethnic differences. Afro-Americans, we often hear, cannot hide or conceal their "blackness," whereas in Irish-WASP or Jewish-Gentile relations such visible markers are absent. Furthermore, "racial" relations are also held to be more intense, conflict ridden, and horrible in their consequences for the believed-to-be inferior "race."

Is any of this true? On the one hand, as the psychoanalyst Michael Vannoy Adams recently noted, "People differ much more culturally than they do naturally. And there is no necessary connection between psychical differences and physical differences. The reason that natural categories like color are so useless (except to racists, for whom they are all too useful) is that they convey very little, if any, information about significant psychical differences. [...]

The simple truth of the matter is that however similar people may look to outsiders, those who believe that there are differences tend to have very little difficulty identifying the believed-in different group and to see gross physical differences that outsiders find it hard to identify. Indeed, the comparative data on inter-group relations strongly suggest that wherever people believe that there are important differences between them, they tend to interpret these differences as biologically grounded. [...]

Not only do people find it easy to make "racial" or believed-in socially meaningful physical distinctions where none seem to exist (to outsiders), but they have an equally powerful capacity not to make these distinctions, even when they seem strikingly obvious to outsiders. The classic case in point here is one we have discussed already: America's one-drop rule. The Afro-American population is somatically extremely varied. Nonetheless, we categorize and perceive of them as a single type in our binary system of racial beliefs. If Afro-Americans and Euro-Americans find it so easy not to see differences where outward differences are so manifestly present, there is no reason to believe that they lack the capacity to see no differences between the groups categorized as "Afro-American" and "white." That they recognize differences is clearly a matter of cultural and political beliefs and of an identity that is, like all others, part chosen and part imposed.

What, then, is the basis of the distinction between the "racial" and the "ethnic"? We must conclude that making this distinction is itself a belief, a distinctively

American belief, an essential part of American racist ideology. The distinction, we now see, plays a crucial role in maintaining the binary conception of "race" that prevails in America, and remains the foundation of racist and purist dividing lines between Americans. This is its only linguistic function. It conceptually bedevils the meaning of integration.

So the question we must now ask is this: If the history of relations between peoples has been, as the distinguished American anthropologist Virginia Dominguez correctly puts it, "the continuous historical pattern of determining race by man-made law rather than by processes of nature," why on earth are American social scientists (presumably the most liberal group in the nation) actively promoting a purist conception of "race"?

Could it be that these emperors of liberalism really have no clothes? Do these mainly Euro-American social scientists find the "racial" identity of "whiteness" so deeply gratifying, so essential a part of their understanding of themselves as true-blue Americans, that they unwittingly promote a distinction that is implicitly racist? Why is it not enough to be simply Jewish-American, Anglo-American, Irish-American, or, if one so chooses, just plain American? Why the added need for "white-Jewish American," "white-Anglo-American" […] unless there remains the age-old American desire to define being truly American as not being that essential contradistinctive definition of oneself as "white": namely, "black." And have Afro-American social scientists and intellectuals so rejected the ideal of integration and so mistakenly committed themselves to a racialized identity that they are prepared to reinforce this racist distinction? Why is it not enough to be simply, and gloriously, Afro-American or, if one so chooses, just plain American, which anyway is already a good deal Afro-American?

We must resolve this paradox if we are serious about achieving the ideal of integration, and we can do so simply by dropping the distinction and all that it implies. All this requires is a little clear thinking. The distinction between "race" and ethnicity is only meaningful if we wish to reinforce the racist belief that Euro-Americans and Afro-Americans are, indeed, biologically and immutably different. The distinction invigorates the salience of "race" in our private and public life. And by legitimizing the binary conception of "race," the distinction perpetuates, to the detriment of Afro-Americans (the self-serving disagreements of their political leadership notwithstanding), the nastiest dogma from our painful ethnic past.

Part VIII

Sociological Theory of Jürgen Habermas

Introduction to Part VIII

30 Modernity: An Unfinished Project

31 The Rationalization of the Lifeworld

32 Civil Society and the Political Public Sphere

Introduction to Part VIII

The importance of Jürgen Habermas for contemporary social theory is in part due to renewed interest in the Frankfurt School in the 1960s and 1970s (see Part VI in *Classical Sociological Theory*). The resurgence of critical theory and the ensuing debates had a number of intellectual consequences. One was that a new field of cultural studies inspired by a linguistic turn emerged that critically analyzed the mass media and the way that the field of cultural representations was shaped by prevailing relations of power. In this new field figures associated with the Frankfurt School's critical theory proved influential, especially Theodor Adorno and Walter Benjamin. The field of cultural studies in turn provided a terrain for the development of a new philosophical movement known as postmodernism (see Part IX in this volume). In his dialogue with these developments, Habermas has become one of the most important theorists of communication in society, of politics after Marxism, and of the role of public discourse in shaping political life.

In the 1970s and 1980s, a new group of postmodern thinkers were critical of what they saw as Enlightenment-inspired philosophical obsessions with reason, universalism, and totality that suppressed social and cultural differences alongside more spontaneous emotional and cultural expression (see Part IX). For them, modern thought had privileged a distinct category of elite actors possessed of the tools of scientific analysis and the techniques of rationalization. This domination was justified by a "regime of truth": scientific discourses and progressivism that promised the improvement of society. Figures such as Jean-François Lyotard and Michel Foucault suggested that in a contemporary world that was increasingly socially and culturally fragmented and in which the manifest irrationality of unchecked scientific reason was plainly evident, modernity's "metanarratives" – the shared stories through which claims to truth are made and modern institutions are legitimated – were being exhausted.

Contemporary Sociological Theory, Third Edition. Edited by Craig Calhoun, Joseph Gerteis, James Moody, Steven Pfaff, and Indermohan Virk. Editorial material and organization © 2012 John Wiley & Sons, Ltd. Published 2012 by John Wiley & Sons, Ltd.

The crisis of the modern metanarratives of progress, universal prosperity, and the objectivity of science meant that the Enlightenment had to be rethought or abandoned. Postmodernism further posed a direct challenge to Western Marxism by rejecting the notion of an objective standpoint of knowledge, that reason was embedded in history, and by casting doubt on discourses of social liberation. In response to these critiques, Habermas warns against the pessimism, conservatism, and exaggerations of much postmodern thought. As he expresses in his address, "Modernity: An Unfinished Project" (excerpted below), we should readily concede the failures and limitations of the Enlightenment, yet see the best hope for human emancipation in its correction and completion rather than in its repudiation by anti-liberal and conservative thinkers. Battling both conservative pessimism and radical critique, Habermas develops a theoretical system devoted to revealing the *possibility* of reason, emancipation, and rational-critical communication embedded in modern liberal institutions and in the human capacities to communicate, deliberate, and pursue rational interests.

Life and Work

Habermas (b. 1929) is closely associated with the second generation of the Frankfurt School (see Part VI of *Classical Sociological Theory*). After completing his dissertation in 1956, he worked at the Institute for Social Research at the University of Frankfurt. At Frankfurt he studied under Theodor Adorno and hoped to write his *Habilitation*, or second dissertation, which is required for the position of professor in the German university system. In spite of his evident abilities, however, Adorno and Max Horkheimer considered Habermas's work too politically engaged and insufficiently critical for their support. Habermas, too, apparently had serious intellectual differences with these leading lights of the Frankfurt School, who in his view had become paralyzed with political skepticism and by disdain for modern culture. This estrangement occurred in spite of the fact that Habermas considers Adorno and Horkheimer's *The Dialectic of Enlightenment* to be one of the most influential books in his philosophical development.

Habermas went on to do work firmly rooted in the German philosophical tradition, drawing not only on the Frankfurt School and Western Marxism, but also on the thought of Max Weber (see Part IV of *Classical Sociological Theory*), Wilhelm Dilthey and the neo-Kantians, systems theorists such as Talcott Parsons (see Part VII in the same volume) and Niklas Luhmann. Moving away from what he saw as the *dis*engagement of Adorno and Horkheimer, Habermas embarked on the lifelong project of reshaping critical theory along the lines of its original intentions as a "theory of society conceived with a practical intention." Habermas's thought has developed in two principal directions. The first has been to develop a more comprehensive theory of reason, intersubjective communication, and practical understanding. The second has been to elaborate and defend a conception of the rational or emancipated society.

In many ways, Habermas's work begins with the sociology of knowledge. In *Knowledge and Human Interests* (1972) Habermas is critical of how ideology distorts communication and undercuts the validity of knowledge. Unlike Marx, however, Habermas maintains that a purely objective, unmediated "purely scientific" knowledge is impossible. Nevertheless, he identifies three cognitive areas where interests generate knowledge. These may be *instrumental* knowledge linked to science and oriented towards reliability, prediction, and causal analysis, *practical* knowledge linked to communication, understanding, and interpretation, and *emancipatory* knowledge linked to criticism, self-reflection, liberation, and utopian visions.

Habermas contends that philosophy plays a vital role in the social sciences. It furnishes the capacity to construct ethical claims and to introduce normative considerations into the practice of science. Through social science, philosophy abandons its remove from society and becomes an applied discipline. But this is not enough. Philosophy has a hermeneutical function in understanding experience and practical knowledge alongside the abstract, rational knowledge that is the domain of science. The task of a critical theorist is to move between the empirical facts of the social world and the normative and philosophical motives that inspire social inquiry.

Social change in contemporary industrial societies has also been an area of lifelong concern for Habermas. In his magnum opus *The Theory of Communicative Action* (2 volumes, 1984), excerpted below, Habermas criticizes the one-sided process of modernization led by forces of economic and administrative rationalization. Humans are endowed with the capacity for language and the basic normative consensus that is implied by the structure of language and in speech rules. Reconstructing this competence allows Habermas to escape the trap of relativism, in which there are an endless number of possible standpoints and competing truth claims. He points out that there is an underlying presumption of validity invested in the act of intersubjective communication in which actors observe practical rules of conversation. Habermas points out that in everyday situations actors routinely seek to convince others who do not share their standpoint and that these others are sometimes persuaded. This suggests that actors in communication do recognize that there is a truth that is not reducible to the identity of the speaker. In their efforts to make their interests and identities known and recognized, actors thus make rational collective action and self-determination possible.

Habermas traced the growing intervention of formal systems in the everyday lives of people. As rationalizing technologies and agencies penetrate the "lifeworld" centered on social reproduction, cultural transmission, and socialization, crises result. This increasing regulation and reorganization of private life, the family, and intimate relations is caused by the parallel development of the administrative functions of the welfare state, on the one hand, and, on the other, to the expanding power and influence of corporate capitalism and mass consumption. Under attack from transformed material and administrative relations, the lifeworld's ability to generate intersubjective understanding decays. The modern crisis is thus often misidentified as a crisis whose roots are cultural rather than as one that takes expression through the lifeworld but originates in the rationalization of formal systems.

Analysis of Politics and Society

Much of Habermas's work is concerned with achieving a rational and emancipated society. In an important early work, *The Structural Transformation of the Public Sphere*, Habermas explored the origins, radical potential, and ultimate degeneration of the bourgeois public sphere of the eighteenth century. It was this public sphere of rational debate on matters of political importance that helped to make parliamentary democracy possible and which promoted Enlightenment ideals of equality, human rights, and justice. Habermas described this sphere in terms of both the actual infrastructure that supported it and the norms and practices that helped critical political discourse flourish. The European public sphere formed in the urban culture of the seventeenth century with its coffee houses, intellectual and literary salons, and the print news media. In this nascent public sphere communication was guided by a norm of rational argumentation and critical discussion in which the strength of argument was more important than the identity of the speaker. Although Habermas tracked the decay of the public sphere as an institution with industrialization and the rise of the mass popular media, it nevertheless provided him with a historical example of a public culture guided by the exercise of reason.

As Habermas observes in "Civil Society and the Political Public Sphere," excerpted here, democratic political life only thrives where institutions enable citizens to debate matters of public importance. What is necessary then, is to craft norms and institutions in a way that supports free communication. Habermas evokes the counterfactual "ideal speech situation" in which actors are equally endowed with the capacities of discourse, recognize each other's basic social equality, and in which their speech is completely undistorted by ideology or misrecognition. Habermas is not claiming that this ideal ever fully obtains in practice but rather that it provides a heuristic tool that empowers critical analysis of actual social communication and provides a utopian ideal after which people can strive.

Indeed, Habermas contends that as routinized political parties and interest groups substitute for personal autonomy and participation, society is increasingly administered at a level remote from the input of citizens. As a result, the boundaries between public and private, the individual and society, the system and the lifeworld, begin to collapse. Habermas saw the student revolt of the 1960s, feminism and civil rights, and ecology and the New Social Movements of the 1980s as attempts by citizens to resist the penetration of the system into everyday life and to assert demands for public recognition. Against the rule of expert administrators and executives, these were efforts by citizens to exert an influence over society, to steer government in a more humane direction, and to empower the disenfranchised by changing public opinion.

In recent work such as *Between Facts and Norms*, Habermas defends Kant's ethical vision of the liberal state as a "community of free citizens". Habermas sees the law as an instrument with which principles of universalism and individual rights are pratically – if not always happily – reconciled. In modern liberal societies in which tightly knit communal relations and religious world-views pluralize and fray, law becomes the principal medium through which stability and social control are exercised. But alongside this regulatory function, the law also provides a set of discourses and practices that are designed to ensure individual rights and the limits of governmental authority. Although universal adherence to like world-views and norms is impossible in a secular world, law provides a new foundation for society by providing a common idiom of communication, contending between competing claims to validity and promoting the practical resolution of conflicts. Given rational deliberation and protection of individual rights, a society of free subjects can be achieved as long as individuals defer to the rules of legal contention. Habermas believes that law – strictly bound by constitutional norms – can thus help to overcome the old dualism between individual autonomy and the maintenance of community.

Today, the threat to democratic polities and the social welfare arises in the struggle for capitalist globalization. Citizens can only defend themselves from the decay of national welfare-state institutions and a globalizing capitalism, Habermas contends, by moving towards a new model of social solidarity beyond the nation-state. This "cosmopolitan solidarity" recognizes that the shared community of fate obtains between diverse peoples confronted with common risks of exploitation, domination, and ecological degradation. Hope lies in a new era of political community that transcends ethnic and cultural likenesses for one based on the equal rights and obligations of vested citizens. This requires more than just a "constitutional patriotism" whereby citizens pledge to honor the political community on the basis of their joint normative and practical investment of the law and deliberative government. Essential to this is an activist public sphere where matters of common interest can be discussed, political issues deliberated, and the force of public opinion brought to bear on the administrative-political system. These matters are not merely abstractions for Habermas; he has been an important advocate for the development of a democratic European Union that would move beyond economic integration to form a new transnational polity.

Habermas's Continuing Influence

Habermas has been criticized for inadequate exploration of the problem of difference in social theory. The ideal speech situation that Habermas imagines is one in which actors "bracket" their social differences and cultural identities in favor of impersonal reason. Critics counter that this simply reproduces liberalism's public–private dualism and argue that to do so would mean renouncing much of what is meaningful about communication and do nothing to address the persistent inequalities among actors that constrain their actual exercise of voice. Others maintain that Habermas's ideal of citizenship privileges a certain type of deliberative and critical discourse over other forms of expression, thereby narrowing the range, content, and creativity of the public sphere. Still others claim that his efforts to resolve the problem of reason through communication ethics remain idealistic and unconvincing.

Against these criticisms Habermas contends that the ideal speech situation is not a reality but a useful counterfactual against which distortion can be measured. And he insists that the logic of self-discovery is primarily a private and intimate process of the lifeworld but is always in dialogue with other voices in the public sphere. The "politics of recognition" have become a chief concern of public culture and provide some opportunity for the discussion of matters of universal concern.

For Habermas, this means the challenge of rescuing Enlightenment from its decay into the oppressive forces of rationalization that Adorno and Horkheimer (and Weber before them, see Parts VI and VII respectively, in *Classical Sociological Theory*) decried. He contends that reason needs to be recovered not only from the forces of rationalization and disenchantment, conformity and order, but also from the reaction against it that takes flight in relativism, nihilism, political romanticism, and hedonism. In Habermas's view the implications of contemporary philosophical debates are of dire importance. His ideas are used not only to explore philosophical and theoretical issue, but also in analytical studies of communications and media, the sociology of law, and political sociology. Habermas is a much-read essayist and public critic, particularly in his native Germany. With the rise of the Internet and discussion of "virtual" communities and cyber democracy, Habermas's work takes on special importance as we debate the meaning and ethics of new forms of communication and new indirect social relationships.

His work reminds us of the ongoing importance of philosophically informed politics, an orientation obvious in Habermas's involvement in public debates on questions relating to politics, social reform, European integration, and an honest confrontation with the crimes of Germany's past. In a sense, this is the hallmark of critical theory properly understood: the philosopher not only interpreting the world but being fully of it and in it.

SUGGESTED READINGS

Benhabib, Seyla (ed.). 1997. *Habermas and the Unfinished Project of Modernity*. Cambridge, MA: MIT Press. (This edited volume contains Habermas's address of the same title along with essays on the theme by a number of sympathetic critics.)

Berstein, Richard J. (ed.). 1985. *Habermas and Modernity*. Cambridge, MA: MIT Press. (A valuable collection of essays on the social and political thought of Habermas.)

Calhoun, Craig (ed.). 1992. *Habermas and the Public Sphere*. Cambridge, MA: MIT Press. (An excellent introduction to Habermas's theory of the public sphere, including critical commentary from a number of important authors. Valuable also for Habermas's thoughtful response to his critics in the conclusion of the volume.)

Dews, Peter (ed.). 1999. *Habermas: A Critical Reader*. London: Basil Blackwell. (An introductory essay provides a useful summary of Habermas's philosophical contribution along with essays on a wide variety of topics by some of the most important critics.)

Habermas, Jürgen. 1972. *Knowledge and Human Interests*. Boston, MA: Beacon Press. (Habermas's key statement on epistemology and the sociology of knowledge.)

Habermas, Jürgen. 1984. *The Theory of Communicative Action* (two volumes). Boston, MA: Beacon Press. (In this two-volume work, Habermas examines reason and the rationalization of society and the lifeworld as a site of practical knowledge, experience, and resistance.)

Habermas, Jürgen. 1987. *The Philosophical Discourse of Modernity*. Cambridge, MA: MIT Press. (In these twelve essays, Habermas criticizes postmodernism and an array of critics of modern society ranging from Horkheimer and Adorno to Michel Foucault.)

Habermas, Jürgen. 1991. *The Structural Transformation of the Public Sphere*. Cambridge, MA: MIT Press. (Habermas's most historical work, tracing the rise and fall of a democratic, bourgeois public culture in the Age of Enlightenment.)

Habermas, Jürgen. 1996. *Between Facts and Norms*. Cambridge, MA: MIT Press. (In a fascinating and wide-ranging study, Habermas develops his discursive theory of law and democracy and points to constitutional patriotism, pluralism, and the institution of law as foundations for a rational society.)

McCarthy, Thomas A. 1978. *The Critical Theory of Jürgen Habermas*. Cambridge, MA: MIT Press. (One of the best single-volume introductions to the philosophy of Habermas by one of the most prominent scholars and translators of his work.)

Chapter 30

Modernity: An Unfinished Project [1980]

Jürgen Habermas

[...]

The Old and the New

Anyone who, like Adorno, conceives of "modernity" as beginning around 1850 is perceiving it through the eyes of Baudelaire and avant-garde art. Let me elucidate this concept of cultural modernity with a brief look at its long prehistory, which has already been illuminated by Hans Robert Jausse.[1] The word "modern" was first employed in the late fifth century in order to distinguish the present, now officially Christian, from the pagan and Roman past. With a different content in each case, the expression "modernity" repeatedly articulates the consciousness of an era that refers back to the past of classical antiquity precisely in order to comprehend itself as the result of a transition from the old to the new. This is not merely true for the Renaissance, with which the "modern age" begins *for us*; people also considered themselves as "modern" in the age of Charlemagne, in the twelfth century, and in the Enlightenment – in short, whenever the consciousness of a new era developed in Europe through a renewed relationship to classical antiquity. In the process culminating in the celebrated *querelle des anciens et des modernes*, the dispute with

Jürgen Habermas, "Modernity: An Unfinished Project," pp. 39–40, 42–6, 53–5 from Jürgen Habermas, *Habermas and the Unfinished Project of Modernity*, edited by Maurizio Passerin d'Entrèves and Seyla Benhabib. Cambridge: Polity Press, 1996. Copyright © 1996. Reprinted by permission of The MIT Press and Polity Press.

Contemporary Sociological Theory, Third Edition. Edited by Craig Calhoun, Joseph Gerteis, James Moody, Steven Pfaff, and Indermohan Virk. Editorial material and organization © 2012 John Wiley & Sons, Ltd. Published 2012 by John Wiley & Sons, Ltd.

the protagonists of a classicistic aesthetic taste in late seventeenth-century France, it was always *antiquitas*, the classical world, which was regarded as the normative model to be imitated. It was only the French Enlightenment's ideal of perfection and the idea, inspired by modern science, of the infinite progress of knowledge and the advance towards social and moral improvement that gradually lifted the spell exercised on the spirit of these *early* moderns by the classical works of antiquity. And finally, in opposing the classical and the romantic to one another, modernity sought its own past in an idealized vision of the Middle Ages. In the course of the nineteenth century *this* Romanticism produced a radicalized consciousness of modernity that detached itself from all previous historical connection and understood itself solely in abstract opposition to tradition and history as a whole.

At this juncture, what was considered modern was what assisted the spontaneously self-renewing historical contemporaneity of the *Zeitgeist* to find its own objective expression. The characteristic feature of such works is the moment of novelty, the New, which will itself be surpassed and devalued in turn by the innovations of the next style. Yet whereas the merely modish becomes outmoded once it is displaced into the past, the modern still retains a secret connection to the classical. The "classical" has always signified that which endures through the ages. The emphatically "modern" artistic product no longer derives its power from the authority of a past age, but owes it solely to the authenticity of a contemporary relevance that has now become past. This transformation of contemporary relevance into a relevance now past has both a destructive and a constructive aspect. As Jauss has observed, it is modernity itself that creates its own classical status – thus we can speak today of "classical modernity" as if such an expression were obvious. Adorno opposes any attempted distinction between "modernity" and "modernism" because he believes that "without the characteristic subjective mentality inspired by the New no objective modernity can crystallize at all."[2]

[…]

Cultural Modernity and Social Modernization

Of course, it is not possible simply to conjure up authoritative beliefs from nowhere. That is why analyses of this kind only give rise, as the sole practical recommendation, to the sort of postulate we have also seen in Germany: namely, an intellectual and political confrontation with the intellectual representatives of cultural modernity. And here I quote Peter Steinfels, a perceptive observer of the new style which the neoconservatives succeeded in imposing on the intellectual scene in the 1970s:

> The struggle takes the form of exposing every manifestation of what could be considered an oppositionist mentality and tracing its "logic" so as to link it to various expressions of extremism: drawing the connection between modernism and nihilism … between government regulation and totalitarianism, between criticism of arms expenditures and subservience to Communism, between women's liberation or homosexual rights and the destruction of the family … between the Left generally and terrorism, anti-Semitism, and fascism.[3]

Peter Steinfels is referring here only to the United States, but the parallels with our situation are very obvious. The personalizing of debate and the degree of bitterness that characterize the abuse of intellectuals stirred up by those hostile to the Enlightenment cannot adequately be explained in psychological terms, since they are grounded rather in the internal conceptual weakness of neoconservative thought itself.

Neoconservatism displaces the burdensome and unwelcome consequences of a more or less successful capitalist modernization of the economy on to cultural modernity. It obscures the connections between the processes of social modernization, which it welcomes, on the one hand, and the crisis of motivation, which it laments, on the other, and fails to reveal the sociostructural causes of transformed attitudes to work, of consumer habits, of levels of demand and of the greater emphasis given to leisure time. Thus neoconservatism can directly attribute what appear to be hedonism, a lack of social identification, an incapacity for obedience, narcissism, and the withdrawal from competition for status and achievement to a culture which actually plays only a very mediated role in these processes. In place of these unanalysed causes, it focuses on those intellectuals who still regard themselves as committed to the project of modernity. It is true that Daniel Bell does perceive a further connection between the erosion of bourgeois values and the consumerism characteristic of a society which has become orientated towards mass production. But even Bell, seemingly unimpressed by his own argument, traces the new permissiveness back first and foremost to the spread of a lifestyle which originally emerged within the elite countercultures of bohemian artists. This is obviously only another variation on a misunderstanding to which the avant-garde itself had already fallen prey – the idea that the mission of art is to fulfill its implicit promise of happiness by introducing into society as a whole that artistic lifestyle that was defined precisely as its opposite.

Concerning the period in which aesthetic modernity emerged, Bell remarks that "radical in economics, the bourgeoisie became conservative in morals and cultural taste."[4] If this were true, one might see neoconservatism as a return to the old reliable pattern of the bourgeois mentality. But that is far too simple: the mood to which neoconservatism can appeal *today* by no means derives from a discontent with the antinomian consequences of a culture that has transgressed its boundaries and escaped from the museum back into life. This discontent is not provoked by the modernist intellectuals, but is rooted rather in much more fundamental reactions to a process of social modernization which, under pressure from the imperatives of economic growth and state administration, intervenes further and further into the ecology of developed forms of social life, into the communicative infrastructure of the historical lifeworlds. Thus neopopulist protests are merely giving forceful expression to widespread fears concerning the possible destruction of the urban and the natural environments, and the destruction of humane forms of social life. Many different occasions for discontent and protest arise wherever a one-sided process of modernization, guided by criteria of economic and administrative rationality, invades domains of life which are centred on the task of cultural transmission, social integration, socialization and education, domains orientated towards quite *different* criteria, namely towards those of communicative rationality. But it is from just these social processes that the neoconservative doctrines distract our attention, only to project the causes which they have left shrouded in obscurity on to an intrinsically subversive culture and its representatives.

It is quite true that cultural modernity also generates its own aporias. And those intellectual positions which hasten to proclaim postmodernity, to recommend a return to premodernity, or which radically repudiate modernity altogether, all appeal to these aporias. Thus, apart from the problematic social consequences of *social* modernization, it is true that certain reasons for doubt or despair concerning the project of modernity *also* arise from the *internal perspective* of cultural development.

The Project of Enlightenment

The idea of modernity is intimately bound up with the development of European art, but what I have called the project of modernity only comes into clear view when we abandon the usual concentration on art. Max Weber characterized cultural modernity in terms of the separation of substantive reason, formerly expressed in religious and metaphysical world-views, into three moments, now capable of being connected only formally with one another (through the form of argumentative justification). In so far as the world-views have disintegrated and their traditional problems have been separated off under the perspectives of truth, normative rightness and authenticity or beauty, and can now be treated in each case as questions of knowledge, justice or taste respectively, there arises in the modern period a differentiation of the value spheres of science and knowledge, of morality and of art. Thus scientific discourse, moral and legal enquiry, artistic production and critical practice are now institutionalized within the corresponding cultural systems as the concern of experts. And this professionalized treatment of the cultural heritage in terms of a single abstract consideration of validity in each case serves to bring to light the autonomous structures intrinsic to the cognitive-instrumental, the moral-practical and the aesthetic-expressive knowledge complexes. From now on there will also be *internal* histories of science and knowledge, of moral and legal theory, and of art. And although these do not represent linear developments, they none the less constitute learning processes. That is one side of the issue.

On the other side, the distance between these expert cultures and the general public has increased. What the cultural sphere gains though specialized treatment and reflection does not *automatically* come into the possession of everyday practice without more ado. For with cultural rationalization, the lifeworld, once its traditional substance has been devalued, threatens rather to become *impoverished*. The project of modernity as it was formulated by the philosophers of the Enlightenment in the eighteenth century consists in the relentless development of the objectivating sciences, of the universalistic foundations of morality and law, and of autonomous art, all in accord with their own immanent logic. But at the same time it also results in releasing the cognitive potentials accumulated in the process from their esoteric high forms and attempting to apply them in the sphere of praxis, that is, to encourage the rational organization of social relations. Partisans of the Enlightenment such as Condorcet could still entertain the extravagant expectation that the arts and sciences would not merely promote the control of the forces of nature, but also further the understanding of self and world, the progress of morality, justice in social institutions, and even human happiness.

Little of this optimism remains to us in the twentieth century. But the problem has remained, and with it a fundamental difference of opinion as before: should we continue to hold fast to the intentions of the Enlightenment, however fractured they may be, or should we rather relinquish the entire project of modernity? If the cognitive potentials in question do not merely result in technical progress, economic growth and rational administration, should we wish to see them checked in order to protect a life praxis still dependent on blind traditions from any unsettling disturbance?

Even among those philosophers who currently represent something of an *Enlightenment rearguard*, the project of modernity appears curiously fragmented. Each thinker puts faith in only one of the moments into which reason has become differentiated. Karl Popper, and I refer here to the theorist of the open society who has not yet allowed himself to be appropriated by the neoconservatives, holds firmly to the potentially enlightening capacity of scientific criticism when extended into the political domain. But for this he pays the price of a general moral scepticism and a largely indifferent attitude to the aesthetic dimension. Paul Lorenzen is interested in the question as to how an artificial language methodically constructed in accordance with practical reason can effectively contribute to the reform of everyday life. But his approach directs all science and knowledge along the narrow path of justification analogous to that of moral practice and he too neglects the aesthetic. In Adorno, on the other hand, the emphatic claim to reason has withdrawn into the accusatory gesture of the esoteric work of art, morality no longer appears susceptible to justification, and philosophy is left solely with the task of revealing, in an indirect fashion, the critical content sealed up within art.

The progressive differentiation of science and knowledge, morality and art, with which Max Weber characterized the rationalism of Western culture, implies *both* the specialized treatment of special domains *and* their detachment from the current of tradition, which continues to flow on in a quasi-natural fashion in the hermeneutic medium of everyday life. This detachment is the problem which is generated by the autonomous logic of the differentiated value spheres. And it is this detachment which has also provoked abortive attempts to "sublate" the expert cultures which accompany it, a phenomenon most clearly revealed in the domain of art.

[...]

Three Conservatisms

Unless I am mistaken, the prospects for this are not encouraging. Virtually throughout the Western world a climate of opinion has arisen which promotes tendencies highly critical of modernism. The disillusionment provoked by the failure of programmes for the false sublation of art and philosophy, and the openly visible aporias of cultural modernity, have served as a pretext for various conservative positions. Let me briefly distinguish here the antimodernism of the Young Conservatives from the premodernism of the Old Conservatives, on the one hand, and the postmodernism of the New Conservatives, on the other.

The *Young Conservatives* essentially appropriate the fundamental experience of aesthetic modernity, namely the revelation of a decentred subjectivity liberated from all the constraints of cognition and purposive action, from all the imperatives of labour and use value, and with this they break out of the modern world altogether. They establish an implacable opposition to modernism precisely through a modernist attitude. They locate the spontaneous forces of imagination and self-experience, of affective life in general, in what is most distant and archaic, and in Manichaean fashion oppose instrumental reason with a principle accessible solely to evocation, whether this is the will to power or sovereignty, Being itself or the Dionysian power for the poetic. In France this tradition leads from Georges Bataille through Foucault to Derrida. Over all these figures hovers, of course, the spirit of Nietzsche, newly resurrected in the 1970s.

The *Old Conservatives* do not allow themselves to be contaminated by cultural modernity in the first place. They observe with mistrust the collapse of substantive reason, the progressive differentiation of science, morality and art, the modern understanding of the world and its purely procedural canons of rationality, and recommend instead a return to positions *prior* to modernity (something which Max Weber regarded as a regression to the stage of material rationality). Here it is principally contemporary neo-Aristotelianism which has enjoyed some success, encouraged by the ecological question to renew the idea of a cosmological ethic. This tradition, which begins with Leo Strauss, has produced the interesting works of Hans Jonas and Robert Spaemann, for example.

It is the *New Conservatives* who relate most affirmatively to the achievements of modernity. They welcome the development of modern science so long as it only oversteps its own sphere in order to promote technological advance, capitalist growth and a rational form of administration. Otherwise, they recommend a politics directed essentially at defusing the explosive elements of cultural modernity. According to one claim, science, once properly understood, has already become meaningless as far as orientation in the lifeworld is concerned. According to another, politics should be immunized as much as possible from the demands of moral-practical legitimation. And a third claim affirms the total immanence of art, contests the idea of its utopian content, and appeals to its fictive character, precisely in order to confine aesthetic experience to the private sphere. One could mention the early

Wittgenstein, Carl Schmitt in his middle period, and the later Gottfried Benn in this connection. With the definitive segregation of science, morality and art into autonomous spheres split off from the lifeworld and administered by specialists, all that remains of cultural modernity is what is left after renouncing the project of modernity itself. The resulting space is to be filled by traditions which are to be spared all demands for justification. Of course, it remains extremely difficult to see how such traditions could continue to survive in the modern world without the governmental support of ministries of culture.

Like every other typology, this too is a simplification, but it may be of some use for the analysis of contemporary intellectual and political controversies. For I fear that antimodernist ideas, coupled with an element of premodernism, are gaining ground in the circles of the greens and other alternative groups. On the other hand, in the changing attitudes within the political parties there is evidence of a similar turn, namely of an alliance between the advocates of postmodernity and those of premodernity. It seems to me that no one political party has a monopoly on neoconservative attitudes and the abuse of intellectuals. [...]

NOTES

This is the first complete English translation of the original version of a speech given by Habermas in September 1980, when he was awarded the Adorno Prize by the City of Frankfurt. The German text was published in Habermas's *Kleine Politische Schriften I–IV* (Frankfurt: Suhrkamp, 1981). Translated by Nicholas Walker.

1 "Literarische Tradition und gegenwärtiges Bewusstsein der Moderne", in H. R. Jauss, *Literaturgeschichte als Provokation* (Frankfurt: Suhrkamp, 1970), pp. 11ff.
2 T. W. Adorno, "Ästhetische Theorie", in *Gesammelte Werke*, vol. 7 (Frankfurt: Suhrkamp, 1970), p. 45.
3 Peter Steinfels, *The Neoconservatives* (New York: Simon & Schuster, 1979), p. 65.
4 Daniel Bell, *The Cultural Contradictions of Capitalism* (London: Heinemann, 1979), p. 17.

Chapter 31

The Rationalization of the Lifeworld [1981]

Jürgen Habermas

1 The Concept of the Lifeworld and the Hermeneutic Idealism of Interpretive Sociology

I would like to explicate the concept of the lifeworld, and to this end I shall pick up again the threads of our reflection on communication theory. It is not my intention to carry further our formal-pragmatic examination of speech acts and of communicative action; rather, I want to build upon these concepts so far as they have already been analyzed, and take up the question of how the lifeworld – as the horizon within which communicative actions are "always already" moving – is in turn limited and changed by the structural transformation of society as a whole.

I have previously introduced the concept of the lifeworld rather casually and only from a reconstructive research perspective. It is a concept complementary to that of communicative action. Like the phenomenological lifeworld analysis of the late Husserl,[1] or the late Wittgenstein's analysis of forms of life (which were not, to be sure, carried out with a systematic intent),[2] formal-pragmatic analysis aims

---

Jürgen Habermas, "The Rationalization of the Lifeworld," pp. 119–26, 136–45, 147–8, 150–2 from Jürgen Habermas, *The Theory of Communicative Action*, vol. 2: *Lifeworld and System: A Critique of Functionalist Reason*. Boston, MA: Beacon Press, 1981 by Jürgen Habermas. Translator's preface and translation © 1987 by Beacon Press. Originally published as *Theorie des kommunikativen Handelns, Band 2: Zur Kritik der funktionalistischen Vernunft*. © 1981 by Suhrkamp Verlag, Frankfurt am Main. Reprinted with permission of Beacon Press, Boston and Polity Press UK.

Contemporary Sociological Theory, Third Edition. Edited by Craig Calhoun, Joseph Gerteis, James Moody, Steven Pfaff, and Indermohan Virk. Editorial material and organization © 2012 John Wiley & Sons, Ltd. Published 2012 by John Wiley & Sons, Ltd.

at structures that, in contrast to the historical shapes of particular lifeworlds and life-forms, are put forward as invariant. With this first step we are taking into the bargain a separation of form and content. So long as we hold to a formal-pragmatic research perspective, we can take up questions that have previously been dealt with in the framework of transcendental philosophy – in the present context, we can focus our attention on structures of the lifeworld in general.

I should like to begin by (A) making clear how the lifeworld is related to those three worlds on which subjects acting with an orientation to mutual understanding base their common definitions of situations. (B) I will then elaborate upon the concept of the lifeworld present as a context in communicative action and relate it to Durkheim's concept of the collective consciousness. Certainly, it is not a concept that can be put to empirical use without further ado. (C) The concepts of the lifeworld normally employed in interpretive [*verstehenden*] sociology are linked with everyday concepts that are, to begin with, serviceable only for the narrative presentation of historical events and social circumstances. (D) An investigation of the functions that communicative action takes on in maintaining a structurally differentiated world originates from within this horizon. In connection with these functions, we can clarify the necessary conditions for a rationalization of the lifeworld. (E) This takes us to the limit of theoretical approaches that identify society with the lifeworld. I shall therefore propose that we conceive of society simultaneously as a system and as a lifeworld.

A. – In examining the ontological presuppositions of teleological, normatively regulated, and dramaturgical action in Chapter I, I distinguished three different actor-world relations that a subject can take up to something in a world – to something that either obtains or can be brought about in the one objective world, to something recognized as obligatory in the social world supposedly shared by all the members of a collective, or to something that other actors attribute to the speaker's own subjective world (to which he has privileged access). These actor-world relations turn up again in the pure types of action oriented to mutual understanding. By attending to the modes of language use, we can clarify what it means for a speaker, in performing one of the standard speech acts, to take up a pragmatic relation

- to something in the objective world (as the totality of entities about which true statements are possible); or
- to something in the social world (as the totality of legitimately regulated interpersonal relations); or
- to something in the subjective world (as the totality of experience to which a speaker has privileged access and which he can express before a public);

such that what the speech act refers to appears to the speaker as something objective, normative, or subjective. In introducing the concept of communicative action, I pointed out that the pure types of action oriented to mutual understanding are merely limit cases. In fact, communicative utterances are always embedded in various world relations at the same time. Communicative action relies on a cooperative process of interpretation in which participants relate simultaneously to something in the objective, the social, and the subjective worlds, even when they *thematically stress only one* of the three components in their utterances. Speaker and hearer use the reference system of the three worlds as an interpretive framework within which they work out their common situation definitions. They do not relate point-blank to something in a world but relativize their utterances against the chance that their validity will be contested by another actor. Coming to an understanding [*Verständigung*] means that participants in communication reach an agreement [*Einigung*] concerning the validity of an utterance; agreement [*Einverständnis*] is the intersubjective recognition of the validity claim the speaker raises for it. Even when an utterance clearly belongs only to one mode of communication and sharply thematizes one corresponding validity claim, all three modes of communication and the validity claims corresponding to them are internally related to each other. Thus, it is a rule of communicative action that when a hearer assents to a thematized validity claim, he acknowledges the other two implicitly raised validity claims as well – otherwise, he is supposed to make known his dissent. Consensus does not come about when, for example, a hearer accepts the *truth of an assertion* but at the same time doubts the sincerity of the speaker or the normative appropriateness of his utterance; the same holds for the case in which a speaker accepts the *normative validity of a command* but suspects the seriousness of the intent thereby expressed or has his doubts about the existential presuppositions of the action commanded (and thus about the possibility of carrying it out). The example of a command that the addressee regards as unfeasible reminds us that participants are always expressing themselves in situations that they have to define in common so far as they are acting with an orientation to mutual understanding. An older construction worker who sends a younger and newly arrived co-worker to fetch some beer, telling him to hurry it up and be back in a few minutes, supposes that the situation is clear to everyone involved – here, the younger worker and any other workers within hearing distance. The *theme* is the upcoming midmorning snack; taking care of the drinks is a *goal* related to this theme; one of the older workers comes up with the *plan* to send the "new guy," who, given his status, cannot easily get around this request. The informal group hierarchy of the workers on the construction site is the *normative framework* in which the one is allowed to tell the other to do something. The action situation is defined *temporally* by the upcoming break and *spatially* by the distance from the site to the nearest store. If the situation were such that the nearest store could not be reached by foot in a few minutes, that is, that the plan of action of the older worker could – at least under the conditions specified – only be carried out with an automobile (or other means of transportation), the person addressed might answer with: "But I don't have a car."

The background of a communicative utterance is thus formed by situation definitions that, as measured against the actual need for mutual understanding have to overlap to a sufficient extent. If this commonality cannot be presupposed, the actors have to draw upon the means of strategic action, with an orientation toward coming to a mutual understanding, so as to bring about a common definition of the situation or to negotiate one directly – which occurs in everyday communicative practice primarily in the form of "repair work." Even in cases where this is not necessary, every new utterance is a test: the definition of the situation implicitly proposed by the speaker is either confirmed, modified, partly suspended, or generally placed in question. This continual process of definition and redefinition involves correlating contents to worlds – according to what counts in a given instance as a consensually interpreted element of the objective world, as an intersubjectively recognized normative component of the social world, or as a private element of a subjective world to which someone has privileged access. At the same time, the actors demarcate themselves from these three worlds. With every common situation definition they are determining the boundary between external nature, society, and inner nature; at the same time, they are renewing the demarcation between themselves as interpreters, on the one side, and the external world and their own inner worlds, on the other.

So, for instance, the older worker, upon hearing the other's response, might realize that he has to revise his implicit assumption that a nearby shop is open on Mondays. It would be different if the younger worker had answered: "I'm not thirsty." He would then learn from the astonished reaction that beer for the midmorning snack is a norm held to independent of the subjective state of mind of one of the parties involved. Perhaps the newcomer does not understand the normative context in which the older man is giving him an order, and asks whose turn to get the beer it will be tomorrow. Or perhaps he is missing the point because he is from another region where the local work rhythm, that is, the custom of midmorning snack, is not familiar, and thus responds with the question: "Why should I interrupt my work *now*?" We can imagine continuations of this conversation indicating that one or the other of the parties changes his initial definition of the situation and brings it into accord with the situation definitions of the others. In the first two cases described above, there would be a regrouping of the individual elements of the situation, a Gestalt-switch: the presumed fact that a nearby shop is open becomes a subjective belief that turned out to be false; what is presumed to be a desire to have beer with the midmorning snack turns out to be a collectively recognized norm. In the other two cases, the interpretation of the situation gets supplemented with respect to elements of the social world: the low man on the pole gets the beer; in this part of the world one has a midmorning snack at 9:00 A.M. These *redefinitions* are based on suppositions of commonality in respect to the objective, social, and each's own subjective world. With this reference system, participants in communication suppose that the situation definitions forming the background to an actual utterance hold intersubjectively.

Situations do not get "defined" in the sense of being sharply delimited. They always have a horizon that shifts with the theme. A *situation* is a segment of *lifeworld contexts of relevance* [*Verweisungszusammenhänge*] that is thrown into relief by themes and articulated through goals and plans of action; these contexts of relevance are concentrically ordered and become increasingly anonymous and diffused as the spatiotemporal and social distance grows. Thus, as regards our little scene with the construction workers, the construction site located on a specific street, the specific time – a Monday morning shortly before midmorning snack – and the reference group of co-workers who are at this site constitute the null point of a spatiotemporal and social reference system, of a world that is "within my actual reach." The city around the building site, the region, the country, the continent, and so on, constitute, as regards space, a "world within my potential reach"; corresponding to this, in respect to time, we have the daily routine, the life history, the epoch, and so forth; and in the social dimension, the reference groups from the family through the community, nation, and the like, to the "world society." Alfred Schutz again and again supplied us with illustrations of these spatiotemporal and social organizations of the lifeworld.[3]

The *theme* of an upcoming midmorning snack and the *plan* of fetching some beer, with regard to which the theme is broached, mark off a situation from the lifeworld of those directly involved. This action situation presents itself as a field of actual needs for mutual understanding and of actual options for action: the expectations the workers attach to midmorning snack, the status of a newly arrived younger co-worker, the distance of the store from the construction site, the availability of a car, and the like, belong to the elements of the situation. The facts that a single-family house is going up here, that the newcomer is a foreign "guest worker" with no social security, that another co-worker has three children, and that the new building is subject to Bavarian building codes are circumstances irrelevant to the given situation. There are, of course, shifting boundaries. That becomes evident as soon as the homeowner shows up with a case of beer to keep the workers in a good mood, or the guest worker falls from the ladder as he is getting ready to fetch the beer, or the theme of the new government regulations concerning child subsidies comes up, or the architect shows up with a local official to check the number of stories. In such cases, the theme shifts and with it the horizon of the situation, that is to say, the segment of the lifeworld relevant to the situation for which mutual understanding is required in view of the options for action that have been actualized. Situations have boundaries that can be overstepped at any time – thus Husserl introduced the image of the *horizon* that shifts according to one's position and that can expand and shrink as one moves through the rough countryside.[4]

For those involved, the action situation is the center of their lifeworld; it has a movable horizon because it points to the complexity of the lifeworld. In a certain sense, the lifeworld to which participants in communication belong is always present, but only in such a way that it forms the background for an actual scene. As soon as a *context of relevance* of this sort is brought into a situation, becomes part of a situation, it loses its triviality and unquestioned solidity. If, for instance, the fact that the new worker is not insured against accidental injury suddenly enters the domain of relevance of a thematic field, it can be explicitly mentioned – and in various illocutionary roles: a speaker can state that p; he can deplore or conceal that p; he can blame someone for the fact that p, and so on. When it becomes part of the situation, this state of affairs can be known and problematized as a fact, as the content of a norm or of a feeling, desire, and so forth. Before it becomes relevant to the situation, the same circumstance is given only in the mode of something taken for granted in the lifeworld, something with which those involved are intuitively familiar without anticipating the possibility of its becoming problematic. It is not even "known," in any strict sense, if this entails that it can be justified and contested. Only the limited segments of the lifeworld brought into the horizon of a situation constitute a thematizable context of action oriented to mutual understanding; only they appear under the category of *knowledge*. From a perspective turned toward the situation, the lifeworld appears as a reservoir of taken-for-granteds, of unshaken convictions that participants in communication draw upon in cooperative processes of interpretation. Single elements, specific taken-for-granteds, are, however, mobilized in the form of consensual and yet problematizable knowledge only when they become relevant to a situation.

If we now relinquish the basic concepts of the philosophy of consciousness in which Husserl dealt with the problem of the lifeworld, we can think of the lifeworld as represented by a culturally transmitted and linguistically organized stock of interpretive patterns. Then the idea of a "context of relevance" that connects the elements of the situation with one another, and the situation with the lifeworld, need no longer be explained in the framework of a phenomenology and psychology of perception.[5] Relevance structures can be conceived instead as interconnections of meaning holding between a given communicative utterance, the immediate context, and its connotative horizon of meanings. Contexts of relevance are based on *grammatically regulated* relations among the elements of a *linguistically organized* stock of knowledge.

If, as usual in the tradition stemming from Humboldt,[6] we assume that there is an internal connection between structures of lifeworlds and structures of linguistic worldviews, language and cultural tradition take on a certain transcendental status in relation to everything that can become an element of a situation. Language and culture neither coincide with the formal world concepts by means of which participants in communication together define their situations, nor do they appear as something innerworldly. Language and culture are constitutive for the lifeworld itself. They are neither one of the formal frames, that is, the worlds to which participants assign elements of situations, nor do they appear as something in the objective, social, or subjective worlds. In performing or understanding a speech act, participants are very much moving within their language, so that they cannot bring a present utterance *before themselves* as "something intersubjective," in the way they experience an event as something objective, encounter a pattern of behavior as something normative, experience or ascribe a desire or feeling as something subjective. The very medium of mutual understanding abides in a peculiar *half-transcendence*. So long as participants maintain their performative attitudes, the language actually in use remains *at their backs*. Speakers cannot take up an extramundane position in relation to it. The same is true of culture – of those patterns of interpretation transmitted in language. From a semantic point of view, language does have a peculiar affinity to linguistically articulated worldviews. Natural languages conserve the contents of tradition, which persist only in symbolic forms, for the most part in linguistic embodiment. For the semantic capacity of a language has to be adequate to the complexity of the stored-up cultural contents, the patterns of interpretation, valuation, and expression.

This stock of knowledge supplies members with unproblematic, common, background convictions that are assumed to be guaranteed; it is from these that contexts for processes of reaching understanding get shaped, processes in which those involved use tried and true situation definitions or negotiate new ones. Participants find the relations between the objective, social, and subjective worlds already preinterpreted. When they go beyond the horizon of a given situation, they cannot step into a void; they find themselves right away in another, now actualized, yet *preinterpreted* domain of what is culturally taken for granted. In everyday communicative practice there are no completely unfamiliar situations. Every new situation appears in a lifeworld composed of a cultural stock of knowledge that is "always already" familiar. Communicative actors can no more take up an extramundane position in relation to their lifeworld than they can in relation to language as the medium for the processes of reaching understanding through which their lifeworld maintains itself. In drawing upon a cultural tradition, they also continue it.

The category of the lifeworld has, then, a different status than the normal world-concepts dealt with above. Together with criticizable validity claims, these latter concepts form the frame or categorial scaffolding that serves to order problematic situations – that is, situations that need to be agreed upon – in a lifeworld that is already substantively interpreted. With the formal world-concepts, speakers and hearers can qualify the possible referents of their speech acts so that they can relate to something objective, normative, or subjective. The lifeworld, by contrast, does not allow for analogous assignments; speakers and hearers cannot refer by means of it to something as "something intersubjective." Communicative actors are always moving *within* the horizon of their lifeworld; they cannot step outside of it. As interpreters, they themselves belong to the lifeworld, along with their speech acts, but they cannot refer to "something in the lifeworld" in the same way as they can to facts, norms, or experiences. The structures of the lifeworld lay down the forms of the intersubjectivity of possible understanding. It is to them that participants in communication owe their extramundane positions vis-à-vis the innerworldly items about which they can come to an understanding. The lifeworld is, so to speak, the transcendental site where speaker and hearer meet, where they can reciprocally raise claims that their utterances fit the world (objective, social, or subjective), and where they can criticize and confirm those validity claims, settle their disagreements, and arrive at agreements. In a sentence: participants cannot assume *in actu* the same distance in relation to language and culture as in relation to the totality of facts, norms, or experiences concerning which mutual understanding is possible.

[...]

This intuitively accessible *concept of the sociocultural lifeworld* can be rendered theoretically fruitful if we can develop from it a reference system for descriptions and explanations relevant to the lifeworld as a whole and not merely to occurrences within it. Whereas narrative presentation refers to what is innerworldly, theoretical presentation is intended to explain the reproduction of the lifeworld itself. Individuals and groups maintain themselves by mastering situations; but how is the lifeworld, of which each situation forms only a segment, maintained? A narrator is already constrained grammatically, through the form of narrative presentation, to take an interest in the identity of the persons acting as well as in the integrity of their life-context. When we tell stories, we cannot avoid also saying indirectly how the subjects involved in them are faring, and what fate the collectivity they belong to is experiencing. Nevertheless, we can make harm to personal identity or threats to social integration visible only indirectly in narratives. While narrative presentations do point to higher-level reproduction processes – to the maintenance imperatives of lifeworlds – they cannot take as their theme the structures of a lifeworld the way they do with what happens in it. The everyday concept of the lifeworld that we bring to narrative presentation as a reference system has to be worked up for theoretical purposes in such a way as to make possible statements about the reproduction or self-maintenance of communicatively structured lifeworlds.

Whereas the lifeworld is given from the *perspective of participants* only as the horizon-forming context of an action situation, the everyday concept of the lifeworld presupposed in the *perspective of narrators* is already being used for cognitive purposes. To make it theoretically fruitful we have to start from those basic functions that, as we learned from Mead, the medium of language fulfills for the reproduction of the lifeworld. In coming to an understanding with one another about their situation, participants in interaction stand in a cultural tradition that they at once use and renew; in coordinating their actions by way of intersubjectively recognizing criticizable validity claims, they are at once relying on membership in social groups and strengthening the integration of those same groups; through participating in interactions with competently acting reference persons, the growing child internalizes the value orientations of his social group and acquires generalized capacities for action.

Under the functional aspect of *mutual understanding*, communicative action serves to transmit and renew cultural knowledge; under the aspect of *coordinating action*, it serves social integration and the establishment of solidarity; finally, under the aspect of *socialization*, communicative action serves the formation of personal identities. The symbolic structures of the lifeworld are reproduced by way of the continuation of valid knowledge, stabilization of group solidarity, and socialization of responsible actors. The process of reproduction connects up new situations with the existing conditions of the lifeworld; it does this in the *semantic* dimension of meanings or contents (of the cultural tradition), as well as in the dimensions of *social space* (of socially integrated groups), and *historical time* (of successive generations). Corresponding to these processes of *cultural reproduction, social integration*, and *socialization* are the structural components of the lifeworld: culture, society, person.

I use the term *culture* for the stock of knowledge from which participants in communication supply themselves with interpretations as they come to an understanding about something in the world. I use the term *society* for the legitimate orders through which participants regulate their memberships in social groups and thereby secure solidarity. By *personality* I understand the competences that make a subject capable of speaking and acting, that put him in a position to take part in processes of reaching understanding and thereby to assert his own identity. The dimensions in which communicative action extends comprise the semantic field of symbolic contents, social space, and historical time. The interactions woven into the fabric of every communicative practice constitute the medium through which culture, society, and person get reproduced. These reproduction processes cover the symbolic structures of the lifeworld. We have to distinguish from this the maintenance of the material substratum of the lifeworld.

Material reproduction takes place through the medium of the purposive activity with which sociated individuals intervene in the world to realize their aims. As Weber pointed out, the problems that actors have to deal with in a given situation can be divided into problems of "inner need" and problems of "outer need." To these categories of tasks as viewed from the perspective of action, there correspond, when the matter is viewed from the perspective of lifeworld maintenance, processes of symbolic and material reproduction.

I would like now to examine how different approaches to interpretative sociology conceive of society as a lifeworld. The structural complexity of a lifeworld, as it has revealed itself to our communication-theoretical analysis, does not come into view along this path. Whenever "the lifeworld" has been made a fundamental concept of social theory – whether under this name, as in Husserl and his followers, or under the title of "forms of life," "cultures," "language communities," or whatever – the approach has remained selective; the strategies of concept formation usually connect up with only one of the three structural components of the lifeworld.

Even the communication-theoretical reading I gave to Schutz's analysis suggests a concept of the lifeworld limited to aspects of mutual understanding and abridged in a culturalistic fashion. On this model, participants actualize on any given occasion some of the background convictions drawn from the cultural stock of knowledge; the process of reaching understanding serves the negotiation of common situation definitions, and these must in turn meet the critical conditions of an agreement accepted as reasonable. Cultural knowledge, insofar as it flows into situation definitions, is thus exposed to a test: it has to prove itself "against the world," that is, against facts, norms, experiences. Any revisions have an indirect effect on nonthematized elements of knowledge internally connected with the problematic contents. From this view, communicative action presents itself as an interpretive mechanism through which cultural knowledge is reproduced. The reproduction of the lifeworld consists essentially in a continuation and renewal of tradition, which moves between the extremes of a mere reduplication of and a break with tradition. In the phenomenological tradition stemming from Husserl and Schutz, the social theory based on such a culturalistically abridged concept of the lifeworld, when it is consistent, issues in a *sociology of knowledge*. This is the case, for instance, with Peter Berger and Thomas Luckmann, who state the thesis of *The Social Construction of Reality* as follows: "The basic contentions of the argument of this book are implicit in its title and subtitle, namely, that reality is socially constructed and that the sociology of knowledge must analyze the processes in which this occurs."[7]

The one-sidedness of the culturalistic concept of the lifeworld becomes clear when we consider that communicative action is not only a process of reaching understanding; in coming to an understanding about something in the world, actors are at the same time taking part in interactions through which they develop, confirm, and renew their memberships in social groups and their own identities. Communicative actions are not only processes of interpretation in which cultural knowledge is "tested against the world"; they are at the same time processes of social integration and of socialization. The lifeworld is "tested" in quite a different manner in these latter dimensions: these tests are not measured directly against criticizable validity claims or standards of rationality, but against standards for the solidarity of members and for the identity of socialized individuals. While participants in interaction, turned "toward the world," reproduce through their accomplishment of mutual understanding the cultural knowledge upon which they draw, they simultaneously reproduce their memberships in collectivities and their identities. When one of these other aspects shifts into the foreground, the concept of the lifeworld is again given a one-sided formulation: it is narrowed down either in an *institutionalistic* or in a *sociopsychological* fashion.

In the tradition stemming from Durkheim, social theory is based on a concept of the lifeworld reduced to the aspect of social integration. Parsons chooses for this expression "societal community"; he understands by it the lifeworld of a social group. It forms the core of every society, where "society" is understood as the structural component that determines the status – the rights and duties – of group members by way of legitimately ordered interpersonal relations. Culture and personality are represented only as functional supplements of the "social community": culture supplies society with values that can be institutionalized, and socialized individuals contribute motivations that are appropriate to normed expectations.

By contrast, in the tradition stemming from Mead, social theory is based on a concept of the lifeworld reduced to the aspect of the socialization of individuals. Representatives of symbolic interactionism, such as Herbert Blumer, A. M. Rose, Anselm Strauss, or R. H. Turner, conceive of the lifeworld as the sociocultural milieu of communicative action represented as role playing role taking, role defining, and the like. Culture and society enter into consideration only as media for the self-formative processes in which actors are involved their whole lives long. It is only consistent when the theory of society shrinks down then to *social psychology*.[8]

If, by contrast, we take the concept of symbolic interaction that Mead himself made central and work it out in the manner suggested above – as a concept of linguistically mediated, normatively guided interaction – and thereby gain access to phenomenological lifeworld analyses, then we are in a position to get at the complex interconnection of all three reproduction processes.

D. – The cultural reproduction of the lifeworld ensures that newly arising situations are connected up with existing conditions in the world in the semantic dimension: it secures a *continuity* of tradition and *coherence* of knowledge sufficient for daily practice. Continuity and coherence are measured by the *rationality* of the knowledge accepted as valid. This can be seen in disturbances of cultural reproduction that get manifested in a loss of meaning and lead to corresponding legitimation and orientation crises. In such cases, the actors' cultural stock of knowledge can no longer cover the need for mutual understanding that arises with new situations. The interpretive schemes accepted as valid fail, and the resource "meaning" becomes scarce.

The social integration of the lifeworld ensures that newly arising situations are connected up with existing conditions in the world in the dimension of social space: it takes care of coordinating actions by way of legitimately regulated interpersonal relations and stabilizes the identity of groups to an extent sufficient for everyday practice. The coordination of actions and the *stabilization of group identities* are measured by the *solidarity* among members. This can be seen in disturbances of social integration, which manifest themselves in *anomie* and corresponding conflicts. In such cases, actors can no longer cover the need for coordination that arises with new situations from the inventory of legitimate orders. Legitimately regulated social memberships are no longer sufficient, and the resource "social solidarity" becomes scarce.

Finally the socialization of the members of a lifeworld ensures that newly arising situations are connected up with existing situations in the world in the dimension of historical time: it secures for succeeding generations the acquisition of *generalized competences for action* and sees to it that *individual life histories are in harmony with collective forms of life*. Interactive capacities and styles of life are measured by the *responsibility of persons*. This can be seen in disturbances of the socialization process, which are manifested in psychopathologies and corresponding phenomena of alienation. In such cases, actors' competences do not suffice to maintain the intersubjectivity of commonly defined action situations. The personality system can preserve its identity only by means of defensive strategies that are detrimental to participating in social interaction on a realistic basis, so that the resource "ego strength" becomes scarce.

Once one has drawn these distinctions, a question arises concerning the contribution of the individual reproduction processes to maintaining the structural components of the lifeworld. If culture provides sufficient valid knowledge to cover the given need for mutual understanding in a lifeworld, the contributions of cultural reproduction to maintaining *the two other* components consist, on the one hand, in *legitimations* for existing institutions and, on the other hand, in *socialization patterns* for the acquisition of generalized competences for action. If society is sufficiently integrated to cover the given need for coordination in a lifeworld, the contribution of the integration process to maintaining *the two other* components consist, on the one hand, in *legitimately regulated social memberships* of individuals and, on the other, in moral duties or *obligations*: the central stock of cultural values institutionalized in legitimate orders is incorporated into a normative reality that is, if not criticism-proof, at least resistant to criticism and to this extent beyond the reach of continuous testing by action oriented to reaching understanding. If, finally,

Structural components / Reproduction processes	Culture	Society	Personality
Cultural reproduction	Interpretive schemes fit for consensus ("valid knowledge")	Legitimations	Socialization patterns Educational goals
Social integration	Obligations	Legitimately ordered interpersonal relations	Social memberships
Socialization	Interpretive accomplishments	Motivations for actions that conform to norms	Interactive capabilities ("personal identity")

Figure 31.1 Contributions of reproduction processes to maintaining the structural components of the lifeworld.

personality systems have developed such strong identities that they can deal on a realistic basis with the situations that come up in their lifeworld, the contribution of socialization processes to maintaining *the other two* components consists, on the one hand, in *interpretive accomplishments* and, on the other, in *motivations for actions that conform to norms* (see Figure 31.1).

The individual reproduction processes can be evaluated according to standards of the *rationality of knowledge*, the *solidarity of members*, and the *responsibility of the adult personality*. Naturally, the measurements within each of these dimensions vary according to the degree of structural differentiation of the lifeworld. The degree of differentiation also determines how great the need for consensual knowledge, legitimate orders, and personal autonomy is at any given time. Disturbances in reproduction are manifested in their own proper domains of culture, society, and personality as loss of meaning, anomie, and mental illness (psychopathology). There are corresponding manifestations of deprivation in the other domains (see Figure 31.2).

Structural components / Disturbances in the domain	Culture	Society	Person	Dimension of evaluation
Cultural reproduction	Loss of meaning	Withdrawal of legitimation	Crisis in orientation and education	Rationality of knowledge
Social integration	Unsettling of collective identity	Anomie	Alienation	Solidarity of memberships
Socialization	Rupture of tradition	Withdrawal of motivation	Psycho-pathologies	Personal responsibility

Figure 31.2 Manifestations of crisis when reproduction processes are disturbed (pathologies).

On this basis we can specify the functions that communicative action takes on in the reproduction of the lifeworld (see Figure 31.3). The highlighted areas along the diagonal in Figure 31.3 contain the characterizations with which we first demarcated cultural reproduction, social integration, and socialization from one another. In the meantime we have seen that *each* of these reproduction processes contributes in maintaining *all* the components of the lifeworld. Thus we can attribute to the medium of language, through which the structures of the lifeworld are reproduced, the functions set forth in Figure 31.3.

With these schematically summarized specifications, our communication-theoretical concept of the lifeworld has not yet attained the degree of explication of its phenomenological counterpart. Nonetheless, I shall leave it with this outline to return to the question of whether the concept of the lifeworld proposed here is fit to serve as a basic concept of social theory. Despite his many reservations, Schutz continued to hold to the approach of transcendental phenomenology. If one considers the method developed by Husserl to be unobjectionable, the claim to universality of

Reproduction processes \ Structural components	Culture	Society	Person
Cultural reproduction	Transmission, critique, acquisition of cultural knowledge	Renewal of knowledge effective for legitimation	Reproduction of knowledge relevant to child rearing, education
Social integration	Immunization of a central stock of value orientations	Coordination of actions via intersubjectively recognized validity claims	Reproduction of patterns of social membership
Socialization	Enculturation	Internalization of values	Formation of identity

Figure 31.3 Reproductive functions of action oriented to mutual understanding.

lifeworld analysis carried out phenomenologically goes without saying. However, once we introduce the concept of the lifeworld in communication-theoretical terms, the idea of approaching any society whatsoever by means of it is not at all trivial. The burden of truth for the universal validity of the lifeworld concept – a validity reaching across cultures and epochs – shifts then to the complementary concept of communicative action.

Mead attempted to reconstruct a sequence of stages of forms of interaction for the transition from the animal to the human. According to this reconstruction, communicative action is anthropologically fundamental; there are empirical reasons – and not merely methodological prejudgments – for the view that the structures of linguistically mediated, normatively guided interaction determine the starting point of sociocultural development. This also determines the range within which historical lifeworlds can vary. Questions of *developmental dynamics* cannot, of course, be answered by identifying structural restrictions of this sort. They can be dealt with only if we take contingent boundary conditions into account and analyze the interdependence between sociocultural transformations and changes in material reproduction. Nevertheless, the fact that sociocultural developments are subject to the structural constraints of communicative action can have a systematic effect. We can speak of a developmental logic – in the sense of the tradition stemming from Piaget, a sense that calls for further clarification – if the structures of historical lifeworlds vary within the scope defined by the structural constraints of communicative action not accidentally but directionally, that is, in dependence on learning processes. For instance, there would be a *directional variation of lifeworld structures* if we could bring evolutionary changes under the description of a structural differentiation between culture, society, and personality. One would have to postulate learning processes for such a structural differentiation of the lifeworld if one could show that this meant an increase in rationality.

The idea of the linguistification of the sacred has served us as a guiding thread for basing an interpretation of this sort on Mead and Durkheim. We can now reformulate this idea as follows: the further the structural components of the lifeworld and the processes that contribute to maintaining them get differentiated, the more interaction contexts come under conditions of rationally motivated mutual understanding, that is, of consensus formation that rests *in the end* on the authority of the better argument. Up to this point, we have considered Mead's utopian projection of a universal discourse in the special form of a communication community that allows for both self-realization and moral argumentation. Behind this, however, stands the more general idea of a situation in which the reproduction of the lifeworld is no longer merely routed *through* the medium of communicative action, but is saddled *upon* the interpretative accomplishments of the actors themselves. Universal discourse points to an idealized lifeworld reproduced through processes of mutual understanding that have been largely detached from normative contexts and transferred over to rationally motivated yes/no positions. This sort of growing autonomy can come to pass only to the extent that the constraints of material reproduction no longer hide behind the mask of a rationally impenetrable, basic, normative consensus, that is to say, behind the authority of the sacred. A lifeworld rationalized in this sense would by no means reproduce itself in conflict-free forms. But the conflicts would appear in their own names; they would no longer be concealed by convictions immune from discursive examination. Such a lifeworld would gain a singular transparency, inasmuch as it would allow only for situations in which adult actors distinguished between success-oriented and understanding-oriented actions just as clearly as between empirically motivated attitudes and rationally motivated yes/no positions.

[...]

Naturally, the progressive rationalization of the lifeworld, as it is described under different aspects by Weber, Mead, and Durkheim, does not at all guarantee that processes of reproduction will be free of disturbances. It is only the level at which disturbances can appear that shifts with the degree of rationalization. As his theses concerning the loss of meaning and freedom indicate, Weber geared his theory of rationalization precisely to diagnosing negative developments. In Mead we find echoes of a critique of instrumental reason,[9] though his studies in the theory of communication are primarily concerned with the orthogenesis of contemporary societies. Their pathogenesis was the stated target of Durkheim's theory of the division of labor. However, he was not able to connect the changing forms of social integration with stages of system differentiation so clearly as to be able to explain the "anomic division of labor," that is, the modern forms of anomie. If we understand the conflicts that Durkheim attributed to social disintegration more generally than he did, that is, as disturbances of reproduction in structurally quite differentiated lifeworlds, "organic solidarity" represents the normal form of social integration in a rationalized lifeworld. It lies on the plane of the symbolic structures of the lifeworld, as do the "abnormal forms" to which Durkheim dedicated Book 3 of *The Division of Labor in Society*.

The systemic mechanisms that Durkheim introduced under the rubric of "the division of labor" lie at another level. This raises the possibility of treating modern forms of anomie in connection with the question of how processes of system differentiation affect the lifeworld and possibly cause disturbances of its symbolic reproduction. In this way, phenomena of reification can also be analyzed along the lines of lifeworld deformations. The counter-Enlightenment that set in immediately after the French Revolution grounded a critique of modernity that has since branched off in different directions.[10] Their common denominator is the conviction that loss of meaning, anomie, and alienation – the pathologies of bourgeois society, indeed of posttraditional society generally – can be traced back to the rationalization of the lifeworld itself. This backward-looking critique is in essence a critique of bourgeois culture. By contrast, the Marxist critique of bourgeois society is aimed first at the relations of production, for it accepts the rationalization of the lifeworld and explains its deformation by the conditions of material reproduction. This materialist approach to disturbances in the symbolic reproduction of the lifeworld requires a theory that operates on a broader conceptual basis than that of "the lifeworld." It has to opt for a theoretical strategy that neither identifies the lifeworld with society as a whole, nor reduces it to a systemic nexus.

My guiding idea is that, on the one hand, the dynamics of development are steered by imperatives issuing from problems of self-maintenance, that is, problems of materially reproducing the lifeworld; but that, on the other hand, this societal development draws upon structural *possibilities* and is subject to structural *limitations* that, with the rationalization of the lifeworld, undergo systematic change in dependence upon corresponding learning processes. Thus the systems-theoretical perspective is relativized by the fact that the rationalization of the lifeworld leads to a directional variation of the structural patterns defining the maintenance of the system.

[...]

If we understand the integration of society exclusively as *social integration*, we are opting for a conceptual strategy that, as we have seen, starts from communicative action and construes society as a lifeworld. It ties social-scientific analysis to the internal perspective of members of social groups and commits the investigator to hermeneutically connect up his own understanding with that of the participants. The reproduction of society then appears to be the maintenance of the symbolic structures of the lifeworld. Problems of material reproduction are not simply filtered out of this perspective; maintenance of the material substratum of the lifeworld is a necessary condition for maintaining its symbolic structures. But processes of material reproduction come into view only from the perspective of acting subjects who are dealing with situations in a goal-directed manner; what gets filtered out are all the counterintuitive aspects of the nexus of societal reproduction. This limitation suggests an immanent critique of the hermeneutic idealism of interpretive sociology.

If, on the other hand, we understand the integration of society exclusively as *system integration*, we are opting for a conceptual strategy that presents society after the model of a self-regulating system. It ties social-scientific analysis to the external perspective of an observer and poses the problem of interpreting the concept of a system in such a way that it can be applied to interconnections of action. In Chapter VII we shall examine the foundations of social-scientific systems research; for now I want only to note that action systems are considered to be a special case of living systems. Living systems are understood as open systems, which maintain themselves vis-à-vis an unstable and hypercomplex environment through interchange processes across their boundaries. States of the system are viewed as fulfilling functions with respect to its maintenance.[11]

However, the conceptualization of societies cannot be so smoothly linked with that of organic systems, for, unlike structural patterns in biology, the structural patterns of action systems are not accessible to [purely external] observation; they have to be gotten at hermeneutically, that is, from the internal perspective of participants. The entities that are to be subsumed under systems-theoretical concepts from the external perspective of an observer must be identified beforehand as the lifeworlds of social groups and understood in their symbolic structures. The inner logic of the symbolic reproduction of the lifeworld, which we discussed from the standpoints of cultural reproduction, social integration, and socialization, results in *internal limitations* on the reproduction of the societies we view from the outside as boundary-maintaining systems. Because they are structures of a lifeworld, the structures important for the maintenance of a [social] system, those with which the identity of a society stands or falls, are accessible only to a reconstructive analysis that begins with the members' intuitive knowledge.

The fundamental problem of social theory is how to connect in a satisfactory way the two conceptual strategies indicated by the notions of "system" and "lifeworld." I shall leave this to one side for now and take it up again in the context of discussing Parson's work. Until then, we shall have to be content with a provisional concept of society as a system that has to fulfill conditions for the maintenance of sociocultural lifeworlds. The formula – societies are *systemically stabilized* complexes of action of *socially integrated* groups – certainly requires more detailed explanation; for the present, it may stand for the heuristic proposal that we view society as an entity that, in the course of social evolution, gets differentiated both as a system and as a lifeworld. Systemic evolution is measured by the increase in a society's steering capacity,[12] whereas the state of development of a symbolically structured lifeworld is indicated by the separation of culture, society, and personality.

NOTES

1. On the phenomenological concept of the lifeworld see L. Landgrebe, *Phänomenologie und Metaphysik* (Heidelberg, 1949), pp. 10ff.; and idem, *Philosophie der Gegenwart* (Bonn, 1952), pp. 65ff.; A. Gurwitsch, *The Field of Consciousness* (Pittsburg, 1964); G. Brand, *Welt, Ich und Zeit* (The Hague, 1955); H. Hohl, *Lebenswelt und Geschichte* (Freiburg, 1962); W. Lippitz, "Der phänomenologische Begriff der Lebenswelt," *Zeitschrift für Philosophische Forschung* 32 (1978): 416ff.; K. Ulmer, *Philosophie der modernen Lebensweht* (Tübingen, 1972).
2. On the sociological analysis of forms of life see P. Winch, *The Idea of a Social Science* (London, 1958); R. Rhees, *Without Answers* (New York, 1969); D. L. Phillips and H. O. Mounce, *Moral Practices* (London, 1970); H. Pitkin, *Wittgenstein and Justice* (Berkeley, 1972); P. McHugh et al., *On the Beginning of Social Inquiry* (London, 1974).
3. Alfred Schutz, *Collected Papers I: The Problem of Social Reality*, ed. M. Natanson (The Hague, 1962).
4. Cf. H. Kuhn, "The Phenomenological Concept of Horizon," in M. Faber, ed., *Philosophical Essays in Memory of E. Husserl* (Cambridge, MA, 1940), pp. 106ff.
5. E. Husserl, *Experience and Judgment* (Evanston, 1973). For a critique of the foundation in consciousness of Schutz's phenomenological ontology of the social, see Michael Theunissen, *The Other: Studies in the Social Ontology of Husserl, Heidegger, Sartre and Buber* (Cambridge, MA, 1984), pp. 345–52.
6. L. Weisgerber, *Die Muttersprache im Aufbau unserer Kultur* (Düsseldorf, 1957); R. Hoberg, *Die Lehre vom sprachlichen Feld* (Düsseldorf, 1970); H. Gipper, *Gibt es ein sprachliches Relativitätsprinzip?* (Frankfurt, 1972).
7. P. Berger and T. Luckmann, *The Social Construction of Reality* (Garden City, NY, 1967), p. 1.
8. Cf. A. M. Rose, ed., *Human Behavior and Social Processes* (Boston, 1962). The above-mentioned debate between ethnomethodology and symbolic interactionism can be traced back to the competition between one-sided, culturalistic and socialization-theoretical concepts of the lifeworld; see N. K. Denzin, "Symbolic Interactionism and Ethnomethodology," in Jack D. Douglas, ed., *Understanding Everyday Life* (London, 1971), pp. 259–84, versus D. H. Zimmerman and D. L. Wieder, "Ethnomethodology and the Problem of Order," ibid., pp. 285–98.
9. G. H. Mead, *Selected Writings*, ed. A. Reck (Chicago, 1964), p. 296.
10. Between the world wars this tradition was represented by such thinkers as Heidegger, Gehlen, Konrad Lorenz, and Carl Schmitt; today it is continued at a comparable level only in French poststructuralism.
11. T. Parsons, "Some Problems of General Theory," in J. C. McKinney and E. A. Tiryakian, eds., *Theoretical Sociology* (New York, 1970), p. 34. See also H. Willke, "Zum Problem der Interpretation komplexer Sozialsysteme," *Kölner Zeitschrift für Soziologie und Sozialpsychologie* 30 (1978): 228ff.
12. A. Etzione, "Elemente einer Makrosoziologie," in W. Zapf, ed., *Theorien des Sozialen Wandels* (Cologne, 1969), pp. 147ff.; and idem, *The Active Society* (New York, 1968), pp. 135ff.

Chapter 32

Civil Society and the Political Public Sphere [1996]

Jürgen Habermas

Civil Society, Public Opinion, and Communicative Power

Up to now, I have generally dealt with the public sphere as a communication structure rooted in the lifeworld through the associational network of civil society. I have described the political public sphere as a sounding board for problems that must be processed by the political system because they cannot be solved elsewhere. To this extent, the public sphere is a warning system with sensors that, though unspecialized, are sensitive throughout society. From the perspective of democratic theory, the public sphere must, in addition, amplify the pressure of problems, that is, not only detect and identify problems but also convincingly and *influentially* thematize them, furnish them with possible solutions, and dramatize them in such a way that they are taken up and dealt with by parliamentary complexes. Besides the "signal" function, there must be an effective problematization. The capacity of the public sphere to solve problems *on its own* is limited. But this capacity must be utilized to oversee the further treatment of problems that takes place inside the political system. I can provide only a broad estimate of the extent to which this is possible. I start by clarifying the contested concepts of the public sphere and civil

---

Jürgen Habermas, "Civil Society and the Political Public Sphere," pp. 359–87 from Jürgen Habermas, *Between Facts and Norms: Contributions to a Discourse Theory of Law and Democracy.* Cambridge, MA: MIT Press, 1996. Copyright © 1996 Massachusetts Institute of Technology. This book was originally published as *Faktizität und Geltung. Beiträge zur Diskurstheorie des Rechts und des demokratischen Rechtsstaats.* Copyright © 1992 Suhrkamp Verlag, Frankfurt am Main, Germany. Reprinted with permission of MIT Press and Polity Press.

society. This allows me to sketch some barriers and power structures inside the public sphere. These barriers, however, can be overcome in critical situations by escalating movements. I then summarize those elements the legal system must take into consideration when it forms its picture of a complex society like ours.

1

The public sphere is a social phenomenon just as elementary as action, actor, association, or collectivity, but it eludes the conventional sociological concepts of "social order." The public sphere cannot be conceived as an institution and certainly not as an organization. It is not even a framework of norms with differentiated competences and roles, membership regulations, and so on. Just as little does it represent a system; although it permits one to draw internal boundaries, outwardly it is characterized by open, permeable, and shifting horizons. The public sphere can best be described as a network for communicating information and points of view (i.e., opinions expressing affirmative or negative attitudes); the streams of communication are, in the process, filtered and synthesized in such a way that they coalesce into bundles of topically specified *public* opinions. Like the lifeworld as a whole, so, too, the public sphere is reproduced through communicative action, for which mastery of a natural language suffices; it is tailored to the *general comprehensibility* of everyday communicative practice. We have become acquainted with the "lifeworld" as a reservoir for simple interactions; specialized systems of action and knowledge that are differentiated within the lifeworld remain tied to these interactions. These systems fall into one of two categories. Systems like religion, education, and the family become associated with general reproductive functions of the lifeworld (that is, with cultural reproduction, social integration, or socialization). Systems like science, morality, and art take up different validity aspects of everyday communicative action (truth, rightness, or veracity). The public sphere, however, is specialized in neither of these two ways; to the extent that it extends to politically relevant questions, it leaves their specialized treatment to the political system. Rather, the public sphere distinguishes itself through a *communication structure* that is related to a third feature of communicative action: it refers neither to the *functions* nor to the *contents* of everyday communication but to the *social space* generated in communicative action.

Unlike success-oriented actors who mutually observe each other as one observes something in the objective world, persons acting communicatively encounter each other in a *situation* they at the same time constitute with their cooperatively negotiated interpretations. The intersubjectively shared space of a speech situation is disclosed when the participants enter into interpersonal relationships by taking positions on mutual speech-act offers and assuming illocutionary obligations. Every encounter in which actors do not just observe each other but take a second-person attitude, reciprocally attributing communicative freedom to each other, unfolds in a linguistically constituted public space. This space stands open, in principle, for potential dialogue partners who are present as bystanders or could come on the scene and join those present. That is, special measures would be required to prevent a third party from entering such a linguistically constituted space. Founded in communicative action, this spatial structure of simple and episodic encounters can be expanded and rendered more permanent in an abstract form for a larger public of present persons. For the public infrastructure of such *assemblies*, performances, presentations, and so on, architectural metaphors of structured spaces recommend themselves: we speak of forums, stages, arenas, and the like. These public spheres still cling to the concrete locales where an audience is physically gathered. The more they detach themselves from the public's physical presence and extend to the virtual presence of scattered readers, listeners, or viewers linked by public media, the clearer becomes the abstraction that enters when the spatial structure of simple interactions is expanded into a public sphere.

When generalized in this way, communication structures contract to informational content and points of view that are uncoupled from the thick contexts of simple interactions, from specific persons, and from practical obligations. At the same time, context generalization, inclusion, and growing anonymity demand a higher degree of explication that must dispense with technical vocabularies and special codes. Whereas the *orientation to laypersons* implies a certain loss in differentiation, uncoupling communicated opinions from concrete practical obligations tends to have an *intellectualizing* effect. Processes of opinion-formation, especially when they have to do with political questions, certainly cannot be separated from the transformation of the participants' preferences and attitudes, but they can be separated from putting these dispositions into action. To this extent, the communication structures of the public sphere *relieve* the public *of the burden of decision making*; the postponed decisions are reserved for the institutionalized political process. In the public sphere, utterances are sorted according to issue and contribution, whereas the contributions are weighted by the affirmative versus negative responses they receive. Information and arguments are thus worked into focused opinions. What makes such "bundled" opinions into *public opinion* is both the controversial way it comes about and the amount of approval that "carries" it. Public opinion is not representative in the statistical sense. It is not an aggregate of individually gathered, privately expressed opinions held by isolated persons. Hence it must not be confused with survey results. Political opinion polls provide a certain reflection of "public opinion" only if they have been preceded by a focused public debate and a corresponding opinion-formation in a mobilized public sphere.

The diffusion of information and points of view via effective broadcasting media is not the only thing that matters in public processes of communication, nor is it the most important. True, only the broad circulation of comprehensible, attention-grabbing messages arouses a sufficiently inclusive participation. But the rules of a *shared* practice of communication are of greater significance for structuring public opinion. Agreement on issues and contributions *develops* only as the result of more or less exhaustive controversy in which proposals, information, and reasons can be more or less rationally dealt with. In general terms, the *discursive level* of opinion-formation and the "quality" of the outcome vary with this "more or less" in the "rational" processing of "exhaustive" proposals, information, and reasons. Thus the success of public communication is not intrinsically measured by the requirement of inclusion either but by the formal criteria governing how a qualified public opinion comes about. The structures of a power-ridden, oppressed public sphere exclude fruitful and clarifying discussions. The "quality" of public opinion, insofar as it is measured by the procedural properties of its process of generation, is an empirical variable. From a normative perspective, this provides a basis for measuring the legitimacy of the influence that public opinion has on the political system. Of course, actual influence coincides with legitimate influence just as little as the belief in legitimacy coincides with legitimacy. But conceiving things this way at least opens a perspective from which the relation between actual influence and the procedurally grounded quality of public opinion can be empirically investigated.

Parsons introduced "influence" as a symbolically generalized form of communication that facilitates interactions in virtue of conviction or persuasion. For example, persons or institutions can enjoy a reputation that allows their utterances to have an influence on others' beliefs without having to demonstrate authority or to give explanations in the situation. "Influence" feeds on the resource of mutual understanding, but it is based on advancing trust in beliefs that are not currently tested. In this sense, public opinion represents political potentials that can be used for influencing the voting behavior of citizens or the will-formation in parliamentary bodies, administrative agencies, and courts. Naturally, political *influence* supported by public opinion is converted into political *power* – into a potential for rendering binding decisions – only when it affects the beliefs and decisions of *authorized* members of the political system and determines the behavior of voters, legislators, officials, and so forth. Just like social power, political influence based on public opinion can be transformed into political power only through institutionalized procedures.

Influence develops in the public sphere and becomes the object of struggle there. This struggle involves not only the political influence that has already been acquired (such as that enjoyed by experienced political leaders and officeholders, established parties, and well-known groups like Greenpeace and Amnesty International). The reputation of groups of persons and experts who have acquired their influence in special public spheres also comes into play (for example, the authority of religious leaders, the public visibility of literary figures and artists, the reputation of scientists, and the popularity of sports figures and movie stars). For as soon as the public space has expanded beyond the context of simple interactions, a differentiation sets in among organizers, speakers, and hearers; arenas and galleries; stage and viewing space. The *actors' roles* that increasingly professionalize and multiply with organizational complexity and range of media are, of course, furnished with unequal opportunities for exerting influence. But the political influence that the actors gain through public communication must *ultimately* rest on the resonance and indeed the approval of a lay public whose composition is egalitarian. The public of citizens must be *convinced* by comprehensible and broadly interesting contributions to issues it finds relevant. The public audience possesses final authority, because it is *constitutive* for the internal structure and reproduction of the public sphere, the *only* place where actors can appear. There can be no public sphere without a public.

To be sure, we must distinguish the actors who, so to speak, emerge from the public and take part in the reproduction of the public sphere itself from actors who occupy an already constituted public domain in order to use it. This is true, for example, of the large and well-organized interest groups that are anchored in various social subsystems and affect the political system *through* the public sphere. They cannot make any manifest use in the public sphere of the sanctions and rewards they rely on in bargaining or in nonpublic attempts at pressure. They can capitalize on their social power and convert it into political power only insofar as they can advertise their interests in a language that can mobilize convincing reasons and shared value orientations – as, for example, when parties to wage negotiations inform the public about demands, strategies, or outcomes. The contributions of interest groups are, in any case, vulnerable to a kind of criticism to which contributions from other sources are not exposed. Public opinions that can acquire visibility only because of an undeclared infusion of money or organizational power lose their credibility as soon as these sources of social power are made public. Public opinion can be manipulated but neither publicly bought nor publicly blackmailed. This is due to the fact that a public sphere cannot be "manufactured" as one pleases. Before it can be captured by actors with strategic intent, the public sphere together with its public must have developed as a structure that stands on its own and reproduces itself *out of itself*. This lawlike regularity governing the formation of a public sphere remains latent in the constituted public sphere – and takes effect again only in moments when the public sphere is mobilized.

The political public sphere can fulfill its function of perceiving and thematizing encompassing social problems only insofar as it develops out of the communication taking place among *those who are potentially affected*. It is carried by a public recruited from the entire citizenry. But in the diverse voices of this public, one hears the echo of private experiences that are caused throughout society by the externalities (and internal disturbances) of various functional systems – and even by the very state apparatus on whose regulatory activities the complex and poorly coordinated subsystems depend. Systemic deficiencies are experienced in the context of individual life histories; such burdens accumulate in the lifeworld. The latter has the appropriate antennae, for in its horizon are intermeshed the private life histories of the "clients" of functional systems that might be failing in their delivery of services. It is only for those who are immediately affected that such services are paid in the currency of "use values." Besides religion, art, and literature, only the spheres of "private" life have an existential language at their disposal, in which such socially generated problems can be *assessed in terms of one's own life history*. Problems voiced in the public sphere first become visible when they are mirrored in personal life experiences. To the extent that these experiences find their concise expression in the languages of religion, art, and literature, the "literary" public sphere in the broader sense, which is specialized for the articulation of values and world disclosure, is intertwined with the political public sphere.

As both bearers of the political public sphere and as *members of society*, citizens occupy two positions at once. As members of society, they occupy the roles of employees and consumers, insured persons and patients, taxpayers and clients of bureaucracies, as well as the roles of students, tourists, commuters, and the like; in such complementary roles, they are especially exposed to the specific requirements and failures of the corresponding service systems. Such experiences are first assimilated "privately," that is, are interpreted within the horizon of a life history intermeshed with other life histories in the contexts of shared lifeworlds. The communication channels of the public sphere are linked to private spheres – to the thick networks of interaction found in families and circles of friends as well as to the looser contacts with neighbors, work colleagues, acquaintances, and so on – and indeed they are linked in such a way that the spatial structures of simple interactions are expanded and abstracted but not destroyed. Thus the orientation to reaching understanding that is predominant in everyday practice is also preserved for a *communication among strangers* that is conducted over great distances in public spheres whose branches are quite complex. The threshold separating the private sphere from the public is not marked by a fixed set of issues or relationships but by *different conditions of communication*. Certainly these conditions lead to differences in the accessibility of the two spheres, safeguarding the intimacy of the one sphere and the publicity of the other. However, they do not seal off the private from the public but only channel the flow of topics from the one sphere into the other. For the public sphere draws its impulses from the private handling of social problems that resonate in life histories. It is symptomatic of this close connection, incidentally, that a modern bourgeois public sphere developed in the European societies of the seventeenth and eighteenth centuries as the "sphere of private persons come together as a public." Viewed historically, the connection between the public and the private spheres is manifested in the clubs and organizational forms of a reading public composed of bourgeois private persons and crystallizing around newspapers and journals.

2

This sphere of civil society has been rediscovered today in wholly new historical constellations. The expression "civil society" has in the meantime taken on a meaning different from that of the "bourgeois society" of the liberal tradition, which Hegel conceptualized as a "system of needs," that is, as a market system involving social labor and commodity exchange. What is meant by "civil society" today, in contrast to its usage in the Marxist tradition, no longer includes the economy as constituted by private law and steered through markets in labor, capital, and commodities. Rather, its institutional core comprises those nongovernmental and non-economic connections and voluntary associations that anchor the communication structures of the public sphere in the society component of the lifeworld. Civil society is composed of those more or less spontaneously emergent associations, organizations, and movements that, attuned to how societal problems resonate in the private life spheres, distill and transmit such reactions in amplified form to the public sphere. The core of civil society comprises a network of associations that institutionalizes problem-solving discourses on questions of general interest inside the framework of organized public spheres. These "discursive designs" have an egalitarian, open form of organization that mirrors essential features of the kind of communication around which they crystallize and to which they lend continuity and permanence.

Such associations certainly do not represent the most conspicuous element of a public sphere dominated by mass media and large agencies, observed by market and opinion research, and inundated by the public relations work, propaganda, and advertising of political parties and groups. All the same, they do form the organizational substratum of the general public of citizens. More or less emerging from the private sphere, this public is made of citizens who seek acceptable interpretations for their social interests and experiences and who want to have an influence on institutionalized opinion- and will-formation.

One searches the literature in vain for clear definitions of civil society that would go beyond such descriptive characterizations. S. N. Eisenstadt's usage reveals a certain continuity with the older theory of pluralism when he describes civil society as follows:

> Civil society embraces a multiplicity of ostensibly "private" yet potentially autonomous public arenas distinct from the state. The activities of such actors are regulated by various associations existing within them, preventing the society from degenerating into a shapeless mass. In a civil society, these sectors are not embedded in closed, ascriptive or corporate settings; they are open-ended and overlapping. Each has autonomous access to the central political arena, and a certain degree of commitment to that setting.

Jean Cohen and Andrew Arato, who have presented the most comprehensive study on this topic, provide a catalog of features characterizing the civil society that is demarcated from the state, the economy, and other functional systems but coupled with the core private spheres of the lifeworld:

> (1) *Plurality*: families, informal groups, and voluntary associations whose plurality and autonomy allow for a variety of forms of life; (2) *Publicity*: institutions of culture and communication; (3) *Privacy*: a domain of individual self-development and moral choice; (4) *Legality*: structures of general laws and basic rights needed to demarcate plurality, privacy, and publicity from at least the state and, tendentially, the economy. Together, these structures secure the institutional existence of a modern differentiated civil society.

The *constitution of this sphere through basic rights* provides some indicators for its social structure. Freedom of assembly and freedom of association, when linked with freedom of speech, define the scope for various types of associations and societies: for voluntary associations that intervene in the formation of public opinion, push topics of general interest, and act as advocates for neglected issues and underrepresented groups; for groups that are difficult to organize or that pursue cultural, religious, or humanitarian aims; and for ethical communities, religious denominations, and so on. Freedom of the press, radio, and television, as well as the right to engage in these areas, safeguards the media infrastructure of public communication; such liberties are thereby supposed to preserve an openness for competing opinions and a representative diversity of voices. The political system, which must remain sensitive to the influence of public opinion, is intertwined with the public sphere and civil society through the activity of political parties and general elections. This intermeshing is guaranteed by the right of parties to "collaborate" in the political will-formation of the people, as well as by the citizens' active and passive voting rights and other participatory rights. Finally, the network of associations can assert its autonomy and preserve its spontaneity only insofar as it can draw support from a mature pluralism of forms of life, subcultures, and worldviews. The constitutional protection of "privacy" promotes the integrity of private life spheres: rights of personality, freedom of belief and of conscience, freedom of movement, the privacy of letters, mail, and telecommunications, the inviolability of one's residence, and the protection of families circumscribe an untouchable zone of personal integrity and independent judgment.

The tight connection between an autonomous civil society and an integral private sphere stands out even more clearly when contrasted with totalitarian societies of bureaucratic socialism. Here a panoptic state not only directly controls the bureaucratically desiccated public sphere, it also undermines the private basis of this public sphere. Administrative intrusions and constant supervision corrode the communicative structure of everyday contacts in families and schools, neighborhoods and local municipalities. The destruction of solidary living conditions and the paralysis of initiative and independent engagement in overregulated yet legally uncertain sectors go hand in hand with the crushing of social groups, associations, and networks; with indoctrination and the dissolution of cultural identities; with the suffocation of spontaneous public communication. Communicative rationality is thus destroyed *simultaneously* in both public and private contexts of communication. The more the bonding force of communicative action wanes in private life spheres and the embers of communicative freedom die out, the easier it is for someone who monopolizes the public sphere to align the mutually estranged and isolated actors into a mass that can be directed and mobilized in a plebiscitarian manner.

Basic constitutional guarantees alone, of course, cannot preserve the public sphere and civil society from deformations. The communication structures of the public sphere must rather be kept intact by an energetic civil society. That the political public sphere must in a certain sense reproduce and stabilize itself from its own resources is shown by the odd *self-referential character of the practice of communication in civil society*. Those actors who are the carriers of the public sphere put forward "texts" that always reveal the same subtext, which refers to the critical function of the public sphere in general. Whatever the manifest content of their public utterances, the performative meaning of such public discourse at the same time actualizes the function of an undistorted political public sphere as such. Thus, the institutions and legal guarantees of free and open opinion-formation rest on the unsteady ground of the political communication of actors who, in making use of them, at the same time interpret, defend, and radicalize their normative content. Actors who know they are involved in the *common* enterprise of reconstituting and maintaining structures of the public sphere as they contest opinions and strive for influence differ from actors who merely use forums that already exist. More specifically, actors who support the public sphere are distinguished by the *dual orientation* of their political engagement: with their programs, they directly influence the political system, but at the same time they are also reflexively concerned with revitalizing and enlarging civil society and the public sphere as well as with confirming their own identities and capacities to act.

Cohen and Arato see this kind of "dual politics" especially in the "new" social movements that simultaneously pursue offensive and defensive goals. "Offensively," these movements attempt to bring up issues relevant to the entire society, to define ways of approaching problems, to propose possible solutions, to supply new information, to interpret values differently, to mobilize good reasons and criticize bad ones. Such initiatives are intended to produce a broad shift in public opinion, to alter the parameters of organized political will-formation, and to exert pressure on parliaments, courts, and administrations in favor of specific policies. "Defensively," they attempt to maintain existing structures of association and public influence, to generate subcultural counterpublics and counterinstitutions, to consolidate new collective identities, and to win new terrain in the form of expanded rights and reformed institutions:

> On this account, the "defensive" aspect of the movements involves preserving *and developing* the communicative infrastructure of the lifeworld. This formulation captures the dual aspect of movements discussed by Touraine as well as Habermas's insight that movements can be the carriers of the potentials, of cultural modernity. This is the sine qua non for successful efforts to redefine identities, to reinterpret norms, and to develop egalitarian, democratic associational forms. The expressive, normative and communicative modes of collective action ... [also involve] efforts to secure *institutional* changes within civil society that correspond to the new meanings, identities, and norms that are created.

In the self-referential mode of reproducing the public sphere, as well as in the Janus-faced politics aimed at the political system and the self-stabilization of public sphere and civil society, the space is provided for the extension and radicalization of existing rights: "The combination of associations, publics, and rights, when supported by a political culture in which independent initiatives and movements represent an ever-renewable, legitimate, political option, represents, in our opinion, an effective set of bulwarks around civil society within whose limits much of the program of radical democracy can be reformulated."

In fact, the *interplay* of a public sphere based in civil society with the opinion- and will-formation institutionalized in parliamentary bodies and courts offers a good starting point for translating the concept of deliberative politics into sociological terms. However, we must not look on civil society as a focal point where the lines of societal self-organization as a whole would converge. Cohen and Arato rightly emphasize the *limited scope for action* that civil society and the public sphere afford to noninstitutionalized political movements and forms of political expression. They speak of a structurally necessary "self-limitation" of radical-democratic practice:

First, a robust civil society can develop only in the context of a liberal political culture and the corresponding patterns of socialization, and on the basis of an integral private sphere; it can blossom only in an already rationalized lifeworld. Otherwise, populist movements arise that blindly defend the frozen traditions of a lifeworld endangered by capitalist modernization. In their forms of mobilization, these fundamentalist movements are as modern as they are antidemocratic.

Second, within the boundaries of the public sphere, or at least of a liberal public sphere, actors can acquire only influence, not political power. The influence of a public opinion generated more or less discursively in open controversies is certainly an empirical variable that can make a difference. But public influence is transformed into communicative power only after it passes through the filters of the institutionalized *procedures* of democratic opinion- and will-formation and enters through parliamentary debates into legitimate lawmaking. The informal flow of public opinion issues in beliefs that have been *tested* from the standpoint of the generalizability of interests. Not influence per se, but influence transformed into communicative power legitimates political decisions. The popular sovereignty set communicatively aflow cannot make itself felt *solely* in the influence of informal public discourses – not even when these discourses arise from autonomous public spheres. To generate political power, their influence must have an effect on the democratically regulated deliberations of democratically elected assemblies and assume an authorized form in formal decisions. This also holds, mutatis mutandis, for courts that decide politically relevant cases.

Third, and finally, the instruments that politics has available in law and administrative power have a limited effectiveness in functionally differentiated societies. Politics indeed continues to be the addressee for all unmanaged integration problems. But political steering can often take only an indirect approach and must, as we have seen, leave intact the modes of operation internal to functional systems and other highly organized spheres of action. As a result, democratic movements emerging from civil society must give up holistic aspirations to a self-organizing society, aspirations that also undergirded Marxist ideas of social revolution. Civil society can directly transform only itself, and it can have at most an indirect effect on the self-transformation of the political system; generally, it has an influence only on the personnel and programming of this system. But in no way does it occupy *the position* of a macrosubject supposed to bring society as a whole under control and simultaneously act for it. Besides these limitations, one must bear in mind that the administrative power deployed for purposes of social planning and supervision is not a suitable medium for fostering emancipated forms of life. These can *develop* in the wake of democratization processes but they cannot be *brought about* through intervention.

The self-limitation of civil society should not be understood as incapacitation. The knowledge required for political supervision or steering, a knowledge that in complex societies represents a resource as scarce as it is desirable, can certainly become the source of a new systems paternalism. But because the administration does not, for the most part, itself produce the relevant knowledge but draws it from the knowledge system or other intermediaries, it does not enjoy a natural monopoly on such knowledge. In spite of asymmetrical access to expertise and limited problem-solving capacities, civil society also has the opportunity of mobilizing counter-knowledge and drawing on the pertinent forms of expertise to make *its own* translations. Even though the public consists of laypersons and communicates with ordinary language, this does not necessarily imply an inability to differentiate the essential questions and reasons for decisions. This can serve as a pretext for a technocratic incapacitation of the public sphere only as long as the political initiatives of civil society fail to provide sufficient expert knowledge along with appropriate and, if necessary, multilevel translations in regard to the managerial aspects of public issues.

3

The concepts of the political public sphere and civil society introduced above are not mere normative postulates but have empirical relevance. However, additional assumptions must be introduced if we are to use these concepts to translate the discourse-theoretic reading of radical democracy into sociological terms and reformulate it in an empirically falsifiable manner. I would like to defend the claim that *under certain circumstances* civil society can acquire influence in the public sphere, have an effect on the parliamentary complex (and the courts) through its own public opinions, and compel the political system to switch over to the official circulation of power. Naturally, the sociology of mass communication conveys a skeptical impression of the power-ridden, mass-media-dominated public spheres of Western democracies. Social movements, citizen initiatives and forums, political and other associations, in short, the groupings of civil society, are indeed sensitive to problems, but the signals they send out and the impulses they give are generally too weak to initiate learning processes or redirect decision making in the political system in the short run.

In complex societies, the public sphere consists of an intermediary structure between the political system, on the one hand, and the private sectors of the lifeworld and functional systems, on the other. It represents a highly complex network that branches out into a multitude of overlapping international, national, regional, local, and subcultural arenas. Functional specifications, thematic foci, policy fields, and so forth, provide the points of reference for a substantive differentiation of public spheres that are, however, still accessible to laypersons (for example, popular science and literary publics, religious and artistic publics, feminist and "alternative" publics, publics concerned with health-care issues, social welfare, or environmental policy).

Moreover, the public sphere is differentiated into levels according to the density of communication, organizational complexity, and range – from the *episodic* publics found in taverns, coffee houses, or on the streets; through the *occasional* or "arranged" publics of particular presentations and events, such as theater performances, rock concerts, party assemblies, or church congresses; up to the *abstract* public sphere of isolated readers, listeners, and viewers scattered across large geographic areas, or even around the globe, and brought together only through the mass media. Despite these manifold differentiations, however, all the partial publics constituted by ordinary language remain porous to one another. The one text of "the" public sphere, a text continually extrapolated and extending radially in all directions, is divided by internal boundaries into arbitrarily small texts for which everything else is context; yet one can always build hermeneutical bridges from one text to the next. Segmented public spheres are constituted with the help of exclusion mechanisms; however, because publics cannot harden into organizations or systems, there is no exclusion rule without a proviso for its abolishment.

In other words, boundaries inside the universal public sphere as defined by its reference to the political system remain permeable in principle. The rights to unrestricted inclusion and equality built into liberal public spheres prevent exclusion mechanisms of the Foucauldian type and ground a *potential for self-transformation*. In the course of the nineteenth and twentieth centuries, the universalist discourses of the bourgeois public sphere could no longer immunize themselves against a critique from within. The labor movement and feminism, for example, were able to join these discourses in order to shatter the structures that had initially constituted them as "the other" of a bourgeois public sphere.

The more the audience is widened through mass communications, the more inclusive and the more abstract in form it becomes. Correspondingly, the *roles of the actors* appearing in the arenas are, to an increasing degree, sharply separated from the roles of the spectators in the galleries. Although the "success of the actors in the arena is ultimately decided in the galleries," the question arises of how autonomous the public is when it takes a position on an issue, whether its affirmative or negative stand reflects a process of becoming informed or in fact only a more or less concealed game of power. Despite the wealth of empirical investigations, we still do not have a well-established answer to this cardinal question. But one can at least pose the question more precisely by assuming that public processes of communication can take place with less distortion the more they are left to the internal dynamic of a civil society that emerges from the lifeworld.

One can distinguish, at least tentatively, the more loosely organized actors who "emerge from" the public, as it were, from other actors merely "appearing before" the public. The latter have organizational power, resources, and sanctions available *from the start*. Naturally, the actors who are more firmly anchored in civil society and participate in the reproduction of the public sphere also depend on the support of "sponsors" who supply the necessary resources of money, organization, knowledge, and social capital. But patrons or "like-minded" sponsors do not necessarily reduce the authenticity of the public actors they support. By contrast, the collective actors who merely enter the public sphere from, and utilize it for, a specific organization or functional system have *their own* basis of support. Among these political and social actors who do not have to obtain their resources from other spheres, I primarily include the large interest groups that enjoy social power, as well as the established parties that have largely become arms of the political system. They draw on market studies and opinion surveys and conduct their own professional public-relations campaigns.

In and of themselves, organizational complexity, resources, professionalization, and so on, are admittedly insufficient indicators for the difference between "indigenous" actors and mere users. Nor can an actor's pedigree be read directly from the interests actually represented. Other indicators are more reliable. Thus actors differ in how they can be identified. Some actors one can easily identify from their functional background; that is, they represent political parties or pressure groups; unions or professional associations; consumer-protection groups or rent-control organizations, and so on. Other actors, by contrast, must first *produce* identifying features. This is especially evident with social movements that initially go through a phase of self-identification and self-legitimation; even after that, they still pursue a self-referential "identity politics" parallel to their goal-directed politics – they must continually reassure themselves of their identity. Whether actors merely use an already constituted public sphere or whether they are involved in reproducing its structures is, moreover, evident in the above-mentioned sensitivity to threats to communication rights. It is also shown in the actors' willingness to go beyond an interest in self-defense and take a universalist stand against the open or concealed exclusion of minorities or marginal groups. The very existence of social movements, one might add, depends on whether they find organizational forms that produce solidarities and publics, forms that allow them to fully utilize and radicalize existing communication rights and structures as they pursue special goals.

A third group of actors are the journalists, publicity agents, and members of the press (i.e., in the broad sense of *Publizisten*) who collect information, make decisions about the selection and presentation of "programs," and to a certain extent control the entry of topics, contributions, and authors into the mass-media-dominated public sphere. As the mass media become more complex and more expensive, the effective channels of communication become more centralized. To the degree this occurs, the mass media face an increasing pressure of selection, on both the supply side and the demand side. These selection processes become the source of a new sort of power. This *power of the media* is not sufficiently reined in by professional standards, but today, by fits and starts, the "fourth branch of government" is being subjected to constitutional regulation. In the Federal Republic, for example, it is both the legal form and the institutional structure of television networks that determine whether they depend more on the influence of political parties and public interest groups or more on private firms with large advertising outlays. In general, one can say that the image of politics presented on television is predominantly made up of issues and contributions that are professionally produced as media input and then fed in via press conferences, news agencies, public-relations campaigns, and the like.

These official producers of information are all the more successful the more they can rely on trained personnel, on financial and technical resources, and in general on a professional infrastructure. Collective actors operating outside the political system or outside large organizations normally have fewer opportunities to influence the content and views presented by the media. This is especially true for messages that do not fall inside the "balanced," that is, the centrist and rather narrowly defined, spectrum of "established opinions" dominating the programs of the electronic media.

Moreover, before messages selected in this way are broadcast, they are subject to *information-processing strategies* within the media. These are oriented by reception conditions as perceived by media experts, program directors, and the press. Because the public's receptiveness, cognitive capacity, and attention represent unusually scarce resources for which the programs of numerous "stations" compete, the presentation of news and commentaries for the most part follows market strategies. Reporting facts as human-interest stories, mixing information with entertainment, arranging material episodically, and breaking down complex relationships into smaller fragments – all of this comes together to form a syndrome that works to depoliticize public communication. This is the kernel of truth in the theory of the culture industry. The research literature provides fairly reliable information on the institutional framework and structure of the media, as well as on the way they work, organize programs, and are utilized. But, even a generation after Paul Lazarsfeld, propositions concerning the *effects of the media* remain controversial. The research on effect and reception has at least done away with the image of passive consumers as "cultural dopes" who are manipulated by the programs offered to them. It directs our attention to the *strategies of interpretation* employed by viewers, who communicate with one another, and who in fact can be provoked to criticize or reject what programs offer or to synthesize it with judgments of their own.

Even if we know something about the internal operation and impact of the mass media, as well as about the distribution of roles among the public and various actors, and even if we can make some reasonable conjectures about who has privileged access to the media and who has a share in media power, it is by no means clear how the mass media intervene in the diffuse circuits of communication in the political public sphere. The *normative reactions* to the relatively new phenomenon of the mass media's powerful position in the competition for public influence are clearer. Michael Gurevitch and Jay G. Blumler have summarized the tasks that the media *ought* to fulfill in democratic political systems:

1 surveillance of the sociopolitical environment, reporting developments likely to impinge, positively or negatively, on the welfare of citizens;
2 meaningful agenda-setting, identifying the key issues of the day, including the forces that have formed and may resolve them;
3 platforms for an intelligible and illuminating advocacy by politicians and spokespersons of other causes and interest groups;
4 dialogue across a diverse range of views, as well as between power-holders (actual and prospective) and mass publics;

5 mechanisms for holding officials to account for how they have exercised power;
6 incentives for citizens to learn, choose, and become involved, rather than merely to follow and kibitz over the political process;
7 a principled resistance to the efforts of forces outside the media to subvert their independence, integrity and ability to serve the audience;
8 a sense of respect for the audience member, as potentially concerned and able to make sense of his or her political environment.

Such principles orient the professional code of journalism and the profession's ethical self-understanding, on the one hand, and the formal organization of a free press by laws governing mass communication, on the other. In agreement with the concept of deliberative politics, these principles express a simple idea: the mass media ought to understand themselves as the mandatary of an enlightened public whose willingness to learn and capacity for criticism they at once presuppose, demand, and reinforce; like the judiciary, they ought to preserve their independence from political and social pressure; they ought to be receptive to the public's concerns and proposals, take up these issues and contributions impartially, augment criticisms, and confront the political process with articulate demands for legitimation. The power of the media should thus be neutralized and the tacit conversion of administrative or social power into political influence blocked. According to this idea, political and social actors would be allowed to "use" the public sphere only insofar as they make convincing contributions to the solution of problems that have been perceived by the public or have been put on the public agenda with the public's consent. In a similar vein, political parties would have to participate in the opinion- and will-formation from the public's own perspective, rather than patronizing the public and extracting mass loyalty from the public sphere for the purposes of maintaining their own power.

The sociology of mass communication depicts the public sphere as infiltrated by administrative and social power and dominated by the mass media. If one places this image, diffuse though it might be, alongside the above normative expectations, then one will be rather cautious in estimating the chances of civil society having an influence on the political system. To be sure, this estimate pertains only to a *public sphere at rest*. In periods of mobilization, the structures that actually support the authority of a critically engaged public begin to vibrate. The balance of power between civil society and the political system then shifts.

4

With this I return to the central question of who can place issues on the agenda and determine what direction the lines of communication take. Roger Cobb, Jennie-Keith Ross, and Marc Howard Ross have constructed models that depict how new and compelling issues develop, from the first initiative up to formal proceedings in bodies that have the power to decide. If one suitably modifies the proposed models – inside access model, mobilization model, outside initiative model – from the viewpoint of democratic theory, they present basic alternatives in how the public sphere and the political system influence each other. In the first case, the initiative comes from officeholders or political leaders, and the issue continues to circulate inside the political system all the way to its formal treatment, while the broader public is either excluded from the process or does not have any influence on it. In the second case, the initiative again starts inside the political system, but the proponents of the issue must mobilize the public sphere, because they need the support of certain groups, either to obtain formal consideration or to implement an adopted program successfully. Only in the third case does the initiative lie with forces at the periphery, outside the purview of the political system. With the help of the mobilized public sphere, that is, the pressure of public opinion, such forces compel formal consideration of the issue:

> The outside initiative model applies to the situation in which a group outside the government structure 1) articulates a grievance, 2) tries to expand interest in the issue to enough other groups in the population to gain a place on the public agenda, in order to 3) create sufficient pressure on decision makers to force the issue onto the formal agenda for their serious consideration. This model of agenda building is likely to predominate in more egalitarian societies. Formal agenda status, ... however, does not necessarily mean that the final decisions of the authorities or the actual policy implementation will be what the grievance group originally sought.

In the normal case, issues and proposals have a history whose course corresponds more to the first or second model than to the third. As long as the informal circulation of power dominates the political system, the initiative and power to put problems on the agenda and bring them to a decision lies more with the Government leaders and administration than with the parliamentary complex. As long as in the public sphere the mass media prefer, contrary to their normative self-understanding, to draw their material from powerful, well-organized information producers and as long as they prefer media strategies that lower rather than raise the discursive level of public communication, issues will tend to start in, and be managed from, the center, rather than follow a spontaneous course originating in the periphery. At least, the skeptical findings on problem articulation in public arenas accord with this view. In the present context, of course, there can be no question of a conclusive empirical evaluation of the mutual influence that politics and public have on each other. For our purposes, it suffices to make it plausible that in a perceived crisis situation, the *actors in civil society* thus far neglected in our scenario *can* assume a surprisingly active and momentous role. In spite of a lesser organizational complexity and a weaker capacity for action, and despite the structural disadvantages mentioned earlier, at the critical moments of an accelerated history, these actors get the chance to *reverse* the normal circuits of communication in the political system and the public sphere. In this way they can shift the entire system's mode of problem solving.

The communication structures of the public sphere are linked with the private life spheres in a way that gives the civil-social periphery, in contrast to the political center, the advantage of greater sensitivity in detecting and identifying new problem situations. The great issues of the last decades give evidence for this. Consider, for example, the spiraling nuclear-arms race; consider the risks involved in the peaceful use of atomic energy or in other large-scale technological projects and scientific experimentation, such as genetic engineering; consider the ecological threats involved in an overstrained natural environment (acid rain, water pollution, species extinction, etc.); consider the dramatically progressing impoverishment of the Third World and problems of the world economic order; or consider such issues as feminism, increasing immigration, and the associated problems of multiculturalism. Hardly any of these topics were *initially* brought up by exponents of the state apparatus, large organizations, or functional systems. Instead, they were broached by intellectuals, concerned citizens, radical professionals, self-proclaimed "advocates," and the like. Moving in from this outermost periphery, such issues force their way into newspapers and interested associations, clubs, professional organizations, academies, and universities. They find forums, citizen initiatives, and other platforms before they catalyze the growth of social movements and new subcultures. The latter can in turn dramatize contributions, presenting them so effectively that the mass media take up the matter. Only through their controversial presentation in the media do such topics reach the larger public and subsequently gain a place on the "public agenda." Sometimes the support of sensational actions, mass protests, and incessant campaigning is required before an issue can make its way via the surprising election of marginal candidates or radical parties, expanded platforms of "established" parties, important court decisions, and so on, into the core of the political system and there receive formal consideration.

Naturally, there are other ways in which issues develop, other paths from the periphery to the center, and other patterns involving complex branchings and feedback loops. But, in general, one can say that even in more or less power-ridden public spheres, the power relations shift as soon as the perception of relevant social problems evokes a *crisis consciousness* at the periphery. If actors from civil society then join together, formulate the relevant issue, and promote it in the public sphere, their efforts can be successful, because the endogenous mobilization of the public sphere activates an otherwise latent dependency built into the internal structure of every public sphere, a dependency also present in the normative self-understanding of the mass media: the players in the arena owe their influence to the approval of those in the gallery. At the very least, one can say that insofar as a rationalized lifeworld supports the development of a liberal public sphere by furnishing it with a solid foundation in civil society, the authority of a position-taking public is strengthened in the course of escalating public controversies. Under the conditions of a *liberal* public sphere, informal public communication accomplishes two things in cases in which mobilization depends on crisis. On the one hand, it prevents the accumulation of indoctrinated masses that are seduced by populist leaders. On the other hand, it pulls together the scattered critical potentials of a public that was only abstractly held together through the public media, and it helps this public have a political influence on institutionalized opinion- and will-formation. Only in *liberal* public spheres, of course, do subinstitutional political movements – which abandon the conventional paths of interest politics in order to boost the constitutionally regulated circulation of power in the political system – take this direction. By contrast, an authoritarian, distorted public sphere that is brought into alignment merely provides a forum for plebiscitary legitimation.

This sense of a reinforced demand for legitimation becomes especially clear when subinstitutional protest movements reach a high point by escalating their protests. The last means for obtaining more of a hearing and greater media influence for oppositional arguments are acts of civil disobedience. These acts of nonviolent, symbolic rule violation are meant as expressions of protest against binding decisions that, their legality notwithstanding, the actors consider illegitimate in the light of valid constitutional principles. Acts of civil disobedience are directed simultaneously to two addressees. On the one hand, they appeal to officeholders and parliamentary representatives to reopen formally concluded political deliberations so that their decisions may possibly be revised in view of the continuing public criticism. On the other hand, they appeal "to the sense of justice of the majority of the community," as Rawls puts it, and thus to the critical judgment of a public of citizens that is to be mobilized with exceptional means. Independently of the current object of controversy, civil disobedience is also always an implicit appeal to connect organized political will-formation with the communicative processes of the public sphere. The message of this subtext is aimed at a political system that, as constitutionally organized, may not detach itself from civil society and make itself independent vis-à-vis the periphery. Civil disobedience thereby refers to its own origins in a civil society that in crisis situations actualizes the normative contents of constitutional democracy in the medium of public opinion and summons it against the systemic inertia of institutional politics.

This *self-referential character* is emphasized in the definition that Cohen and Arato have proposed, drawing on considerations raised by Rawls, Dworkin, and me:

> Civil disobedience involves illegal acts, usually on the part of collective actors, that are public, principled, and symbolic in character, involve primarily nonviolent means of protest, and appeal to the capacity for reason and the sense of justice of the populace. The aim of civil disobedience is to persuade public opinion in civil and political society ... that a particular law or policy is illegitimate and a change is warranted. Collective actors involved in civil disobedience invoke the utopian principles of constitutional democracies, appealing to the ideas of fundamental rights or democratic legitimacy. Civil disobedience is thus a means for reasserting the link between civil and political society ... , when legal attempts at exerting the influence of the former on the latter have failed and other avenues have been exhausted.

This interpretation of civil disobedience manifests the self-consciousness of a civil society confident that at least in a crisis it can increase the pressure of a mobilized public on the political system to the point where the latter switches into the conflict mode and neutralizes the unofficial countercirculation of power.

Beyond this, the justification of civil disobedience relies on a *dynamic understanding* of the constitution as an unfinished project. From this long-term perspective, the constitutional state does not represent a finished structure but a delicate and sensitive – above all fallible and revisable – enterprise, whose purpose is to realize the system of rights *anew* in changing circumstances, that is, to interpret the system of rights better, to institutionalize it more appropriately, and to draw out its contents more radically. This is the perspective of citizens who are actively engaged in realizing the system of rights. Aware of, and referring to, changed contexts, such citizens want to overcome in practice the tension between social facticity and validity. Although legal theory cannot adopt this participant perspective as its own, it can reconstruct the paradigmatic *understanding* of law and democracy that guides citizens whenever they form an idea of the structural constraints on the self-organization of the legal community in their society.

5

From a reconstructive standpoint, we have seen that constitutional rights and principles merely explicate the performative character of the self-constitution of a society of free and equal citizens. The organizational forms of the constitutional state make this practice permanent. Every historical example of a democratic constitution has a double temporal reference: as a historic document, it recalls the foundational act that it interprets – it marks a beginning in time. At the same time, its normative character means that the task of interpreting and elaborating the system of rights poses itself *anew* for each generation; as the project of a just society, a constitution articulates the horizon of expectation opening on an ever-present future. From this perspective, as an *ongoing* process of constitution making set up for the long haul, the democratic procedure of legitimate lawmaking acquires a privileged status. This leads to the pressing question of whether such a demanding procedure can be implemented in complex societies like our own and, if it can, how this can be done effectively, so that a constitutionally regulated circulation of power actually prevails in the political system. The answers to this question in turn inform our own paradigmatic understanding of law. I note the following four points for elucidating such a historically situated understanding of the constitution.

(a) The constitutionally organized political system is, on the one hand, specialized for generating collectively binding decisions. To this extent, it represents only one of several subsystems. On the other hand, in virtue of its internal relation to law, politics is responsible for problems that concern society as a whole. It must be possible to interpret collectively binding decisions as a realization of rights such that the structures of recognition built into communicative action are transferred, via the medium of law, from the level of simple interactions to the abstract and anonymous relationships among strangers. In pursuing what in each case are particular collective goals and in regulating specific conflicts, politics simultaneously deals with general problems of integration. Because it is constituted in a legal form, a politics whose mode of operation is functionally specified still refers to society-wide problems: it carries on the tasks of social integration at a reflexive level when other action systems are no longer up to the job.

(b) This asymmetrical position explains the fact that the political system is subject to constraints on two sides and that corresponding standards govern its achievements and decisions. As a functionally specified action system, it is limited by other functional systems that obey their own logic and, to this extent, bar direct political interventions. On this side, the political system encounters limits on the effectiveness of administrative power (including legal and fiscal instruments). On the other side, as a constitutionally regulated action system, politics is connected with the public sphere and depends on lifeworld sources of communicative power. Here the political system is not subject to the external constraints of a social environment but rather experiences its internal dependence on enabling conditions. This is because the conditions that make the production of legitimate law possible are ultimately not at the disposition of politics.

(c) The political system is vulnerable on both sides to disturbances that can reduce the *effectiveness* of its achievements and the *legitimacy* of its decisions, respectively. The regulatory competence of the political system fails if the implemented legal programs remain ineffective or if regulatory activity gives rise to disintegrating effects in the action systems that require regulation. Failure also occurs if the instruments deployed overtax the legal medium itself and strain the normative composition of the political system. As steering problems become more complex, irrelevance, misguided regulations, and self-destruction can accumulate to the point where a "regulatory trilemma" results. On the other side, the political system fails as a guardian of social integration if its decisions, even though effective, can no longer be traced back to legitimate law. The constitutionally regulated circulation of power is nullified if the administrative system becomes independent of communicatively generated power, if the social power of functional systems and large organizations (including the mass media) is converted into illegitimate power, or if the lifeworld resources for spontaneous public communication no longer suffice to guarantee an uncoerced articulation of social interests. The independence of illegitimate power, together with the weakness of civil society and the public sphere, can deteriorate into a "legitimation dilemma," which in certain circumstances can combine with the steering trilemma and develop into a vicious circle. Then the political system is pulled into the whirlpool of legitimation deficits and steering deficits that reinforce one another.

(d) Such crises can at most be explained historically. They are not built into the structures of functionally differentiated societies in such a way that they would intrinsically compromise the project of self-empowerment undertaken by a society of free and equal subjects who bind themselves by law. However, they are symptomatic of the peculiar position of political systems as asymmetrically embedded in highly complex circulation processes. Actors must form an idea of this context whenever, adopting the performative attitude, they want to engage successfully as citizens, representatives, judges, or officials, in realizing the system of rights. Because these rights must be interpreted in various ways under changing social circumstances, the light they throw on this context is refracted into a spectrum of changing legal paradigms. Historical constitutions can be seen as so many ways of construing one and the *same* practice – the practice of self-determination on the part of free and equal citizens – but like every practice this, too, is situated in history. Those involved must start with their *own current* practice if they want to achieve clarity about what such a practice means *in general*.

Part IX

Modernity

Introduction to Part IX

33 The Social Constraint towards Self-Constraint

34 Modernity and the Holocaust

35 The Consequences of Modernity

36 We Have Never Been Modern

Introduction to Part IX

In recent years, there has been a rather sterile debate between self-proclaimed "modernists" and "postmodernists." Theorists in both camps generally agree that something has fundamentally changed in the patterns of social relations, economic flows, and moral regulation in modern societies. The question at the center of the debate has been whether these changes should best be considered part and parcel of the same ever-transforming "modern" era that the founding figures of sociology spent their lives studying, or whether it is best to conceive of this as a new "postmodern" era. It has been a heated exchange to be sure, but it has not produced many fruitful outcomes.

Rather than attempting to reproduce this debate, this section is designed to move beyond it by taking postmodernist claims seriously but avoiding problematic historicist assumptions. This introduction will outline the different trends in "postmodern" social theory, but it will also emphasize how its style and substance were immediately linked to its historical and social context. The goal is to suggest that the concepts of modernity and postmodernity are deeply linked. On the one hand, "postmodernity is undoubtedly part of the modern," as Jean-François Lyotard has claimed (1984: 79). On the other hand, postmodernism has actually been beneficial in helping us reinterpret our understanding of the modern (see Calhoun, 1995).

Postmodernism as an intellectual and cultural movement gained momentum in the late twentieth century. Any attempt to date the exact emergence of this movement is elusive as it spans a large number of academic and cultural domains. Following Lemert (1997: p. 103), however, it may be safe to say that, for social theorists, the 1979 publication of Jean-François Lyotard's *The Postmodern Condition* and Richard Rorty's *Philosophy and the Mirror of Nature* marks its inauguration as a subject of academic inquiry. Because it is not a coherent intellectual movement, postmodernism does not lend itself to easy description. Instead, it draws its inspiration from different social and cultural contexts.

Contemporary Sociological Theory, Third Edition. Edited by Craig Calhoun, Joseph Gerteis, James Moody, Steven Pfaff, and Indermohan Virk. Editorial material and organization © 2012 John Wiley & Sons, Ltd. Published 2012 by John Wiley & Sons, Ltd.

Postmodernism and the Social Landscape

Postmodernism perhaps finds its clearest expression as an aesthetic movement in the cultural sphere. It arose as a rejection of modernism, especially "high modernism," a movement in the late nineteenth and early twentieth century that sought to redefine literature, music, architecture, and the visual arts. While modernism rejects formal aesthetic theories in favor of the functional, postmodernism questions the adequacy of the functional as an inspiration of artistic expression. According to Charles Jencks, a proponent of postmodern architecture, this shift from modernism to postmodernism in architecture, for instance, occurred symbolically with the demolition of the modernist low-income Pruitt-Igoe housing project in 1972. This act is considered to be a statement of the failure of the modernist faith in the redemptive ability to improve human life through the construction of the best "machine for modern life." Signification and intertextuality replace the functional as the aesthetic principles of postmodernism. One of the distinguishing features of postmodern architecture, for instance, has been the juxtaposition of symbols and forms from different historical and design periods. In general, it may be said that where modernists tend to think in terms of totality, genre, or system, postmodernists think in terms of fragmentation, ephemerality, and discontinuity. While it is the case that this emphasis on fragmentation and discontinuity. While it is the case that this emphasis on fragmentation and discontinuity in postmodernist thought is carried over from modernism, the distinction between the two has more to do with attitude. While modernism laments the fragmentary and the chaotic, postmodernism accepts, and even valorizes it.

Theoretically, postmodernism has its roots in, although it is not coterminous with, poststructuralism, an intellectual movement that emerged in France following the political and social events of May 1968. Central figures associated with this movement are Foucault, Lacan, Barthes, and Kristeva, among others. Following structuralists, poststructuralists seek to decenter the subject. This theoretical position poses a challenge to the modernist belief in subject-centered reason. In other words, it questions the assumption that the rational mind (*any* rational mind) is capable of understanding and depicting the "real" world around us. In general, the postmodernist position is critical of truth claims and monological texts or readings. An important component of this critique is to question the very status of knowledge in modern discourse. Modernism privileges science, above all, as the source of objective knowledge and truth. Poststructuralism (and postmodernism) makes the claim instead that language is central to the production of knowledge, including scientific knowledge, which is also a form of discourse. This linguistic turn is central to the work of postmodern theorists. Jacques Derrida, whose name is associated with deconstruction, suggests that it is "*différance*" that marks writing, a differing and deferring of the linguistic presence of meaning. Texts must be treated as linguistic products, independent of authors with specific intentions. Thus, it may be said that postmodernism is suspicious of the modernist faith in the straightforward relationship between the signifier and the signified.

Postmodern thought critiques the kind of grand narratives that it associates with modernism, in particular humanism and the Enlightenment. As Jean-François Lyotard (1984: p. xxiv), one of the leading theorists of postmodernism, puts it, postmodernism may be characterized as "incredulity toward meta-narratives." These meta-narratives refer to grand theories about, for instance, the Spirit, Man, the rational subject, the proletariat, etc. Such grand theories, like those associated with Marx and Freud, are taken to have at their center a category (or a set of categories) that is assumed to be universal, thereby masking any internal differentiation. Instead, postmodernism favors more small-scale, local narratives that take into account the contingent, provisional, and unstable nature of the social world. An example of such an approach is Foucault's conceptualization of power. Moving away from the idea that power is most importantly vested in the state, Foucault traces the micro-politics of power in multiple locations and social contexts. In a similar vein, Lyotard argues that, in a postmodern world, people live at the intersection of numerous "language games." In fact, he proposes that the social bond is ultimately linguistic, following different discursive rules in different situations.

Modernism and Postmodernism

Having noted some of the main characteristics associated with postmodernism, the question remains whether these theoretical and cultural approaches arose in response to radical changes in our social world. Is postmodernism a theory of postmodernity? In considering these changes, postmodern theory assimilated other theories from the 1970s and 1980s that engaged the same question. Earlier versions of such theories were Daniel Bell's and Alain Touraine's accounts of a postindustrial society. They base their analysis of postindustrial society on the increasing dominance of information and knowledge in the economic sphere. Theorists of post-modernity continue to pursue this interest in the implications of new communication technologies and media, making more radical pronouncements than those made by scholars like Bell and Touraine. For instance, Jean Baudrillard, reflecting on the power of mass communication media, questions the notion of reality in postmodern societies. The power of mediated images, he argues, has led to the production of the "hyperreal" in which it becomes impossible to differentiate between the imaginary and the real. The world becomes a world of simulation, of images without an original. Since the postmodern world has come to be characterized largely by consumption and seduction, Baudrillard suggests that relations of production have now given way to relations of signs.

Admittedly, our social world has experienced some significant structural changes in the past few decades. The economy, for instance, has witnessed deindustrialization and the increasing dominance of post-Fordist practices in which capital has become more flexible and disorganized. In other words, capital accumulation increasingly occurs through flexible work practices that have resulted in significant spatial deconcentration of work and labor. Consumption dominates this "new" economy. Global information and communication technologies have come to assume a powerful role in our world. Manuel Castells, in his influential book *The Network Society*, examines the economic and technological changes that have occurred in our "informational society." He argues that capitalism has evolved in its organizational logic due to the speed and scope with which information is transmitted in this global network society. In a society in which business projects are embedded in global networks, the space of flows supersedes (to some extent) the space of places, with important implications for social relations. Communication networks allow organizations to disperse spatially. In other words, while high-level executives live in "world cities," they manage to remain "connected," and thus control, the actual management of their operations anywhere in the world. In addition to the transformations noted by Castells, other globalizing impulses, for instance migrations, have imbricated us in new social networks that bring to fore the play of difference in contemporary life.

In response to the changes transforming our contemporary world, Wallerstein, in his book *World Systems Analysis*, extends his earlier work on the unequal exchange characterizing the world-system. He traces much of our present-day global situation to certain historical developments, namely, the emergence of the capitalist world-economy in the sixteenth century, the political ideas resulting from the French Revolution, and what he refers to as the "world revolution of 1968" that resulted in the decline of the liberal world-view. While the world-system has historically extended beyond, and been affected by forces outside, the boundaries of any nation-state, he argues that the conditions of the current capitalist global order have become particularly unstable, resulting in more unpredictable ideological responses.

Having made a note of these changes, it is worth considering, however, whether these changes amount to an epochal shift that renders redundant the categories (especially Marxist) of industrial, capitalist societies. David Harvey (1989) argues that, while there have indeed been recent changes in political economic practices, the underlying logic of capitalism remains the same. An acknowledgment of these changes does not lead Harvey to conclude the end of modernity. Rather, he sees them as internal shifts in the organization of capitalism. Calhoun (1995) makes the case that, despite obvious changes, there is no evidence that capital accumulation does not continue to be basic to economic activity today. In fact, he argues that the cultural orientation of society still remains primarily productivist. These accounts, then, advance the view that postmodernity is merely another phase of modernity. In fact, Giddens (1990) argues that what we are witnessing is the radicalization of modernity rather than the emergence of postmodernity.

Also acknowledging that postmodernity is a part of modernity, Lyotard sees it as a vantage point for the rewriting of modernity. In a similar vein, Zygmunt Bauman argues that postmodernity has not replaced modernity. Rather, it is the stage that may be characterized as the culmination of modernity. It is a position from which we can reflect upon modernity. For instance, in his 1989 book *Modernity and the Holocaust*, Bauman explores the limits of modernity witnessed in the Holocaust. The Holocaust, according to him, was a product of the modernist faith in progress embodied in bureaucracy and technocracy. It was the desire to remake the world that motivated the Nazi project. While generally believing that postmodernity does not replace modernity, Bauman suggests that it is a new phase. Like Baudrillard, he is of the opinion that capitalism has evolved from a system based on production to one based on consumption. In such a society, freedom has come to be associated with the freedom to consume.

While there is perhaps more agreement on the beginnings of modernity in the eighteenth century, there is less agreement on those of postmodernity. An example of an historical examination of the emergence of modernity as a social and political form is Norbert Elia's *The Civilizing Process*. It is a rigorous social history of the process of civilization. Elias examines the modern social *habitus*, or personality, which has increasingly come to be dominated by manners, or self-restraint and self-approbation. Through the formation of gradually more effective monopolies of force, the threat which one person represents for another is subjected to control. He also shows how the emergence of this "civilized" behavior is closely interrelated to the sociogenesis of the state. The exercise of force, which was earlier the privilege of rival warriors, becomes increasingly more centralized in the organization of modern states. Similar accounts of the beginnings of postmodernity are harder to find. Calhoun (1995) attributes this difficulty to the fact that postmodernism is more "pseudohistory" than a historically and culturally specific account of postmodernity. It is even more difficult to establish the link between postmodernism and postmodernity. Some, like Jameson (1992), argue that postmodernism arose as an aesthetic movement in response to economic and social changes. He proposes that postmodern cultural formations are associated with the stage of late capitalism, which he characterizes as multinational or consumer capitalism. Others point out, however, that postmodernism is merely an extension of modernism rather than a theory associated with some real empirical changes. As a critique of modernism, it comprises less a stylistic shift than a carry-over from counter-movements within modernity, itself represented by, for instance, Dadaism, Surrealism, the Bauhaus movement, or Russian formalism. In this sense, it bears a "family resemblance" with antimodernism, the critique of modernity within modernity. Habermas makes a stronger claim. Following in the tradition of other Frankfurt School critical theorists like Horkheimer and Adorno, Habermas is critical of Englishtement rationality. However, he believes that this is a tradition that can be traced back to modern thinkers like Schiller, Fichte, the Young Hegelians, and Nietzsche. Rather than abandoning the modern project, Habermas proposes "communicative reason" in place of "subject-centered reason." Communicative reason refers to the idea that consensual agreement can be dialogically arrived at through the articulation of validity claims.

Taking a slightly different approach on the subject of modernism, Latour, in his book *We Have Never Been Modern*, suggests, as the title indicates, that we have never really been modern. He bases this claim on one of the foundational dichotomies underlying modern thought, the dichotomy of nature and society. Latour argues that, in fact, these two realms have never been separate; "nature-cultures" have always existed in hybrid form, thereby casting doubt on the very legitimacy of modernity. Following the same logic, Latour is suspicious of the postmodern project as it also fails to question the premise of this dualism at the heart of the "modern Constitution." He proposes instead the alternative of adopting a non-modern or amodern position, which would acknowledge the legitimacy of hybrids.

In the final analysis, the debate about whether we live in a modern or postmodern world is largely an empty one, and we have seen the difficulty of defining definitively what a "postmodern" society looks like. What can be said, however, is that, as Kumar (1995: 178–9) states, postmodernism provides a valuable corrective to the standard accounts of modernity. Perhaps most importantly, it has brought into the scholarly and popular discourse, for instance, the "problem" of difference.

BIBLIOGRAPHY

Baudrillard, Jean. 1988. *Selected Writings*. Edited by Mark Poster. Cambridge: Polity Press. (An important voice that has come to be associated with postmodernism.)
Beck, Ulrich, Anthony Giddens and Scott Lash (eds.). 1994. *Reflexive Modernization, Politics, Tradition and Aesthetics in the Modern Social Order*. Cambridge: Polity Press. (A useful collection of essays on "late" modernity.)
Calhoun, Craig. 1995. *Critical Social Theory*. Cambridge, MA: Blackwell. (Includes a critique of postmodernism's historical claims.)
Derrida, Jacques. 1978. *Writing and Difference*. Chicago, IL: University of Chicago Press. (A key text by the leading proponent of deconstruction.)
Giddens, Anthony. 1990. *Modernity and Its Discontents*. Palo Alto, CA: Standford University Press. (A notable contribution to thinking on the transformation of modernity.)
Habermas, Jürgen. 1987. *The Philosophical Discourse of Modernity: Twelve Lectures*. Trans. Frederick Lawrence. Cambridge, MA: MIT Press. (An important contribution to the discussions on modernity and postmodernity.)
Harvey, David. 1989. *The Condition of Postmodernity: An Inquiry into the Origins of Cultural Change*. Oxford: Basil Blackwell. (An engaging book on the postmodern condition in the social, cultural, and political realm.)
Jameson, Frederic. 1992. *Postmodernism, or, The Cultural Logic of Late Capitalism*. London: Verso. (A Marxist account that figures prominently in discussions of postmodernism.)
Kilminster, Richard (ed.). 1996. *Culture, Modernity and Revolution: Essays in Honor of Zygmunt Bauman*. London: Routledge. (One of the most comprehensive collection of essays on Bauman.)
Kumar, Krishan. 1995. *From Post-Industrial to Post-Modern Society: New Theories of the Contemporary World*. Cambridge, MA: Blackwell. (A sophisticated account of modernity and postmodernity that is based in historical and theoretical explorations.)
Lemert, Charles. 1997. *Postmodernism Is Not What You Think*. Cambridge, MA: Blackwell. (An insightful account of postmodernism and its implications for the practice of sociology.)
Lyotard, Jean-François. 1984. *The Postmodern Condition: A Report on Knowledge*. Trans. G. Bennington and B. Massumi. Minneapolis, MN: University of Minnesota Press. (One of the most influential works on postmodernism.)
Seidman, Steven and David Wagner (eds.). 1992. *Postmodernism and Social Theory: The Debate over General Theory*. Cambridge, MA: Blackwell. (A collection of essays on the practice of sociology from a modernist, postmodernist, and a "between-modernist-and-postmodernist" position.)

Chapter 33

The Social Constraint towards Self-Constraint [1937]

Norbert Elias

What has the organization of society in the form of "states", what have the monopolization and centralization of taxes and physical force over a large area, to do with "civilization"?

The observer of the civilizing process finds himself confronted by a whole tangle of problems. To mention a few of the most important at the outset, there is, first of all, the most general question. We have seen that the civilizing process is a change of human conduct and sentiment in a quite specific direction. But, obviously, individual people did not at some past time intend this change, this "civilization", and gradually realize it by conscious, "rational", purposive measures. Clearly, "civilization" is not, any more than rationalization, a product of human "ratio" or the result of calculated long-term planning. How would it be conceivable that gradual "rationalization" could be founded on pre-existing "rational" behaviour and planning over centuries? Could one really imagine that the civilizing process had been set in motion by people with that long-term perspective, that specific mastery of all short-term affects, considering that this type of long-term perspective and self-mastery already presuppose a long civilizing process?

In fact, nothing in history indicates that this change was brought about "rationally", through any purposive education of individual people or groups. It happened by and large unplanned; but it did not happen, nevertheless, without a specific type of

Norbert Elias, "The Social Constraint towards Self-Constraint," pp. 443–8, 450–6 from Norbert Elias, *The Civilizing Process: The History of Manners and State Formation and Civilization*. Oxford: Basil Blackwell, 1978. Originally translated by Edmund Jephcott. Copyright © 1978 by Norbert Elias. Reprinted by permission of Blackwell Publishing Ltd.

Contemporary Sociological Theory, Third Edition. Edited by Craig Calhoun, Joseph Gerteis, James Moody, Steven Pfaff, and Indermohan Virk. Editorial material and organization © 2012 John Wiley & Sons, Ltd. Published 2012 by John Wiley & Sons, Ltd.

order. It has been shown in detail above how constraints through others from a variety of angles are converted into self-restraints, how the more animalic human activities are progressively thrust behind the scenes of men's communal social life and invested with feelings of shame, how the regulation of the whole instinctual and affective life by steady self-control becomes more and more stable, more even and more all-embracing. All this certainly does not spring from a rational idea conceived centuries ago by individual people and then implanted in one generation after another as the purpose of action and the desired state, until it was fully realized in the "centuries of progress". And yet, though not planned and intended, this transformation is not merely a sequence of unstructured and chaotic changes.

What poses itself here with regard to the civilizing process is nothing other than the general problem of historical change. Taken as a whole this change is not "rationally" planned; but neither is it a random coming and going of orderless patterns. How is this possible? How does it happen at all that formations arise in the human world that no single human being has intended, and which yet are anything but cloud formations without stability or structure?

It is simple enough: plans and actions, the emotional and rational impulses of individual people, constantly interweave in a friendly or hostile way. *This basic tissue resulting from many single plans and actions of men can give rise to changes and patterns that no individual person has planned or created. From this interdependence of people arises an order sui generis, an order more compelling and stronger than the will and reason of the individual people composing it.* It is this order of interweaving human impulses and strivings, this social order, which determines the course of historical change; it underlies the civilizing process.

This order is neither "rational" – if by "rational" we mean that it has resulted intentionally from the purposive deliberation of individual people; nor "irrational" – if by "irrational" we mean that it has arisen in an incomprehensible way. It has occasionally been identified with the order of "Nature"; it was interpreted by Hegel and some others as a kind of supra-individual "Spirit", and his concept of a "cunning of reason" shows how much he too was preoccupied by the fact that all the planning and actions of people give rise to many things that no one actually intended. But the mental habits which tend to bind us to opposites such as "rational" and "irrational", or "spirit" and "nature", prove inadequate here. In this respect, too, reality is not constructed quite as the conceptual apparatus of a particular standard would have us believe, whatever valuable services it may have performed in its time as a compass to guide us through an unknown world. *The immanent regularities of social figurations are identical neither with regularities of the "mind", of individual reasoning, nor with regularities of what we call "nature", even though functionally all these different dimensions of reality are indissolubly linked to each other.* [...] Civilization is not "reasonable"; not "rational", any more than it is "irrational". It is set in motion blindly, and kept in motion by the autonomous dynamics of a web of relationships, by specific changes in the way people are bound to live together. But it is by no means impossible that we can make out of it something more "reasonable", something that functions better in terms of our needs and purposes. For it is precisely in conjunction with the civilizing process that the blind dynamics of men intertwining in their deeds and aims gradually leads towards greater scope for planned intervention into both the social and individual structures – intervention based on a growing knowledge of the unplanned dynamics of these structures.

But which specific changes in the way people are bonded to each other mould their personality in a "civilizing" manner? The most general answer to this question too, an answer based on what was said earlier about the changes in Western society, is very simple. From the earliest period of the history of the Occident to the present, social functions have become more and more differentiated under the pressure of competition. The more differentiated they become, the larger grows the number of functions and thus of people on whom the individual constantly depends in all his actions, from the simplest and most commonplace to the more complex and uncommon. As more and more people must attune their conduct to that of others, the web of actions must be organized more and more strictly and accurately, if each individual action is to fulfil its social function. The individual is compelled to regulate his conduct in an increasingly differentiated, more even and more stable manner. That this involves not only a conscious regulation has already been stressed. Precisely this is characteristic of the psychological changes in the course of civilization: the more complex and stable control of conduct is increasingly instilled in the individual from his earliest years as an automatism, a self-compulsion that he cannot resist even if he consciously wishes to. The web of actions grows so complex and extensive, the effort required to behave "correctly" within it becomes so great, that beside the individual's conscious self-control an automatic, blindly functioning apparatus of self-control is firmly established. This seeks to prevent offences to socially acceptable behaviour by a wall of deep-rooted fears, but, just because it operates blindly and by habit, it frequently indirectly produces such collisions with social reality. But whether consciously or unconsciously, the direction of this transformation of conduct in the form of an increasingly differentiated regulation of impulses is determined by the direction of the process of social differentiation, by the progressive division of functions and the growth of the interdependency chains into which, directly or indirectly, every impulse, every move of an individual becomes integrated. [...]

The pattern of self-constraints, the template by which drives are moulded, certainly varies widely according to the function and position of the individual within this network, and there are even today in different sectors of the Western world variations of intensity and stability in the apparatus of self-constraint that seem at face value very large. At this point a multitude of particular questions are raised, and the sociogenetic method may give access to their answers. But when compared to the psychological make-up of people in less complex societies, these differences and degrees within more complex societies become less significant, and the main line of transformation, which is the primary concern of this study, emerges very clearly: as the social fabric grows more intricate, the sociogenic apparatus of individual self-control also becomes more differentiated, more all-round and more stable.

But the advancing differentiation of social functions is only the first, most general of the social transformations which we observe in enquiring into the change in psychological make-up known as "civilization". Hand in hand with this advancing division of functions goes a total reorganization of the social fabric. It was shown in detail earlier why, when the division of functions is low, the central organs of societies of a certain size are relatively unstable and liable to disintegration. It has been shown how, through specific figurational pressures, centrifugal tendencies, the mechanisms of feudalization, are slowly neutralized and how, step by step, a more stable central organization, a firmer monopolization of physical force, are established. The peculiar stability of the apparatus of mental self-restraint which emerges as a decisive trait built into the habits of every "civilized" human being, stands in the closest relationship to the monopolization of physical force and the growing stability of the central organs of society. Only with the formation of this kind of relatively stable monopolies do societies acquire those characteristics as a result of which the individuals forming them get attuned, from infancy, to a highly regulated and differentiated pattern of self-restraint; only in conjunction with these monopolies does this kind of self-restraint require a higher degree of automaticity, does it become, as it were, "second nature".

When a monopoly of force is formed, pacified social spaces are created which are normally free from acts of violence. The pressures acting on individual people within them are of a different kind than previously. Forms of non-physical violence that always existed, but hitherto had always been mingled or fused with physical force, are now separated from the latter; they persist in a changed form internally within the more pacified societies. They are most visible so far as the standard thinking of our time is concerned as types of economic violence. In reality, however, there is a whole set of means whose monopolization can enable men as groups or as individuals to enforce their will upon others. The monopolization of the means of production, of "economic" means, is only one of those which stand out in fuller relief when the means of physical violence become monopolized, when, in other words, in a more pacified state society the free use of physical force by those who are physically stronger is no longer possible.

In general, the direction in which the behaviour and the affective make-up of people change when the structure of human relationships is transformed in the manner described, is as follows: societies without a stable monopoly of force are always societies in which the division of functions is relatively slight and the chains of action binding individuals together are comparatively short. Conversely, societies with more stable monopolies of force, always first embodied in a large princely or royal court, are societies in which the division of functions is more or less advanced, in which the chains of action binding individuals together are longer and the functional dependencies between people greater. Here the individual is largely protected from sudden attack, the irruption of physical violence into his life. But at the same time he is himself forced to suppress in himself any passionate impulse urging him to attack another physically. And the other forms of compulsion which now prevail in the pacified social spaces pattern the individual's conduct and affective impulses in the same direction. The closer the web of interdependence becomes in which the individual is enmeshed with the advancing division of functions, the larger the social spaces over which this network extends and which become integrated into functional or institutional units – the more threatened is the social existence of the individual who gives way to spontaneous impulses and emotions, the greater is the social advantage of those able to moderate their affects, and the more strongly is each individual constrained from an early age to take account of the effects of his own or other people's actions on a whole series of links in the social chain. The moderation of spontaneous emotions, the tempering of affects, the extension of mental space beyond the moment into the past and future, the habit of connecting events in terms of chains of cause and effect – all these are different aspects of the same transformation of conduct which necessarily takes place with the monopolization of physical violence, and the lengthening of the chains of social action and interdependence. It is a "civilizing" change of behaviour. [...]

As the structure of human relations changes, as monopoly organizations of physical force develop and the individual is held no longer in the sway of constant feuds and wars but rather in the more permanent compulsions of peaceful functions based on the acquisition of money or prestige, affect-expressions too slowly gravitate towards a middle line. The fluctuations in behaviour and affects do not disappear, but are moderated. The peaks and abysses are smaller, the changes less abrupt.

We can see what is changing more clearly from its obverse. Through the formation of monopolies of force, the threat which one man represents for another is subject to stricter control and becomes more calculable. Everyday life is freer of sudden reversals of fortune. Physical violence is confined to barracks; and from this store-house it breaks out only in extreme cases, in times of war or social upheaval, into individual life. As the monopoly of certain specialist groups it is normally excluded from the life of others; and these specialists, the whole monopoly organization of force, now stand guard only in the margin of social life as a control on individual conduct.

Even in this form as a control organization, however, physical violence and the threat emanating from it have a determining influence on individuals in society, whether they know it or not. It is, however, no longer a perpetual insecurity that it brings into the life of the individual, but a peculiar form of security. It no longer throws him, in the swaying fortunes of battle, as the physical victor or vanquished, between mighty outbursts of pleasure and terror; a continuous, uniform pressure is exerted on individual life by the physical violence stored behind the scenes of everyday life, a pressure totally familiar and hardly perceived, conduct and drive economy having been adjusted from earliest youth to this social structure. It is in fact the whole social mould, the code of conduct which changes; and accordingly with it changes, as has been said before, not only this or that specific form of conduct but its whole pattern, the whole structure of the way individuals steer themselves. The monopoly organization of physical violence does not usually constrain the individual by a direct threat. A strongly predictable compulsion or pressure mediated in a variety of ways is constantly exerted on the individual. This operates to a considerable extent through the medium of his own reflection. It is normally only potentially present in society, as an agency of control; the actual compulsion is one that the individual exerts on himself either as a result of his knowledge of the possible consequences of his moves in the game in intertwining activities, or as a result of corresponding gestures of adults which have helped to pattern his own behaviour as a child. The monopolization of physical violence, the concentration of arms and armed men under one authority, makes the use of violence more or less calculable, and forces unarmed men in the pacified social spaces to restrain their own violence through foresight or reflection; in other words it imposes on people a greater or lesser degree of self-control.

This is not to say that every form of self-control was entirely lacking in medieval warrior society or in other societies without a complex and stable monopoly of physical violence. The agency of individual self-control, the super-ego, the conscience or whatever we call it, is instilled, imposed and maintained in such warrior societies only in direct relation to acts of physical violence; its form matches this life in its greater contrasts and more abrupt transitions. Compared to the self-control agency in more pacified societies, it is diffuse, unstable, only a slight barrier to violent emotional outbursts. The fears securing socially "correct" conduct are not yet banished to remotely the same extent from the individual's consciousness into his so-called "inner life". As the decisive danger does not come from failure or relaxation of self-control, but from direct external physical threat, habitual fear predominantly takes the form of fear of external powers. And as this fear is less stable, the control apparatus too is less encompassing, more one-sided or partial. In such a society extreme self-control in enduring pain may be instilled; but this is complemented by what, measured by a different standard, appears as an extreme form of freewheeling of affects in torturing others. Similarly, in certain sectors of medieval society we find extreme forms of asceticism, self-restraint and renunciation, contrasting to a no less extreme indulgence of pleasure in others, and frequently enough we encounter sudden switches from one attitude to the other in the life of an individual person. The restraint the individual here imposes on himself, the struggle against his own flesh, is no less intense and one-sided, no less radical and passionate than its counterpart, the fight against others and the maximum enjoyment of pleasures.

What is established with the monopolization of physical violence in the pacified social spaces is a different type of self-control or self-constraint. It is a more dispassionate self-control. The controlling agency forming itself as part of the individual's personality structure corresponds to the controlling agency forming itself in society at large. The one like the other tends to impose a highly differentiated regulation upon all passionate impulses, upon men's conduct all around. Both – each to a large extent mediated by the other – exert a constant, even pressure to inhibit affective outbursts. They damp down extreme fluctuations in behaviour and emotions. As the monopolization of physical force reduces the fear and terror one man must have for another, but at the same time reduces the possibility of causing others terror, fear or torment, and therefore certain possibilities of pleasurable emotional release, the constant self-control to which the individual is now increasingly accustomed seeks to reduce the contrasts and sudden switches in conduct, and the affective charge of all self-expression. The pressures operating upon the individual now tend to produce a transformation of the whole drive and affect economy in the direction of a more continuous, stable and even regulation of drives and affects in all areas of conduct, in all sectors of his life.

And it is in exactly the same direction that the unarmed compulsions operate, the constraints without direct physical violence to which the individual is now exposed in the pacified spaces, and of which economic restraints are an instance. They too are less affect-charged, more moderate, stable and less erratic than the constraints exerted by one person on another in a monopoly-free warrior society. And they, too, embodied in the entire spectrum of functions open to the individual in society, induce incessant hindsight and foresight transcending the moment and corresponding to the longer and more complex chains in which each act is now automatically enmeshed. They require the individual incessantly to overcome his momentary affective impulses in keeping with the longer-term effects of his behaviour. Relative to the other standard, they instil a more even self-control encompassing his whole conduct like a tight ring, and a more steady regulation of his drives according to the social norms. Moreover, as always, it is not only the adult functions themselves which immediately produce this tempering of drives and affects; partly automatically, partly quite consciously through their own conduct and habits, adults induce corresponding behaviour-patterns in children. From earliest youth the individual is trained in the constant restraint and foresight that he needs for adult functions. This self-restraint is ingrained so deeply from an early age that, like a kind of relay-station of social standards, an automatic self-supervision of his drives, a more differentiated and more stable "super-ego" develops in him, and a part of the forgotten drive impulses and affect inclinations is no longer directly within reach of the level of consciousness at all.

Earlier, in warrior society, the individual could use physical violence if he was strong and powerful enough; he could openly indulge his inclinations in many directions that have subsequently been closed by social prohibitions. But he paid for this greater opportunity of direct pleasure with a greater chance of direct and open fear. Medieval conceptions of hell give us an idea of how strong this fear between man and man was. Both joy and pain were discharged more openly and freely. But the individual was their prisoner; he was hurled back and forth by his own feelings as by forces of nature. He had less control of his passions; he was more controlled by them.

Later, as the conveyor belts running through his existence grow longer and more complex, the individual learns to control himself more steadily; he is now less a prisoner of his passions than before. But as he is now more tightly bound by his functional dependence on the activities of an ever-larger number of people, he is much more restricted in his conduct, in his chances of directly satisfying his drives and passions. Life becomes in a sense less dangerous, but also less emotional or pleasurable, at least as far as the direct release of pleasure is concerned. And for what is lacking in everyday life a substitute is created in dreams, in books and pictures. So, on their way to becoming courtiers, the nobility read novels of chivalry; the bourgeois contemplate violence and erotic passion in films. Physical clashes, wars and feuds diminish, and anything recalling them, even the cutting up of dead animals and the use of the knife at table, is banished from view or at least subjected to more and more precise social rules. But at the same time the battlefield is, in a sense, moved within. Part of the tensions and passions that were earlier directly released in the struggle of man and man, must now be worked out within the human being. The more peaceful constraints exerted on him by his relations to others are mirrored within him; an individualized pattern of near-automatic habits is established and consolidated within him, a specific "super-ego", which endeavours to control, transform or suppress his affects in keeping with the social structure. But the drives, the passionate affects, that can no longer directly manifest themselves in the relationships *between* people, often struggle no less violently *within* the individual against this supervising part of himself. And this semi-automatic struggle of the person with himself does not always find a happy resolution; not always does the self-transformation required by life in this society lead to a new balance between drive-satisfaction and drive-control. Often enough it is subject to major or minor disturbances, revolts of one part of the person against the other, or a permanent atrophy, which makes the performance of social functions even more difficult, or impossible. The vertical oscillations, if we may so describe them, the leaps from fear to joy, pleasure to remorse are reduced, while the horizontal fissure running right through the whole person, the tension between "super-ego" and "unconscious" – the wishes and desires that cannot be remembered – increases.

Here too the basic characteristics of these patterns of intertwining, if one pursues not merely their static structures but their sociogenesis, prove to be relatively simple. Through the interdependence of larger groups of people and the exclusion of physical violence from them, a social apparatus is established in which the constraints between people are lastingly transformed into self-constraints. These self-constraints, a function of the perpetual hindsight and foresight instilled in the individual from childhood in accordance with his integration in extensive chains of action, have partly the form of conscious self-control and partly that of automatic habit. They tend towards a more even moderation, a more continuous restraint, a more exact control of drives and affects in accordance with the more differentiated pattern of social interweaving. But depending on the inner pressure, on the condition of society and the position of the individual within it, these constraints also produce peculiar tensions and disturbances in the conduct and drive economy of the individual. In some cases they lead to perpetual restlessness and dissatisfaction, precisely because the person affected can only gratify a part of his inclinations and impulses in modified form, for example in fantasy, in looking-on and overhearing, in daydreams or dreams. And sometimes the habituation to affect-inhibition goes so far – constant feelings of boredom or solitude are examples of this – that the individual is no longer capable of any form of fearless expression of the modified affects, or of direct gratification of the repressed drives. Particular branches of drives are as it were anaesthetized in such cases by the specific structure of the social framework in which the child grows up. Under the pressure of the dangers that their expression incurs in the child's social space, they become surrounded with automatic fears to such an extent that they can remain deaf and unresponsive throughout a whole lifetime. In other cases certain branches of drives may be so diverted by the heavy conflicts which the rough-hewn, affective and passionate nature of the small human being unavoidably encounters on its way to being moulded into a "civilized" being, that their energies can find only an unwanted release through bypasses, in compulsive actions and other symptoms of disturbance. In other cases again, these energies are so transformed that they flow into uncontrollable and eccentric attachments and repulsions, in predilections for this or that peculiar hobby-horse. And in all these cases a permanent, apparently groundless inner unrest shows how many drive energies are dammed up in a form that permits no real satisfaction.

Until now the individual civilizing process, like the social, runs its course by and large blindly. Under the cover of what adults think and plan, the relationship that forms between them and the young has functions and effects in the latter's personalities which they do not intend and of which they scarcely know. Unplanned in that sense are those results of social patterning of individuals to which one habitually refers as "abnormal"; psychological abnormalities which do not result from social patterning but are caused by unalterable hereditary traits need not be considered here. But the psychological make-up which keeps within the social norm and is subjectively more satisfying comes about in an equally unplanned way. It is the same social mould from which emerge both more favourably and more unfavourably structured human beings, the "well-adjusted" as well as the "mal-adjusted", within a very broad spectrum of varieties. The automatically reproduced anxieties which, in the course of each individual civilizing process and in connection with the conflicts that form an integral part of this process, attach themselves to specific drives and affect impulses sometimes lead to a permanent and total paralysis of these impulses, and sometimes only to a moderate regulation with enough scope for their full satisfaction. Under present conditions it is from the point of view of the individuals concerned more a question of their good or bad fortune than that of anybody's planning whether it is the one or the other. In either case it is the web of social relations in which the individual lives during his most impressionable phase, during childhood and youth, which imprints itself upon his unfolding personality where it has its counterpart in the relationship between his controlling agencies, super-ego and ego, and his libidinal impulses. The resulting balance between controlling agencies and drives on a variety of levels determines how an individual person steers himself in his relations with others; it determines that which we call, according to taste, habits, complexes or personality structure. However, there is no end to the intertwining, for although the self-steering of a person, malleable during early childhood, solidifies and hardens as he grows up, it never ceases entirely to be affected by his changing relations with others throughout his life. The learning of self-controls, call them "reason" or "conscience", "ego" or "super-ego", and the consequent curbing of more animalic impulses and affects, in short the civilizing of the human young, is never a process entirely without pain; it always leaves scars. If the person is lucky – and as no one, no parent, no doctor, and no counsellor, is at present able to steer this process in a child according to a clear knowledge of what is best for its future, it is still largely a question of luck – the wounds of the civilizing conflicts incurred during childhood heal; the scars left by them are not too deep. But in less favourable cases the conflicts inherent in the civilizing of young humans – conflicts with others and conflicts within themselves – remain unsolved, or, more precisely, though perhaps buried for a while, open up once more in situations reminiscent of those of childhood; the suffering, transformed into an adult form, repeats itself again and again, and the unsolved conflicts of a person's childhood never cease to disturb his adult relationships. In that way, the interpersonal conflicts of early youth which have patterned the personality structure continue to perturb or even destroy the interpersonal relationships of the grown-up. The resulting tensions may take the form either of contradictions between different self-control automatisms, sunk-in memory traces of former dependencies and needs, or of recurrent struggles between the controlling agencies and the libidinal impulses. In the more fortunate cases, on the other hand, the contradictions between different sections and layers of the controlling agencies, especially of the super-ego structure, are slowly reconciled; the most disruptive conflicts between that structure and the libidinal impulses are slowly contained. They not only disappear from waking consciousness, but are so thoroughly assimilated that, without too heavy a cost in subjective satisfaction, they no longer intrude unintentionally in later interpersonal relationships. In one case the conscious and unconscious self-control always remains diffuse in places and open to the breakthrough of socially unproductive forms of drive energy; in the other this self-control, which even today in juvenile phases is often more like a confusion of overlapping ice-floes than a smooth and firm sheet of ice, slowly becomes more unified and stable in positive correspondence to the structure of society. But as this structure, precisely in our times, is highly mutable, it demands a flexibility of habits and conduct which in most cases has to be paid for by a loss of stability.

Theoretically, therefore, it is not difficult to say in what lies the difference between an individual civilizing process that is considered successful and one that is considered unsuccessful. In the former, after all the pains and conflicts of this process, patterns of conduct well adapted to the framework of adult social functions are finally formed, an adequately functioning set of habits and at the same time – which does not necessarily go hand-in-hand with it – a positive pleasure balance. In the other, either the socially necessary self-control is repeatedly purchased, at a heavy cost in personal satisfaction, by a major effort to overcome opposed libidinal energies, or the control of these energies, renunciation of their satisfaction is not achieved at all; and often enough no positive pleasure balance of any kind is finally possible, because the social commands and prohibitions are represented not only by other people but also by the stricken self, since one part of it forbids and punishes what the other desires.

In reality the result of the individual civilizing process is clearly unfavourable or favourable only in relatively few cases at each end of the scale. The majority of civilized people live midway between these two extremes. Socially positive and negative features, personally gratifying and frustrating tendencies, mingle in them in varying proportions.

The social moulding of individuals in accordance with the structure of the civilizing process of what we now call the West is particularly difficult. In order to be reasonably successful it requires with the structure of Western society, a particularly high differentiation, an especially intensive and stable regulation of drives and affects, of all the more elementary human impulses. It therefore generally takes up more time, particularly in the middle and upper classes, than the social moulding of individuals in less complex societies. Resistance to adaptation to the prevailing standards of civilization, the effort which this adaptation, this profound transformation of the whole personality costs the individual, is always very considerable. And later, therefore, than in less complex societies the individual in the Western world attains with his adult social function the psychological make-up of an adult, the emergence of which by and large marks the conclusion of the individual civilizing process.

But even if in the more differentiated societies of the West the modelling of the individual self-steering apparatus is particularly extensive and intense, processes tending in the same direction, social and individual civilizing processes, most certainly do not occur only there. They are to be found wherever, under competitive pressures, the division of functions makes large numbers of people dependent on one another, wherever a monopolization of physical force permits and imposes a cooperation less charged with emotion, wherever functions are established that demand constant hindsight and foresight in interpreting the actions and intentions of others. What determines the nature and degree of such civilizing spurts is always the extent of interdependencies, the level of the division of functions, and within it, the structure of these functions themselves.

Chapter 34

Modernity and the Holocaust [1989]

Zygmunt Bauman

"Wouldn't you be happier if I had been able to show you that all the perpetrators were crazy?" asks the great historian of the Holocaust, Raul Hilberg. Yet this is precisely what he is *unable* to show. The truth he does show brings no comfort. It is unlikely to make anybody happy. "They were educated men of their time. That is the crux of the question whenever we ponder the meaning of Western Civilization after Auschwitz. Our evolution has outpaced our understanding; we can no longer assume that we have a full grasp of the workings of our social institutions, bureaucratic structures, or technology."[1]

This is certainly bad news for philosophers, sociologists, theologians and all the other learned men and women who are professionally concerned with understanding and explaining. Hilberg's conclusions mean that they have not done their job well; they cannot explain what has happened and why, and they cannot help us to understand it. This charge is bad enough as far as the scientists go (it is bound to make the scholars restless, and may even send them, as they say, back to the drawing board), but in itself it is not a cause for public alarm. There have been, after all, many other important events in the past that we feel we do not fully understand. Sometimes this makes us angry; most of the time, however, we do not feel particularly perturbed. After all – so we console ourselves – these past events are matters of *academic interest*.

But are they? It is not the Holocaust which we find difficult to grasp in all its monstrosity. *It is our Western Civilization which the occurrence of the Holocaust has*

Zygmunt Bauman, "Modernity and the Holocaust," pp. 83–6, 86–95, 95–102, 103–4, 106–9, 111–13, 217–18 from Zygmunt Bauman, *Modernity and the Holocaust*. Ithaca, NY: Cornell University Press, 1989. Copyright © 1989 by Zygmunt Bauman. Reprinted by permission of Polity Press and Cornell University Press.

Contemporary Sociological Theory, Third Edition. Edited by Craig Calhoun, Joseph Gerteis, James Moody, Steven Pfaff, and Indermohan Virk. Editorial material and organization © 2012 John Wiley & Sons, Ltd. Published 2012 by John Wiley & Sons, Ltd.

made all but incomprehensible – and this at a time when we thought we had come to terms with it and seen through its innermost drives and even through its prospects, and at a time of its world-wide, unprecedented cultural expansion. If Hilberg is right, and our most crucial social institutions elude our mental and practical grasp, then it is not just the professional academics who ought to be worried. True, the Holocaust occurred almost half a century ago. True, its immediate results are fast receding into the past. The generation that experienced it at first hand has almost died out. But – and this is an awesome, sinister "but" – these once-familiar features of our civilization, which the Holocaust had made mysterious again, are still very much part of our life. They have not gone away. Neither has, therefore, the *possibility* of the Holocaust.

We shrug off such a possibility. We pooh-pooh the few obsessed people riled by our balance of mind. We have a special, derisive name for them – "prophets of doom". It comes easy to dismiss their anguished warnings. Are we not vigilant already? Do we not condemn violence, immorality, cruelty? Do we not muster all our ingenuity and considerable, constantly growing resources to fight them? And besides, is there anything at all in our life that points to the sheer possibility of a catastrophe? Life is getting better and more comfortable. On the whole, our institutions seem to cope. Against the enemy, we are well protected, and our friends surely won't do anything nasty. Granted, we hear from time to time of atrocities that some not particularly civilized, and for this reason spiritually far-away people, visit upon their equally barbaric neighbours. Ewe massacre a million Ibos, having first called them vermin, criminals, money-grabbers and subhumans without culture;[2] Iraqis poison-gas their Kurdish citizens without even bothering to call them names; Tamils massacre Singhalese; Ethiopians exterminate Eritreans; Ugandans exterminate themselves (or was it the other way round?). It is all sad, of course, but what can it possibly have to do with us? If it proves anything at all, it certainly proves how bad it is to be unlike us, and how good it is to be safe and sound behind the shield of our superior civilization.

Just how untoward our complacency may prove in the end becomes apparent once we recall that still in 1941 the Holocaust was not expected; that, given the extant knowledge of the "facts of the case", it was not expectable; and that, when it finally came to pass one year later, it met with universal incredulity. People refused to believe the facts they stared at. Not that they were obtuse or ill-willed. It was just that nothing they had known before had prepared them to believe. For all they had known and believed, the mass murder for which they did not even have a name yet was, purely and simply, unimaginable. In 1988, it is unimaginable again. In 1988, however, we know what we did not know in 1941; that also *the unimaginable ought to be imagined.*

The Problem

There are two reasons for which the Holocaust, unlike many other topics of academic study, cannot be seen as a matter of solely academic interest; and for which the problem of the Holocaust cannot be reduced to the subject-matter of historical research and philosophical contemplation.

The first reason is that the Holocaust, even if it is plausible that, "as a central historical event – not unlike the French Revolution, the discovery of America, or the discovery of the wheel – it has changed the course of subsequent history,"[3] has most certainly changed little, if anything, in the course of the subsequent history of our collective consciousness and self-understanding. It made little visible impact on our image of the meaning and historical tendency of modern civilization. It left the social sciences in general, and sociology in particular, virtually unmoved and intact, except for the still marginal regions of specialist research, and some dark and ominous warnings of the morbid proclivities of modernity. Both exceptions are consistently kept at a distance from the canon of sociological practice. For these reasons, our understanding of the factors and mechanisms that once made the Holocaust possible has not significantly advanced. And with the understanding not much improved over that of half a century ago, we could be once more unprepared to notice and decode the warning signs – were they now, as they had been then, blatantly displayed all around.

The second reason is that whatever happened to the "course of history", nothing much happened to those products of history which in all probability contained the potentiality of the Holocaust – or at least we cannot be sure that it did. For all we know (or, rather, for all we do not know) they may still be with us, waiting for their chance. We can only suspect that the conditions that once before gave birth to the Holocaust have not been radically transformed. If there was something in our social order which made the Holocaust possible in 1941, we cannot be sure that it has been eliminated since then. [...]

> Within certain limits set by political and military power considerations, the modern state may do anything it wishes to those under its control. There is no moral-ethical limit which the state cannot transcend if it wishes to do so, because there is no moral-ethical power higher than the state. In matters of ethics and morality, the situation of the individual in the modern state is in principle roughly equivalent to the situation of the prisoner in Auschwitz: either act in accord with the prevailing standards of conduct enforced by those in authority, or risk whatever consequences they may wish to impose [...]
>
> Existence now is more and more recognizably in accord with the principles that governed life and death in Auschwitz. (George M. Kren and Leon Rappoport)[4]

Overwhelmed by the emotions which even a perfunctory reading of the Holocaust records cannot but arouse, some of the quoted authors are prone to exaggerate. Some of their statements sound incredible – and certainly unduly alarmist. They may be even counterproductive; if everything we know is like Auschwitz, then one can live with Auschwitz, and in many a case live reasonably well. If the principles that ruled over life and death of Auschwitz inmates were like these that rule our own, then what has all this outcry and lamentation been about? Truly, one would be well advised to avoid the temptation to deploy the inhuman imagery of the Holocaust in the service of a partisan stance towards larger or smaller, but on the whole routine and daily human conflicts. Mass destruction was the extreme form of antagonism and oppression, yet not all cases of oppression, communal hatred and injustice are "like" the Holocaust. Overt, and hence superficial similarity is a poor guide to causal analysis. Contrary to what Kren and Rappoport suggest, having to choose between conformity and bearing the consequences of disobedience does not necessarily mean living in Auschwitz, and the principles preached and practised by most contemporary states do not suffice to make their citizens into Holocaust victims.

The real cause for concern, one that cannot be easily argued away, nor dismissed as a natural yet misleading outcome of post-Holocaust trauma, lies elsewhere. It can be gleaned from two related facts.

First, ideational processes that by their own inner logic may lead to genocidal projects, and the technical resources that permit implementation of such projects, not only have been proved fully compatible with modern civilization, but have been conditioned, created and supplied by it. The Holocaust did not just, mysteriously, avoid clash with the social norms and institutions of modernity. It was these norms and institutions that made the Holocaust feasible. Without modern civilization and its most central essential achievements, there would be no Holocaust.

Second, all those intricate networks of checks and balances, barriers and hurdles which the civilizing process has erected and which, as we hope and trust, would defend us from violence and constrain all [our] ambitious and unscrupulous powers, have been proven ineffective. When it came to mass murder, the victims found themselves alone. Not only had they been fooled by an apparently peaceful and humane, legalistic and orderly society – their sense of security became a most powerful factor of their downfall.

To put it bluntly, there are reasons to be worried because we know now that *we live in a type of society that made the Holocaust possible, and that contained nothing which could stop the Holocaust from happening.* For these reasons alone it is necessary to study the lessons of the Holocaust. Much more is involved in such a study than the tribute to the memory of murdered millions, settling the account with the murderers and healing the still-festering moral wounds of the passive and silent witnesses.

Obviously, the study itself, even a most diligent study, is not a sufficient guarantee against the return of mass murderers and numb bystanders. Yet without such a study, we would not even know how likely or improbable such a return may be.

Genocide Extraordinary

Mass murder is not a modern invention. History is fraught with communal and sectarian enmities, always mutually damaging and potentially destructive, often erupting into overt violence, sometimes leading to massacre, and in some cases resulting in extermination of whole populations and cultures. On the face of it, this fact denies the uniqueness of the Holocaust. In particular, it seems to deny the intimate link between the Holocaust and modernity, the "elective affinity" between the Holocaust and modern civilization. It suggests instead that murderous communal hatred has always been with us and will probably never go away; and that the only significance of modernity in this respect is that, contrary to its promise and to the widespread expectations, it did not file smooth the admittedly rough edges of human coexistence and thus has not put a definite end to man's inhumanity to man. Modernity has not delivered on its promise. Modernity has failed. But modernity bears no responsibility for the episode of the Holocaust – as genocide accompanied human history from the start.

This is not, however, the lesson contained in the experience of the Holocaust. No doubt the Holocaust was another episode in the long series of attempted mass murders and the not much shorter series of accomplished ones. It also bore features that it did not share with any of the past cases of genocide. It is these features which deserve special attention. They had a distinct modern flavour. Their presence suggests that modernity contributed to the Holocaust more directly than through its own weakness and ineptitude. It suggests that the role of modern civilization in the incidence and the perpetration of the Holocaust was active, not passive. It suggests that the Holocaust was as much a product, as it was a failure, of modern civilization. Like everything else done in the modern – rational, planned, scientifically informed, expert, efficiently managed, co-ordinated – way, the Holocaust left behind and put to shame all its alleged pre-modern equivalents, exposing them as primitive, wasteful and ineffective by comparison. Like everything else in our modern society, the Holocaust was an accomplishment in every respect superior, if measured by the standards that this society has preached and institutionalized. It towers high above the past genocidal episodes in the same way as the modern industrial plant towers above the craftsman's cottage workshop, or the modern industrial farm, with its tractors, combines and pesticides, towers above the peasant farmstead with its horse, hoe and hand-weeding.

On 9 November 1938 an event took place in Germany which went down in history under the name of *Kristallnacht*. Jewish businesses, seats of worship, and homes were attacked by an unruly, though officially encouraged and surreptitiously controlled, mob; they were broken down, set on fire, vandalized. About one hundred persons lost their lives. *Kristallnacht* was the only large-scale pogrom that occurred on the streets of German towns throughout the duration of the Holocaust. It was also the one episode of the Holocaust that followed the established, centuries-old tradition of anti-Jewish mob violence. It did not differ much from past pogroms; it hardly stood out from the long line of crowd violence stretching from ancient time, through the Middle Ages and up to the almost contemporary, but still largely pre-modern, Russia, Poland or Rumania. Were the Nazis treatment of the Jews composed only of *Kristallnächte* and suchlike events, it would hardly add anything but an extra paragraph, a chapter at best, to the multi-volume chronicle of emotions running amok, of lynching mobs, of soldiers looting and raping their way through the conquered towns. This was not, however, to be.

This was not to be for a simple reason: one could neither conceive of, nor make, mass murder on the Holocaust scale of no matter how many *Kristallnächte*.

Consider the numbers. The German state annihilated approximately six million Jews. At the rate of 100 per day this would have required nearly 200 years. Mob violence rests on the wrong psychological basis, on violent emotion. People can be manipulated into fury, but fury cannot be maintained for 200 years. Emotions, and their biological basis, have a natural time course; lust, even blood lust, is eventually sated. Further, emotions are notoriously fickle, can be turned. A lynch mob is unreliable, it can sometimes be moved by sympathy – say by a child's suffering. To eradicate a "race" it is essential to kill the children.

Thorough, comprehensive, exhaustive murder required the replacement of the mob with a bureaucracy, the replacement of shared rage with obedience to authority. The requisite bureaucracy would be effective whether manned by extreme or tepid anti-Semites, considerably broadening the pool of potential recruits; it would govern the actions of its members not by arousing passions but by organizing routines; it would only make distinctions it was designed to make, not those its members might be moved to make, say, between children and adults, scholar and thief, innocent and guilty; it would be responsive to the will of the ultimate authority through a hierarchy of responsibility – whatever that will might be.[5]

Rage and fury are pitiably primitive and inefficient as tools of mass annihilation. They normally peter out before the job is done. One cannot build grand designs on them. Certainly not such designs as reach beyond momentary effects like a wave of terror, the breakdown of an old order, clearing the ground for a new rule. Ghengis Khan and Peter the Hermit did not need modern technology and modern, scientific methods of management and co-ordination. Stalin or Hitler did. It is the adventurers and dilettantes like Ghengis Khan and Peter the Hermit that our modern, rational society has discredited and, arguably, put paid to. It is the practitioners of cool, thorough and systematic genocide like Stalin and Hitler for whom the modern, rational society paved the way.

Most conspicuously, the modern cases of genocide stand out for their sheer scale. On no other occasion but during Hitler's and Stalin's rule were so many people murdered in such a short time. This is not, however, the only novelty, perhaps not even a primary one – merely a by-product of other, more seminal features. Contemporary mass murder is distinguished by a virtual absence of all spontaneity on the one hand, and the prominence of rational, carefully calculated design on the other. It is marked by an almost complete elimination of contingency and chance, and independence from group emotions and personal motives. It is set apart by merely sham or marginal – disguising or decorative – role of ideological mobilization. But first and foremost, it stands out by its purpose.

Murderous motives in general, and motives for mass murder in particular, have been many and varied. They range from pure, cold-blooded calculation of competitive gain, to equally pure, disinterested hatred or heterophobia. Most communal strifes and genocidal campaigns against aborigines lie comfortably within this range. If accompanied by an ideology, the latter does not go much further than a simple "us or them" vision of the world, and a precept "There is no room for both of us", or "The only good injun is a dead injun". The adversary is expected to follow mirror-image principles only if allowed to. Most genocidal ideologies rest on a devious symmetry of assumed intentions and actions.

Truly modern genocide is different. *Modern genocide is genocide with a purpose.* Getting rid of the adversary is not an end in itself. It is a means to an end: a necessity that stems from the ultimate objective, a step that one has to take if one wants ever to reach the end of the road. *The end itself is a grand vision of a better, and radically different, society.* Modern genocide is an element of social engineering, meant to bring about a social order conforming to the design of the perfect society.

To the initiators and the managers of modern genocide, society is a subject of planning and conscious design. One can and should do more about the society than change one or several of its many details, improve it here or there, cure some of its troublesome ailments. One can and should set oneself goals more ambitious and radical: one can and should remake the society, force it to conform to an overall, scientifically conceived plan. One can create a society that is objectively better than the one "merely existing" – that is, existing without conscious intervention. Invariably, there is an aesthetic dimension to the design: the ideal world about to be built conforms to the standards of superior beauty. Once built, it will be richly satisfying, like a perfect work of art; it will be a world which, in Alberti's immortal words, no adding, diminishing or altering could improve.

This is a gardener's vision, projected upon a world-size screen. The thoughts, feelings, dreams and drives of the designers of the perfect world are familiar to every gardener worth his name, though perhaps on a somewhat smaller scale. Some gardeners hate the weeds that spoil their design – that ugliness in the midst of beauty, litter in the midst of serene order. Some others are quite unemotional about them: just a problem to be solved, an extra job to be done. Not that it makes a difference to the weeds; both gardeners exterminate them. If asked or given a chance to pause and ponder, both would agree; weeds must die not so much because of what they are, as because of what the beautiful, orderly garden ought to be.

Modern culture is a garden culture. It defines itself as the design for an ideal life and a perfect arrangement of human conditions. It constructs its own identity out of distrust of nature. In fact, it defines itself and nature, and the distinction between them, through its endemic distrust of spontaneity and its longing for a better, and necessarily artificial, order. Apart from the overall plan, the artificial *order* of the garden needs tools and raw materials. It also needs defence – against the unrelenting danger of what is, obviously, a disorder. The order, first conceived of as a design, determines what is a tool, what is a raw material, what is useless, what is irrelevant, what is harmful, what is a weed or a pest. It classifies all elements of the universe by their relation to itself. This relation is the only meaning it grants them and tolerates – and the only justification of the gardener's actions, as differentiated as the relations themselves. From the point of view of the design all actions are instrumental, while all the objects of action are either facilities or hindrances.

Modern genocide, like modern culture in general, is a gardener's job. It is just one of the many chores that people who treat society as a garden need to undertake. If garden design defines its weeds, there are weeds wherever there is a garden. And weeds are to be exterminated. Weeding out is a creative, not a destructive activity. It does not differ in kind from other activities which combine in the construction and sustenance of the perfect garden. All visions of society-as-garden define parts of the social habitat as human weeds. Like all other weeds, they must be segregated, contained, prevented from spreading, removed and kept outside the society boundaries; if all these means prove insufficient, they must be killed.

Stalin's and Hitler's victims were not killed in order to capture and colonize the territory they occupied. Often they were killed in a dull, mechanical fashion with no human emotions – hatred included – to enliven it. They were killed because they did not fit, for one reason or another, the scheme of a perfect society. Their killing was not the work of destruction, but creation. They were eliminated, so that an objectively better human world – more efficient, more moral, more beautiful – could be established. A Communist world. Or a racially pure, Aryan world. In both cases, a harmonious world, conflict-free, docile in the hands of their rulers, orderly, controlled. People tainted with ineradicable blight of their past or origin could not be fitted into such unblemished, healthy and shining world. Like weeds, their nature could not be changed. They could not be improved or re-educated. They had to be eliminated for reasons of genetic or ideational heredity – of a natural mechanism, resilient and immune to cultural processing.

The two most notorious and extreme cases of modern genocide did not betray the spirit of modernity. They did not deviously depart from the main track of the civilizing process. They were the most consistent, uninhibited expressions of that spirit. They attempted to reach the most ambitious aims of the civilizing process most other processes stop short of, not necessarily for the lack of good will. They showed what the rationalizing, designing, controlling dreams and efforts of modern civilization are able to accomplish if not mitigated, curbed or counteracted.

These dreams and efforts have been with us for a long time. They spawned the vast and powerful arsenal of technology and managerial skills. They gave birth to institutions which serve the sole purpose of instrumentalizing human behaviour to such an extent that any aim may be pursued with efficiency and vigour, with or without ideological dedication or moral approval on the part of the pursuers. They legitimize the rulers' monopoly on ends and the confinement of the ruled to the role of means. They define most actions as means, and means as subordination – to the ultimate end, to those who set it, to supreme will, to supra-individual knowledge.

Emphatically, this does not mean that we all live daily according to Auschwitz principles. From the fact that the Holocaust is modern, it does not follow that modernity is a Holocaust. The Holocaust is a by-product of the modern drive to a fully designed, fully controlled world, once the drive is getting out of control and running wild. Most of the time, modernity is prevented from doing so. Its ambitions clash with the pluralism of the human world; they stop short of their fulfilment for the lack of an absolute power absolute enough and a monopolistic agency monopolistic enough to be able to disregard, shrug off, or overwhelm all autonomous, and thus countervailing and mitigating, forces.

Peculiarity of Modern Genocide

When the modernist dream is embraced by an absolute power able to monopolize modern vehicles of rational action, and when that power attains freedom from effective social control, genocide follows. A modern genocide – like the Holocaust. The short circuit (one almost wishes to say: a chance encounter) between an ideologically obsessed power elite and the tremendous facilities of rational, systemic action developed by modern society, may happen relatively seldom. Once it does happen, however, certain aspects of modernity are revealed which under different circumstances are less visible and hence may be easily "theorized away".

Modern Holocaust is unique in a double sense. *It is unique among other historic cases of genocide because it is modern. And it stands unique against the quotidianity of modern society because it brings together some ordinary factors of modernity which normally are kept apart.* In this second sense of its uniqueness, only the combination of factors is unusual and rare, not the factors that are combined. Separately, each factor is common and normal. And the knowledge of saltpetre, sulphur or charcoal is not complete unless one knows and remembers that, if mixed, they turn into gunpowder.

The simultaneous uniqueness and normality of the Holocaust has found excellent expression in the summary of Sarah Gordon's findings:

> systematic extermination, as opposed to sporadic pogroms, could be carried out only by extremely powerful government, and probably could have succeeded only under the cover of wartime conditions. It was only the advent of Hitler and his radical anti-Semitic followers and their subsequent centralization of power that made the extermination of European Jewry possible [...]
>
> the process of organized exclusion and murder required cooperation by huge sections of the military and bureaucracy, as well as acquiescence among the German people, whether or not they approved of Nazi persecution and extermination.[6]

Gordon names several factors which had to come together to produce the Holocaust; radical (and [...] modern: racist and exterminatory) antisemitism of the Nazi type; transformation of that antisemitism into the practical policy of a powerful, centralized state; that state being in command of a huge, efficient bureaucratic apparatus; "state of emergency" – an extraordinary, wartime condition, which allowed that government and the bureaucracy it controlled to get away with things which could, possibly, face more serious obstacles in time of peace; and the non-interference, the passive acceptance of those things by the population at large. Two among those factors (one can argue that the two can be reduced to one: with Nazis in power, war was virtually inevitable) could be seen as coincidental – not necessary attributes of a modern society, though always its possibility. The remaining factors, however, are fully "normal". They are constantly present in every modern society, and their presence has been made both possible and inescapable by those processes which are properly associated with the rise and entrenchment of modern civilization.

[…] Here I intend to focus on […] arguably the most crucial among the constituent factors of the Holocaust: the typically modern, technological-bureaucratic patterns of action and the mentality they institutionalize, generate, sustain and reproduce.

There are two antithetical ways in which one can approach the explanation of the Holocaust. One can consider the horrors of mass murder as evidence of the fragility of civilization, or one can see them as evidence of its awesome potential. One can argue that, with criminals in control, civilized rules of behaviour may be suspended, and thus the eternal beast always hiding just beneath the skin of the socially drilled being may break free. Alternatively, one can argue that, once armed with the sophisticated technical and conceptual products of modern civilization, men can do things their nature would otherwise prevent them from doing. To put it differently; one can, following the Hobbesian tradition, conclude that the inhuman pre-social state has not yet been fully eradicated, all civilizing efforts notwithstanding. Or one can, on the contrary, insist that the civilizing process has succeeded in substituting artificial and flexible patterns of human conduct for natural drives, and hence made possible a scale of inhumanity and destruction which had remained inconceivable as long as natural predispositions guided human action. I propose to opt for the second approach, and substantiate it in the following discussion.

The fact that most people (including many a social theorist) instinctively choose the first, rather than the second, approach, is a testimony to the remarkable success of the etiological myth which, in one variant or another, Western civilization has deployed over the years to legitimize its spatial hegemony by projecting it as temporal superiority. Western civilization has articulated its struggle for domination in terms of the holy battle of humanity against barbarism, reason against ignorance, objectivity against prejudice, progress against degeneration, truth against superstition, science against magic, rationality against passion. It has interpreted the history of its ascendance as the gradual yet relentless substitution of human mastery over nature for the mastery of nature over man. It has presented its own accomplishment as, first and foremost, a decisive advance in human freedom of action, creative potential and security. It has identified freedom and security with its own type of social order: Western, modern society is defined as *civilized* society, and a civilized society in turn is understood as a state from which most of the natural ugliness and morbidity, as well as most of the immanent human propensity to cruelty and violence, have been eliminated or at least suppressed. The popular image of civilized society is, more than anything else, that of the absence of violence; of a gentle, polite, soft society.

Perhaps the most salient symbolic expression of this master-image of civilization is the sanctity of the human body: the care which is taken not to invade that most private of spaces, to avoid bodily contact, to abide by the culturally prescribed bodily distance; and the trained disgust and repulsion we feel whenever we see or hear of that sacred space being trespassed on. Modern civilization can afford the fiction of the sanctity and autonomy of the human body thanks to the efficient mechanisms of self-control it has developed, and on the whole successfully reproduced in the process of individual education. Once effective, the reproduced mechanisms of self-control dispose of the need of subsequent external interference with the body.

On the other hand, privacy of the body underlines personal responsibility for its behaviour, and thus adds powerful sanctions to the bodily drill. (In recent years the severity of sanctions, keenly exploited by the consumer market, have finally produced the tendency to interiorize demand for the drill; development of individual self-control tends to be itself self-controlled, and pursued in a DIY fashion.) Cultural prohibition against coming into too close a contact with another body serves therefore as an effective safeguard against diffuse, contingent influences which may, if allowed, counteract the centrally administered pattern of social order. Non-violence of the daily and diffuse human intercourse is an indispensable condition, and a constant output, of the centralization of coercion.

All in all, the overall non-violent character of modern civilization is an illusion. More exactly, it is an integral part of its self-apology and self-apotheosis; in short, of its legitimizing myth. It is not true that our civilization exterminates violence due to the inhuman, degrading or immoral character of the latter. If modernity

> is indeed antithetical to the wild passions of barbarism, it is not at all antithetical to efficient, dispassionate destruction, slaughter, and torture [...] As the quality of thinking grows more rational, the quantity of destruction increases. In our time, for example, terrorism and torture are no longer instruments of passions; they have become instruments of political rationality.[7]

What in fact has happened in the course of the civilizing process, is the redeployment of violence, and the re-distribution of access to violence. Like so many other things which we have been trained to abhor and detest, violence has been taken out of sight, rather than forced out of existence. It has become invisible, that is, from the vantage point of narrowly circumscribed and privatized personal experience. It has been enclosed instead in segregated and isolated territories, on the whole inaccessible to ordinary members of society; or evicted to the "twilight areas", off-limits for a large majority (and the majority which counts) of society's members; or exported to distant places which on the whole are irrelevant for the life-business of civilized humans (one can always cancel holiday bookings).

The ultimate consequence of all this is the concentration of violence. Once centralized and free from competition, means of coercion would be capable of reaching unheard of results even if not technically perfected. Their concentration, however, triggers and boosts the escalation of technical improvements, and thus the effects of concentration are further magnified. As Anthony Giddens repeatedly emphasized (see, above all, his *Contemporary Critique of Historical Materialism* (1981), and *The Constitution of Society* (1984)), the removal of violence from the daily life of civilized societies has always been intimately associated with a thoroughgoing militarization of inter-societal exchange and inner-societal production of order; standing armies and police forces brought together technically superior weapons and superior technology of bureaucratic management. For the last two centuries, the number of people who have suffered violent death as the result of such militarization has been steadily growing to reach a volume unheard of before.

The Holocaust absorbed an enormous volume of means of coercion. Having harnessed them in the service of a single purpose, it also added stimulus to their further specialization and technical perfection. More, however, than the sheer quantity of tools of destruction, and even their technical quality, what mattered was the way in which they were deployed. Their formidable effectiveness, relied mostly on the subjection of their use to purely bureaucractic, technical considerations (which made their use all but totally immune to the countervailing pressures, such as they might have been submitted to if the means of violence were controlled by dispersed and unco-ordinated agents and deployed in a diffuse way). Violence has been turned into a technique. Like all techniques, it is free from emotions and purely rational. "It is, in fact, entirely reasonable, if 'reason' means instrumental reason, to apply American military force, B-52s, napalm, and all the rest to 'communist-dominated' Viet-Nam (clearly an 'undesirable object'), as the 'operator' to transform it into a 'desirable object'."[8]

Effects of the Hierarchical and Functional Divisions of Labour

Use of violence is most efficient and cost-effective when the means are subjected to solely instrumental-rational criteria, and thus dissociated from moral evaluation of the ends. [...] such dissociation is an operation all bureaucracies are good at. One may even say that it provides the essence of bureaucratic structure and process, and with it the secret of that tremendous growth of mobilizing and co-ordinating potential, and of the rationality and efficiency of action, which modern civilization has achieved thanks to the development of bureaucratic administration. The dissociation is by and large an outcome of two parallel processes, which are both central to the bureaucratic model of action. The first is the *meticulous functional division of labour* (as additional to, and distinct in its consequences, from linear graduation of power and subordination); the second is the *substitution of technical for a moral responsibility*.

All division of labour (also such division as results from the mere hierarchy of command) creates a distance between most of the contributors to the final outcome of collective activity, and the outcome itself. Before the last links in the bureaucratic chain of power (the direct executors) confront their task, most of the preparatory operations which brought about that confrontation have been already performed by persons who had no personal experience, and sometimes not the knowledge either, of the task in question. Unlike in a pre-modern unit of work, in which all steps of the hierarchy share in the same occupational skills, and the practical knowledge of working operations actually grows towards the top of the ladder (the master knows the same as his journeyman or apprentice, only more and better), persons occupying successive rungs of modern bureaucracy differ sharply in the kind of expertise and professional training their jobs require. They may be able to put themselves imaginatively into their subordinates' position; this may even help in maintaining "good human relations" inside the office – but it is not the condition of proper performance of the task, nor of the effectiveness of the bureaucracy as a whole. In fact, most bureaucracies do not treat seriously the romantic recipe that requires every bureaucrat, and particularly those who occupy the top, to "start from the bottom" so that on the way to the summit they should acquire, and memorize, the experience of the entire slope. Mindful of the multiplicity of skills which the managerial jobs of various magnitudes demand, most bureaucracies practise instead separate avenues of recruitment for different levels of the hierarchy. Perhaps it is true that each soldier carries a marshal's baton in his knapsack, but few marshals, and few colonels or captains for that matter, keep soldiers' bayonets in their briefcases.

What such practical and mental distance from the final product means is that most functionaries of the bureaucratic hierarchy may give commands without full knowledge of their effects. In many cases they would find it difficult to visualize those effects. Usually, they only have an abstract, detached awareness of them; the kind of knowledge which is best expressed in statistics, which measure the results without passing any judgement, and certainly not moral ones. In their files and their minds the results are at best diagramatically represented as curves or sectors of a circle; ideally, they would appear as a column of numbers. Graphically or numerically represented, the final outcomes of their commands are devoid of substance. The graphs measure the *progress* of work, they say nothing about the nature of the operation or its objects. The graphs make tasks of widely different character mutually exchangeable; only the quantifiable success or failure matter, and seen from that point of view, the tasks do not differ.

All these effects of distance created by the hierarchical division of labour are radically magnified once the division becomes functional. Now it is not just the lack of direct, personal experience of the actual execution of the task to which successive command contribute their share, but also the lack of similarity between the task at hand and the task of the office as a whole (one is not a miniature version, or an icon, of the other), which distances the contributor from the job performed by the bureaucracy of which he is a part. The psychological impact of such distantiation is profound and far-reaching. It is one thing to give a command to load bombs on the plane, but quite different to take care of regular steel supply in a bomb factory. In the first case, the command-giver may have no vivid, visual impression of the devastation the bomb is about to cause. In the second case, however, the supply manager does not, if he chooses to, have to think about the use to which bombs are put at all. Even in abstract, purely notional knowledge of the final outcome is redundant, and certainly irrelevant as far as the success of his own part of the operation goes. In a functional division of labour, everything one does is in principle *multifinal*; that is, it can be combined and integrated into more than one meaning-determining totality. By itself, the function is devoid of meaning, and the meaning which will be eventually bestowed on it is in no way pre-empted by the actions of its perpetrators. It will be "the others" (in most cases anonymous and out of reach) who will some time, somewhere, decide that meaning. "Would workers in the chemical plants that produced napalm accept responsibility for burned babies?" ask Kren and Rappoport.

"Would such workers even be aware that others might reasonably think they were responsible?"⁹ Of course they wouldn't. And there is no bureaucratic reason why they should. The splitting of the baby-burning process in minute functional tasks and then separating the tasks from each other have made such awareness irrelevant – and exceedingly difficult to achieve. Remember as well that it is chemical plants that produce napalm, not any of their individual workers [...]

The second process responsible for distantiation is closely related to the first. The substitution of technical for moral responsibility would not be conceivable without the meticulous functional dissection and separation of tasks. At least it would not be conceivable to the same extent. The substitution takes place, to a degree, already within the purely linear graduation of control. Each person within the hierarchy of command is accountable to his immediate superior, and thus is naturally interested in his opinion and his approval of the work. However much this approval matters to him, he is still, though only theoretically, aware of what the ultimate outcome of his work is bound to be. And so there is at least an abstract chance of one awareness being measured against the other; benevolence of superiors being confronted with repulsiveness of the effects. And whenever comparison is feasible, so is the choice. Within a purely linear division of command, technical responsibility remains, at least in theory, vulnerable, It may still be called to justify itself in moral terms and to compete with moral conscience. A functionary may, for instance, decide that by giving a particular command his superior overstepped his terms of reference, as he moved from the domain of purely technical interest to that charged with ethical significance (shooting soldiers is OK; shooting babies is a different matter); and that the duty to obey an authoritative command does not extend so far as to justify what the functionary considers as morally unacceptable deeds. All these theoretical possibilities disappear, however, or are considerably weakened, once the linear hierarchy of command is supplemented, or replaced, by functional division and separation of tasks. The triumph of technical responsibility is then complete, unconditional, and for all practical purposes, unassailable.

Technical responsibility differs from moral responsibility in that it forgets that the action is a means to something other than itself. As outer connections of action are effectively removed from the field of vision, the bureaucrat's own act becomes an end in itself. It can be judged only by its intrinsic criteria of propriety and success. Hand-in-hand with the vaunted relative autonomy of the official conditioned by his functional specialization, comes his remoteness from the overall effects of divided yet co-ordinated labour of the organization as a whole. Once isolated from their distant consequences, most functionally specialized acts either pass moral test easily, or are morally indifferent. When unencumbered by moral worries, the act can be judged on unambiguously rational grounds. What matters then is whether the act has been performed according to the best available technological know-how, and whether its output has been cost-effective. Criteria are clear-cut and easy to operate.

For our topic, two effects of such context of bureaucratic action are most important. First is the fact that the skills, expert knowledge, inventiveness and dedication of actors, complete with their personal motives that prompted them to deploy these qualities in full, can be fully mobilized and put to the service of the overall bureaucratic purpose even if (or perhaps because) the actors retain relative functional autonomy towards this purpose and even if this purpose does not agree with the actors' own moral philosophy. To put it bluntly, *the result is the irrelevance of moral standards for the technical success of the bureaucratic operation.* The instinct of workmanship, which according to Thorstein Veblen is present in every actor, focuses fully on proper performance of the job in hand. The practical devotion to the task may be further enhanced by the actor's craven character and severity of his superiors, or by the actor's interest in promotion, the actor's ambition or disinterested curiosity, or by many other personal circumstances, motives, or character features – but, on the whole, workmanship will suffice even in their absence. By and large, the actors want to excel; whatever they do, they want to do well. Once, thanks to the complex functional differentiation within bureaucracy, they have been distantiated from the ultimate outcomes of the operation to which they contribute, their moral concerns can concentrate fully on the good performance of the job at hand. Morality boils down to the commandment to be a good, efficient and diligent expert and worker.

Dehumanization of Bureaucratic Objects

Another, equally important effect of bureaucratic context of action is *dehumanization of the objects of bureaucratic operation*; the possibility to express these objects in purely technical, ethically neutral terms.

We associate dehumanization with horrifying pictures of the inmates of concentration camps – humiliated by reducing their action to the most basic level of primitive survival, by preventing them from deploying cultural (both bodily and behavioural) symbols of human dignity, by depriving them even of recognizably human likeness. As Peter Marsh put it, "Standing by the fence of Auschwitz, looking at these emaciated skeletons with shrunken skin and hollowed eyes – who could believe that these were really people?"[10] These pictures, however, represent only an extreme manifestation of a tendency which may be discovered in all bureaucracies, however benign and innocuous the tasks in which they are currently engaged. I suggest that the discussion of the dehumanizing tendency, rather than being focused on its most sensational and vile, but fortunately uncommon, manifestations, ought to concentrate on the more universal, and for this reason potentially more dangerous, manifestations.

Dehumanization starts at the point when, thanks to the distantiation, the objects at which the bureaucratic operation is aimed can, and are, reduced to a set of quantitative measures [...]

Reduced, like all other objects of bureaucratic management, to pure, quality-free measurements, human objects lose their distinctiveness. They are already dehumanized – in the sense that the language in which things that happen to them (or are done to them) are narrated, safeguards its referents from ethical evaluation. In fact, this language is unfit for normative-moral statements. It is only humans that may be objects of ethical propositions. [...]

Dehumanization is inextricably related to the most essential, rationalizing tendency of modern bureaucracy. As all bureaucracies affect in some measure some human objects, the adverse impact of dehumanization is much more common than the habit to identify it almost totally with its genocidal effects would suggest. Soldiers are told to shoot *targets*, which *fall* when they are *hit*. Employees of big companies are encouraged to destroy *competition*. Officers of welfare agencies operate *discretionary awards* at one time, *personal credits* at another. Their objects are *supplementary benefit recipients*. It is difficult to perceive and remember the humans behind all such technical terms. The point is that as far as the bureaucratic goals go, they are better not perceived and not remembered.

Once effectively dehumanized, and hence cancelled as potential subjects of moral demands, human objects of bureaucratic task-performance are viewed with ethical indifference, which soon turns into disapprobation and censure when their resistance, or lack of co-operation, slows down the smooth flow of bureaucratic routine. [...]

The overall conclusion is that the bureaucratic mode of action, as it has been developed in the course of the modernizing process, contains all the technical elements which proved necessary in the execution of genocidal tasks. This mode can be put to the service of a genocidal objective without major revision of its structure, mechanisms and behavioural norms.

Moreover, contrary to widespread opinion, bureaucracy is not merely a tool, which can be used with equal facility at one time for cruel and morally contemptible, at another for deeply humane purposes. Even if it does move in any direction in which it is pushed, bureaucracy is more like a loaded dice. It has a logic and a momentum of its own. It renders some solutions more, and other solutions less, probable. Given an initial push (being confronted with a purpose), it will – like the brooms of the sorcerer's apprentice – easily move beyond all thresholds at which many of those who gave it the push would have stopped, were they still in control of the process they triggered. Bureaucracy is programmed to seek the optimal solution. It is programmed to measure the optimum in such terms as would not distinguish between one human object and another, or between human and inhuman objects. What matters is the efficiency and lowering of costs of their processing.

[...]

Bureaucracy is intrinsically *capable* of genocidal action. To *engage* in such an action, it needs an encounter with another invention of modernity: a bold design of a better, more reasonable and rational social order – say a racially uniform, or a classless society – and above all the capacity of drawing such designs and determination to make them efficacious. Genocide follows when two common and abundant inventions of modern times meet. It is only their meeting which has been, thus far, uncommon and rare.

Bankruptcy of Modern Safeguards

Physical violence and its threat

> is no longer a perpetual insecurity that it brings into the life of the individual, but a peculiar form of security [...] a continuous, uniform pressure is exerted on individual life by the physical violence stored behind the scenes of everyday life, a pressure totally familiar and hardly perceived, conduct and drive economy having been adjusted from earliest youth to this social structure.[11]

In these words, Norbert Elias restated the familiar self-definition of civilized society. Elimination of violence from daily life is the main assertion around which that definition revolves. As we have seen, the apparent elimination is in fact merely an eviction, leading to the reassembly of resources and disposition of centres of violence in new locations within the social system. According to Elias, the two developments are closely interdependent. The area of daily life is comparatively free from violence precisely because somewhere in the wings physical violence is stored – in quantities that put it effectively out of the control of ordinary members of society and endow it with irresistible power to suppress unauthorized outbursts of violence. Daily manners mellowed mainly because people are now threatened with violence in case they are violent – with violence they cannot match or reasonably hope to repel. The disappearance of violence from the horizon of daily life is thus one more manifestation of the centralizing and monopolizing tendencies of modern power; violence is absent from individual intercourse because it is now controlled by forces definitely outside the individual reach. But the forces are not outside *everybody's* reach. Thus the much vaunted mellowing of manners (which Elias, following the etiological myth of the West, celebrates with such a relish), and the cosy security of daily life that follows have their price. A price which we, dwellers in the house of modernity, may be called to pay at any time. Or made to pay, without being called first.

Pacification of daily life means at the same time its defencelessness. By agreeing, or being forced to renounce the use of physical force in their reciprocal relations, members of modern society disarm themselves in front of the unknown and normally invisible, yet potentially sinister and always formidable managers of coercion. Their weakness is worrying not so much because of the high probability that the managers of coercion will indeed take advantage of it and hurry to turn the means of violence they control against the disarmed society, as for the simple fact that whether such advantage will or will not be taken, does not in principle depend on what ordinary men and women do. By themselves, the members of modern society cannot prevent the use of massive coercion from happening. Mellowing of manners goes hand-in-hand with a radical shift in control over violence.

Awareness of the constant threat which the characteristically modern imbalance of power contains would make life unbearable, were it not for our trust in safeguards which we believe have been built into the fabric of modern, civilized society. Most of the time we have no reason to think that the trust is misguided. Only on a few dramatic occasions a doubt is cast on the reliability of the safeguards. Perhaps the main significance of the Holocaust lies in its having been one of the most redoubtable of such occasions to date. *In the years leading to the Final Solution the most trusted of the safeguards had been put to a test. They all failed – one by one, and all together.*

Perhaps the most spectacular was the failure of science – as a body of ideas, and as a network of institutions of enlightenment and training. The deadly potential of the most revered principles and accomplishments of modern science has been exposed. The emancipation of reason from emotions, of rationality from normative pressures, of effectiveness from ethics have been the battle-cries of science since its inception. Once implemented, however, they made science, and the formidable technological applications it spawned, into docile instruments in the hands of unscrupulous power. The dark and ignoble role which science played in the perpetuation of the Holocaust was both direct and indirect.

Indirectly (though centrally to its general social function), science cleared the way to genocide through sapping the authority, and questioning the binding force, of all normative thinking, particularly that of religion and ethics. Science looks back at its history as the long and victorious struggle of reason over superstition and irrationality. In as far as religion and ethics could not rationally legitimize the demands they made on human behaviour, they stood condemned and found their authority denied. As values and norms had been proclaimed immanently and irreparably subjective, instrumentality was left as the only field where the search for excellence was feasible. Science wanted to be value-free and took pride in being such. By institutional pressure and by ridicule, it silenced the preachers of morality. In the process, it made itself morally blind and speechless. It dismantled all the barriers that could stop it from co-operating, with enthusiasm and abandon, in designing the most effective and rapid methods of mass sterilization or mass killing; or from conceiving of the concentration camps' slavery as a unique and wonderful opportunity to conduct medical research for the advancement of scholarship and – of course – of mankind.

Science (or this time, rather the scientists) helped the Holocaust perpetrators directly as well. Modern science is a gigantic and complex institution. Research costs dear, as it requires huge buildings, expensive equipment and large teams of highly paid experts. Thus science depends on a constant flow of money and non-monetary resources, which only equally large institutions are able to offer and to guarantee. Science is not, however, mercantile, nor are the scientists avaricious. Science is about truth, and scientists are about pursuing it. Scientists are overwhelmed with curiosity and excited by the unknown. If measured by all other earthly concerns, including monetary, curiosity is disinterested. It is only the value of knowledge and truth which scientists preach and search. It is just a coincidence, and preferably a minor irritant, that curiosity cannot be sated, and the truth found, without ever-growing funds, ever-more costly laboratories, ever-larger salary bills. What scientists want is merely to be allowed to go where their thirst for knowledge prompts them.

A government who stretches its helpful hand and offers just that can count on the scientists' gratitude and co-operation. Most scientists would be prepared in exchange to surrender quite a long list of lesser precepts. They would be prepared, for instance, to make do with the sudden disappearance of some of their colleagues with the wrong shape of nose or biographical entry. If they object at all, it will be that taking all these colleagues away in one swoop may put the research schedule in jeopardy. (This is not a slur nor a squib; this is what the protests of German academics, medics and engineers, if recorded at all, boiled down to. Less still was heard from their Soviet equivalents during the purges.) With relish, German scientists boarded the train drawn by the Nazi locomotive towards the brave, new, racially purified and German-dominated world. Research projects grew more ambitious by the day, and research institutes grew more populous and resourceful by the hour. Little else mattered.

[...]

Conclusions

If we ask now what the original sin was which allowed this to happen, the collapse (or non-emergence) of democracy seems to be the most convincing answer. In the absence of traditional authority, the only checks and balances capable of keeping the body politic away from extremities can be supplied by political democracy. The latter is not, however, quick to arrive, and it is slower still to take root once the hold of the old authority and system of control had been broken – particularly if the breaking was done in a hurry. Such situations of interregnum and instability tend to occur during and after deep-reaching revolutions, which succeed in paralysing old seats of social power without as yet replacing them with new ones – and create for this reason a state of affairs in which *political and military forces are neither counterbalanced nor restrained by resourceful and influential social ones.*

Such situations emerged, arguably, in pre-modern times as well – in the wake of bloody conquests or protracted internecine strifes which led on occasion to well-nigh complete self-annihilation of established elites. The expectable consequences of such situations were, however, different. A general collapse of the larger social order normally followed. War destruction seldom reached as low as the grass-root, communal networks of social control; communally regulated local islands of social order were now exposed to erratic acts of violence and pillage, but they had themselves to fall back upon once the social organization above the local level disintegrated. In most cases, even the most profound blows to traditional authorities in pre-modern societies differed from modern unheavals in two crucial aspects; first, they left the primeval, communal controls of order intact or at least still viable; and second, they weakened, rather than strengthened the possibility of organized action on a supra-communal level, as the social organization of the higher order fell apart and whatever exchange was left between localities was once again subjected to a free play of unco-ordinated forces.

Under modern conditions, on the contrary, upheavals of a similar kind occur, on the whole, after communal mechanisms of social regulation have all but disappeared and local communities ceased to be self-sufficient and self-reliant. Instead of an instinctive reflex of "falling back" upon one's own resources, the void tends to be filled by new, but again supra-communal, forces, which seek to deploy the state monopoly of coercion to impose a new order on the societal scale. Instead of collapsing, political power becomes therefore virtually the only force behind the emerging order. In its drive it is neither stopped nor restrained by economic and social forces, seriously undermined by the destruction or paralysis of old authorities.

This is, of course, a theoretical model, seldom implemented in full in historical practice. Its use consists however in drawing attention to those social dislocations that seem to make the surfacing of genocidal tendencies more likely. Dislocations may differ in form and intensity, but they are united by the general effect of *the pronounced supremacy of political over economic and social power, of the state over the society*. They went perhaps deepest and farthest in the case of the Russian Revolution and the subsequent prolonged monopoly of the state as the only factor of social integration and order-reproduction. Yet also in Germany they went farther and deeper than it is popularly believed. Arriving after the brief Weimar interlude, the Nazi rule undertook and completed the revolution that the Weimar Republic – that uneasy interplay of old and new (but immature) elites which only at the surface resembled political democracy – was, for various reasons, incapable of administering. Old elites were considerably weakened or pushed aside. One by one, the forms of articulation of economic and social forces were dissembled and replaced with new, centrally supervised forms emanating from, and legitimized by, the state. All classes were profoundly affected, but the most radical blow was delivered to the classes that can carry non-political power only collectively, i.e. to the non-proprietary classes, and to the working class above all. Etatization or disbanding of all autonomous labour institutions coupled with the subjection of local government to almost total central control, left the popular masses virtually powerless and, for all practical purposes, excluded from the political process. Resistance of social forces was prevented additionally by the surrounding of state activity with an impenetrable wall of secrecy – indeed, the state conspiracy of silence against the very population it ruled. The overall and ultimate effect was the replacement of traditional authorities not by the new vibrant forces of self-governing citizenship, but by an almost total monopoly of the political state, with social powers prevented from self-articulation, and thus from forming a structural foundation of political democracy.

Modern conditions made possible the emergence of a resourceful state, capable of replacing the whole network of social and economic controls by political command and administration. More importantly still, modern conditions provide substance for that command and administration. Modernity, as we remember, is an age of artificial order and of grand societal designs, the era of planners, visionaries, and – more generally – "gardeners" who treat society as a virgin plot of land to be expertly designed and then cultivated and doctored to keep to the designed form.

[...]

NOTES

1. Raul Hilberg, "Significance of the Holocaust", in *The Holocaust: Ideology, Bureaucracy, and Genocide*, ed. Henry Friedlander and Sybil Milton (Millwood, NY: Kraus International Publications, 1980), pp. 101–2.
2. Cf. Colin Legum in *The Observer*, 12 October 1966.
3. Henry L. Feingold, "How Unique is the Holocaust?" in *Genocide: Critical Issues of the Holocaust*, ed. Alex Grobman and David Landes (Los Angeles, CA: Simon Wiesenthal Centre, 1983), p. 397.
4. George M. Kren and Leon Rappoport, *The Holocaust and the Crisis of Human Behaviour* (New York: Holmes & Meier, 1980), pp. 130, 143.
5. John P. Sabini and Mary Silver, "Destroying the Innocent with a Clear Conscience: A Sociopsychology of the Holocaust", in *Survivors, Victims, and Perpetrators: Essays in the Nazi Holocaust*, ed. Joel E. Dinsdale (Washington: Hemisphere Publishing Corporation, 1980), pp. 329–30.
6. Sarah Gordon, *Hitler, Germans, and the "Jewish Question"* (Princeton, NJ: Princeton University Press, 1984), pp. 48–9.
7. Kren and Rappoport, *The Holocaust and the Crisis*, p. 140.
8. Joseph Weizenbaum, *Computer Power and Human Reason: From Judgment to Calculation* (San Francisco, CA: W. H. Freeman, 1976), p. 252.
9. Kren and Rappoport, *The Holocaust and the Crisis*, p. 141.
10. Peter Marsh, *Aggro: The Illusion of Violence* (London: J. M. Dent & Sons, 1978), p. 120.
11. Norbert Elias, *The Civilising Process: State Formation and Civilization*, trans. Edmund Jephcott (Oxford: Basil Blackwell, 1982), pp. 238–9.

Chapter 35

The Consequences of Modernity [1990]

Anthony Giddens

Abstract Systems and the Transformation of Intimacy

Abstract systems have provided a great deal of security in day-to-day life which was absent in pre-modern orders. A person can board a plane in London and reach Los Angeles some ten hours later and be fairly certain that not only will the journey be made safely, but that the plane will arrive quite close to a predetermined time. The passenger may perhaps only have a vague idea of where Los Angeles is, in terms of a global map. Only minimal preparations need to be made for the journey (obtaining passport, visa, air-ticket, and money) – no knowledge of the actual trajectory is necessary. A large amount of "surrounding" knowledge is required to be able to get on the plane, and this is knowledge which has been filtered back from expert systems to lay discourse and action. One has to know what an airport is, what an air-ticket is, and very many other things besides. But security on the journey itself does not depend upon mastery of the technical paraphernalia which make it possible.

Compare this with the task of an adventurer who undertook the same journey no more than three or four centuries ago. Although he would be the "expert," he might have little idea of where he was traveling *to* – and the very notion of "traveling" sounds oddly inapplicable. The journey would be fraught with dangers, and the risk of disaster or death very considerable. No one could participate in such an expedition who was not physically tough, resilient, and possessed of skills relevant to the conduct of the voyage.

Every time someone gets cash out of the bank or makes a deposit, casually turns on a light or a tap, sends a letter or makes a call on the telephone, she or he implicitly recognises the large areas of secure, coordinated actions and events that make modern social life possible. Of course, all sorts of hitches and breakdowns can also happen, and attitudes of scepticism or antagonism develop which produce the disengagement of individuals from one or more of these systems. But most of the time the taken-for-granted way in which everyday actions are geared into abstract systems bears witness to the effectiveness with which they operate (within the contexts of what is expected from them, because they also produce many kinds of unintended consequences).

Trust in abstract systems is the condition of time-space distanciation and of the large areas of security in day-to-day life which modern institutions offer as compared to the traditional world. The routines which are integrated with abstract systems are central to ontological security in conditions of modernity. Yet this situation also creates novel forms of psychological vulnerability, and trust in abstract systems is not psychologically rewarding in the way in which trust in persons is. I shall concentrate on the second of these points here, returning to the first later. To begin, I want to advance the following theorems: that there is a direct (although dialectical) connection between the globalising tendencies of modernity and what I shall call the *transformation of intimacy* in contexts of day-to-day life; that the transformation of intimacy can be analysed in terms of the building of trust mechanisms; and that personal trust relations, in such circumstances, are closely bound up with a situation in which the construction of the self becomes a reflexive project. [...]

Trust and Personal Relations

With the development of abstract systems, trust in impersonal principles, as well as in anonymous others, becomes indispensable to social existence. Nonpersonalised trust of this sort is discrepant from basic trust. There is a strong psychological need to find others to trust, but institutionally organised personal connections are lacking, relative to pre-modern social situations. The point here is *not* primarily that many social characteristics which were previously part of everyday life or the "life-world" become drawn off and incorporated into abstract systems. Rather, the tissue and form of day-to-day life become reshaped in conjunction with wider social changes. Routines which are structured by abstract systems have an empty, unmoralised character – this much is valid in the idea that the impersonal increasingly swamps the personal. But this is not simply a diminishment of personal life in favour of impersonally organised systems – it is a genuine transformation of the nature of the personal itself. Personal relations whose main objective is sociability, informed by loyalty and authenticity, become as much a part of the social situations of modernity as the encompassing institutions of time-space distanciation.

It is quite wrong, however, to set off the impersonality of abstract systems against the intimacies of personal life as most existing sociological accounts tend to do. Personal life and the social ties it involves are deeply intertwined with the most far-reaching of abstract systems. It has long been the case, for example, that Western diets reflect global economic interchanges: "every cup of coffee contains within it the whole history of Western imperialism." With the accelerating globalisation of the past fifty years or so, the connections between personal life of the most intimate kind and disembedding mechanisms have intensified. As Ulrich Beck has observed, "The most intimate – say, nursing a child – and the most distant, most general – say a reactor accident in the Ukraine, energy politics – are now suddenly *directly* connected."[1]

What does this mean in terms of personal trust? The answer to this question is fundamental to the transformation of intimacy in the twentieth century. Trust in persons is not focused by personalised connections within the local community and kinship networks. Trust on a personal level becomes a project, to be "worked at" by the parties involved, and demands the *opening out of the individual to the other*. Where it cannot be controlled by fixed normative codes, trust has to be *won*, and the means of doing this is demonstrable warmth and openness. Our peculiar concern with "relationships," in the sense which that word has now taken on, is expressive of this phenomenon. Relationships are ties based upon trust, where trust is not pre-given but worked upon, and where the work involved means *a mutual process of self-disclosure*.

Given the strength of the emotions associated with sexuality, it is scarcely surprising that erotic involvements become a focal point for such self-disclosure. The transition to modern forms of erotic relations is generally thought to be associated with the formation of an ethos of romantic love, or with what Lawrence Stone calls "affective individualism." The ideal of romantic love is aptly described by Stone in the following way:

> the notion that there is only one person in the world with whom one can unite at all levels; the personality of that person is so idealised that the normal faults and follies of human nature disappear from view; love is like a thunderbolt and strikes at first sight; love is the most important thing in the world, to which all other considerations, particularly material ones, should be sacrificed; and lastly, the giving of full rein to personal emotions is admirable, no matter how exaggerated and absurd the resulting conduct might appear to others.[2]

Characterised in this way, romantic love incorporates a cluster of values scarcely ever realisable in their totality. Rather than being an ethos associated in a continuous way with the rise of modern institutions, it seems essentially to have been a transitional phenomenon, bound up with a relatively early phase in the dissolution of the older forms of arranged marriage. Aspects of the "romantic love complex" as described by Stone have proved quite durable, but these have become increasingly meshed with the dynamics of personal trust described above. Erotic relations involve a progressive path of mutual discovery, in which a process of self-realisation on the part of the lover is as much a part of the experience as increasing intimacy with the loved one. Personal trust, therefore, has to be established through the process of self-enquiry: the discovery of oneself becomes a project directly involved with the reflexivity of modernity.

Interpretations of the quest for self-identity tend to divide in much the same way as views of the decline of community, to which they are often linked. Some see a preoccupation with self-development as an offshoot of the fact that the old communal orders have broken down, producing a narcissistic, hedonistic concern with the ego. Others reach much the same conclusion, but trace this end result to forms of social manipulation. Exclusion of the majority from the arenas where the most consequential policies are forged and decisions taken forces a concentration upon the self; this is a result of the powerlessness most people feel. In the words of Christopher Lasch:

> As the world takes on a more and more menacing appearance, life becomes a never-ending search for health and well-being through exercise, dieting, drugs, spiritual regimens of various kinds, psychic self-help, and psychiatry. For those who have withdrawn interest from the outside world except in so far as it remains a source of gratification and frustration, the state of their own health becomes an all-absorbing concern.[3]

Is the search for self-identity a form of somewhat pathetic narcissism, or is it, in some part at least, a subversive force in respect of modern institutions? Most of the debate about the issue has concentrated upon this question, and I shall return to it toward the end of this study. But for the moment we should see that there is something awry in Lasch's statement. A "search for health and well-being" hardly sounds compatible with a "withdrawal of interest in the outside world." The benefits of exercise or dieting are not personal discoveries but came from the lay reception of expert knowledge, as does the appeal of therapy or psychiatry. The spiritual regimens in question may be an eclectic assemblage, but include religions and cults from around the world. The outside world not only enters in here; it is an outside world vastly more extensive in character than anyone would have had contact with in the pre-modern era.

To summarise all this, the transformation of intimacy involves the following:

1 An intrinsic relation between the *globalising tendencies* of modernity and *localised events* in day-to-day life – a complicated, dialectical connection between the "extensional" and the "intensional."
2 The construction of the self as a *reflexive project*, an elemental part of the reflexivity of modernity; an individual must find her or his identity amid the strategies and options provided by abstract systems.
3 A drive towards self-actualisation, founded upon *basic trust*, which in personalised contexts can only be established by an "opening out" of the self to the other.

4 The formation of personal and erotic ties as "relationships," guided by the *mutuality of self-disclosure*.
5 *A concern for self-fulfilment*, which is not just a narcissistic defence against an externally threatening world, over which individuals have little control, but also in part a *positive appropriation* of circumstances in which globalised influences impinge upon everyday life.

Risk and Danger in the Modern World

How should we seek to analyse the "menacing appearance" of the contemporary world of which Lasch speaks? To do so means looking in more detail at the specific risk profile of modernity, which may be outlined in the following way:

1 *Globalisation of risk* in the sense of *intensity*: for example, nuclear war can threaten the survival of humanity.
2 *Globalisation of risk* in the sense of the *expanding number of contingent events* which affect everyone or at least large numbers of people on the planet: for example, changes in the global division of labour.
3 Risk stemming from the *created environment*, or *socialised nature*: the infusion of human knowledge into the material environment.
4 The development of *institutionalised risk environments* affecting the life-chances of millions: for example, investment markets.
5 *Awareness of risk* as *risk*: the "knowledge gaps" in risks cannot be converted into "certainties" by religious or magical knowledge.
6 The *well-distributed awareness of risk*: many of the dangers we face collectively are known to wide publics.
7 *Awareness of the limitations of expertise*: no expert system can be wholly expert in terms of the consequences of the adoption of expert principles.

[...]

In what ways does this array of risks impinge upon lay trust in expert systems and feelings of ontological security? The baseline for analysis has to be the *inevitability* of living with dangers which are *remote* from the control not only of individuals, but also of large organisations, including states; and which are *of high intensity* and *life-threatening* for millions of human beings and potentially for the whole of humanity. The facts that these are not risks anyone *chooses* to run and that there are, in Beck's terms, no "others" who could be held responsible, attacked, or blamed reinforce the sense of foreboding which so many have noted as a characteristic of the current age.[4] Nor is it surprising that some of those who hold to religious beliefs are inclined to see the potential for global disaster as an expression of the wrath of God. For the high consequence global risks which we all now run are key elements of the runaway, juggernaut character of modernity, and no specific individuals or groups are responsible for them or can be constrained to "set things right."

How can we constantly keep in the forefront of our minds dangers which are enormously threatening, yet so remote from individual control? The answer is that most of us cannot. People who worry all day, every day, about the possibility of nuclear war, as was noted earlier, are liable to be thought disturbed. While it would be difficult to deem irrational someone who was constantly and consciously anxious in this way, this outlook would paralyse ordinary day-to-day life. Even a person who raises the topic at a social gathering is prone to be thought hysterical or gauche. In Carolyn See's novel *Golden Days*, which finishes in the aftermath of a nuclear war, the main character relates her fear of a nuclear holocaust to another guest at a dinner party:

> Her eyes were wide. She gazed at me with terrific concentration. "Yes", she said, "I understand what you're saying. I get it. But isn't it true that your fear of nuclear war is a metaphor for all the *other* fears that plague us today?"
>
> My mind has never been exactly fine. But sometimes it has been good. "No", I said. I may have shouted it through the beautiful, sheltered room. "It's my view that the other fears, all those of which we have spoken, are a metaphor of my fear of nuclear war!"
>
> She stared at me incredulously, but was spared the difficulty of a response when we were all called to a very pleasant late supper.[5]

The incredulity of the dinner party guest has nothing to do with the argument expressed; it registers disbelief that anyone should become emotional about such an issue in such a setting.

The large majority of people do not spend much of their time, on a conscious level at least, worrying about nuclear war or about the other major hazards for which it may or may not be a metaphor. The need to get on with the more local practicalities of day-to-day life is no doubt one reason, but much more is involved psychologically. In a secular environment, low-probability high-consequence risks tend to conjure up anew a sense of *fortuna* closer to the pre-modern outlook than that cultivated by minor superstitions. A sense of "fate," whether positively or negatively tinged – a vague and generalised sense of trust in distant events over which one has no control – relieves the individual of the burden of engagement with an existential situation which might otherwise be chronically disturbing. Fate, a feeling that things will take their own course anyway, thus reappears at the core of a world which is supposedly taking rational control of its own affairs. Moreover, this surely exacts a price on the level of the unconscious, since it essentially presumes the repression of anxiety. The sense of dread which is the antithesis of basic trust is likely to infuse unconscious sentiments about the uncertainties faced by humanity as a whole.[6]

Low-probability high-consequence risks will not disappear in the modern world, although in an optimal scenario they could be minimised. Thus, were it to be the case that all existing nuclear weapons were done away with, no other weapons of comparable destructive force were invented, and no comparably catastrophic disturbances of socialised nature were to loom, a profile of global danger would still exist. For if it is accepted that the eradication of established technical knowledge could not be achieved, nuclear weaponry could be reconstructed at any point.

Moreover, any major technological initiative could thoroughly disturb the overall orientation of global affairs. The juggernaut effect is inherent in modernity, for reasons I shall amplify in the next section of this work.

The heavily counterfactual character of the most consequential risks is closely bound up with the numbness that a listing of them tends to promote. In mediaeval times, the invention of hell and damnation as the fate of the unbeliever in the afterlife was "real." Yet things are different with the most catastrophic dangers which face us today. The greater the danger, measured not in terms of probability of occurrence but in terms of its generalised threat to human life, the more thoroughly counterfactual it is. The risks involved are necessarily "unreal," because we could only have clear demonstration of them if events occurred that are too terrible to contemplate. Relatively small-scale events, such as the dropping of atomic bombs on Hiroshima and Nagasaki or the accidents at Three Mile Island or Chernobyl, give us some sense of what could happen. But these do not in any way bear upon the necessarily counterfactual character of other, more cataclysmic happenings – the main basis of their "unreality" and the narcotising effects produced by the repeated listing of risks. As Susan Sontag remarks, "A permanent modern scenario: apocalypse looms – and it doesn't occur. And still it looms. [...] Apocalypse is now a long-running serial: not 'Apocalypse Now', but 'Apocalypse from now on'."[7]

A Phenomenology of Modernity

Two images of what it feels like to live in the world of modernity have dominated the sociological literature, yet both of them seem less than adequate. One is that of Weber, according to which the bonds of rationality are drawn tighter and tighter, imprisoning us in a featureless cage of bureaucratic routine. Among the three major founders of modern sociology, Weber saw most clearly the significance of expertise in modern social development and used it to outline a phenomenology of modernity. Everyday experience, according to Weber, retains its colour and spontaneity, but only on the perimeter of the "steel-hard" cage of bureaucratic rationality. The image has a great deal of power and has, of course, featured strongly in fictional literature in the twentieth century as well as in more directly sociological discussions. There are many contexts of modern institutions which are marked by bureaucratic fixity. But they are far from all-pervasive, and even in the core settings of its application, namely, large-scale organisations, Weber's characterisation of bureaucracy is inadequate. Rather than tending inevitably towards rigidity, organisations produce areas of autonomy and spontaneity – which are actually often less easy to achieve in smaller groups. We owe this counterinsight to Durkheim, as well as to subsequent empirical study of organisations. The closed climate of opinion within some small groups and the modes of direct sanction available to its members fix the horizons of action much more narrowly and firmly than in larger organisational settings.

The second is the image of Marx – and of many others, whether they regard themselves as Marxist or not. According to this portrayal, modernity is seen as a monster. More limpidly perhaps than any of his contemporaries, Marx perceived how shattering the impact of modernity would be, and how irreversible. At the same time, modernity was for Marx what Habermas has aptly called an "unfinished project." The monster can be tamed, since what human beings have created they can always subject to their own control. Capitalism, simply, is an irrational way to run the modern world, because it substitutes the whims of the market for the controlled fulfilment of human need.

For these images I suggest we should substitute that of the juggernaut[8] – a runaway engine of enormous power which, collectively as human beings, we can drive to some extent but which also threatens to rush out of our control and which could rend itself asunder. The juggernaut crushes those who resist it, and while it sometimes seems to have a steady path, there are times when it veers away erratically in directions we cannot foresee. The ride is by no means wholly unpleasant or unrewarding; it can often be exhilarating and charged with hopeful anticipation. But, so long as the institutions of modernity endure, we shall never be able to control completely either the path or the pace of the journey. In turn, we shall never be able to feel entirely secure, because the terrain across which it runs is fraught with risks of high consequence. Feelings of ontological security and existential anxiety will coexist in ambivalence.

The juggernaut of modernity is not all of one piece, and here the imagery lapses, as does any talk of a single path which it runs. It is not an engine made up of integrated machinery, but one in which there is a tensionful, contradictory, push-and-pull of different influences. Any attempt to capture the experience of modernity must begin from this view, which derives ultimately from the dialectics of space and time, as expressed in the time-space constitution of modern institutions. I shall sketch a phenomenology of modernity in terms of four dialectically related frameworks of experience, each of which connects in an integral way with the preceding discussion in this study:

Displacement and reembedding: the intersection of estrangement and familiarity.
Intimacy and impersonality: the intersection of personal trust and impersonal ties.
Expertise and reappropriation: the intersection of abstract systems and day-to-day knowledgeability.
Privatism and engagement: the intersection of pragmatic acceptance and activism.

Modernity "dis-places" in the sense previously analysed – place becomes phantasmagoric. Yet this is a double-layered, or ambivalent, experience rather than simply a loss of community. We can see this clearly only if we keep in mind the contrasts between the pre-modern and the modern described earlier. What happens is not simply that localised influences drain away into the more impersonalised relations of abstract systems. Instead, the very tissue of spatial experience alters, conjoining proximity and distance in ways that have few close parallels in prior ages. There is a complex relation here between familiarity and estrangement. Many aspects of life in local contexts continue to have a familiarity and ease to them, grounded in the day-to-day routines individuals follow. But the sense of the familiar is one often mediated by time-space distanciation. It does not derive from the particularities of localised place. And this experience, so far as it seeps into general awareness, is simultaneously disturbing and rewarding. The reassurance of the familiar, so important to a sense of ontological security, is coupled with the realisation that what is comfortable and nearby is actually an expression of distant events and was "placed into" the local environment rather than forming an organic development within it. The local shopping mall is a milieu in which a sense of ease and security is cultivated by the layout of the buildings and the careful planning of public places. Yet everyone who shops there is aware that most of the shops are chain stores, which one might find in any city, and indeed that innumerable shopping malls of similar design exist elsewhere.

A feature of displacement is our insertion into globalised cultural and information settings, which means that familiarity and place are much less consistently connected than hitherto. This is less a phenomenon of estrangement from the local than one of integration within globalised "communities" of shared experience. The boundaries of concealment and disclosure become altered, since many erstwhile quite distinct activities are juxtaposed in unitary public domains. The newspaper and the sequence of television programmes over the day are the most obvious concrete examples of this phenomenon, but it is generic to the time-space organisation of modernity. We are all familiar with events, with actions, and with the visible appearance of physical settings thousands of miles away from where we happen to live. The coming of electronic media has undoubtedly accentuated these aspects of displacement, since they override presence so instantaneously and at such distance. As Joshua Meyrowitz points out, a person on the telephone to another, perhaps on the opposite side of the world, is more closely bound to that distant other than to another individual in the same room (who may be asking, "Who is it? What's she saying?" and so forth).

The counterpart of displacement is reembedding. The disembedding mechanisms lift social relations and the exchange of information out of specific time-space contexts, but at the same time provide new opportunities for their reinsertion. This is another reason why it is a mistake to see the modern world as one in which large, impersonal systems increasingly swallow up most of personal life. The self-same processes that lead to the destruction of older city neighbourhoods and their replacement by towering office-blocks and skyscrapers often permit the gentrification of other areas and a recreation of locality. Although the picture of tall, impersonal clusters of city-centre buildings is often presented as the epitome of the landscape of modernity, this is a mistake. Equally characteristic is the recreation of places of relative smallness and informality. The very means of transportation which help to dissolve the connection between locality and kinship provide the possibility for reembedding, by making it easy to visit "close" relatives who are far away.

Parallel comments can be made about the intersection of intimacy and impersonality in modern contexts of action. It is simply not true that in conditions of modernity we live increasingly in a "world of strangers." We are not required more and more to exchange intimacy for impersonality in the contacts with others we routinely make in the course of our day-to-day lives. Something much more complex and subtle is involved. Day-to-day contacts with others in pre-modern settings were normally based upon a familiarity stemming in part from the nature of place. Yet contacts with familiar others probably rarely facilitated the level of intimacy we associate with personal and sexual relations today. The "transformation of intimacy" of which I have spoken is contingent upon the very distancing which the disembedding mechanisms bring about, combined with the altered environments of trust which they presuppose. There are some very obvious ways in which intimacy and abstract systems interact. Money, for example, can be spent to purchase the expert services of a psychologist who guides the individual in an exploration of the inner universe of the intimate and the personal.

A person walks the streets of a city and encounters perhaps thousands of people in the course of a day, people she or he has never met before – "strangers" in the modern sense of that term. Or perhaps that individual strolls along less crowded thoroughfares, idly scrutinising passersby and the diversity of products for sale in the shops – Baudelaire's *flâneur*. Who could deny that these experiences are an integral element of modernity? Yet the world "out there" – the world that shades off into indefinite time-space from the familiarity of the home and the local neighbourhood – is not at all a purely impersonal one. On the contrary, intimate relationships can be sustained at distance (regular and sustained contact can be made with other individuals at virtually any point on the earth's surface – as well as some below and above), and personal ties are continually forged with others with whom one was previously unacquainted. We live in a *peopled* world, not merely one of anonymous, blank faces, and the interpolation of abstract systems into our activities is intrinsic to bringing this about.

In relations of intimacy of the modern type, trust is always ambivalent, and the possibility of severance is more or less ever present. Personal ties can be ruptured, and ties of intimacy returned to the sphere of impersonal contacts – in the broken love affair, the intimate suddenly becomes again a stranger. The demand of "opening oneself up" to the other which personal trust relations now presume, the injunction to hide nothing from the other, mix reassurance and deep anxiety. Personal trust demands a level of self-understanding and self-expression which must itself be a source of psychological tension. For mutual self-revelation is combined with the need for reciprocity and support; yet the two are frequently incompatible. Torment and frustration interweave themselves with the need for trust in the other as the provider of care and support.

Deskilling and Reskilling in Everyday Life

Expertise is part of intimacy in conditions of modernity, as is shown not just by the huge variety of forms of psychotherapy and counseling available, but by the plurality of books, articles, and television programmes providing technical information about "relationships." Does this mean that, as Habermas puts it, abstract systems "colonise" a pre-existing "life-world," subordinating personal decisions to technical expertise? It does not. The reasons are twofold. One is that modern institutions do not just implant themselves into a "life-world," the residues of which remain much the same as they always were. Changes in the nature of day-to-day life also affect the disembedding mechanisms, in a dialectical interplay. The second reason is that technical expertise is continuously reappropriated by lay agents as part of their routine dealings with abstract systems. No one can become an expert, in the sense of the possession either of full expert knowledge or of the appropriate formal credentials, in more than a few small sectors of the immensely complicated knowledge systems which now exist. Yet no one can interact with abstract systems without mastering some of the rudiments of the principles upon which they are based.

Sociologists often suppose that, in contrast to the pre-modern era, where many things were mysteries, today we live in a world from which mystery has retreated and where the way "the world works" can (in principle) be exhaustively known. But this is not true for either the lay person or the expert, if we consider their experience as individuals. To all of us living in the modern world things are specifically *opaque*, in a way that was not the case previously. In pre-modern environments the "local knowledge," to adapt a phrase from Clifford Geertz,[9] which individuals possessed was rich, varied, and adapted to the requirements of living in the local milieu. But how many of us today when we switch on the light know much about where the electricity supply comes from or even, in a technical sense, what electricity actually is?

Yet, although "local knowledge" cannot be of the same order as it once was, the sieving off of knowledge and skill from everyday life is not a one-way process. Nor are individuals in modern contexts less knowledgeable about their local milieux than their counterparts in pre-modern cultures. Modern social life is a complex affair, and there are many "filter-back" processes whereby technical knowledge, in one shape or another, is reappropriated by lay persons and routinely applied in the course of their day-to-day activities. As was mentioned earlier, the interaction between expertise and reappropriation is strongly influenced, among other things, by experiences at access points. Economic factors may decide whether a person learns to fix her or his car engine, rewire the electrical system of the house, or fix the roof; but so do the levels of trust that an individual vests in the particular expert systems and known experts involved. Processes of reappropriation relate to all aspects of social life – for example, medical treatment, child-rearing, or sexual pleasure.

For the ordinary individual, all this does not add up to feelings of secure control over day-to-day life circumstances. Modernity expands the arenas of personal fulfilment and of security in respect of large swathes of day-to-day life. But the lay person – and *all* of us are lay persons in respect of the vast majority of expert systems – must ride the juggernaut. The lack of control which many of us feel about some of the circumstances of our lives is real.

It is against this backdrop that we should understand patterns of privatism and engagement. A sense of "survival," in Lasch's use of this term, cannot be absent from our thoughts all of the time in a world in which, for the indefinite future, survival is a real and inescapable issue. On the level of the unconscious – even, and perhaps especially, among those whose attitude is one of pragmatic acceptance towards high-consequence risks – the relation to survival probably exists as existential dread. For basic trust in the continuity of the world must be anchored in the simple conviction that it will continue, and this is something of which we cannot be entirely sure. Saul Bellow remarks in the novel *Herzog*, "The revolution of nuclear terror returns the metaphysical dimension to us. All practical activity has reached this culmination: everything may go now, civilisation, history, nature. Now to recall Mr. Kierkegaard's question [...]"[10] "Mr. Kierkegaard's question" is, how do we avoid the dread of nonexistence, considered not just as individual death but as an existential void? The possibility of global calamity, whether by nuclear war or other means, prevents us from reassuring ourselves with the assumption that the life of the species inevitably surpasses that of the individual.

How remote that possibility is, literally no one knows. So long as there is deterrence, there must be the chance of war, because the notion of deterrence only makes sense if the parties involved are in principle prepared to use the weaponry they hold. Once again, no one, no matter how "expert" about the logistics of weapons and military organisation or about world politics, can say whether deterrence "works," because the most that can be said is that so far there has been no war. Awareness of these inherent uncertainties does not escape the lay population, however, vague that awareness might be.

Balanced against the deep anxieties which such circumstances must produce in virtually everyone is the psychological prop of the feeling that "there's nothing that I as an individual can do," and that at any rate the risk must be very slight. Business-as-usual, as I have pointed out, is a prime element in the stabilising of trust and ontological security, and this no doubt applies in respect of high-consequence risks just as it does in other areas of trust relations.

Yet obviously even high-consequence risks are not only remote contingencies, which can be ignored in daily life, albeit at some probable psychological cost. Some such risks, and many others which are potentially life-threatening for individuals or otherwise significantly affect them, intrude right into the core of day-to-day activities. This is true, for example, of any pollution damage which affects the health of adults or children, and anything which produces toxic contents in food or affects its nutritional properties. It is also true of a multitude of technological changes that influence life chances, such as reproductive technologies. The mix of risk and opportunity is so complex in many of the circumstances involved that it is extremely difficult for individuals to know how far to vest trust in particular prescriptions or systems, and how far to suspend it. How can one manage to eat "healthily," for example, when all kinds of food are said to have toxic qualities of one sort or another and when what is held to be "good for you" by nutritional experts varies with the shifting state of scientific knowledge?

Trust and risk, opportunity and danger – these polar, paradoxical features of modernity permeate all aspects of day-to-day life, once more reflecting an extraordinary interpolation of the local and the global. Pragmatic acceptance can be sustained towards most of the abstract systems that impinge on individuals' lives, but by its very nature such an attitude cannot be carried on all the while and in respect of all areas of activity. For incoming expert information is often fragmentary or inconsistent,[11] as is the recycled knowledge which colleagues, friends, and intimates pass on to one another. On a personal level, decisions must be taken and

Table 35.1   A comparison of conceptions of "Post-Modernity" (PM) and "Radicalised Modernity" (RM)

PM	RM
1. Understands current transitions in epistemological terms or as dissolving epistemology altogether.	1. Identifies the institutional developments which create a sense of fragmentation and dispersal.
2. Focuses upon the centrifugal tendencies of current social transformations and their dislocating character.	2. Sees high modernity as a set of circumstances in which dispersal is dialectically connected to profound tendencies towards global integration.
3. Sees the self as dissolved or dismembered by the fragmenting of experience.	3. Sees the self as more than just a site of intersecting forces; active processes of reflexive self-identity are made possible by modernity.
4. Argues for the contextuality of truth claims or sees them as "historical."	4. Argues that the universal features of truth claims force themselves upon us in an irresistible way given the primacy of problems of a global kind. Systematic knowledge about these developments is not precluded by the reflexivity of modernity.
5. Theorises powerlessness which individuals feel in the face of globalising tendencies.	5. Analyses a dialectic of powerlessness and empowerment, in terms of both experience and action.
6. Sees the "emptying" of day-to-day life as a result of the intrusion of abstract systems.	6. Sees day-to-day life as an active complex of reactions to abstract systems, involving appropriation as well as loss.
7. Regards coordinated political engagement as precluded by the primacy of contextuality and dispersal.	7. Regards coordinated political engagement as both possible and necessary, on a global level as well as locally.
8. Defines post-modernity as the end of epistemology/the individual/ethics.	8. Defines post-modernity as possible transformations moving "beyond" the institutions of modernity.

policies forged. Privatism, the avoidance of contestatory engagement – which can be supported by attitudes of basic optimism, pessimism, or pragmatic acceptance – can serve the purposes of day-to-day "survival" in many respects. But it is likely to be interspersed with phases of active engagement, even on the part of those most prone to attitudes of indifference or cynicism. For, to repeat, in respect of the balance of security and danger which modernity introduces into our lives, there are no longer "others" – no one can be completely outside. Conditions of modernity, in many circumstances, provoke activism rather than privatism, because of modernity's inherent reflexivity and because there are many opportunities for collective organisation within the polyarchic systems of modern nation-states.

Objections to Post-Modernity

I have sought to develop an interpretation of the current era which challenges the usual views of the emergence of post-modernity. As ordinarily understood, conceptions of post-modernity – which mostly have their origin in post-structuralist thought – involve a number of distinct strands. I compare this conception of post-modernity (PM) with my alternative position, which I shall call radicalised modernity (RM) in Table 35.1.

NOTES

1. Ulrich Beck, "The Anthropological Shock: Chernobyl and the Contours of the Risk Society," *Berkeley Journal of Sociology* 32 (1987).
2. Lawrence Stone, *The Family, Sex and Marriage in England 1500–1800* (London: Weidenfeld, 1977), p. 282.
3. Christopher Lasch, *Haven in a Heartless World* (New York: Basic, 1977), p. 140. See also his *The Minimal Self* (London: Picador, 1985), in which the formulation of narcissism is sharpened, and the theme of "survivalism" developed further.
4. Cf. W. Warren Wagar, *Terminal Visions* (Bloomington: University of Indiana Press, 1982).
5. Carolyn See, *Golden Days* (London: Arrow, 1989), p. 126.
6. Robert Jay Lifton and Richard Falk, *Indefensible Weapons* (New York: Basic Books, 1982).
7. Susan Sontag: *AIDS and Its Metaphors* (Harmondsworth: Penguin, 1989).
8. The term comes from the Hindi *Jagann th*, "lord of the world," and is a title of Krishna; an idol of this deity was taken each year through the streets on a huge car, which followers are said to have thrown themselves under, to be crushed beneath the wheels.
9. Clifford Geertz, *Local Knowledge* (New York: Basic Books, 1983).
10. Saul Bellow, *Herzog* (Harmondsworth: Penguin, 1964), p. 323.
11. Consider, as one among an indefinite range of examples, the case of cyclamate, an artificial sweetener, and the U.S. authorities. Cyclamate was widely used in the United States until 1970, and the Food and Drug Administration classified it as "generally recognised as safe." The attitude of the FDA changed when scientific research concluded that rats given large doses of the substance were prone to certain types of cancer.

Cyclamate was banned from use in food-stuffs. As more and more people began to drink low-calorie beverages in the 1970s and early 1980s, however, manufacturers exerted pressure on the FDA to change its stance. In 1984, a committee of the FDA decided that cyclamate was not after all a cancer-producing agent. A year later, the National Academy of Sciences intervened, reaching yet a different conclusion. In its report on the subject, the Academy declared that cyclamate is unsafe when used with saccharin, although probably harmless when used on its own as a sweetener. See James Bellini, *High Tech Holocaust* (London: Tarrant, 1986).

Chapter 36

We Have Never Been Modern [1991]

Bruno Latour

[…]

The Impossible Modernization

[…]

Modernization, although it destroyed the near-totality of cultures and natures by force and bloodshed, had a clear objective. Modernizing finally made it possible to distinguish between the laws of external nature and the conventions of society. The conquerors undertook this partition everywhere, consigning hybrids either to the domain of objects or to that of society. The process of partitioning was accompanied by a coherent and continuous front of radical revolutions in science, technology, administration, economy and religion, a veritable bulldozer operation behind which the past disappeared for ever, but in front of which, at least, the future opened up. The past was a barbarian medley; the future, a civilizing distinction. To be sure, the moderns have always recognized that they too had blended objects and societies, cosmologies and sociologies. But this was in the past, while they were still only premodern. By increasingly terrifying revolutions, they have been able to tear themselves away from that past. Since other cultures still mix the constraints of rationality with the needs of their societies, they have to be helped to emerge from

Bruno Latour, "We Have Never Been Modern," pp. 130–45 from Bruno Latour, *We Have Never Been Modern*. Cambridge, MA: Harvard University Press, 1993. Copyright © 1993 by Harvester Wheatsheaf and the President and Fellows of Harvard College. Reprinted by permission of Harvard University Press. Originally translated by Catherine Porter.

that confusion by annihilating their past. Modernizers know perfectly well that even in their own midst islands of barbarianism remain, in which technological efficacity and social arbitrariness are excessively intertwined. But before long they will have achieved modernization, they will have liquidated those islands, and we shall all inhabit the same planet; we shall all be equally modern, all equally capable of profiting from what, alone, forever escapes the tyranny of social interest: economic rationality, scientific truth, technological efficiency.

Certain modernizers continue to speak as if such a fate were possible and desirable. However, one has only to express it to see how self-contradictory this claim is. How could we bring about the purification of sciences and societies at last, when the modernizers themselves are responsible for the proliferation of hybrids thanks to the very Constitution that makes them proliferate by denying their existence? For a long time, this contradiction was hidden by the moderns' very increase. Permanent revolutions in the State, and sciences, and technologies, were supposed to end up absorbing, purifying and civilizing the hybrids by incorporating them either into society or into nature. But the double failure that was my starting point, that of socialism – at stage left – and that of naturalism – at stage right – has made the work of purification less plausible and the contradiction more visible. There are no more revolutions in store to impel a continued forward flight. There are so many hybrids that no one knows any longer how to lodge them in the old promised land of modernity. Hence the postmoderns' abrupt paralysis.

Modernization was ruthless toward the premoderns, but what can we say about postmodernization? Imperialist violence at least offered a future, but sudden weakness on the part of the conquerors is far worse for, always cut off from the past, it now also breaks with the future. Having been slapped in the face with modern reality, poor populations now have to submit to postmodern hyperreality. Nothing has value; everything is a reflection, a simulacrum, a floating sign; and that very weakness, they say, may save us from the invasion of technologies, sciences, reasons. Was it really worth destroying everything to end up adding this insult to that injury? The empty world in which the postmoderns evolve is one they themselves, and they alone, have emptied, because they have taken the moderns at their word. Postmodernism is a symptom of the contradiction of modernism, but it is unable to diagnose this contradiction because it shares the same upper half of the Constitution – the sciences and the technologies are extrahuman – but it no longer shares the cause of the Constitution's strength and greatness – the proliferation of quasi-objects and the multiplication of intermediaries between humans and nonhumans allowed by the absolute distinction between humans and nonhumans.

However, the diagnosis is not very difficult to make, now that we are obliged to consider the work of purification and the work of mediation symmetrically. Even at the worst moments of the Western imperium, it was never a matter of clearly separating the Laws of Nature from social conventions once and for all. It was always a matter of constructing collectives by mixing a certain type of nonhumans and a certain type of humans, and extracting in the process Boyle-style objects and Hobbes-style subjects (not to mention the crossed-out God) on an ever-increasing scale. The innovation of longer networks is an interesting peculiarity, but it is not sufficient to set us radically apart from others, or to cut us off for ever from our past. Modernizers are not obliged to continue their revolutionary task by gathering their forces, ignoring the postmoderns' predicament, gritting their teeth, and continuing to believe in the dual promises of naturalism and socialism no matter what, since that particular modernization has never got off the ground. It was never anything but the official representation of another much more profound and different work that had always been going on and continues today on an ever-increasing scale. Nor are we obliged to struggle against modernization – in the militant manner of the antimoderns or the disillusioned manner of the postmoderns – since we would then be attacking the upper half of the Constitution alone, which we would merely be reinforcing while remaining unaware of what has always been the source of its vitality.

But does this diagnosis allow any remedy for the impossible modernization? If [...] the Constitution allows hybrids to proliferate because it refuses to conceptualize them as such, then it remains effective only so long as it denies their existence. Now, if the fruitful contradiction between the two parts – the official work of purification and the unofficial work of mediation – becomes clearly visible, won't the Constitution cease to be effective? Won't modernization become impossible? Are we going to become – or go back to being – premodern? Do we have to resign ourselves to becoming antimodern? For lack of any better option, are we going to have to continue to be modern, but without conviction, in the twilight zone of the postmods?

Final Examinations

To answer these questions, we must first sort out the various positions I have outlined in the course of this essay, to bring the nonmodern to terms with the best those positions have to offer. What are we going to retain from the moderns? Everything, apart from exclusive confidence in the upper half of their Constitution, because this Constitution will need to be amended somewhat to include its lower half too. The moderns' greatness stems from their proliferation of hybrids, their lengthening of a certain type of network, their acceleration of the production of traces, their multiplication of delegates, their groping production of relative universals. Their daring, their research, their innovativeness, their tinkering, their youthful excesses, the ever-increasing scale of their action, the creation of stabilized objects independent of society, the freedom of a society liberated from objects – all these are features we want to keep. On the other hand, we cannot retain the illusion (whether they deem it positive or negative) that moderns have about themselves and want to generalize to everyone: atheist, materialist, spiritualist, theist, rational, effective, objective, universal, critical, radically different from other communities, cut off from a past that is maintained in a state of artificial survival due only to historicism, separated from a nature on which subjects or society would arbitrarily impose categories, denouncers always at war with themselves, prisoners of an absolute dichotomy between things and signs, facts and values.

Westerners felt far removed from the premoderns because of the External Great Divide – a simple exportation [...] of the Internal Great Divide. When the latter is dissolved, the former disappears, to be replaced by differences in size. Symmetrical anthropology has redistributed the Great Divide. Now that we are no longer so far removed from the premoderns – since when we talk about the premoderns we have to include a large part of ourselves – we are going to have to sort them out as well. Let us keep what is best about them, above all: the premoderns' inability to differentiate durably between the networks and the pure poles of Nature and Society, their obsessive interest in thinking about the production of hybrids of Nature and Society, of things and signs, their certainty that transcendences abound, their capacity for conceiving of past and future in many ways other than progress and decadence, the multiplication of types of nonhumans different from those of the moderns. On the other hand, we shall not retain the set of limits they impose on the scaling of collectives, localization by territory, the scapegoating process, ethnocentrism, and finally the lasting nondifferentiation of natures and societies.

But the sorting seems impossible and even contradictory in the face of what I have said above. Since the invention of longer networks and the increase in size of some collectives depends on the silence they maintain about quasi-objects, how can I promise to keep the changes of scale and give up the invisibility that allows them to spread? Worse still, how could I reject from the premoderns the lasting nondifferentiation of natures and societies, and reject from the moderns the absolute dichotomy between natures and societies? How can size, exploration, proliferation be maintained while the hybrids are made explicit? Yet this is precisely the amalgam I am looking for: *to retain the production of a nature and of a society that allow changes in size through the creation of an external truth and a subject of law, but without neglecting the co-production of sciences and societies.* The amalgam consists in using the premodern categories to conceptualize the hybrids, while retaining the moderns' final outcome of the work of purification – that is, an external Nature distinct from subjects. I want to keep following the gradient that leads from unstable existences to stabilized essences – and vice versa. To accomplish the work of purification, but as a particular case of the work of mediation. To maintain all the advantages of the moderns' dualism without its disadvantages – the clandestineness of the quasi-objects. To keep all the advantages of the premoderns' monism without tolerating its limits – the restriction of size through the lasting confusion of knowledge and power.

The postmoderns have sensed the crisis of the moderns and attempted to overcome it; thus they too warrant examination and sorting. It is of course impossible to conserve their irony, their despair, their discouragement, their nihilism, their self-criticism, since all those fine qualities depend on a conception of modernism that modernism itself has never really practised. As soon, however, as we add the lower part of the Constitution to the upper part, many of the intuitions of postmodernism are vindicated. For instance, we can save deconstruction – but since it no longer has a contrary, it turns into constructivism and no longer goes hand in hand with self-destruction. We can retain the deconstructionists' refusal of naturalization – but since Nature itself is no longer natural, this refusal no longer distances us from the sciences

	What is retained	**What is rejected**
From the moderns	• long networks • size • experimentation • relative universals • final separation between objective nature and free society	• separation between nature and society • clandestineness of the practices of mediation • external Great Divide • critical denunciation • universality, rationality
From the premoderns	• non-separability of things and signs • transcendence without a contrary • multiplication of nonhumans • temporality by intensity	• obligation always to link the social and natural orders • scapegoating mechanism: ethnocentrism territory • limits on scale
From the postmoderns	• multiple times • constructivism • reflexivity • denaturalization	• belief in modernism • critical deconstruction • ironic reflexivity • anachronism

Figure 36.1 What is retained and what is rejected.

but, on the contrary, brings us closer to sciences in action. We can keep the postmoderns' pronounced taste for reflexivity – but since that property is shared among all the actors, it loses its parodic character and becomes positive. Finally, we can go along with the postmoderns in rejecting the idea of a coherent and homogeneous time that would advance by goose steps – but without retaining their taste for quotation and anachronism which maintains the belief in a truly surpassed past. Take away from the postmoderns their illusions about the moderns, and their vices become virtues – nonmodern virtues!

Regrettably, in the antimoderns I see nothing worth saving. Always on the defensive, they consistently believed what the moderns said about themselves and proceeded to affix the opposite sign to each declaration. Antirevolutionary, they held the same peculiar views as the moderns about time past and tradition. The values they defended were never anything but the residue left by their enemies; they never understood that the moderns' greatness stemmed, in practice, from the very reverse of what the antimoderns attacked them for. Even in their rearguard combats, the antimoderns never managed to innovate, occupying the minor role that was reserved for them. It cannot even be said in their favour that they put the brakes on the moderns' frenzy – those moderns for whom the antimoderns were always, in effect, the best of stooges.

The balance sheet of this examination is not too unfavourable [Figure 36.1]. We can keep the Enlightenment without modernity, provided that we reintegrate the objects of the sciences and technologies into the Constitution, as quasi-objects among many others – objects whose genesis must no longer be clandestine, but must be followed through and through, from the hot events that spawned the objects to the progressive cool-down that transforms them into essences of Nature or Society.

Is it possible to draw up a Constitution that would allow us to recognize this work officially? We must do this, since old-style modernization can no longer absorb either other peoples or Nature; such, at least, is the conviction on which this essay is based. For its own good, the modern world can no longer extend itself without becoming once again what it has never ceased to be in practice – that is, a nonmodern world like all the others. This fraternity is essential if we are to absorb the two sets of entities that revolutionary modernization left behind: the natural crowds that we no longer master, the human multitudes that no one dominates any longer. Modern temporality gave the impression of continuous acceleration by relegating ever-larger masses of humans and nonhumans together to the void of the past. Irreversibility has changed sides. If there is one thing we can no longer get rid of, it is those natures and multitudes, both equally global. The political task starts up again, at a new cost. It has been necessary to modify the fabric of our collectives from top to bottom in order to absorb the citizen of the eighteenth century and the worker of the nineteenth. We shall have to transform ourselves just as thoroughly in order to make room, today, for the nonhumans created by science and technology.

Humanism Redistributed

Before we can amend the Constitution, we first have to relocate the human, to which humanism does not render sufficient justice. Here are some of the magnificent figures that the moderns have been able to depict and preserve: the free agent, the citizen builder of the Leviathan, the distressing visage of the human person, the other of a relationship, consciousness, the *cogito*, the hermeneut, the inner self, the thee and thou of dialogue, presence to oneself, intersubjectivity. But all these figures remain asymmetrical, for they are the counterpart of the object of the sciences – an object that remains orphaned, abandoned in the hands of those whom epistemologists, like sociologists, deem reductive, objective, rational. Where are the Mouniers of machines, the Lévinases of animals, the Ricoeurs of facts? Yet the human, as we now understand, cannot be grasped and saved unless that other part of itself, the share of things, is restored to it. So long as humanism is constructed through contrast with the object that has been abandoned to epistemology, neither the human nor the nonhuman can be understood.

Where are we to situate the human? A historical succession of quasi-objects, quasi-subjects, it is impossible to define the human by an essence, as we have known for a long time. Its history and its anthropology are too diverse for it to be pinned down once and for all. But Sartre's clever move, defining it as a free existence uprooting itself from a nature devoid of significance, is obviously not one we can make, since we have invested all quasi-objects with action, will, meaning, and even speech. There is no longer a practico-inert where the pure liberty of human existence can get bogged down. To oppose it to the crossed-out God (or, conversely, to reconcile it with Him) is equally impossible, since it is by virtue of their common opposition to Nature that the modern Constitution has defined all three. Must the human be steeped in Nature, then? But if we were to go looking for specific results of specific scientific disciplines that would clothe this robot animated with neurons, impulses, selfish genes, elementary needs and economic calculations, we would never get beyond monsters and masks. The sciences multiply new definitions of humans without managing to displace the former ones, reduce them to any homogeneous one, or unify them. They add reality; they do not subtract it. The hybrids that they invent in the laboratory are still more exotic than those they claim to break down.

Must we solemnly announce the death of man and dissolve him in the play of language, an evanescent reflection of inhuman structures that would escape all understanding? No, since we are no more in Discourse than we are in Nature. In any event, nothing is sufficiently inhuman to dissolve human beings in it and announce their death. Their will, their actions, their words are too abundant. Will we have to avoid the question by making the human something transcendental that would distance us for ever from mere nature? This would amount to falling back on just one of the poles of the modern Constitution. Will we have to use force to extend some provisional and particular definition inscribed in the rights of man or the preambles of constitutions? This would amount to tracing out once again the two Great Divides, and believing in modernization.

If the human does not possess a stable form, it is not formless for all that. If, instead of attaching it to one constitutional pole or the other, we move it closer to the middle, it becomes the mediator and even the intersection of the two. The human is not a constitutional pole to be opposed to that of the nonhuman. The two expressions "humans" and "nonhumans" are belated results that no longer suffice to designate the other dimension. The scale of value consists not in shifting the definition of the human along the horizontal line that connects the Object pole to the Subject pole, but in sliding it along the vertical dimension that defines the nonmodern world. Reveal its work of mediation, and it will take on human form. Conceal it again, and we shall have to talk about inhumanity, even if it is draping itself in the Bill of Rights. The expression "anthropomorphic" considerably underestimates our humanity. We should be talking about morphism. Morphism is the place where technomorphisms, zoomorphisms, phusimorphisms, ideomorphisms, theomorphisms, sociomorphisms, psychomorphisms, all come together. Their alliances and their exchanges, taken together, are what define the *anthropos*. A weaver of morphisms – isn't that enough of a definition? The closer the *anthropos* comes to this distribution, the more human it is. The farther away it moves, the more it takes on multiple forms in which its humanity quickly becomes indiscernible, even if its figures are those of the person, the individual or the self. By seeking to isolate its form from those it churns together, one does not defend humanism, one loses it.

How could the *anthropos* be threatened by machines? It has made them, it has put itself into them, it has divided up its own members among their members, it has built its own body with them. How could it be threatened by objects? They have all been quasi-subjects circulating within the collective they traced. It is made of them as much as they are made of it. It has defined itself by multiplying things. How could it be deceived by politics? Politics is its own making, in that it reconstructs the collective through continual controversies over representation that allow it to say, at every moment, what it is and what it wants. How could it be dimmed by religion? It is through religion that humans are linked to all their fellows, that they know themselves as persons. How could it be manipulated by the economy? Its provisional form cannot be assigned without the circulation of goods and obligations, without the continuous distribution of social goods that we concoct through the goodwill of things. *Ecce homo*: delegated, mediated, distributed, mandated, uttered. Where does the threat come from? From those who seek to reduce it to an essence and who – by scorning things, objects, machines and the social, by cutting off all delegations and senders – make humanism a fragile and precious thing at risk of being overwhelmed by Nature, Society, or God.

Modern humanists are reductionist because they seek to attribute action to a small number of powers, leaving the rest of the world with nothing but simple mute forces. It is true that by redistributing the action among all these mediators, we lose the reduced form of humanity, but we gain another form, which has to be called irreducible. The human is in the delegation itself, in the pass, in the sending, in the continuous exchange of forms. Of course it is not a thing, but things are not things either. Of course it is not a merchandise, but merchandise is not merchandise either. Of course it is not a machine, but anyone who has seen machines knows that they are scarcely mechanical. Of course it is not of this world, but this world is not of this world either. Of course it is not in God, but what relation is there between the God above and the God below? Humanism can maintain itself only by sharing itself with all these mandatees. Human nature is the set of its delegates and its representatives, its figures and its messengers. That symmetrical universal is worth at least as much as the moderns' doubly asymmetrical one. This new position, shifted in relation to the subject/society position, now needs to be underwritten by an amended Constitution.

The Nonmodern Constitution

In the course of this essay, I have simply reestablished symmetry between the two branches of government, that of things – called science and technology – and that of human beings. I have also shown why the separation of powers between the two branches, after allowing for the proliferation of hybrids, could no longer worthily represent this new third estate. A constitution is judged by the guarantees it offers. The moderns' Constitution [...] included four guarantees that had meaning only when they were taken together but also kept strictly separate. The first one guaranteed Nature its transcendent dimension by making it distinct from the fabric of Society – thus contrary to the continuous connection between the natural order and the social order found among the premoderns. The second guaranteed Society its immanent dimension by rendering citizens totally free to reconstruct it artificially – as opposed to the continuous connection between the social order and the natural order that kept the premoderns from being able to modify the one without modifying the other. But as that double separation allowed in practice for the mobilization and construction of Nature (Nature having become immanent through mobilization and construction) – and, conversely, made it possible to make Society stable and durable (Society having become transcendent owing to the enrolment of ever more numerous nonhumans), a third guarantee assured the separation of powers, the two branches of government being kept in separate, watertight compartments: even though it is mobilizable and constructed, Nature will remain without relation to Society; Society, in turn, even though it is transcendent and rendered durable by the mediation of objects, will no longer have any relation to Nature. In other words, quasi-objects will be officially banished – should we say taboo? – and translation networks will go into hiding, offering to the work of purification a counterpart that will nevertheless continue to be followed and monitored – until the postmoderns obliterate it entirely. The fourth guarantee of the crossed-out God made it possible to stabilize this dualist and asymmetrical mechanism by ensuring a function of arbitration, but one without presence or power. [...]

In order to sketch in the nonmodern Constitution, it suffices to take into account what the modern Constitution left out, and to sort out the guarantees we wish to keep. We have committed ourselves to providing representation for quasi-objects. It is the third guarantee of the modern Constitution that must therefore be suppressed, since that is the one that made the continuity of their analysis impossible. Nature and Society are not two distinct poles, but one and the same production of successive states of societies-natures, of collectives. The first guarantee of our new draft thus becomes the nonseparability of quasi-objects, quasi-subjects. Every concept, every institution, every practice that interferes with the continuous deployment of collectives and their experimentation with hybrids will be deemed dangerous, harmful, and – we may as well say it – immoral. The work of mediation becomes the very centre of the double power, natural and social. The networks come out of hiding. The Middle Kingdom is represented. The third estate, which was nothing, becomes everything.

As I have suggested, however, we do not wish to become premoderns all over again. The nonseparability of natures and societies had the disadvantage of making experimentation on a large scale impossible, since every transformation of nature had to be in harmony with a social transformation, term for term, and vice versa. Now we seek to keep the moderns' major innovation: the separability of a nature that no one has constructed – transcendence – and the freedom of manœuvre of a society that is of our own making – immanence. Nevertheless, we do not seek to inherit the clandestineness of the inverse mechanism that makes it possible to construct Nature – immanence – and to stabilize Society durably – transcendence.

Can we retain the first two guarantees of the old Constitution without maintaining the now-visible duplicity of its third guarantee? Yes, although at first this looks like squaring the circle. Nature's transcendence, its objectivity, and Society's immanence, its subjectivity, stem from the work of mediation without depending on their separation, contrary to what the Constitution of the moderns claims. The work of producing a nature or producing a society stems from the durable and irreversible accomplishment of the common work of delegation and translation. At the end of the process, there is indeed a nature that we have not made, and a society that we are free to change; there are indeed indisputable scientific facts, and free citizens, but once they are viewed in a nonmodern light they become the double consequence of a practice that is now visible in its continuity, instead of being, as for the moderns, the remote and opposing causes of an invisible practice that contradicts them. The second guarantee of our new draft thus makes it possible to recover the first two guarantees of the modern Constitution but without separating them. All concepts, all institutions, all practices that interfere with the progressive objectivization of Nature – incorporation into a black box – and simultaneously the subjectivization of Society – freedom of manœuvre – will be deemed harmful, dangerous and, quite simply, immoral. Without this second guarantee, the networks liberated by the first would keep their wild and uncontrollable character. The moderns were not mistaken in seeking objective nonhumans and free societies. They were mistaken only in their certainty that that double production required an absolute distinction between the two terms and the continual repression of the work of mediation.

Historicity found no place in the modern Constitution because it was framed by the only three entities whose existence it recognized. Contingent history existed for humans alone, and revolution became the only way for the moderns to understand their past [...] by breaking totally with it. But time is not a smooth, homogeneous flow. If time depends on associations, associations do not depend on time. We are no longer going to be confronted with the argument of time that passes for ever based on a regrouping into a coherent set of elements that belong to all times and all ontologies. If we want to recover the capacity to sort that appears essential to our morality and defines the human, it is essential that no coherent temporal flow comes to limit our freedom of choice. The third guarantee, as important as the others, is that we can combine associations freely without ever confronting the choice between archaism and modernization, the local and the global, the cultural and the universal, the natural and the social. Freedom has moved away from the social pole it had occupied exclusively during the modern representation into the middle and lower zones, and becomes a capacity for sorting and recombining sociotechnological imbroglios. Every new call to revolution, any epistemological break, any Copernican upheaval, any claim that certain practices have become outdated for ever, will be deemed dangerous, or – what is still worse in the eyes of the moderns – outdated!

But if I am right in my interpretation of the modern Constitution, if it has really allowed the development of collectives while officially forbidding what it permits in practice, how could we continue to develop quasi-objects, now that we have made their practice visible and official? By offering guarantees to replace the previous ones, are we not making impossible this double language, and thus the growth of collectives? That is precisely what we want to do. This slowing down, this moderation, this regulation, is what we expect from our morality. The fourth guarantee – perhaps the most important – is to replace the clandestine proliferation of hybrids by their regulated and commonly-agreed-upon production. It is time, perhaps, to speak of

Modern Constitution	Nonmodern Constitution
1st guarantee: Nature is transcendent but mobilizable (immanent).	*1st guarantee:* nonseparability of the common production of societies and natures.
2nd guarantee: Society is immanent but it infinitely surpasses us (transcendent).	*2nd guarantee:* continuous following of the production of Nature, which is objective, and the production of Society, which is free. In the last analysis, there is indeed a transcendence of Nature and an immanence of Society, but the two are not separated.
3rd guarantee: Nature and Society are totally distinct, and the work of purification bears no relation to the work of mediation.	*3rd guarantee:* freedom is redefined as a capacity to sort the combinations of hybrids that no longer depend on a homogeneous temporal flow.
4th guarantee: the crossed-out God is totally absent but ensures arbitration between the two branches of government.	*4th guarantee:* the production of hybrids, by becoming explicit and collective, becomes the object of an enlarged democracy that regulates or slows down its cadence.

Figure 36.2 Modern/nonmodern constitution.

democracy again, but of a democracy extended to things themselves. We are not going to be caught by Archimedes' coup again.

Do we need to add that the crossed-out God, in this new Constitution, turns out to be liberated from the unworthy position to which He had been relegated? The question of God is reopened, and the nonmoderns no longer have to try to generalize the improbable metaphysics of the moderns that forced them to believe in belief [Figure 36.2].

The Parliament of Things

We want the meticulous sorting of quasi-objects to become possible – no longer unofficially and under the table, but officially and in broad daylight. In this desire to bring to light, to incorporate into language, to make public, we continue to identify with the intuition of the Enlightenment. But this intuition has never had the anthropology it deserved. It has divided up the human and the nonhuman and believed that the others, rendered premoderns by contrast, were not supposed to do the same thing. While it was necessary, perhaps, to increase mobilization and lengthen some networks, this division has now become superfluous, immoral, and – to put it bluntly – anti-Constitutional! We have been modern. Very well. We can no longer be modern in the same way. When we amend the Constitution, we continue to believe in the sciences, but instead of taking in their objectivity, their truth, their coldness, their extraterritoriality – qualities they have never had, except after the arbitrary withdrawal of epistemology – we retain what has always been most interesting about them: their daring, their experimentation, their uncertainty, their warmth, their incongruous blend of hybrids, their crazy ability to reconstitute the social bond. We take away from them only the mystery of their birth and the danger their clandestineness posed to democracy.

Yes, we are indeed the heirs of the Enlightenment, whose asymmetrical rationality is just not broad enough for us. Boyle's descendants had defined a parliament of mutes, the laboratory, where scientists, mere intermediaries, spoke all by themselves in the name of things. What did these representatives say? Nothing but what the things would have said on their own, had they only been able to speak. Outside the laboratory, Hobbes's descendants had defined the Republic in which naked citizens, unable to speak all at once, arranged to have themselves represented by one of their number, the Sovereign, a simple intermediary and spokesperson. What did this representative say? Nothing but what the citizens would have said had they all been able to speak at the same time. But a doubt about the quality of that double translation crept in straight away. What if the scientists were talking about themselves instead of about things? And if the Sovereign were pursuing his own interests instead of reciting the script written for him by his constituents? In the first case, we would lose Nature and fall back into human disputes; in the second, we would fall back into the State of Nature and into the war of every man against every man. By defining a total separation between the scientific and political representations, the double translation-betrayal became possible. We shall never know whether scientists translate or betray. We shall never know whether representatives betray or translate.

During the modern period, the critics will continue to sustain themselves on that double doubt and the impossibility of ever putting an end to it. Modernism consisted in choosing that arrangement, nevertheless, but in remaining constantly suspicious of its two types of representatives without combining them into a single problem. Epistemologists wondered about scientific realism and the faithfulness of science to things; political scientists wondered about the representative system and the relative faithfulness of elected officials and spokespersons. All had in common a hatred of intermediaries and a desire for an immediate world, emptied of its mediators. All thought that this was the price of faithful representation, without ever understanding that the solution to their problem lay in the other branch of government.

In the course of this essay, I have shown what happened once science studies re-examined such a division of labour. I have shown how fast the modern Constitution broke down, since it no longer permitted the construction of a common dwelling to shelter the societies-natures that the moderns have bequeathed us. There are not two problems of representation, just one. There are not two branches, only one, whose products can be distinguished only late in the game, and after being examined together. Scientists appear to be betraying external reality only because they are constructing their societies and their natures at the same time. The Sovereign appears to be betraying his constituents only because he is churning together both citizens and the enormous mass of nonhumans that allow the Leviathan to hold up. Suspicion about scientific representation stemmed only from the belief that without social pollution Nature would be immediately accessible. 'Eliminate the social and you will finally have a faithful representation,' said some. 'Eliminate objects and you will finally have a faithful representation,' declared others. Their whole debate arose from the division of powers enforced by the modern Constitution.

Let us again take up the two representations and the double doubt about the faithfulness of the representatives, and we shall have defined the Parliament of Things. In its confines, the continuity of the collective is reconfigured. There are no more naked truths, but there are no more naked citizens, either. The mediators have the whole space to themselves. The Enlightenment has a dwelling-place at last. Natures are present, but with their representatives, scientists who speak in their name. Societies are present, but with the objects that have been serving as their ballast from time immemorial. Let one of the representatives talk, for instance, about the ozone hole, another represent the Monsanto chemical industry, a third the workers of the same chemical industry, another the voters of New Hampshire, a fifth the meteorology of the polar regions; let still another speak in the name of the State; what does it matter, so long as they are all talking about the same thing, about a quasi-object they have all created, the object-discourse-nature-society whose new properties astound us all and whose network extends from my refrigerator to the Antarctic by way of chemistry, law, the State, the economy, and satellites. The imbroglios and networks that had no place now have the whole place to themselves. They are the ones that have to be represented; it is around them that the Parliament of Things gathers henceforth. 'It was the stone rejected by the builders that became the keystone' (Mark 12:10).

However, we do not have to create this Parliament out of whole cloth, by calling for yet another revolution. We simply have to ratify what we have always done, provided that we reconsider our past, provided that we understand retrospectively to what extent we have never been modern, and provided that we rejoin the two halves of the symbol broken by Hobbes and Boyle as a sign of recognition. Half of our politics is constructed in science and technology. The other half of Nature is constructed in societies. Let us patch the two back together, and the political task can begin again.

Is it asking too little simply to ratify in public what is already happening? Should we not strive for more glamorous and more revolutionary programmes of action, rather than underlining what is already dimly discernible in the shared practices of scientists, politicians, consumers, industrialists and citizens when they engage in the numerous sociotechnological controversies we read about daily in our newspapers? As we have been discovering throughout this essay, the official representation is effective; that representation is what allowed, under the old Constitution, the exploration and proliferation of hybrids. Modernism was not an illusion, but an active performing. If we could draft a new Constitution, we would, similarly, profoundly alter the course of quasi-objects. Another Constitution will be just as effective, but it will produce different hybrids. Is that too much to expect of a change in representation that seems to depend only on the scrap of paper of a Constitution? It may well be; but there are times when new words are needed to convene a new assembly. The task of our predecessors was no less daunting when they invented rights to give to citizens or the integration of workers into the fabric of our societies. I have done my job as philosopher and constituent by gathering together the scattered themes of a comparative anthropology. Others will be able to convene the Parliament of Things.

We scarcely have much choice. If we do not change the common dwelling, we shall not absorb in it the other cultures that we can no longer dominate, and we shall be forever incapable of accommodating in it the environment that we can no longer control. Neither Nature nor the Others will become modern. It is up to us to change our ways of changing. Or else it will have been for naught that the Berlin Wall fell during the miraculous year 1989, offering us a unique practical lesson about the conjoined failure of socialism and naturalism.

Part X

Crisis and Change

Introduction to Part X

37 Systemic and Antisystemic Crises

38 Reconfiguring Territory, Authority, and Rights

39 The Modern World-System in Crisis

Introduction to Part X

Sociology as a formal discipline emerged in response to the changes experienced by eighteenth-century European societies. These changes were catapulted by the forces of modernity, such as capitalism, industrialism, and urbanization. All of these developments resulted in momentous structural transformations in society that changed the way life was lived and experienced. Most of the theorists we read in *Classical Sociological Theory* (volume 1) were reflecting upon these changes in one way or another.

Theoretical discussions of crisis and change in sociological theory have been shaped, in particular, by Marx's theory (see volume 1). He argued that the contradictions of capitalism will inevitably lead to a crisis in capitalist societies and that revolutionary change will ensue. In fact, Marx suggested that crises are endemic to the capitalist system. The contradictory class interests of the bourgeoisie and the proletariat will inevitably widen the gap between the two classes. These class antagonisms will eventually result in a proletarian revolution and the transformation of capitalism into socialism. Within capitalism, thus, lie the seeds of its own destruction. In articulating this theory, Marx confronted the confidence expressed by classical liberal economists like Adam Smith in the self-regulatory powers of the market. He questioned their assumption that any crises in capitalism will be automatically resolved in the best manner possible.

Subsequent analyses of crisis and change have engaged in some fashion or another with Marx's theories. These analyses have addressed the historical transformations of the economies of capitalist societies and the resultant restructuring of the social and political realms. The industrial capitalism of Marx's time grew through the first half of the twentieth century, although the 1930s witnessed a crisis of severe economic downturn. The Great Depression led to a serious examination of the economic system that had reverberations in the political realm as well. In the United States, the state initiated more protections from the market in the form of social welfare, public works, and industrial regulation.

Contemporary Sociological Theory, Third Edition. Edited by Craig Calhoun, Joseph Gerteis, James Moody, Steven Pfaff, and Indermohan Virk. Editorial material and organization © 2012 John Wiley & Sons, Ltd. Published 2012 by John Wiley & Sons, Ltd.

Around the 1960s, theorists, like Daniel Bell, began to notice that there had been a decline of industrial growth in the core capitalist societies. This decline in industrial production in the United States has been subsequently accompanied by a concurrent growth in the service economy. With deindustrialization and the increasing dominance of post-Fordist practices, capital has become more flexible and disorganized. In other words, capital accumulation increasingly occurs through flexible work practices that have resulted in significant spatial de-concentration of work and labor. Capital has vigorously explored global markets and labor in its pursuit of increased accumulation. Corporations, for instance, have cast their production and business networks on a global scale. And, in this globalizing economic landscape, the United States has played a dominant role. The second half of the twentieth century, then, was a period of US ascendancy in the economic and world-political stage. Needless to say, these economic trends have had a profound impact on the political-economic landscape of advanced capitalist societies.

Much popular and academic discourse has been devoted in recent decades to exploring the contours of globalization and the implication of these transnational economic relations for the nation-state and individuals. This discussion has problematized the relationship between the nation-state and markets. Issues of power and sovereignty are integral to the interplay of these two domains; for instance, whose interests, state or market, ought to prevail in situations where there are competing claims and interests?

Discussions of crisis and change have emerged afresh in our world today. On the one hand, there has been a renewed interest in evaluating the relationship between the state and the market following the 2008 recession. A vigorous debate continues to be conducted on the merits of government regulation of market institutions and the limits of market self-regulation. The economic downturn has thus led to serious questions about the future face of capitalism. On the other hand, there has emerged a potential challenge to the position of the United States as the most important economic force in the world. Several Asian economies have experienced significant growth, with China being the most notable. This has raised questions about the nature of the existing balance of power in future years.

Yet, the crises social theorists have examined have not been limited to the economic sphere alone. Modernity has been shaped radically, for instance, by critical political events, such as the French Revolution. Aside from changes in the immediate local context, such political revolutions (including the American Revolution) have had long-term consequences, ushering in the modern liberal, democratic, nation-state on the political landscape. It introduced the idea of popular sovereignty to conceptions of governance. While the idea of a sovereign nation-state gradually took firm roots in the post-Revolutionary period, it has faced fresh challenges in recent decades. The growth in the globalization of capital during the late twentieth century (discussed above) has tested the territorial boundaries of the nation-state and its sovereignty vis-à-vis the operations of multinational corporations.

The theorists in this section address many of these developments in one form or another.

Crises of Capitalist Development

Immanuel Wallerstein (1930–) is an American sociologist best known for his contribution of the idea of a world-system to sociological theory. In proposing this concept, Wallerstein was challenging modernization theory, the prevailing dominant explanation of economic development. Modernization theory assumes that the model of progress and development experienced by Western societies is one that all "traditional" societies will follow. Once integrated into the global market, traditional societies will be transformed into modern, industrial societies. Wallerstein challenged this assumption of modernization theory for offering a simplistic analysis of the course of progress. Instead, he proposed the idea of a world-system, in which the world economy consists of a core and a periphery, both inextricably tied into a global economic system. The core, societies that occupy a dominant position in the economy, are comprised predominantly of Western, industrial nations whose economy is capital-intensive. The periphery, on the other hand, comprises the less productive, labor-intensive societies that are dependent upon the core. Classically, the periphery has served as the primary supplier of raw materials to the core. In between the core and the periphery is the semi-periphery. An unequal exchange of resources occurs between these sectors of the global economy, an exchange that occurs in favor of the core. Shaped by Marxist thought, Wallerstein argues that this relationship is clearly one of exploitation and hegemonic power.

In response to the changes transforming our contemporary world, Wallerstein, in his book *World Systems Analysis*, extends his earlier work on the unequal exchange characterizing the world-system. He traces much of our present-day global situation to certain historical developments, namely, the emergence of the capitalist world-economy in the sixteenth century, the political ideas resulting from the French Revolution, and what he refers to as the "world revolution of 1968" that resulted in the decline of the liberal world-view.

Applying a *longue durée* approach, Wallerstein explores the relationship between capitalism and state structures. Core states, he argues, develop strong states. However, regardless of the form of state structures or cultural forms, societies are tied together in a world economic system. While the world-system has historically extended beyond, and been affected by forces outside, the boundaries of any nation-state, he argues that the conditions of the current capitalist global order have become particularly unstable, resulting in more unpredictable ideological responses. One can expect to see the emergence of more extreme ideologies on the left and the right.

Giovanni Arrighi (1937–2009), an Italian sociologist, taught most recently at Johns Hopkins University. Arrighi was a scholar of global capitalism. In his influential work, *The Long Twentieth Century*, Arrighi discusses the expansion of capitalism over the course of several centuries. He notes that alliances between state and business organizations result in successive "systemic cycles of accumulation." These cycles of accumulation contribute to the expansion of capitalism. At stages when this expansion faces limits, capital enters the competitive world of high finance, with the support of militarized states.

Arrighi traces the emergence of capitalism in the Italian city-states of the thirteenth and fourteenth century. He argues that these states exhibit characteristics of modern capitalism: the desire for accumulation, the pursuit of balance of power, a protection-producing industry (that is, militarized state-making), and the use of diplomacy in all of these pursuits. Arrighi also studies the case of Dutch trading interests, British hegemony, and the emergence of the United States as a world power.

In *Adam Smith in Beijing*, Arrighi continues his exploration of global capitalism. He conducts an examination of the decline of Western dominance and the emergence of China as a power center in global finance. Arrighi argues that historically Western dominance has been the result of a combined deployment of financial and military capabilities. The weakening of US power began in the 1960s and 1970s with the burdens of the failed Vietnam War and the global oil crisis. It has since been further precipitated by the limits on surplus accumulation through internal institutional constraints and as a result of international competition. By the late twentieth century, the US had become dependent on foreign investors. In particular, Arrighi attributes the decline of US power to what he argues was the misjudged and ineffective handling of the Iraq War by George W. Bush.

The crisis of the weakening US hegemony in the global political-economic arena has been accompanied by the simultaneous emergence of China as a powerful force in international affairs. Although Arrighi notes that Chinese trade and markets were well-developed through the eighteenth century, its present economy approximates Adam Smith's idea of a market economy. In Smith's thought, a strong state that prevented the operation of state or private monopolies was favorable to a competitive market economy. China's government has actively pursued growth in domestic and foreign policies that advance its positioning as a leader in the global economy. Its economic robustness has had echoes in the international arena as well. The shifting of power from the West to the East, according to Arrighi, offers an opportunity for a "commonwealth of civilizations truly respectful of cultural differences." What happens in the future remains to be seen.

Global Capitalism and the State

Saskia Sassen (1949–) is a professor of sociology at Columbia University. Sassen is a scholar of globalization, migration, and urbanization. In *The Mobility of Capital and Labor* (1988), Sassen examines transnational migrations. Her argument is that the increased mobility of capital and the globalization of production have created conditions for the transnational mobility of labor. In *The Global City* (1991), she proposes that the global flows of money, information, and people are occurring through a network of cities. These "global cities" are the centers of global banks, accounting, and financial firms. While they are spatially dispersed, global cities are also tightly integrated in a network of exchange.

In *Territory, Authority, Rights: From Medieval to Global Assemblages*, Sassen argues that our present world is undergoing some epochal transformations. She addresses the relationship between nation-states and the economic forces of globalization. Her main argument in the book is that globalization has not caused the redundancy of nation-states. Rather, reconfigured state apparatuses have come to serve global market forces. The assemblages of territory, authority, and rights (TAR) in this context have experienced some unique arrangements. For instance, the borders of territorial authority have become more fluid and complex with the global operations of foreign firms, electronic media, and international humanitarian efforts. Such transnational processes have indeed raised procedural questions of authority and rights not only for economic actors, but for citizens and migrants as well.

Sassen traces the emergence of the nation-state from the feudal political landscape of medieval Europe. During this stage of state development, authority was territorially delimited by national boundaries even as capitalism advanced through imperialist expansion. She discusses the disassembling tendencies of the national that began to emerge in the eighteenth and nineteenth centuries. These tendencies, however, were more fully embodied in the establishment of Bretton Woods in 1944, when international norms for the regulation of international monetary and trade relations were constituted. The 1980s witnessed the launching of a global phase of history. This phase was marked by declining state control over the economic realm and the rising role of stock markets and private actors in the global economy, trends that refashioned understandings of the national. While these trends contribute to "denationalization," Sassen's argument is that the global is tied inextricably with the local and the national. She shows that this period was also market by denationalization in the form of the privatization of executive power in the United States.

SELECTED BIBLIOGRAPHY

Arrighi, Giovanni. 1994. *The Long Twentieth Century*. London: Verso.
Arrighi, Giovanni 2007. *Adam Smith in Beijing*. London: Verso.
Bell, Daniel. 1973. *The Coming of Post-Industrial Society*. New York: Basic Books.
Brenner, Neil. 1999. "Beyond State Centrism? Space, Territoriality, and Geographical Scale in Globalization Studies." *Theory and Society*. 29(1). (Builds the claim that (social) space is being rescaled; at different rates across different domains, including political and economic spaces.)
Castells, Manuel. 1989. *The Informational City*. Blackwell.
Castells, Manuel. 1999. *The Rise of the Network Society*. Blackwell. (A leader in the movement for thinking about the global as a social system, these are key pieces expressing that places become manifestations of global flows, intertwining information, technology, state and military prowess.)
Friedman, Jonathan. 1982. "World City Formation: An Agenda for Research and Action." *International Journal of Urban and Regional Research*. 6(3). (Argues that world cities integrate territorial economies into the world system and reflect the power of those territories, and that nation-states project national power through world cities, using them to secure standing in the global economic system.)

Hall, Peter. 1999. "The Future of Cities." *Computers, Environment and Urban Systems*. 23(1). (Argues that the significance of face-to-face contract and the benefit of agglomeration economies prevent the death of location. Instead, cities come to occupy unique roles in a complex global political and economic system.)

Levitt, Peggy. 2001. *The Transnational Villagers*. University of California Press. (Migrants as simultaneously embedded in both destination and origin societies, creating sociological, cultural, political, and economic bridges between societies; creating a globalized world as a world of simultaneous embeddedness across such systems.)

Mann, Michael. 1997. "Has Globalization Ended the Rise of the Nation-State?" *Review of International Political Economy*. 4(3). (The evidence is not as clear as some proponents would argue for a decreasing role of the nation state.)

Porter, Michael E. 1990. "The Competitive Advantage of Nations." *Harvard Business Review*. (Argues the nation has become more important in a globalized world, proposing a new logic to production based on location endowments. Agglomeration economies and regional governance structures both localize conditions and are key drivers of global competitiveness.)

Sassen, Saskia. 1988. *The Mobility of Labor and Capital*. Cambridge, Cambridge University Press.

Sassen, Saskia. 2001. *The Global City*. Princeton, Princeton University Press (2nd edn; orig 1991).

Sassen, Saskia. 2006. *Territory, Authority, Rights: From Medieval to Global Assemblages*. Princeton, Princeton University Press.

Wallerstein, Immanuel. 2004. *World Systems Analsyis: An Introduction*. Durham, Duke University Press (*One of the founders of world systems theory provides a nice overview and introduction to the field. For more details, see his 4-volume set on* The Modern World-System [*1974, 1980, 1989, 2011*]).

Chapter 37

Systemic and Antisystemic Crises [2007]

Giovanni Arrighi

Introduction

"When the twentieth century opened," wrote Geoffrey Barraclough in the mid 1960s, "European power in Asia and Africa stood at its zenith; no nation, it seemed, could withstand the superiority of European arms and commerce. Sixty years later only the vestiges of European domination remained.... Never before in the whole of human history had so revolutionary a reversal occurred with such rapidity." The change in the position of the peoples of Asia and Africa "was the surest sign of the advent of a new era." Barraclough had few doubts that when the history of the first half of the twentieth century – which for most historians was still dominated by European wars and problems – came to be written in a longer perspective, "no single theme will prove to be of greater importance than the revolt against the west."[1] The contention of this book is that, when the history of the *second* half of the twentieth century will be written in such a longer perspective, the chances are that no single theme will prove to be of greater significance than the economic renaissance of East Asia. The revolt against the West created the political conditions for the social and economic empowerment of the peoples of the non-Western world. The economic renaissance of East Asia is the first and clearest sign that such an empowerment has begun.

We speak of renaissance because – in Gilbert Rozman's words – "East Asia is a great region of the past, having been in the forefront of world development for at

Giovanni Arrighi, "Systemic and Antisystemic Crises," pp. 1–2, 379–89 from Giovanni Arrighi, *Adam Smith in Beijing: Lineages of the Twenty-First Century*. (London: Verso, 2007). Reprinted with the permission of Verso.

Contemporary Sociological Theory, Third Edition. Edited by Craig Calhoun, Joseph Gerteis, James Moody, Steven Pfaff, and Indermohan Virk. Editorial material and organization © 2012 John Wiley & Sons, Ltd. Published 2012 by John Wiley & Sons, Ltd.

least two thousand years, until the sixteenth, seventeenth, or even the eighteenth century, after which it suffered a relatively brief but deeply felt eclipse."[2] The renaissance has occurred through a snowballing process of connected economic "miracles" in a succession of East Asian states, starting in Japan in the 1950s and 1960s, rolling on in South Korea, Taiwan, Hong Kong, Singapore, Malaysia, and Thailand in the 1970s and 1980s, and culminating in the 1990s and early 2000s in the emergence of China as the world's most dynamic center of economic and commercial expansion. According to Terutomo Ozawa – who first introduced the notion of a snowballing process to describe the East Asian ascent – "the Chinese miracle, though still in its inchoate phase, will be no doubt ... the *most* dramatic in terms of its impact on the rest of the world ... especially on neighboring countries."[3] In a similar vein, Martin Wolf has proclaimed that

> Should [Asia's rise] proceed as it has over the last few decades, it will bring the two centuries of global domination by Europe and, subsequently, its giant North American offshoot to an end. Japan was but the harbinger of an Asian future. The country has proved too small and inward-looking to transform the world. What follows it – China, above all – will prove neither. ... Europe was the past, the US is the present and a China-dominated Asia the future of the global economy. That future seems bound to come. The big questions are how soon and how smoothly it does so.[4]

The Asian future envisaged by Wolf may not be as inevitable as he implies. But even if he is only in part right, the East Asian renaissance suggests that Adam Smith's prediction of an eventual equalization of power between the conquering West and the conquered non-West might finally come true.

[...]

Epilogue

The central question from which we began is whether, and under what conditions, the Chinese ascent, with all its shortcomings and likely future setbacks, can be taken as the harbinger of that greater equality and mutual respect among peoples of European and non-European descent that Smith foresaw and advocated 230 years ago. The analysis developed in this book points towards a positive answer but with some major qualifications.

[...]

The emergence of China as the true winner of the United States' War on Terror has resulted in a reversal of the two countries' influence in East Asia and in the world at large. One expression of this reversal has been what Joshua Cooper Ramo has called the Beijing Consensus – the China-led emergence of "a path for other nations around the world" not simply to develop but also "to fit into the international order in a way that allows them to be truly independent, to protect their way of life and political choices." Ramo points to two features of the new Consensus that are especially appealing to the nations of the global South. One is "localization" – the recognition of the importance of tailoring development to local needs, which necessarily differ from one location to another – in sharp contrast to the one-size-fits-all prescriptions of the increasingly discredited Washington Consensus; and the other is "multilateralism" – the recognition of the importance of interstate cooperation in constructing a new global order based on economic interdependence but respectful of political and cultural differences – in sharp contrast to the unilateralism of US policies. As Arif Dirlik has pointed out, these features of the Beijing Consensus may lead the world in radically different directions. They may lead to the formation of a new Bandung – i.e., a new version of the Third World alliance of the 1950s and 1960s – aimed, like the old, at countering economic and political subordination but suited to an age of unprecedented global economic integration. Or they may lead in the direction of a co-optation of Southern states in North–South alliances aimed at containing the China-led subversion of the global hierarchy of wealth.[5]

The more "realistic" alternatives to the failed neo-conservative strategy aimed at containing China [...] point to three different kinds of North–South alliance. Each alternative strategy, we argued, has problems of its own, which have resulted in incoherent US policies towards China. As long as the United States is bogged down militarily in West Asia, the incoherence will probably persist regardless of who rules the roost in Washington. But whether pursued coherently or not, all three strategies have the potential to detail the formation of a new Southern alliance capable of countering Northern domination.

The most disastrous derailment would be the one implicit in Pinkerton's "happy-third" strategy, which advocates a rerun of the first half of the twentieth century – when the US grew rich and powerful by financing and provisioning European states at war with one another – with the difference that the states at war would now be Asian rather than European. The least disastrous derailment would be the one implicit in Kissinger's strategy – which envisages the co-optation of China into a reformed US-centered world order – because, if successful, it would preserve Northern dominance but at least it would not plunge Asia and the global South into the chaos and wars that would ensue from the success of the happy-third strategy. The costs and risks for the South of Kaplan's strategy of encircling China with a US-led military alliance – which advocates a rerun of the Cold War but centered on Asia instead of Europe – would fall somewhere in between. It would provoke deep divisions among Asian and Southern countries and risk the nuclear holocaust that the old Cold War managed to avoid, but it would force the United States to treat with some respect and make concessions to its Southern allies and to be cautious in provoking wars that would involve the US directly. There are, of course, other possibilities, some of which are already being practiced; but they are all variants or combinations of the "third-happy," "co-optation" and "cold-war" strategies.[6]

We should not underestimate the temptation for China to settle for co-optation in a US- or Northern-dominated world order and for other Southern countries to seek or accept US support for their mutual jealousies. But neither should we overestimate the power of the United States, even in collusion with Europe, to succeed in the pursuit of these strategies. Not only has the Iraqi debacle confirmed the limits of coercive means in enforcing the Northern will against Southern resistance; more important in a capitalist world, the financial underpinnings of US and Northern dominance rest on increasingly shaky grounds.

A crucial turning point in this respect has been the Asian financial crisis of 1997–98. Wade and Veneroso have claimed that this crisis confirmed the validity of the dictum, attributed to Andrew Mellon, that "in a depression assets return to their rightful owners."

> The combination of massive devaluations, IMF-pushed financial liberalization, and IMF-facilitated recovery may have precipitated the biggest peacetime transfer of assets from domestic to foreign owners in the past fifty years anywhere in the world, dwarfing the transfers from domestic to US owners in Latin America in the 1980s or in Mexico after 1994.[7]

Correct in identifying the immediate effects of the crisis, the diagnosis missed entirely its longer-term effects on North–South relations and on the capacity of the IMF to further facilitate the transfer of Southern assets to Northern owners. [...] The 1997–98 crisis marks the beginning of a huge bifurcation between the Northern deficit and the rest-of-the world's surplus in the current-accounts of their respective balances of payments. The bifurcation reflects the fact that there are less and less goods and services that the North, especially the United States, can produce at lower prices than the rest of the world. Much of the rest of the world's surplus still flows to the US financial entrepôt, both to finance the escalating US deficit and to be reinvested around the world, including the global South. But a significant and growing portion of that surplus is bypassing the US entrepôt, both to build up currency reserves and to flow directly to other Southern destinations, thereby relaxing the hold of the IMF and other Northern-controlled financial institutions on Southern countries.[8]

Flush with cash and eager to regain control over their economic policies, Southern countries have bought back their debts reducing the IMF's loan portfolio to the lowest level since the 1980s. A shrinking loan portfolio, notes the *Wall Street Journal*, "greatly diminishes the IMF's influence over global economic policy;" forces it to switch from "arm-twisting" to "persuasion;" and reduces its interest income and cash reserves. "In an irony that has provoked tittering among many [Southern] finance ministers, the agency that has long preached belt-tightening now must practice it itself."[9]

In spite of its massive purchases of US Treasury bonds, China has played a leading role both in rerouting the Southern surplus to Southern destinations and in providing neighboring and distant Southern countries with attractive alternatives to the trade, investment, and assistance of Northern countries and financial institutions. [...]

Supplementing and complementing Chinese initiatives, oil-rich countries have also redirected their surpluses to the South. Of great political and symbolic significance has been Venezuela's use of windfall proceeds from high oil prices to free Latin American countries from subordination to Northern interests.

> When Argentina needed loans so that it could say goodbye to the International Monetary Fund, Venezuela committed $2.4 billion. Venezuela bought $300 million in bonds from Ecuador. Washington has historically had enormous influence over economic policy in Latin America through its control over the major sources of credit, including the IMF, the World Bank and the Inter-American Development Bank. Venezuela's role as a new "lender of last resort" has reduced that influence.[10]

Equally important, and potentially more disruptive of Northern financial dominance, has been the interest that Saudi Arabia and other West Asian countries have recently shown in rerouting at least part of their surpluses from the United States and Europe to East and South Asia. According to Western bankers, "We're definitely seeing a big jump in terms of deal flow between the Middle East and Asia, and Southeast Asia and China in particular." Although, for the time being, West Asian investors are not withdrawing money from the United States, "a lot of new money from higher oil prices is not going to North America." The reasons are partly political: the unpopularity of the war in Iraq and things like the backlash in the US that forced Dubai's port company to sell off American holdings after it bought the British port operator P&O. But the most compelling reason is strictly economic: China and all fast growing Asian economies want West Asian oil, and the West Asian capital and liquidity generated by that oil are searching for investments with higher returns than US Treasury bonds.[11]

When, in May 2006, India's prime minister, Manmohan Singh, urged Asian nations at the annual meeting of the ADB to redirect Asian surpluses towards Asian development projects, one US observer found the speech "stunning" – "the harbinger of the end of the dollar and of American hegemony."[12] [...] US hegemony, as opposed to sheer domination, in all likelihood has already ended; but, just as the pound sterling continued to be used as an international currency three to four decades after the end of British hegemony, so may the dollar. The really important issue here, however, is not whether Asian and other Southern countries will continue to use US dollars as a means of exchange – which, to an unknown extent, they probably will for a long time to come. Rather, it is whether they will continue to put the surpluses of their balances of payments at the disposal of US-controlled agencies, to be turned into instruments of Northern domination; or will instead use them as instruments of Southern emancipation. From this standpoint, there is nothing stunning about Singh's statement, which merely lends support to a practice that is already in place. What is truly stunning is the lack of awareness – in the South no less than in the North – of the extent to which the monetarist counterrevolution of the early 1980s has backfired, creating conditions more favorable than ever before for a new Bandung to bring into existence the commonwealth of civilizations that Smith envisioned long ago.

For a new Bandung can do what the old could not: it can mobilize and use the global market as an instrument of equalization of South–North power relations.

The foundations of the old Bandung were strictly political-ideological and, as such, were easily destroyed by the monetarist counterrevolution. The foundations of the Bandung that may be emerging now, in contrast, are primarily economic and, as such, far more solid. [...]

Under these circumstances, Northern resistance to the subversion of the global hierarchy of wealth and power can only succeed with widespread Southern collaboration. Crucial in this respect is what China and India – which by themselves account for more than one-third of the world population – will choose to do. Commenting in the *International Herald Tribune* on news of huge investments by China and India in each other's economies, Howard French aptly asked: "If one places any stock in the notion of creative destruction, what could be more disruptive to the global status quo?"

> With more than 2.3 billion people between them, agreement between India and China on almost any standard makes that item an instant contender for global standard status. What does this mean in practical terms? That the successor to a ubiquitous product like Microsoft Office could very well be Chinese. ... It could mean that the mobile phone standards of the future are decided jointly in Asia, and not in Europe or the United States. ... What it clearly means already is that the day when a cozy club of the rich – the United States, the strongest economies of Western Europe and Japan – sets the pace for the rest of world, passing out instructions and assigning grades, is fast drawing to a close.[13]

Yes, it does mean that but on condition that the ruling groups of the global South in general, and of China and India in particular, open up a path capable of emancipating not just their nations but the entire world from the social and ecological devastations entailed in Western capitalist development. An innovation of such world-historical significance requires some awareness of the impossibility of bringing the benefits of modernization to the majority of the world's population unless – to paraphrase Sugihara – the Western developmental path converges with the East Asian path, not the other way round. This is no new discovery. Almost eighty years ago, in December 1928, Mohandas Gandhi wrote:

> God forbid that India should ever take to industrialization after the manner of the West. The economic imperialism of a single tiny island kingdom [England] is today keeping the world in chains. If an entire nation of 300 million [India's population at the time] took to similar economic exploitation, it would strip the world like locusts.[14]

Gandhi already knew then what many leaders of Southern emancipation have yet to learn or have forgotten: Western success along the extroverted, Industrial Revolution path was based upon the exclusion of the vast majority of the world's population from access to the natural and human resources needed to benefit rather than bear the costs of global industrialization. As such, it never was an option for that majority. Elvin's considerations concerning the developmental advantages and disadvantages of China's huge national market in the eighteenth century demonstrate the absurdity of the contrary view, still dominant among historians and social scientists across the ideological spectrum. The huge size of China's market created opportunities for the social division of labor that were not available in smaller markets, but it also ruled out innovations that were feasible in a smaller economy. Between 1741 and the early 1770s, for example, the introduction of machine-spinning tripled Britain's consumption of raw cotton.

> To accomplish this tripling for China in a similar space of thirty-odd years would have been beyond the cotton-production resources of the entire eighteenth-century world. Between 1785 and 1833, the single province of Kwang-tung imported on average from India each year six times as much cotton as all Britain used annually at the time of Arkwright's first water-frame. Again, an expansion of Chinese exports of cotton cloth comparable to eighteenth-century Britain's both in its speed and in its relative size to the domestic market would have been too great for the available purchasing power of the world at that time.[15]

The economic success of Britain's Industrial Revolution, in other words, was dependent both on the relative and absolute small size of the British economy. A small absolute size meant that a given increase in the import of raw cotton and in the export of cotton manufactures translated into a much higher rate of growth of the economy than it would have in an economy of China's size. And a small size relative to the global economy meant that the rest of the world could supply the natural resources and purchase the products necessary to sustain a high rate of growth to an extent that was inconceivable for China. Had the rulers of Qing China been so insane as to follow in the footsteps of Britain's extroverted Industrial Revolution path, they would have been brought back to their senses by escalating import prices, collapsing export prices, and unbearable social tensions at home, long before they had a chance to "strip the world like locusts."

Two hundred years later China and India face the same problem with a vengeance. The displacement of the tiny UK island by the continental US island as the leader of the Industrial Revolution path has resulted in a further massive increase in the natural-resource intensity, not just of production, but of consumption as well. This massive increase was possible because the vast majority of world population was excluded from the production and consumption standards established by the United States. But as soon as a small minority of the Chinese population (and an even smaller one of the Indian population) gained partial access to those standards, the validity of Gandhi's contention has become obvious to all but the most obtuse defenders of the American way of life. "The world, as it turns out, cannot afford two countries [with a large population] behaving like the United States. It lacks the atmosphere ... and it also may lack the resources." Bill McKibben calls this a "tragedy" because

> China is actually accomplishing some measurable good with its growth. People are enjoying some meat, sending their [children] to school, heating their huts. Whereas we're burning nine times as much energy per capita so that we can: air-condition game

rooms and mow half-acre lots, drive SUVs on every errand, eat tomatoes flown in from Chile.... Which is why it seems intuitively obvious when you're in China that the goal of the twenty-first century must somehow be to simultaneously develop the economies of the poorest parts of the world and *undevelop* those of the rich ... with us using less energy so that they can use more, and eating less meat so that they can eat more.... But try to imagine the political possibilities in America ... of acknowledging that there isn't room for two of us to behave in this way, and that we don't own the rights to our lifestyle simply because we got there first. The current president's father [George Bush Senior] announced, on his way to the parley in Rio that gave rise to the Kyoto treaty, that "the American way of life is not up for negotiation." That's what defines a tragedy.[16]

As it turns out, the latest act of the tragedy, played out in Iraq, has shown that the United States does not have the power to impose coercively upon the world its right to an extravagant way of life and must therefore pay an increasing price for the preservation of that right.[17] But the fact remains that not even a quarter of China's and India's population can adopt the American way of producing and consuming without choking themselves and everybody else to death. Also in this respect, the PRC's new leadership has shown greater awareness than its predecessors of the environmental problems of energy-intensive economic growth. "Model cities" focusing specifically on environmental protection have been established; forests are replanted; the Five Year Plan for 2006–10 has set the ambitious objective of a 20 percent reduction in the energy intensity of the economy and, to this end, a far-reaching industrial policy, banning 399 industrial sub-sectors and restricting another 190 has been announced. It nonetheless remains unclear how these and other measures can restore a seriously compromised ecological balance if, as expected, over the next fifteen years 300 million rural residents or more will move into cities where growing fleets of motor vehicles are crowding bicycles out.[18]

In short, by relying too heavily on the energy-consuming Western path, China's rapid economic growth has not yet opened up for itself and the world an ecologically sustainable developmental path. This reliance does not just threaten to bring the "economic miracle" to a premature end, because of pressure on scarce resources (including clean air and water). More important, it is both a result and a cause of the widening cleavage between those who have been in a position to appropriate the benefits of rapid economic growth and those who had to bear its costs. [...] This cleavage has resulted in a major wave of popular unrest, in which ecological grievances loomed large and which has prompted a major reorientation of Chinese policies towards a more balanced development between rural and urban areas, between regions, and between economy and society. All we need to add to bring our study to a close is that the eventual outcome of this reorientation is of crucial importance for the future not just of Chinese society but of world society as well.

If the reorientation succeeds in reviving and consolidating China's traditions of self-centered market-based development, accumulation *without* dispossession, mobilization of human rather than non-human resources, and government through mass participation in shaping policies, then the chances are that China will be in a position to contribute decisively to the emergence of a commonwealth of civilizations truly respectful of cultural differences. But, if the reorientation fails, China may well turn into a new epicenter of social and political chaos that will facilitate Northern attempts to re-establish a crumbling global dominance or, to paraphrase once again Schumpeter, help humanity burn up in the horrors (or glories) of the escalating violence that has accompanied the liquidation of the Cold War world order.

NOTES

1 Geoffrey Barraclough, *An Introduction to Contemporary History* (Harmondsworth, Penguin, 1967), pp. 153–4.
2 Gilbert Rozman, *The East Asian Region: Confucian Heritage and its Modern Adaptation* (Princeton, NJ, Princeton University Press, 1991), p. 6.
3 Terutomo Ozawa, "Pax Americana-Led Macro-Clustering and Flying-Geese-Style Catch-Up in East Asia: Mechanisms of Regionalized Endogenous Growth," *Journal of Asian Economics*, 13 (2003), p. 700, emphasis in the original. The "snowballing" metaphor was first introduced in Terutomo Ozawa, "Foreign Direct Investment and Structural Transformation: Japan as a Recycler of Market and Industry," *Business and the Contemporary World*, 5, 2 (1993), pp. 30–1.
4 "Asia Is Awakening," *Financial Times*, September 22, 2003.
5 Joshua Cooper Ramo, *The Beijing Consensus: Notes on the New Physics of Chinese Power* (London, Foreign Affairs Policy Centre, 2004), pp. 3–4; Arif Dirlik, "Beijing Consensus: Beijing 'Gongshi': Who Recognizes Whom and to What End?" *Globalization and Autonomy Online Compendium*, available at http://www.globalautonomy.ca/global1/position.jsp?index=PP_Dirlik_Beijing Consensus.xml.
6 These strategies, of course, may be directed not just against China but against other states or against South–South links in general. Thus, the US offer of cooperation in dual-use nuclear and space technologies with India apparently had the immediate objective of blocking the Iran–Pakistan–India gas pipeline so as to isolate Iran and simultaneously break up a South–South connection of great symbolic and material value. See R. Palat, "India Suborned: The Global South and the Geopolitics of India's Vote against Iran," *Japan Focus*, October 24, 2005. Similarly, the US and EU co-optation of India and Brazil into an informal grouping known as the Five Interested Parties (FIPS), consisting of the four of them and Australia, was aimed at turning these two countries from leaders of an emerging Southern alliance into partners of a North–South alliance at the upcoming 2005 Hong Kong meeting of the WTO. Focus on the Global South, "The End of an Illusion. WTO Reform, Global Civil Society and the Road to Hong Kong," *Focus on Trade*, no. 108, April 2005.
7 Robert Wade and Frank Veneroso, "The Asian Crisis: The High Debt Model versus the Wall Street – Treasury – IMF Complex," *New Left Review*, 1/228 (1998).
8 The ravages of past financial crises contributed decisively to the build-up of currency reserves in low- and middle-income countries. For most of these countries, "these reserves are simply insurance against financial disaster. A long list of developing countries have experienced devastating crises in the last 15 years: Mexico in 1994; Thailand, Indonesia and other Asian countries in 1997; Russia in 1998; Brazil in 1999; and Argentina in 2002. ... As the dust settled over the ruins of many former 'emerging' economies, a new creed took hold among policy makers in the developing world: Pile up as much foreign-exchange as possible" (E. Porter, "Are Poor Nations Wasting their Money

on Dollars?" *New York Times*, April 30, 2006); "Another Drink? Sure. China Is Paying," *New York Times*, June 5, 2005; F. Kempe, "Why Economists Worry about Who Holds Foreign Currency Reserves," *Wall Street Journal*, May 9, 2006.

9 M. Moffett and B. Davis, "Booming Economy Leaves the IMF Groping for Mission," *Wall Street Journal*, April 21, 2006.

10 M. Weisbrot, "The Failure of Hugo-Bashing," *Los Angeles Times*, March 9, 2006. See also N. Chomsky, "Latin America and Asia Are Breaking Free of Washington's Grip," *Japan Focus*, March 15, 2006.

11 H. Timmons, "Asia Finding Rich Partner in Mideast," *New York Times*, December 1, 2006.

12 A. Giridharadas, "Singh Urges Asian Self-Reliance," *International Herald Tribune*, May 5, 2006.

13 H.W. French, "The Cross-Pollination of India and China," *International Herald Tribune*, November 10, 2005.

14 Quoted in Ramachandra Guha, *Environmentalism: A Global History* (New York, Longman, 2000), p. 22.

15 Mank Elvin, *The Pattern of the Chinese Past* (Stanford, CA, Stanford University Press, 1973), pp. 313–14.

16 Bill McKibben, "The Great Leap: Scenes from China's Industrial Revolution," *Harper's Magazine* (December 2005), p. 52.

17 In avidly supporting the war against Iraq, newspaper baron Rupert Murdoch observed that a reduction of the price of oil from $30 to $20 a barrel would have been a good thing for the US economy: D. Kirkpatrick, "Mr. Murdoch's War," *New York Times*, April 7, 2003. The fact that four years into the war the price of oil has instead doubled provides a good measure of the failure of the US attempt to coercively impose its right to extravagant energy consumption.

18 Lester R. Brown, "A New World Order," *Guardian*, January 25, 2006; *Quarterly Update*, World Bank Office, Beijing, February 2006, pp. 13–16; K. Bradsher, "China Set to Act on Fuel Economy," *New York Times*, November 18, 2003; J. Kynge, "New Agenda for a New Generation," *Financial Times*, December 16, 2003; A. Lorenz, "China's Environmental Suicide: A Government Minister Speaks," *openDemocracy*, April 5, 2005.

Chapter 38

Reconfiguring Territory, Authority, and Rights [2006]

Saskia Sassen

From National Borders to Embedded Borderings: Implications for Territorial Authority

State sovereignty is usually conceived of as a monopoly of authority in a particular territory. Today it is becoming evident that state sovereignty articulates both its own and external conditions and norms. Sovereignty remains a systemic property but its institutional insertion and its capacity to legitimate and absorb all legitimating power, to be the source of law, have become unstable. The politics of contemporary sovereignties are far more complex than notions of mutually exclusive territorialities can capture.

The question of territory as a parameter for authority and rights has entered a new phase. State exclusive authority over its territory remains the prevalent mode of final authority in the global political economy. But it is less absolute formally than it once was meant to be and […] prevalence is not to be confused with dominance. In addition, critical components of this authority that may still have a national institutional form and location are no longer national in the historically constructed sense of that term. One way of deciphering some of these issues and opening them up to a research agenda is by singling out the capability represented by the power of the geographic border in the modern nation-state project.

Saskia Sassen, "Reconfiguring Territory, Authority, and Rights," pp. 415–23 from Saskia Sassen, *Territory. Authority. Rights: From Medieval to Global Assemblages*. (Princeton: Princeton University Press, 2006). Reprinted with permission of Princeton University Press.

We are seeing the formation of global, partly territorial alignments that incorporate what were once protections encased in border regimes [...] Insofar as the state has historically had the capability to encase its territory through administrative and legal instruments, it also has the capability to change that encasement – for instance, deregulate its borders and open up to foreign firms and investment. The question that concerns me here is whether this signals that the capabilities entailed by territoriality, a form of exclusive and final authority, can be detached from geographic territory. Such detachment is conceivably partial and variable, depending on what is to be subjected to authority. This in turn raises a question about how the issue of borderings can function inside the nation-state.

[...] This detachment today assumes two forms broadly speaking. One is that the border is embedded in the product, the person, and the instrument: a mobile agent endogenizes critical features of the border. The other is that there are multiple locations for the border, whether inside firms or in long transnational chains of locations that can move deep inside national territorial and institutional domains. Global cities account for a disproportionate concentration of such border locations; the latter are mostly institutional locations that assume a territorial correlate, for example, the large concentration of international banking facilities in New York City. Institutional locations in principle need not have territorial correlates. The locations of bordering capabilities are in a phase of sharp unsettlement, which opens up a whole new research agenda. If there is one sector where we can begin to discern new stabilized bordering capabilities and their geographic and institutional locations it is in the corporate economy [...].

Thus, rather than conceiving of the much noted new mobilities as a function of globalization and the new information and communication technologies, I argue that these new types of mobilities also arise from a third critical dimension: the fact that state border capabilities centered on nineteenth- and twentieth-century geographic concepts of the border could switch into nongeographic bordering capabilities operating both transnationally and subnationally. In this process, particular legal protections get detached from their national territorial jurisdictions and become incorporated into a variety of often highly specialized or partial global regimes and thereby often become transformed into far more specialized rights and obligations. I also see in this dynamic capabilities jumping tracks and becoming lodged into a novel organizing logic. One example is the bundle of rights granted by host states to foreign firms under the WTO which unsettles older national regimes. Many of these rights and guarantees derive from what were once national rights and guarantees used precisely to distinguish national firms from foreign firms; these rights and guarantees were also one critical component in the building up of the state's exclusive authority over its national territory.

Such shifts from geographic borders to embedded bordering capabilities have been far more common and formalized in the case of major corporate economic actors than they have, for example, for citizens and migrants. Firms and markets have seen their advantages shift toward new types of institutionalized protections while for citizens this has not been the case. The international human rights regime is a weaker system of protections than the WTO provisions protecting the cross-border circulation of professionals [...]. It is also weaker, though far broader, than the specialized visas for business people and the increasingly common visas for high-tech workers. As national states are directly and indirectly involved in both the human rights and these business regimes, one question this raises is how much divergence in critical regimes a system can accommodate.

While this detachment and re-embedding in new types of bordering regimes has been formalized and institutionalized for corporate economic actors but not for citizenship, a systemic perspective would posit corresponding pressures on the institution of citizenship also moving toward particular types of detachments. This would be a type of pressure freeing citizenship from state capture – escaping the highly formalized and institutionalized relation between the citizen and the state, one typically characterized as inevitable in much of the standard scholarship. [...] I discussed both formal and informal ways that signal such a partial shift out of the historically produced correspondence between the nation-state and citizenship. I argued that such dynamics are taking place and that they are not confined to the much noted postnational and transnational citizenship identities but also include complex formalizations inside the state that partly denationalize various features of citizenship.

One of the modes in which the embedded borderings discussed above function is through specialized geographies that do involve particular forms of reterritorialization. For instance, some of the capabilities entailed by bordering operate through the variety of norms, standards, and subcultures of financial centers [...]. In the case of the new types of bordering for individual rights entailed by the international human rights regime, we can conceive of a national court (as distinct from an international court) using such instruments to adjudicate a case as also representing a particular type of reterritorializing of bordering functions. I identify a type of reterritorializing even in digital space, a transboundary space that in principle should be nongeographic and escape all territorial authority [...]. Yet the state can also be shown to exercise authority over digital networks through the indirect venue of hardware standards and whatever regulations of content circulation and intellectual property rights might be involved.

Are these specialized types of reterritorializing a reinsertion into the exclusive territorial authority of the state? The processes presented above do not have the territorial parameters underlying territoriality but could, nonetheless, represent a form of state authority. Territoriality, understood as exclusive institutionalized authority over its territory, was foundational for the nation-state. It is not clear that [...] territorial insertions [...] are constitutive of the state even though they do articulate state authority. My interpretation of the matter is that these territorial insertions – for instance, of electronic financial markets – do not necessarily entail subsumption under exclusive state authority because they are predicated on specific denationalizations in law and policy in the service of a global regime. While such circulate through the national institutional apparatus – or specific components of the latter – and hence are subject to state authority they cannot be seen as constitutive of the state's exclusive territoriality. This is a type of framing of the relationship between territory and state authority that comprises forms of globality constituted via localized actors encased in local places. The relationship between territory and state authority today can accommodate the existence inside national territory of denationalized spatialities. That relationship also encases the types of differential temporal orders [...]. This contrasts with the aims of the Bretton Woods regime. Bretton Woods illuminates a particular set of issues about territorial boundaries precisely because it was an international regime and as such aimed at strengthening national boundaries and state territorial authority, protecting national economies from external forces, and developing supranational authority. In the current period, the aim is the opposite – not to protect, but to open up, and, more significantly, to ensure strategic denationalizations.

Authority with territorial parameters can take many different forms: the historical territorial exclusivity associated with the nation-state should be conceived of as just one of these. [...] I posited that late medieval cities constituted a type of urban political economy of territoriality. Can we make this more abstract so as to accommodate particular forms of territorial authority we see emerge today? Some of these get constituted as denationalized territories inside ongoing national territorial regimes. Global cities are such entities as compared to electronic financial networks, which are not. Insofar as some components of historical borders are evolving into long chains with multiple locations inside national territories, the resulting denationalized domains inside those territories create a new type of internal bordering. One question for research is whether these internal borderings bring particular types of advantages to some actors and institutions – for instance, do they entail capacities akin to arbitraging in finance? These are all issues that complicate the question of state authority: it remains critical but corresponds less to its representation in national and international law than it did before the current transformation.

Another specific type of state territorial authority is extraterritoriality, an interesting capability in this context. It was and remains critical to an international system made up of nation-states, where the "community" of nation-states basically accounts for the system. What happens with extraterritoriality in a global context. Are the new global regimes a variant of extraterritorial authority, as some scholars posit? But even as this older form persists, the emergent dynamic is one whereby territorial insertions in a foreign country denationalize rather than produce an extension of national territorial authority.

It is interesting to recall that in feudal times, the capabilities for a future formation marked by unitary authority – the territorial sovereign – were being developed through organizational modes that would have seemed incompatible with those of the territorial state. We need to ask if today we might have a similar situation of ambiguity and illegibility – albeit moving in the opposite direction. The nation-state remains the prevalent organizational source of authority and to variable extents the dominant one. But, as I argued above and in this book generally, critical components of authority deployed in the making of the territorial state are shifting toward becoming strong capabilities for detaching that authority from its exclusive territory and onto multiple bordering systems. Insofar as many of these systems are operating inside the nation-state, they may be obscuring the fact that a significant switch has happened. It may take a while to become legible in its aggregate impact. At its most extreme this may entail a shift of capabilities historically associated with the nation-state onto global digital assemblages; given their extreme form, such assemblages may make the switch more visible than other types of transformations that might be foundational.

Toward a Multiplication of Specialized Orders: Assemblages of Tar

One of the arguments developed in the book is that much of the globalization literature has focused on what are at best bridging events in the process of foundational transformation, rather than the transformation itself or "the event," in Sewell's terms. Many of the global formations that have received much attention, such as the new roles of the IMF or the creation of the WTO are, from the perspective of this book, bridging events that function as indications of and capabilities for a foundational change. But the actual dynamics getting shaped are far deeper and more radical than such entities as the WTO or IMF per se. The latter are powerful capabilities for the making of a new order – they are instruments for, not the new order itself. Similarly, the Bretton Woods system was a powerful capability that facilitated some of the new global formations but was not itself the beginning of the new order as is so often asserted in the globalization literature. These are not the core of the transformation itself, no matter how powerful they are as foot soldiers. The transformation is partly an outcome of these powerful capabilities but is in itself far more complex and radical, albeit not all-encompassing. If anything, it is the new literature on empire (D. Harvey 2003; Hardt and Negri 2000), more so than those focusing on the IMF and WTO, that is closer to conveying the depth of the potential changes even when I have my disagreements with some of these analyses. Let us recall that even as industrial capitalism was becoming the dominant dynamic, most people, most firms, and most political debates were not centered on it. Objectively the prevalent condition remained agriculture and trade.

At the heart of this foundational transformation I see a sharp proliferation of subassemblages bringing together elements that used to be part of more diffuse institutional domains within the nation-state or, at times, the institutionalized supranational system. The novel types of bordering capabilities posited above play a critical role in the forming of these particularized assemblages. These are partial and often highly specialized formations centered in particular utilities and purposes. This trend brings with it several significant consequences even though it is a partial, not an all-encompassing development. While these are for now still mostly incipient formations, they are potentially profoundly unsettling of what are still the prevalent institutional arrangements – nation-states and the supranational system. In this regard, it is reminiscent in its analytic status of what I specified for the early development of industrial capitalism: even as it was the dominant form it was not (yet) the prevalent form [...].

One of the consequences of the sharpening differentiation among domains once suffused with the national, or the supranational, is that at the limit this can enable a proliferation of temporal and spatial framings and a proliferation of normative orders where once the dominant logic was toward producing unitary spatial, temporal, and normative framings. Even though this is a partial rather than all-encompassing development, its character is strategic.

There are, clearly, features of this development that resonate with the multiple systems of rule of the Middle Ages. But an interpretation of current developments along the lines posited above – the proliferation of particular kinds of specialized assemblages – points to a critical difference. At the heart of this difference is that these new assemblages produce a new type of segmentation that entails, in some of its components, a kind of inequality that can cut across every scale, nation-state, major city, and state apparatus. It is not the intrasystemic inequality that emerges out of a unitary, albeit highly differentiated system, such as is a nation-state. Nor is it the kind of inequality that exists among countries and among developed and less developed regions of the world. Those are two types of recognized and named inequalities and we have developed massive institutional and discursive domains to address them; although all this effort has only partly reduced those inequalities, they are a target for efforts and resources. The proliferation of specialized assemblages that cut across the master units that continue to organize our geopolity and that segment once unitary components produces a kind of inequality we might conceive of as multiplying intersystemic segmentations, where the systems are these particularized assemblages. It is then a kind of inequality that coexists with older forms of differentiation inside countries and across countries but is to be distinguished from these.

What distinguishes this multiplying intersystemic segmentation is both the possibility of exiting what are today still ruling normative orders and, equally important if not more so, the constituting of particularized novel normative orders internal to each assemblage. This is still a minor process in the larger scale of our geopolity. But it may well be the beginning of a multisited disruption of its existing formal architecture. This is not akin to the battles between old empires. It is multisited and often endogenous. It lifts territorial segments out of their unitary state normative framing. It is strategic and particular, and hence often illegible. For instance, I would include the internal transformation of the liberal state [...] the growing inequality between the power of the executive and that of the legislature, and the trends toward the partial privatizing of particular components of executive authority – as one such emergent segmentation at the heart of an assemblage where there is not meant to be any.

Herein lies a foundational difference with the medieval period, when there were strong broadly encompassing normative orders (the church, the empire) and the disaggregations (the feuds, the cities) each contained within them a fairly complete structure involving many if not most aspects of life (different classes, norms, systems of justice, and so forth). Today these assemblages are not only highly specialized, partial, and without much internal differentiation, but not even the state can quite counteract the particularized normativities each contains. The norm-making power of the global capital market [...] illustrates this well. Finally, these assemblages tend to have rules for governance wired into the structures of their system in a way reminiscent of how free markets function in that these are not explicated rules and norms, as distinct from formalized systems for governance, that are meant to be explicated and outside the system itself. Again, the new forms of unaccountable power within the executive [...] and the global market for capital [...] illustrate this; but so does the world of NGOs.

This type of analysis suggests a disaggregating of the glue that for a long time held possibly different normative orders together under the somewhat unitary dynamics of nation-states. I see in this proliferation of specialized assemblages a tendency toward a remixing of constitutive rules, for instance in the shifts of the private-public division [...] and in the microtransformations of the relationship of citizens to the state and vice versa [...] A second tendency is the multiplication of partial systems, each with a small set of sharply distinctive constitutive rules, amounting to a type of simple system. Not all of these new specialized assemblages contain such constitutive rules, but it is evident in a number of those that constitute themselves precisely as disembedded from state authority and normativity and as private systems of justice and authority [...]. In contrast, the localized and limited world of the manor or the fief of the medieval lord was a complex world encompassing constitutive rules that addressed the full range of spheres of social life. This is, then, a very different formation from that of the Middle Ages, and it is a fallacy and a deeply erroneous – albeit it common – parallel. One synthesizing image we might use to capture these dynamics is that we see a movement from centripetal nation-state articulation to a centrifugal multiplication of specialized assemblages. We come to see how foundational the centripetal power of the nation-state has been, and to variable extents, remains. Thinking that this resembles feudalism is a genuine error of interpretation and far too easy a representation and explanation of the transformation.

The multiplication of partial, specialized, and applied normative orders is unsettling and produces distinct normative challenges in the context of a still prevalent world of nation-states. Just to mention one instance, I would induce from these trends that normative orders such as religion reassume great importance where they had been confined to distinct specialized spheres by the secular normative orders of states. I would posit that this is not a fallback on older cultures but is, on the contrary, a systemic outcome of cutting-edge developments. This is not pre-modern but a new type of modernity. It arises out of the partial unbundling of what had been dominant and centripetal normative orders into multiple particularized segmentations.

A second issue is, however, the considerable illegibility, ultimately, of this shift to a centrifugal logic. We cannot quite see that it has replaced important segments of the centripetal logic of the nation-state. This is partly because the administrative capability represented by the nation-state remains critical also for significant elements of the new centrifugal logic [...] and because war and militarized border controls mark the geopolitical landscape have mostly been sharpened rather than diluted in much of the world. The ongoing prevalence of strong state politics and policies may well increasingly be a matter more of raw power than the more complex category that is authority – as the new types of wars, whether "civil" or international, suggest. Even as the raw power of national states in many cases has increased, this may not necessarily mean that sovereign territorial authority has become more significant. This distinction is critical to the analysis in this book. It is grounded in the weight and gravitational pull of the centripetal logic that feeds the ascendance of the nation-state. As the unitary character of the nation-state disaggregates, even if only partially, sovereign authority is itself subject to partial disaggregations [...] As this centripetal dynamic of the nation-state becomes less significant, we also see exit options for the disadvantaged.

Denationalization is the category through which I attempt to capture this foundational difference. This is a historicizing categorization with the double intent of de-essentializing the national by confining it to a historically specific configuration and making it a reference point by positing that its enormous complexity and large capture of society and the geopolity make it a strategic site for the transformation – the latter cannot simply come from the outside. What this categorization does not entail is the notion that the nation-state as a major form will disappear but rather that, in addition to being the site for key transformations, it will itself be a profoundly changed entity.

REFERENCES

Hardt, M. and Negri, A. 2000. *Empire*. Cambridge, MA: Harvard University Press.
Harvey, D. 2003. *The New Imperialism*. Oxford: Oxford University Press.

Chapter 39

The Modern World-System in Crisis [2004]

Immanuel Wallerstein

We have said that historical systems have lives. They come into existence at some point in time and space, for reasons and in ways that we can analyze. If they survive their birth pangs, they pursue their historical life within the framework and constraints of the structures that constitute them, following their cyclical rhythms and trapped in their secular trends. These secular trends inevitably approach asymptotes that aggravate considerably the internal contradictions of the system: that is, the system encounters problems it can no longer resolve, and this causes what we may call systemic crisis. Most often, people use the word crisis loosely, simply to mean a difficult period in the life of any system. But whenever the difficulty can be resolved in some way, then there is not a true crisis but simply a difficulty built into the system. True crises are those difficulties that *cannot* be resolved within the framework of the system, but instead can be overcome only by going outside of and beyond the historical system of which the difficulties are a part. To use the technical language of natural science, what happens is that the system bifurcates, that is, finds that its basic equations can be solved in two quite different ways. We can translate this into everyday language by saying that the system is faced with two alternative solutions for its crisis, both of which are intrinsically possible. In effect, the members of the system collectively are called upon to make a historical choice about which of the alternative paths will be followed, that is, what kind of new system will be constructed.

Immanuel Wallerstein, "The Modern World-System in Crisis," pp. 76–90 from Immanuel Wallerstein, *World-Systems Analysis: An Introduction*. Durham, NC: Duke University Press, 2004. Copyright © 2004 Duke University Press. Reprinted by permission of the author.

Contemporary Sociological Theory, Third Edition. Edited by Craig Calhoun, Joseph Gerteis, James Moody, Steven Pfaff, and Indermohan Virk. Editorial material and organization © 2012 John Wiley & Sons, Ltd. Published 2012 by John Wiley & Sons, Ltd.

Since the existing system can no longer function adequately within its defined parameters, making a choice about the way out, about the future system (or systems) which are to be constructed, is inevitable. But which choice the participants collectively will make is inherently unpredictable. The process of bifurcating is chaotic, which means that every small action during this period is likely to have significant consequences. We observe that under these conditions, the system tends to oscillate wildly. But eventually it leans in one direction. It normally takes quite some time before the definitive choice is made. We can call this a period of transition, one whose outcome is quite uncertain. At some point, however, there is a dear outcome and then we find ourselves ensconced in a different historical system.

The modern world-system in which we are living, which is that of a capitalist world-economy, is currently in precisely such a crisis, and has been for a while now. This crisis may go on another twenty-five to fifty years. Since one central feature of such a transitional period is that we face wild oscillations of all those structures and processes we have come to know as an inherent part of the existing world-system, we find that our short-term expectations are necessarily quite unstable. This instability can lead to considerable anxiety and therefore violence as people try to preserve acquired privileges and hierarchical rank in a very unstable situation. In general, this process can lead to social conflicts that take a quite unpleasant form.

When did this crisis start? Geneses of phenomena are always the most debatable topic in scientific discourse. For one can always find forerunners and forebodings of almost anything in the near past, but also of course in the very far past. One plausible moment at which to start the story of this contemporary systemic crisis is the world revolution of 1968, which unsettled the structures of the world-system considerably. This world revolution marked the end of a long period of liberal supremacy, thereby dislocating the geoculture that had kept the political institutions of the world-system intact. And dislocating this geoculture unhinged the underpinnings of the capitalist world-economy and exposed it to the full force of political and cultural shocks to which it had always been subject, but from which it had previously been somewhat sheltered.

The shock of 1968 to which we shall return is not, however, enough to explain a crisis in the system. There have to have been long-existing structural trends which were beginning to reach their asymptotes, and therefore made it no longer possible to overcome the repeated difficulties into which any system gets itself because of its cyclical rhythms. Only when we have perceived what these trends are and why the recurrent difficulties can no longer be easily resolved can we then understand why and how the shock of 1968 precipitated an unraveling of the geoculture which had been binding the system together.

In the ceaseless quest for accumulation, capitalists are constantly seeking ways of increasing the sales prices of their products and reducing the costs of production. Producers cannot however arbitrarily raise sales prices to just any level. They are constrained by two considerations. The first is the existence of competitive sellers. This is why the creation of oligopolies is so important, because they reduce the number of alternative sellers. The second is the level of effective demand – how much money buyers have in total – and the choices that consumers make because their buying-power is limited.

The level of effective demand is affected primarily by the world distribution of income. Obviously, the more money each buyer has, the more he or she can buy. This simple fact creates an inherent and continuing dilemma for capitalists. On the one hand, they want as much profit as possible, and therefore wish to minimize the amount of surplus that goes to anyone else, for example their employees. On the other hand, at least some capitalists must allow for some redistribution of the surplus-value created, or there would normally be too few buyers overall for the products. So, intermittently at least some producers in fact favor increased remuneration for employees to create a higher effective demand.

Given the level of effective demand at any given time, the choices that consumers make are decided by what economists call the elasticity of demand. This refers to the value that each buyer places on alternate uses of his or her money. Purchases vary in the eyes of the buyer from the indispensable to the totally optional. These valuations are the result of an interplay between individual psychologies, cultural pressures, and physiological requirements. The sellers can only have a limited impact on the elasticity of demand, although marketing (in the broadest sense) is designed precisely to affect consumer choice.

The net consequence for the seller is that the seller can never raise the price to a level where (a) competitors can sell more cheaply, (b) buyers do not have the money to purchase the product, or (c) buyers are not ready to allocate that much of their money to the purchase. Given the inbuilt ceiling to sales price levels, producers usually spend most of their energy in the effort to accumulate capital in finding ways to reduce the costs of production, something which is often termed efficiency of production. To understand what is happening in the contemporary world-system, we have to look at the reasons why the costs of production have been rising worldwide over time despite all the efforts of producers, thereby reducing the margin between the costs of production and the possible sales prices. In other words, we need to understand why there has been a growing squeeze on the average worldwide rate of profits.

There are three main costs of production for any producer. The producer must remunerate the personnel who work in the enterprise. The producer must purchase the inputs of the production process. And the producer must pay the taxes that are levied by any and all governmental structures which have the authority to levy them on the particular production process. We need to examine each of these three costs in turn, and in particular to see why each has been steadily rising over the *longue durée* of the capitalist world-economy.

How does an employer decide how much to remunerate an employee? There may be laws, which set minimum levels. There are certainly customary wages at any given time and place, although these are subject to constant revision. Basically, the employer would almost always like to offer a figure lower than the employee would like to receive. Producer and worker negotiate about this; they struggle over this question, constantly and repeatedly. The outcome of any such negotiation or struggle depends on the strengths of each side – economic, political, and cultural.

Employees may grow stronger in the bargaining because their skills are rare. There is always a supply-and-demand element in determining levels of remuneration. Or the employees may grow stronger because they organize with each other and engage in syndical action. This applies not only to the production workers (both skilled technicians and unskilled workers) but also to managerial personnel (both senior managers and middle-level cadres). This is the part of the question of economic strength internal to each productive enterprise. There is also an external part. The overall state of the economy, locally and worldwide, determines the level of unemployment and therefore how desperate each side of each production unit is to come to a remuneration arrangement.

The political strengths derive from a combination of the political machinery and arrangements in the state-structure, the strength of syndical organization by the workers, and the degree to which employers need to secure the support of managers and middle-level cadres to hold off the demands of ordinary workers. And what we mean by cultural strength – the mores of the local and national community – is usually the result of prior political strengths.

In general, in any production area the syndical power of workers will tend to increase over time, by dint of organization and education. Repressive measures may be used to limit the effects of such organization, but then there are costs attached to this too – perhaps higher taxes, perhaps higher remuneration to cadres, perhaps the need to employ and pay for repressive personnel. If one looks at the most profitable loci of production – oligopolistic firms in leading sectors – there is a further factor at play, in that highly profitable firms do not wish to lose production time because of workers' discontent. As a result, remuneration costs in such firms tend to rise as time goes on, but sooner or later these same production units come to face increased competition and therefore may need to restrain price increases, resulting in lower rates of profit.

There is only one significant counter to the consequent creeping rise in remuneration costs – runaway factories. By moving production to places where the current costs of production are much lower, the employer not only gets lower costs of remuneration but gains political strength in the zone out of which the enterprise is partially moving, in that existing employees may be willing to accept lower rates of remuneration to prevent further "flight" of jobs. Of course, there is a negative in this for the employer. If there weren't, the production site would have moved much earlier. There are the costs of moving. And in these other zones, the transaction costs are normally higher – because of the increased distance from eventual customers, poorer infrastructure, and higher costs of "corruption" – that is, unavowed remuneration to non-employees.

The trade-off between remuneration costs and transactions costs plays itself out in a cyclical manner. Transactions costs tend to be the primary consideration in times of economic expansion (Kondratieff A-phases) while remuneration costs are the primary consideration in times of economic stagnation (B-phases). Still, one has to ask why there exist zones of lower remuneration at all. The reason has to do with the size of the non-urban population in a given country or region. Wherever the non-urban population is large, there are large pockets of persons who are partially, even largely, outside the wage-economy. Or changes in land use in the rural areas are forcing some persons to leave. For such persons, the opportunity of wage-employment in urban areas usually represents a significant increase in the overall income of the household of which they are a part, even if the wages are significantly below the worldwide norm of remuneration. So, at least at first, the entry of such persons into a local wage-force is a win-win arrangement – lower costs of remuneration for the employer, higher income for the employees. Wages are lower there not only for unskilled workers but for cadres as well. Peripheral zones usually are lower-price, lower-amenity zones and the wages of cadres are accordingly below the norm of core zones.

The problem is that the political strengths of employer and employee are not fixed in stone. They evolve. If at first the newly urbanized employees have difficulty adjusting to urban life and are unaware of their potential political strengths, this state of ignorance does not last forever. Certainly, within twenty-five years the employees or their descendants become adjusted to the realities of the new situation and become aware of the low level of their remuneration in terms of world norms. The reaction is to begin to engage in syndical action. The employer then rediscovers the conditions from which the enterprise had sought to escape by moving its production operation in the first place. Eventually, in a future period of economic downturn, the producer may again try the "runaway factory" tactic.

Over time, however, the number of zones in which this particular solution to rising remuneration costs can be effectuated in the capitalist world-economy has become ever fewer. The world has been deruralizing, in large part precisely because of this mode of restraining remuneration costs by relocating production processes. In the last half of the twentieth century, there was a radical reduction in the share of the world population that lives in rural areas. And the first half of the twenty-first century threatens to eliminate the remaining pockets of serious rural concentration. When there are no zones into which the factories can run away, there will be no way to reduce seriously the levels of remuneration for employees worldwide.

The steadily rising level of remuneration is not the only problem which producers are facing. The second is the cost of inputs. By inputs, I include both machinery and materials of production (whether these are so-called raw materials or semi-finished and finished products). The producer of course buys these on the market and pays what must be paid for them. But there are three hidden costs for which producers do not necessarily pay. They are the costs of disposal of waste (especially toxic materials), the costs of renewing raw materials, and what are generically called infrastructural costs. The ways of evading these costs are manifold, and not paying for these costs has been a major element in keeping down the cost of inputs.

The primary mode of minimizing the costs of disposal is dumping, that is, placing waste in some public area with minimal or no treatment. When these are toxic materials, the result, in addition to clutter, is noxious consequences for the ecosphere. At some point, the consequences of clutter and noxious effects become perceived as a social problem, and the collectivity is forced to address it. But clutter and noxious effects behave a bit like the absence of rural zones nearby. A producer can always move on to a new area, thereby eliminating the problem, until these "unspoiled" areas are exhausted. Worldwide, this is what has been happening in the capitalist world-economy. It is only really in the second half of the twentieth century that the potential exhaustion of dumping grounds has come to be perceived as a social problem.

The problem of renewal of raw materials is a parallel problem. The purchaser of raw materials is normally uninterested in their long-run availability. And sellers are notoriously ready to subordinate long-run viability to short-run gains. Over five hundred years, this has led to successive exhaustions and increases in the costs of obtaining such resources. These trends have only partially been counteracted by technological advances in creating alternative resources.

The two exhaustions – of dumping space and natural resources – have become the subject of a major social movement of environmentalists and Greens in recent decades, who have sought governmental intervention to meet collective needs. To meet these needs however requires money, a great deal of money. Who will pay? There are only two real possibilities – the collectivity, through taxation, and the producers who use the raw materials. To the extent that the producers are being required to pay for them – economists call this internalization of costs – the costs of production are rising for individual producers.

Finally, there is the issue of infrastructure, a term which refers to all those physical institutions outside the production unit which form a necessary part of the production and distribution process – roads, transport services, communications networks, security systems, water supply. These are costly, and ever more costly. Once again, who is footing the bill? Either the collectivity, which means taxation, or the individual firms, which means increased costs. It should be noted that to the degree the infrastructure is privatized, the bill is paid by the individual firms (even if other firms are making profits out of operating the infrastructure, and even if individual persons are paying increased costs for their own consumption).

The pressure to internalize costs represents for productive firms a significant increase in the costs of production which, over time, has more than overcome the cost advantages that improvements in technology have made possible. And this internalization of costs omits the growing problem that these firms are having as a result of penalties imposed by the courts and legislatures for damages caused by past negligence.

The third cost that has been rising over time is that of taxation. Taxes are a basic element in social organization. There have always been and always will be taxes of one sort or another. But who pays, and how much, is the subject of endless political struggle. In the modern world-system, there have been two basic reasons for taxation. One is to provide the state structures with the means to offer security services (armies and police forces), build infrastructure, and employ a bureaucracy with which to provide public services as well as collect taxes. These costs are inescapable, although obviously there can be strong and wide differences in views as to what should be spent and how.

There is however a second reason to tax, which is more recent (it has arisen only in the last century to any significant degree). This second reason is the consequence of political democratization, which has led to demands by the citizenry on the states to provide them with three major benefits, which have come to be seen as entitlements: education, health, and guarantees of lifetime income. When these benefits were first provided in the nineteenth century, state expenditures were quite small and only existed in a few countries. Throughout the twentieth century, the definition of what the states were expected to provide and the number of states which provided something steadily grew in each of these domains. It seems virtually impossible today to push the level of expenditures back in the other direction.

As a result of the increasing cost (not merely in absolute terms but as a proportion of world surplus) of providing security, building infrastructure, and offering the citizenry benefits in education, health, and lifetime guarantees of income, taxation as a share of total costs has been steadily rising for productive enterprises everywhere, and will continue to rise.

Thus it is that the three costs of production – remuneration, inputs, and taxation – have all been rising steadily over the past five hundred years and particularly over the past fifty years. On the other hand, the sales prices have not been able to keep pace, despite increased effective demand, because of a steady expansion in the number of producers and hence of their recurring inability to maintain oligopolistic conditions. This is what one means by a squeeze on profits. To be sure, producers seek to reverse these conditions constantly, and are doing so at present. To appreciate the limits of their ability to do so, we must return to the cultural shock of 1968.

The world-economy in the years after 1945 saw the largest expansion of productive structures in the history of the modern world-system. All the structural trends of which we have been speaking – costs of remuneration, costs of inputs, taxation – took a sharp upward turn as a result. At the same time, the antisystemic movements, which we previously discussed, made extraordinary progress in realizing their immediate objective – coming to power in the state structures. In all parts of the world, these movements seemed to be achieving step one of the two-step program. In a vast northern area from central Europe to East Asia (from the Elbe to the Yalu Rivers), Communist parties governed. In the pan-European world (western Europe, North America, and Australasia), social democratic parties (or their equivalents) were in power, or at least in alternating power. In the rest of Asia and most of Africa, national liberation movements had come to power. And in Latin America, nationalist/populist movements gained control.

The years after 1945 thus became a period of great optimism. The economic future seemed bright, and popular movements of all kinds seemed to be achieving their objectives. And in Vietnam, a little country struggling for its independence seemed to be holding the hegemonic power, the United States, in check. The modern world-system had never looked so good to so many people, a sentiment that had an exhilarating effect, but in many ways also a very stabilizing effect.

Nonetheless, there was an underlying and growing disillusion with precisely the popular movements in power. The second step of the two-step formula – change the world – seemed in practice much further from realization than most people had anticipated. Despite the overall economic growth of the world-system, the gap between core and periphery had become greater than ever. And despite the coming to power of the antisystemic movements, the great participatory élan of the period of mobilization seemed to die out once the antisystemic movements came to power in any given state. New privileged strata emerged. Ordinary people were now being asked not to make militant demands on what was asserted to be a government that represented them. When the future became the present, many previously ardent militants of the movements began to have second thoughts, and eventually began to dissent.

It was the combination of long-existing anger about the workings of the world-system and disappointment with the capacity of the antisystemic movements to transform the world that led to the world revolution of 1968. The explosions of 1968 contained two themes repeated virtually everywhere, whatever the local context. One was the rejection of US hegemonic power, simultaneously with a complaint that the Soviet Union, the presumed antagonist of the United States, was actually colluding in the world order that the United States had established. And the second was that the traditional antisystemic movements had not fulfilled their promises once in power. The combination of these complaints, so widely repeated, constituted a cultural earthquake. The many uprisings were like a phoenix and did not put the multiple revolutionaries of 1968 in power, or not for very long. But they legitimated and strengthened the sense of disillusionment not only with the old antisystemic movements but also with the state structures these movements had been fortifying. The long-term certainties of evolutionary hope had become transformed into fears that the world-system might be unchanging.

This shift in worldwide sentiment, far from reinforcing the status quo, actually pulled the political and cultural supports from under the capitalist world-economy. No longer would oppressed people be sure that history was on their side. No longer could they therefore be satisfied with creeping improvements, in the belief that these would see fruition in the lives of their children and grandchildren. No longer could they be persuaded to postpone present complaints in the name of a beneficent future. In short, the multiple producers of the capitalist world-economy had lost the main hidden stabilizer of the system, the optimism of the oppressed. And this of course came at the very worst moment, when the squeeze on profits was beginning to be felt in a serious way.

The cultural shock of 1968 unhinged the automatic dominance of the liberal center, which had prevailed in the world-system since the prior world revolution of 1848. The right and the left were liberated from their role as avatars of centrist liberalism and were able to assert, or rather reassert, their more radical values. The world-system had entered into the period of transition, and both right and left were determined to take advantage of the increasing chaos to ensure that their values would prevail in the new system (or systems) that would eventually emerge from the crisis.

The immediate effect of the world revolution of 1968 seemed to be a legitimation of left values, most notably in the domains of race and sex. Racism has been a pervasive feature of the modern world-system for all of its existence. To be sure, its legitimacy has been called into question for two centuries. But it was only after the world revolution of 1968 that a widespread campaign against racism – one led by the oppressed groups themselves, as distinguished from those previously led primarily by liberals among the dominant strata – became a central phenomenon on the world political scene, taking the form both of actively militant "minority" identity movements everywhere and of attempts to reconstruct the world of knowledge, to make the issues deriving from chronic racism central to intellectual discourse.

Along with the debates about racism, it would have been hard to miss the centrality of sexuality to the world revolution of 1968. Whether we are speaking of policies related to gender or to sexual preferences, and eventually to transgender identity, the impact of 1968 was to bring to the forefront what had been a slow transformation of sexual mores in the preceding half-century and allow it to explode onto the world social scene, with enormous consequences for the law, for customary practice, for religions, and for intellectual discourse.

The traditional antisystemic movements had emphasized primarily the issues of state power and of economic structures. Both issues receded somewhat in the militant rhetoric of 1968 because of the space given the issues of race and sexuality. This posed a real problem for the world right. Geopolitical and economic issues were easier for the world right to deal with than the sociocultural issues. This was because of the position of the centrist liberals, who were hostile to any undermining of the basic political and economic institutions of the capitalist world-economy, but were latent, if less militant, supporters of the sociocultural shifts advocated by the militants in the revolutions of 1968 (and afterward). As a result, the post-1968 reaction was actually split, between on the one hand an Establishment attempt to restore order and solve some of the immediate difficulties of the emerging profit squeeze and on the other a more narrowly based but much more ferocious cultural counterrevolution. It is important to distinguish the two sets of issues and therefore the two sets of strategic alignments.

As the world-economy entered at this time into a long Kondratieff B-phase, the coalition of centrist and rightist forces attempted to roll back rising costs of production in all three components of costs. They sought to reduce remuneration levels. They sought to re-externalize the costs of inputs. They sought to reduce taxation for the benefit of the welfare state (education, health, and lifetime guarantees of income). This offensive took many forms. The center abandoned the theme of developmentalism (as a mode of overcoming global polarization) and replaced it with the theme of globalization, which called essentially for the opening of all frontiers to the free flow of goods and capital (but not of labor). The Thatcher regime in the United Kingdom and the Reagan regime in the United States took the lead in promoting these policies, which were called "neoliberalism" as theory and "the Washington consensus" as policy. The World Economic Forum at Davos was the locus for promoting the theory, and the International Monetary Fund (IMF) and the newly established World Trade Organization (WTO) became the chief enforcers of the Washington consensus.

The economic difficulties faced by governments everywhere from the 1970s onward (particularly in the South and in the former communist zone) made it extremely difficult for these states, governed by old antisystemic movements, to resist the pressures for "structural adjustment" and opening frontiers. As a result, a limited amount of success in rolling back costs of production worldwide was achieved, but a success far below what the promoters of such policies had hoped for, and far below what was necessary to end the squeeze on profits. More and more, capitalists sought profits in the arena of financial speculation rather than in the arena of production. Such financial manipulations can result in great profits for some players, but it renders the world-economy very volatile and subject to swings of currencies and of employment. It is in fact one of the signs of increasing chaos.

In the world political arena, the world political left would increasingly make electoral objectives secondary, and began the organization rather of a "movement of movements" – what has come to be identified with the World Social Forum (WSF), which met initially in Porto Alegre and is often referred to by that symbol. The WSF is not an organization, but a meeting-ground of militants of many stripes and persuasions, engaging in a variety of actions from collective demonstrations that are worldwide or regional to local organizing across the globe. Their slogan, "another world is possible," is expressive of their sense that the world-system is in a structural crisis, and that political options are real. The world is facing increasingly a struggle on many fronts between the spirit of Davos and the spirit of Porto Alegre.

The dramatic attack by Osama bin Laden on the Twin Towers on September 11, 2001, marked a further indication of world political chaos and a turning-point in political alignments. It allowed those on the right who wished to cut their links with the center to pursue a program centered around unilateral assertions by the United States of military strength combined with an attempt to undo the cultural evolution of the world-system that occurred after the world revolution of 1968 (particularly in the fields of race and sexuality). In the process, they have sought to liquidate many of the geopolitical structures set in place after 1945, which they have seen as constraining their politics. But these efforts threatened to worsen the already-increasing instability in the world-system.

This is the empirical description of a chaotic situation in the world-system. What can we expect in such a situation? The first thing to emphasize is that we can expect, we are already seeing, wild fluctuations in all the institutional arenas of the world-system. The world-economy is subject to acute speculative pressures, which are escaping the control of major financial institutions and control bodies, such as central banks. A high degree of violence is erupting everywhere in smaller and larger doses, and over relatively long periods. No one has any longer the power to shut down such eruptions effectively. The moral constraints traditionally enforced both by states and by religious institutions are finding their efficacy considerably diminished.

On the other hand, just because a system is in crisis does not mean that it does not continue to try to function in its accustomed ways. It does. Insofar as the accustomed ways have resulted in secular trends that are approaching asymptotes, continuing in customary ways simply aggravates the crisis. Yet continuing to act in customary ways will probably be the mode of behavior of most people. It makes sense in the very short run. The customary ways are the familiar ways, and they promise short-run benefits, or they would not be the customary ways. Precisely because the fluctuations are wilder, most people will seek their security by persisting in their behavior.

To be sure, all sorts of people will seek middle-run adjustments to the system, which they will argue will mitigate the existing problems. This too is a customary pattern, and in the memory of most people one that has worked in the past and should therefore be tried again. The problem is that in a systemic crisis, such middle-run adjustments have little effect. This is after all what we said defined a systemic crisis.

And others will seek to pursue more transformative paths, often in the guise of middle-run adjustments. They are hoping to take advantage of the wild swings of the period of transition to encrust major changes in operating modes, which will push the process toward one side of the bifurcation. It is this last form of behavior which will be the most consequential. In the present situation, it is the one to which we referred as the struggle between the spirit of Davos and the spirit of Porto Alegre. This struggle is perhaps not yet at the center of most people's attention. And of course, many most active in the struggle may find it useful to divert attention from the intensity of the struggle and its real stakes, in the hope of achieving some of their objectives without arousing the opposition which the open proclamation of these objectives might arouse.

There is only so much that can be said about a struggle that is just beginning to unfold, one of whose central characteristics is the total uncertainty of its outcome, and another of whose characteristics is the opacity of the struggle. One might think of it as a clash of fundamental values, even of "civilizations," just as long as we don't identify the two sides with existing peoples, races, religious groups, or other historic groupings. The key element of the debate is the degree to which any social system, but in this case the future one we are constructing, will lean in one direction or the other on two long-standing central issues of social organization – liberty and equality – issues that are more closely intertwined than social thought in the modern world-system has been willing to assert.

The issue of liberty (or "democracy") is surrounded by so much hyperbole in our modern world that it is sometimes hard to appreciate what the underlying issues are. We might find it useful to distinguish between the liberty of the majority and the liberty of the minority. The liberty of the majority is located in the degree to which collective political decisions reflect in fact the preferences of the majority, as opposed to those of smaller groups who may in practice control the decision-making processes. This is not merely a question of so-called free elections, although no doubt regular, honest, open elections are a necessary if far from sufficient part of a democratic structure. Liberty of the majority requires the active participation of the majority. It requires access to information on the part of the majority. It requires a mode of translating majority views of the populace into majority views in legislative bodies. It is doubtful that any existing state within the modern world-system is fully democratic in these senses.

The liberty of the minority is a quite different matter. It represents the rights of all individuals and groups to pursue their preferences in all those realms in which there is no justification for the majority to impose its preferences on others. In principle, most states in the modern world-system have given lip service to these rights to exemption from majority preferences. Some have even lauded the concept not merely as a negative protection but as a positive contribution to the construction of a historical system of many different strands. The traditional antisystemic movements placed priority on what we are calling the liberty of the majority. The world revolutionaries of 1968 placed great emphasis rather on expanding the liberty of the minorities.

Even if we assume that everyone is in fact in favor of liberty, which is a rash assumption, there is the enormous and never-ending difficulty of deciding what is the line between the liberty of the majority and the liberty of the minorities – that is, in what spheres and issues one or the other takes precedence. In the struggle over the system (or systems) that will succeed our existing world-system, the fundamental cleavage will be between those who wish to expand both liberties – that of the majority and that of the minorities – and those who will seek to create a non-libertarian system under the guise of preferring either the liberty of the majority or the liberty of the minorities. In such a struggle, it becomes clear what the role of opacity is in the struggle. Opacity leads to confusion, and this favors the cause of those who wish to limit liberty.

Equality is often posed as a concept in conflict with that of liberty, especially if we mean relative equality of access to material goods. In fact, it is the reverse side of the same coin. To the degree that meaningful inequalities exist, it is inconceivable that equal weight be given to all persons in assessing the preferences of the majority. And it is inconceivable that the liberty of the minorities will be fully respected if these minorities are not equal in the eyes of everyone – equal socially and economically in order to be equal politically. What the emphasis on equality as a concept does is point to the necessary positions of the majority to realize its own liberty and to encourage the liberty of the minorities.

In constructing the successor system (or systems) to our existing one, we shall be opting either for a hierarchical system bestowing or permitting privileges according to rank in the system, however this rank is determined (including meritocratic criteria), or for a relatively democratic, relatively egalitarian system. One of the great virtues of the existing world-system is that although it has not resolved any of these debates – far from it! – it has increasingly brought the debate to the fore. There is little question that across the world, people are more fully aware of these issues today than a century ago, not to speak of five centuries ago. They are more aware, more willing to struggle for their rights, more skeptical about the rhetoric of the powerful. However polarized the existing system, this at least is a positive legacy.

The period of transition from one system to another is a period of great knowledge. We need first of all to try to understand clearly what is going on. We need then to make our choices about the directions in which we want the world to go. And we must finally figure out how we can act in the present so that it is likely to go in the direction we prefer. We can think of these three tasks as the intellectual, the moral, and the political tasks. They are different, but they are closely interlinked. None of us can opt out of any of these tasks. If we claim we do, we are merely making a hidden choice. The tasks before us are exceptionally difficult. But they offer us, individually and collectively, the possibility of creation, or at least of contributing to the creation of something that might fulfill better our collective possibilities.

Index

abstract public spheres 480
abstract systems 531–3, 543
abstracted empiricism 17–18
academic credibility 409–11, 412–13
ad hoc category systems 197
Adam Smith in Beijing (Arrighi) 566, 569–78
adjudication 263–4
administrative organizations
   Habermas, Jürgen 440
   power 227, 236, 259–60, 262–4, 279–80, 283
Adorno, Theodor 437, 438, 445, 448
affective individualism 533
agents of knowledge 412–13
Alchian, Armen 181
Alexander, Jeffrey 2
allocative resources 282
alternative groups 134
Althusser, Louis 289, 291
altruism 95
anatomo-politics of human body 298
anchorage of opinions 104
Anderson, Benedict 89
anthropology 11–12, 16, 403
anticipatory socialization 58, 184

anti-economies 363
antimodernism 548, 550
antiracist racism 428
Anti-Semite and Jew (Sartre) 421
anti-Semitism 421–2
antisystemic crises 569–78, 593–8
appearance 50
approval 102
Arato, Andrew 475, 477–8
The Archaeology of Knowledge (Foucault) 290
Arrighi, Giovanni 565–6, 569–78
art for art's sake 333, 363, 364
artistic production 332–3, 359–74, 446–50
Asian financial crisis 572
aspirations 48
atomistic action theory 160–1, 168–9
authenticity 363
authoritative resources 282–4
autonomy
   Bourdieu, Pierre 348–50, 362–5, 368–70, 378, 384
   Habermas, Jürgen 440
   power 274, 279
   structural 217–19
aversive stimulation 100–1

Contemporary Sociological Theory, Third Edition. Edited by Craig Calhoun, Joseph Gerteis, James Moody, Steven Pfaff, and Indermohan Virk. Editorial material and organization © 2012 John Wiley & Sons, Ltd. Published 2012 by John Wiley & Sons, Ltd.

baby boom generation 4
Bachrach, P. 267–70, 273
Back, K. 101–2
balanced net systems 194–5, 203
Bandung 571, 573–4
bankruptcy of modern safeguards 526–8
Baratz, M.S. 267–70, 273
Barkey, Karen 214–15
Barraclough, Geoffrey 569
Barthes, Roland 291
Baudrillard, Jean 495, 497
Bauman, Zygmunt 496–7, 510–30
because-motives 41–2
Beck, Ulrich 533, 535
behaviorist theory 94, 100–2
Beijing Consensus 570–1
belief
　Bourdieu, Pierre 381–2
　interaction ritual chains 79
　in the part one is playing 46–9
Bell, Daniel 5, 446–7, 564
Bell, David 495
benefit-rich networks 206
Benjamin, Walter 437
Bentham, Jeremy 314–17, 319–21
Berger, Peter 6–7, 28
Bernhard, Thomas 375–6
Between Facts and Norms
　(Habermas) 440–1
bias, mobilization of 268–9
Bierstedt, Robert 400–1
bifurcation of consciousness 404–6
bin Laden, Osama 596
bio-history 300
bio-politics of populations 298
bio-power 298–301
The Birth of the Clinic (Foucault) 292, 305
Black Feminist Thought: Knowledge, Consciousness and the Politics of Empowerment (Collins) 393–4, 407–16
Black Skin, White Masks (Fanon) 395, 417–25
Blau, Peter 19–20, 95–6, 98, 108–9, 112–23
blocs 253–4

blood relations 302–4
Blumer, Herbert 27, 30–1, 62–74
border zones 379
Bourdieu, Pierre 323–86
　anti-economies 363
　bureaucratic field 375–85
　collective histories 336, 350–2
　cultural production 332–3, 359–74
　early works 323–4
　false dichotomies 327–8
　fields and capital 330–1, 360–8, 379
　genesis of states 378–80
　habitus and misrecognition 328–30, 332, 340–1, 345–58, 371–3
　hierarchization 362–3, 364–6, 368–9
　historical context 8–9, 20
　homologies 366–8
　interaction ritual chains 77–8
　logic of classes 342–4
　The Logic of Practice 326, 332
　minds of state 380–4
　monopoly and state nobility 384–5
　operational definition 365–6
　positions and dispositions 368–73, 381–2
　positions in social space 328–30, 337–9, 360–1, 367–73, 383–4
　radical doubt 377–8
　real as relational 337–41
　relational analysis 328–30
　social space and symbolic space 332, 335–44
　structure and action 327–8
　structure and practice in social life 332–3
bourgeoisie
　Bourdieu, Pierre 337–9, 360–1, 364–5, 368–70
　crisis and change 563
　Habermas, Jürgen 440, 446, 474, 480
Bowles, Samuel 167–8
branches of drives 506–7
Briggs, Jean 402–3
Brown, E.H.Phelps 167
Bruderhof community 130–1
Bubois, W.E.B. 9
Burckhardt, Jacob 229

bureaucracies
  Bourdieu, Pierre 375–85
  modernity 521–5, 537
  organizational fields 175–6, 178
Burt, Ronald 159, 162, 204–19

Calhoun, Craig 496, 497
capital
  Bourdieu, Pierre 323–4, 330–1, 337–9, 360–8, 379
  coercion 255–9, 265
  Foucault, Michel 319
capital punishment 297
capital volume 331, 337–9
capitalism
  Bourdieu, Pierre 326, 351
  crisis and change 563–4, 565–7, 584, 588–99
  Foucault, Michel 298–9, 306, 312
  Habermas, Jürgen 441, 446, 478
  historical context 2–6, 10, 13–14
  institutions 175–6
  modernity 496, 497, 538
  overproduction 2
  power 223–4, 227, 231, 256–8, 264
capitalized coercion 265
caste systems 135
Castells, Manuel 496
categories and category systems 195–202
catnets 193–203
  categories 195–7
  category systems 197–202
  frames 202–3
  limited systems 195
  net systems 194–5
  nets 193–4
causality
  Bourdieu, Pierre 356
  Holocaust 513
  power 246, 274
celebrity 233
census data 15, 429–31
centralization
  organizational fields 186
  power 230–2
  violence 520–1
childhood socialization 79
children, sexualization of 302, 308

China 566, 569–78
Churches 244–6
cities and city-states 251–3, 255–8, 261
citizenship 2
  crisis and change 581
  difference 395, 409
  Habermas, Jürgen 441, 474
civil disobedience 486–7
civil rights 395, 409
civil-service reforms 177–8
The Civilizing Process (Elias) 497, 499–509
civil society 440, 474–9
class
  Bourdieu, Pierre 331, 336, 337–40, 343, 352–3, 367
  crisis and change 563
  Foucault, Michel 306
  power 223–6, 227, 284
Class and Class Conflict in Industrial Society (Dahrendorf) 224
Class Counts: Comparative Studies in Class Analysis 224
classical sociological theory 1–2, 5
Classical Sociological Theory (Marx) 223
classification principle 337–44, 380–1
cliques 216–17
coercion
  capital and coercion 255–9, 265
  cities and states in world history 251–62
  crisis and change 576
  domination 258–9
  exchange theory 114, 120–1
  exploitation 256–8
  extraction and protection 262–3
  modernity 520–1, 526
  power 227, 251–65
  states and citizens 262–5
  war driving state formation and transformation 259–65
Coercion, Capital and European States (Tilly) 227, 251–65
coercive isomorphism 161, 178–80, 186
cognitive structures 380–3
Cohen, Jean 475, 477–8
coherence of knowledge 461
cohesion 208–10, 218
cohesiveness 101–2

Cold War 2–3
Cold War strategy 571–2
Coleman, James 93–4, 97, 145, 159–60
collective action 124–8
   competitive market analogy 124–6
   interaction ritual chains 89
   participation 96
   power 269
   solidarity 96–7
   symbolic interactionism 70–1, 74
collective approval/disapproval of
   power 115
collective consciousness 452
collective goods 128
collective histories 336, 350–2
collective mobilization 352
collective rationality 175–92
Collins, Patricia Hill 393–4, 407–16
Collins, Randall 32–3, 75–90
colonialism
   difference 394–5, 417–25
   fact of blackness 418–22
   language 417–18
   recognition 422–5
combat sports 327, 330
commission 385
common mood/experience 80–1
common sense 237–48, 349
communal lending 150–4
communal norms 148–50
communication
   ambiguities in understanding another
     person 35
   exchange theory 102
   Habermas, Jürgen 437–9, 441–2, 446–7,
     452–8, 463–4, 470–89
   interaction ritual chains 84–8
   intersubjectivity 36–8, 438, 453–4,
     456–7, 470–1
   meaning-context 41–3
   meaning-establishment and
     meaning-interpretation 38–40
   product and evidence 43–5
   subjective and objective meaning 38–40,
     43–5
communicative power 470–4, 488
communism 290
compensation 130–1, 138

competence 108–9
competitive markets
   exchange theory 124–6, 132–3
   institutions 162, 166–7, 175–6, 204–19
   modernity 525
compliance
   with demands 114–15, 118
   with obligations 96–7, 129, 136–40
   power 279
compulsory payments 127–8
Comte, Auguste 15
The Conceptual Practices of Power: A
   Feminist Sociology of Knowledge
   (Smith) 393, 398–406
concrete arrangements 298
conflict
   economic embeddedness 172–3
   exchange theory 116
   historical context 9–10
   modernity 508
   power 224–5, 269–71
conflicts of interests 273
conformity 102, 103
connectedness 177
consensual authority 273
consensus 453
The Consequences of Modernity
   (Giddens) 531–45
constitutions
   civil society 475–6, 487–8
   modernity 498, 547–8, 551–9
constraints 302
constructionist position 392
consumerism
   cultural production 361
   Habermas, Jürgen 446
   historical context 5–6
contact clusters 212–13, 216–17
contexts of relevance 455–6
contextual category systems 199–200
continuity of tradition 461
contrivance 57–61
control
   Foucault, Michel 311
   modernity 528–9
   power 279–80
   structural holes 213–19
control capacity 136–40, 149–50

conventions 130, 148–50
Cook, Karen 97–8, 142–56
Cooley, Charles 53
cooperation
   communal lending 150–4
   communal norms and
     responsibility 148–50
   law and trust 97–8, 142–56
   reputational effects 143–4
   social capital 144–8
co-optation strategy 571–2
costs of production 589–93
counter-laws 320–1
credit associations 151–2
crisis and change 561–99
   capitalism 563–4, 565–7, 584, 588–99
   denationalization 567, 582–6
   globalization 564, 566–7, 580, 583, 595
   modernity 564, 565
   multiplication of specialized
     orders 583–6
   nation-states 564, 567, 579–86
   systemic and antisystemic crises 569–78, 593–8
   territory, authority and rights 566–7, 579–86
   world systems 565, 587–99
crisis consciousness 485
cross-tabulation category systems 197–9, 201
crossed-out God 547, 551, 554–6
crowd behaviors 80–1, 85–7
cult behavior 63
cultural capital 9, 330–1, 337–9, 356–7, 364
cultural construction of knowledge 6–9
cultural difference 11–12, 21–2
cultural modernity 445–7
cultural movements 239–40, 244
cultural production
   Bourdieu, Pierre 332–3, 359–74
   Habermas, Jürgen 446–50
cultural theory 2
culture and language 247

Dahl, R.A. 267, 270
Dahrendorf, Ralf 224–5
danger, modernity 535–7, 542–3
Darwin, Charles 15

dating 4–5
de Beauvoir, Simone 54
de Sade, Marquis 303–4
de Saussure, Ferdinand 8
de Tocqueville, Alexis 13
debt 206–7
deduction 296
degree of specific consecration 362
dehumanization of bureaucratic
   objects 524–5
democracies
   crisis and change 593, 597
   exchange theory 139
   Habermas, Jürgen 478, 484, 487–8
   historical context 3, 13–14
   modernity 528
democratic philosophers 248
denationalization 567, 582–6
dependence 133–9
   see also interdependency
Derrida, Jacques 291
deskilling 540–4
determinism 69, 348, 350
developmental dynamics 464–5
deviates 102, 137
dialectic of control 280
The Dialectic of Enlightenment
   (Habermas) 438
dictatorships 3–4
difference 387–433
   agents of knowledge 412–13
   antiracist racism 428
   bifurcation of consciousness 404–6
   Bourdieu, Pierre 341, 343
   colonialism 394–5, 417–25
   crisis and change 594–5
   epistemologies 408–11, 412–15
   exclusion from governing conceptual
     mode 401
   fact of blackness 418–22
   historical context 9–14
   humanity 427–8
   identity 391–3, 432–3
   ideology and interpretation 428–33
   integration 395–6, 426–33
   knowing society from within 402–3
   language 417–18

liberal racialization in academic and
public discourse 431–3
one-drop rule 429–31
power 393, 398–406
recognition 422–5
ruling and objectified
knowledge 399–401
structuring relations between subject and
object 403–4
theorizing difference 389–91
truth 413–15
differentiation principles 339–44, 380–1
differentiation of social functions 501–2,
509
DiMaggio, P.J. 159–61, 175–92
Dirlik, Arif 571
disciplinary societies 316–21
discipline 314–21
Discipline and Punish (Foucault) 290,
292–3, 307, 310, 314–21
disciplines of human body 298, 301–2
disembedding mechanisms 538–41
disinterestedness 363, 384–5
dispossession 337
distantiation 522–3, 524, 532
Distinction (Bourdieu) 335–6, 337–9, 341–2
distribution 263
distributive justice 107–8
diversity
Bourdieu, Pierre 353
difference 415
organizational theory 176–85
division of labor
Bourdieu, Pierre 384
crisis and change 575
difference 400
Foucault, Michel 319
Habermas, Jürgen 466
modernity 521–4
domestic control 259–60, 262–4
domination
Bourdieu, Pierre 331, 367, 382
coercion 258–9
difference 392, 428
modernity 519
power 224, 227, 277–84
dramatic realization 50–2

dramaturgical approach 31
see also performance
Dreyfus, Hubert 291
Duchamp, Marcel 373
dumping grounds 591–2
Durkheim, Emile 1–2, 8, 15–17
habitus 349
institutions 159
interaction ritual chains 77, 79, 81–2, 86,
88–9
micro-sociological analysis 28, 31, 53
modernity 537
rationalization of the lifeworld 452,
465–6

economic capital *see* financial capital
economic embeddedness 159, 161,
165–74
generalized morality 170–3
over- and undersocialized action 161,
166–9
trust and malfeasance 169–73
economic instruments 150–4
economic organization 2
economic policy 571–7
economic power 230–2, 234–6
EEC *see* European Economic Community
effect of universality 383–5
effective demand 357–8
efficient-effective networks 210–13
egoism 95
Eisenstadt, S.N. 475
Elias, Norbert 497, 499–509, 526
elite theory 225–6, 229–36
Ellickson, Robert 143
emancipatory knowledge 439
embedded borderings 579–83
embeddedness *see* economic embeddedness;
social embeddedness
embodied knowledge 329, 349–50
emotional behavior 78–9, 81, 85–6
empathy, projective theory of 36–7
empires 259–61
see also imperialism
empirical indicators 208–10
empirical research 14–20
empty rituals 83–4

enforcement 132–3
Engels, Friedrich 13, 14–15
Enlightenment 445–8, 495, 556–7
entertainment events 86–7
episodic public spheres 480
epistemologies 408–11, 412–15
equilibrium 103–7, 109, 117, 120
essential tension 215
essentialist position 392
ethics
　Habermas, Jürgen 441–2
　hegemony 241
ethnicity *see* race/ethnicity
ethnography 336, 402–3
ethnomethodology 28, 33
eugenics 303–4
Eurocentric knowledge validation
　processes 408–11, 413
European Economic Community
　(EEC) 253–4
excessive reciprocation 122
exchange theory
　basic social processes 112–20
　cooperation 148–9
　criticisms 98
　distributive justice 107–8
　influence process 101–2
　paradigm of social behavior 100–1
　power in social life 95–6, 112–23
　practical equilibrium 103–7, 109, 117, 120
　profit and social control 104–8
　social behavior 93–4, 100–11
　social structures 108–9, 115–17
　unspecified obligations and trust 120–3
exclusion
　difference 401, 411
　from groups 136–7, 149–50
exercise of power 317–18
exit costs 133–4
exogamy 135
exploitation 120, 256–8
expressive function 38–40
extensiveness of group/corporate
　obligations 96–7, 129, 130–6
extraction process 263–4
extraterritoriality 582–3

fact of blackness 418–22
failed rituals 83–4
faith 243–4
faithful representation 557–8
false dichotomies 327–8
false performance 55, 57–61
Fanon, Frantz 394–5, 417–25
fascism 16–17
feminist theory
　agents of knowledge 412–13
　bifurcation of consciousness 404–6
　Black feminist thought 393–4, 407–16
　civil society 479–80
　epistemologies 408–11, 412–15
　exclusion from governing conceptual
　　mode 401
　historical context 12–13
　identity 392
　knowing society from within 402–3
　micro-sociological analysis 33
　power 393, 398–406
　ruling and objectified
　　knowledge 399–401
　sociological theory 393–4
　structuring relations between subject and
　　object 403–4
　theorizing difference 390–1
　truth 413–15
Fennell, Mary 185
Festinger, L. 101–2
field-level predictors 187–9
field of positions 330–1, 360–8
filtering of personnel 183
financial capital
　Bourdieu, Pierre 330–1, 337–9, 356–7, 364, 366
　structural holes 204–5
focused crowds 89–90
forced rituals 83–4
formal-pragmatic analysis 451–2
formal rituals 81–2
Foucault, Michel 287–321
　Discipline and Punish 290, 292–3, 307, 310, 314–21
　early writings 291, 293
　education 289–90

The History of Sexuality 290, 292–3,
    295–304
  legacy 293
  life and intellectual context 289–92
  Madness and Civilization 292, 305,
    307
  political action 300–1
  postmodernism 437, 495
  social and cultural construction of
    knowledge 7–8
  truth and power 305–13
The Foundations of Social Theory
  (Coleman) 93–4, 97
frames 202–3
Frankfurt School 437
fraud 172
free will 348
Freeman, John 177–8
free-riding 96, 97
French Revolution 299–301, 317
Freudian theory 79
frictionless markets 132–3
front 49–50, 55
functional division of labor 521–4
functionalism
  exchange theory 94
  historical context 1–2, 10, 12
  power 224–5

games 86, 329, 363
garden culture analogy 516–17, 529
Garfinkel, Harold 29
gender
  agents of knowledge 412–13
  bifurcation of consciousness 404–6
  Black feminist thought 393–4,
    407–16
  crisis and change 595
  epistemologies 408–11, 412–15
  exclusion from governing conceptual
    mode 401
  historical context 9–13
  identity 391–3
  knowing society from within 402–3
  power 393, 398–406
  ruling and objectified
    knowledge 399–401

  sociological theory 393–6
  structuring relations between subject and
    object 403–4
  theorizing difference 389–91
  truth 413–15
generalizable social factors 21
generalized morality 170–3
generalized other 68
generic category systems 197
genesis of states 378–80
genetic structuralism 328
genocide *see* Holocaust
gentrification 539
Gerard, H.B. 104
Ghandi, Mohandas 574–5
Giddens, Anthony 227, 272, 277–85, 496,
    520, 531–45
Gilroy, Paul 21
Gintis, Herbert 167–8
The Global City (Sassen) 566
globalization
  Bourdieu, Pierre 326
  crisis and change 564, 566–7, 573, 580,
    595
  Habermas, Jürgen 441
  historical context 4, 14
  modernity 533, 535, 539
Goffman, Erving 4–5, 28, 30, 31–2,
    46–61, 76
Golden Days (See) 536
Gordon, Sarah 518
Gouldner, Alvin 20
governing conceptual mode 401
government price-support programs
    125–6
Grameen bank 152–4
Gramsci, Antonio 9–10, 226, 237–50
grand theory 17–18
Granovetter, Mark 159, 161, 165–74
Great Depression 2–3, 17, 563
group action
  interaction ritual chains 89
  participation 96
  solidarity 96–7, 129–41
  symbolic interactionism 70–1, 74
group cohesiveness 101–2
group identity 460–2

Habermas, Jürgen 2, 435–89
    analysis of politics and society 438, 440–1
    civil society and the political public
        sphere 440, 469–89
    continuing influence 441–2
    cultural modernity and social
        modernization 445–7
    hermeneutic idealism 451–67
    interpretive sociology 451–67
    life and work 438–9
    modernity 439, 444–50, 538, 541
    postmodernism 437–8
    project of Enlightenment 447–8
    public opinion and communicative
        power 470–4
    rationalization of the lifeworld 451–68
    three Conservatisms 449–50
Habilitation (Habermas) 438
habitus 328–30, 332, 340–1, 345–58,
    371–3, 497
Hannan, Michael 177–80
happy-third strategy 571–2
Hardin, Russell 142–56
Harvey, David 496
Hechter, Michael 96–7, 129–41
Hegel, G.W.F. 280
hegemony
    crisis and change 566, 573
    Foucault, Michel 299
    languages and common sense 246–8
    philosophy and politics 237–48
    power 226, 237–50
    science, religion and common
        sense 237–46
Hemmings, Sally 408
Henry, Patrick 390
hermeneutic idealism 451–67
Herzog (Bellow) 542
hierarchical division of labor 521–4
hierarchization 362–3, 364–6, 368–9
hierarchy of texts 332
high-attraction groups 104–6
Hilberg, Raul 510–11
historical context
    classical sociological theory 1–2, 5
    controversy and resistance 20–2
    empirical research 14–20

individual and society 4–9, 19–20
inequality, power and difference 9–14,
    21–2
mid-twentieth century
    transformations 2–4
social and cultural construction of
    knowledge 6–9
The History of Sexuality (Foucault) 290,
    292–3, 295–304
Hitler, Adolf 515, 517
Hobbes, Thomas 142, 165–7, 169, 172–3,
    295–6, 547, 557
Holocaust 496–7, 510–30
    bankruptcy of modern safeguards 526–8
    bureaucracies 521–5
    causal analysis 513
    centralization of violence 520–1
    civilizing process 517, 519
    dehumanization of bureaucratic
        objects 524–5
    division of labor 521–4
    historical impact 511–13
    modern genocide 513–21
    modernity 521–4
    motives 515–16
    social impact 511–13
Homans, George 19–20, 94, 100–11
homogeneity 351–3
homologies 366–8
homosexuality 308
    see also sexual orientation
honest performance 57–61
Horkheimer, Max 438
human capital 204–5
humanism 495, 551–3
Hume, David 143, 382
Husserl, E. 455–6, 459
hyperbolic doubt 376

idealism 239–40
idealization 52–4
identity
    crisis and change 595
    difference 391–3, 432–3
    Habermas, Jürgen 460–2, 464
    modernity 534
identity politics 481

identity thieves 6
ideological mobilization 515
ideologies
   Bourdieu, Pierre 329, 381–2
   difference 428–33
   Foucault, Michel 298, 307, 312–13
   power 239, 244–5, 284
imagined communities 89
imbalances of power 118–19
IMF *see* International Monetary Fund
immanence 554
immanent goods 131–2
immanentist philosophies 239–40
immigration
   cooperation 150–1
   crisis and change 566
   historical context 10–11, 13
imperialism 533, 547
impersonality mechanisms 538–40
impersonation 55–6
in-order-to motives 41–2
inborn complexes 421
India 574–5
indications, interpretation of 64, 66–8, 69
indifference 337, 341
indirect relations 202–3
individual civilizing process 507–9
individualism
   historical context 4–9, 19–20
   institutions 160
   micro-sociological analysis 33
Industrial Revolution 574–5
inequality
   Bourdieu, Pierre 326–7
   crisis and change 598
   historical context 9–14
   power 223–8
influence 101–2, 472–3
informal economic instruments 150–4
information benefits 215–16
information-processing strategies 482
infra-laws 320
infrastructure 592
initial category systems 200
innovation 181, 242–3
input costs 591–2
inside access model 484

institutional isomorphism 159, 161, 175–92
   coercive isomorphism 161, 178–80, 186
   mechanisms of change 178–85
   mimetic isomorphism 161, 179, 180–2, 186–7
   normative isomorphism 161, 179, 182–5, 187
   organizational theory and diversity 176–85
   predictors of change 185–9
institutional mediation of power 279–80
institutionalization
   Bourdieu, Pierre 369
   catnets 202
   crisis and change 581
   exchange theory 117
   Habermas, Jürgen 447, 460, 477–8
institutions 159–219
   catnets 193–203
   economic embeddedness 159, 161, 165–74
   individualism 160
   institutional isomorphism 159, 161, 175–92
   network theory 161–2
   rationalization and competition 160–1, 175–6
   structural holes 204–19
institutions of power 299
instrumental knowledge 439
integration
   difference 395–6, 426–33
   social 460–3, 466–7, 488
intelligentsias 239–44, 247–8
interaction ritual chains 32–3, 75–90
   bodily presence 84–8
   central mechanism 77–9
   failed, empty and forced rituals 83–4
   formal and natural rituals 81–2
   individuals and situations 75, 76
   ingredients, processes and outcomes 80–1
   nature of rituals 75, 77
   solidarity 88–90
   symbols 81, 82, 88–90
Interaction Ritual Chains (Collins) 32–3, 75–90

interdependency
  institutions 160, 185–6
  modernity 500, 503, 506, 509
  system behavior 93
interests 274–5
inter-group relations 431–3
internal consistency 186
internalization of costs 592
International Monetary Fund (IMF) 572–3, 583, 595
interorganizational structures 177
interpretation of indications 64, 66–8, 69
interpretation strategies 482
interpretive accomplishments 462
interpretive sociology 451–67
intersubjectivity 6–7
  communication 438, 453–4, 456–7, 470–1
  understanding 29, 36–8, 79
intimacy, transformation of 531–2, 538–40
intrinsic attraction 114
The Iron Cage Revisited (DiMaggio and Powell) 175–92
isomorphism *see* institutional isomorphism

Jameson, Frederic 497
Japanese culture 335–6
Jausse, Hans Robert 444
Jefferson, Thomas 408
Junker capitalism 15–16

Kant, Immanuel 440
KcKibben, Bill 575–6
Keynes, John Maynard 2, 5
kinship 161–2, 533
knowledge
  agents of 412–13
  difference 392–3, 399–401, 403, 407–16
  embodied 329, 349–50
  Foucault, Michel 321
  Habermas, Jürgen 439, 448–50, 456, 458–61
  hegemony 245
  modernity 494, 541
  social and cultural construction of 6–9
  validation processes and power relations 408–11, 412

Knowledge and Human Interests (Habermas) 439
knowledge-power 300
Kristallnachte 514
Kumar, Krishan 498

labeling theory 6, 331
labor markets 167–8
labor movements 480
labor unions 126, 133
Lamont, Michele 78
landlordism 261
language
  Bourdieu, Pierre 341, 376
  difference 417–18
  Habermas, Jürgen 456–7
  hegemony 246–8
  modernity 494
Lasch, Christopher 534–5, 541–2
latent conflicts 270
Latour, Bruno 497–8, 546–59
law
  cooperation and trust 142–56
  Foucault, Michel 300–1, 304, 320–1
  Habermas, Jürgen 487
  institutions 179–80
Le Play, Frédéric 15
leadership and power 119–20
learned behavior 100–1
legitimacy
  Bourdieu, Pierre 382–3, 384
  difference 409–11, 412–13
  Habermas, Jürgen 461–2, 472, 486–8
  of power 115–17, 120
Leifer, Eric 98
Levi, Margaret 142–56
Lévi-Strauss, Claude 8, 291, 327
Leviathan (Hobbes) 167
levying-violence principle 318
liberal racialization 431–3
liberal states 440–1
liberty of minority/majority 597–8
lifeworld analysis 451–68
limited systems 195
literary production 332–3, 359–74
lobbying organizations 125–6
local knowledge 541

locales 281–2
localization 570–1
The Logic of Collective Action (Olson) 96, 124–8
The Logic of Practice (Bourdieu) 326, 332
The Long Twentieth Century (Arrighi) 565–6
Lorenzen, Paul 448
low-attraction groups 104–6
Luckman, Thomas 6–7, 28
Luhmann, Niklas 2
Lukes, Steven 226–7, 266–76
Lyotard, Jean-François 437, 493, 495, 496

MacIver, R.M. 128
macrostructures 115–17
Madness and Civilization (Foucault) 292, 305, 307
maintenance of personal integrity 106
malfeasance 169–73
Malinowski, Bronislaw 122
Mallarmé, Stéphane 372–3
manner 50
manners 341, 353
mapping neighborhood systems 201
Marcuse, Herbert 5
Markets from Networks (White) 162
Marsh, Peter 524
Marshall, Thomas 2
Marx, Karl
   crisis and change 563
   modernity 537–8
   power 223–5, 269, 278
Marxism
   Bourdieu, Pierre 342–3, 383–4
   difference 415
   Foucault, Michel 291, 306–7
   Habermas, Jürgen 437–8
   historical context 2–3, 9–10, 17–18
   interaction ritual chains 77
   power 223–5
mass-audience productions 362–3
mass communication
   civil society 479–80, 483
   crisis and change 580
   modernity 495–6
mass media 481–3

mass murder *see* Holocaust
mass phenomena 318–19
material reproduction 459
Mead, George Herbert 6, 7, 15–16, 27, 29, 31, 66–9, 332, 465
meaning-context 41–3
meaning-establishment 38–40
meaning-interpretation 38–40
meanings of objects 64–6
measurability of contributions 138
media representations 481–3
Merelman, R. 267
Merton, Robert 18
Mesopotamia 251–2
metanarratives 437–8, 495
Meyer, John 179–80
Meyer, Marshall 177–8, 182
Meyrowitz, Joshua 539
micro-sociological analysis 25–90
   challenges 28–9
   development and approaches 27–8, 30–3
   legacy 33
   performance 31–2, 46–61
   phenomenology 27–8, 30–1, 33, 35–45
   ritual participation 32–3, 75–90
   symbolic interactionism 27, 31, 33, 62–74
microlending 152–4
microstructures 115–17
middle class aspirations 48
middle-range theories 18–19
mildness-production-profit principle 318
militarization 520
military power 230–2, 234–6
Mills, C. Wright 17–18, 225–6, 229–36
mimetic isomorphism 161, 179, 180–2, 186–7
minds of state 380–4
misrecognition 328–30
misrepresentation 54–7
mob violence 514–15
The Mobility of Capital and Labor (Sassen) 566
mobilization
   of bias 268–9
   civil society 484, 485–6
   collective 352

modernity 491–559
　abstract systems 531–3, 543
　bankruptcy of modern safeguards
　　526–8
　bureaucracies 521–5
　centralization of violence 520–1
　civilizing process 499–509, 517, 519
　consequences 531–45
　crisis and change 564, 565
　dehumanization of bureaucratic
　　objects 524–5
　deskilling and reskilling in everyday
　　life 540–4
　division of labor 521–4
　final examinations 548–51
　Foucault, Michel 300
　Habermas, Jürgen 439, 444–50
　historical context 13–14, 493
　Holocaust 496–7, 510–30
　humanism redistributed 495, 551–3
　impossible modernization 546–8
　nonmodern constitutions 553–9
　objections to postmodernity 543–4
　Parliament of Things 556–9
　phenomenology 537–40
　physical violence 502–5, 526
　radicalised 543–4
　relation to postmodernism 495–8
　risk and danger 535–7, 542–3
　social constraint towards
　　self-constraint 499–509
　transformation of intimacy 531–2,
　　538–40
　trust and personal relations 532–5, 540,
　　542–3
　what is retained and rejected 550
　see also postmodernism
Modernity and the Holocaust
　(Bauman) 496–7, 510–30
monarchies 308–9
monitoring capacity 137, 140
monopolies
　bureaucratic field 384–5
　modernity 502–4, 517
Moore, Barrington 3
moral passivity 241
moral responsibility 523

morality
　Foucault, Michel 299
　Habermas, Jürgen 448–50
　interaction ritual chains 81
multiculturalism 11, 430, 485
multilateralism 571
multinational corporations 564
multiplication of specialized orders
　583–6
multiplicities 318–19
Murdoch, Peter 12
mutual attraction 113–14, 117–18
mutual exteriority 339
mutual understanding 458

narrative presentations 457–8
Nation State and Violence (Giddens) 227,
　277–85
national borders 579–83
national states
　collective action 127
　crisis and change 564, 567, 579–86
　power 253–4, 260–1, 277–85
nationality 389–90
NATO *see* North Atlantic Treaty
　Organization
natural resources 591–2
natural rituals 81–2
natural systems 2
naturalism 548–51, 559
naturalistic inquiry 62–3
nazism 304
negative freedom 347
neighborhood category systems 200–2,
　203
neoconservatism 446
neofunctionalism 2
neoliberalism 595
nets and net systems 193–5
network expansion 207–8, 210
network optimization 210–13
The Network Society (Castells) 496
network theory
　cooperation 146–7
　historical context 19
　institutions 161–2
　social capital 97

New Conservatives 449–50
New Deal 2, 17
Nietzsche, Friedrich 313, 425
noble sports 337–9
noblesse oblige 107–8
noncollective goods 128
non-cooperation 97–8
non-decision-making 226–7, 278–9
nonmodern constitution 553–9
nonredundant contacts 211–13
norm of reciprocity 20
normative isomorphism 161, 179, 182–5, 187
normative validity 453
North Atlantic Treaty Organization (NATO) 253–4
nuclear families 12

objectified knowledge 399–401
objective meaning 38–40, 43–5
objectivism 327–8, 344, 345–8, 350–1, 356–8, 378
objectivity 402, 403–4, 411, 423
obligations
    extensiveness of group/corporate 96–7, 129, 130–6
    Habermas, Jürgen 461–2
    minimizing 132–3
    of neutrality/disinterestedness 384–5
    probability of compliance 96–7, 136–40
    unspecified 120–3
occasional public spheres 480
occupational socialization 183–4, 187, 188–9
Old Conservatives 449
Olson, Mancur 96, 124–8
one-dimensional view of power 266–7, 271, 273, 275
one-drop rule 429–31
operant conditioning 94, 100–1
operational definition 365–6
opportunity 204–8
opportunity costs 208
optimization 93–4
The Ordeal of Integration: Progress and Resentment in America's "Racial" Crisis (Patterson) 395–6

The Order of Things (Foucault) 292
organizational behavior
    coercion 254
    diversity 176–85
    domination 281
organizational fields 177, 183–5, 187–8
organizational-level predictors 185–7
organizational modeling 181–2, 186–8
organizational power 480–1
orthography 376
Outline of a Theory of Practice (Bourdieu) 326
outside initiative model 484
overproduction 2
oversocialized action 161, 166–9
Ozawa, Terutomo 570

pacified societies 504, 526–8
Panopticon (Bentham) 314–17, 319–21
Park, Robert Ezra 48, 71
Parkinson, C. Northcote 254
Parliament of Things 556–9
parody 360–1
Parsons, Talcott 1–3, 9–10
    civil society 460, 472
    exchange theory 94
    institutions 159–60
    micro-sociological analysis 28
    power 272
Pascalian Meditations (Bourdieu) 325, 326
passions 505–6, 520
patriotism 127
patterns of exchange 96
Patterson, Orlando 395–6, 426–33
peasants 261
performance 31–2, 46–61
    belief in the part one is playing 46–9
    dramatic realization 50–2
    front 49–50, 55
    idealization 52–4
    misrepresentation 54–7
    reality and contrivance 57–61
personal ties 135
personality systems 459, 461–3
perversions 302

phenomenology 27–8, 30–1, 33, 35–45
  ambiguities in understanding another person 35
  Bourdieu, Pierre 383
  Foucault, Michel 306–7
  Habermas, Jürgen 456, 460, 463–4
  historical context 7
  intersubjective understanding 29, 36–8
  meaning-context 41–3
  meaning-establishment and meaning-interpretation 38–40
  modernity 537–40
  product and evidence 43–5
  subjective and objective meaning 38–40, 43–5
The Phenomenology of the Social World (Schutz) 30–1, 35–45
philanthropic contributions 127
philosophy
  experts and the common man 242–6
  Habermas, Jürgen 439
  hegemony 237–48
  language 246–8
  political action 237–42, 248
Philosophy and the Mirror of Nature (Rorty) 493
physical violence 502–5, 526
Piore, Michael 167
pluralist approach to power 266–7, 271
political action
  difference 428
  Foucault, Michel 300–1, 319–20
  hegemony 237–42, 248
  power 269–70
political campaigns 87
political indifference 337, 341
political influence 472–3
political passivity 241
political public sphere 440, 469–89
political revolution 309–10
political theory
  Foucault, Michel 309, 312
  Habermas, Jürgen 438, 440–1
  power 230–2, 234–6, 267–8
Polsby, N.W. 267
Popper, Karl 448
popular culture 21

Popular Universities 239–40, 245–6
positions in social space 328–30, 337–40, 360–1, 367–73, 383–4
positivism 410–11
postindustrial society 495
The Postmodern Condition (Lyotard) 493
postmodernism
  final examinations 549–50
  Habermas, Jürgen 437–8, 450
  historical context 493
  impossible modernization 547–8
  objections to 543–4
  radicalised modernity 543–4
  relation to modernity 495–8
  social landscape 494–5
poststructuralism 8–9, 289, 291, 494
Powell, W.W. 159–61, 175–92
power 221–85
  administrative organizations 227, 236
  basic social processes 112–20
  Bourdieu, Pierre 323–4, 331, 362–8, 383
  centralization 230–2
  civil society 481–3
  class 223–6, 227, 284
  coercion 227, 251–65
  collective approval/disapproval 115–17
  communicative 470–4, 488
  decision-making 226–7, 278–9
  difference 393, 398–406
  discipline and punishment 314–21
  domination 224, 227, 277–84
  elite theory 225–6, 229–36
  exchange theory 95–6, 112–23
  Foucault, Michel 295–304, 305–13, 314–21
  hegemony 226, 237–50
  historical context 9–14, 21–2
  imbalances 118–19
  inequality 223–8
  interests 274–5
  leadership 119–20
  life and death 295–301
  locales 281–2
  mobilization of bias 268–9
  one-dimensional view 266–7, 271, 273, 275
  pluralist approach 266–7, 271

rational persuasion 272–4
reciprocity in exchange 113–15, 118–19, 121–2
repression 307–8, 310
sexuality 295–304
social structures 115–17
society and modern history 277–85
surveillance 282–4
three-dimensional view 268–71, 273, 275
tradition 280–1
truth 305–13
two-dimensional view 267–8, 271, 273, 275
underlying concept 271–4
unspecified obligations and trust 120–3
wealth 232–3
Power: A Radical View (Lukes) 226–7, 266–76
The Power Elite (Mills) 225–6, 229–36
practical equilibrium 103–7, 109, 117, 120
practical knowledge 439
practical understanding 438
pragmatism 7, 247
praxis 240–2, 246
The Presentation of Self in Everyday Life (Goffman) 31–2, 46–61
prestige 108–9, 233, 362
price-support programs 125–6
principle of least interest 95
Principles of Group Solidarity (Hechter) 96–7, 129–41
Prison Notebooks (Gramsci) 226
Prisoner's Dilemmas 171–2
probability of compliance with obligations 96–7, 136–40
probable classes 343
production
  Bourdieu, Pierre 332–3, 359–74
  coercion and capital 263–4
  crisis and change 589–93
  cultural 332–3, 359–74
  Foucault, Michel 311
professionalization
  cultural production 366
  Habermas, Jürgen 447, 481
  organizational fields 182–5, 187, 188–9
profit
  Bourdieu, Pierre 356–7

exchange theory 104–8, 125
institutions 205, 217–18
projective theory of empathy 36–7
propaganda 245
property 351
protection 263–4
The Protestant Ethic and the Spirit of Capitalism (Weber) 5, 175–6
psychoanalysis 304
psychodrama 58
psychological disorders 507
psychological processes 112
public goods 128
public opinion 440, 470–4
punishment 314–21

quasi-objects 548–9, 554–6
quasi-simultaneity 38, 44

Rabinow, Paul 291
race/ethnicity
  agents of knowledge 412–13
  antiracist racism 428
  Black feminist thought 393–4, 407–16
  colonialism 394–5, 417–25
  crisis and change 594–5
  epistemologies 408–11, 412–15
  fact of blackness 418–22
  Foucault, Michel 304
  historical context 10–13, 21–2
  humanity 427–8
  identity 391–3
  ideology and interpretation 428–33
  integration 395–6, 426–33
  language 417–18
  liberal racialization in academic and public discourse 431–3
  one-drop rule 429–31
  recognition 422–5
  sociological theory 393–6
  theorizing difference 389–91
  truth 413–15
radical doubt 377–8
radicalised modernity 543–4
Ramo, Joshua Cooper 570–1
rational choice theory 19–20, 98
rational egoists 133, 136

rational persuasion 272–4
rationalization and competition 160–1, 175–6
rationalization of the lifeworld 451–68
Rawls, John 165
real performance 57–61
reason 437, 438, 440
reasons of state 384
reciprocity in exchange 113–15, 118–19, 121–2, 148–9
recognition 422–5
redefinitions 454
redundancy by cohesion 208–10, 218
reembedding mechanisms 538–41
regulatory control 298, 301–2
    see also law
reinforcement behavior 101–2, 106
relational analysis 328–30
religion and hegemony 237–46
religious cults 63
religious fundamentalism 14
religious gatherings 87
religious sects 131
remote communication 84–8
remuneration costs 589–91
repetition of arguments 244
representation of categories 195–202
repression 307–8, 310
reproduction processes 458–67
reputational effects 143–4
reskilling 540–4
responsibility 148–50, 523
reterritoriality 581–2
revolutions
    crisis and change 594–5
    truth and power 309–10
Rieff, Philip 5
right to kill 297
rights of knowledge 245
risk 535–7, 542–3
rites of institution 381
ritual participation see interaction ritual chains
ritual performance 59–60
romantic love
    exchange theory 95, 113–14, 117–18
    modernity 533–4
Rorty, Richard 493

rotating credit associations 151–2
ruling knowledge 399–401
Russian Revolution 529

sacred objects 81, 89
sanctioning capacity 136–7, 140, 149–50, 283–4
Santayana, George 46, 53–4
Sartre, Jean-Paul 52, 60–1, 421, 428, 551
Sassen, Saskia 566–7 579–86
Schachter, S. 101–2
Schutz, Alfred 6–7, 27–8, 30–1, 35–45, 455, 459
science
    Foucault, Michel 311–13, 321
    Habermas, Jürgen 448–50
    hegemony 237–46
    modernity 494, 527–8, 556–9
    symbolic interactionism 63–4
secondary holes 216–17
security 132–3
segmented labor markets 167–8
selecting contacts 206–7
self-belief 48
self-consciousness 422–5
self-constraint 499–509
self-control 501, 504, 507, 519
self-criticism 248
self-deception 238
self-expression 505
self-indication 67–8, 69
self-interest
    economic embeddedness 169
    presentation of self 47
    system behavior 97–8
self-limitation of civil society 478–9
self-referential character 476–7, 481, 486–7
serfdom 261
setting 49–50
sexual orientation
    crisis and change 595
    historical context 9–12
    theorizing difference 389–90
sexuality 8
    crisis and change 595
    difference 394
    Foucault, Michel 290, 292–3, 295–304, 308

sexualization of children 302, 308
shared mood/experience 80–1
sign-using 42
signatum 42
significative function 38–40
Simmel, Georg 162, 213–16
simultaneity 38, 44
sincere performance 57–61
siting contacts 207–8
situational behavior 78–9
Skinner, B.F. 94, 100
slavery 395, 423–4, 426–33
Slavery and Social Death (Patterson) 395
Smith, Adam 135, 143, 166–7, 563, 566, 570
Smith, Dorothy 12–13, 393, 398–406
social actions 64, 68–72
social approval 102
social attraction 113–14, 116
social behavior
    distributive justice 107–8
    exchange theory 93–4, 100–11
    influence process 101–2
    optimization 93–4
    paradigm of exchange 100–1
    practical equilibrium 103–7, 109
    profit and social control 104–8
    social structures 108–9
social capital
    Bourdieu, Pierre 330–1, 372
    cooperation 144–8, 153–4
    network theory 97
    structural holes 204–8
social change
    Bourdieu, Pierre 323–4
    power 278
    symbolic interactionism 73
social constraint 499–509
social construction
    bureaucratic field 380–1
    difference 402
    of knowledge 6–9
social control 104–7
social differentiation 501–2, 509
social dynamics 77–8
social embeddedness 159
social institutions 2
social integration 1, 460–3, 466–7, 488

social modernization 445–7
social organization 64, 71–3
social positions 328–30, 337–40, 360–1, 367–73, 383–4
social production 311
social space 328–30, 332, 335–44, 470
social stratification 223, 227
social structures 64, 71–3, 108–9, 115–17
socialism
    Bourdieu, Pierre 378
    Foucault, Michel 306, 312
    modernity 548, 559
    power 263–4
socialization 458, 460–3
socialized performance 52–4, 58–9, 79
society as symbolic interaction 66–74
sociogenetic method 501, 506
sociological determinism 69
solidarity 129–41
    dependence 133–9
    exchange theory 96–7
    extensiveness of group/corporate obligations 96–7, 129, 130–6
    Habermas, Jürgen 441, 459, 462
    interaction ritual chains 88–90
    probability of compliance 96–7, 136–40
Sontag, Susan 537
SOP *see* standard operating procedures
sovereignty
    Foucault, Michel 295–7, 300–4, 309–10, 319
    power 260
specialization 379
Spencer, Herbert 15
sports events 86
Stalin, Josef 515, 517
standard operating procedures (SOP) 180
standpoint theory 393–4, 414–15
state bureaucracies 375–85
state control 214–15
State of Nature 557
state nobility 384–5
state power
    Bourdieu, Pierre 383
    coercion 251–65
    domination 277–85
    Foucault, Michel 309–10

state regulation 142–56
statist capital 379
status congruence 107
Steinfels, Peter 445–6
stigma 31
Stone, Lawrence 533
structural autonomy 217–19
structural equivalence 177
structural holes 204–19
   benefit-rich networks 206
   control and the *tertius gaudens* 213–19
   distinguishing social capital 205–6
   efficient-effective networks 210–13
   empirical indicators 208–10
   essential tension 215
   information benefits 215–16
   network expansion 207–8, 210
   network optimization 210–13
   opportunity and capital 204–8
   secondary holes 216–17
   selecting contacts 206–7
   siting contacts 207–8
   structural autonomy 217–19
Structural Holes (Burt) 159, 162, 204–19
The Structural Transformation of the Public Sphere (Habermas) 440–1
structuralism 8
   Bourdieu, Pierre 327–8, 332–3, 344, 345
   Foucault, Michel 290–1
structuration
   Bourdieu, Pierre 326
   organizational fields 177, 188–9
The Structure of Social Action (Parsons) 2
structuring structures 380–3
struggle of classifications 343
subject-centered reason 494
subjective meaning 38–40, 43–5
subjectivism 327–8, 344, 348, 356, 378
subjectivity 401, 403–4, 411, 423
subordination
   coercion 258–9
   difference 392, 408
   domination 280
   exchange theory 96, 115, 120
substantialist position 328–9, 337–8
substitutable goods 134

suicide 297
super-ego 505–8
supranational states 583–4
surveillance 282–4
symbolic interactionism 27, 31, 33, 62–74
   interpretation of indications 64, 66–8, 69
   meanings of objects 64–6
   methodological orientation 63–6
   methodological position 62–6
   social actions 64, 68–72
   social organization and structures 64, 71–3
   society as symbolic interaction 66–74
Symbolic Interactionism (Blumer) 31, 62–74
symbolic space 332, 335–44
symbolic violence 331, 341
symbols 81, 82, 88–90
system behavior
   interdependence 93
   self-interest 97
system integration 467
systematic knowledge 403
systemic crises 569–78, 597
systemic cycles of accumulation 565–6
systems of states 254, 262

tabular representation of categories 198–9
taxation
   crisis and change 592–3
   exchange theory 127–8, 130
   power 264–5
technical responsibility 523
techniques of power 299
technology of power 301–2, 311
technology of sex 302
territorial insertions 581–2
Territory, Authority, Rights: From Medieval to Global Assemblages (Sassen) 566–7, 579–86
terrorism 596
tertius gaudens 213–19
theoretical classes 342–4
theoretical consciousness 241
The Theory of Communicative Action (Habermas) 439, 451–68

theory-practice nexus 241–2
third-happy strategy 571–2
Thomas, W.I. 71
three-dimensional view of power 268–71, 273, 275
Tilly, Charles 227, 251–65
totalitarianism 306, 446
Touraine, Alain 495
trade associations 184, 187
trade unions 126, 133
tradition
   Bourdieu, Pierre 323–4
   continuity 461
   power 280–1
transcendence 554
transfer costs 134
transformation of intimacy 531–2, 538–40
triad representation of categories 196
tribute-making empires 260–1
trust
   cooperation 97–8, 142–56
   difference 426
   economic embeddedness 169–73
   exchange theory 120–3
   modernity 532–5, 540, 542–3
truth
   difference 413–15
   five traits 311–12
   Foucault, Michel 305–13
   Habermas, Jürgen 453
   power 305–13
Tsai, Kellee 151–2
two-dimensional view of power 267–8, 271, 273, 275

undersocialized action 161, 166–9
understanding another person 35, 36–8
unilateral services/power 118–19
unions 126, 133
United States power relations 408–11
universal validity 336
universality 383–5
unspecified obligations 120–3
untouchables 135
urban renewal 539

urbanization
   Bourdieu, Pierre 323–4
   crisis and change 591
   power 257–8

value consensus 2, 116
Veblen, Thorstein 524
Venn diagrams 198–9
violation of conventions 130, 149–50
violence
   centralization 520–1
   interaction ritual chains 89
   modernity 502–5, 514–15, 520–1, 526
   symbolic 331, 341
visibility 314–15
voluntary contributions 127–8

Wallerstein, Immanuel 3–4, 496, 565, 587–99
war
   crisis and change 571, 576
   Foucault, Michel 296–7, 310
   modernity 542
   state formation and transformation 259–65
warrior societies 504–5, 520
Warwaw Pact 253–4
Washington Consensus 571, 595
waste disposal 591–2
We Have Never Been Modern (Latour) 497–8, 546–59
wealth and power 232–3
Weber, Max 1, 5, 15–17
   Bourdieu, Pierre 356, 378–9, 383
   modernity 447–8, 465–6, 537
   organizational fields 175–6
   phenomenology 29
   power 223–4, 269, 283
White Collar (Mills) 225
White, Harrison 161–2, 193–203
white supremacists 429–31
The Will to Power (Nietzsche) 425
Williamson, Oliver 160, 169–70
Wittgenstein, Ludwig 8, 326, 450
Wolf, Martin 570
Wolstonecraft, Mary 390

World Social Forum (WSF) 596–7
World Systems Analysis (Wallerstein) 496, 565, 587–99
world systems theory 3–4
World Trade Organization (WTO) 580–1, 583, 595
The Wretched of the Earth (Fanon) 394
Wright, Eric Olin 224

Wrong, Dennis 166–7
WSF *see* World Social Forum
WTO *see* World Trade Organization

Young Conservatives 449
Yunus, Muhammad 152–4

Zeitgeist 445